EIGHTH EDITION
EFFECTIVE SELLING

Joseph F. Hair, Jr.

Chair, Department of Marketing
Louisiana State University
Baton Rouge, Louisiana

Francis L. Notturno

Division of Business Administration
College Misericordia
Dallas, Pennsylvania

Frederick A. Russ

Head, Department of Marketing
University of Cincinnati
Cincinnati, Ohio

COLLEGE DIVISION South-Western Publishing Co.

CINCINNATI   DALLAS   LIVERMORE

S57

Copyright © 1991
by SOUTH-WESTERN PUBLISHING CO.
Cincinnati, Ohio

Publisher: James R. Sitlington, Jr.
Production Editor: Rhonda Eversole
Production House: Carnes-Lachina Publication Services, Inc.
Cover Designer: Elaine Lagenaur
Interior Designers: Elaine Lagenaur and Joseph Devine
Photo Researcher: Diana Fears
Staff Photographer: Diana Fleming
Marketing Manager: Dave Shaut

Library of Congress Cataloging-in-Publication Data

Hair, Joseph F.
   Effective selling / Joseph F. Hair, Jr., Francis L. Notturno, Frederick A. Russ. —
8th ed.
      p.   cm.
   Eighth ed. of: Effective selling / Charles A. Kirkpatrick, Frederick A. Russ.
7th ed.
   ISBN 0-538-19570-3
   1. Selling.   I. Notturno, Francis L.   II. Russ, Frederick A.   III. Kirkpatrick,
Charles Atkinson.   Effective selling.   IV. Title.
HF5438.25.K57   1991
658.8′5—dc20
                                                                   90-9540
                                                                      CIP

1 2 3 4 5 6 7 8 MT 7 6 5 4 3 2 1 0

Printed in the United States of America

BRIEF CONTENTS

CONTENTS

PART 7   SALES MANAGEMENT

DEDICATION

The Eighth Edition of EFFECTIVE SELLING is dedicated to the memory of C. A. Kirkpatrick and his many contributions to sales education over the years.

PREFACE

For nearly 30 years, *Effective Selling* has graced the classrooms of colleges and universities across the United States. The text has also been used within the sales training programs of some of the world's most successful selling organizations. What has made *Effective Selling* a top seller over the years? Its exhaustive coverage of the selling profession and easy-to-understand presentation! Why have the authors of the Eighth Edition of *Effective Selling* chosen to revise this text? Because the selling profession is undergoing many changes in the 1990s that will affect the way corporations and salespeople do business well into the 21st century.

Personal selling expenditures by all marketers have increased dramatically in the past decade. Since the cost of food, travel, and lodging will continue to climb, selling organizations must seek to train their salespeople on the most effective techniques of selling, and the most efficient means of time and territory management. The role of the salesperson is to use this training, along with the latest technologies, to become a productive seller and time manager.

FOCUSES OF THE EIGHTH EDITION

The Eighth Edition focuses on continuing the success *Effective Selling* has had in developing successful sales professionals, and in educating college and university business students throughout the country. It is targeted toward beginning sales and marketing students. However, it is beneficial to anyone interested in persuasive communications. As with past editions, it contains a comprehensive coverage of the selling profession and is written in an easy-to-understand manner. What sets the Eighth Edition apart from past editions is its practical and realistic presentation of the subject matter and its attention to visuals that help reinforce the text. Examples of real companies and the techniques they use are featured in highlights throughout the text to bring the material to life to the student. The reader should complete the text with a more thorough understanding and, hopefully, a better appreciation of the selling profession, its techniques, and its opportunities.

SPECIAL ATTENTION

The text includes many of the same topics contained in other introductory sales texts, with special attention given to such topics as computer technology and telecommunications and how they are used for time and territory management, telemarketing, the SPIN Approach to selling, adaptive selling, and the psychological aspects of selling. These topics are presented to show the dynamic nature of sales in the 1990s, and the excitement that has been created by the development of these new sales productivity aids.

ORGANIZATION AND FEATURES OF CHAPTERS

Each chapter in the Eighth Edition of *Effective Selling* starts with a set of learning objectives, contains key terms that are set in bold type throughout the text, and concludes with expanded end-of-chapter material, including a summary, a list of key terms, an expanded and more strenuous set of review and discussion questions, and cases that reinforce the chapter's material. Within each chapter real-life examples, charts, graphs, and figures are used to aid the student's understanding and to bring excitement to the subject matter.

TEXT CASES

A special feature of the Eighth Edition is the addition of text cases that have been adapted for use with a Lotus®-based[1] spreadsheet approach, and a template disk is provided free of charge to instructors at educational institutions that adopt *Effective Selling*. These cases are designated by a diskette icon next to the problems. The instructor may choose either to have students execute the Lotus exercises by using the pre-prepared templates or to obtain the solutions provided in the *Instructor's Manual* and use them as a basis of discussion. In the text cases, suggestions are also provided for developing original templates for other "what if" scenarios. At the end of the User's Guide section of the *Instructor's Manual* three new cases are included to provide more spreadsheet application.

SUPPLEMENTS

Instructors who have used previous editions of *Effective Selling* will note the material provided in the *Instructor's Manual* has been substantially expanded. Expansions include more detailed answers to the chapter review and discussion questions as well as for the case problems, and an improved test bank. Tests are also available in disk format, which allows modification for individual class instruction and coverage. In addition, there are transparency masters, many of which do not duplicate material already presented in the text. Finally, a user's guide, pro-

---

[1]Lotus® and Lotus 1-2-3® are registered trademarks of Lotus Development Corporation.

vided in a special section of the *Instructor's Manual*, explains how to use most effectively the Lotus-based cases.

PERSONAL SELLING—A MUST

Today's marketing and business students would be well-advised to take a course in personal selling. It is a must for anyone attempting to enter the sales profession in the 1990s. Gone are the days when just anyone can get a sales position. As selling increases its level of professionalism, so do the qualifications for such positions increase.

A personal selling course would also be beneficial to anyone planning to take a job with a corporation or to own his or her own business. It provides an understanding of how to relate to others in business terms, whether they are customers, business associates, or fellow employees.

Finally, familiarity with the selling process is vital to anyone who plans to interview for a position. Future employees must sell themselves and their abilities to prospective employers! Students should prospect for potential employers, and qualify them as to whether they provide the necessary and preferred benefits, atmosphere, and opportunities. Next and prior to the interview, students should gather as much information as possible about the interviewer and the company to adjust their sales strategy to attaining that particular position.

When students enter the interview, they must approach the recruiter with a firm handshake, professional appearance, and a confident attitude. *Corporations want to hire winners*, just as customers want to buy from well-known companies! In presenting themselves to the recruiter, students will use their sales brochure (resume and/or portfolio) to feature their abilities, show the advantages they have over others being considered for the job, and relate how the company will benefit from hiring them. Along the way, students will have to satisfy all of the prospective employers' questions and objections. When the prospective employer is ready to end the interview, it is imperative for students to find out the number of interviews required for that corporation's recruiting process so they can properly close the interview. Just as salespeople must ask for the sale, so should recruits ask for the second interview or the job!

Finally, no recruit should end the selling process without following up with a prospective employer to determine whether they are satisfied with the recruit's abilities. A brief letter a day or two after the interview followed by a telephone call a week or two later can provide recruits with the opportunity to say "Thank you for your time and consideration." A follow-up can also help determine what went wrong and what mistakes to avoid a second time. Also, a follow-up can be an effective means of reselling recruits' abilities to that prospective employer.

Please enjoy the Eighth Edition of *Effective Selling*.

Joseph F. Hair, Jr.   Francis L. Notturno
Louisiana State University   College Misericordia

ACKNOWLEDGMENTS

A number of people have read and commented on various chapters of this text. In particular, we would like to thank:

Rosemary R. Lagace
University of Kentucky

Abraham Axelrud
Queensborough Community
    College

Eugene F. Grape
Northern Arizona University

Randall D. Mertz
Mesa Community College

G. Dean Kortge
Central Michigan University

Charles T. Harrington
Pasadena City College

James J. Alling
Augusta Technical Institute

Leroy M. Buckner
Florida Atlantic University

Joel Katz
Davenport College

Reginald A. Graham
Fort Lewis College

Debbie Easterling
Bentley College

K. Randall Russ
SSA Consultants

Norman Cohn
Milwaukee Area Technical
    College

Willis Galer
Lake Superior State
    University

Thomas Leitzel
Chesapeake College

Bobbe Horton
Ferris State College

Charles Pettijohn
Southwest Missouri State
    University

Charles W. Hockert
Oklahoma City Community
    College

James F. Wolter
Grand Valley State University

Corinthian Fields
Tarrant County Junior
    College

Elaine McCain
Lee College

Sheri Marquette
Louisiana State University

Sandy Franklin
Louisiana State University

Nora Fierro
Louisiana State University

PART 1

Personal Selling Basics

CHAPTER 1

The Role of
Personal Selling

After studying this chapter, you should be able to:

- Explain why sales is an exciting career
- Discuss the modern sales attitude toward professionalism
- Tell why selling offers an attractive career
- Show how selling benefits our economy and our society
- Discuss the roles salespeople play within the firm.
- Argue that a person can learn how to sell.

What do you really think about a career in personal selling? If you are like most college students, you probably have not had much of an opportunity to learn about careers in general or one in personal selling in particular. In this book, we will share with you the many interesting and exciting aspects of a career in sales. In the first section of this chapter we describe the sales position of Lisa Brown to show you some of the things today's salespeople do. Next we review examples of the latest technology in selling and how they have made an impact on sales careers. The third section provides an overview of past and present attitudes toward the sales profession, and of what is in store for the future. The fourth section covers the attractiveness of sales as a career. The fifth section deals with the way in which sales fits into the company and society. The sixth, and final, section discusses how one learns to sell.

LISA BROWN: CAREER SALESPERSON

Lisa Brown is the international sales representative for a computer software developer. Because she handles the overseas territory and cannot visit her customers, Lisa does her selling via telemarketing.

Lisa starts a typical day by checking her facsimile (fax) machine to see if any messages were sent to her overnight. Although she works from 8:30 A.M. to 6 P.M., her overseas clients are in different time zones. Tuesday afternoon in some countries is Wednesday morning in others. Just because Lisa's office has closed for the night does not mean her customers are not communicating with her — international business goes on 24 hours a day.

When Lisa comes to work in the morning, her first task is to sort through her messages to determine which ones are urgent. Hans, her West German **reseller**, has a potential corporate customer who needs 75 copies of a particular software program. Hans wants to know if he can give the prospect a 30 percent discount instead of the usual 22 percent. He says there is the possibility that the company will buy another 250 copies within the next year or two. He wants Lisa to call him at his home at 9:30 A.M., her time, so she can advise him on how to handle the situation. Before calling Hans, she must check with her sales manager because the exchange rate for the U.S. dollar may not permit this much additional discount.

Pierre, a prospect from France, is still very interested in her product, but he wants to know if research and development can modify the package slightly to meet his needs. He will be in his office until 11 A.M., Lisa's time.

Lisa records these two calls with the others in her "Daily Calendar" and her day is set, as shown in Figure 1-1.

At 9 A.M. Lisa calls Merrick in England. Merrick is the Director of Communications for a large international company. He purchased 95 copies of the software package and they were supposed to have been delivered last week. Lisa is calling to see if Merrick has received the product and if his systems analysts have been able to get it working on their computers. After talking for about ten minutes, Lisa learns that Merrick has not yet received the copies. He will call Lisa when they do arrive. This shorter-than-expected call gives Lisa time to talk to her boss, Dan, about whether or not they will let Hans offer the 30 percent discount. They decide that a **conference call** might be best.

Lisa's 9:30 A.M. call to Isabelle finds the South African executive in a meeting. Though this phone meeting was arranged a day earlier, circumstances arose to force a postponement. Lisa uses this time to confirm Isabelle's shipment and to ensure that there are no problems.

Lisa and Dan call Hans at 10:30 A.M. from her office. Lisa's telephone is equipped with a speakerphone so that both Dan and Lisa can talk to Hans at the same time. They advise Hans to get a commitment for those 250 additional copies before consenting to the 30 percent discount. Hans will call back with his results.

Lisa's two other calls this morning go well. And she still has about half an hour before she goes to lunch. So Lisa enters the results of her morning calls onto each customer's computer file. This will allow each customer's file to be up-to-date.

After lunch, Lisa spends two hours "power dialing." Power dialing is Lisa's term for making phone calls, one after the other, to potential cus-

DAILY CALENDAR

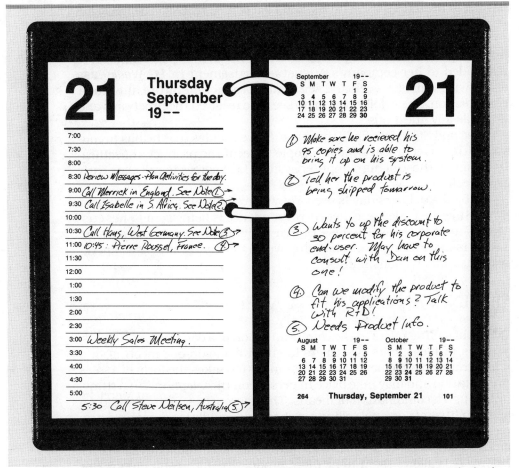

Figure 1-1 Daily calendars enable salespeople to organize their time effectively.

tomers who have shown an interest in the company and its products. Lisa accesses her computer's inquiry database to obtain the names of 55 potential customers in her territory who have phoned or written to the company in the last month seeking information. In two hours Lisa can contact approximately 10 to 15 potential customers, determine their level of interest, answer any questions they might have, and send out product literature if requested. Finally, she will enter the information gathered from these calls into the database and rank them from high to low, according to their level of interest.

The weekly sales meeting at 3:00 P.M. lasts an hour. Lisa spends the rest of her afternoon writing to four customers whose business day starts after hers has finished. The letters will be sent via the fax machine, and they will be at the customers' places of business when they start the day. All of the letters list a time when Lisa can be reached the following day if something needs clarification.

Lisa calls Steve Neilsen at 5:30 P.M. (7:30 A.M. in Australia). She brings up Steve Neilsen's **prospect file** on her computer screen. Steve responded to her company's August advertisement in *PC Week.* Lisa spoke with him last week and sent some product literature after their conversation. She is following up to see if he received the brochures and if he has any questions.

Lisa and Steve talk for 20 minutes. Steve decides that he has to consult with his technical support people to see if the product's specifications match those of his computer system. Lisa agrees to call back early next week.

At 5:45 P.M. Lisa's day is over. Yet while she is at home relaxing, or even while she is sleeping, her correspondence is being sent to her customers around the world. Lisa Brown is living proof that sales in the 1990s is an exciting, ever-changing world of new technologies, methodologies, and responsibilities.

SELLING: AN EXCITING CAREER

Personal selling refers to the communication of a company's products, services, or ideas to its customers in either a one-on-one meeting, or a small group arrangement. The communication takes the form of a sales presentation and may take place in person, on the telephone, in writing, or through a combination of means. The approaches, methods, and responsibilities of personal selling are changing rapidly in response to new technologies and a changing business environment. These changes enable salespeople to perform their duties far more efficiently than ever before. This allows them to be more productive and results in greater career satisfaction. Several of the new technologies and methods are discussed briefly in the following sections.

NEW TECHNOLOGIES

The major new technologies affecting the selling profession include: (1) personal computers, (2) computer software, (3) facsimile machines, and (4) mobile communications equipment.

PERSONAL COMPUTERS

The use of personal computers in selling increased tremendously in the late 1980s and continues to increase in the 1990s. Salespeople who sell via telemarketing (such as Lisa Brown), or inside a store or office, have the advantage of having their own personal computers on their desks. But traveling sales representatives are not at a disadvantage. Many computer manufacturers sell portable personal computers (as

Figure 1-2 Advances in microcomputer technology have made access to information portable.

Source: Courtesy of Radio Shack, a division of Tandy Corporation.

shown in Figure 1-2) that can be carried in the salespersons' cars, taken into their hotel rooms, into their customers' offices, and even on board airplanes.

COMPUTER SOFTWARE

Numerous types of software are available that enable salespeople to manage the selling process more efficiently. For example, **word processing** software helps salespeople prepare letters, customer files, and reports. Once these documents are prepared they can be saved on a disk, and, when needed, be updated or modified. This saves a tremendous amount of time normally spent typing and creating similar reports and form letters. It also speeds up response time to customers, because the salesperson does not have to get a secretary to type the letter. Many word processing packages even correct spelling and punctuation.

A second type of software is the **database manager**. The database manager allows salespeople to put the information usually kept in paper files onto a computer disk. Customer files, prospecting cards, competitive information, product information, and past sales records can all be stored on a convenient 3½- or 5¼-inch computer disk, thus eliminating the need for paper files. Once a database of information has been created, salespeople can search the database and display specific items or general categories of interest by issuing simple software commands. For example, if you want to know which customers have not purchased from you within the last six months, the database manager will search through the files, locate those customers, and display them on the screen or print them out. You can then call on these customers to find out why they have stopped purchasing.

Spreadsheet analysis is a third type of software. It is designed to perform arithmetic calculations and to display these calculations in a grid format (columns and rows). Spreadsheets can save hours normally spent doing calculations by hand, and can point out relationships among the numbers. Knowledge of these relationships can help salespeople in planning, forecasting sales, calculating discounts, determining customer pricing strategies, and in doing many other tasks.

A fourth type of software provides salespeople with graphic capabilities. **Graphics software** enables salespeople to develop sophisticated sales presentations using pie charts, bar graphs, and XY plots. For example, salespeople use graphics such as bar graphs to show customers the profit levels they could attain by using their product at varying time intervals (see Figure 1-3).

Another type of software available to salespeople allows them to keep in touch with their sales managers or the "home office" through the use

GRAPHICS SOFTWARE HELP TO VISUALIZE THE PRESENTATION

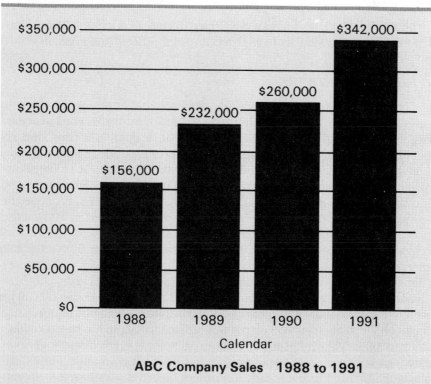

ABC Company Sales   1988 to 1991

Figure 1-3 The use of a bar graph illustrates clearly ABC Company's sales growth. With the help of a graphics software program, salespeople can develop professional charts and graphs in minutes.

of **electronic mail**. Salespeople can check their computer mailbox at a central computer for any messages, and can also send messages to other sales representatives, managers, or sales support people. Electronic mail reduces the hassle of trying to keep in touch when on the road, and eliminates the problem of missing people when calling. Communications software also allows salespeople to check product inventory levels, delivery schedules, and pricing information immediately.

The final type of sales-oriented software is called **vertical software**. Vertical software provides scenarios or situations that salespeople can review by filling in the needed characteristics. For example, one program can be used to help salespeople prepare for a specific customer. The salesperson inputs information on the customer's personality and their own personality. The software then displays a profile on how the salesperson could approach the customer and how he or she could succeed in selling to that customer. The scenarios are specific to the selling process but not to each type of selling organization. The company must adapt its situation to the software in order to use it effectively.

FACSIMILE MACHINES

Facsimile (or **"fax"**) **machines** enable salespeople to send copies of important papers to customers in a matter of minutes. The salesperson feeds the documents into the fax machine, dials the customer's special fax number, and, in minutes, the paper is reproduced on the customer's fax machine. This is significantly faster and less expensive than both

Figure 1-4 Many sales are won or lost on the speed in which facts are transmitted to the buyer. Fax machines are essential when time is short.
Source: Photo courtesy of Xerox Corporation.

express mail and regular mail service. Salespeople find out which customers have a fax machine by looking in the "fax directory." (The original fax phone book is a subscription service that includes dial-a-fax directory assistance. The fax directory is published by Dial-A-Fax Directories Corporation.) This directory lists thousands of companies from around the world that have fax machines. Salepeople use fax machines to confirm appointments, transmit sales information, solicit new prospects, and many other things. The latest fax innovation, the personal facsimile and answering system, represents increased versatility over previous fax machines, and a significant reduction in price.

MOBILE COMMUNICATIONS EQUIPMENT

The surging popularity of **cellular phones, pagers**, and **airfones** is expected to continue throughout the 1990s. Many salespeople carry pagers to maintain contact with the office, a customer, a vendor, or anyone else who knows their number. The pager is somewhat limited because the salesperson still must find a telephone to return the call.

Cellular mobile phones are popular with salespeople because calls can be placed or received from the car. In the case of portable cellular phones, calls can be made almost anywhere. The cellular phone system uses a network of antennas that divide service areas into cells. A switching office shifts the call from one cell to another until the call is completed. Studies conducted by the manufacturers of cellular phones have shown that salespeople significantly increase their sales in a period of time as short as six months by using cellular phones.

Airfones are telephones on airplanes. To make a call while airborne, callers put a credit card in a slot, detach the phone from the wall, and take it to their seats. Weak signals, interference, and busy phone lines are a

Figure 1-5 Car phones enable salespeople to alter their sales call schedules without having to return to the office. This added efficiency holds great potential for increasing sales.

few of the problems that need to be worked out before the airfone will be considered commonplace. The use of airfones is increasing, however, because it increases sales productivity.

NEW METHODS

The latest trend in selling methods is **telemarketing**. Telemarketing can be defined as the use of the telephone in conjunction with traditional marketing methods and techniques. The skyrocketing cost of a personal sales call, up 9.5 percent from 1985 to 1987 to an average of over $250,[1] has encouraged companies to use telemarketing as a less expensive alternative. Salespeople such as Lisa Brown can use the telephone to solicit new accounts, follow up on sales leads, set appointments, close sales, and maintain strong customer relations. The telephone enables salespeople to contact more people in a shorter period of time than could be done traveling to and from each customer's place of business. More important, telemarketing is far less expensive than a personal sales visit.

NEW RESPONSIBILITIES

Salespeople in the 1990s must do more than just sell. They must manage their territories in a cost-effective way, thus requiring them to stay up-to-date with new technologies and new methods. They must also coordinate these technologies into a systematic approach aimed at satisfying the customer. Salespeople like Lisa Brown are in high demand because they are skilled at using computer software, fax machines, cellular phones, and telemarketing to satisfy a wide range of customers in an effective manner. They are able to reach overlooked market segments and be successful in them. This is evident in the fact that Ms. Brown made sales of over half-a-million dollars in 1989 in a territory that was not marketed to in 1987. This was achieved with a minimum amount of money (less than $10,000) spent on international advertising.

SELLING: A PROFESSIONAL CAREER

In recent years the sales profession has struggled to overcome the negative image that has been ingrained in the minds of customers by overzealous salespeople of past decades. Selling today is not made up of jokes and drinks, backslapping and smiles, high pressure and high living, gifts, shady deals, and expense accounts. The advent of new technologies has reduced the time salespeople spend away from home and family. Salespeople do not have to resign themselves to lives that are less full, less satisfying, or less happy than those other individuals enjoy.

---

[1]*Marketing News*, "Average Business-to-Business Sales Call Increases to 9.5%" (September 12, 1988): 5.

THE MODERN SALES ATTITUDE

Today's salespeople seek a more professional image by putting their customers' needs ahead of what they are selling, by providing excellent service after the sale, and by not overstating the quality or performance capabilities of their products. The new sales attitude of businesses focuses on the **marketing concept**, which is based solely on finding out what consumers want and need and providing that product or service to customers at a reasonable price.

The marketing concept has arisen because customers are no longer forced to buy only what the seller offers. Consumers now live in a **buyer's market** (where supply exceeds demand), which has been created by the increased competition in the marketplace. Where has this competition come from?

First, many products are imported into the United States every year from Japan, Germany, Taiwan, and many other countries. The automobile industry, for example, has only three American competitors: General Motors, Ford, and Chrysler. The increased competition in this industry comes primarily from Japan and Germany.

A second reason for increased competition in today's marketplace is that the availability of inexpensive communication equipment enables companies to talk to customers in faraway markets. A third reason is the low cost of transportation. The ready combination of communications and transportation allows small companies to do business nationwide, and even worldwide, rather than being limited to local or regional markets.

Finally, our foreign competitors have simply done a better job of marketing their products than we have in the United States. In the book *The New Competition*, Philip Kotler et al. point out that the Japanese in particular have gone to great lengths to determine what their consumers want and to satisfy those wants. In short, the Japanese have researched American consumers, and then provided more value per dollar spent than their American counterparts.

Apart from the automotive industry, another example of the modern sales attitude is the firm Swiss Colony Farms, a small company that does business nationwide. Swiss Colony is known for its holiday gift packages of smoked meats, cheeses, fruit, nuts, and baked goods. Using mail-order catalogs, an 800 number, telemarketing, and the low cost of transportation, Swiss Colony began offering nationwide service from its Wisconsin home office. This sales approach enabled them to provide customers all across the United States with numerous holiday gift-giving ideas.

In today's highly competitive marketplace, salespeople must satisfy consumers' wants and needs completely to establish a long-term buyer-seller relationship. Otherwise, salespeople will almost certainly become former salespeople.

SALESPEOPLE ARE NEEDED

Many salespeople gain satisfaction from the challenge of selling. They thrive on excelling in their field and take pride in their work and in satisfying the needs of their customers. They realize selling is essential to the economy and offers something productive to society.

SELLING IS ESSENTIAL

Nothing happens in our economy until somebody sells something. Thus, to consider personal selling an optional economic activity is a serious mistake. The products of our manufacturing, service, and agriculture sectors will not sell themselves, no matter how good or how big they are. The advice that all one needs to do to succeed is to build a better mousetrap is as treacherous as it is untrue. Informative and persuasive face-to-face selling is necessary to move much of the volume of goods that comes from our factories and farms. As for services, how many people buy life insurance without a little nudging from a salesperson?

Selling is essential for high employment. Salespeople make possible in part the massive production that contributes greatly to our national independence and security. One study has shown that the typical salesperson of a manufacturer is responsible for the steady employment of 31 factory workers. The combination of those factory workers and their dependents, and the salesperson's dependents, add up to 109 consumers. Furthermore, salespeople contribute to the continued operation of other enterprises. For instance, when manufacturers' salespeople sell their products transportation firms get the business of shipping the products. Wholesalers, retailers, storage companies, banks, advertising agencies, and advertising media stay in business because salespeople are out making sales.

New products are not alone in requiring personal selling. Established products, too, must be sold year after year. Continual changes in the marketplace require a continued sales effort. For example, suppose a manufacturer decides to enter a new market, or new competitors appear, or established competitors take away some dealers. Advertising alone will almost never keep a product on the market. The manufacturer must make use of salespeople indefinitely. What would happen if personal selling were abandoned? Sales would drop, production would have to be cut back, workers would be laid off, inventories would rise, and, eventually, the manufacturer would face bankruptcy.

SELLING IS PRODUCTIVE

It is a misconception to think selling adds no value to the goods and services it markets, or to think it is a parasitic form of promotion. Selling is productive because the product being sold must benefit the buyer as well as the seller, or it won't sell. Practically all sellers must receive repeat orders and purchases from their customers if they are to be profitable. Most sellers must hold a customer's patronage through many successive purchases and over many years. Clearly, no sensible buyer makes repeat purchases from a seller if those purchases are of no benefit to that buyer.

SELLING IS A PROUD ACTIVITY

Every sincere, competent salesperson is entitled to a feeling of pride from a career in selling. Certainly, it is a satisfying experience for the salesperson who guides buyers to better products and services. Buyers, whether they are consumers, middlemen, members of a profession, or purchasing agents, benefit from competent salespeople.

SELLING IS EDUCATION

Salespeople provide information to their customers. The more complex the product or service, the greater the need for educating the prospect. Salespeople can take great pride in educating the public.

SELLING: AN ATTRACTIVE CAREER

The aspects of selling that probably will be most important to a person who is contemplating a career in sales are: the opportunity for advancement, expected earnings, personal satisfaction from the job, security, respect, independence, variety, and interesting work. For many of you, these advantages will overcome any negative attitudes you may have about a sales career.

OPPORTUNITY FOR ADVANCEMENT

Few activities offer individuals the bright future that personal selling offers. As buyers demand new products, and manufacturers comply, more salespeople are needed to match the demand with the supply. The increase in the amount of leisure time each customer enjoys is opening up new markets, especially in the service sectors of our economy.

Salespeople are more apt to get promoted as a result of their efforts than are many individuals in other phases of business. The majority of marketing students begin their careers in sales because it provides the necessary exposure to the product/service, the customer, the competition, the distribution channels, and the marketing environment, which they will need to make good decisions as managers. Hard work and resourcefulness will move them up faster and farther than would be possible in many other types of work. Good salespeople, regardless of their age or sex, do not have to wait long for management to recognize their worth. They can stand on their records of successful performance, rather than relying on seniority as a reason for advancement.

Where does promotion lead? Successful salespeople often chart one of two career paths: being the top salesperson, or securing a position in management. These two paths can be pursued, of course, within either the salesperson's own company or in other organizations. Salespeople advance in selling careers largely by taking on expanding territories or bigger accounts. Advancement in management might be through jobs such as sales supervisor, branch manager, district or zone manager, regional manager, divisional manager, assistant sales manager, sales manager, director of marketing, and even president. Advancement in retailing might be to head of stock, assistant buyer, buyer, or selling supervisor. There also are several related activities in marketing into which salespeople might move — advertising, sales promotion, market analyst, and market research. One example of the opportunities available for salespeople is described in Highlight 1-1.

HIGHLIGHT 1-1   *Sales and Sales Management Careers at Procter & Gamble*

Procter & Gamble is one of the most successful consumer packaged-goods companies in the world. P&G operates in 38 different product categories and is the sales leader in 21 of them. Needless to say, Procter & Gamble employs thousands of sales representatives and each is trained to be the best.

The P&G sales career starts at the sales representative level, where each salesperson is responsible for managing a territory of approximately 125 accounts and $4 million in annual sales. The salesperson must be a creative merchandiser entrusted with the task of creating enthusiasm for P&G products and promotions. They are also problem solvers, developing new ways of meeting their customers' needs. P&G salespeople introduce new brands and sizes, and develop plans for managing and expanding their business. P&G salespeople are compensated with a salary and a potential group bonus based on performance. Also, salespeople receive a company car and funds to cover all business expenses.

P&G salespeople are promoted into sales management on the basis of individual merit, and promotion is always from within the organization. The first step up from sales representative is the district field representative and then unit manager. Each promotion brings new assignments and increased responsibilities. Sales management at P&G involves two primary responsibilities: increasing sales volume and hiring and managing a sales staff.

P&G sales managers are responsible for two to five key accounts in their territories. They are required to work with their accounts' entire management group: advertising and merchandis-

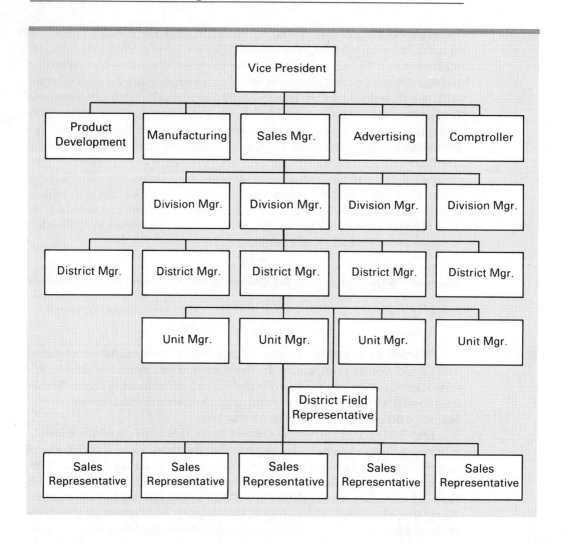

ing managers, buyers, store operations managers, warehousing
managers, and top executives. From these interactions the sales
managers are expected to develop analyses such as sales forecasts,
market trend analyses, and reports on competitors' activities.

The personnel side of the sales manager's job at P&G involves
recruiting and hiring sales trainees, leading and motivating these
sales reps, and developing them into future P&G sales managers. At
each level of sales management these two responsibilities are present. The higher up on the ladder one goes, the more responsibilities
and rewards are available.

Source: Procter & Gamble *Sales Management*, rev. October 1987.

Business used to staff its senior management from the fields of production, law, and finance. Today, however, many top managers are coming from the ranks of salespeople. The personal qualities one needs in management and leadership everywhere, such as the ability to get along with others and to influence people, are often the same traits exhibited by salespeople. Through contact with all types of people, those in sales learn to sell not only products but their company and themselves. For individuals planning to enter business for themselves, the future is brighter if they have learned to sell.

THE REWARDS OF SELLING

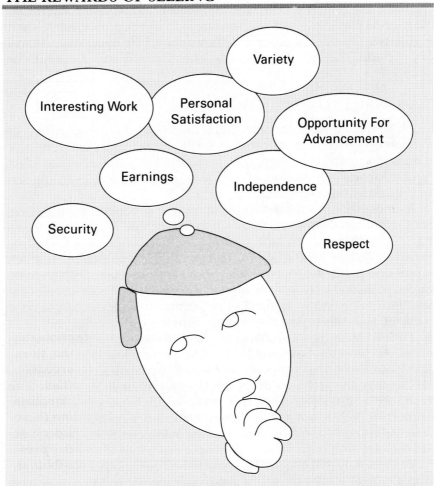

Figure 1-6 A sales career can provide an individual with many rewards, both financial and psychological.

EARNINGS

Good salespeople are paid well. Studies of college and university classes consistently show that within five years after graduation, salespeople earn more than almost any other group. In fact, some of the highest incomes in business are found in selling. In addition, selling ranks highest among many fields in above-average earnings.

Practically all salespeople are paid a salary or commission, or some combination of the two. But some people flatly refuse to enter selling strictly on a commission basis, demanding straight salary compensation. This group considers factors such as steady salary, fringe benefits, size of the company, and prestige of the company as more desirable than incentive, opportunity, or even amount of pay. The significant point is that most salespeople set their own compensation, whether they are on salary or on commission. Their income is in direct proportion to their productivity, which is measured by how much, how hard, and how well they perform. The equation is simple: The more one sells, the more one earns.

PERSONAL SATISFACTION

Dollar income is not the only kind of income a person must earn to be and feel successful. Unless a person's livelihood provides psychic income in addition to dollar income, that person is likely to feel dissatisfied. **Psychic income** is a measure of one's level of satisfaction regarding personal growth and development.

As most successful salespeople know, the process of selling offers many opportunities for one to earn psychic income. Most people find a degree of satisfaction in both meeting the needs of others and being needed. At its best, selling is a mutually profitable relationship in which buyers find better solutions to their problems and salespeople are rewarded with long-lasting accounts. On a personal level, salespeople cannot afford to be narrow-minded or self-centered if they expect to communicate with the buyers they will encounter.

The thrill of accomplishment goes beyond simply meeting the needs of a buyer, however. Salespeople also find personal satisfaction in the experience of locating buyers who will benefit from using their products. They analyze the problems of prospective buyers in order to be able to make specific proposals. Then they persuade the buyers to take advantage of their products or services. The completion of each sale is actually the recognition by the customer that the salesperson has fulfilled the purpose of selling.

To see clearly that one's efforts have benefitted another is truly gratifying. Being of service to others makes salespeople feel that they have contributed to society, making it more pleasant, more convenient, and easier for their customers. By selling satisfaction, salespeople find their own satisfaction in return.

SECURITY

Almost everyone wants a good measure of security. Some students consider a career in sales to be risky and uncertain. They contend that they can take a long-shot chance at success and enter selling, or they can choose security. But companies continue operating only if their salespeople make sales. When a recession develops, does a company fire its salespeople? As times get tougher, does the need for productive salespeople decline? Sales executives say that for people who like to sell and can sell, there is no job more secure. There have never been enough good salespeople. Consequently, the ability to sell at a profit is the most effective type of security. Indeed, it is during depressions that demand for competent salespeople is greatest. When times are bad, ineffective salespeople may be fired along with production and office personnel, but productive salespeople usually suffer no more than a drop in earnings.

INDEPENDENCE

Selling is an independent way of life. Salespeople have considerable control over their time and activities. They have so much freedom that often they are virtually in business for themselves. Each may work in a single territory, handling products, prospects, and customers in the most effective way possible. There is some supervision, of course, but salespeople, in a sense, are generally expected to develop a schedule of work and plan their call pattern to meet their customers' needs and location.

VARIETY

The very nature of selling ensures considerable variety for salespeople. Many sales jobs involve at least some travel, and this means getting out of the office and seeing new places and things. Customers and competitors change over time so salespeople get to meet and know many different people over their sales careers. The circumstances will always vary, as surely as today differs from yesterday or tomorrow and each market differs from city to city or product to product. But because no two buyers are alike and no two calls the same, salespeople find each buyer a new challenge, each call a new test.

In a broader sense, stimulating variety can be found in different markets. Sales expectations and the potential of individual markets can change overnight. Prices, for example, vary from market to market, from time to time, and even from buyer to buyer. Products often change, or they may become dated or obsolete. Promotional strategy and tactics are always being revised and improved to increase their effectiveness. New types of middlemen appear and may be added to a manufacturer's distribution channels. Selling is certainly not monotonous.

ANNUAL COMPENSATION IN 1989 FOR SALESPEOPLE COMPENSATED BY SALARY PLUS INCENTIVE

Salespeople's Average Annual Compensation

Definitions of Sales Personnel

Sales Trainee: Anyone at an entry level who is in the process of learning about the company's products, services, and policies in preparation for a regular sales assignment.

Middle-Level Salesperson: A "regular" salesperson with selling experience ranging from a beginner, who primarily contacts already established customers and accounts, to more experienced sales personnel who have a broad knowledge of products and/or services and are selling in established territories as well as developing new prospects.

Top-Level Salesperson: A salesperson at the highest level of selling responsibility who is completely familiar with the company's products, services, and policies. A salesperson at this level usually has many years of experience and is assigned to a company's major accounts or territories.

Sales Supervisor: A veteran who, due to his ability and experience, leads others. Although his primary function is to direct the activities of the sales force (and, in some cases, to train salespeople), he may also retain certain key accounts.

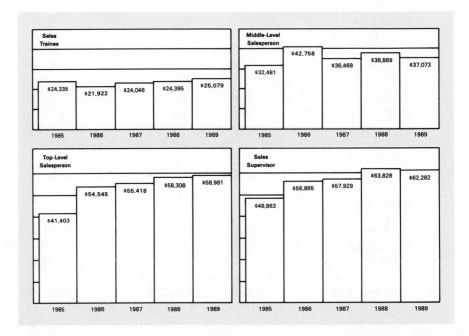

Note: Compensation equals salary plus commissions and incentives but excludes T&E (travel and entertainment) expenses. Figures for the year **1985** apply to consumer goods, industrial goods, and "other" (insurance, transportation, utilities, and services), and represent medians as calculated by Executive Compensation Service, a subsidiary of the Wyatt Co. Figures for **1986-89** represent averages compiled by Sales & Marketing Management in a survey of consumer, industrial, and service companies. CAUTION: Due to the differences between the ECS and S&MM surveys, direct comparisons between 1986-89 figures and those from previous years should not be made, since the methods involved in gathering these data differ.

SOURCES: 1985 data: Executive Compensation Service. 1986-89 data: Sales & Marketing Management

Figure 1-7a Selling ranks highest among many fields in above average earnings.

Source: "1989 Survey of Selling Costs," *Sales and Marketing Management* (February 6, 1990): 75–76. Used with permission of Bill Communications, Inc. All rights reserved.

Compensation by Industry Group

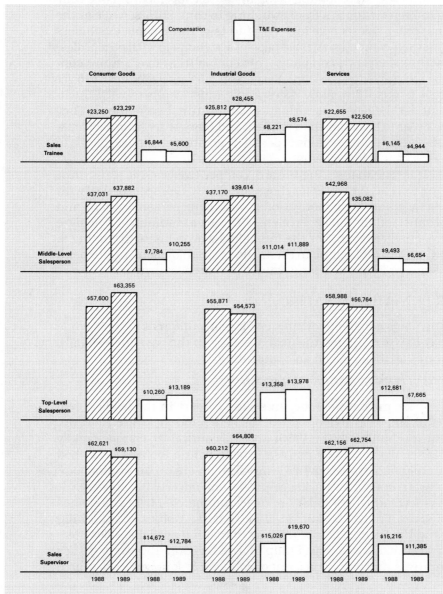

Notes: **Compensation** includes base salary, commission, and bonus. **T&E Expenses** include travel, entertainment, and food.
SOURCE: Sales & Marketing Management; *1990 Survey of Selling Costs*.

Figure 1-7b.

INTERESTING WORK

The most challenging aspect of selling is the competitive nature of salespeople. In one sense, salespeople compete with buyers as to who will influence whom. Competition is also the essence of the relationship between salespeople of competing companies. Salespeople from one company try to keep customers from switching to competitors, while at the same time other salespeople are trying to take those same customers away from their competitors. Salespeople also compete with other salespeople within their own company. This competition may involve contests to be recognized as the "top salesperson," or merely the desire to get the largest bonus. Ultimately, salespeople must compete with themselves, against their past performances and future expectations. They want each year to be better than the last, and every order from each customer to be larger than previous orders. The greatest challenge may be to exceed one's past achievements.

While it is true that selling is hard, competitive work, it is the most interesting work in the world for those who like it. Salespeople deal with human beings and their motivations, work with personal values and personal satisfaction, and experiment with various stimuli and analyze buyers' reactions to each. For the individual who delights in coming to grips with buyers and selling to them, the basic enjoyment, excitement, and satisfaction found in selling cannot be matched anywhere else.

OPPORTUNITIES IN SALES

Selling offers career opportunities for many different groups. While males may have dominated the field of selling in the past, increasingly, other groups are being given an opportunity.

OPPORTUNITIES IN SALES FOR WOMEN

In the past, most women began selling careers in the fields of real estate, retail, and door-to-door sales of cosmetics and cookware. However, opportunities changed in the 1980s and will continue to change rapidly in the 1990s. Women, such as Lisa Brown, whose job was described earlier in this chapter, are now making sales careers in computers, computer software, consumer packaged-goods, and advertising space.

In fact, few industries today are male-dominated. Major companies such as Xerox, Procter & Gamble, IBM, General Motors, Alcoa, Philip Morris, and Unisys are leading the way in making available sales positions for women. For example, Philip Morris has over 150 women sales representatives, and over 30 percent of Johnson & Johnson's sales force is female.[2]

---

[2]Rayna Skolnik, "A Woman's Place Is on the Sales Force," *Sales & Marketing Management* (April 1, 1985): 34-37.

There have been myths about women and sales. At one time, sales was thought to be too "tough" for women. However, women have proved they can be just as tough and just as persuasive in negotiations as their male counterparts. Another myth, that customers prefer to deal with men, has faded as more and more women enter the sales force. While myths fade, there are still some problems female sales representatives face. Sales, as a profession, is not immune to the problem of sexual harassment. Some male buyers may still look down on women in a sales situation and may be abusive. Others may tend to lace conversation with sexual overtones. In such instances, the buyer-seller relationship is an uncomfortable one. However, these instances are becoming much less frequent.

OPPORTUNITIES IN SALES FOR MINORITIES

Women are not the only group that is growing in the sales profession. The number of minorities, among them blacks, Hispanics, Asians, and handicapped, is also increasing in today's sales force. There are two reasons for this occurrence: first, moral and legal pressure from the civil rights laws to provide opportunities for minorities and, second, shifting population trends.

While the 1964 Civil Rights Act prompted employers to consider and hire minorities, the increased numbers of minorities on college campuses and in business degree programs now provide companies with qualified applicants. This trend is expected to continue in the 1990s.

OPPORTUNITIES FOR OLDER PEOPLE

Among the fastest growing segments of the population in the 1990s will be those 40 years old and older. Some companies are beginning to recognize the opportunity this creates and are recruiting older people who can relate better to older prospects. Companies that employ older salespeople indicate they are satisfied with their performances. In fact, it is not uncommon for salespeople 50 and older to report the highest sales volumes. Thus, good sales managers are always interested in interviewing older applicants, especially those who have been successful in sales.

Experience, knowledge, and hard work do pay; and many sales opportunities are available for older salespeople. Examples of areas where they have found success include real estate, insurance, building materials, sporting goods, health-care services, and retailing in general. Many salespeople remain very active in sales careers in their 70s and some in their 80s.

OPPORTUNITIES IN SALES FOR COLLEGE STUDENTS

Today's sales profession is very much interested in expanding interest in sales courses among college students. It not only actively recruits on college campuses, but it also provides opportunities for college students who are still in school. Many major companies such as Carnation,

IBM, Procter & Gamble, Sherwin Williams Paints, and Xerox offer opportunities to students in their internship programs. College students can combine their course work with practical, on-the-job experience that can provide compensation as well as college credit.

One internship program that has been highly successful is sponsored by IBM. After the salesperson has made the sale, college students work as sales support people and train the customer's employees on proper product usage and care. This program gives the student the experience of dealing with customers and the IBM products, while the salesperson can spend more time selling. The college student gets one advantage: the ability to list this internship on a resume as work experience. In today's competitive recruiting wars, this experience gives these students an edge on others looking for jobs.

NEGATIVE ATTITUDES

For many salespeople, much of the challenge to selling is overcoming the demands of the position. Some selling positions demand considerable travel and time away from home and family. This aspect of selling creates a pattern of irregular hours, sleep, meals, and travel. Salespeople also must see buyers at their convenience. Life insurance agents can testify to sales made in strange settings and at odd hours.

An obstacle that all salespeople encounter sometimes is buyer hostility. Some buyers raise their defenses the moment a salesperson appears. They believe they are being imposed on, and they worry the salesperson will try to take advantage of them. Some buyers have little confidence in their own abilities to analyze products, prices, and proposals. They fear making an unsound decision and an unhappy selection. This fear is converted into a fear of the salesperson. Selling to buyers who are insecure and, as a result, distrust the salesperson is not easy work, yet this is a situation that many salespeople find challenging and enjoyable.

Another common negative view is the misconception that personal selling lacks the glamour, prestige, and social status of professions such as medicine and law. Some students believe that a career in selling would be a waste of a college education. There are many students, however, who realize that selling is an attractive and lucrative profession.

Perhaps the most negative aspect is the disappointment when a sales presentation fails. Salespeople are under pressure to exceed last month's and last year's volume. Some students may think that for salespeople to succeed, they must stoop to deception, false promises, trickery, and misrepresentation. This book will dispel that notion.

Finally, many students develop negative attitudes because they lack confidence in themselves. Unfortunately, sales does involve rejection. The student must realize, however, that all professions have their level of rejection. Lawyers lose cases, doctors lose patients, and in baseball, they give million-dollar contracts to .300 hitters who fail to get a hit 70 percent of the time.

SELLING BENEFITS OUR ECONOMY AND OUR SOCIETY

Selling benefits more than just salespeople and the companies they represent. Personal selling plays a vital role in our free enterprise system and thus has an influence on our entire society.

PRODUCT/SERVICE INNOVATIONS

Competition in the marketplace exerts strong, even irresistible, pressure on sellers to produce better products and/or services. Businesses must constantly ask if they should bring out any new products or services, if there are improvements that can be made, or if there are any new uses for their present products/services. If there are unmet customer needs that can be served profitably, then business must respond.

Salespeople encourage, and often demand, the improvement of current products/services and the invention of new ones. Their plea is for products that will enable them to meet consumer needs, thereby giving them an advantage over the competition. In effect, they are asking the inventor to create and improve products, urging the engineers and production managers to manufacture the items, and encouraging the advertising manager to promote the end result.

HIGH STANDARD OF LIVING

In a real way the activities of salespeople help raise our standard of living. Salespeople influence our way of life by changing our consumption patterns. They start by helping potential customers understand how their situation could improve if they change their present habits, decisions, and products. In this particular undertaking, salespeople function as both informer and reformer.

Most people approach new products with caution, hesitation, and skepticism. People are often reluctant to accept change, preferring the old and familiar. New ideas and new products may be resisted because they disrupt routines. Customers know the old; they are not quite sure of the new; so they often delay change. That delay is ended usually by salespeople who convince consumers to spend some of their money for new and better ways of living. Price cuts, advertising, and other promotions will not prove to homeowners that they need air conditioning, trash compactors, microwave ovens, or food processors. Telephones, automobiles, vacuum cleaners, TV sets, VCRs, and clothes dryers all had to be sold.

Consumers in the United States are the best-fed, best-housed, best-clothed, best-transported, and best-entertained consumers in the world. There are more comforts of life available to more people in our economy than anywhere else. Our high standard of living relies on selling. No product or service can affect a consumer's living standard and increase that consumer's satisfaction until the consumer buys that product or service.

ECONOMIC GROWTH

The second half of the twentieth century deserves to be called the "Age of Marketing" just as much as the first half of the century can be thought of as the "Age of Production." Marketing is a major element in our economy today. As needs are identified, products and services are developed and communicated to the public at a pace that normally exceeds our demand.

Economic growth assumes continued investment because investment causes the production of additional products and services. This means more jobs, and more jobs means greater consumer buying power. Growth feeds on buying power. The cycle is something like this: marketing determines what products/services will sell; sales demand production; production forces capital investment; capital investment creates jobs; people with jobs earn income; and people with income make purchases and sales. Investors invest because salespeople assure a market for the product, thus reducing the investors' risks to an acceptable level. New companies and new products would never be financed unless salespeople could find markets for the products.

Personal selling and advertising are our two basic promotional forces. Though advertising is both desirable and necessary, it cannot do the entire marketing job for our products and services. Indeed, the greater portion of this task must be assigned to personal selling, because salespeople not only communicate a company's offerings, but they also ensure that that offering is in the right place at the right time.

ECONOMIC RECESSION

It is tempting to say that the role of salespeople diminishes when there are fewer products (shortages) or fewer buyers (recession), but this is not the case. Studies consistently show that during recessionary periods many companies continue to expand the size of their sales forces. There are at least four reasons for this expansion:

1. When there are fewer buyers, competition is even more intense. The firm that survives hard times (even just barely) will be in an excellent position once good times return.
2. Shortages of raw materials and reluctance to increase capital expenditures (on new plants or machinery) mean that most of the

competition will come not from new products but from new and better ways of selling.
3.   Neither the buyer nor the seller can afford any slack. Both must become lean and efficient. The seller cannot afford to produce something that will not sell. The buyer needs to know what will be available. The salesperson is a major source of information both for the buyer and seller.
4.   Salespeople can help the buyer make intelligent purchases and decisions by informing the buyer about: (a) other products that can substitute for products in short supply, (b) ways to use the products more efficiently, and (c) sources of financing.

SELLING LINKS THE COMPANY TO ITS CUSTOMERS

Salespeople provide a personal link between their companies and their customers (and often the rest of the outside world). The behavior and skills of salespeople reflect on the image of the company and do much to determine its success. More specifically, salespeople play three roles in the link between the company and its customers: a persuasion role, a service role, and an information role.

A PERSUASION ROLE

As the name implies, salespeople sell. That is, salespeople persuade buyers to meet their needs with the products or the service offered by the salesperson's company. How well salespeople play this role will depend on their understanding of the art of selling, which is the major focus of this text.

A SERVICE ROLE

It is not enough for salespeople simply to persuade buyers to buy products. Unless buyers get satisfaction from the products, the salesperson and the company represented will lose any chance of repeat business, and repeat business is the cornerstone of long-term success for all companies. This means that salespeople must provide service after the sale: showing the customer how to make effective and efficient use of the product, providing assistance if the product fails to perform well, and showing how the product can be used in new and better ways. This benefit to the customer results in increased sales and loyal customers for the seller.

AN INFORMATION ROLE

No matter what the product or service is, salespeople should be the most important source of information for the customer. For example,

THE SALESPERSON IS THE LINK BETWEEN MANUFACTURER AND CUSTOMER

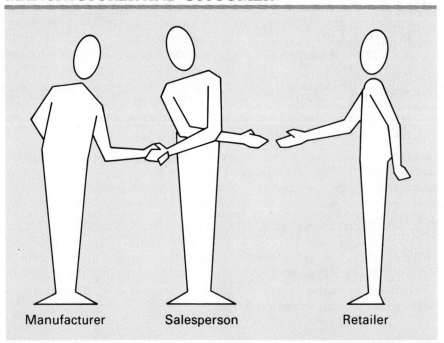

Manufacturer   Salesperson   Retailer

Figure 1-8 Manufacturers produce products that customers need and want to use. Salespeople help to make sure manufacturers can sell the products they produce and that customers can find and buy the products and services they need.

salespeople for drug manufacturers tell doctors about new drugs or new methods of using them. Grocery sales agents tell chain-store buyers about new products that will increase their gross margin per square foot of selling space. Sales associates for office equipment companies tell office managers about new word processing systems that will promote greater secretarial efficiency. Sales representatives for book publishers tell professors about new books that will help the learning process.

Salespeople are also important sources of information for the seller. They help the company plan new products by identifying and reporting customers' needs that aren't being adequately filled. And they help the company adjust its current operations by providing feedback about what the customer likes or dislikes about the way the company is doing business, and what competitors are doing.

LEARNING TO SELL

Some people believe that an individual cannot learn how to sell. This contention is based on their conception of the nature of selling and the nature of individuals. On the first point, the argument is that selling is an art and not a science, so it cannot be taught and learned. On the second point, it is believed that some individuals are born salespeople, while others just are not endowed with the ability to sell and there is little or nothing they can do about it.

The facts indicate, however, that there are certain sound principles of selling that are so long-established and proven that they are difficult to challenge. These principles can be examined and understood in a classroom and can be proven by pragmatic testing in the real world.

There are some people who are naturally better suited to sales than others. Still those without "natural" sales ability can improve the quality and increase the quantity of their sales through increased motivation and hard work. People are not born successful, whether they are farmers, doctors, merchants, manufacturers, or salespeople. Much of their success must be attributed to hard work, practice, and a fierce determination to improve. Even the innate qualities and characteristics of those with an aptitude for selling need cultivating and developing. Companies would not conduct elaborate and expensive sales training programs if the principles of personal selling could not be taught and learned.

ADVANTAGES OF COLLEGE COURSES

It certainly seems reasonable to assume that a person who enters the field of selling with no sales training would be at a disadvantage. College courses in selling can be helpful to you in several ways.

One major benefit is that you will recognize the need for training in selling. You will see that selling is a demanding, specialized activity for which preparation is necessary. Through training, one quickly discards the idea that salespeople succeed automatically because of their personal charm, a well-known name, or their "connections."

Another major benefit is that college courses serve as an introduction to selling. You learn something about what to expect, which reduces the number of situations for which you are completely unprepared. This form of preparation can help you as a future salesperson to work more intelligently and satisfactorily with your supervisor and with the sales training personnel of your company because you will know what they are trying to do. College coursework offers you the opportunity to acquire in a short time much of the fundamental selling knowledge that has been accumulated by others through years of experience. As for lesser advantages, college courses can help uncertain individuals decide whether selling is the proper field to enter. It may help all students to become better buyers. And it is a valuable adjunct to other business courses.

LIMITATIONS OF COLLEGE COURSES

Despite the need for and the value of college courses in selling, this type of instruction has limitations, as would a classroom study of swimming, for example. Schools cannot turn out salespeople in the same way that schools turn out typists, mechanics, or accountants.

The fact that a sales situation involves human beings means there are always some differences between any two sales calls, prospects, or conditions. Therefore, salespeople are called on to exercise and demonstrate originality, mental agility, and ingenuity. Experience is needed to give meaning to the principles learned in the classroom. Proficiency in selling can be acquired in no other way. For maximum progress, it is best to combine study and instruction with experimentation and practice.

NEED FOR CONTINUOUS STUDY

There is no specific time period within which selling can be learned, whether it is a quarter, two semesters, a year, or a decade. The obvious inference is that salespeople can never afford to stop learning. The minute they become complacent, they begin to stagnate and slip. Instead of feeling they have mastered the process of selling and are entitled to coast for a while, salespeople must search for new and more effective techniques if they want to ensure lasting success. They must check books and trade papers for whatever material may be of value to them. Observation and practice must not be neglected. Constructive suggestions about beneficial changes should always be welcome. By adopting and maintaining an inquiring, experimental attitude, the salesperson may avoid drifting into mental stagnation.

SUMMARY

Selling is an exciting, ever-changing profession filled with new technologies and changing methods and responsibilities. Salespeople have an obligation to keep up-to-date with these technological and methodological advances.

The modern sales attitude attempts to dismiss a negative past by focusing on the marketing concept: finding consumers' needs, and developing products/services to satisfy these needs. This modern sales attitude is the result of the increasing number of alternatives entering into the marketplace, and creating a "buyer's market." Selling must benefit both sellers and buyers!

Selling can be an attractive career because of promotional opportunities, financial rewards, the thrill of accomplishment, and the satisfaction of personal growth and development. Some of the drawbacks include irregular travel, odd hours, occasional buyer hostility, and pressure to succeed.

Selling is a noble profession because it involves introducing new products to society and educating consumers of these new products. Also, selling helps to keep the economy running by increasing consumption, encouraging production, and raising the level of employment.

Selling requires hard work, practice, determination, and continual learning of new methods and technologies. College courses can teach the basic principles of selling and can introduce salespeople to new methods and technologies, but they cannot provide the salesperson with the mental agility and ingenuity that are necessary for success in sales.

KEY TERMS

reseller	cellular phones
conference call	pagers
prospect file	airfones
personal selling	telemarketing
word processing	marketing concept
database manager	buyer's market
spreadsheet analysis	psychic income
graphics software	consumption
electronic mail	production
vertical software	employment
facsimile (fax) machines	

REVIEW QUESTIONS

1. What are the new technologies that are being used in selling?
2. Why is telemarketing becoming popular?
3. What new responsibilities face today's salespeople?
4. What is meant by the *modern sales attitude*?
5. What has happened to cause today's buyer's market?
6. Why is personal selling an essential activity?
7. Why is sales an attractive career?
8. Why do salespeople push for new and better products?
9. How do salespeople raise our standard of living?
10. Where does selling fit into the cycle of economic growth?
11. What information do salespeople provide their employers?
12. What are the two primary compensation methods for salespeople?
13. How can your college courses help you become a better salesperson?
14. What are the limitations of college courses?

DISCUSSION QUESTIONS

1. Given the ever-changing nature of sales in the 1990s, what should you, the potential salesperson, do now while in college to separate you from your competition (other college graduates)?
2. Can you locate any other technologies, methods, and responsibili-

ties in the trade journals and business periodicals that may change the face of sales in the year 2000 and beyond?

3. Think of the salespeople you know personally. Do they conduct themselves under the modern sales attitude? What do you like/dislike about those who adhere to the modern sales attitude, and what do you like/dislike about those who still conduct themselves under the old sales attitude?

4. How do the promotional opportunities of salespeople compare to those in other professions?

CASE 1-1   IS SALES A CHALLENGING CAREER?

Jim Longwell has almost completed the requirements for his Associate of Arts Degree at Miami-Dade Junior College in Miami, Florida. He was born in New Jersey but moved to Miami when his father was transferred there. His father is a computer technician with IBM.

Jim is trying to decide what career he should follow when he gets his degree. He has interviewed with about ten companies and has several job offers. While in school he worked part-time as a sales clerk in a retail department store and was a waiter at Bennigan's Restaurant. He also belonged to a couple of school clubs but still managed to make good grades. Jim has been impressed by most of the companies he has talked to, but the jobs that are paying the most are in sales. Jim likes to work with people and is attracted to the flexibility and challenge of a sales career. He also likes the fact that part of his income from a sales job will be on commission; so, if he works harder he will make more money. Two of the companies are providing a car; and since his is a seven-year-old clunker, it would be nice to be given one by the company he goes to work for.

Jim's problem is his dad. He has discussed the different jobs with his dad several times; and every time Jim mentions sales jobs, his dad says: "Can't you find something better than sales? You didn't need to go to college to get a sales job." Jim has come to Professor Neidel, head of the Business Administration Division, to ask his advice.

CASE QUESTIONS

1. Did Jim need to get his degree at the community college to be a success in sales?

2. Is sales a prestigious enough career for a person with an Associate of Arts Degree? Why?

3. What can Professor Neidel tell Jim about a sales career that will help him convince his father to accept sales as a good career option?

CHAPTER 2
The Job of Personal Selling: Traits and Tasks

After studying this chapter, you should be able to:

- Name and explain the obligations of salespeople
- Distinguish among different types of selling jobs
- List eight psychological characteristics that are commonly mentioned as essential to successful selling
- Point out social characteristics that help salespeople
- Comment on the physical characteristics of salespeople
- Define a great salesperson

The modern sales attitude that characterizes today's salesperson is based on the increasingly sophisticated sales position descriptions adopted by most successful selling organizations. All salespeople have some similar obligations for which they are responsible. These will be discussed in the first section. The second section discusses job descriptions of several different types of sales representatives. The third section looks at the characteristics shared by successful salespeople. And finally, the chapter concludes by looking at how great salespeople are made.

ALL SALESPEOPLE HAVE SIMILAR OBLIGATIONS

We begin by examining the basic duties that apply to every person in the selling field.

JOB DUTIES

A salesperson's basic duties fall into three major areas: direct selling duties, auxiliary selling duties, and nonselling duties. Figure 2-1 provides examples of each.

DIRECT SELLING DUTIES

The basic responsibility of salespeople is to satisfy the needs of their customers. If salespeople can do this effectively, they will make sales in

OUTLINE FOR A JOB DESCRIPTION HAVING GENERAL APPLICATION

Sales:
Make regular calls.
Sell the line, demonstrate.
Handle questions and objections.
Check stock—discover possible product uses.
Interpret selling points and features and benefits of the product/service to customers.
Ascertain customers' potential needs.
Emphasize quality.
Explain company policies on price, delivery, and credit.
Get the order.
Follow up on the sale.

Services:
Install product or display.
Report product weaknesses, complaints.
Handle adjustments, returns, and allowances.
Handle requests for credit.
Handle special orders for customers.
Establish priorities, if any.
Analyze local conditions for customers.

Territory Management:
Arrange route for best coverage.
Balance effort with customer against potential.
Maintain sales portfolio, samples, kits.

Sales Promotion:
Develop new prospects and new accounts.
Distribute home office literature, catalogs, desk pieces.
Make calls with customers' salespeople.
Train jobbers' personnel.
Present survey reports, layouts, and proposals.

Executive:
Each night make a daily work plan for the next day.
Organize field activity for minimum travel and maximum calls.
Prepare and submit special reports on trends, competition.
Prepare and submit daily reports to home office.
Collect and submit statistical data requested by home office.
Investigate lost sales and the reasons for loss.
Prepare reports on developments, trends, new objections, and new ideas on meeting objections.
Attend sales meetings.
Build a prospect list.

Collect overdue accounts; report faulty accounts.
Collect credit information.

Goodwill:
Counsel customers on their problems.
Maintain loyalty and respect for firm represented.
Attend local sales meetings held by customers.

Figure 2-1 This outline—taken from *Sales Training for the Smaller Manufacturer*, a Small Business Administration publication by Kenneth Lawyer—gives a good summary of a salesperson's duties and responsibilities.

spite of their competitor's selling efforts, which will result in achieving their sales quota. In order to do this, salespeople must gather information to use in approaching customers, sell to them via a presentation and demonstration, answer their questions, and get them to commit to buying the product or service. Salespeople must show ultimate consumers how to enhance their self-concept and business buyers how to increase their companies' sales or reduce their costs. They must attract new customers, and maintain and increase sales to present customers. Both customer and salesperson must benefit from sales transactions; this usually involves a period of time and a number of transactions. To make sales, an individual must have the need and the will to succeed at selling, and must be a successful communicator. Simply said, the salesperson's selling responsibility refers to all of those activities that are directed toward selling to a particular customer.

AUXILIARY SELLING DUTIES

To succeed in selling, most salespeople must perform certain auxiliary, or indirect, selling duties. Practically all salespeople perform such services for buyers, perhaps before the first sale, sometimes after getting an order. For example, manufacturers' salespeople help their retailers by building and maintaining displays and by checking inventories. Some calls by salespeople are literally service calls. By following up first sales, by counseling buyers on their problems, and by working with their customers whenever possible, salespeople establish loyal customers and friends, not just sales. Salespeople handle most complaints and make some adjustments. In conclusion, auxiliary selling duties are those that improve the image of the company and the salesperson, by showing an interest in their customer outside of the sale.

NONSELLING DUTIES

All salespeople must manage and develop themselves through sound planning and control, which often means cooperating with company sales trainers and supervisors. Most salespeople must attend sales meetings, trade shows, and conventions (see Figure 2-2).

Communication takes time. Salespeople in the field should read communications sent out by their firms, and their reports to their sales managers should be correct and prompt. The credit manager may expect the salespeople to collect financial information about buyers and even collect on past-due accounts. The sales manager will want information about what competitors are doing, so other market research tasks may be assigned. Finally, some salespeople are expected to be active in public relations, at trade shows or in the community. The ultimate goal is to increase goodwill.

THE SALESPERSON'S OBLIGATIONS TO THE EMPLOYER

Salespeople are responsible to their employers and to their prospects and customers. This section and the next review these obligations.

SELLING AT A PROFIT

From the company's point of view, the salesperson's primary long-range duty is to sell at a profit. The company wants to continue in business, and this will not be possible unless its operation is profitable. Salespeople can best serve personal interests and those of the employer by being of maximum benefit and assistance to the customers.

Selling at a profit demands that the salesperson explore the assigned territory and analyze it to find out just how much opportunity is present. Having determined the sales potential of an area, the salesperson proceeds to draft a specific, detailed program for developing profitable sales. If a new territory is being opened, prospects must first be identified and converted into customers. In an established territory, the program involves maintaining present customers, increasing their purchasing level, and adding new customers.

WORKING INDUSTRIOUSLY

In hiring a salesperson, the company assumes the risks involved with any new employee; the salesperson should justify this risk. In training the salesperson, the company spends both time and money; the salesperson should justify this expenditure. Salespeople must put forth the effort necessary to do a successful job. They must be efficient managers—always in control, purposeful, and active. Their time and energy should be budgeted wisely in order to get the greatest possible return from their efforts.

When working at peak efficiency and keeping fit and busy, the salesperson can rely on the law of averages. This is possible because few relationships are more basically sound than the one between calls and presentations, and presentations and sales. In this case, the law of averages says, if the salesperson makes enough calls on properly qualified prospects, there will be a satisfactory number of presentations and an acceptable volume of sales.

COOPERATING WITH OTHERS

Salespeople should try to fit into the culture and spirit of the organization, learning as much about the company as possible. They must work in harmony with the rest of the organization so that a healthy team spirit of cooperation can prevail. Numerous situations require cooperation: the credit manager and the opening of new accounts, the sales promotion manager and the influencing of dealers to use display material, the advertising manager and the letters of inquiry from prospects, and the production manager and the scheduling of a rush order.

THE SALESPERSON'S OBLIGATIONS TO CUSTOMERS

Salespeople have the primary obligations of providing fair treatment to customers and assisting them in finding answers to their needs.

GIVING FAIR TREATMENT TO CUSTOMERS

The relationship between a salesperson and a customer must be characterized by mutual loyalty, trust, and dependence. Salespeople must respect the customer's position, policies, and time. In return, the salesperson hopes to earn the customer's confidence and goodwill.

To treat customers fairly, a salesperson should truly believe the customer will benefit from the purchase before offering the product or service. Here's a good "fair-treatment" test: If a salesperson can assume the role of customer and buy what is being offered, the purchase can be recommended. Otherwise, the salesperson should find another prospect who truly needs the product/service.

Sometimes fair treatment to the customer competes with fair treatment to the salesperson's company. In the case of a complaint or a request for an adjustment, salespeople may find themselves in the middle of a conflict of interest, owing something to both the customer and the company. There is no universally applicable rule. Whatever action is taken, the salesperson must be honest and fair to both, doing nothing to damage personal independence and self-respect.

GIVING ASSISTANCE TO CUSTOMERS

Because individuals have unlimited desires with limited purchasing power, they need assistance in approaching their level of satisfaction. In general, consumers want increased gratification, whereas business buyers want to make or save more money. In providing assistance, salespeople must be qualified to serve. If they plan to act as experts, they should be experts. If they want to function as advisers on purchasing, they should have enough information to perform that function adequately.

In fulfilling the obligation to help prospects and customers, the salesperson must give whatever assistance is available, regardless of whether the prospect buys or not. Prospects and customers have problems, and they need help in solving them on nonbuying days as well as on days when purchases are made. Whether there is a large order or no order at all, the salesperson should be a friendly counselor, and work to build a firm long-term relationship.

PERSONAL SELLING JOB DESCRIPTIONS

Personal selling jobs can be divided into trade selling, which includes both selling to middlemen and missionary selling, selling to purchasing agents, and selling to ultimate consumers.

TRADE SELLING

The primary objective for trade salespeople is to increase the sales of their companies' products to wholesalers and retailers. Wholesalers and retailers often are called middlemen because they are in the middle of the channel of distribution, between manufacturers and consumers. This is shown in Figure 2-2.

Three principal relationships exist when selling merchandise to middlemen for resale. First, a manufacturer's salesperson can sell to **wholesalers**. Second, a manufacturer's salesperson can sell to **retailers**. Third, a wholesaler's salesperson can sell to retailers. Often the same individual will sell to more than one type of buyer. Thus, a manufacturer's representative (salesperson) may sell to both wholesalers and retailers, to wholesalers and institutions, or to wholesalers and chain store warehouses. A wholesaler's salesperson may sell to retailers, to business and industrial buyers, and may even sell to other wholesalers.

CHANNEL OF DISTRIBUTION

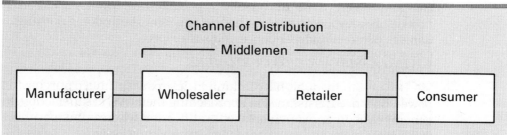

Figure 2-2 Wholesalers and retailers are middlemen in the channel of distribution.

Middlemen display a wide range of buying skills, but in one respect they are identical: they buy mainly in response to rational, not emotional, motivation. Their principal concern is to make a profit, and they know that the only way to increase profits is to increase sales volume and to reduce costs. Wholesalers and retailers think in terms of inventory requirements, turnover, unit and dollar sales volume, markdowns, and margins. The manufacturer, the wholesaler, and the retailer all know that merchandise is completely and satisfactorily sold only when the ultimate consumer buys, consumes, and returns to buy more. Thus, middlemen are serving ultimate consumers and themselves when they buy with **rational motivation**.

Selling to middlemen for resale sometimes consists of more **service selling** than **creative selling**. Service selling is little more than finding buyers who know what they want, and taking their orders.

In creative selling, the salesperson discovers a customer need of which the customer was unaware and sells a product as the answer to that need. The salesperson must have the foresight to recognize this need and to point this need out to the customer in such a way that the customer does not feel uneasy. Then, the salesperson must promote his or her product or service as the solution to the customer's need.

REGULAR MIDDLEMAN-SELLING SALESPEOPLE

A salesperson who sells to middlemen may work for a manufacturer and call on wholesalers and retailers, or may work for a wholesaler and call on retailers. The products sold to these two types of middlemen are **items for resale**, not for use by the wholesaler or the retailer in the operation of the business. For example, this type of salesperson sells toothpaste, not a cash register, to a drugstore, or sells canned food, not refrigeration equipment or display racks, to a grocery store.

Features of the Job. The regular middleman-selling salesperson travels over a planned route in a sequence. Through a pattern of regular visits, each buyer knows when to expect the salesperson. This salesperson may make numerous calls each day. The job provides the individual with a considerable amount of security in the form of a regular daily pattern and often a straight salary.

The regular salesperson who sells to middlemen does practice a modest amount of creative selling, such as identifying prospects and converting them into customers. Occasionally, a salesperson may discover an overlooked need of a regular buyer and then sell the product that best fills that need. This, too, is creative selling. Finally, getting promotional support from a wholesaler or retailer often requires creative selling. Manufacturers pay for product displays, prime shelf space, and other promotional advantages through special deals and other incentives. With so many companies fighting for the best displays and prime shelf space, it is not always easy for salespeople to convince retailers to carry their products.

For the most part, however, a middleman-selling salesperson writes up reorders of products for established customers. In one sense, this service selling makes the salesperson's call more of a friendly visit than a product-promoting conference. Clearly, friendship between buyer and seller plays a vital role in this type of selling.

Creative Selling Duties.   Besides the creative selling to wholesalers and retailers that was previously mentioned, there is one area of selling to middlemen for resale in which creative selling ability is most essential—the new-product area. Products can be new in regard to the name of the product or the nature of the product. When the name of the product is new to buyers, the salesperson must sell against a group of brands already known and established. For example, creative selling would be useful in introducing to the Pacific Coast market a product formerly marketed only east of the Rockies. An example of placing a new product on the market was Panasonic's addition of a facsimile machine to its line of office products and other electronic equipment.

When the nature of the product is new to buyers, the demand for creative selling is even stronger. Salespeople must maintain sufficient knowledge of the new product. For example, both videocassette recorders and personal computers, when first offered to middlemen, were so revolutionary that educational brochures, product demonstrations, and extensive middleman training were necessary before middlemen would stock them. Middlemen stock new types of products with reluctance. They may fear that the item is ahead of its time, overpriced, a fad, or defective. Placing a different type of product on the market takes a pioneering effort. Effective creative selling along with informative advertising can open new markets.

Service Selling Duties.   As mentioned, service selling is a big part of a regular middleman-selling salesperson's job. Usually the seller and the buyer have been doing business with each other for some time, so the products are generally well known to the middleman and, more important, to the middleman's customers. The salesperson's job is largely one of regular contact and service. The customers are steady, and the salesperson's task is to retain them, by keeping the middlemen stocked at all times with an adequate supply of merchandise. Much of the salesperson's time is occupied with writing up reorders after checking the middleman's stock and looking at the middleman's **want book**, when available. (A want book is a notebook, or with more advanced retailers a computerized order file, in which the retailer lists the items that will soon need to be replenished.) Thus, while it is true that the service salesperson hopes to expand present accounts, his or her main concern is for continued patronage.

Nonselling Duties.   Middleman-selling salespeople perform a variety of nonselling duties, because either they think they should or their companies require them to. Collecting past-due accounts is one such duty. Handling complaints is another. Counseling is a broader nonselling duty that may have to do with any of the buyer's problems. Another, even more general, duty of the salesperson would be striving for goodwill, for both company and self.

Selling to Retailers for Wholesalers.   Salespeople who work for a wholesaler typically call on three types of buyers: retailers, industrial buyers, and other wholesalers. Their interest is in selling merchandise to wholesalers and retailers for resale. When salespeople sell to industrial buyers, they are dealing with purchasing agents, and that area of selling will be discussed later.

Wholesalers stock thousands of items. In the grocery field, the number is often 120,000 or more; in pharmaceuticals, 70,000 is not uncommon; in hardware, a figure of 60,000 is not unusual. This means, of course, that the wholesaler's salespeople must know something about an extremely wide range of products. Furthermore, they cannot take much time selling any specific product because of time constraints.

In the pharmaceuticals field, most retail druggists want advice and assistance from wholesalers on various problems concerning retail store operation. The type of assistance they most want is in selling merchandise to the consumer. This typically includes two major services: sales promotion assistance and help in training retail store clerks. Others will request information about successful promotions by other druggists, and some will ask salespeople to advise them on what to display and how to display it.

A primary function of the wholesaler's salesperson is to keep reorders coming in. Because products and prices are nearly identical to those of competing wholesalers, the salesperson must find some unique selling points to stress.

· ***Requirements.***   For any creative selling, salespeople who sell to middlemen will need to be confident and, in some cases, aggressive. These salespeople must have initiative, enthusiasm, and resourcefulness to be successful. Service selling, on the other hand, calls for a different set of requirements. Since service is not tangible, salespeople who sell a service must develop a stronger degree of trust and credibility with the customer through examples of their expertise. Because of the repetitive nature of the calling, sincerity and dependability are also necessary for success, as well as persistence. The most obvious example of a trade salesperson is the consumer packaged-goods sales representative. These salespeople represent such well-known companies as Procter & Gamble, Beecham, and Nabisco.

Figure 2-3 Salespeople often are responsible for setting up and maintaining large store displays of their products.

At Beecham, the sales representative has four main responsibilities when on a sales call, and each relates to one of the four marketing mix variables. Figure 2-4 shows how the Beecham sales representative views the marketing mix. All companies are concerned with these four variables, although they may use different terminology to describe it. At Nabisco, sales representatives are shown a target as to where their Nabisco products should be located on the grocer's shelf, including the implied degree of attractiveness that is expected. Moreover, as described in Figure 2-6, they are given specific instructions on selling and merchandising in their sales manuals.

MISSIONARY SALESPEOPLE

Missionary salespeople work for manufacturers and are relatively prominent in the marketing of pharmaceuticals, tobacco, food, textbooks, and hardware products. The primary duty of the missionary sales-

THE MARKETING MIX ACCORDING TO BEECHAM

Product:	To Beecham salespeople, the actual product is an afterthought; it has already been produced. Their responsibility is to make sure that all sizes and styles of their product have been distributed and are on the shelves in each store.
Place:	Placement to Beecham sales reps means shelf position. Their responsibility is to maximize the amount of shelf space allocated to their product, and to get the prime position (eye level) on the shelf. If Beecham has a 15 percent market share in the toothpaste category, the sales reps should achieve at least 15 percent of the shelf space allocated to toothpaste in that store.
Price:	The pricing responsibility has lessened in recent years because of the universal pricing code (UPC) and unit pricing. The price of the product is on computer and is not likely to change week to week as in the past.
Promotion:	Beecham sales reps are required to sell two promotions on each sales call. This could be a coupon, a display, a deal, etc.

Figure 2-4 The responsibilities of salespeople at Beecham relate to each of the four marketing mix variables: product, place, price, and promotion.
Source: Information provided courtesy of Beecham Products.

person is to move the manufacturer's products faster and in larger volume through the use of techniques that are more indirect than direct. These salespeople work to promote their customers' sales, thus increasing their company's sales.

Features of the Job.   The most common situation finds a manufacturer's missionary salesperson calling on wholesalers to develop greater interest in and support for the manufacturer's line of goods. Arrangements may be made for the missionary salesperson to talk to the wholesaler's salespeople. The follow-up might well be for the missionary salesperson to travel for a short time with each of the wholesaler's salespeople, making calls on the wholesaler's prospects and customers.

Another situation finds the missionary salesperson calling alone on retailers who might, or do, stock the manufacturer's merchandise. Still another possibility is found in industrial selling. A manufacturer who supplies fabricating materials or parts to other manufacturers might employ missionary salespeople to keep in close touch with those manufacturers.

Creative Selling Duties.   Another objective of the missionary salesperson is to stimulate the wholesaler's business by writing up a

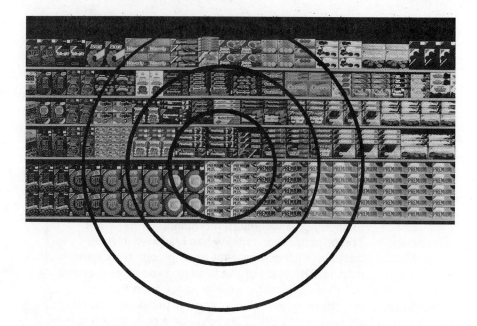

Figure 2-5 Nabisco wants the salesperson to make its products look attractive on the shelf.

Source: Courtesy of Nabisco Biscuit Company

larger order than the wholesaler's salesperson would have written by calling alone. In other words, the objective is to improve, at least temporarily, a circumstance common to many manufacturers—the failure of wholesalers to push the manufacturer's products.

To achieve these goals, the missionary salesperson in most instances must persuade the retailer to stock a larger quantity of the manufacturer's goods. This can be quite a challenge when the manufacturer is launching new products on the market. In this case, the missionary salesperson wants to obtain the best location in the store for the line and to be given excellent shelf position in that location. Finally, the missionary salesperson wants as much retail support as can be obtained. This includes displaying the merchandise, advertising the merchandise, and putting stronger personal selling behind it.

Service Selling Duties. Service selling is obviously neither an adequate nor an appropriate assignment for a missionary salesperson. Of course, the missionary salesperson can write up an order for a retailer's needs while the wholesaler's salesperson is busy with other matters, but then the missionary salesperson must move immediately into creative selling or into performing services for the retailer.

NABISCO BISCUIT COMPANY SALES REPRESENTATIVES SELLING AND MERCHANDISING RESPONSIBILITIES

BASIC

Promote the sales of Nabisco Biscuit Company products to the trade in a designated geographical area assigned by management. This responsibility also includes the maintenance or expansion of customer/consumer relations to perpetuate the positive image of the company.

SPECIFICS — SELLING

- Establish positive communications with all levels of your trade—from Store Supervisor through all levels of employees.
- Learn to use communication and diplomacy in overcoming and handling customer objections.
- Maintain total knowledge of product line features and benefits **as well as competitive lines** necessary to sell the customer on **your** products.
- Study the geography of the district, present and potential customer locations.
- Identify account needs relative to Nabisco products and services.
- Develop efficient routing of calls, deliveries, call levels, etc., for a smooth running district.
- Get to know customers to determine proper approach for each.
- Write orders.
- Familiarize yourself with allowances, contracts, or other ''deal'' information.
- Establish sales objectives with every key account.
- Organize what you **want** to sell prior to each call **before** you call.
- Present your sales story enthusiastically!
- Use **Merchandising Proposals** as selling aids to communicate your sales plans more clearly to customers.
- Follow up **after** the sale or promotion using **Profit Feedback** or **results** of the sale. This ''tool'' becomes an ideal ''opener'' for your next presentation!
- Compute Gross Margin/Markup as it relates to reporting pricing and profit. Be familiar with the difference and how to use each in presenting the Nabisco profit story.

SPECIFICS — MERCHANDISING

- Sell and maintain the ''vertical by brand/company'' concept of merchandising the Nabisco product line.
- Sell and maintain ''out of department'' items.
- Sell and maintain ''multiple'' facings, plus all regional programs.

- Sell and maintain total stock rotation, shelves, store rooms, displays.
- Analyze and sell order control/inventory records.
- Sell "best-in-store locations" for departments, displays.
- Know each account's store "traffic" flow.
- Use POS (point of sale) materials including signs, posters, dumps, easels, etc.
- Sell "another" display, never settle on a specific number of displays! Always room for "one more"!
- Sell and maintain "tie-in" displays, promotions with other products.
- Sell and maintain the leadership role in setting, remodeling of departments with the customer.
- Develop **written** Plan-O-Grams to sell the concept of department resets.
- Know the "best food days" in your store.
- Sell allowances or other incentives.
- Use and care for: sales builder kit, hand-held computer terminal, marking equipment, and other tools.
- Express appreciation for all business obtained.

Figure 2-6 The responsibilities of the Nabisco Biscuit Company sales representative include specific selling and merchandising responsibilities.
Source: Courtesy of Nabisco Biscuit Company

Nonselling Duties.   Missionary salespeople must be merchandising salespeople and, to some degree, management salespeople. If they build store traffic and sales volume for retailers, and if they are able to improve their management techniques, they build goodwill, confidence, and profits for their employers.

One of the most effective techniques for the missionary salesperson is the **service approach**. (This is not to be confused with service selling, which is little more than filling the retailers' requests.) In calling on retailers, the missionary salesperson has an excellent opportunity to offer services such as point-of-purchase materials, even going so far as to change a retailer's window display or to build a floor display of the products. The salesperson can help retailers with their advertising and can teach the retailer and its sales staff about the merchandise, especially how to sell more of it more profitably. As an adviser on management problems, the missionary salesperson may analyze some of the retailer's problems and make recommendations. Such problems might involve store equipment, store layout, organization, credit, records, special promotion events, or customer services.

Requirements.   Missionary salespeople must be broadly informed and highly competent salespeople for two reasons. First, their assignments are varied and challenging. They must be experts in their product line; and know more than a little about the buyer's business. Second, the buyers seen by a missionary salesperson present a special type of challenge. Retailers may feel they are in for a matching of wits with a high-powered specialist when faced with an accompanied salesperson. As for calling on wholesalers, getting them to show even a bit more interest in a manufacturer's products is not easy.

SELLING TO PURCHASING AGENTS

Purchasing agents are professional buyers who are responsible for the procurement function in their organization. The authority and activities of purchasing agents vary from organization to organization depending on management philosophy. A salesperson must sell to the person who makes the organization's purchases—the purchasing agent.

FEATURES OF THE JOB

In selling to purchasing agents, the salesperson considers three important areas: the market, the nature of purchasing agents' buying, and the general nature of selling to purchasing agents.

The Market.   Many of the industries for which purchasing agents buy are actually very limited markets. The automotive industry, the aluminum industry, and the tobacco industry are examples of markets consisting of a relatively small number of buyers. Because buyers are few, 65 to 70 percent of an industry often is found in just a few locations.

The individual buyers making up the industrial market are experts in buying. The contrast between their purchasing skill and that of the typical consumer is impressive. Purchasing agents normally are trained thoroughly for their roles. In addition, most of them are experienced, cost-conscious buyers. Spending a company's money makes their accountability for purchases more serious and stricter than that of a consumer.

Purchasing agents are also rational buyers. Whereas consumers can gratify some or many of their emotional desires, purchasing agents generally cannot. Because their purchases are considered good or bad depending on whether profits go up or down, purchasing agents must try to act only on rational motivations. Unfortunately, advertising and sales promotion are usually more effective in appealing to a person's emotions than to reason, so they are of limited use to salespeople who sell to the industrial market. Purchasing agents are less influenced by these two marketing forces than are consumers or even middlemen buying for resale.

Nature of Purchasing Agents' Buying.   Purchasing agents buy from a number of suppliers: manufacturers, industrial distributors, mill supply firms, and sometimes wholesalers. There is much more direct buying from the manufacturer and less buying from middlemen than is found in the marketing of consumer goods. Several vendors are usually considered before a purchase is made.

The nature of the buying done by purchasing agents is based on a **derived demand**, or the result of actual or anticipated buying by consumers. If the sales force of the buyer's company is not moving merchandise, no salesperson on earth can persuade the purchasing agent of that company to buy on a larger scale. In the case of capital items, the purchasing agent may not buy anything new for years. This makes infrequent purchase a feature for certain types of products. For many industrial goods, the business cycle is a significant factor. The natural longevity of some items, such as railroad cars or turbines, can be extended even further by a relatively small increase in maintenance costs. As a result, replacement of such items can be postponed when times are bad.

The fact that certain purchases are made by a group of company officials suggests a few other features of purchasing agents' buying. For example, the determination of need can originate in one or more departments. When a salesperson does not know which individuals can request a particular type of product and does not know the relative influence of the members of the buying group, the question is one of whom to see. Suppose the salesperson is selling industrial lubricants. What voice does the production manager have in such a purchase? What about the chief engineer, the plant engineer, and the plant superintendent?

General Nature of Selling to Purchasing Agents.   Selling efforts directed at purchasing agents are influenced by the buyers themselves and by the character of their buying. With many product lines, the salesperson makes only a few sales, but each one is large. Often the salesperson can predict when a certain buyer will be buying and can even make a shrewd guess as to when this buyer will begin thinking seriously about buying. Because buyers can postpone certain purchases for years, the negotiation phase can extend over a long period of time.

Prices must be quoted or negotiated when a product is to be built to the specifications of a single buyer. If the salesperson's customer is also a manufacturer, that customer can be the salesperson's most dangerous competition in the sale of products such as parts. The customer has the choice of producing certain parts or of buying them.

Often the salesperson is active with the account both before and after the actual sale. The first task in many situations is to determine the buyer's need. Where appropriate, the salesperson may ask for permission to make a survey of the buyer's circumstances. If she or he finds a need exists, the salesperson might convince the customer of the need for a demonstration, hoping thereby to make a sale. After the sale, the salesperson could install or help to install the product and supervise the product's maintenance. If the buyer's employees must be trained to use the product, the salesperson might conduct the training. Finally, the salesperson must help the buyer solve problems involving the product.

Requirements.   For most selling to purchasing agents, the salesperson needs a dual background consisting of a technical specialty plus marketing training. Engineering, accounting, chemistry, or electronics

---

HIGHLIGHT 2-1   *Industrial Sales Description: CMS-Gilbreth Packaging Systems*

At CMS-Gilbreth Packaging Systems, the company's sales agents work with sales support people to satisfy their client's production needs. CMS-Gilbreth manufactures assembly-line machines that apply polyvinyl chloride shrink wrap to the lids of such products as Hellmann's Mayonnaise, Light & Lively Yogurt, and Häagen-Dazs Ice Cream. Shrink wrap provides the consumer with evidence that the product has not been opened or tampered with. If the shrink wrap is secure, the product has not been opened. It provides the company with an added measure to keep their product's lid on and the product fresh, and a means of showing their customers that they care about consumer protection.

The CMS-Gilbreth sales agent must work with each customer to customize the machine for its assembly line. Thus, the sales agent needs to be able to read blueprints and develop specifications for modifying the machine to fit the customer's needs. This involves calling on different levels within the buyer's company besides the purchasing agent, developing product specifications, and relating these specifications to the sales support person who works with CMS-Gilbreth engineers to determine if the machine can be modified. The sales support person then advises the sales agent on how to further advance toward the sale.

As you can imagine, these machines are very expensive and the process of selling them to a company can go on for months before a decision has been made. Salespeople need to be patient, and must be able to deal not only with many buyers within the customer's organization, but also with support people within their own organization.

Source: Information received from Lisa Notturno, Sales Coordinator for CMS-Gilbreth Packaging Systems.

might be the specialty which must be understood to complement the selling function. In some lines, a person with a marketing background can be taught by the employer much of the specialized knowledge required. In other lines, specialists or technicians can be hired and given the necessary training in selling. If the item being sold is very complex, the salesperson should be accompanied on sales calls by experts from his

---

HIGHLIGHT 2-2 *Pharmaceutical Sales Description: Merrell Dow Pharmaceuticals*

Salespeople who work for Merrell Dow Pharmaceuticals are detailers. They call on doctors to promote their prescription drugs, and on druggists to make sure that the product is available for those patients coming in with prescriptions.

The real challenge facing Merrell Dow salespeople, according to Bob Ott, sales manager for the Louisiana district, is getting to see the doctors. Doctors are very busy people and can rarely offer the salespeople more than five minutes if they can see them at all. To complicate matters, there are two levels of barriers shielding representatives from the doctors. The first line of protection for doctors is the receptionist. Salespeople must cultivate relationships with receptionists, or they will never get to see the doctor.

After the receptionist, the second barrier is often the nurse. The nurse is there to provide further insulation for the physician. Again, the nurse must be treated with respect. Simply said, few salespeople get to see the doctor. Those who do have earned it by befriending those in charge of protecting the doctor's time. Meeting this challenge brings great pride to those who consistently see the doctor.

To improve their chances of seeing the doctor, the Merrell Dow sales representatives are provided with sales support items to use to befriend the receptionist and the nurse. Note pads, posters, nutrition books, diet guides, and other such items are offered to show appreciation. These are not considered "gifts" because they are not given in a personal context. Instead, these items are provided to aid the receptionist and the nurse in doing their jobs. Diet guides and nutrition books, for example, can be used to take better care of patients.

Source: Information received from Bob Ott, sales manager, Merrell Dow Pharmaceuticals.

or her company, and may even be asked to serve a lengthy apprenticeship before taking over a territory.

In selling to purchasing agents, salespeople need a thorough understanding of what their technical products or intangibles can do for buyers. They need the ingenuity necessary to see how their present products can be adapted to provide better solutions to buyers' problems. And the salespeople must be keen enough to spot waste, inefficiency, and unnecessary expense of which the buyer is unaware. This requires an analytical mind and a knowledge of the production, equipment, and operating problems of plants.

SELLING TO ULTIMATE CONSUMERS

Salespeople who sell to ultimate consumers may perform their selling activities either in retail stores or in the consumer's home or office.

SELLING IN RETAIL STORES

Of all types of selling, the least complex type is found inside most retail stores. There are some retailers that require salespeople who have

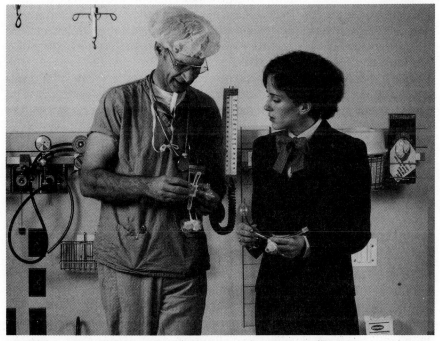

Figure 2-7 Pharmaceutical representatives must make good use of their time with the doctor.

Source: Photo courtesy of Mallinckrodt Division, Avon Products, Inc.

strong creative selling skills and product expertise. These retailers handle high-priced products such as personal computers, computer software, and furniture. However, the bulk of the transactions over the counter are purchases rather than sales.

Typically, customers seek out the retail store in which they expect to find what they want and may even seek out a favorite salesperson. For instance, a customer comes in, selects two ties, tells a salesclerk that he wants them, pays for them, gets the ties and a "thank you" from the salesclerk, and the purchase is completed. This is another example of service selling. If the same retail salesclerk had sold a better-quality tie to the customer, had sold three ties instead of two, or had sold three shirts to the customer in addition to the ties, that would have been creative selling.

Many retailers expect their salespeople to practice service selling, whereby the salesperson acts primarily as an attendant. However, there are some retailers, such as Nordstrom's, a large department store chain on the West Coast, who encourage their salespeople to practice creative selling. Competition appears to be pushing retail selling more in this direction.

Duties of Retail Salespeople.   The selling duties of retail salespeople can be stated briefly. First, the salesperson must greet the customer, determining the customer's needs and wants. Next, merchandise is selected that is thought most suitable in light of the customer's stated intentions. Third, the customer is told why and shown how particular merchandise will best fill the requirements. Fourth, the sale is completed. Then, if it seems reasonable, an attempt may be made at **suggestion selling**—recommending some product the customer had not asked about. Finally, the salesperson makes a bid for the customer's goodwill so that the customer will be inclined to return for future purchases.

In addition, certain nonselling duties are usually assigned to retail salespeople. Activities such as making change, operating the cash register, writing up a salescheck, and bagging the merchandise are integral phases of the selling process. Salespeople also must know the location of stock throughout the store, must see that their own department's stock is always adequate, and must keep their stock in place and their selling area neat. Many retail salespeople are asked to participate in taking inventory and to set up store displays.

Features of the Job.   On the plus side, retail selling does not require salesclerks to do extensive traveling to find customers. Instead, the customer comes to the retail outlet, usually with an interest in the products sold in that store. Consequently, salespeople can spend more of their valuable time involved in selling, instead of nonselling duties. Another benefit of retail selling is that in most cases, all of the products the store sells are located in the store. Thus, the salesperson has a product to show and demonstrate to the customer. A customer who can see the benefits of the product immediately is more likely to make a commitment to buy that product than someone who is relying on a salesperson's presentation or a product brochure. Unfortunately, many traveling salespeople do not have the physical capacity to stock all of their products in their cars or in their homes. They must make greater use of promotional materials such as brochures, pamphlets, flyers, and videotapes.

Retail selling is good preparation for other types of selling and for marketing jobs other than selling. The duties one performs at this level of selling make a retail position almost a prerequisite for people who plan to open their own stores.

SELLING IN CONSUMERS' HOMES

A salesperson can call on an ultimate consumer at home, a place of business, or even in a restaurant over lunch. Because customers do not always visit sellers' places of business often enough to buy or be sold, some salespeople take the initiative by going to the buyers. Such salespeople can be working entirely for themselves, for a retailer, or for a manufacturer. They may sell intangibles such as insurance, securities, or travel tours. Or they may sell physical products such as appliances, shoes, books, brushes, or cosmetics. Calling may be as mechanical and unscientific as going from house to house, or it may be highly selective and done only by appointment.

Consumers might look upon house-to-house salespeople with either favor or disfavor, depending on the product and the person selling that product. The family can make a group purchase with little inconvenience if the salesperson will call at their home at an appointed hour. Homemakers can experiment with and operate certain products under the same conditions as they will be used. Instruction is typically available from the salesperson. The homemaker may well feel under less pressure at home than in a retail store. Unfortunately, many people have knowledge of or have had experience with dishonest and otherwise objectionable house-to-house salespeople. Many have been subjected to the rude behavior or the almost insulting aggressiveness of high-pressure salespeople selling everything from brushes to encyclopedias. Therefore, a "cooling off" law was enacted enabling consumers to void an agreement within 72 hours of purchase.

Certain aspects of selling to consumers on their own ground deserve special mention. Locating prospective buyers is often a considerable undertaking. There is also the problem of getting in to see the buyer. Homemakers needn't open the door when a stranger rings the bell, and requests for appointments can be refused. These two aspects mean that there is a high percentage of failure in nonselective calling. Also, in house-to-house or office-to-office selling, the salesperson has little specific information about the person being interviewed. If a salesperson can persuade a prospect to hold a "house party" to which other prospects are invited, send out direct mail to a large list and offer an incentive to prospects, or request appointments with individuals whose names were acquired from satisfied customers, the number of unproductive calls and the amount of wasted time will be reduced.

HIGHLIGHT 2-3   *Ultimate Consumer Sales Description: Northwestern Mutual*

Northwestern Mutual Life Insurance agents use a low-key approach to selling. They realize that most consumers are a little anxious when it comes to life insurance. Instead of pushing their way into a conversation with the consumer, they choose to ease into the interview by asking several questions. This serves to gather information, as well as to make the consumer feel at ease.

The Northwestern Mutual sales agent is trained to develop a relationship with prospects—to get to know them—before trying to sell to them. This approach is designed to form a trust between the agent and the prospect, allowing for a smoother buyer-seller relationship. According to John Battaglia, a district manager for Northwestern Mutual, sales agents must sell themselves to the prospect as individuals before the prospect will allow them to sell insurance.

Battaglia spends a lot of time recruiting sales agents. He does not want salespeople to enter prospects' homes with dollar signs in their eyes. After all, this is a reflection on him, as district manager. Besides the industry-wide insurance examinations that are given to measure sales aptitude, Battaglia's recruits take several Northwestern Mutual exams following an intensive training program. One of the exams involves administering a questionnaire to ten "strangers." Battaglia says this serves two purposes. First, it shows whether or not the recruit has what it takes to deal with consumers at their homes. And second, the recruit may develop one or two prospects, and hopefully future customers from this exercise.

Battaglia makes certain his recruits know the score. A career with Northwestern Mutual has many rewards. However, if they are looking to take advantage of the customer, Battaglia has no use for them. Northwestern Mutual and John Battaglia are trying to erase the negative image of ultimate consumer salespeople that has grown over the years.

Source: Courtesy of John Battaglia, Northwestern Mutual Life Insurance Company. This was based on a sales class presentation at LSU.

CHARACTERISTICS OF SUCCESSFUL SALESPEOPLE

A dynamic personality is one of the basic needs of all salespeople. Complete product knowledge is eminently desirable, as are other features such as strict obedience to company instructions, long hours of work, determination to keep up-to-date, accurate records on all prospects, and a mastery of selling fundamentals and techniques. Though these are examples of things the salesperson should try to achieve, they and other similar accomplishments are not enough. To be a successful salesperson, an individual also must have a superior sales personality. Finally, the salesperson must enjoy meeting and interacting with people.

PSYCHOLOGICAL CHARACTERISTICS

A pleasing personality by itself is not enough. Popularity and an engaging personality alone will not enable a salesperson to sell anything to anybody. Salespeople who rely solely on personality are at a disadvantage when competing with a professional salesperson.

Personality is a broad concept that cannot be easily defined. A sales personality may be thought of as the impression prospects get of the salesperson. It is the attitude and level of desire the salesperson shows the customers. The sales personality is what the prospect likes or dislikes about the salesperson as a human being. No salesperson can afford to be indifferent to or negligent about the cultivation of a superior sales attitude and personality because these characteristics influence prospects. Every impression the salesperson makes helps or hurts the chance of making a sale. If the reaction elicited is unfavorable, or even neutral, the sale will be more difficult.

In implementing a program of attitude and personality development, the salesperson starts with self-analysis. It is necessary to work largely through control and change of habits because methods of operation, selling techniques, and even attitudes are matters of habit. The habit pattern is what has good or bad effects on prospects, customers, the company, and oneself. A superior sales personality is largely the result of certain habits and ways of thinking, certain practices and policies that fortunately can be acquired by experimentation and effort. It is not easy to develop a more pleasing personality. Most individuals are reluctant to admit even to themselves that something about them is wrong and needs to be changed, because such an admission deflates the ego, and that tends to be avoided. People with whom the salesperson comes in contact are hesitant to point out habits that need correction. With a determined effort, however, a more favorable sales personality can be developed.

Eight psychological characteristics are commonly mentioned as essential to successful selling. They are optimism, enthusiasm, confidence, sincerity, determination, dependability, initiative, and imagination.

OPTIMISM

Optimism is a characteristic of success-minded salespeople—those who, within reasonable limits, do not admit to themselves the possibility of failing to reach the objective. The first thing salespeople are optimistic about is themselves. They are confident they are going to better themselves as time passes. Second, they are optimistic about the products they sell. They feel that each one is an excellent value in its own price class and each will give satisfaction to the proper user. A third source of optimism is a firm belief in their company's service to its customers and the quality of its products.

ENTHUSIASM

Enthusiasm is a combination of interest and belief, and energy and activity. Salespeople need a broad curiosity about the products being sold, the prospects, themselves, and even matters unrelated to selling. Enthusiasm leads a salesperson to become acquainted with the work from all possible angles. Enthusiasm plays a dominant role in the sales presentation in helping secure the interest and confidence of the prospect. When translated into animated and persuasive delivery, enthusiasm prevents the sales story from being a dull recital. If the salesperson is to inspire the prospect's enthusiasm over the proposition, the only safe course to follow is to carry infectious enthusiasm into the presentation.

CONFIDENCE

Confidence is the result of knowledge plus experience, and for this reason it can be developed and is acquired more easily than optimism and enthusiasm. Confidence is a belief in oneself, a healthy respect for one's own capabilities and powers. It is the motivation that causes salespeople to be not merely willing but eager to encounter hard-to-sell prospects. Confident salespeople inspire confidence in prospects.

SINCERITY

Nothing is so vital to the continued trust and confidence of prospects as a sincere interest in their problems and well-being. Salespeople who are known to be high-powered individuals determined to sell at all costs, who have concern for their own interests above the interests of their prospects and customers, who make claims that will not be lived up to, who resort to half-truths and false information to influence customers, cannot expect to hold customers long. Prospects usually have little trouble in detecting an insincere presentation. Salespeople cannot hope to make other people believe that which they themselves know to be untrue.

DETERMINATION

Successful salespeople are those who have the will to succeed. Their driving ambition makes them industrious individuals who are willing to work long hours under discouraging circumstances. This same ambition is responsible for their aggressive, competitive spirit and for their pride in wanting to be the best people on the sales force.

Patience and perseverance, which are facets of determination, do not allow salespeople to give up easily, but instead make them stick to their jobs. The persevering salesperson makes calls on a desirable prospect repeatedly and regularly, knowing that the first order will come eventually.

DEPENDABILITY

Buyers are always in search of elements of certainty in an area which is largely one of perpetual change. One such welcome element is a dependable salesperson. Every buyer knows too many salespeople who have proven to be unworthy of confidence. Consequently, the salesperson who can be relied upon is received enthusiastically by buyers.

INITIATIVE

Salespeople with initiative learn to rely on themselves, to make their own plans, and then to follow those plans. These are the self-starters, who stay active even when not under close supervision. In their constant search for methods of increasing their value to the company, these salespeople are a fertile source of new ideas, suggestions, and challenging questions.

IMAGINATION

If the sales presentation is not imaginative, it becomes boring. Because ideas are the real stock in trade, regardless of what the physical product or service may be, the salesperson makes greatest use of imagination when painting word pictures. Consider, for example, an annuity. An annuity is a plan for saving money for retirement. The imaginative salesperson does not present it merely as a legal document, or even as a certain number of dollars each month. Instead, the salesperson paints a picture of retirement, one of trips and touring, of hobbies and longings to be gratified, of the feeling of security. Using imagination, the salesperson is able to translate the product into those exact benefits the prospect wants.

SOCIAL CHARACTERISTICS

A salesperson's chances of long-term success are slight if a pronounced social inclination and a basic liking for people are lacking. One must be eager to meet new individuals and be friendly by nature.

FRIENDLY NATURE

The salesperson encounters all types of prospects in all types of situations. Prospects vary in point of view, age, pattern of living, background, ideals, knowledge, and in many other respects, yet the salesperson must be a friend to all. This demands extreme social adaptability. The only lasting basis for friendship between salesperson and prospect is the salesperson's genuine interest in the prospect and an accompanying desire to help with any problems. To be liked, the salesperson must be genuine, and to know the prospect is to take a long step toward liking and becoming friends with the prospect.

SOCIAL GRACE

The mannerly salesperson tries to make each sales call a pleasant, enjoyable visit, marred by no violation of social custom. Tact and diplomacy should be used in arranging and opening the interview and in handling objections, interruptions, and other obstacles to purchasing. Courtesy must be evidenced from the moment of entering the prospect's office until it is time to go. Prospects should not be the only ones granted this social grace. Salespeople should also be courteous to clerks, receptionists, secretaries, assistant buyers, and all other personnel contacted in the prospect's place of business.

CONVERSATIONAL ABILITY

To be a good conversationalist, the salesperson should focus on four concerns. First, the salesperson must assume prospects are basically interested in only one subject, themselves, and in what the salesperson's products can do for them. This point of view requires a sympathetic understanding of the prospect's buying problems, together with a spirit of tolerance. It also demands that the salesperson be attentive to what the prospect says.

The salesperson's second concern is to make the prospect feel important, which calls for deferring to and complimenting the prospect. The salesperson should find something to congratulate the prospect about; ask for the prospect's advice and opinions; or hold the prospect's judgment and experience in high regard.

The third concern is to control the conversation with finesse. By exercising subtle control over the subject matter and direction of the conversation, the salesperson prevents arguments, interruptions, undesirable domination by the prospect, and discussion of unnecessary topics.

A fourth concern is to guard against overusing certain words or expressions. This practice restricts the salesperson's ability to express a precise meaning. In addition, excess repetition becomes monotonous and annoying. The salesperson with an inadequate vocabulary cannot express thoughts intelligently.

WHY SALESPEOPLE FAIL

Cause of Failure	Percent
Lack of initiative	55
Poor planning and organization	39
Inadequate product knowledge	37
Lack of enthusiasm	31
Salesperson not customer-oriented	30
Lack of proper training	23
Inability to get along with buyers	21
Lack of personal goals	20
Inadequate knowledge of market	19
Lack of knowledge of company	16
Lack of job satisfaction	15
Unsuited for selling career	14
Lack of adequate background	13
Insufficient self-discipline	12
Salesperson not company-oriented	12
No interest in self-development	11
Failure to follow instructions	11
Lack of self-confidence	11
Improper supervision	9
Inability to improvise	8
Lack of imagination	7
Personal problems	6
Difficulties in communicating	6
Dishonesty	5
Unfortunate appearance	5
Improper attitude	5
Failure to ask buyers to buy	3
Lack of tact and courtesy	2
Gambling and drinking	2

Table 2-1 In a survey conducted by the authors, sales managers of Fortune 500 companies were asked what, in their experience, were the causes of salespeople's failure on the job. Their composite answers appear in this table, with the percent mentioning each cause.

POISE

Poise is the characteristic that permits people to be in command of themselves—physically, mentally, and emotionally. Nothing is more essential to a salesperson's personality than self-confidence, and that confidence permits poise. Poised salespeople are recognized immediately. Their bearing reflects maturity and emotional stability. At least on the surface, the poised salesperson takes criticism or praise, disappointment or success, with the same even manner.

How can one become a poised salesperson? Salespeople acquire poise in several ways. The first step involves thorough preparation for a selling career. This same painstaking preparation should be applied to each sales presentation. If salespeople know themselves, their products, their company, and their buyers, and if they know how to sell, they should be confident and poised. But a rehearsal, in which the salesperson runs through a presentation before actually making it to a buyer, can also be a helpful device. Over the long run, the salesperson will recognize that experience will provide in large measure the competence and confidence that result in poise.

PHYSICAL CHARACTERISTICS

The physical image of the salesperson is the first factor to register on the prospect. The salesperson must appear to be both trustworthy and able, and must advise with authority. To do this, personal appearance must instill confidence and respect in the prospect. The salesperson pays dearly for any indifference or inattention to appearance, for such neglect will cost sales. To be a success, the salesperson must look successful. A personal appearance that is beyond reproach goes hand in hand with success in selling.

GROOMING, CLOTHING, AND BEARING

The ability to sell is not limited to any one physical type. Tall or short, obese or slim, fair or dark, bald or bushy—each group has its share of outstanding salespeople. It is good that such physical differences are unimportant, for one is limited in what can be done about such matters as build, features, or vision. One is not limited, however, in what can be done about such controllable factors as grooming, clothing, and bearing.

The first controllable factors include the cut and grooming of hair, the condition of hands and nails, and the appearance of the teeth. Even the new salesperson knows from experience what is pleasing about these and should need no instruction. Clothes constitute the second group of controllable factors. The main requirement is neatness. Clean and neat clothes bear silent but powerful witness to the attention and care they receive. Personality is expressed in the choice of clothes. Extremes should be avoided. Clothes plus grooming do for a salesperson what a package does for the product.

Posture and bearing are also subject to control. Sitting or standing, the salesperson should display both respect and assurance. The physical manner should be of such vigor and power that it bespeaks authority and gets attention. Because posture and bearing are revealing, the salesperson should see that they are a positive force rather than a negative one. The salesperson's walk is also important. It should be energetic and businesslike, with head erect and shoulders back. It should connote authority and purpose.

MANNERISMS

Many salespeople acquire unconscious habits, such as tugging at earlobes, fidgeting with glasses, scratching the head, constantly adjusting clothing, or rubbing a hand over the face repeatedly. Tapping with a pencil, cracking the knuckles, chewing gum, or even talking with food in the mouth are other undesirable mannerisms. The trouble with such mannerisms is that they make concentration harder for the prospect and, in more extreme cases, create an impression that is definitely unfavorable. This, of course, hinders the salesperson in making the sale.

The salesperson must be constantly alert to detect such mannerisms and eliminate them so that there is complete, conscious control over the physical self. If feasible, the salesperson should encourage some associate, the sales manager, or even some long-established customer to observe a sales presentation and to suggest desirable changes.

GOOD HEALTH

The sales job is exacting and exhausting. The daily grind of selling makes heavy demands on a salesperson, requiring considerable physical effort. Yet the salesperson is expected to be the personification of vitality at all times. Because appearance depends in large measure on physical condition, one's health should be guarded.

NONVISUAL PHYSICAL FACTORS

The prospect's sense of hearing ranks second to the sense of sight in registering a favorable impression of the salesperson. The salesperson's voice should be pleasing, well modulated, clear, and warm. The tone should be both courteous and respectful. The job of persuasion requires a voice that is convincing, emphatic, firm, and purposeful.

Since effective expression is the goal, the salesperson must work to eliminate vocal defects and improve vocal versatility. A monotone is lifeless and boring and will not persuade a prospect to buy. Practice is required until voice, enunciation, and expression are all acceptable.

Distracting and irritating oral mannerisms can no more be permitted than can visual distractions. An odd-sounding laugh, a nervous cough, an objectionable clearing of the throat, resorting to "ahs" or "uhs" as prefaces to remarks, or a habit of humming or whistling should be avoided, for some prospects and customers will certainly find these habits offensive.

THE MAKING OF GREAT SALESPEOPLE

The psychological, social, and physical characteristics discussed in this chapter are all important to the development of a successful, professional salesperson. The proper use of these skills and characteristics are necessary for the salesperson to be successful. But what makes great salespeople? Great salespeople become great because of two reasons. First, they are more efficient than other salespeople. And second, they are more industrious than other salespeople.

EFFICIENCY

Great salespeople are those who spend their free time researching the latest techniques and technologies for making their job more efficient and more effective. They maximize the time spent on the road and waiting in offices. Efficiency does not happen by accident. One must be organized and spend many hours planning one's actions.

Great salespeople have the ability to empathize. That is, they put their customers first by asking questions to determine customers' needs, and by listening to their customers' responses. This reduces the time wasted in miscommunication and results in satisfied customers, and more time to call on other customers.

Finally, great salespeople are never closed-minded to learning. Every day is a new learning experience with new situations and new obstacles to overcome. Great salespeople take note of new situations and record their occurrences. They analyze these situations and practice overcoming them.

INDUSTRY

Great salespeople are more industrious than other salespeople. That is, they work harder and make more of their opportunities than other salespeople.

One of the benefits of a sales career, as discussed in Chapter 1, is independence. Salespeople have the freedom of working on their own, without constant, daily supervision. This benefit is often abused. It is very easy for salespeople to get away with sleeping late, extending lunch breaks, stopping work early, and taking an occasional day off. Of course, these salespeople run the risk of having their jobs terminated should they be caught. In any case, it is obvious that this salesperson is likely to "just get by" as a sales representative.

Great salespeople refuse to give in to these temptations. They are highly motivated self-starters who get up every morning and make the first call early. They are also the ones who go out of their way to make those one or two extra calls at the end of the day before calling it quits. They know the more calls they make, the more sales they will make. They also have respect for themselves, their company and customers, and pride in the way they do their jobs. Great salespeople are true professionals. An example of one great salesperson is in Highlight 2-4.

HIGHLIGHT 2-4   *Joe Girard: The World's Greatest Salesperson?*

The **Guinness Book of World Records** *lists Joe Girard as the world's greatest salesperson. Girard, the top car salesman in America for over a decade, sold nearly a thousand cars a year from a Detroit Chevrolet dealership. Today, he makes even more money by writing books (e.g.,* **How to Sell Anything to Anybody***), making videotapes, and conducting training courses for salespeople.*

Girard has great confidence in himself and works at keeping it. Every morning when he gets out of bed, he looks in the mirror and says: "You are the most terrific, most beautiful person in the whole world." He even wears a gold pin on his lapel proclaiming himself as No. 1, and as he puts it: "I am the best. Numero uno. And you know why I'm the best? I believe in myself. If you want to sell anything, you have to sell yourself, you must have self-respect, that is, you must believe you're number one."

When he sold cars, he used two full-time assistants. The assistants greeted prospective customers and took them on demonstration rides. Once the customers were prepped, Joe Girard took over. Each customer was taken into a tiny office where they sat two-and-a-half feet from each other. As Girard explains, "You've got to keep the electricity going, maintain close eye contact, shut everything out but me and what I've got to say." He explains that people always look at salespeople as though they're liars or cheats and are out to rob them of their money. "But I'm their friend. I give everyone this button which says: " 'I like you.' "

Joe Girard pays close attention to prospects' body language. If their eyes narrow or they perspire or cross and uncross their legs, he changes the subject and talks about the football game or politics—anything to make them relax. And then he moves back in. Girard insists that he's not a phony. People sniff out phoniness, he claims, and "no one who's insincere will ever be a successful salesman." Sixty-five percent of his customers are repeats. That's because he treats them the way they want to be treated. He takes care of them because if he treats them right, they'll send him more customers. (To increase the chances that they will, he pays a $25 commission for any referral of a potential car buyer.) "I never stop working," says Girard, "I'm the best, but I can be better."

Joe Girard's Tips on Good Selling Techniques:

1. *Let customers know you want to be their friend—and don't give them a chance to decline your offer of friendship. Never ask questions that can be answered yes or no.*

2. *Let the customer try the product until they are satisfied. In Girard's case, he tells prospective customers to take any car they want and drive the car by their house to show it to their spouse. Once one spouse sees the other in a brand new car, a certain excitement starts to grow. At that point, it's really tough to bring the car back to the dealership.*

3. *Use flattery, but be certain the flattery is sincere. "How can anyone walk away from someone who's interested in them?"*

4. *Never interrupt or attempt to upstage a prospective customer.*

5. *Make your customers work for you. The most important selling begins after the sale when you make sure that the customer is satisfied.*

6. *Follow through after your sale. "I'll go all the way to the top people at General Motors to help someone who got stuck with a lemon," says Girard.*

7. *Quote a reasonable price, regardless of the customer's savvy. Sooner or later, the customer is going to find out whether or not the price is fair. If you want repeat business and a good reputation, treat all customers fairly.*

8. *Never pressure a customer, and not just because it isn't nice to do. "I don't use hard-sell techniques," Girard claims, "because they don't work."*

Source: Joe Girard and Stanley H. Brown, *How to Sell Anything to Anybody* (New York: Warner Books, Inc., 1979).

SUMMARY

The salesperson's job responsibilities fall into three categories: (1) selling activities; (2) auxiliary activities; and (3) nonselling activities. Selling activities are directly related to a sale, auxiliary activities help foster goodwill and future sales, and nonselling activities help management to manage, evaluate, and control the salesperson.

Salespeople have a responsibility to maximize profits, work industriously, and properly represent their employers. Buyers must be treated fairly; this means aggressive selling, not high-pressure selling.

Salespeople can sell to wholesalers, retailers, purchasing agents, professionals, and ultimate consumers. Wholesalers and retailers are middlemen who buy products from manufacturers and resell them to consumers for a profit. Middleman-selling salespeople do both service selling and creative selling, and they call on middlemen. Missionary salespeople work for the manufacturer by promoting goodwill in order to generate sales. Salespeople who sell directly to the ultimate consumer do so either in a retail store, or in the consumer's home. Purchasing agents are professional buyers who are experts in buying for the company.

Successful salespeople are dynamic. They exhibit technical expertise and a superior sales personality. Their physical appearance is important also, because it is the first thing the prospect notices. Great salespeople are great because they are more efficient and industrious than other salespeople.

KEY TERMS

middlemen

wholesalers

retailers

rational motivation

service selling

creative selling

items for resale

want book

missionary salespeople

service approach

derived demand

detailers

suggestion selling

REVIEW QUESTIONS

1. What characteristics are shared by great salespeople?
2. List eight psychological characteristics essential to successful selling.
3. Why do some salespeople fail?
4. What factors are important for good conversational ability?
5. What traits must good salespeople avoid?
6. What physical traits can people improve?
7. What are some auxiliary selling duties?
8. What is service selling?
9. How is creative selling different from service selling?
10. Why must salespeople use creative selling for new products?
11. What is a missionary salesperson?
12. What are the special requirements for selling to purchasing agents?
13. What are the responsibilities of a pharmaceutical detailer?
14. Why is selling in retail stores considered to be the least complex type of selling?
15. What advantages does the buyer have when a salesperson comes to his or her home?

DISCUSSION QUESTIONS

1. Gross margin and total profit from sales are the best measures of a salesperson's performance. Do most companies really measure

these, or is total sales the variable that most firms use to evaluate performance?

2. Salespeople act as the link between sellers and buyers. One of the salesperson's responsibilities is to provide the seller with information. How in performing one's duties as a salesperson can that be accomplished? What information should be gathered?

3. What type of selling would you like to do? What are the attractions of that alternative?

4. Would your approach to a purchasing agent be different from your approach to a professional? If so, how?

CASE 2-1   ZENON CORPORATION*

Judy Evans recently interviewed with Zenon Corporation for a position as a Technical Sales Representative for the Northeast region. Zenon is a major international chemical company selling mostly to other chemical companies and to the plastics industry. If Judy Evans took the position with Zenon, she would be a member of Zenon's Specialty Additives Division, which supplies the polymer industry with products to improve the quality and performance of finished plastic products. A key to serving this industry successfully is an understanding of the formulation of resin products—especially the impact of additives on the chemical and physical properties of the finished plastics. Because of the technical nature of the products, chemists and engineers dominate the industry. Salespeople, such as Judy, have only recently made inroads into this male bastion.

General Polymers is a major worldwide producer of plastics for use in consumer appliances, electronic equipment, aircraft and a host of other applications. For several years Zenon has targeted General Polymers as a major account, but has been unsuccessful in securing a significant share of their business. As in many industrial selling situations, a few key accounts represent a large majority of potential sales. Typically, four or five customers account for 80 percent of industry sales. General Polymers was one of these key customers.

The information in Exhibit 2-1 shows the current and potential sales for the Zenon Corporation accounts in the Northwest region. Zenon's management staff prepared the information with the help of its sales force and accounting department. It was provided to Judy to help her understand the sales position for which she was applying, and she intended to use it to impress Mr. Rodriguez, the Zenon sales manager for the Northeast Region.

---

*Case prepared by Chuck Nielson. Used with permission.

EXHIBIT 2-1
ZENON CORPORATION
Specialty Additives Division: Northwest Region
Sales by Account

Customer	Sales Current	Potential
Abbott Chemicals	$812	$1,037
Alliance Chemicals	$79	$790
Beckner Products	$4,247	$5,000
Calmes Inc.	$124	$170
General Polymers	$3,029	$4,700
Great Lakes Polymers	$533	$600
Guarisco Chemical Div/UGA	$612	$795
Manchester Chemicals Inc.	$313	$350
Nesbit Industries	$547	$738
Process Management Chemicals	$5,060	$5,090
PSA Polymers International	$321	$409
Quaid Industries	$4,700	$5,190
Quality Copolymers	$1,645	$2,200
Remco Products & Chemicals	$826	$1,100
Reynolds Chemicals Ltd	$434	$598
Riverside Industries	$3,121	$4,232
Russell Chemicals	$89	$95
Sargon Div./MPC Corp.	$167	$189
Slade Industries	$333	$450
Tri-Plastics Inc.	$607	$2,100
Total	$27,599	$35,833

At the time she interviewed for the position, Judy recognized the special challenges facing women in the traditionally male-dominated industrial sales profession. These challenges are based on a number of common misperceptions about women in sales, including:

Myth #1: Sales jobs are too tough for women.

Myth #2: Customers prefer to deal with men.

Myth #3: Women are unreliable because of marriage, pregnancy, or other "women's problems."

Myth #4: Women take advantage of their sex in selling situations or might cause sex-related problems within the sales force.

Myth #5: Women cannot sell as well as men.

Judy's experience over the past several years with another firm demonstrated that these difficult challenges could be met successfully by careful sales planning and persistent effort. She also recognized she would need help and understanding from Mr. Rodriguez. As she prepared for her second interview, she was outlining the issues she needed to talk about so she could decide whether or not to accept the new position.

CASE QUESTIONS

1. How do you feel about the misperceptions about women in sales? What percent of people have these misperceptions? Do they differ by male versus female? Can you think of any other misperceptions about women?
2. If Judy is confronted with a manager who holds one or more of these perceptions, what can she do to overcome them?
3. What issues should Judy discuss in the second interview?
4. Should Judy take this new position if she has a favorable second interview?

5. Using Lotus: (a) rank order the customers by total sales and create a separate column indicating each company's ranking; (b) rank order the customers by potential and create a separate column indicating each company's ranking on potential; and (c) create a formula to calculate sales as a percent of potential and calculate this percentage for each customer. Then answer the following questions:

   - What percent of total sales are accounted for by the top five customers?
   - Which five firms have the lowest sales as a percent of potential?
   - How well exploited are the opportunities at General Polymer compared to the other major accounts?
   - Which five firms have been the best exploited, in terms of potential?
   - How could Judy use this information to impress Mr. Rodriguez?

PART 2

Background for Selling

CHAPTER 3
Buying Behavior

After studying this chapter, you should be able to:

- Explain the difference between consumers, resellers, and organizational buyers

- Explain the influences culture, social classes, reference groups, and family have on behavior

- Discuss self-concept, perception, learning, motivation, and attitudes as they relate to behavior

- Explain the stages of the consumer buying process

- Explain the stages in the organizational buying process

- Discuss the roles organizational members play in the decision-making process

Salespeople need to understand why buyers behave the way they do. To explain the "why" of buying behavior, many marketers and sellers draw on the principles of three behavioral sciences: psychology, sociology, and anthropology. Behavioral sciences are concerned with the study of human thought and behavior. Psychology concentrates on individuals and their mental processes and behavior. Sociology is the study of the development, structure, and function of human groups in a society. Anthropology is concerned with the study of total cultures comprised of individuals and groups of individuals.

One who considers the broad dimensions of consumer buying behavior is concerned with the nature of culture, social class, reference groups, and family. Each of these factors has considerable influence on "why" and "what" consumers buy.

By understanding culture, sellers can better appeal to the goals and respect the values of buyers from that culture. The social class of a buyer is something that most salespeople should know about, because social class membership influences what consumers buy, and from whom. Salespeople need to identify the *reference groups* (especially the smaller, more intimate groups) of which a consumer is a member. Family, the most influential reference group, greatly affects the buying actions of its

70

members, both individually and as a unit. There are individual aspects of a consumer's buying behavior that are of great interest to salespeople. These include *self-concept, perception, personality, learning, motivation,* and *attitudes.*

Most consumers do not make voluntary purchases unless they believe that the product or service will do good things for their self-concept. What a buyer does about a stimulus involves perception. A salesperson's presentation is an example of a stimulus. Learning usually affects subsequent behavior. A buyer senses a need, buys, then learns whether or not the purchase filled the need. Those needs that initiate behavior or action represent motivation. Each consumer has many needs. Attitudes are the opinions, views, beliefs, or convictions a person holds about some object. Most attitudes influence whether the person takes favorable or unfavorable action toward purchasing a product or using a service.

Our discussion of buying behavior will begin with an overview of three types of markets: *consumers, resellers,* and *industrial buyers.* Next, the chapter focuses on the social and individual characteristics that influence consumer buying decisions, including a model that illustrates the consumer buying process. Finally, the chapter reviews the organizational buying process. Included in each review are tactics and techniques salespeople may use to influence each type of decision.

TYPES OF BUYERS

There are three types of buyers: consumers, resellers (including both wholesalers and retailers), and industrial buyers.

CONSUMERS

Consumers are people who buy products and/or services for their own use or for use in their households by household members. Groceries, home cleaning services, appliance repair, clothing and sporting equipment are all examples of products and services that are purchased for personal or household use. The person(s) who are to use these products/services are usually the ones who make the decision on which one to buy and use. Obviously, salespeople should be concerned with satisfying this person's needs, and the needs of those in the household who influence decisions.

RESELLERS

Resellers are wholesalers and retailers who purchase products in order to sell them for a profit. In exchange for this profit, resellers provide various services. For example, retailers such as department stores and supermarkets provide a convenient location for the manufacturer's products to be sold to the consumer. Retailers also will buy a large volume of

Figure 3-1 **A potential customer tries out exercise equipment before purchase.**

products and store them in warehouses. By paying their bills quickly retailers receive a discount. This early payment serves a financing function for the manufacturer who quickly puts the money to use in further production. Retailers also promote the manufacturer's products in the store and in their advertising.

Wholesalers provide many of the same services as retailers. They buy in large quantities, pay their bills quickly, store the products in their warehouses, and promote the manufacturer's products. While they do not provide a convenient location for consumers to purchase the products, wholesalers do act as the manufacturer's sales force when selling their products to retailers. The wholesaler also may transport the manufacturer's product, stock the store, and set up displays. Perhaps the most important service wholesalers can provide is the function of buying products in large quantities, dividing them into smaller amounts, and then combining them with other products into an assortment. When a wholesaler contacts a retail outlet, the wholesaler may represent as many as 25 manufacturers. The wholesaler presents the retailer with an assortment of products from all of these manufacturers.

In selling to resellers, manufacturer's salespeople must be aware of the benefits sought by the reseller. For example, the ultimate consumer may be seeking the benefit of an improved self-image, such as an attractive appearance from the purchase of a sweater. But the reseller's interest in that sweater is somewhat different. The benefits they would receive from purchasing and reselling that sweater are a satisfied customer, an improved store image, a demand for that sweater and perhaps for some of their other products, and a profit.

Resellers think differently than other buyers when purchasing products. Typically, they are more rational and logical in making purchase decisions. They must be able to resell the product in order for them to consider buying it. Thus, the salesperson must provide proof of the product's performance and ability to sell. Proof may come in many forms. For example, some retailers base their decision to buy on the amount of advertising dollars spent by the manufacturer to support the product. Others insist on knowing the test marketing results to determine sales potential. And many demand manufacturers' coupons before they purchase the product. Still others expect the manufacturer to offer sales or specials to ensure the product's sale. On top of this proof, resellers usually want an assurance that the manufacturer will help them sell the product by training their salespeople, setting up point-of-purchase displays, and stocking the product on shelves. The manufacturer and the salesperson must provide these assurances in return for the many services resellers provide.

INDUSTRIAL BUYERS

Industrial buyers purchase products and services for use in making their own products/services, or for use in their daily operations. Examples of these products include machinery, components, and supplies. As with resellers, industrial buyers also buy products based more on rational decision making. Performance, service, quality, and price are very important to the industrial buyer because these factors will be reflected in the customer's product or service. A product of poor quality or performance may reduce the perceived quality and performance not only for that product, but for the customer's product as well. Finally, the higher the cost of the product, the higher the price of the customer's product. This may also affect the demand for the customer's product/service.

When selling to industrial buyers, salespeople often must satisfy several decision makers who are involved in the industrial buying decision. At one level, salespeople encounter purchasing agents who screen sales representatives, work as the liaisons between their companies and the salespeople, and are involved in negotiating the terms of the deal. The next level may be a group of engineers who examine the product's performance, evaluate its reliability, and field test the product. Finally, the financial personnel must be convinced the product is sound, because they determine how to pay for the product before top management (president or vice-president) will approve the purchase.

Industrial buyers, besides being relatively more rational concerning the product's capabilities, are likely to examine several alternatives and spend considerable time evaluating each competitor's product. Often, there are many procedures and restrictions imposed by the buying company to ensure that the appropriate product or service is purchased.

The complexity of the industrial buying decision places enormous pressure on the salesperson. The sales representative must be able to work with a variety of different people, and possess a multitude of skills, from technical expertise to financial planning and human relations. For example, in selling assembly-line machinery, the salesperson must know the product's technical and economic benefits, and be able to deal successfully with the production, product development, legal, and quality-control personnel in the customer's company. Organizational buying will be discussed in more depth later in this chapter, as well as in Chapter 17.

SOCIAL INFLUENCES ON BUYING BEHAVIOR

Some of the **social influences** that affect our buying behavior are *culture, social class, reference groups*, and *families*.

CULTURE

Culture is the set of basic values, perceptions, wants, and behaviors that are passed on from one generation to another within a society. A culture includes a broad grouping of people and the geographic area the group occupies. Every culture is identified by the material and nonmaterial elements it reflects. Material items such as personal computers, cars, stereos, and water beds establish the pattern of daily living. Nonmaterial aspects such as ideas, attitudes, values, and beliefs serve to influence human behavior.

Successive generations learn about their culture through the symbolism, artifacts, and behavior patterns that an older generation passes on to them using language and systems of abstract thought. Individuals in a society can accept all that is transmitted, reject all, or accept some elements and reject others. In short, individuals can conform, deviate, or do some of each. In addition to learning how to behave from others, individuals also can learn by evaluating the results of their own personal behavior.

Although all cultures are different, each has its own set of beliefs and attitudes concerning social structure and organization, sex, age groupings, kinship, marriage, social stratification and status, economic relations, rituals, political relations, and social control.

SUBCULTURES

As the total population of a society or a culture grows in number and inhabits a larger geographical area, the homogeneity of its identity changes, and subcultures appear. A **subculture** can be defined as a grouping of people who exhibit patterns of behavior sufficient to distinguish them from the overall culture or society. These subgroupings occur because individuals feel the need for more personal and satisfying identification than is possible with the total population.

The basis on which subcultures develop varies. Many subcultures are based on race, religion, or national origin. In New York City, for example, there are at least six major subcultures based on ethnicity: Italian, Jewish, Black, Hispanic, Chinese, and Puerto Rican. Subcultures also develop from language differences, age groups, and social classes. Awareness of a subculture's effect on an individual buyer can help salespeople become more effective.

NORMS OF BEHAVIOR

The customary, approved modes of behavior that develop over time as a result of personal interaction within a culture are known as **norms**. Every culture, subculture, social class, and group has its own norms of behavior. Individuals tend to learn, accept, and respect the norms of their particular culture. The norms may be questioned, but rarely are they abandoned or replaced. As reflections of allowed or approved behavior, norms set standards that can be used as behavioral guides.

SOCIAL CLASS

Whether we admit it or not, society is made of different social classes. For the sake of discussion, a **social class** can be described as a relatively homogeneous and permanent segment of society to which individuals and families belong. Yet the differences are often a matter of perception, rather than reality. As a result, members of one social class have only limited social contact with social classes other than their own. The common classifications, including a few generalized features of each class, are shown in Figure 3-2.

Each **social class** has its own norms of behavior, its own consumption patterns, its own tastes. The norms of each social class influence individual behavior in two ways. First, the typical person feels pressure to conform to the norms of his or her own class. Second, the socially ambitious person feels pressure to conform to the norms of the social class just above the present class, the class to which the person aspires. The person whose ambition is quite strong may even flout some of the norms of the peer group.

Within any social class, the members tend to have the same hopes, attitudes, and preferences; feel the same needs; share the same values, tastes, and emotions; consume the same goods and services; and buy from the same sellers. Members want the approval of their social class so that they can feel good about themselves.

SEVEN SOCIAL CLASSES IN THE UNITED STATES

1. **Upper upper.** Old wealth passed on through the generations. Family is well respected and looked up to by the rest of society. Examples of such families include the Kennedys, Rockefellers, and Vanderbilts.

2. **Lower upper.** Those who have attained their wealth in their lifetime through exceptional business, professional, or athletic abilities; very status-conscious.

3. **Upper middle.** Owners of medium-size firms. Managers. Successful but not top professionals. Want to appear successful. Ambitious for their children. Expensive status symbols such as large houses. College graduates.

4. **Middle.** Ambitious; encourage college for their children. Owners of small firms; highly paid blue-collar workers; salaried white-collar workers. Small homes or multifamily dwellings. Strong on respectability.

5. **Working.** Average-pay blue collar workers, and those who lead a "working class" lifestyle regardless of income, educational background, and occupation. Rely heavily on relatives for emotional and financial support. Very sharp divisions on sexual roles and responsibilities.

6. **Upper lower.** Working, but living just above poverty level. Poorly educated, unskilled. Work for low wages. Strive toward respectability.

7. **Lower lower.** Sporadic employment. Unskilled workers. Low pay. Battle for life's necessities. Slums. Welfare.

Figure 3-2 Social scientists have detected seven social classes in the United States. Salespeople should try to understand these social classes, as they do have an effect on the individual's buying habits.

Source: Adapted from Kotler and Armstrong, *Principles of Marketing*, 4th ed. (Englewood Cliffs, NJ: Prentice-Hall, 1989): 122.

CRITERIA FOR SOCIAL STRATIFICATION

Perhaps the three most common criteria for assigning individuals to certain social classes are income, occupation, and education. Other criteria used include type of residence, neighborhood, kinship, ethnicity, political position or power, source of income, friends and associates, public service, and property ownership. The criteria for grouping individuals in social classes change over time, as do the weights given to each, although occupation is generally identified as the major factor determining social class.

Social mobility is the movement of an individual from one social position to another, either upward or downward. The term is most commonly used in connection with upward movement, however. In theory, our society offers complete mobility, but in practice there is relatively little mobility. There is no agreement on the degree of mobility in our social class structure, but rarely does an individual rise more than one social class. Mobility is more restricted at the top and bottom of the social class structure.

REFERENCE GROUPS

A **reference group** consists of two or more individuals who have something in common. Members of the more influential reference groups communicate and interact in group activities on a continuing basis. Because members refer (and defer) to the group for guidance and direction, we call them reference groups. The "something in common" usually includes experiences, problems, interests, and goals. Its members form and change attitudes as a group. The group serves its members as a model, a standard of comparison, and a source of approval. It influences its members' tastes, beliefs, and behavior.

There are reference groups everywhere, because individuals tend to gravitate together for support rather than remain apart or alone. For example, there are work groups (job associates) and there are play groups (nonwork groups). Much of human behavior is influenced by groups. Indeed, our behavior cannot be understood or explained without reference to the groups of which we are members.

CHOICE OF REFERENCE GROUPS

The reference groups to which an individual may belong include family, friends, neighbors, professional and work associates, relatives, political groups, fraternities and sororities, civic clubs, church groups, PTA, athletic groups, country clubs, student body, classmates, and service organizations. Reference groups can be either membership groups (family), aspirational groups (country club), formal membership groups (labor union), informal groups (coffee-break associates), or groups consisting of categories (based on age or vocation). Some reference groups exert a positive influence, some a negative influence, and some even evoke both types of reactions from different people.

Some reference groups are primarily concerned with the continuation or survival of the group—bridge or garden clubs, for example. Other groups are primarily concerned with the successful accomplishment of some project—a research and development unit or a district sales force, for example. Certain features of social class are also features of reference groups, but it must be remembered that some reference groups cut across social class lines.

Affiliation with some groups is more automatic and unavoidable than is true of others, but there is considerable freedom to exercise personal membership preferences. Many people use one, two, or three groups as the main points of reference, identifying closely with and depending heavily on those particular ones even though they are also members of other groups.

USE OF REFERENCE GROUPS BY AN INDIVIDUAL

Individuals use reference groups to provide identification. Almost everyone feels a need to belong, to be accepted and approved by other people. Reference groups provide support, comfort, and well-being. They enhance one's sense of personal worth, provide stability, and reduce the risk of being perceived as "different" or being left alone. One contributes to the group and also draws from the group.

Individuals use reference groups as a source of information. Members assume that other members have information they will pass on to the group.

Individuals also use reference groups as their major source of norms. By respecting the norms and by holding the attitudes that are common in a reference group, each member's conformity contributes to the group's uniformity. Individuals use reference groups to satisfy their social needs and permit social fulfillment. Reference groups provide association and fellowship.

The typical reference group establishes its qualifications for membership and its standards of proper behavior in order to screen prospects for membership. The group rewards those who observe its norms and punishes those who criticize them. It is important for salespeople to understand the dynamics of reference groups because group preferences often prevail over personal preferences. This is the trade-off the individual makes in being a member of or aspiring to belong to a reference group. Reference groups do provide the individual with certain benefits; however, the individual must conform to the group's norms in order to remain a member. Thus, much of an individual's behavior cannot be understood apart from the behavior of some reference group.

POSITION AND ROLE

Where an individual stands in the structure of a reference group is usually determined by the individual's reputation or particular talent. Position determines status within the group. Each position has its own rank and measure of prestige, which influences who says what and to whom. Each position has its own rights—the demands its occupant can make on others—and its own responsibilities—the obligations its occupant owes to others. Position implies some specialization and ability. The more ability demanded and the larger the number of persons the occupant supervises, the higher the status of the position. A position requiring unusual talents obviously should be filled by an individual with such talents. The status of each member is always relative to the status of each of the other members. Many positions in many reference groups continue over time but are filled by different individuals as time passes. For example, last year's purchasing agent in XYZ Company may not be the purchasing agent this year.

Role, in turn, is based on position. Role is that behavior considered acceptable for a specific position. For each position, certain types of behavior are appropriate and other types are not. Each occupant of a position is under pressure to see that his or her behavior is in harmony with the position and with what is expected of its occupant. Roles must be learned, sometimes from instruction, sometimes from trial and error. Each person plays many roles, because each individual is many different persons in different groups and in different situations. The purchasing agent plays one role when speaking to a salesperson, another role when dealing with his or her supervisor, and still another role when speaking to the product's user(s). The individual tries to play each role satisfactorily. Most role playing is done in situations of personal interaction, and the individual stays alert for indications of how his or her performance is being received and evaluated by the other members of the reference group.

OPINION LEADERS

Most reference groups consist of **opinion leaders** and opinion followers. Those who lead do so because their tastes tend to be adopted by the other members of the group. By definition, followers look to leaders for leadership. Opinion followers ask their opinion leader for information and advice, for recommendations, and even for instruction in the leader's area of specialization. If the leader is inclined to "sell" personal attitudes, this influence can be quite powerful. The direction of this influence is largely horizontal (meaning it comes from those on an equal level) because individuals wanting guidance usually look for it inside their own reference groups. Only the socially ambitious are inclined to follow leaders in a higher social class or in an aspirational reference group.

There are opinion leaders in every social stratum, income level, and reference group. In business firms, opinion leaders can be found in any department and hold any title. For example, picture four accountants who are co-workers and close friends. One has taken many steamship cruises, the others none. Another is a wizard at bridge. One's golfing skills are the envy of the other three. The fourth builds wooden tables and chairs that are a joy to behold. In each specialty, one communicates, informs, recommends, persuades, and may even exert a bit of social pressure. An opinion leader in one field is seldom an opinion leader in another field. Indeed, the typical opinion leader is quite similar to followers in almost every context except their specialty.

There is no simple, satisfactory technique by which outsiders can identify the opinion leaders in a reference group. Position, of course, sometimes helps, because certain positions imply a type of leadership by requiring particular competence in the specialty. The very fact that a certain person is the golf pro (position) at a country club automatically makes that person an authority (opinion leader) on golf.

In reference groups of the social type, opinion leaders are usually gregarious, easy to reach, and easy to communicate with. In many types of reference groups, an opinion leader will have contacts and sources of information outside of the group. Who they are, what they own, what their great interest is, what they have done, what they can do, what they know, and who they know may all be clues to the identity of opinion leaders.

The identification of opinion leaders has great implication for sellers. Communication is often made more effective if, instead of trying to communicate directly with the total audience, a seller tries to communicate with opinion leaders in the hope that they will pass both the seller's message and their influence on to their followers.

FAMILY

For most individuals, the **family** is the most influential reference group. It is so powerful that we treat it separately.

Technically, a family is two or more people who live together and are related by marriage, blood, or adoption. By way of contrast, a household is a person who lives alone, or two or more people who are unrelated but live together. Traditionally, a family was thought of as consisting of a father, a mother, and their children. But today we have many single-parent families. Most individuals start life as a child in their parents' family. In later life, many persons marry, become parents, and head their own families.

From birth, individuals have needs. As they grow older, they have more to say about what is bought to fill their needs, and later family needs. As consumers, both children and teenagers make certain individual buying decisions and influence certain family buying decisions. The family as a group may decide where to go on vacation, or which house to buy.

The family is a major influence on its members' attitudes, motivations, values, decisions, norms, and habits. Year after year, children find their values, consumption patterns, and habits shaped by others in the family. For instance, if one member is treated to some expensive item, the other members expect to receive something comparable later. What you experience, absorb, adopt, and learn as a child is not easily abandoned when you become an adult.

The role of each family member varies, and has been changing in recent years. Women used to dominate decision making in the areas of food, household supplies, and clothing. But the emergence of househusbands and seven-day-a-week, 24-hour-a-day retailing have resulted in men playing a larger role in those areas. In contrast, men have traditionally dominated the buying decisions involving high-priced, "big-ticket" items, such as automobiles, insurance, and investments. But this is changing too.

The concept of the family as a consuming unit has assimilated three relatively recent developments: working spouses, single-parent households, and single people. With both spouses earning income, many families have increased their purchases of products and services. Just as more husbands are shopping with their wives in retail stores, wives are joining their husbands in making buying decisions involving such items as automobiles, TVs, and insurance.

The emergence of single-parent households, most of which are headed by females, has increased the number of women as decision makers for many products and services they had had little involvement in previously.

Finally, about 28 percent of the 95 million U.S. households consist of single persons. The buying behavior of single people is characterized by heavy spending for such services as entertainment, travel, and domestic help. Single people are also buying houses and condominiums.

INDIVIDUAL ASPECTS OF BUYING BEHAVIOR

The individual aspects of buying behavior include self-concept, perception, learning, motivation, and attitudes.

SELF-CONCEPT

As an individual, your voluntary behavior is influenced by your **self-concept.** Your actions also reflect how you wish to be perceived by others.

The most obvious dimensions of self-concept are physical traits. Are you thin or heavy? Tall or short? Coordinated or clumsy? There are also moral dimensions. Do you tell only the truth? Do you "cut corners"? Further, there are social dimensions. What social class are you in? Are you married? Are you a leader? Finally, there are mental dimensions. What is your IQ? Your grade-point average? Your views of yourself are truly complex and powerful. Your self-concept is a valued possession for it influences your feelings of worth, your motivation, and your initiative.

THE IMPACT OF SELF-CONCEPT

The formation of self-concept starts very early in life. Family, friends, circumstances, and experiences can all be determinants of it. Many facets of self-concept remain virtually unchanged over long periods of time, often throughout life. Self-concept is a significant feature of a person because it is the key to behavior. The individual is anxious to avoid any behavior that downgrades self-concept, and is alert for opportunities to improve self-concept.

Each person tries to live according to a concept of self and tries to project certain personality traits. If a person succeeds in these two endeavors, behavior is in harmony with self-concept. If you sense at some point that others do not attribute to you the same image as you attribute to yourself, this discrepancy may force you to revise your behavior.

ENVIRONMENT

Environment must be included whenever behavior is examined, because at any given time, the individual is behaving in the environment of that moment. There is continuous interaction between a person and environment because they are mutually dependent variables, each capable of changing the other and being changed by the other. Actions are taken within the context of the situation or environment. An individual's behavior reflects how the total environment of the moment is seen. Obviously, the way one person evaluates a situation may be quite different from the way someone else evaluates it. For example, the optimistic salesperson may see the slimmest opportunity to persuade a reluctant prospect as a reason for persisting in his or her presentation. But the pessimistic salesperson has given up and is contemplating the next prospect. In all instances, individuals try to integrate self-concept with their environment.

Other persons are often present in an individual's environment. They can be very influential because interpersonal relations have a powerful effect on behavior. For example, you have shopped many times alone and many times with another person. You know that there were differences in your behavior in each situation. And consider the difference between your topics of conversation when with your peers and topics of conversation when with your parents. Whom you are with has much to do with how you behave.

There are other environmental elements besides people. Some are animate—dogs and cats, for example—and others are inanimate—tables, books, clothes. Some are even less obvious but are still influential: hour of the day, temperature, season, and geographic location, for example.

The awareness one has of one's environment is highly selective. How many items in a supermarket attract your attention? How much of the bulk of a Sunday newspaper do you notice? In most situations, a person can be conscious of only a small portion of the elements of, or potential stimuli in, the environment. One's awareness could always be greater. You may note some objects or people in passing, then pay no further attention; such items may never gain your genuine awareness. Occasionally, however, a person seeks out some environmental elements. A generalization is that individuals pay attention to a potential stimulus only if that stimulus is thought to affect self-concept.

PERCEPTION

The **perception** process is based mostly on stimulus-response relationships. An external stimulus is something in a person's physical environment that excites a sense organ enough to cause a response. The stimulus can be a physical element, an act, a situation, a change, or an event. Each of these stimulates the senses because of some attribute such as size, intensity, color, movement, position, contrast, or isolation. An internal stimulus originates inside the individual. Examples of internal stimuli may include pain, fear, discomfort, hunger, and thirst. A response is a person's reaction to a stimulus.

STEPS IN THE PERCEPTION PROCESS

There are several kinds of perception, each of which leads to the formation of concepts. A concept is a thought, an opinion, or an idea that grows out of a stimulus-response pattern. A concept can be an image or an inner representation of an act, an object, a person, an event, a condition, or a relationship. In the most common type of perception, the individual takes in some stimulus through one or more of the five senses—hearing, sight, touch, taste, and smell. There may be a simple stimulus (a police officer raises an arm to halt a line of automobiles), which leads to perception (in this case, by sight), which leads to the formation of a concept (my line of traffic is to stop).

Another kind of perception is called unconscious perception. For example, imagine a student starting to write a term paper but facing the basic problem of how to organize it. Suddenly, perhaps during some other activity, the sections fall into place in a logical sequence. There were stimuli that eventually resulted in the concept of how to organize the paper, but they were not consciously defined.

Perception does not stop with the awareness of some outside stimulus, however. Perception includes the individual's selection of stimuli for attention, her or his interpretation of that stimuli, and the coherent organization of these concepts into the individual's personal world. Perception is the major determinant of how you adapt to your world.

PERCEPTUAL FIELD

Everything that a person sees or knows about the world is included in the **perceptual field**. The dimensions of the perceptual field depend on an individual's past experiences, needs and wants, emotional makeup, mental set (readiness to react almost automatically to a stimulus), membership in a particular social class and in various reference groups, and the physical environment.

Your self-concept controls much of what enters into your perceptual field. It determines whether you reject or accept certain stimuli instantly and automatically. For example, your perceptual field may pick up any announcement of an upcoming quiz, but reject what someone is saying in the seat beside you. Your perceptual field does not function on the basis of chance, or on the basis of random selection. Rather, it hunts and accepts stimuli that can affect self-concept.

No two perceptual fields are alike, because no two people are alike. Our perceptual fields reflect everywhere we have ever been; everything we have seen, heard, tasted, smelled, and touched; everything we have experienced, thought, and learned. The differences between individual perceptions pose a great problem to sellers. For example, imagine how the different perceptual fields of the following people would cause them to perceive a television commercial: marketing student, English instructor, advertising instructor, Better Business Bureau investigator, copywriter, advertiser's lawyer, media representative, artist, and prospective buyer.

LEARNING

Although learning is a complicated process, and one which is not fully understood, we must acquire some basic facts about it because of its influence on behavior. The stimulus-response relationship is the essence of learning. To learn is to accumulate associations or relationships between certain behavior patterns (including the purchase and consumption of specific products or services), and the satisfaction or dissatisfaction that results. When the probability increases that a certain act will be repeated, or when the probability decreases that some other act will be repeated, something has been learned.

REINFORCEMENT

Reinforcement is necessary if learning is to take place. When a person experiences gratification because of a particular response to a stimulus, there has been positive reinforcement. The greater the satisfaction, the stronger the stimulus-response relationship and the incentive to repeat it. Continuing positive reinforcement encourages automatic reaction to the stimulus involved and recommends that the selection of response be based more and more on habit.

Reinforcement also leads to the assigning of ratings to concepts. Ratings may range from very positive to very negative. Those valued as "very positive" are approved and sought. Those valued as "very negative" are unpleasant and avoided. Ratings can be assigned to concepts concerning such things as persons, institutions, activities, services, and products.

HABIT-BASED AND PROBLEM-SOLVING BEHAVIOR

Positive reinforcement and positive concept values lead to repetition, and over time repetition becomes habit. The relationship between a stimulus and its most satisfactory response becomes largely fixed, usually operating below the conscious level. In habitual, routine behavior, little or no consideration is given to other possible responses.

More of a person's behavior is of the habitual type than of the problem-solving type. In problem-solving behavior, the individual makes a conscious choice from among several options. The more serious or infrequent the situation, the more likely problem-solving behavior will be used. Sometimes habitual behavior is not possible. If a store is sold out of your regular product brand, for example, you are forced into problem-solving behavior.

MOTIVATION

Psychologists do not agree on just how **motivation** operates. We do know, however, that each individual has needs, and as soon as one need is satisfied, another appears.

A motive is an impetus for an individual to act. It results from a recognized need or want. An individual's overall motivation is to maintain a certain self-concept by behaving in accordance with it. When a situation demands the protection of self-concept or when it offers an opportunity to enhance self-concept, the individual experiences a feeling of need. This prompts the individual to initiate and direct behavior in a particular direction; a direction determined by the perception of self and the environment.

THE HIERARCHY OF NEEDS

The hierarchy of needs was developed by psychologist Abraham Maslow in an attempt to classify those needs that fueled one's motives. Maslow suggested that people have five basic needs and they are ordered from bottom to top based on those that are most important to the person. This hierarchical model is shown in Figure 3-3.

The most basic needs according to Maslow are the person's physiological needs. These needs include hunger, thirst, and sleep. The second group of needs are safety and security. The third group of needs represents one's social needs: the need to love and be loved, to belong, and to have friends. The fourth group of needs is for self-esteem and status. The person has a need to be recognized by others. And the final group of needs is for self-actualization. This is the need to be "all you can be," to realize all of one's self-development goals.

Maslow suggests that individuals satisfy first those needs that are most important to them, and then work on satisfying the others. Thus, working from the bottom up, the person is likely first to satisfy those needs for hunger and thirst in order to survive. Beyond survival, individuals will satisfy their need to be safe and secure. Once an individual feels

MASLOW'S HIERARCHY OF NEEDS

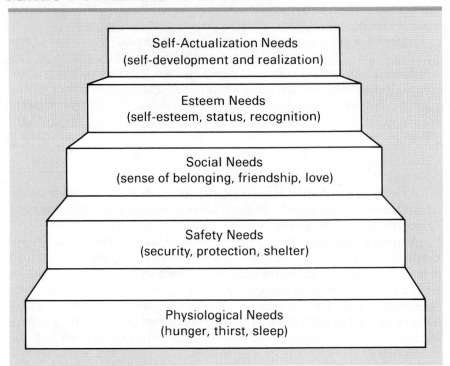

Figure 3-3 Salespeople's ability to understand the customer's motives may help to increase their effectiveness.

Source: Abraham Maslow, *Motivation and Personality* (New York: Harper & Row, 1954).

secure, she or he will attempt to develop friends, to join groups, to fall in love and to be loved by someone. The hierarchy suggests that this continues until all of the person's needs are met.

Must one level of needs be totally satisfied before going on to the next? No! Individuals, it is recognized, may be motivated to satisfy several groups of needs at the same time. If individuals' lower order needs are not satisfied, often they will focus their attention on satisfying them, while de-emphasizing the others. However, over time, the degree of emphasis a person places on each of his or her needs is dependent upon the relative level of each of these needs at a given point in time.

Salespeople can make use of Maslow's hierarchy of needs if they can determine which set of needs is more important for each particular customer. For example, if the salesperson knows a customer's motivation for buying an automobile is not travel or safety, but rather status or self-esteem, a presentation can be adapted to add certain words or phrases that would appeal to that particular need. For instance, the salesperson might talk about the prestigious styling of the car, or the "look of confidence" one might exude when riding in it. Of course, if the automobile is being purchased for travel or safety, the salesperson might emphasize the car's comfort and stability. The words the salesperson uses create a mental picture in the customer's mind. And these clues may be enough to trigger the customer's motives.

VARIATIONS IN BUYING MOTIVES

Motivation is an intensely personal matter. No two persons have exactly the same needs or buying motives because no two persons are identical. Each individual establishes goals and decides, subject to personal limitations, what he or she is willing to pay to achieve those goals. Consumers decide which benefits and advantages they want to enjoy, then buy those products and services that promise the chosen benefits.

A seller quickly discovers that buying motives vary in strength and that this variation can be from person-to-person and time-to-time. Person-to-person variations in buying motivation reflect the fact that no two individuals are alike. Hereditary background is one factor which helps explain why one person's buying motives are different from another's. "Hereditary background" refers to a person's culture, subculture, and family history; all of these are uncontrollable by the individual and affect socialization and development of motives. Other important factors are personality, capabilities, training, education, experience, environment, social status, occupation, and income.

Time-to-time variations in buying motivation reflect the fact that each individual buyer experiences changes in the pattern of motivation. Age is obviously a variable that affects desires and abilities. Seasons of the year, business cycles, moods, and immediate circumstances can also cause variations in an individual's buying motivation.

LIFESTYLES

Lifestyle is total behavior. The lifestyle of an individual can be determined with great accuracy if one learns how that individual spends money, particularly for status symbols, and how he or she spends time. Sometimes a lifestyle is adopted by a group, a family, or some other reference group. A group's lifestyle may be unusual—even bizarre. However, more consumers conform to common lifestyles than deviate. Whatever your lifestyle, it expresses you or you would change it.

GOALS AND GOAL-OBJECTS

Goals are the conditions, objects, experiences, or activities that motivate behavior. All voluntary behavior is goal-directed behavior. A goal reflects the concept of a desired state of affairs. A **goal-object** is a specific item which will help to produce that state. Consumption or use of a goal-object allows one to achieve a goal. For example, if one feels thirsty, the goal is alleviation of that thirst; the goal-object is some type of beverage.

The typical goal-object is an assortment of features, some of which are positive and some of which are negative. For example, a product of high quality (positive) usually has a high price (negative). Most products, when they function as goal-objects, consist of physical features plus various attributes such as credit terms, store location, manufacturer's image, buying assistance, design, and status. The best goal-object is the one with the best assortment of features for the need in question.

RATIONALIZATION

In studying motivation, the concept of **rationalization** is an important one to consider. Rationalization is the individual's attempt to justify behavior on logical and proper bases. The outcome of some behavior is embarrassing because it is disappointing. Also, the motivation for some behavior may be unethical or illegal. The self-concept, when it is healthy, rejects behavior that fails in its undertaking and denies motivation that incriminates. Both are unacceptable to the self-concept and to other individuals. Thus, an individual may resort to the practice of assigning respectable explanations to the behavior in question so as to disguise the truth.

Figure 3-4 Through personal attention, a salesperson helps a customer feel good about his purchase.

Suppose a retailer enters a manufacturer's window display contest but does not win a prize. Instead of admitting that the display did not deserve to win, the retailer rationalizes by saying that the manufacturer awarded the prizes to friends. Or suppose that because of the faulty buying of a purchasing agent, a small hand tool used by certain production employees turns out to be unsatisfactory. Instead of admitting that the buying proposition was not carefully evaluated, the purchasing agent claims to have been misled by the tools salesperson. A cruise taken for fun could be claimed to be for the traveler's health. An executive whose expensive wardrobe is bought for pride may say business demands it. Rationalization helps reduce mental anguish by helping to protect one's self-concept.

ATTITUDES

The views or convictions a person holds about or toward something are called **attitudes**. Every person brings to every situation an assortment of predispositions—needs, interests, goals, motives, opinions, values, beliefs, and preferences. They are the expectations that reflect the person's anticipation of events or experiences. They are the evaluation, feeling, and inclination to take favorable or unfavorable action toward an object. Attitudes are similar to what we call tastes. Here is a list of objects of which buyers form attitudes that are of particular interest to salespeople:

- Product type
- Retailer
- Salesperson
- Sellers' policies
- Brand or make
- Manufacturer
- Advertising
- Ideas

Attitudes vary in basic ways. They can be positive (favorable), neutral, or negative (hostile). They can be easy or difficult to change, but most strongly held attitudes cannot be changed quickly. An attitude can be powerful or weak as a determinant of behavior.

HOW ATTITUDES DEVELOP

An individual acquires attitudes from experience. Social interaction, experimentation and trial, and interpersonal communication are powerful determinants of one's attitudes. The odds are that many of your attitudes were learned while you were growing up.

Attitudes are formed whenever a buyer examines or tries a new type of product, brand, or retail store. When a friend, neighbor, or opinion leader reports on purchase and consumption of a product or service, the buyer's attitude is likely to be affected. The promotional communication of sellers affects the buyer's attitude.

ATTITUDES AND BEHAVIOR

Attitudes influence total behavior. They incline a person to look with favor or disfavor on elements in the perceptual field. They influence an individual to be ready to respond in a predetermined way to certain experiences. Attitudes influence reaction to all communication—exposure (attention), learning (decoding), perception (grasp), and remembering (retention). Generally, changes in attitudes cause behavioral changes.

Buying behavior is greatly influenced by a buyer's current attitude toward types of products, brands, salespeople, manufacturers, retailers, prices, etc. Buyers interpret and respond to sellers' promotions favorably or unfavorably, usually in accordance with the buyer's experience, values, and expectations. Sometimes, a change in attitude can trigger a change in buying behavior. For example, an impressive advertisement or a persuasive presentation by a salesperson can induce a buyer to try a product or a brand for the first time. Sometimes such a change in buying behavior can change an attitude. If a skeptical buyer tries a new product or brand and likes it, skepticism may change to favorable enthusiasm.

A seller may try to change unfavorable attitudes or may try to strengthen favorable attitudes. It is possible to revise the product offering more easily than it is to change an unfavorable attitude. The revised product offering may increase the number of favorable attitudes.

MODEL OF CONSUMER BUYING BEHAVIOR

Our glance at motivation leads naturally into an attempt to build a model of what actually takes place when an ultimate consumer considers buying a product. Salespeople must influence buyers to buy. Purchase-sale transactions are the core of all business because each business firm must sell at a profit if it is to survive. Only if salespeople have adequate understanding of the steps or phases of the buying process can they persuade individuals to become buyers. A diagram of a consumer buying process model is shown in Figure 3-5.

NEED IDENTIFICATION

A sense of need appears when an individual perceives either a threat to self-concept or an opportunity to enhance self-concept. Both of these cause tension or disequilibrium and put pressure on the individual to take appropriate action. Both make the individual aware of a difference

MODEL OF THE CONSUMER BUYING PROCESS

```
┌─────────────────┐
│      Need       │
│  Identification │
└─────────────────┘
          │
          ▼
┌─────────────────┐
│   Information    │
│     Search       │
└─────────────────┘
          │
          ▼
┌─────────────────┐
│   Evaluation    │
│       of        │
│   Alternatives  │
└─────────────────┘
          │
          ▼
┌─────────────────┐
│    Purchase     │
│    Decision     │
└─────────────────┘
          │
          ▼
┌─────────────────┐
│  Postpurchase   │
│   Evaluation    │
└─────────────────┘
```

Figure 3-5 Salespeople can persuade individuals to become buyers if they have a proper understanding of the steps the individual goes through in making buying decisions.

between the actual condition and a better condition which is possible to obtain.

The realization that one has unsatisfied needs will trigger a motive to satisfy that need. Maslow's hierarchy of needs, discussed earlier in this chapter, illustrates some of the needs that might be identified. The salesperson can be effective here by helping customers recognize their needs.

INFORMATION SEARCH

When potential buyers recognize that an unsatisfied need exists, they are likely to search for alternative ways to rectify the situation. The length of time spent in searching for information will depend on (1) how much information is needed; (2) how important satisfaction or immediate gratification is to that person; and (3) where the consumer must go to find the information.

AMOUNT OF INFORMATION NEEDED

The amount of information to be gathered depends on what consumers already know. In terms of information search, there are three types of decisions:

1. **Extensive Problem Solving:** When customers have little or no information about the product or any of the brands that are available, it is likely that they will have to do an extensive search for information. For example, the customer has recognized the need for a personal computer but has never purchased one before, and only knows what he or she has seen on television commercials. It is likely that the person, given his or her lack of knowledge and the high level of risk involved in purchasing a costly personal computer, will probably spend a great deal of time searching for information in order to make an intelligent decision. First of all, the customer will have to learn about computers in general, then about the features that are available, and then about the brands that are offered.
2. **Limited Problem Solving:** When customers have a good level of knowledge concerning a product category, they may only have to learn about the new product features or new brands that are available. In this situation, the customer probably has purchased the product before, or maybe has used the product at work. In either case, the customer has a good working knowledge of the product offerings and may even have developed attitudes about some of the brands. Thus the level of information search required is limited.
3. **Routinized Behavior:** When customers purchase a product regularly, they have well-defined attitudes concerning all of the brands that are available. These customers have as close to "perfect knowledge" as possible, and probably will not search at all. Instead, they will buy based on habit. The act of buying brand X has become routine for these customers, and the product is often bought without considering the alternatives.

Salespeople can have a strong influence on customers during the information search stage by providing information when it is needed. Sales representatives are vital sources of information to consumers, and can have a strong effect on decisions if they present the information in a satisfactory manner.

LEVEL OF PRODUCT IMPORTANCE

The level of importance of a product or a concept determines the degree of "involvement." When customers are very interested in a product/service, or when that product/service is very important to them, they are said to be "highly involved." When they have little interest in the product/service, they are said to have a low level of involvement.

Salespeople can influence low-involvement customers merely by making their product or service available as a sample or as a demonstration. Because they are not very involved with the product/service, customers may opt for the first brand that satisfies their needs, and with continued satisfaction will likely make subsequent purchases a routinized decision. Thus, by being the first to approach these customers, and by making the product/service readily available, the salesperson may be establishing long-term customers.

Highly involved customers present a different challenge to the salesperson. The salesperson must prove superiority of his or her product/service over other alternatives. In doing so, the salesperson must be cooperative in providing the customer with as much information as possible in order for the customer to make a good decision.

WHERE TO FIND INFORMATION

Product or service information is obtained from two different sources: internal and external. Internal sources are those that are part of the customer's memory. A person develops attitudes and learns product information based on past experiences with the product. When that information is needed, it is retrieved from memory and combined with any new information that has been found.

Figure 3-6 Information from *Consumer Reports* helps consumers evaluate purchases.

External sources, on the other hand, are the ones consumers must go out and actively search for, or be exposed to. Examples of this type of information are the salesperson's presentation, advertisements, promotional materials such as catalogs, brochures, packaging information, and publicity. Sometimes the consumer will go out and buy information from an external source. These include special-interest magazines that rate products and rating-service publications, such as *Consumer Reports*, which rate and compare brands in product categories against each other.

Salespeople are another external source of information. Good salespeople provide exact information in an honest fashion to their customers. It is important for the salesperson to provide this information honestly, since, as we will see later, customers will recognize an over-exaggerated product and will probably not purchase from that salesperson again. Being honest with the customer is a sign of "class," which is a credit to the salesperson, the company, and the product. If customers perceive the salesperson to be dishonest, they will not buy from that salesperson. Customers only trust those they perceive to be credible sources of information.

EVALUATION OF ALTERNATIVES

When customers have finished collecting information on the various alternatives, they will evaluate each and select the one that best satisfies their needs. Some consumers evaluate each alternative on a very rational basis. That is, selecting those features that are most important to them, assigning an importance weight to each feature, and then rating each alternative on each particular feature. The brand that has the highest cumulative score is the brand that will be selected. This method of evaluating alternatives is shown in Table 3-1.

In Table 3-1, the customer has limited shelf space and is deciding among three brands of gourmet popping corn. The most important features are consumer demand and profit margin, which are represented by importance weights of "10"; least important is product image with a weight of "5." Each of the three brands is then given a performance rating from 1 to 10, with 10 being the highest. To determine each brand's score, the customer would multiply the importance weight for each feature by the performance rating for each feature, and then add all of the scores together to get a total score. Thus, Brand X is scored as follows:

Consumer Demand	$10 \times 7 = 70$
Profit Margin	$10 \times 8 = 80$
Promotional Support	$8 \times 5 = 40$
Service/Availability	$7 \times 8 = 56$
Product Image	$5 \times 7 = 35$
Total Score	281

EVALUATING COMPETING BRANDS OF GOURMET POPPING CORN TO BE STOCKED IN A SUPERMARKET

Weight × Rating = Score

Features	Importance Weight	Performance Rating		
		Brand X	*Brand Y*	*Brand Z*
Consumer Demand	10	7 (70)	8 (80)	10 (100)
Profit Margin	10	8 (80)	4 (40)	7 (70)
Promotional Support	8	5 (40)	10 (80)	8 (64)
Service/Availability	7	8 (56)	7 (49)	6 (42)
Product Image	5	7 (35)	8 (40)	5 (25)
Total Score		281	289	301

Table 3-1 Buyers, especially in industrial markets, sometimes make use of multiattribute rating models to help them make the best rational decision.

Brand Z in this example is the obvious choice, even though Brand X and Brand Y have superior ratings to Brand Z on three of the five features. Brand Z's high ratings on the more important features make up for the difference.

Of course, this type of rational evaluation is not done by all consumers for every product/service. In fact, most people do this type of calculation in their heads, if they do it at all. Many consumer products/services are selected for emotional reasons. Style, prestige, status, and self-concept are all emotional reasons consumers buy certain products. Consider all the status-symbol products that are purchased merely to impress others or to make one "look good."

Salespeople fit into the consumer's rational evaluation by, first, being one of the alternatives to be rated; second, making sure that their brand's strength (feature) is given a high importance weight; and third, making sure that their brand is rated highly on performance. How does one do this? First, they must enter the buying process early, when the consumers are doing their search. By providing an abundance of information, and developing a rapport with the customer, salespeople are almost assured of being considered. Second, salespeople improve the importance weight for their strong feature by pointing out how important that feature is to the customer. The customer might not realize how important that feature is until someone points it out. That someone is the salesperson. Finally, salespeople can improve their brand's rating on these features by providing the product to the consumer for a demonstration or a sample. Many consumers have prior perceptions about a product/service based on what they have heard, or read, or seen on television. They do not know any better until they gain some experience with that product/service. The salesperson's job is to give the consumer the experience.

Salespeople can influence the consumer's emotional evaluation of their product/service by appealing to the consumer's emotions. If the consumer wants status and prestige, talk status and prestige! If they want safety, talk safety. If style is important, stress your product's style. If the salesperson's product does not fit into the prestigious, stylish, or status-symbol category, the salesperson must downplay these emotional variables and stress the rational, thus trying to change the consumer's evaluation from an emotional one to a rational one. This will enable their product to be one of those being considered.

PURCHASE DECISION

The purchase decision is many decisions wrapped into one. First, to buy or not to buy? The decision, itself, is not always to purchase. Instead, the individual might postpone the purchase until later, or not purchase at all. Once the decision has been made to purchase, the next decision is, which brand? Based on the evaluation of alternatives consumers might decide on a certain brand to purchase. However, the decision is not finished. The next part of the decision is from which store they should buy the brand, and which form of payment they will use—cash, credit card, or check. All of these factors go into the purchase decision.

The salesperson, in dealing with a customer at this stage, should make the customer feel as comfortable as possible. The sale should be the natural result of the customer's evaluation and decision. Where appropriate, the salesperson should have the purchase order filled out and ready to be signed. A pen should be on hand, as well as any financing or credit information that may be needed in closing the deal.

POSTPURCHASE EVALUATION

The consumer's buying process does not end when the purchase has been made, because a customer will almost always evaluate whether the choice was a wise one or not. If the product satisfies his or her expectations, the consumer will likely validate that choice. However, if the product or service fails to satisfy those expectations, the customer will start to question whether or not he or she should have bought another brand, or if anything should have been purchased at all. This latter situation is known as **postpurchase dissonance**.

One technique that buyers use to combat postpurchase dissonance is to initiate interpersonal communication soon after buying. A consumer may talk with a member of the family or a friend. Ads promoting the item bought may be thoroughly read. Reassurance and support are needed, particularly for more expensive items, and information consistent with the buying decision is welcome.

Sometimes a consumer obtains information that would have caused different buying behavior if it had been received sooner and if the decision had been made on that basis alone. After the purchase, the consumer may learn of better products or services, lower prices, negative case histories, or hostile attitudes and norms. If postpurchase dissonance is strong, an order may be canceled, payment on the check stopped, or the product may be returned.

When a discrepancy develops between a buyer's expectations and a subsequent experience, or a state of disharmony is detected among actions and attitudes, or it is sensed that the purchase was inconsistent with one of his or her reference group's norms, then there is the psychological discomfort called postpurchase dissonance. In general, individuals try to avoid any experience that will knowingly cause postpurchase dissonance and welcome experiences that will cause postpurchase consonance.

The salesperson can influence the customer's postpurchase evaluation prior to and after the purchase being made. By being honest with the customer, and not overexaggerating the product's capabilities during the information search stage, the salesperson is doing his or her part to develop realistic expectations within the customer. Postpurchase dissonance is likely to happen only when the customer has unrealistic expectations. Though the salesperson often confronts the dilemma of "overexaggerate and make the sale; be honest and lose the sale," he or she is well advised that "honesty is the best policy." Salespeople must understand that eventually a customer will realize that he or she has been lied to. When that happens, the customer loses all trust in the salesperson, the company, and the product/service, and is likely to voice his or her displeasure to friends and relatives. Word-of-mouth communication can be a tremendous advertising tool, but it can also be the "kiss of death" to a salesperson. Much of the success salespeople enjoy depends on the trust customers have in them. Once that trust is shattered, customers and those they have an influence over are lost forever.

After the sale, the salesperson can minimize postpurchase dissonance by following up and ensuring that the customer is satisfied by showing the product's proper usage, how to care for the product, and by providing quick and effective service.

THE ORGANIZATIONAL BUYING PROCESS

Organizations also go through a buying process in making their purchasing decisions. Industrial purchases, however, are far more complex than consumer purchases. Industrial purchase decisions require not only more prepurchase activities, but more people are involved in such decisions. This section discusses the organizational buying process, the types of organizational buying decisions, and the roles organizational members play within the decision process.

STAGES OF THE ORGANIZATIONAL BUYING PROCESS

The buying process for many industrial purchases can be viewed through a sequence of eight stages. These are shown in Figure 3-7, which includes a description of what is going on during each stage.

TYPES OF ORGANIZATIONAL BUYING DECISIONS

Just as there are different types of consumer buying decisions based on their current knowledge, so are there different types of organizational buying decisions.

NEW BUY

A new buy situation is one in which the company has never purchased this type of product or service before, and thus has little or no current knowledge of the choices. An example of a new buy might be a small company's purchase of a personal computer in order to automate its accounting system. Because it is a new buy, the company is likely to go through all eight stages of the decision process.

The salesperson should get involved early in the decision process of a new buy product/service. Since the organization has little knowledge, the sales representative who provides the most honest and helpful information is likely to have an edge over those sales representatives who enter the scene later.

MODIFIED REBUY

In a modified rebuy situation, the customer has ordered the product or service in the past but is interested in finding out more about the other alternatives. This usually happens because the current product is not performing up to expectations, or because new technology has created new products.

If this is the case, the salesperson must find out why the customer is not satisfied and try to correct the problem. Otherwise, the salesperson must make sure that his or her product/service is one of the products/services being considered for the change.

STRAIGHT REBUY

The straight rebuy is a routine reorder process that may even be automated. Salespeople whose product/service is being routinely reordered each time must make sure that the customer is satisfied. They can do this by ensuring on-time delivery and top performance. This salesperson does not want the customer to look elsewhere.

STAGES OF THE ORGANIZATIONAL BUYING PROCESS

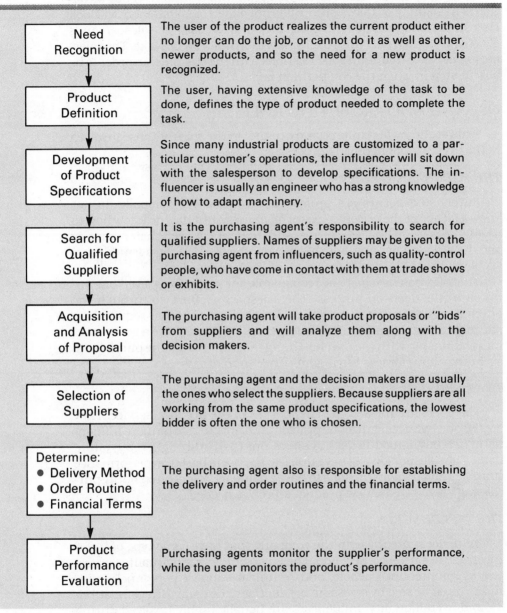

Need Recognition	The user of the product realizes the current product either no longer can do the job, or cannot do it as well as other, newer products, and so the need for a new product is recognized.
Product Definition	The user, having extensive knowledge of the task to be done, defines the type of product needed to complete the task.
Development of Product Specifications	Since many industrial products are customized to a particular customer's operations, the influencer will sit down with the salesperson to develop specifications. The influencer is usually an engineer who has a strong knowledge of how to adapt machinery.
Search for Qualified Suppliers	It is the purchasing agent's responsibility to search for qualified suppliers. Names of suppliers may be given to the purchasing agent from influencers, such as quality-control people, who have come in contact with them at trade shows or exhibits.
Acquisition and Analysis of Proposal	The purchasing agent will take product proposals or "bids" from suppliers and will analyze them along with the decision makers.
Selection of Suppliers	The purchasing agent and the decision makers are usually the ones who select the suppliers. Because suppliers are all working from the same product specifications, the lowest bidder is often the one who is chosen.
Determine: • Delivery Method • Order Routine • Financial Terms	The purchasing agent also is responsible for establishing the delivery and order routines and the financial terms.
Product Performance Evaluation	Purchasing agents monitor the supplier's performance, while the user monitors the product's performance.

Figure 3-7 Organizational buyers go through a more involved process since their purchases tend to be much larger and more expensive than consumers'. Many industrial products are customized; thus, product definition and specification development stages are needed. Also, industrial buyers usually need to determine financing, delivery, and order-routine terms.

The salesperson who is trying to break into a straight rebuy situation is in an unfavorable position. It is not likely that customers will look elsewhere if they are currently satisfied. In this case, the salesperson is effectively "locked out" until the competition makes a mistake. The salesperson needs to maintain good relations with the customer in order to be able to step in when the competition fails.

ORGANIZATIONAL BUYING ROLE

This section will reinforce and expand on the roles of those involved in the organizational buying process.

THE PURCHASING AGENT

Purchasing agents are professional buyers. They usually do not know a lot about the various types of machinery, but they do know how to negotiate, develop financial terms, and interact between their company and the seller's company. For this reason, the purchasing agent is most visible in the initial and later stages of the process.

The purchasing agent is responsible for organizing everyone involved in the decision process. The salesperson must go through the purchasing agent, who directs the salesperson to the other required departments. For this reason, the salesperson must cultivate a good working relationship with the purchasing agent even though the purchasing agent may have far less buying influence than others.

THE USERS

The users are the actual beneficiaries of the product/service. They are the ones who recognize the problem and are likely to be more influential in new buy or modified rebuy situations than in straight rebuy situations. The salesperson will have to sell to the users based on performance statistics and demonstrations to have an impact. Users often notify purchasing agents that a new product search is needed.

THE INFLUENCERS

Influencers are those in the company that have some type of influence over the purchase decision. These can be engineers, quality-control people, maintenance people, and technical support personnel. Influencers must be sold by stressing product/service reliability, compatibility, and overall quality. Influencers are usually highly involved during new buy and modified rebuy situations.

THE DECISION MAKERS

The last group of people involved are the decision makers. It is often very difficult to determine who has the most say or who are the real decision makers in an organization. For straight rebuys and other small orders, the purchasing agent may serve as the decision maker. For larger orders, however, especially new buys, the decision maker is likely to be the president, vice-president, or vice-president of finance of the buying company.

To the top executives of the buying company, the salesperson would probably stress the potential long-term profitability from purchasing the product/service. These executives are involved in the decision because of the amount of money being spent on the purchase. Industrial purchases, on average, are far more expensive than consumer purchases. Thus, the top executives must approve the deal before it is consummated.

In dealing with organizational buyers, the salesperson must learn to interact with people of differing backgrounds, to understand the roles that each of these people play in the buying process, to realize how and when to get involved in the decision process, and to develop an edge over the competition based on the type of purchase decision. Though the stages of the decision process are similar for organizations and consumers, the organizational sale is a far more complex and time consuming task than the consumer sale. Thus, the salesperson will have to work a lot harder to be successful.

SUMMARY

There are three types of buyers: (1) consumers, (2) resellers, and (3) industrial or organizational buyers. Consumers buy goods and services for their own personal or household consumption; resellers buy products in order to resell them for a profit; industrial or organizational buyers purchase products to use in making their own products or for use in their everyday operations.

Buyer behavior is influenced by culture, social class, reference groups, and family. Culture is a broad grouping of people in a specific geographic area. Subcultures are smaller groups within the overall culture. A social class is a relatively homogeneous and permanent segment of society to which individuals and families belong. Reference groups consist of individuals who have something in common, such as experiences, goals, and attitudes. The family unit is the most influential reference group. It shapes everyone's attitudes, values, norms, and buying habits.

Individual aspects of buying behavior include self-concept, perception, goals, and attitudes. One's self-concept, or view of self, controls his or her voluntary behavior. A motive is an impetus to behave and is created by needs. Perception is based in large part on stimulus-response relationships; stimuli can be external or internal. Goals are the conditions, objects, experiences, or activities that motivate behavior. Attitudes are the views a person holds about something. They are the sum of needs, interests, goals, motives, opinions, values, beliefs, and preferences.

The consumer buying process itself consists of five stages: (1) need identification, (2) information search, (3) evaluation of alternatives, (4) purchase decision, and (5) postpurchase evaluation. The organizational buying process has six stages: (1) need recognition, (2) product definition, (3) development of product specifications, (4) search for qualified suppliers, (5) acquisition and analysis of proposal, and (6) selection of supplier.

KEY TERMS

consumers
resellers
industrial buyers
social influences
culture
subculture
norms
social class
social mobility
reference groups
opinion leaders

family
self-concept
perception
perceptual field
reinforcement
motivation
goal-object
rationalization
attitudes
postpurchase dissonance

REVIEW QUESTIONS

1. What are the three types of buyers?
2. What types of services do wholesalers and retailers provide the manufacturer?
3. What is a subculture?
4. What are the three general types of norms?
5. List the seven different social classes.
6. How are social classes determined?
7. How do individuals use reference groups?
8. How is a person's position in a reference group determined?
9. Who are opinion leaders?
10. How does self-concept affect behavior?
11. What is the difference between external and internal stimuli?
12. What is a perceptual field?
13. What are the five classifications of Maslow's hierarchy of needs?
14. Describe four types of nonphysiological motives.
15. How can a salesperson determine a prospect's lifestyle?
16. Why do people rationalize?
17. How is buying behavior influenced by attitudes?
18. How can the salesperson influence the consumer's evaluation of alternatives?

19. How can the salesperson reduce the chance of consumer postpurchase dissonance before they purchase?
20. What are the main responsibilities of the purchasing agent?

DISCUSSION QUESTIONS

1. In what fields are you an opinion leader? In what fields are you an opinion follower?
2. If you were a sales representative, what words might you use to appeal to someone you knew was trying to satisfy a:
   - physiological need?
   - safety need?
   - social need?
   - esteem need?
   - self-actualization need?
3. In your opinion, does every consumer go through all five stages of the buying process every time they buy a product or service? If not, what stages do they eliminate, and why?
4. Discuss your attitude toward the last salesperson you dealt with face to face. Did you buy anything from that salesperson? Why or why not?

CASE 3-1   SUNSHINE BOATS, INC.*

Sam Benson has been a retail salesperson for televisions, automobiles, stereos, and home appliances for the past fifteen years. Having been a fisherman and boat owner for most of that time, he has decided to open a store selling boats, outboard motors, and marine accessories for recreational boaters. With the cost of some boat and motor combinations running from $8,000 to $10,000 or higher, Sam figures he will have to identify his target market carefully.

Sam has narrowed his planned boat distributorship to a certain section of San Diego, California. While the San Diego trade area has about 2.5 million residents, the per capita income of the suburbs may vary considerably. Sam has secured the exclusive distributorship for a popular line of boats and motors (Glastron boats and Evinrude motors) and would be one of the few recreational powerboat distributors in the part of the city where he is considering locating.

San Diego is located on a large bay with numerous rivers and small lakes within a short distance of the city. Also, the Pacific Ocean is close by and there are many public port facilities throughout the region. Sam has

---

*Case prepared by Dan Sherrell. Used with permission.

tentatively decided to try to locate his store somewhere in the neighborhood of Mission Bay Park or the area immediately to its north. This area is shown on the Census Tract map in Exhibit 3-1. Sam has also obtained some Census Tract data for the area he is considering (shown in Exhibit 3-2).

    Sam feels there is an unserved segment of the recreational boating public in the area of San Diego he is considering. The existing marine

EXHIBIT 3-1
SAN DIEGO CENSUS TRACTS

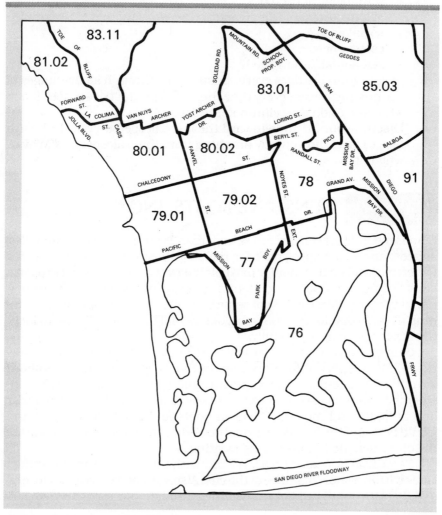

Source: U.S. Bureau of the Census

EXHIBIT 3-2
CENSUS DATA FOR PROSPECTIVE MARKET AREA

Characteristic	Census Tract					
	77	78	79.01	79.02	80.01	80.02
Households	3,949	2,399	2,743	4,771	3,450	1,022
Mean Income/ Household	$14,119	$10,620	$10,558	$9,475	$9,662	$12,305
Households With 3 or More Vehicles	540	389	203	369	428	310

Source: 1980 Census of Population & Housing

stores cater primarily to the fishing enthusiast, both freshwater and saltwater. A few stores in the city carry several boat models suitable for either fishing or pleasure boating (i.e., water skiing, cruising, etc.), but no firm in the part of town he is considering currently carries a full inventory of boats designed for the recreational segment of the boating public that has little interest in fishing. Sam is presently developing plans for his store, including considerations for location and merchandising and promotion (such as distribution of fliers and/or direct mail programs) that might be directed to particular neighborhoods.

CASE QUESTIONS

1. Using the Census data and Lotus, construct a set of indexes for households, mean income per household, and households with three or more vehicles. For each index, the base should be 100, representing the census tract with the lowest value in that series. Then create a "total index"—that is, the sum of the three indexes for each tract. Using these indexes as a guide to neighborhood marketing potential for Sam's boating equipment:
    * What tract has the greatest potential?
    * What tract has the least potential?
2. What are the advantages of this approach to solving Sam's marketing problems? What are the shortcomings?
3. What sales techniques that work successfully in the selling of automobiles might be used to sell boats and outboard motors?
4. What elements of consumer behavior might help determine buyer motives?
5. Do you think boating and boat ownership is a status symbol? Why or why not?
6. What buying motives do you think Sam might appeal to most successfully in his sales presentation?

CASE 3-2 QUALITY TV RENTAL COMPANY*

Jim Lawrence, owner of the Quality TV Rental Company of San Francisco, California, was in disagreement with his sales manager, Bob Kenison, about the buying motives of the firm's customers. Jim felt that the sales presentation used by the company's sales force was based on the wrong motivation. Bob has designed a sales presentation for apartment dwellers using the motive of economy: "Why worry about big down payments, credit checks, and large monthly notes? Instead, rent your TV from us for just the first week's rent and charge it to your credit card. All rental payments apply toward purchase. No credit-check hassles and no service problems. If your set breaks down, we'll fix it or replace it at no charge to you. Don't tie all your money up in a TV, rent from us and keep your cash."

Jim thought more emphasis should be placed on the convenience aspects of their offer for apartment dwellers. Since people in apartments move more often than those in single-family housing, Jim felt that apartment dwellers would be more likely to think of TVs as appliances, similar to refrigerators or dishwashers, which usually stay with the apartment. In addition, the ability to rent newer or larger model television sets might appeal to those who liked to show off their apartments to their friends. He was convinced that a sales presentation based on an appeal to convenience, ego, or status motives would be more effective with apartment dwellers than an appeal based strictly on economy.

Jim told Bob, "Pushing the economy motive for this group of apartment customers assumes they buy TVs for the same reasons as people who live in single-family homes or condominiums. I'm not so sure that is correct. Anyway, this is an expensive way to buy a TV. There is no way to justify renting a TV on an economic basis. The less we say about money the better off we are."

Bob disagreed, "People don't usually rent TVs unless they are short on money to buy one. Our plan makes it easy to get a TV for only the cost of a week's rent. I think the cost of buying a TV is one of the most important reasons people consider renting."

CASE QUESTIONS

1. What do you think are the main reasons or motives for people living in apartments to rent TV sets?
2. Who has the better argument, Jim or Bob? Why?
3. What kind of sales presentation would you recommend to Jim?

---

*Case prepared by Dan Sherrell. Used with permission.

CHAPTER 4
The Communication System

After studying this chapter, you should be able to:

- Identify the elements in a communication system

- Discuss sources of communication and receivers of communication

- Understand the encoding process and the transmitting process

- Demonstrate familiarity with the receiving and decoding of messages

- Present a clear picture of responses to messages

- Understand the importance of developing communication skills

- Discuss adaptive selling and its benefits through the use of adaptive selling approaches

- Understand the negotiation process and its importance in personal selling

The primary function of the salesperson is to communicate—to relate the company's offerings to prospective and existing customers. This can be done verbally—in person, on the telephone, or in writing—and through body movements, facial expressions, and other nonverbal forms of communication. Although advertising, sales promotions, and publicity are used by companies to communicate, they are all impersonal forms of communication that deny both parties feedback and the assurance of the message being fully understood. The salesperson is the company's personal communicator, and as such is usually more effective than the other forms of communication at ensuring full understanding of the company's messages.

To be an effective communicator, the salesperson must be knowledgeable of the communication process and of communication skills such as questioning, listening, and communicating nonverbally. Salespeople also must learn how to adapt their communication efforts to each prospect or customer in order to enhance their effectiveness as communicators. All of these topics will be discussed within this chapter.

The chapter begins with a description of the communications process. The discussion focuses on a communications process model and how it applies to selling. Next, the chapter reviews the skills of questioning, listening, and using and learning to read nonverbal communications. The chapter then discusses how to adapt one's communications to a particular customer. The final section focuses on the important role of negotiation in the sales process.

THE COMMUNICATIONS PROCESS

In Figure 4-1, the model shows what is happening during the course of communication. The sender is the source of the communication. Senders attempt to put their ideas in a form that is understandable by the receiver of the communication. This process is known as **encoding**. The end result is a **message**. The receiver, or "target," of the communication must take the message and interpret it to give it meaning to a situation. This interpretation process is known as **decoding**. Noise may enter the picture during the encoding and decoding processes, as well as during message transmission. **Noise** is anything that causes an incorrect message to be encoded, or a properly encoded message to be incorrectly decoded. Distractions, misunderstandings, and language differences are all considered to be noise.

The receiver's response to the message provides the sender with **feedback**. Feedback tells the sender that the receiver has understood the message correctly or that the receiver interpreted the message incorrectly. Feedback in the form of customer questions or statements is known as **two-way communication**. This form of communication is vital to the success of a sales situation, because customer involvement is essential for determining needs. If feedback is in the form of a purchase, the sender, though receiving positive results, does not know if the message has been communicated effectively. If feedback is in the form of a

A MODEL OF THE COMMUNICATION PROCESS

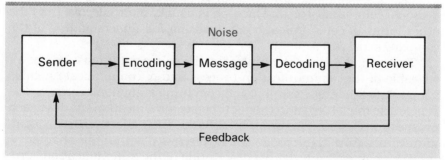

Figure 4-1 Salespeople send messages to their prospects or customers. Feedback may take the form of a purchase/nonpurchase or a question. Effective communication depends on proper encoding and decoding.

nonpurchase, the sender may have communicated effectively, but what was offered was not needed. In the latter two cases, two-way communication had not been achieved. The following section examines all phases of the communication process and discusses the importance of two-way communication to the salesperson.

SENDERS/SOURCES OF COMMUNICATION

Sources of communication are almost limitless. Individuals, groups of people, business enterprises, and other institutions try to communicate with potential customers on a daily basis. One study concluded that the typical person in the United States is exposed to over 2,000 promotional messages each day.

THE SALESPERSON AND THE COMPANY ARE SOURCES OF COMMUNICATION

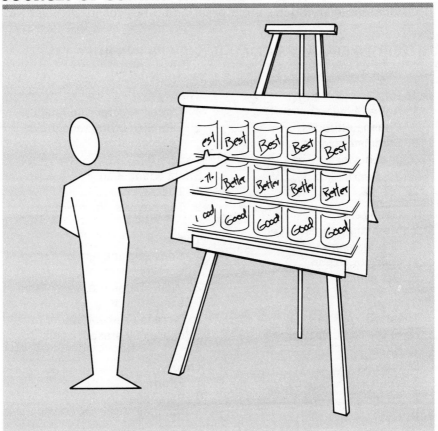

Figure 4-2 The presentation is the primary source of communication for the salesperson. Some companies also provide product literature to aid in the communication process.

On first calls, the salesperson usually is viewed by customers as an agent who delivers the company's sales message; the company is considered the source of the message. After mutually satisfactory dealings, the salesperson tends to become the source. Customers judge messages according to their sources, and salespeople need to be considered trustworthy sources by their customers.

OBJECTIVES OF SOURCES

In selling, the overall objective of sources is to influence the attitudes and behavior of buyers and people who influence buying. But several theories see sources as having more specific objectives, as shown in Figure 4-3. Some experts see the seller as trying to achieve awareness, change attitudes, and stimulate favorable behavior (Theory 1). To others, the seller tries to move the potential buyer through the definite stages of attention, interest, desire, conviction, and action (Theory 2). To still others, the seller tries to obtain affirmative answers to the five buying decisions—need, product, source, price, and time (Theory 3). Some pic-

THEORIES OF SALES COMMUNICATION OBJECTIVES

Theory 1
1. Achieve awareness
2. Change attitudes
3. Stimulate favorable actions or behavior

Theory 2
1. Get attention
2. Maintain interest
3. Create desire
4. Gain conviction
5. Get action

Theory 3
Have the customer agree to:
1. Need
2. Product
3. Source
4. Price
5. Time

Theory 4
1. Establish corporate image
2. Establish brand recognition

Theory 5
Effect changes in:
1. The buyer
2. The buyer's environment

Theory 6
1. Convert nonusers of a product into users
2. Woo customers away from competitors
3. Increase the volume of purchases by present users

Theory 7
1. Inform
2. Persuade
3. Remind

Figure 4-3 Salespeople may choose from many different theories of objectives when developing their communication.

ture the seller as communicating to establish a brand image and corporate image (Theory 4). Others see the seller as trying to effect changes in the buyer, in the buyer's environment, or in both (Theory 5). A seller also has been described as communicating for the purposes of converting nonusers of a product into users, of wooing customers away from competitors, and of increasing the volume of purchases by present users (Theory 6). Finally, some state that the seller communicates to inform, persuade, and remind (Theory 7).

The common theme in all these theories is that the seller tries to influence perceptions, attitudes, and behaviors—either by changing them or perhaps more often by reinforcing them. Whatever their specific objectives, successful persuasive communications from a source cause an internal response in the receiver that predisposes a prospect to buy and a customer to continue buying.

The objective of every salesperson (who is essentially a communicator) is to present to each customer an "offer" (information, knowledge, assurance) that will be so appealing that the customer will take the action the salesperson desires. The heart of every sales presentation is an offering. Indeed, one can say, confidently and correctly, that every sales presentation (and every ad) should be built on and actually be just that—an offer. What is offered? Satisfaction. What is satisfaction? The "disappearance," or reduced intensity, of a feeling of need, the solution to a problem, the gratification of a desire. Unless the communicator promises the receivers something desirable, the promotional communication fails in its effectiveness.

SOURCE CREDIBILITY

The more credible the source, the more likely the receiver is to accept the message. The greater the respect for the source, the more likely it is that the receiver will be persuaded to take the action the source desires. Two basic determinants of source credibility are trustworthiness and expertness in a given area. Firms seek to establish source credibility by building favorable corporate images through their advertising, sales promotion, and salespeople. The credibility standing of a salesperson determines the confidence that a customer has in that salesperson and the believability of the message the salesperson is trying to communicate. The salesperson must project the image of being an expert on the product and the company.

ENCODING THE MESSAGE

A salesperson must identify exactly the attitude and/or behavior to be changed before developing the appropriate message to effect that change. If the salesperson is to influence and persuade and if the customer is to respond favorably, the salesperson must transmit information that reaches the receiver through one or more of the senses. The customer must then take in the data and find the meaning in the message.

When a salesperson undertakes to put an idea into a form that a customer is capable of understanding, the salesperson is encoding a message. Encoding is mainly concerned with meaning—the definitions and effects of words—and communication is faulty unless the meaning of a given message is virtually the same to both the seller and the buyer. The salesperson may have to alter or customize the message for each presentation.

The fundamental element of every encoded message is an offer of satisfaction to customers who buy and use the seller's product. This satisfaction may be in the form of the disappearance of a feeling of need, the solution to a problem, or the gratification of a desire. Unless the source offers the receivers something significant and desirable, the selling communication is likely to be ineffective and will fail in its objective.

COMMUNICATION SYMBOLS

Communication symbols are substitutes for real objects, concepts, actions, or sensations. The most common kind of communication is face-to-face oral exchange, and words are the most basic communication symbols. The salesperson uses words to convey impressions. These word-symbols are stimuli to the customer, and the customer's word-symbols are stimuli to the salesperson. Other commonly used communication symbols are illustrations, numbers, and sounds.

Each communication symbol used must have a common meaning to the seller and the buyer, or the message will not be interpreted as the salesperson desires. In actuality, each customer will interpret symbols somewhat differently, because the meaning of each verbal and nonverbal symbol is determined largely by the dimensions of each customer's perceptual field. It is impossible for any salesperson to be certain that the message will be decoded exactly as it is intended. It is possible, however, to control the decoding process in some measure by understanding the norms and frames of reference of the intended customer and by encoding the message accordingly.

Communication symbols must be suitable for the salesperson, the medium, the intended message, and the customers. The symbols selected should be ones that the intended audience knows and uses.

WORDS AND SENTENCES

Salespeople must choose words carefully. Specific words (*apple pie*) are better than general words (*dessert*). Words that refer to objects (*shoes*) are safer than words that refer to intangible concepts (*security*). Short words are usually superior to long ones (*do* vs. *accomplish*); the same is true of phrases (*because* vs. *for the simple reason that*). Every word should be correct; *infer* is often used when the salesperson means *imply, since* is often used for *because.* The words in parentheses are unnecessary: *consensus* (of opinion), (final) *outcome.*

Though there are 500,000 to 600,000 words in the English language, the average conversational vocabulary consists of only 2,000 words. One-half of the typical consumer's conversation makes use of only 44 words. Some communication experts recommend that about 75 percent of the communicator's words be of one syllable. Of the 66 words in the Lord's Prayer, 48 (72 percent) are of one syllable. In Abraham Lincoln's 268-word Gettysburg Address, 196 (73 percent) are one-syllable words. One study analyzed the lyrics of the most recent top ten music hits and found that over 70 percent of the words were one syllable.

A short, direct sentence is easier to understand than a longer, more complex sentence. Familiar nouns, pronouns, and action verbs strengthen sentences and contribute interest.

WORDLESS COMMUNICATION IN SELLING

The salesperson should be an expert in both verbal and nonverbal communication. Salespeople send wordless (nonverbal) communication to customers and customers do the same to salespeople; signals flow back and forth continuously. Because most customers "read" the salesperson's signals, all of these signals should be positive. The salesperson must be sensitive to the customer's signals, "read" them, and then use them as guides as to what to do and not to do. If salespeople ignore or miss a customer's signals, they can easily lose the sale.

Below are four examples of customer-to-salesperson wordless communications:

1. A customer remains sitting at the desk and does not invite the salesperson to sit.
2. A customer treats the product with care and respect when examining it.
3. A customer gazes out the window as the salesperson moves into the presentation.
4. A customer's voice becomes harsh and the facial expression hostile when the name of the salesperson's firm is heard.

Here are four examples of salesperson-to-customer wordless communications:

1. A door-to-door salesperson takes two steps back as the door is opened.
2. A salesperson makes a totally silent product demonstration.
3. A salesperson's breath, grooming, and dress are not what they should be.
4. A salesperson extends (offers) something for the customer to take (accept).

The salesperson's wordless communication can be less specific than the examples given. The salesperson's mood or frame of mind is usually sensed by the customer; it can help or hurt. Interest in and respect for the customer (or the lack of either) are not easily concealed. The same is true of the desire to help the customer. General demeanor can be either an asset or a liability. Above all, the salesperson's attitudes communicate with powerful impact and have much to do with the salesperson's performance.

Nonverbal communication will be discussed further, later in this section. It is important, however, to know that it can be used to encode, and to transmit, the message.

FIVE CONSTRUCTION QUESTIONS

There are five basic questions a salesperson should consider in constructing, or encoding, the selling message (see Figure 4-4). First, the salesperson must decide where the most important idea should be placed. Should the message begin with it? If the idea is placed first, the salesperson is observing the principle of **primacy**. If it is placed last, the salesperson is observing the rule of **recency**. There is no agreement as to which procedure is better. Communication experts do know that concepts at the beginning and the end are more likely to be remembered than are those concepts placed in the middle of the message. The more powerful the beginning, the more likely it is that the customers' attention will be gained. The more powerful the ending, the more likely customers are to recall the message later.

The second question concerns whether the need or the answer to the need should be featured. Unless customers identify with the need that is being referred to, they will pay little attention to the message. Gaining attention is requisite to gaining acceptance and recall of the message. If the communication is to succeed, the customer must admit to the presence of need and then perceive the salesperson's recommended answer to that need. As far as position within the message is concerned, the statement of need should precede the solution to that need.

THE FIVE MESSAGE CONSTRUCTION QUESTIONS

1. Where should the most important idea be placed?
2. Should the need or the answer to the need be featured?
3. Should there be an appeal to fear?
4. Should the appeal be one-sided or two-sided?
5. Should the message draw conclusions for the receiver?

Figure 4-4 Salespeople should consider these questions when developing their presentations. The construction angles they choose will depend on their customers and the type of product.

What about appeals to fear? Such appeals can be effective in gaining attention, but they can produce an emotion that may cause the customer to reject either the message or the salesperson. There is some indication that strong appeals to fear are not as successful as less extreme appeals. For example, the insurance salesperson who says, "If you do not provide for your family's needs now, when you die they may be left penniless and forced to beg for food just to survive," may be a little too harsh for some customers to handle. If an appeal to fear is used, an escape route should be provided for the customer. This escape route, of course, is the seller's product or service. The effectiveness of the communication will be directly related to how easy the escape route is to implement.

Should salespeople present just one side of an issue (the seller's side), or should both sides be included? Few messages transmitted through nonpersonal channels such as advertising and sales promotion present both sides of an issue. In personal selling, many salespeople are forced at least to admit their products' limitations, because customers generally hear the competitor's side, anyway. Some salespeople present one side only if the audience is friendly and no counterargument is expected, but present both pros and cons if the audience is hostile. The more capable and informed the audience, the more prudent it is to include both sides of an issue.

Should selling communications include the conclusions the salesperson hopes the customer will draw? Because every promotional communication is intended to produce some response favorable to the salesperson, and buyers will sometimes miss some of the salesperson's selling points, the inclination is to include some conclusions. This practice is recommended particularly when the substance of the message is complicated or personal, and when customers' potential interest is likely to be low.

TRANSMITTING THE MESSAGE

Messages can be transmitted from salesperson to customer through several channels. The salesperson, for instance, engages in face-to-face conversation with customers. The advertiser, on the other hand, places ads in newspapers, magazines, television, radio, outdoor signs, and transit media. Many sellers also use direct-mail promotion and point-of-purchase promotion. Informal contacts and word-of-mouth exchanges are other forms of communication. Yet no one channel of communication is best universally. Most high-volume sellers use a combination, because of the many differences in audiences, objectives, messages, and situations.

Generally, personal channels are most effective when the product or service must be tailored to a customer's needs, when it must be demonstrated, when a trade-in is involved, when it is costly or infrequently bought, or when the market segment is small. Nonpersonal channels are

Figure 4-5 Outdoor signs is one channel by which messages are communicated between salespeople and customers.
Source: Foster and Kleiser Outdoor Advertising (A Metromedia Company).

effective when the product/service is well known but the customer must
be periodically reminded of its availability, the differences between competing brands are slight, the product/service is inexpensive, a special
price concession is being offered, or the statement of a single point of
differentiation may influence customers' buying decisions.

RECEIVING AND DECODING THE MESSAGE

Raw data are inputs into the customer's physiological and psychological systems. When the customer takes note of these data and converts
them into concepts, communication takes place. The receiving and decoding of a message involves three basic questions for the salesperson:

1. Did the intended customer pay attention to the message?
2. Did the customer perceive in the communication the same meaning
   the salesperson built into it?
3. Did the customer accept and believe the communication?

SELECTIVITY OF ATTENTION

There is potential reception of a message when an individual is physically able to receive it through one or more of the five senses. Potential

reception becomes actual reception when the message makes contact with one or more of those senses. In an individual's typical sensory environment, various stimuli are always present and bidding for attention. Add the salesperson's message, and there is one more competitor to be recognized. At any given moment, one can attend to only a fraction of the stimuli in one's environment. Thus, the individual exercises power to select those stimuli that will be allowed to reach the senses.

Attention may be either voluntary or involuntary. When one cannot help but notice a gaudy electric spectacle advertising some product, one's attention has been given involuntarily. Most attention related to selling communication is voluntary, however, and a person is inclined to attend to messages about matters of interest. A person is also inclined to pay attention to messages consistent with the role of the moment. A couple who are planning their vacation are more likely to be interested in a message about vacation cruises than a message about garden equipment. The best way to gain a receiver's attention is to appeal to needs and wants of the moment.

PERCEPTION AND MEANING

The way in which the receiver decodes the meaning of a message is a real problem for communicators, because communication is not precise. Perceptual fields differ, and perceptual fields determine the meaning of communication symbols. Symbols have no inherent meaning except that which is given to them by communicators and their audiences, and concepts often differ from person to person. Adding to the imprecision is the fact that many words have several accepted meanings and slightly different meanings to different persons. For example, the 500 most commonly used words in the English language have over 14,000 definitions (an average of 28 meanings per word). Take the word *fast* for instance:

- A person is *fast* when he can run rapidly.
- But he is also *fast* when he is tied down and cannot run at all.
- And colors are *fast* when they do not run.
- One is *fast* when he moves in suspect company.
- But this is not quite the same thing as playing *fast* and loose.
- A racetrack is *fast* when it is in good running condition.
- A friend is *fast* when he is loyal.
- A watch is *fast* when it is ahead of time.
- To be *fast* asleep is to be deep in sleep.
- To be *fast* by is to be near.
- To *fast* is to refrain from eating.
- A *fast* may be a period of noneating—or a ship's mooring line.
- Photographic film is *fast* when it is sensitive (to light).
- But bacteria are *fast* when they are insensitive (to antiseptics).

To determine how a customer decoded a message, three questions must be asked:

1. Did the customer interpret the symbols in the same way the salesperson did? (Interpretation)
2. Did the customer reconstruct the message the same as the message was constructed by the salesperson? (Reconstruction)
3. Is the customer's understanding of the message content the same as the salesperson's? (Understanding)

Unless the answers are yes, communication has been faulty.

One barrier to effective communication is a customer's mental set, which, as you have learned, predisposes one to almost automatic reaction to a certain stimulus. Individuals tend to perceive what they want to perceive and what they expect to perceive. Indeed, of the various determinants of perception, **expectancy** may well be the most important as far as communication is concerned. Salespeople cannot determine each customer's mental set. By understanding the buying behavior of their customers, however, salespeople can learn what mental set customers are likely to have in a given communication situation and can encode their messages accordingly.

Another problem in communicating effectively is the different meaning of symbols, particularly words, to customers. Every word has its literal, or denotative, meaning and its emotional, or connotative, meaning. In encoding their messages, salespeople should consider what connotative meanings their words and symbols are likely to have and then avoid those words and symbols that are likely to have unpleasant connotative meanings. Salespeople run the risk of being misinterpreted when they use vague, general words. The broader the classification to which the general word applies, the wider the range of interpretation. The more precise the words used, the more likely the communication is to be decoded as the salesperson intended.

Noise is a real problem in determining whether a message will be received and decoded as the salesperson intended. Anything that interferes with the communication process, whether by obstructing either sending or receiving, or distorting the message, is a form of noise. At any given moment, every customer has many personal concerns demanding attention. The current emotional state of customers can be a powerful influence on communication; it can keep them from questioning what they want to hear and stop them from hearing what they do not want to hear. In addition to this internal competition, there are competing stimuli of an external nature—the ring of a telephone, the appearance of a third party, or a malfunctioning, such as static, in the channel of communication. Any competing stimulus that distracts the customer from the message constitutes noise. For example, when the salesperson is in the customer's office making a sales presentation and the telephone rings, the customer's attention and interest are drawn to the caller. When the conversation has concluded, the customer may have forgotten the points the salesperson has already made. At this point it is wise for the salesperson to review what had taken place prior to the interruption.

ACCEPTANCE AND BELIEF

Exposure and attention to a message are essential to communicating effectively, but alone they are not enough. Perception and meaning are essential, but they are not enough. Also essential are the customer's acceptance of and belief in the message. When the communication effort is successful, the customer infers that the message is correct and then absorbs the substance of the message so that it becomes an integral part of his or her perceptual field.

How does a person conclude that one communication should be accepted and believed but that another communication should not? First, one must recognize that each person tends to believe what is in agreement with his or her experience. Beliefs tend to be founded not so much on reason as on emotion. Also, an individual acts and reacts in the environment in harmony with the mood of the moment. To be accepted and believed, the meaning of the message must be within the customer's experience and capabilities, and it must be compatible with the customer's attitudes, circumstances, and self-concept.

Just as individuals tend to see and hear what they want to see and hear, so too do they tend to believe what they want to believe. They will not accept what is true if they believe it to be untrue. This has been demonstrated in advertising illustrations which were true-to-life and realistic but were not accepted because consumers thought them too extreme to be possible. On the other hand, those same consumers often believe claims such as an offer of a "free" set of encyclopedias, an "inside" stock market tip, or "irresistible" sex appeal because most of us want to get something for nothing, to get rich quickly, or to overwhelm the opposite sex.

RECEIVERS OF COMMUNICATION

The receiver of the communication is the customer, and it is the customer who determines whether communication takes place, and what is communicated. The salesperson, therefore, must be aware of who his or her customer is. The marketing manager calls this customer the "market." A market consists of those buyers who share certain characteristics of interest to the marketer. The marketer sends persuasive messages to those persons for the purpose of accomplishing some marketing objective. In a selling situation, salespeople typically talk to one buyer at a time while advertisements are carried by mass media to mass audiences.

Those who communicate through the media find the techniques of market segmentation particularly helpful. Communication efforts are more effective if the total market can be broken down into a number of smaller segments. This process consists of three basic steps. First, the total market is defined as specifically as possible. Second, the total market is divided into smaller, reasonably homogeneous segments. Each segment consists of persons who have some similar characteristics, especially concerning circumstances, motivation, and decision making. Ideally, the salesperson wants a minimum of differences within a segment and a maximum of differences between segments. Finally, the salesperson tailors a different message to fit each segment of the market.

A similar procedure is used in personal selling, whereby the total market is divided into an industrial market and a consumer market. Other divisions may be the domestic market and the foreign market, or the government market and the private market.

No segmentation structure lasts indefinitely. Because the number of segments and the characteristics of each are always changing, continual market research is essential.

RESPONSE TO THE MESSAGE: FEEDBACK

The responses, either overt or covert, that a salesperson hopes to achieve with a message may be a new or greater demand for a product or service, increased brand preference or brand insistence, or a favorable association of the advertised product with a concept that has selling value. A salesperson wants a customer to learn from the communication, to be favorably influenced by it, and to recall it for future use. The ultimate response desired, of course, is buying action. Just as attention, perception, and belief are selective, retention is also selective. The individual can keep a concept within the perceptual field so that it can be recalled, or the concept can be discarded. Obviously, every seller wants the messages to be stored and recalled for later use.

If there is to be a favorable response to a seller's message, the communication should produce tension in the buyer. This tension results because the customer senses consciously or subconsciously either a threat to self-concept or an opportunity to enhance self-concept. Buyers feel involved because they identify with a problem or an opportunity. The customer's response must be related to and evaluated against the salesperson's objectives.

In one-way communication, the salesperson transmits but does not receive, and the customer receives but does not transmit. A salesperson in a radio or TV commercial is a one-way communicator. In two-way communication, the salesperson and the customer exchange ideas. There is action and reaction, or transmitting and feedback. Feedback can be communication that flows from the customer back to the salesperson. Some feedback is volunteered by the customer. Some is initiated unintentionally, such as a facial expression, but can still be interpreted as feedback by the salesperson. Some feedback is promoted and brought about by the salesperson. Feedback can be either verbal ("I missed that last point. Will you please repeat it?") or nonverbal (nodding, smiling). Feedback can also be a behavior, such as purchase or nonpurchase.

Salespeople rely on feedback to determine whether they are securing attention, understanding, and acceptance. For example, a salesperson can use feedback as a continuing indicator of success or failure. The salesperson can present a customer-benefit, obtain feedback, revise the presentation, obtain feedback to the revision, take further corrective action, and so on. In personal selling, feedback can be instantaneous. The salesperson and customer are each senders and receivers of communication; each generates and uses feedback. In advertising, however, feedback is delayed and is both difficult to obtain and to interpret.

COMMUNICATION SKILLS

Two-way communication is important to salespeople because it provides them with the evidence of whether or not the communication has been

TWO-WAY COMMUNICATION IS ESSENTIAL FOR DETERMINING A CUSTOMER'S NEEDS

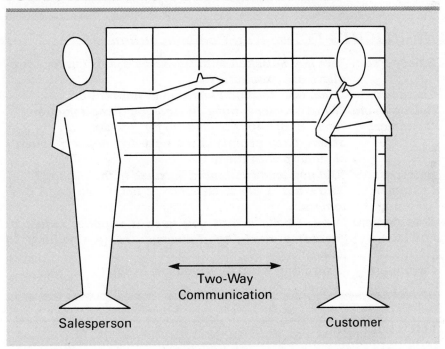

Figure 4-6 When salespeople get their customers involved in two-way communication, needs are uncovered and possible solutions are explored.

understood. If, after the presentation, the customer looks perplexed or has questions, the salesperson knows the message was not understood. This allows the salesperson a second chance to ensure that the message is understood; a chance to clarify. Without two-way communication, this lack of understanding would have continued and likely meant a lost sale.

Two-way communication is essential for the salesperson to determine the customer's needs. Once the needs are identified, the salesperson relates the product's features and benefits to the customer's needs. This improves the effectiveness of the communication by allowing the salesperson to tailor the message to a particular customer. Personalized presentations make customers feel that the salesperson is willing to do something out of the ordinary to satisfy their needs. More important, the salesperson can adhere to the marketing concept. Undoubtedly, customers are more likely to pay closer attention to the message when they are spoken with and not spoken to. Without the customer's participation full satisfaction is impossible.

Effective two-way communication requires skillful questioning and careful listening, of both words and nonverbal communication. The following sections discuss the importance of developing one's questioning and listening skills to improve two-way communications. An example of the two-way communication is shown in Highlight 4-1.

HIGHLIGHT 4-1   *Two-Way Communication*

Salesperson: *"Are you satisfied with the service your current suppliers are providing?"*

Customer: *"Well, now that you mention it, not really."*

Salesperson: *"What problems have caused you dissatisfaction?"*

Customer: *"Well, they kept me waiting for five days on my last order. They promised me next-day delivery when I signed up with them."*

Salesperson: *"Did you lose customers because of their delay?"*

Customer: *"Sure did! I bet it cost me at least two good customers."*

Salesperson: *"Well, I believe that you need a supplier who can guarantee next-day delivery. Are you willing to listen?"*

Customer: *"I sure am! What have you got to say?"*

THE SKILL OF QUESTIONING

Questioning allows salespeople to elicit information from customers regarding their situations, attitudes, and needs. This information is used by salespeople to develop effective presentations for customers. Questioning also allows for participation from customers. Participation develops interest in the product because customers are more likely to be attentive to the salesperson's presentation if they know they will be asked questions about it. This will lead customers to learn more about the product or service than if they were discouraged from actively engaging in the presentation.

GUIDELINES FOR QUESTIONING

When using questions, the salesperson should follow several guidelines to be most effective. First, the salesperson should ask **open-ended questions**. Open-ended questions require customers to answer in their own words. By providing the customer with a choice of answers, the salesperson could be shortchanging him or herself on the amount of information the customer may be willing to give. Second, the salesperson should ask questions that encourage a long response. The salesperson not only wants to know which product/service the customer is currently using, but also "why?" For this situation, the salesperson should ask a question that requires more than just a one-word or a yes-no answer. A good example of such a question is, "What features does your current product/service have that make it appealing to you?"

A third guideline is to space questions throughout the presentation rather than ask questions one after another, which may intimidate the respondent. This spacing allows for a more relaxed atmosphere and helps maintain the customer's attention until the end of the presentation.

Salespeople should be careful of the terms they use in their questions. Complex terminology, as well as complicated sentence structure, may overwhelm the customer. It is best to use short questions and simple terminology so the customer will not have trouble understanding or answering the question.

Finally, salespeople should avoid making assumptions within their questions or leading customers toward a certain response. Customers do not appreciate being forced toward a certain answer. For instance, the question "What do you like about IBM's service?" assumes that the customer likes their service, and may be met with a negative rebuttal. Also, questions that lead prospects to a certain response will mask the prospect's true feelings.

TYPES OF INFORMATION SOUGHT

Questions are used to gather different types of information. First, the salesperson is likely to use certain questions to gain specific, factual information. These questions serve the purpose of determining who, what, where, when, how, and why. This information will give the salesperson a better idea of who the prospects are, what kind of business they are in, who their competition is, and which competitors they currently are considering buying from.

Salespeople will use other questions to get opinionated information. These questions seek the prospect's feelings toward the company, its products, its services, and its competition. This type of information tells salespeople where they stand with prospects.

Prospects may not feel comfortable, however, in revealing their feelings to salespeople. Some might find these questions to be overly personal. Therefore, salespeople may want to ask these questions indirectly, possibly by using a third party. For example, "The last customer I spoke to said he has had some trouble getting his machinery serviced. Are you running into the same problem?"

Finally, a salesperson can use certain questions to clarify and summarize what has been said up to a certain point in the presentation. Clarifying information improves the salesperson's understanding of the prospect's situation, and full understanding is essential for the salesperson to satisfy the prospect's needs. Examples of questions used to obtain all three types of information are shown in Figure 4-7.

EXAMPLES OF QUESTIONS USED TO OBTAIN INFORMATION

1. Obtaining factual information:
   - Which suppliers are you currently dealing with?
   - What problems have you had with these suppliers?
   - How much are you currently paying per case?
   - Where do you stock your excess supplies?
   - Why don't you purchase in smaller quantities?
2. Obtaining opinionated information:
   - How do you feel about buying in such large quantities?
   - What is your attitude concerning the handling of product damages?
   - What is your opinion of the new products being manufactured?
   - Who do you think provides the best service?
   - Why don't you like the new styling?
3. Obtaining further information:
   - Could you show me an example of what you mean?
   - I don't quite understand—how would that affect you?
   - You mean to tell me they refused to reimburse you?
   - I'm sorry, could you repeat that?
   - Well then, do we agree with what has been discussed so far?

Figure 4-7 Salespeople should develop a list of questions they can choose from when trying to ascertain specific information.

THE SKILL OF LISTENING

Listening is essential to effective communication. However, it is one of the toughest skills for people to master. Most salespeople would prefer to talk than to listen, and even when their mouths are closed, it doesn't mean that they are really listening. They are usually worrying about what to say next to the prospect in order to convince her or him to buy. Young salespeople, especially, are unsure of themselves and are more likely trying to remember product facts and selling techniques than actually listening to what the prospect is saying.

Effective listening requires the salesperson to take an active role in the conversation. Passive listeners are those who hear but usually do not understand. Active listeners are those who put themselves into a position to feel what the prospect feels. Active listeners are aware of not only the spoken words, but the tone of voice, and the actions, or nonverbal communication, being used. Together, these provide more information to active listeners than just the words.

WHY LISTEN?

Effective listening provides the salesperson with the information needed to sell to a particular customer. The information obtained reveals the prospect's needs, likes, and dislikes, and what the salesperson must do to satisfy them. Being an active listener can save the salesperson time. Instead of discussing features the prospect is not interested in, the salesperson can instead zero in on those features that the prospect finds important. All of these factors should result in a more effective presentation, and ultimately, more sales.

ACTIVE LISTENING SKILLS

The Xerox Learning System recommends active listening as an effective way to serve one's customers. The system outlines several methods for being an effective active listener. First, salespeople should try to verify the important information they receive. This can be done by repeating the information word for word. When dealing with customers it is necessary to verify all terms, figures, and policies so that few misunderstandings arise.

Another suggestion for active listening is to rephrase information. That is, to put the information into one's own words to get the full meaning. If the salesperson has rephrased the information incorrectly, the prospect is likely to mention the mistake, and get the salesperson back on the right track.

A third suggestion is to clarify information. Clarifying information is designed to clear up misunderstandings by obtaining additional information. Proper usage of this listening skill can help the salesperson to better identify the prospect's problems and needs.

Another method of active listening is to keep a mental summary of key points that have been made during the presentation. Then, at critical times, the salesperson can state these points to provide all concerned with an overview of the situation and an insight into where the rest of the presentation should go. These four listening skills can help the salesperson to be a better active listener.

NONVERBAL COMMUNICATION

Nonverbal communication refers to messages that are sent by a person's eyes, hand and arm gestures, facial expressions, and body angle. Nonverbal communication accounts for more than 60 percent of all communication, so it is important to notice. Also, most people are unaware of the nonverbal messages that they are sending or receiving. For these reasons, it is imperative that salespeople learn how to read, and how to use, nonverbal communication, especially those involving space, eyes, facial expressions, hands, arms, and posture.

The first form of nonverbal communication to examine is space; that is, the difference in distance between the two parties. People engaged in business usually stand farther away from each other than those who are personally involved. This distance, known as **business space**, is important to recognize. If a salesperson is standing too close or tries to invade the prospect's space, the prospect is likely to back off.

The prospect's eyes are another source of nonverbal communication. Eyes can tell a salesperson whether the prospect is actively listening. If the customer is not actively listening, the salesperson's presentation will not be effective. Eyes can also express doubt, interest, and excitement. These emotions are important because they help the salesperson to trigger the prospect's feeling and to get him or her emotionally involved.

Along with the eyes, a person's facial expressions can give away emotions. In fact, these two usually accompany each other. A smiling face and sparkling eyes usually mean a person is pleased. When someone's eyes narrow and forehead furrows, the person is likely confused or doubtful. Only the most professional of customers can truly hold a "poker face" throughout the sales presentation. Comedians such as Charlie Chaplin, Jackie Gleason, Art Carney, and Chevy Chase have made millions of people laugh throughout the years not so much with what they said but with the facial expressions and body movements they made.

Hand gestures are often used to add intensity to what a person is saying. To observant salespeople, hand gestures, such as nervous twitching, might also reveal perhaps that the prospect is not being honest. Salespeople should always keep an eye on their prospect's hands, as these gestures are usually uncontrollable.

The positioning of the prospect's arms is also a good way of "reading" the prospect's intensity. If the customer is waving his or her arms vigorously while expressing an opinion, the customer is showing an emphatic commitment to that opinion. If the customer's arms are crossed, he or she may be showing a sign of defensiveness.

Finally, the angle and posture of the customer's body will communicate certain messages to the salesperson. Slumping, sitting erect, and leaning forward are all signs of the prospect's personality and level of interest in the salesperson's product. For example, someone who is slumping in a chair may be showing a lack of self-confidence. Possibly, such a person might be showing a certain level of disappointment in the salesperson's ability to satisfy his or her needs. Contrariwise, the salesperson who can satisfy this person's needs will notice the prospect's posture straighten up.

The prospect is not the only one who shows nonverbal messages. The facial expressions and body movements of the salesperson can communicate confidence to prospects and encourage them to do business with that salesperson. Thus, the proper use of nonverbal communication can be a selling tool.

ADAPTING TO THE BUYER

Whenever salespeople alter their presentations during a sales call, or use different presentations according to the customer's situation or personality, they are practicing **adaptive selling**. Adapting is less difficult when salespeople are familiar with the customer or when there is a reasonable expectation of how to deal with that particular customer. However, when the customer is completely new, salespeople have to work a lot harder in order to adjust their approach.

Salespeople who use a nonadaptive selling approach are simply memorizing a presentation and repeating it to every prospect, no matter what the situation might be. Obviously, this is a far easier approach than adaptive selling. Adaptive selling, however, is preferred in virtually every instance where the ultimate goal is customer satisfaction and a long-term buyer-seller relationship. This section will talk about the importance of adaptive selling: why adaptive selling is preferred over a non-adaptive approach; how it can be used prior to the sales call; and how it can be used during the sales call. Included in this final section is a brief discussion of the social-style matrix and transactional analysis.[1]

THE IMPORTANCE OF ADAPTIVE SELLING

Consumers are bombarded daily with marketing stimuli designed to inform, persuade, and remind them of certain products. These market-

---

[1]See Eric Berne, *Games People Play* (New York: Ballantine Books, 1978); and Thomas A. Harris, *I'm OK — You're OK* (New York: Harper & Row, 1969).

ing stimuli can range anywhere from television commercials to direct-mail flyers to store signs. Consumers can view the stimulus and absorb its meaning, but cannot immediately respond to it in any form other than by purchasing or not purchasing the product. Thus, the appeal of personal selling. Compared to advertising, sales promotion, and publicity, personal selling is the only form of marketing communication that provides the customer with an immediate response to a marketing stimulus. This allows the marketer (salesperson) to adapt messages to that particular customer's attitudes, personality, and situation. Whereas advertisers and sales promotion people must do market research to determine what the customers want, salespeople only need to ask the customers and then listen to their responses. While advertisers develop messages for the broad masses, salespeople can develop messages for the individual. And while it takes months of monitoring an advertisement to determine its effectiveness, salespeople can determine their presentation's effectiveness and make any necessary adjustments in a matter of minutes.

ADAPTIVE VS. NONADAPTIVE SELLING

There really is little comparison in the effectiveness of adaptive and nonadaptive approaches to selling. Adaptive selling is far better in making the customer feel comfortable and relaxed, because the salesperson is making every effort to adapt. In a nonadaptive approach salespeople are forcing the same presentation on all customers regardless of their situation, the way they feel, or whether or not they even understand. Consequently, the amount of nonadaptive selling that is used has been reduced.

Adaptive selling is preferred over nonadaptive selling because it provides the salesperson with the opportunity to "save" a sales presentation that is heading toward failure. Sometimes a presentation is geared toward a particular benefit, say a cost savings, that does not have an effect on that customer, perhaps because cost is not an issue to her or him. Salespeople using the adaptive approach can detect that the cost-saving benefit is of little concern to that customer, and then relate the features of their product or service to that particular benefit. Under a nonadaptive selling approach, the salesperson would still be stressing cost, and the customer will have given up on that presentation.

Nonadaptive selling does have its place, though. With some products customers will have the same basic needs, or will receive the same basic benefit, so the salesperson can use the same sales pitch repeatedly. In other instances, the salesperson may not be skilled enough to adapt to different customers or different situations. Thus, a nonadaptive approach would be best for the salesperson to simply get the message across. However, it does not provide the salesperson with any flexibility.

ADAPTING ONE'S PRESENTATION

Salespeople can adapt their messages to buyers prior to making a presentation. Before calling on a prospect the salesperson should obtain as much information on that prospect as possible. This is part of the preapproach which is discussed in depth in Chapter 9. The salesperson will conduct a customer profile, which is a collection of background information regarding the buyer and the buyer's company. This information can be collected from the prospect's secretary, other salespeople who deal with that prospect, trade publications, or from the prospect directly when calling for an appointment.

The salesperson then takes the customer profile and tries to determine which product features will appeal to this type of person. Research enables the salesperson to develop a full plan of attack for selling to this particular customer. This plan of attack is known as the *customer benefit plan*. This form of adaptive selling can be very effective, providing all of the information the salesperson has gathered is true. If so, it should result in a very smooth, relaxed selling atmosphere. Also, the better the adaptation prior to the sales call, the less needed during the presentation.

ADAPTING DURING THE PRESENTATION

Adaptation during the presentation is more difficult to achieve successfully than adaptation prior to the presentation because it is primarily reactionary and changes must be made quickly without the benefit of a lot of thought. The term "thinking on your feet" refers to this reactionary form of adaptive selling. It means being able to detect verbal or nonverbal cues or commands that identify the prospect's personality, and immediately adapting oneself to that personality.

A diagram of the adaptive selling process is shown in Figure 4-8. This process illustrates the salesperson's objectives during a sales call. Notice that adjustments can be made at any time during this process. If the presentation is going well, great! No adjustments are needed. However, if the salesperson is stumped on a question concerning the features of the product or service, the salesperson must adapt by assessing his or her credibility. Even if the salesperson is not necessarily stumped by a question, if the customer is showing doubt in a facial expression or is taking a resistant posture, the salesperson must be able to adjust in order to put that customer back at ease.

It has been said that to sell more, salespeople should work harder. Recent studies, however, have shown that most salespeople can be more successful by working "smarter" not harder. Adaptive selling is one way to work smarter and sell more. Salespeople who work smarter are more knowledgeable about different selling approaches and more skillful at selecting the appropriate approach for each situation.

THE ADAPTIVE SELLING PROCESS

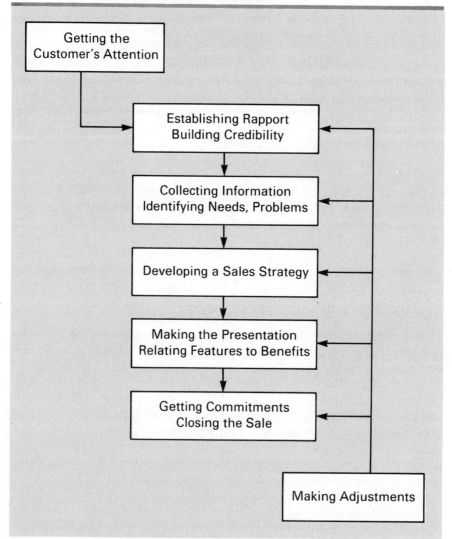

Figure 4-8 The key to adapting one's message is the flexibility to make adjustments when needed.

Source: Barton A. Weitz, "Relationship Between Salesperson Performance and Understanding Customer Decision Process," *Journal of Marketing Research* (November 1978): 501-516; and H. Sujan, B. Weitz, and M. Sujan, "Increasing Sales Productivity by Getting Salespeople to Work Smarter," *Journal of Personal Selling and Sales Management* (August 1988): 9-19.

The ability to be an effective adaptive seller is essential to success. By being able to adapt presentations to the customer, salespeople are realizing their unique advantage as a form of marketing communication over advertising, sales promotion, and publicity. There are two approaches that can assist salespeople in adapting to their customers—**transactional analysis** and the **social-style matrix**.

TRANSACTIONAL ANALYSIS

Transactional analysis is an approach that is useful for determining why people act the way they do. By knowing the customers' motivations, the salesperson can better adapt to the customers.

The central idea behind transactional analysis is that each person has three ego states—the parent, the child, and the adult. These ego states influence a person's behavior.

The parent ego state leads people to behave like their parents when they were young: authoritative, domineering, critical. They talk down to people as though they are lecturing, they emphasize following rules, and they often fail to listen to what others are saying. The nonverbal cues that correspond to these attitudes are folded arms, pointed fingers, and a raised voice. This represents the person's conscience.

The child ego state represents peoples' emotional side. In the child ego state they are happy, carefree, and spontaneous. They can also be selfish and prone to temper tantrums. The nonverbal cues sent by those in the child ego state are rapidly changing facial expressions or emotions and a lack of attention.

The adult ego state represents the rational decision-making processes. These people act deliberately. They are very organized and businesslike.

Generally, salespeople must determine in which of the three ego states their customer is communicating and then adapt themselves to that ego state. If the customer is communicating from the adult ego state, the salesperson should adapt by responding from the adult ego state. Effective communication is only possible from the adult ego state because of the rationality that is involved. If the customer is communicating in the child or parent state, the salesperson should move the customer to the adult state so they can communicate on a rational basis.

One approach that can be effective in moving customers to the adult ego state is listening and empathizing with their parent and child ego states. Thus, by letting customers get these out of their systems through an emotional release the salesperson can ease them into the adult ego state. They let go of their emotions and realize that it is time to get back to business.

A second way of moving customers into the adult ego state is **stroking**. Stroking refers to satisfying the child ego state. Making customers in this state feel good about themselves, that they are important, showing them respect and appreciation, and listening to their viewpoints are all means of stroking. When customers have been stroked to the point of regaining their self-confidence, they will abandon the child or parent state and enter into the adult state, thus allowing for better communication.

THE SOCIAL-STYLE MATRIX

The social-style matrix is another approach that has been used to help salespeople adapt their presentations to the prospect. The approach developed by David Merrill and his associates[2] draws upon the style or pattern of behavior one uses when dealing with others. It assumes that salespeople must first understand their own social style before adapting it to someone else's—namely, the customer's.

The social-style matrix is based on three dimensions: assertiveness, responsiveness, and versatility. Assertiveness refers to the extent to which one will go in order to influence another person's attitudes and behaviors. Assertive people tend to be very straightforward. They have a take-charge questioning attitude, whereas a nonassertive person tends to be more passive. Assertive types try to lead, or assume a position of power, while nonassertive types prefer to follow.

Responsiveness refers to the amount of control one exerts over one's feelings when dealing with others. Responsive people are emotional and are not afraid to show their emotions to others. Nonresponsive people, on the other hand, have learned to control their emotions. They present a cool exterior, usually preferring to be formal in their interactions.

Versatility is the ability to adapt one's social style to match that of others; for example, the salesperson to the customer. People are often more at ease dealing with others who are like themselves. Versatility requires practicing communication skills such as asking questions, listening carefully, and looking for nonverbal communication cues.

The social-style matrix uses responsiveness and assertiveness as the dimensions to form the matrix shown in Figure 4-9. The four quadrants represent four distinct social styles: analytical, driver, amiable, and expressive. Analyticals are low on responsiveness and assertiveness. They are controlled and rational while choosing to avoid risk by following the crowd. Expressives are the complete opposite. They are highly assertive and responsive, and are prone to being take-charge leaders, who are emotional and show great concern for others. In adapting to an expressive, salespeople should be more emotional themselves, while emphasizing the idea that the customer would be one of the first people to own this product or use this service. For the analytical, salespeople would want to reduce their assertiveness and responsiveness by becoming more formal and logical, emphasizing the product's technical features and long-run performance.

---

[2]David W. Merrill and Roger Reid, *Personal Styles and Effective Performance* (Radnor PA: Chilton, 1981).

THE SOCIAL-STYLE MATRIX

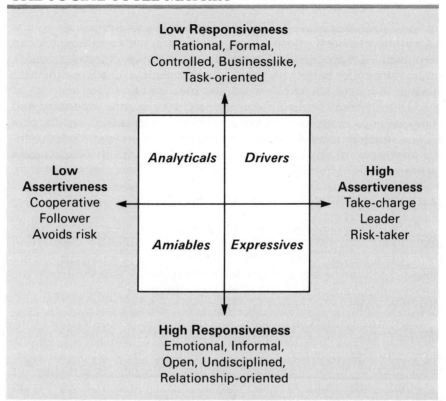

Low Responsiveness
Rational, Formal,
Controlled, Businesslike,
Task-oriented

**Low
Assertiveness**
Cooperative
Follower
Avoids risk

Analyticals   *Drivers*

Amiables   *Expressives*

**High
Assertiveness**
Take-charge
Leader
Risk-taker

High Responsiveness
Emotional, Informal,
Open, Undisciplined,
Relationship-oriented

Figure 4-9 Salespeople should know the signs of each social style type and adapt themselves to that customer's style in order to make the customer more comfortable.

Drivers are low on responsiveness, but high on assertiveness. They prefer to tell people what to do and to control the situation. They like challenges, prefer to work alone, and are driven to success. Amiables, on the other hand, are high on responsiveness and low on assertiveness. They are more likely to ask questions, be good listeners and try to build long-term relationships. When trying to sell to an amiable, salespeople should try to develop a strong mutual trust with their prospect, emphasizing the reduction of risk and assuring product quality. To sell to a driver, salespeople should be direct and to-the-point, stressing on-time delivery and "bottom-line" results.

Versatility is the key to successful adaptive selling when using this approach. Salespeople must ask questions, listen carefully, and note any nonverbal signals in order to quickly determine their prospect's social style. Then they must successfully adapt their own style in order to make the prospect as comfortable and as relaxed as possible.

NEGOTIATION AND PERSONAL SELLING

Professional salespeople understand that skills and knowledge are the keys to success. Having good selling skills usually means salespeople can set objectives, execute an action plan to achieve those objectives, make a professional offer to the customer, build agreement, and close the sale. Having adequate knowledge generally means that salespeople know everything there is to know about the product, customer, industry, and competition: they are experts. But essential to success in the selling profession, and often overlooked in personal selling courses and sales training programs, are the knowledge of and skills in effective **negotiation** techniques.

IMPORTANCE OF NEGOTIATION SKILLS

As with personal selling, effective negotiation involves specific skills and tactics. Otherwise skilled salespeople, untrained in negotiation techniques, may be so concerned about closing the sale that they do not close as *profitable* a sale as might have been possible. Consequently, the salespeople's companies—and likely the salespeople as well—earn less than they could have, and *should have*, on a sale.

Sales negotiation can be defined as the process of working out a purchase and sales program to the point of reaching a mutually satisfactory agreement. Generally, the negotiation session begins after the salesperson's proposal has been submitted and an "agreement in principle," or agreeing to agree, has been achieved with the customer. The negotiation process is then utilized to work out the specific terms and conditions of the sale.

A skilled negotiator understands that the information and power displayed in a negotiation situation are almost always developed long before the actual process begins. It is far more difficult to get information or to enhance one's power position once the respective parties sit down face-to-face. Therefore, an effective negotiator begins to prepare well in advance and often uncovers valuable information from a wide variety of sources, including secretaries, janitors, users, technical-buying influences, and the like. To gain this requisite knowledge, the skilled negotiator asks a lot of questions and listens carefully. A comment made by a worker in a factory, such as, "your company is the only one that met our specifications, and we're down to three days' inventory," can be a piece of information which may significantly enhance one's power in a negotiation.

Professional salespeople must believe that it is in the customer's best interest to purchase their product/service, and in the presentation focus on translating features to benefits which will satisfy the wants and needs of the customer. Therefore, the salesperson demonstrates that the proposed sale should be of mutual benefit, to both parties, and present a wise agreement which will improve or at least not damage the relationship with the customer. However, salespeople often enter a negotiation believing they are in an inferior power position and, therefore, are intimidated by the customer. Figure 4-10 shows a list of several false assumptions commonly made by salespeople entering a negotiation session, which cause them to be intimidated by buyers. Salespeople must become skillful negotiators and avoid making assumptions that cause them to operate from a position of perceived disadvantage.

WHAT TO DO DURING NEGOTIATION

Negotiation is a game of power, whether it is played out by heads of state or buyers and sellers. From the beginning of the process, a salesperson must establish a strong posture and maintain neutrality, meaning that the need to sell is as important as the need to buy. The following text discusses the stages encountered in negotiating situations.

CREATE THE PROPER SETTING

The first thing to do is to select a quiet, comfortable setting where both the salesperson and the customer will not be interrupted. When factors such as uncomfortable physical surroundings, stress or tension, or fatigue interfere with the negotiation process, try to eliminate them.

FALSE ASSUMPTIONS MADE BY SALESPEOPLE IN NEGOTIATION SITUATIONS

1. The customer is all-powerful and holds all the cards. (Rarely, if ever, is this the case.)
2. The customer knows what he or she wants. (Sometimes yes, but often no, particularly for details such as terms, delivery, and peripherals.)
3. You'll make the sale solely on the basis of price, and your only real weapon is the ability to lower the price. (In fact, price is only one variable in the negotiation, and price-cutting is generally not in the salesperson's best interest as a negotiation tool.)
4. Your competition is all around you, with better products and better prices. (Seldom, if ever, is this the case.)

Figure 4-10 Salespeople should never place themselves on a level lower than the customer. Negotiation, to be effective, must be played on equal ground.

Source: G. Karrass, *Negotiate to Close* (New York: Fireside Books, 1985).

IDENTIFY ALL ISSUES FIRST

Get *all* issues on the table *before* you start negotiating. Negotiation is a process of give and take, but giving and taking cannot occur without first identifying all issues of importance to both parties. Skilled negotiators do not talk about issues in isolation, but as components which must be fitted together to make a total package. Therefore, they will probe to identify all the issues and take careful notes, but make no commitments before getting the complete list of issues. In doing so, it is important to maintain close attention and try to understand the real goals and needs that are the basis of the other party's position. Also, good negotiators are careful not to make the most serious negotiation error: trading down with no concession. Any issue may be put on the table, but one should not agree to give up anything without getting something else in return.

SEPARATE FACTS FROM EMOTIONS

Negotiation is a communication process consisting of two dimensions: factual issues, which are logical in nature, and emotional issues, which most often are not logical but are certainly real. Many times one side in a negotiation may be unwilling to agree to factual or substantive issues that might be in their best interest, solely because of negative feelings about the other side. Therefore, a skilled negotiator separates personalities and emotions from the issues of substance. Part of doing this involves acting decently toward the other side, getting them to relate to and identify with you as a person, and trying to work together with them to achieve a win-win agreement. Additionally, in dealing with substantive issues, it is essential to look past stated positions and understand the interests and needs that are the basis of those positions. For example, two people might be trying to negotiate an agreement on where to spend their vacation. One might want to go to Las Vegas and the other to Aspen. Compromising on their positions, they might wind up in eastern Utah, satisfactory to neither party. But looking at the interests and needs behind the positions, one may want to go to Las Vegas to gamble, and the other to Aspen to ski. Compromising on interests and needs, they go to Reno, and both are happy.

CONSIDER ALL OPTIONS

Be sure your agenda covers all the issues that need to be discussed. Brainstorm to develop as many options as possible for achieving mutual gain. Classify each option/issue as win-win, win-lose, or mixed, and rank them in their order of importance. Carefully analyze the relativity of variables: items that are of low cost to you and high benefit to them, and vice versa. Then, make trades from a position of strength and equality where both sides can gain more in benefits than they lose through concessions. Negotiation is a game, albeit a very serious game. But it is a game that two can play and both believe they won.

KNOW WHEN AND HOW TO PLAY "HARDBALL"

For negotiation to be effective and mutually satisfying, both parties must desire to work together to achieve a win-win agreement. At times, however, one party may attempt to impose its will on the other and seek a win-lose resolution. A skilled negotiator must watch for indications that the other side is employing "hardball" tactics. One tactic is to take an extreme opening position to influence the expectations of the other side. For example, the salesperson might have an asking price of $350 for an item, but would be happy getting $325 under certain conditions. The customer may offer $250, a tactic designed to make the salesperson think $300 would be tops, but would feel lucky to get $275.

Another hardball tactic is the use of emotions. At one end of this scale, a customer might flatly tell the salesperson to take it or leave it: the first offer is the only one that will be made. At the other end, the customer may claim he or she is unable to pay more and ask for fairness. In any of these circumstances, concessions made by the salesperson may be viewed as evidence of weakness in the mind of a hardball negotiator. The skilled negotiator will recognize such tactics as just tactics and nothing more, knowing that a tactic perceived is tantamount to no tactic at all.

When faced with hardball tactics, several countermeasures can be employed. For instance, one could throw the tactic right back at the customer and counter the extreme opening position with a very small, almost insignificant concession of one's own. In the preceding example, where the salesperson was asking $350 and the customer offered $250, the salesperson might propose to reduce the price to $347.50 if the customer would pay cash today.

Another potential countermeasure is to say nothing, laugh, or just leave. By indicating a willingness to walk away, salespeople communicate to customers that they are not dealing from a position of weakness in which they would take any offer rather than risk having the deal fall through totally. To prepare for such an eventuality, salespeople must fully evaluate all alternatives, determine their absolute bottom line, the point at which they will go no further, and be prepared to hold their position.

Hardball negotiation is an adversarial, win-lose style approached on the assumption that a gain for one party is seen to be at the expense of the other. Salespeople need to recognize hardball tactics, and be prepared to respond with appropriate tactics of their own. However, hardball negotiation often results in neither party getting as good an agreement as could have been possible through win-win collaborative negotiation. Therefore, when faced with hardball tactics, a skilled negotiator will attempt to shift the discussion to issues and variables on which beneficial compromises can be achieved, laying the foundations for creating a win-win environment.

SUMMARY

The major job of our marketing system is to communicate; this is done through advertising, sales promotion, publicity, and personal selling. Marketers use the communication process to send messages to prospects. Salespeople are the company's communicators. They are the senders of the messages, and the customers are the receivers. The more credible the salesperson, the more likely the customer is to believe the message.

The salesperson should understand the market before sending the message, so the message used will have optimal effect. The salesperson wants the customer to be favorably influenced by the communication. The ultimate response desired is the buying action.

Messages can be transmitted through many media: face-to-face conversation, newspapers, magazines, television, advertising, and others. Wordless communication, including body language, plays an important role in getting the message across. The customer transmits an indication of understanding and an acceptance or rejection of the initial message through feedback.

Two-way communication is necessary in order to get the prospect's full attention and participation. It is also necessary in order to determine the prospect's needs and to satisfy them properly. The salesperson needs to develop communication skills in order to have effective two-way communication. These skills include questioning and listening, and both are vital for adaptive selling. Adaptive selling refers to tailoring the presentation to each particular prospect in order to put him or her at ease and to facilitate a successful sale. In order to adapt oneself to the customer, the salesperson must carefully question the prospect and listen to his or her responses in order to gather the information needed to tailor the presentation. Discovery of the prospect's personality can lead the salesperson to choose either transactional analysis or the social-style matrix as ways to help him or her adapt to the prospect.

The salesperson also needs to develop sales negotiation skills. Sales negotiation is the process of working out a purchase and sales program to the point of reaching a mutually satisfactory agreement. Central to successful negotiations are creating the proper setting, identifying all the issues, separating facts from emotions, considering all options, and knowing when and how to play "hardball."

KEY TERMS

encoding	feedback
message	two-way communication
decoding	primacy
noise	recency

expectancy
open-ended questions
business space
adaptive selling
transactional analysis

social-style matrix
stroking
negotiation
nonpersonal channels of
  communication

REVIEW QUESTIONS

1. What are the parts of the communication process?
2. Explain encoding.
3. Explain decoding.
4. What is the basic job of the salesperson?
5. What are the two determinants of source credibility?
6. How are market segments determined?
7. What factors make written and oral communication effective?
8. What role does wordless communication play in a sales presentation?
9. What are the five questions to consider in encoding a selling message?
10. What media are most popular for advertising?
11. Why is a receiver's mental set sometimes a barrier to communication?
12. Why is connotative meaning important?
13. What factors are important for acceptance and belief of a message?
14. How do salespeople use feedback to improve their presentations?
15. Why does a salesperson want to engage the prospect in two-way communication?
16. What guidelines should be considered when questioning?
17. What type of information is usually sought in questioning?
18. What is meant by "active listening"?
19. How does personal selling differ from other forms of marketing communication?
20. Why is adaptive selling preferred over nonadaptive selling?
21. How can the salesperson adapt to the customer prior to the sales presentation?
22. What are the three ego states used by prospects?
23. What are the four social styles?
24. What are the stages that are used in negotiating situations?

DISCUSSION QUESTIONS

1. Observe your professors while they are teaching class. What nonverbal messages are they sending? What is your interpretation of these signals?

2. Think of the last salesperson you spoke to. In your opinion, how credible was that person? Why?

3. Take a look at the person next to you. What is his or her social style? What cues led you to arrive at this answer? How would you adapt your style to match his or hers?

4. What steps can a salesperson take to ensure that the customer is receiving and decoding the same message the salesperson is transmitting?

CASE 4-1   DELANCY BUSINESS FORMS, INC.

Barbara McGowan, sales representative for DeLancy Business Forms, Inc., has been assigned a sales territory that includes Washington, Oregon, Idaho, and western Montana. DeLancy is a newcomer in the business forms field, and McGowan is its newest sales representative. DeLancy does very little advertising and relies heavily on its salespeople to inform prospective customers about its products. The company hopes that its salespeople can sell complete systems rather than just individual forms. The company has no formal training program for its sales personnel. Instead it expects its salespeople to familiarize themselves with the product features and company services.

McGowan's first selling effort is to a large manufacturer of automobile parts. This company, Marshall-Vollman, Inc., is involved in computerizing its accounting and bookkeeping system. Unfortunately, McGowan is unaware of this. In fact, she has taken very little time to acquaint herself with Marshall-Vollman's operations or the automotive parts industry as a whole.

McGowan enters the office of Marshall-Vollman and asks to see the chief accountant. Although he usually sees salespeople only by appointment, Hal Maples consents to see her. They meet briefly, and Maples calls Rick Findlay, systems analyst, and asks him to join the meeting.

McGowan emphasizes the low price of her products, their convenient size, their practicality, the color coding used to help the accountant, the ease of ordering, prompt delivery service, and easy credit terms. The meeting is interrupted by several phone calls for Maples and Findlay and by a visitor looking for Findlay. McGowan tries to point out the merits of each form but fails to present them as a totally integrated system. Maples and Findlay ask several questions, but McGowan senses that their interest is artificial. When she is ready to leave, she offers some sample forms for Maple and Findlay to examine and use. They decline the offer and tell McGowan they will call her after they have better determined their needs.

CASE QUESTIONS

1. What basic tenet of communication theory did McGowan violate, which, had she observed it, might have saved the situation for her?
2. Identify some of the barriers to effective communication in this case, and suggest ways in which they might have been eliminated or reduced.

CASE 4-2 OFFICE AUTOMATION—A*

Kay Kendall is a sales representative for Office Automation, Inc., a firm that distributes and services word processing equipment. She has just completed a sales presentation to Lea Lewis of the Metro Products Company, proposing a package including equipment, training, and service. They have reached agreement in principle on the proposal, and now are negotiating specific terms and conditions.

Kay: You can see, then, how Office Automation will best serve your needs. Do you have any more questions?

Lea: Yes. What was the total cost figure again?

Kay: $100,000.

Lea: That's just for our office here, is that right?

Kay: Right.

Lea: What if we liked it and decided to put similar systems in each of our four branch offices next year? You'd be able to give us a better price, then, couldn't you?

Kay: I suppose we could.

Lea: How much better?

Kay: (looking through a computer printout) We could do it for $95,000 per office.

Lea: So we're really talking about $95,000, not $100,000.

Kay: Yes, but that's for all five offices.

Lea: Kay, if your system does all you say it does, I can't see any reason why we wouldn't do it everywhere. If it doesn't do all you say it does, your company hasn't lived up to its promises. You can't expect us to be penalized $5,000 in that case, can you?

Kay: Well, no.

Lea: Then your price is really $95,000, isn't it?

Kay: All right. We'll make it $95,000.

Lea: I'm afraid that's still a little more than we can live with.

---

*Case prepared by Bob Kimball. Used with permission.

Kay:	I realize it might sound like a lot. But it meets or beats all the competition.
Lea:	That may be, but you're going to have to do better than that.
Kay:	Well, I guess we could go as low as $92,000.
Lea:	That's better, but not good enough. We only have $80,000 in the budget.
Kay:	$80,000? That's below our cost!
Lea:	Are you sure? Aren't you including some fixed costs in your cost figures?
Kay:	There may be some, but our variable costs are still over $80,000.
Lea:	Tell you what I'll do. I want to be fair to you. I may be able to get some discretionary funds from another department. Let's just split the difference and get this over with: $86,000.
Kay:	I don't know. My sales manager won't be very happy about that.
Lea:	But at that figure, your company will make a profit and you'll earn a commission, won't you?
Kay:	Not much of one.
Lea:	I'm sorry, but it's the best we can do. As it is, I'll have a real tough time securing those discretionary funds. $86,000 is all there is. There isn't any more. Take it or leave it.
Kay:	All right. I guess something is better than nothing.
Lea:	Fine. $86,000 it is. Now what were the payment terms?
Kay:	Net 30 days.
Lea:	That's going to be a problem. We'll need six months.
Kay:	Six months? That's not going to be possible. I won't be able to get approval.
Lea:	What *can* you get approved?
Kay:	Oh, maybe 90 days.
Lea:	What do you say we compromise? Half in 90 days and half in six months.
Kay:	Do you think you could give us the first half in 30 days?
Lea:	Make it 60 days and you've got a deal.
Kay:	OK, half in 60 days and half in six months. Is there anything else?
Lea:	Yes, delivery and set-up. When can you get everything installed?
Kay:	In about two weeks.
Lea:	We've got to have it in next week.
Kay:	Next week? Why that soon?
Lea:	We're closing the office for the holiday. It's the only time we can do it without disrupting our whole routine.

Kay:	But we can't get the equipment with that little lead time.
Lea:	Why not?
Kay:	We don't have it all in stock. Some of it will have to come from our manufacturing facility in Seattle.
Lea:	How do you get it from there?
Kay:	By rail to Chicago, and by truck from there. It takes at least 10 days, often two weeks.
Lea:	What if you air freight it direct? Couldn't everything be here in a day or two?
Kay:	Yes, but the cost would be prohibitive.
Lea:	How you get it here is your problem. You *can* get it here to install everything next week, then, can't you?
Kay:	It *can* be done, but . . . .
Lea:	Good! We'll get started first thing Monday morning. And a week from Monday we'll begin training the operators and supervisors.
Kay:	That will be fine. The training sessions last for five days and you have a total of 24 operators and supervisors. How many people are you going to want to send over for training each week?
Lea:	Send over? What do you mean?
Kay:	To our training facility in Dayton. That's where we conduct all our training activities.
Lea:	You expect us to send all those people over to Dayton?
Kay:	Well, yes. Is that a problem?
Lea:	It certainly is. And a great inconvenience. We'd have to pay everyone $.26 a mile to drive, and there's the potential for a lawsuit against our company if someone were involved in an accident. You'll just have to conduct the training right here in our office.
Kay:	But you don't have adequate meeting room here. We could only do four people at a time.
Lea:	If that's all you can do, then that's all you can do.
Kay:	But we'd have to hook in four additional work stations in your meeting room and tie up a training manager for six weeks.
Lea:	Just do what you have to do.
Kay:	But we don't normally do it that way. Most companies usually just send their people over to Dayton.
Lea:	But, but, but! Then you have conducted training at the customer's place of business in the past, I take it?
Kay:	It has been done under unusual circumstances.
Lea:	So why should we be treated any differently? Are we a less important customer to you or something?
Kay:	No, of course not.

Lea:	Then it's settled. Now one more thing: warranty coverage. I understand we have that in full for two years.
Kay:	Two years? No, that's an extra cost option. The standard coverage is for 90 days.
Lea:	That hardly seems adequate. You expect this equipment to last longer than 90 days, don't you?
Kay:	Certainly, but extended coverage isn't included in the base price. And I'm sure you'll agree you've received a more than favorable base price.
Lea:	That's true. Let's just say one year, then.
Kay:	One year?
Lea:	Yes. That way, I've met you more than halfway. That's a reasonable compromise, isn't it?
Kay:	I guess so. Is there anything else, or is this all we need to agree on?
Lea:	I believe that will do it. I'll summarize everything in writing and submit this proposal to my supervisor. You can then meet with her to iron out the final price, terms, and conditions.
Kay:	Meet with her?
Lea:	Yes, she'll be the one you'll have to negotiate with. Can you be here for a meeting tomorrow morning at 10?
Kay:	Yes, I can.
Lea:	Good. Her name is Hilda Hawkins. Just ask for her when you come in.

CASE QUESTIONS

1. Rate Kay's negotiating skills on a scale of 1 to 10 (1 = terrible negotiating skills; 10 = excellent negotiating skills).
2. What things did Kay do well in working out all the terms and conditions of the sale and negotiating effectively?
3. What things did Kay not do well in working out all the terms and conditions of the sale and negotiating effectively? What should she have done differently?

CASE 4-3   OFFICE AUTOMATION—B*

Peggy Puckett is a sales representative for Office Automation, Inc., a firm which distributes and services word processing equipment. She has just completed a sales presentation to Susan Slade of the Metro Products

---

*Case prepared by Bob Kimball. Used with permission.

Company, proposing a package including equipment, training, and service. They have reached agreement in principle on the proposal, and now are negotiating specific terms and conditions.

Peggy: You can see, then, how Office Automation will best serve your needs. Do you have any more questions?

Susan: Yes. What was the total cost figure again?

Peggy: $100,000.

Susan: That's just for our office here, is that right?

Peggy: Right.

Susan: What if we liked it and decided to put similar systems in each of our four branch offices next year? You'd be able to give us a better price then, couldn't you?

Peggy: It's something we could talk about. Let me make a note of that (making a notation on her order form). Is there something else you were wondering about?

Susan: It all comes down to your price. What you're asking is simply more than we can live with.

Peggy: I realize this is a significant investment, but as I pointed out, it will pay for itself in less than two years. And our package will meet or beat all the competition.

Susan: That may be, but you're going to have to do better than your proposed price of $100,000.

Peggy: Maybe we can do something (making a notation on her order form). Are there any other details you were concerned about?

Susan: Yes. What were the payment terms again?

Peggy: Net 30 days.

Susan: That's going to be a problem. We'll need six months.

Peggy: Six months? (making a notation on her order form). So we'll need to talk about payment terms. What else will we need to discuss?

Susan: Delivery and set-up. When can you get everything installed?

Peggy: In about two weeks.

Susan: We've got to have it in next week.

Peggy: Next week? Why that soon?

Susan: We're closing the office for the holiday. It's the only time we can do it without disrupting our whole routine.

Peggy: Delivery and set-up . . . (making a notation on her order form). Any other details we'll need to finalize?

Susan: Training schedule. We'll want to begin training the operators and supervisors a week from Monday.

Peggy: Training schedule . . . (making a notation on her order form). The training sessions last for five days and you have a total of 24 operators and supervisors. How many people are you going to want to send over for training each week?

Susan: Send over? What do you mean?

Peggy: To our training facility in Dayton. That's where we conduct all our training activities.

Susan: You expect us to send all those people over to Dayton?

Peggy: Most of our customers prefer to do that. Would that present a problem to you?

Susan: It certainly would. And a great inconvenience. We'd have to pay everyone $.26 a mile to drive, and there's the potential for a lawsuit against our company if someone were involved in an accident. You'll just have to conduct the training right here in our office.

Peggy: Training location . . . (making a notation on her order form). Anything else?

Susan: One more thing: warranty coverage. I understand we have that in full for two years.

Peggy: Two year coverage is available, or you may select our standard coverage of 90 days.

Susan: That hardly seems adequate. You expect this equipment to last longer than 90 days, don't you?

Peggy: We certainly do. Then we'll want to discuss warranty coverage (making a notation on her order form). Have we omitted anything, or is this all we need to agree on?

Susan: I believe that will do it.

Peggy: All right, let's see what we can do. You had mentioned that you'd like to make payment in six months rather than 30 days. Is there any particular reason why you wish to pay in six months?

Susan: Yes. We just don't have that kind of money in this year's budget and our new fiscal year begins in six months.

Peggy: And the allocation for this system is in next year's budget?

Susan: That's correct.

Peggy: Will all of this investment have to be allocated into next year's budget or would you be able to get at least a portion of the funds from this year's budget?

Susan: We might be able to pay some, but there's no way we can handle it all this year.

Peggy: Fine. But if we were able to do something on the total price, could you pay at least half the amount now?

Susan: It would depend on the price.

Peggy: Certainly. But it would be feasible?

Susan: It would.

Peggy: Good. Now, you said you wanted installation next week and to have training begin the week after.

Susan: Right.

Peggy: We can arrange to do that. However, we don't have all this equipment in stock. Some of it will have to come from our manufacturing facility in Seattle. Normally, we ship by rail to Chicago, and by truck from there. It takes at least 10 days, often two weeks.

Susan: What if you air freight it direct? Couldn't everything be here in a day or two?

Peggy: Yes, but the cost would be prohibitive.

Susan: How you get it here is your problem. You *can* get it here to install everything next week, then, can't you?

Peggy: If that's what you wish, absolutely. But really, it's *our* problem. Every dollar we have to spend on shipping is one less dollar you could save on total price. I was just thinking about something: your company has its own fleet of trucks, doesn't it?

Susan: We do.

Peggy: How often do you have a truck in or around Seattle?

Susan: We have two trucks a week going to Tacoma.

Peggy: And they're coming back empty?

Susan: Sometimes. No more than half full.

Peggy: So it might be possible to save *all* the shipping costs by having your trucks pick up the equipment in Seattle.

Susan: I guess we could do that.

Peggy: That'll help a lot. Now you were saying you were concerned about disrupting your office schedule while we're installing the equipment.

Susan: Right.

Peggy: I'm concerned it may also be disruptive and inefficient for you to conduct the training here.

Susan: How so?

Peggy: You have a fairly small meeting room. That means we could only train four people at a time.

Susan: If that's all you can do, that's all you can do.

Peggy: But that means your meeting room will be tied up for six weeks. Might that present an inconvenience for you and your management?

Susan: Some inconvenience, yes.

Peggy: And it also means that only four people each week will be able to begin using the equipment. Wouldn't you wish to have them trained sooner so you can start enjoying the benefits of the new system as soon as possible?

Susan: Well, yes.

Peggy: If we could train eight people per week, we could complete all the training in three weeks. Can you spare that many at

	one time, or would six people a week over four weeks be better?
Susan:	This time of year, we could do eight.
Peggy:	(Making notations on her order form and punching in some numbers on her calculator). See what you think of this: We arrange to have your trucks transport the equipment here. Then, we begin installing it two weeks from Monday. We could install eight machines per week for three weeks. There will be a minimum of disruption to your office because we'll do the installations just for those people undergoing training that week. To lower the cost of paying mileage and to address your concerns about liability, you could arrange to have a van drive your people over in the morning and return to pick them up in the evening. Would those arrangements be satisfactory?
Susan:	A possibility...
Peggy:	Under those arrangements, we can give you one system for $94,000. If you wish to consider similar systems in your branch offices, we would be able to give you a volume discount and they would be $89,000 each. That's with 50 percent payment in 10 days, and the remainder in six months. If you wish to have the 90-day warranty instead of the two-year warranty, we could save you an additional $2,000 per system.
Susan:	So it comes out to $87,000 per system.
Peggy:	$92,000 for one system and $87,000 per system for the second system through the fifth.
Susan:	Peggy, if your system does all you say it does, I can't see any reason why we wouldn't do it everywhere. If it doesn't do all you say it does, your company hasn't lived up to its promises. You can't expect us to be penalized $5,000 in that case. And another thing: I don't like having to pay an extra $2,000 for that warranty.
Peggy:	I can understand how you feel. Let me ask you this: If we could give you a price of $88,000 per system, regardless of how many you purchase, including a one-year warranty, would you be able to authorize the paperwork today?
Susan:	If you make it $87,000 with a two-year warranty, I can give you an official purchase order requisition in 30 minutes.
Peggy:	That's a rock bottom price. I don't know. You say you can give me a requisition in 30 minutes?
Susan:	30 minutes.
Peggy:	Then we've got a deal. Just let me be sure I've got everything correct on the order form.

CASE QUESTIONS

1. Rate Peggy's negotiating skills on a scale of 1 to 10 (1 = terrible negotiating skills; 10 = excellent negotiating skills).
2. What things did Peggy do well in working out all the terms and conditions of the sale and negotiating effectively? What were the major differences between this case and the prior case, Office Automation—A?
3. What things did Peggy not do well in working out all the terms and conditions of the sale and negotiating effectively? What should she have done differently?

CHAPTER 5
Knowledge Necessary for Successful Selling

After studying this chapter, you should be able to:

- Tell what salespeople need to know about their industry and their company

- Tell what salespeople need to know about their product(s)/service(s), distribution, and price

- List what salespeople should know about terms of sale

- Indicate what product attributes are of great interest to salespeople

- Answer questions about what information salespeople should have about the distribution system.

One area where information is essential involves the company for which the salesperson works. Company facts should begin with a description of the industry of which the company is a part. Information about the salesperson's company also can play an important role as a basic tool in the selling process. For example, if a prospect has a problem that the salesperson's firm confronted and solved earlier, the salesperson may be of specific help. A suggestion in such a situation may be helpful in making a sale.

A second area involves the product or service that the salesperson is selling. Product information is used mainly to show prospects how they will gain by buying a particular product/service. Essential facts here include product research, the terms of sale (prices, discounts, and credit procedures), the actual product/service (its features, brand name, and packaging), the product/service guarantee, and the follow-up service the company supplies to customers. Salespeople need to know about products and services other than those they sell, such as other products/services sold by their company, and, certainly, competing products/services.

A third area involves distribution systems. The sellers of Xerox copiers, Dial soap, Zenith TVs, cable TV, Merrill Lynch Brokerage Services, and the orange growers of Florida all have a common problem: how to get their products/services to the ultimate consumer. Solving this problem often is accomplished in two steps: (1) the producer selects a marketing channel through which title to the products/services moves to ultimate buyers, and (2) where physical products are involved, the producer plans a physical distribution system to perform storage and transportation functions.

Knowledge of company policies and procedures, the company's products/services, and the marketing channel strategies for those products/services helps the salesperson. It speeds personal progress; increases confidence, enthusiasm, and professional selling skills; and raises income. This knowledge also has benefits for the company, encouraging higher sales performance, greater loyalty to the company, increased cooperation, and better customer relations.

WHAT KNOWLEDGE CAN DO FOR THE SALESPERSON

Increases Confidence: Knowledge provides the salesperson with the right answer. This reduces hesitation and increases assuredness.

Increases Enthusiasm: Knowledge allows the salesperson to talk intelligently on many topics. This encourages openness toward consumers.

Increases Customer Trust: Customers trust people they find to be credible. Credibility is based on the customers' perception of that salesperson as an expert, or as someone who is similar to themselves.

Increases Income: All of these benefits of knowledge work together to make the salesperson feel and look like a winner. And customers love to purchase from winners. Thus, income also increases.

Figure 5-1 Knowledgeable salespeople are effective salespeople.

COMPANY BACKGROUND

Salespeople advance in an organization largely because of their ability to produce a profit, and this ability reflects knowledge and understanding of the company's objectives, policies, and methods. Salespeople also should be aware of the company's relationship with the industry as a whole. Finally, salespeople must have knowledge of their company's history, its hierarchies, and philosophies.

THE INDUSTRY

Salespeople should study the industry of which their company is a unit. A logical starting point would be the beginning of the industry and its evolution. Then salespeople might branch out into the industry's relationship to and dependence on other industries. Knowledge of current developments, particularly those that are being referred to in various news media, and also the activities of the industry's trade association, will most certainly be of interest to customers. If the industry is affected by current legislative proposals or the activities of some outstanding personality, salespeople can count on being asked for the detailed story.

Many individuals will ask salespeople about the future of the particular industry, simply taking for granted that a salesperson connected with the industry is an expert source of information. Salespeople will be expected and encouraged to talk knowledgeably about trends within the industry and about problems and their solutions.

In certain cases, the size and nature of the industry will be interesting to customers. For instance, the national significance of an industry might be impressive. The number of persons it employs and the volume of its output, both in units and dollars, will interest some customers. Likewise, the number of companies making up the industry and the relative rank of the leaders will be important information. Though salespeople learn automatically who their chief competitors are, they should also know where their company fits into the industry picture (market share), what rank it has held in the past, how the company is and has been positioned, and the explanation for its current competitive position. Even more important, salespeople should be able to explain to buyers why they should patronize their company no matter what position the company might hold in the industry.

Most companies provide their sales representatives with sales information binders or **sales books**. These booklets contain considerable information about the industry, the company, the competition, and the company's products, promotion, pricing, and distribution strategies. An example of some of the industry information provided to a major consumer packaged-goods company is shown in Figure 5-2.

COMPANY FEATURES

Three features of the company the salesperson should be familiar with are: the physical aspects, the financial aspects, and its reputation.

PHYSICAL ASPECTS

Nothing is more basic or necessary than for salespeople to be informed about the physical makeup of the company. Salespeople must know the various parts that combine to make the complete physical plant and should know what each part looks like. In addition, salespeople should understand why each of the component parts is needed and how it fits into the broad picture. It may help to know where certain machinery was bought, what it cost, and its principal features. Knowledge of other facilities and holdings, such as office buildings, trucks, component

SPECIFIC INDUSTRY KNOWLEDGE
INCLUDES MARKET SHARE

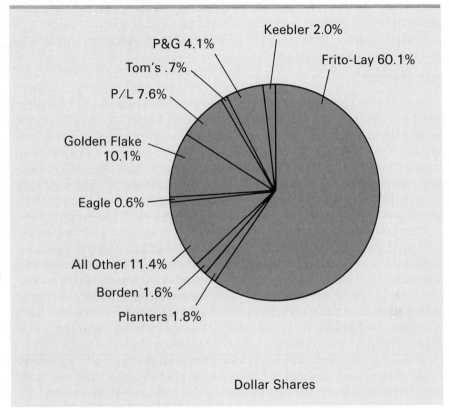

Figure 5-2 Sales organizations often provide such information to their representatives to aid in making a persuasive presentation.
Source: Frito-Lay Sales Representative Information Manual. Courtesy of Frito-Lay.

part suppliers, distribution centers, and other company divisions or subsidiaries is desirable.

These facts about the physical company are of little value unless they are properly presented to prospects. For instance, size is a most impressive feature about many companies. Size can be expressed in terms of daily consumption of raw materials, amount of floor space, daily output, annual output, number of employees, size of payroll, and extent of dealer representation. To be most effective, statistics on such matters should be presented in graphic, understandable style.

FINANCIAL ASPECTS

Financial topics often enter conversations between salespeople and prospects, and prospects are only exercising ordinary caution when requesting information about the financial condition of a possible supplier. Because this is a common salesperson-buyer topic, salespeople must be prepared to answer questions concerning it. Also, some prospects may consider a firm's financial standing to be beneficial or detrimental. For example, sellers who are in fine financial standing provide their customers with the benefit of security that that company will be able to honor its warranties.

REPUTATION

A manufacturer's good reputation with wholesalers and retailers may be indicated in various ways. Prominent dealers may be included among the middlemen handling the manufacturer's line. The relationship between the manufacturer and its better customers may have been established for quite a long time. Belonging to a trade association that is well recognized and respected in the manufacturer's field might be another favorable point. Further, consistently adding new dealers to its list of customers also can speak well for a company's trade reputation.

The company's standing with ultimate consumers is of greater significance than its trade standing because the public helps influence—and may almost determine—what the trade reaction will be. If the public has passed through the early stages of brand recognition and brand acceptance and has moved on to one of the later stages, brand preference or brand insistence, the manufacturer has solved the most serious problem of reputation. Evidence of continued patronage by the consuming public or proof of increased buying may be emphasized by the salesperson as indicating an excellent standing with the consuming public. For an example of how some companies advertise to help establish and maintain their reputations, see the Novacor ad in the color insert to this text.

Finally, the manufacturer's reputation is of vital concern to the industrial and institutional customers to whom it sells. The quality of these customers' products and services depends on the quality of the manufacturer's product/service. Thus, industrial and institutional customers are not likely to take a chance on a manufacturer with a questionable reputation.

PRODUCT KNOWLEDGE

The salesperson should be familiar with the history of the product/service being sold, as well as significant improvements that have been made or are being planned. Each type of knowledge should be customer- and sales-oriented.

PRODUCT RESEARCH

The two types of **product research** that are of interest and value to salespeople are manufacturing research and marketing research. Favorable research results are useful because they can offer evidence that a product is just what the prospect needs and that it is the best quality for the price. When companies use tested methods and build up a store of facts over years of research, salespeople are better able to meet the exact needs and wants of prospects and customers.

MANUFACTURING RESEARCH

Salespeople need to know the nature of manufacturing research; where it is carried on, under whose supervision, with the use of what facilities, and, above all, with what purposes and results. For example, the company might be experimenting with a new type of machine, a change in manufacturing sequence, other methods of storing raw materials, greater utilization of fuel, or the use of substitute raw materials. All this information could be of value to a prospect.

Product quality can be improved as a result of a continuous research program. Reductions in price also can result. Information on manufacturing research assures prospects that a never-ending study of all manufacturing phases is being made and that operating methods and practices are continually being reviewed for the benefit of the customer.

MARKET RESEARCH

Market research can make selling easier and more effective. Examples of market research with product significance include the determination of customer attitudes toward a product/service, acceptance of the package, selection of a brand name, and the identification and evaluation of the market for a new product/service. Salespeople need information about what research projects the company undertakes, why they are undertaken, and whether the projects are handled by the company or turned over to a commercial research organization. Salespeople should learn as much as possible about the studies that are made, and certainly should learn about the findings.

In the interest of staying informed, salespeople must follow the statistics on the trend of public thinking and on the thinking of the trade in regard to the product/service. One must realize market research influences both buyers who use the product/service and those who resell. Salespeople who sell to wholesalers should know not only what wholesalers think, but what retailers and consumers think as well. Those who sell to consumers should know how various types of consumers react. Both buyers and resellers are pleased to know that the manufacturer is selling a popular product/service year after year and that it keeps a sensitive finger on the customer's pulse.

Fortunately for busy salespeople, market research data is collected and reported by market research firms who track customer demographics, attitudes and lifestyles, and purchase behaviors. These firms sell this data to companies who use it to make product-line decisions.

This data is also used by salespeople to support their sales pitches. Some of the companies who provide this information are A. C. Neilsen, Simmons Market Research Bureau, Town and Country Market Research, and SAMI (Selling Area Marketing, Incorporated). An example of this type of information is shown in Figure 5-3.

TERMS OF SALE

When **terms of sale** are discussed, each salesperson should be familiar with product/service prices, allowable discounts, and the credit and collection policies of the company.

PRODUCT PRICES

Prices are of vital interest to customers and consequently to salespeople. A salesperson's ideas about prices are significant to the company in making pricing decisions.

Although salespeople do not establish prices, they must justify prices to customers. If the firm's prices are above the market, the salesperson

MARKET RESEARCH DATA USED BY SALESPEOPLE

Top Selling Supermarket Brands
(Millions of Dollars)

1.	Campbell R & W Soup	$849
2.	Doritos Brand Tortilla Chips	$526
3.	Folger's Coffee	$469
4.	Maxwell House Coffee	$461
5.	Star Kist Tuna	$440
6.	Ruffles Brand Potato Chips	$386
7.	Chicken of the Sea Tuna	$345
8.	Lay's Brand Potato Chips	$322
9.	Similac Baby Food	$311
16.	Purina Dog Chow	$255
17.	Fritos Brand Corn Chips	$252
18.	Lipton Tea	$245
49.	Purina Puppy Chow	$159
50.	Tostitos Brand Tortilla Chips	$158
51.	Brim Coffee	$157
54.	V-8 Juice	$154
55.	Cheetos Brand Cheese Puffs	$152
56.	Kellogg's Corn Flakes	$151

Figure 5-3 Frito-Lay salespeople use market research data like that shown in this chart to improve their sales presentations.

Source: Frito-Lay Representatives Information Manual. Courtesy of Frito-Lay.

would point out the quality of the product and remind the prospect that the lowest-priced item is rarely the most economical. If the firm's prices are at the market level, the salesperson would point out aspects of the product/service that make it superior to the competitors' products/services. If the firm's prices are below the market, the salesperson would emphasize economy, volume, and competitive position. A price structure that gives the merchant a generous markup and a cash-discount inducement is often irresistible to the buyer.

DISCOUNTS

Some of the common discounts granted to customers are quantity discounts, trade discounts, and cash discounts.

Quantity Discounts.   Quantity discounts are offered to customers in return for buying in large volume. They encourage customers to place large orders and discourage hand-to-mouth, small-scale purchasing. Discounts usually are for single orders but may be cumulative, which means that they are applicable to a customer's purchases for a month or even for a year. Quantity discounts permit a seller to share savings in administrative, production, and marketing costs from volume operation with the customers who make that large-scale operation possible.

Trade Discounts.   When a manufacturer sells to different types of middlemen, trade, or functional, discounts may be offered. A manufacturer groups customers according to their position in the distribution channel and the jobs or functions they perform. The status of the customer is the key issue, not the quantity bought. For example, retailers might be allowed a 33-1/3 percent discount on purchases from the wholesaler, and wholesalers might be allowed a larger discount because they perform an extra distribution function for the manufacturer. Discounts for each group are intended to cover the typical middleman's operating costs plus an amount for profit.

Cash Discounts.   Cash discounts are incentives that the seller offers for prompt payment for merchandise bought. A common base is the invoice date. A typical set of terms is 2/10, net 30, meaning the buyer gets a 2 percent discount on payments made within 10 days from the invoice date and the net is due in no more than 30 days from the invoice date. Suppose the order totals $100, and the invoice date is August 1. If the buyer pays by August 11, the seller will accept $98 (reflecting a 2 percent discount) as payment in full. Otherwise, the customer is obligated to pay the full $100 not later than August 31.

CREDIT AND COLLECTION

Every salesperson should understand the fundamentals that underlie sound credit management. Salespeople should comprehend fully the role of the four Cs—character, capacity, capital, and conditions—and should be familiar with financial statements and credit reports. They should keep informed on how their company feels and what their company does about these matters. New salespeople must learn the firm's credit and collection policy, and then follow it, and should never override a company decision without company approval. In some cases, the company has been operating for years and has probably experimented with a variety of credit regulations. New salespeople are seldom in a position to challenge this background of experience.

A credit policy cannot be sound if it is either too conservative or too liberal. Policies that are too strict may keep bad-debt losses down to a very low figure, but they do so at too great a cost in the form of low sales volume. Conversely, an overly lax policy encourages a large sales volume, but at the same time encourages heavy credit losses. A firm, middle-of-the-road policy maximizes sales and minimizes expenses most satisfactorily.

Salespeople also must be knowledgeable about credit procedures. They must know what the credit manager requires prior to the opening of a new account, the credit limit of each customer, and just what the company policy is on credit limits for new customers.

As for collection policy, salespeople first must become acquainted with the collection techniques adopted by the company. Salespeople need to be able to explain and defend them to customers who, as a result of an unhappy credit experience with the company, hesitate to reopen their accounts. New customers should be informed of collection policy. Detailed instructions should be given to salespeople if any collecting is to be handled for the home office. Salespeople must recognize their responsibility for helping the company avoid bad-debt losses, and for keeping the total cost of handling credit as low as possible. It is easy for credit expense to grow and reduce net profit.

PRODUCT/SERVICE ATTRIBUTES

Salespeople must be familiar with the features of the product/service being sold as well as brand names, trademarks, and packaging. Then the features of the product/service must be translated into fulfillment of the buyer's need.

PRODUCT/SERVICE

Salespeople must be able to describe their products/services clearly and adequately in order to translate these features into product/service benefits. For example, the person selling electric blankets might point out that four new and improved precision resistance elements are used to ensure absolute control. The features of the electric blanket then may be translated into the user-benefits of safety, simplicity of operation,

*HIGHLIGHT 5-1   Brand Names: The Origin of
the Name "Kodak"*

The origin of the name "Kodak" has run the gamut of human curiosity. Romance, mystery, superstition, legend—all have been in the minds of thousands of persons who have tried to guess the source of the name.

As a matter of fact, there is nothing obscure about it. The word came straight from the mind of George Eastman, who coined it.

In 1888, George Eastman designed the Kodak camera. The photographic inventor also devised the name for his new instrument by experimenting with the letters of the alphabet in much the same way he tested the various elements of a camera.

The mental processes that went into the name "Kodak" are quite simple. Mr. Eastman wanted a word that was easily spelled and readily pronounced in English or in a foreign tongue. To that end, he arranged the now-famous combination of consonants and vowels so that the word sounds essentially the same in Kansas or Katmandu.

A similar process was used in developing the name "Exxon." The big difference was that a computer processed all the combinations of letters instead of a person.

convenience, and dependability of performance. Similarly, someone selling cable TV might emphasize the large number of cable channels providing a wide variety of programs, including the premium movie channels and the news channels, such as CNN, that provide 24-hour news coverage, and so on.

Two final aspects of product/service concern type and selection. Salespeople need to know how each product/service in the line will perform. The type of product/service available can be matched to the needs of the customer. This calls for knowledge of such things as features, warranties, dimensions, capacity, design, and adaptability. Selection refers to choices available to buyers. It involves models, grades, sizes, colors, styles, quantity per package, minimum orders, and dealer assortments.

BRAND NAMES AND TRADEMARKS

Brand names lend familiarity to the product/service. They are serious, significant, and costly to establish in the marketplace. Brand names can be comprised of personal names, company names, foreign words, numbers, letters, or coined names. Good brand names are usually short, appropriate to the product, and distinctive. They are easy to pronounce, spell, and remember. They are suitable for all types of promotion and for a family of products. They should not be commonplace or negative in connotation and must not infringe or misrepresent.

The term *trademark* is the official legal designation (registered with the U.S. Patent Office) for brand names as well as for certain symbols and devices used with a product. A trademark can be a word, name, symbol, device, or a combination of these. Coke, Ivory, Ford, and Jello are both brand names and trademarks.

Brand names and trademarks are very helpful marketing tools. In fact, as shown in Figure 5-4, some companies specialize in developing names and/or trademarks.

SOME COMPANIES DO NOTHING BUT DEVELOP BRAND NAMES

NAMES ARE MARKETING SHORTHAND

In today's marketplace, your new product's name must communicate a precise benefit or positioning message. At NameSake, we:

1 Help you determine your most important benefit or positioning message.

2 Build that message into scores of names, reflecting different styles and character.

3 Evaluate those names using a set of 15 marketing-based criteria.

4 Test the best names among your customers.

5 Recommend 3-5 tested and precleared name candidates for deep search and registration.

For more information, or a copy of our newsletter, call or write today.

NAMESAKE.

NameSake, Inc.
118 Barrington Commons Ct.
Barrington, IL 60010
(312) 382-6556

Making names

At NameLab, we've made product and company names like *Acura, AutoZone, Compaq, Cycolor, Geo, Sequa* and *Zapmail* by constructional linguistics.

The result of a NameLab project is a report presenting and analyzing registrable names expressing your marketing ideas. We quote costs accurately in advance and complete most projects within 4 weeks.

For information, contact NameLab Inc., 711 Marina Blvd., San Francisco, CA 94123, 415-563-1639.

NAMELAB®

Figure 5-4 A brand name can give a company and/or salesperson an edge over the competition. Thus, many companies select a brand name very carefully or pay professionals for their expertise.

Source: Courtesy of Namelab, Inc. and Namesake.

PACKAGING

A salesperson's interest in how the product is packaged is understandable, because the package is a competitive and a promotional strategy as well as a production concern. The package can have a significant influence on the decision to buy.

The package has three basic functions. It must protect, identify, and promote. But it must not add too much to the selling price. Consumers know what they like and dislike in packages, and the same holds true for retailers.

COMPANY SUPPORT OF THE PRODUCT/SERVICE

When, where, and how a company stands behind its products constitutes essential information. There will be reasonable and unreasonable requests as well as honest and dishonest claims made by customers who regret something about their purchases.

Product guarantees/warranties are one type of company support. Information on guarantees should include the precise terms of the guarantee, the mechanics of handling, and, for the salesperson's own personal knowledge, the strictness with which the company observes the letter of the agreement.

Product service is another type of support. The necessary facts here include the amount, kind, and availability of company service; the details about charges for it; and the time limit for the services.

The handling of defective merchandise is another part of company support. Time limits, repairs, credit memorandums, refunds, replacements, proof of purchase and detection, and transportation charges are typical of the matters involved.

The salesperson's first duty when defective merchandise is involved is to know what the company's policy is and to make sure that every buyer understands this policy clearly so that friction will not be caused by misinterpretation. Salespeople must also know exactly what areas are covered by personal authority and responsibility. Finally, they should transform the company's product support policies into reasons for buying.

CAN SALESPEOPLE KNOW TOO MUCH ABOUT PRODUCTS/SERVICES?

Sometimes the question arises regarding whether or not a salesperson can know too much about the product or service. There are two pitfalls to the dissemination of information by salespeople. The first to be avoided is the mistake of overburdening customers with technical data. The second is stressing product/service features at the expense of user-benefits. Because inexperienced salespeople are apt to be attracted to and impressed by product/service features, they often spend too much time describing them to prospects. Overemphasizing features can be nonproductive because few things are more certain to cause a "So what?" reaction from the prospect. Instead of offering features, salespeople should offer the benefits that result from buying. They should not sell insulation, they should sell economy. They should not sell dancing lessons, they should sell social popularity. They should not sell annuities, they should sell retirement with a comfortable income.

Therefore, salespeople probably cannot know too much about their products or services, providing they use that information properly. Though information does give the salesperson confidence, it is not necessary to memorize every possible fact. The greatest danger is overburdening the sales talk with so much technical data that the customer is either confused or indifferent.

COMPOSITION OF THE PRODUCT/SERVICE LINE

Salespeople also should be familiar with the composition of the product or service line. If the salesperson happens to work for a manufacturer who makes only spark plugs and markets them only under a single brand name, the line is that one brand of plugs. If the company manufactures a family of products/services, the salesperson may benefit from knowing which was the original item, the sequence of additions, and how, when, and why each related item was added to the line.

RELATED PRODUCTS/SERVICES

In learning everything possible about what the product/service will do for its buyers and just how it can be best applied to users' needs, salespeople often must acquire information about complementary or auxiliary products/services. A person who sells computers must know printers and software. Someone selling automobiles needs to have a better-than-casual acquaintance with accessories of various types. Windows should be sold only by an individual who knows something about both architecture and construction.

COMPETITIVE PRODUCTS/SERVICES

Salespeople must know their competitors' products/services almost as well as they know their own. They must identify and study the outstanding features—and the weak points—of competing brands. They also must know about their competitors' market coverage, the customer service they provide, and the prices they charge.

MARKET COVERAGE

All salespeople should know for their territories the market coverage of each competitive seller. The concept of market coverage includes both geography and buyers. The geographical aspect often involves sales organization (districts, territories) and selling effort (areas getting stronger or weaker sales attention). The buyer aspect includes knowing who are the large volume customers of each competitor, the types of buyers given special attention, and the buyers who are neglected. The salesperson needs at least a rough estimate of how the firm and its competitors share the market, how those shares have changed over the last five years, and forecasts of how each major competitor may do over the next five years.

CUSTOMER SERVICE

Sellers compete in providing services to their customers. Examples of services include the following:

1. Superior knowledge about products and their uses
2. Speedy and satisfactory handling of complaints
3. Quick-order handling and delivery by the dates promised
4. Answering buyers' questions fully, accurately, and promptly
5. Installation, maintenance, and repair
6. Handling returned defective merchandise

PRICES

Competitors' prices are not only a major concern, but sometimes the most perplexing problem to salespeople because, in most situations, some competitor is quoting lower prices to buyers than their company. Some competitor mistakenly assumes that quoting the lowest price will result in dominating the market and getting rich almost overnight. Or, a competitive salesperson has authority to quote special discounts or looser credit terms, which put these prices below the salesperson's prices.

THE DISTRIBUTION SYSTEM

Some distribution channels are direct channels. In such cases the producer deals directly with the industrial purchaser or ultimate consumer via the company sales force. Such direct channels involve no middlemen. The producer and the customer perform all the activities necessary to get the products/services distributed.

When channels are indirect, middlemen are involved. In the traditional distribution channel for consumer goods, a producer sells to a wholesaler who sells to a retailer who sells to the ultimate consumer. Growing more popular with the growth of larger retailers (such as Sears, K mart, Safeway, Federated Department Stores) are channels that bypass the wholesaler: producers sell directly to retailers who then sell to the ultimate consumer. But there are some channels for consumer goods in which, in addition to a retailer, two or more wholesalers are involved. Examples of possible distribution channels are shown in Figure 5-5.

CHANNELS OF DISTRIBUTION

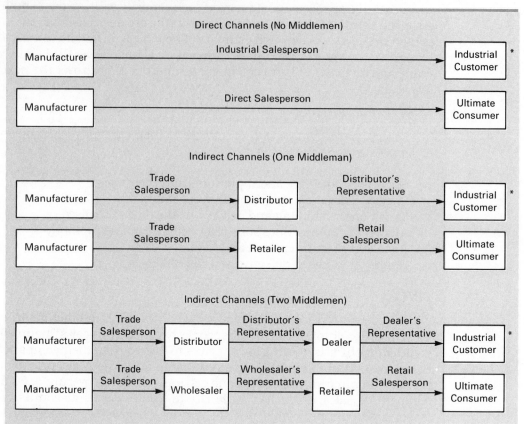

*Industrial goods channels refer to wholesalers and retailers as "distributors" and "retailers," respectively.

Figure 5-5 The number of middlemen involved in placing the product affects the intensity of market coverage and the product's price.

The salesperson's task will depend to a great extent on the length of the distribution channel. In a direct channel, the salesperson will call on the ultimate consumer or the industrial purchaser. In longer channels, it is possible that the salesperson may call on retailers, wholesalers, or both.

Let us now look in more detail at the middlemen with whom a salesperson must interact if the channel of distribution is to be effective.

WHOLESALERS

Wholesaling is selling to buyers (wholesalers, retailers) for resale, to producers (manufacturers, farmers), governments, or to institutional users (universities). The role of the wholesaler is to facilitate the transfer of goods/services between manufacturers and retailers. Some wholesalers perform a full range of functions, others provide only one or two. The various wholesaling functions include buying, selling, extension of credit, consultation and information, title transfer, breaking of bulk, assorting, stocking, delivery, and risk taking. These functions are defined in Figure 5-6.

RETAILERS

Retailers sell to ultimate consumers for personal or household use. Retail organizations can be classified on the basis of their ownership, size, location, service, organizational, merchandise, contractual, and operational characteristics. The complexity and diversity of retailing formats within the industry make it difficult to develop a classification that clearly distinguishes each type of retailer from all other types. Moreover, competition among retailers is no longer just among those of a single type. Rather, specialty stores compete with department stores and both compete with mass merchandisers. Figure 5-7 profiles the various major types of U.S. retailing institutions.

DEPARTMENT STORES

Department stores are large retailing organizations that carry a wide variety of merchandise with a reasonably good selection within each line. Merchandise lines typically carried include: furniture, home furnishings, appliances, audiovisual equipment, family apparel, household linens, and dry goods. The characteristic that distinguishes department stores from other general-line merchandisers is their high degree of "departmentalization." From an operating standpoint, most of the basic functions of buying, selling, servicing, and promoting are handled largely at the departmental level. Also, the accounting and control procedures are organized on a departmental basis.

SUPERMARKETS

A supermarket is a large store specializing in groceries that typically operates on a self-service basis (except, perhaps, in the meat, deli, bakery, or produce sections) and very rarely offers credit or delivery. Because of the large volume of business they do and the absence of much service, supermarkets make a very small profit margin—often only 1 percent on each sales dollar—and sell at low prices. Because of the wide variety of business approaches used in the grocery industry, no commonly accepted definition of a supermarket exists.

FUNCTIONS PERFORMED BY WHOLESALERS

Buying. Wholesalers act as purchasing agents when they anticipate the merchandise needs of retailers and their customers. By locating sources of supply and obtaining merchandise that is suitable to the retailer's needs, wholesalers enhance the retailer's buying and procurement processes.

Selling. Wholesalers simplify buying procedures by having salespeople calling at the retailer's place of business. Wholesaling intermediaries help reduce the retailer's cost of securing goods by: (1) eliminating some trips to the market, and (2) assuming some of the responsibilities (e.g., order follow-up, self-stocking) for getting the merchandise onto the retailer's displays.

Extension of Credit. Many wholesaling intermediaries finance part or all of a retailer's inventory. The most common credit extension is the setting of the date when the net price of an invoice is due in full. By providing 30, 45, 60, or more days to pay an invoice without charges, the wholesaler is in effect financing the retailer's inventory. Consignment and memorandum selling, wherein the retailer does not pay for the merchandise until it is sold, is still another form of extending credit. In addition, many wholesalers make available to retailers short-, intermediate-, and long-term loans that can be used as working and fixed capital.

Consultation and Information. Wholesalers provide their customers with numerous advisory services. Typical consultant services deal with accounting, advertising, personnel training, financial and legal advice, location analysis, inventory control, and facilities planning. Marketing research and other information are two important functions that also may be provided by some wholesalers. Many large wholesaling operations engage in an ongoing effort to determine marketplace needs and conditions. By passing this information on, retailers have comparison points for examining their market performance and adjusting their marketing programs. Wholesalers' unique position within the channel allows them to provide useful information on products, manufacturers' programs, supply sources, and activities of competitors.

Title Transfer. Free-and-clear title to products is essential to the exchange process. Merchant wholesalers that own the goods they deal in assume the responsibility for transfer of payments and the management of title exchange. Agent wholesalers that do not take title to the goods facilitate the exchange of title by providing or arranging for the services necessary to the title-exchange process.

Breaking of Bulk. A quantity gap occurs between the manufacturer's need to produce and sell in large quantities and the retailer's need to buy in smaller quantities. Wholesaling intermediaries help bridge this quantity gap by: (1) buying in car- or truck-load quantities, (2) performing bulk-breaking activities, and (3) selling in smaller quantities (e.g., case lots) to retailers. This bulk-breaking function helps reduce the cost of doing business by reducing inventory carrying and handling costs.

Assorting. An assortment gap exists between manufacturers that need (manufacturing economies of scale) to provide and sell a limited line of identical, or nearly identical, products and retailers that must offer the consumer a wider selection of products. Wholesalers can fill this gap by buying the limited product lines and items of many different manufacturers and combining these lines and items into appropriate assortments. The retailer's desire for either mass- or target-market appeal is greatly enhanced by the availability of diversified product assortments.

Stocking. Retailers often have limited stockroom space and inventory investment capital. Wholesalers provide a valuable service by reducing the space and capital needed for retail stock. This reduces the need for facilities and inventory carrying costs for the retailer. The local nature of wholesalers also enhances the time and place availability of products for restocking purposes.

Delivery. Quick and frequent deliveries by the wholesaler help avoid or replenish out-of-stock conditions that result in lost sales. A timely delivery system is one service a wholesaler provides that helps the retailer to hold down in-store inventories that are required to meet customer expectations. Reliable deliveries also play an integral part in reducing safety stock and the risk and investment associated with such stock.

Risk Taking. Wholesalers also take a risk when dealing with manufacturers and retailers. When the wholesaler buys in bulk from the manufacturer the wholesaler is assuming responsibility for the sale of that product. The manufacturer has been paid and the product is owned by the wholesaler. Also, there is no guarantee that the retailer will buy that product off the wholesaler. If the retailer can no longer sell that product to the consumer, the retailer will not buy from the wholesaler. The wholesaler runs the risk of getting stuck with the product.

Figure 5-6 While some wholesalers perform a full range of functions, others provide limited services.

Source: Adapted from D. Lewison and W. DeLozier, *Retailing*, 3d ed. (Columbus, OH: Merrill Publishing Company, 1989), 472. Reprinted by permission of Merrill Publishing Company.

PROFILES OF U.S. RETAILING INSTITUTIONS

Retail Institution Type	Examples
General-Merchandise Retailers	
Department Stores	Macy's, Dayton Hudson, Bloomingdales
Discount Stores	K mart, Wal-Mart, Target, Sam's Wholesale Club
Mass Merchandisers	Sears, JC Penney, Montgomery Ward
Catalog Showrooms	Best, Service Merchandise
Variety Stores	F. W. Woolworth, Family Dollar, Dollar General
Food Retailers	
Conventional Supermarkets	Albertson, Kroger, Safeway, Winn-Dixie
Warehouse Store	Kash 'N Karry, Pic-N-Pay, Cub
Combination Store	Jewel, Skaggs Alpha-Beta Center
Convenience Store	Southland (7-Eleven), Circle K
Drug Retailers	
Chain	Eckerd, Walgreen's, Revco, Savco
Independent	Gould, Kerr, "mom-and-pop"
Home-Improvement Centers	Home Depot, Wickes, Payless Cashaways
Hardware Stores	True Value, Ace
Apparel Specialty Stores	Kinney Shoes, Petrie, The Limited
Furniture & Appliance Stores	Silo, Levitz, Circuit City
Mail-Order Houses	Spiegel, Fingerhut, L. L. Bean
Miscellaneous Specialty Stores	
Sporting Goods Stores	Sports Unlimited, Oshman's, Herman's
Jewelry Stores	Kay, Gordon, Zale
Hobby, Toy, and Game Stores	Toys "R" Us, Children's Palace
Gift and Novelty Stores	Hallmark, Spencer Gifts
Off-Price Chains	Marshall's, Burlington Coat Factory

Figure 5-7 A wide variety of retailers is found in the United States.

DISCOUNT STORES

These stores are retailing organizations that sell a wide variety of merchandise at lower-than-traditional retail prices. Their retailing strategy is to use mass merchandising techniques, which enable them to offer discount prices. Discount store operations vary with respect to the size of the discount and the nature of the merchandise. **Conventional discount stores** sell name-brand merchandise at prices consumers easily recognize as below traditional prices. In contrast to conventional discount stores, **distressed discount stores** offer merchandise that is either damaged, discontinued, seconds, irregulars, or used at substantially below market prices.

OFF-PRICE RETAILERS

These are specialty retailers that sell primarily fashion apparel and other soft goods discounted 20 percent to 60 percent below regular retail prices. Off-price retailers are a relatively recent phenomenon that are able to offer such low prices because of volume buying and merchandising strategies. As marketing strategies, they typically offer self-service, limited advertising, and fairly modest facilities.

CHAIN STORES

A retail chain is a group of stores that sell similar lines of merchandise operating under single ownership. The *Census of Business*, a U.S. Government publication, considers retail organizations that operate 11 or more units to be chains. Thus, the division of small chains (2 to 10 units) and large chains (11 or more units) is often used. Small chains tend to be local or regional in market coverage and large chains are regional or national in scope. The principal organizational characteristic of chain stores is highly centralized control of product, place, price, and promotional strategies.

The importance of corporate chains to the distribution system of many manufacturers has created two distinct types of selling jobs. The first, and therefore most important, task of salespeople for a manufacturer is to convince buyers for a corporate chain to recommend or require that each store carry their brands. The second task is to help each store in the chain to sell as much of the manufacturer's brands as possible. Some firms have one group of salespeople who specialize in the first task, and another group who specialize in the second task. For example, Armstrong Cork has a Corporate Market Sales Department whose salespeople call at the headquarters of major department store chains, large building contractors, and so on. Then there are other salespeople, specialists in the types of products they sell (floor and wall coverings, residential ceilings, carpet) who act as consultants to the individual stores in each chain. These salespeople will often help to set up displays, provide advice about advertising, and offer assistance in many other areas of the business.

CONVENIENCE STORES

This type of retailer offers consumers a convenient place to shop for a limited number of items. They are typically open longer and during inconvenient early-morning and late-night hours, and offer fast service close to homes or places of business. The basic marketing strategy is to serve emergency and/or convenience items consumers may have forgotten to purchase or run out of unexpectedly, or items consumers want to purchase quickly with a minimum of hassle. Of course, customers must pay higher prices for this type of service, which provides both time and place utilities. Typical examples of convenience stores are 7-Eleven, Minit Market, Jiffy Food Stores, and Stop-And-Go, the names of which suggest the type of retail operations they provide.

CONTRACTUAL CHAINS

In an effort to secure the advantages of corporate chains, independent retailers have organized into chains that are linked by contract rather than common ownership. By entering contractual arrangements, the retailers can formalize the rights and obligations of each party in the contract. Generally, the terms of the contract cover all aspects of the retailer's product, price, place, and promotional strategies. The most common types of contractual chains are retailer-sponsored cooperative groups, wholesaler-sponsored voluntary chains, franchised retailers, and leased departments.

Retailer-sponsored chains are a contractual organization formed by many independent retailers—both large and small. They were originally formed to combat competition from large chain organizations. Typically, retailer-sponsored chains establish a jointly owned warehousing/wholesaling facility, which enables them to purchase in larger, more economical quantities.

Wholesaler-sponsored chains are a reaction to the loss of business that occurs when retail chains purchase directly from the manufacturer. This typically involves persuading independent retailers to join together in a voluntary chain where members guarantee to buy agreed-upon volumes of certain products through the wholesaler forming the chain. In return, they receive lower prices on the merchandise they buy, and operating and marketing help from the wholesaler. The voluntary chain is capable of providing the wholesaler with guaranteed customers and, therefore, significant buying power. IGA, Super-Value Stores, Western Auto Stores, and Walgreen Pharmacies are four good examples of large voluntary chains.

Selling to voluntary chains is similar to selling to corporate chains. The salesperson must convince chain headquarters to adopt the product or there is little chance of getting individual stores to carry it.

A **franchising system** is a contractual form of retailing agreed upon by a franchiser and a franchisee. The franchise agreement grants the franchisee the right to sell the franchiser's brand of product or service in a particular location or market area. The franchiser typically promises to supply managerial assistance, a national or regional advertising program, and some portion of the equipment, products, and supplies necessary for doing business. In return, the franchisee agrees (1) to produce or market the product or service according to procedures established by the franchiser and (2) to pay a franchising fee and, possibly, royalties on the basis of sales or profits.

Franchises of many types have become household words: McDonald's, Kentucky Fried Chicken, Holiday Inn, Hertz, Midas Mufflers, and so on. Most automobile dealerships are franchises, as are soft-drink bottlers.

Leased departments are retailers that operate departments under a contractual arrangement with conventional retail stores. Many department stores and supermarkets lease space to outside organizations to sell merchandise such as magazines, shoes, and auto supplies. The store typically provides space, utilities, and basic in-store services necessary to the leased department's operation. In turn, the leased department provides the personnel, management, and capital necessary to stock and operate a department with specifically defined merchandise. Generally, the leased department pays the store either a flat monthly fee, a commission on sales, or some combination.

WAREHOUSE RETAILING

One of the major retailing trends to emerge in recent years is warehouse retailing. The typical warehouse retailing operation involves some combination of warehouse and showroom display facilities. Sometimes these facilities are combined and sometimes separate. The strategy of warehouse retailers is to reduce operating expenses and thereby offer discount prices.

The four primary types of warehouse retailers are catalog showrooms, warehouse showrooms, home centers, and hypermarkets. Catalog showrooms typically sell hard goods such as housewares, jewelry, watches, toys, sporting goods, small appliances, luggage, stereos, and lawn and garden equipment, at discounted prices. Warehouse showrooms most often are single-line, hard-goods retailers that stock well-known, nationally advertised merchandise such as appliances, carpeting, and furniture. Home centers combine the traditional hardware store and lumberyard to form a self-service home-improvement center. Hypermarkets are general-merchandise warehouse retailers that sell food products and a wide variety of both hard and soft goods. All four types of warehouse retailers have enjoyed substantial success.

MAIL-ORDER RETAILING

Originally, mail-order retailing emerged to serve rural America. But in recent years it has expanded rapidly as consumers began to value the convenience of in-home shopping. Mail-order retailers typically are of three types: general-merchandise retailers, specialty mail-order retailers, and novelty-merchandise sellers. Many of them involve the use of catalogs, but some rely only on smaller brochures or coupons placed in newspapers and magazines.

ELECTRONIC RETAILING

Retailing operations using electronic and video systems are the most recent innovations in the retailing sector. A wide variety of electronic catalog retailing systems are currently being developed and/or tested. Computer networks such as Compuserve and The Source also provide shopping alternatives. Individuals can even make their own airline reservations or reserve rental cars using these networks if they wish. One of the most well-known systems is Videotex. It is an interactive electronic system in which data and graphics are transmitted through a computer network, cable lines, or telephone lines and displayed on a television set or personal computer. This approach to electronic retailing involves the consumer accessing the system, and then making a series of choices about product lines, brands, and services using menus displayed on the screen. With the demand for convenience and more leisure time, it is very likely that this type of retailing will grow considerably in the future.

SALESPEOPLE AND THE DISTRIBUTION SYSTEM

Physical distribution, or logistics, is the physical flow of goods. Physical distribution management has two goals: (1) to maximize the service provided to customers, and (2) to minimize the costs of providing the service. Unfortunately, the better the service the more costly it is likely to be. This often puts the salesperson, who wants to provide rapid, accurate delivery to customers, in conflict with the traffic manager or warehouse manager, who want to use slower, cheaper methods of transportation and materials handling. Thus, it is very important for salespeople to understand the distribution system so customers can be given the best service possible relative to their needs, and conflicts with physical distribution management can be reduced or eliminated. Furthermore, good service is an excellent selling point for salespeople.

Basic to understanding the distribution system is awareness of what affects the length of the order cycle and a knowledge of storage and transportation. These two basic decision areas determine physical distribution costs and service.

THE ORDER CYCLE

The order cycle is the time that elapses between placement of the order by the buyer and the receipt of the products ordered. If a manufacturer's order cycle is rapid and consistent, customers are happy because they can get the products they need when they need them (and don't have to order much in advance of a possible need). Salespeople and middlemen are happy because it gives them an important edge over their competitors. Finally, rapid and consistent order cycles typically reduce the amount of inventory which must be stored throughout the buyer's system.

Order Placement. Salespeople influence the order cycle most during the order-placement stage because they are usually responsible for getting and placing the order. Though customers sometimes place their orders directly with the main office, more often they place orders through the salesperson. Therefore, the salesperson's accessibility is very important: the frequency of calls on customers and the ability of customers to reach the salesperson between calls can mean the difference between rapid order placement and a delay. Order-placement delays have been reduced dramatically in recent years by new technology. Salespeople are accessible virtually 24 hours a day through regional and national pager systems, cellular mobile phones, facsimile machines, and computers. Salespeople who do not use this new technology have a significant competitive disadvantage because they cannot service their customers as well.

Order Processing. Order processing involves paperwork and the physical assembly and packaging of the order. The main office may need to run credit checks and make credit-granting decisions. Work orders must be transmitted to the warehouse or plant indicating what should be assembled or produced. Also, invoices must be prepared so the customer is properly billed. The order-processing cycle has been reduced substantially in recent years. Increasingly, orders are transmitted, received, and processed electronically. It is not uncommon for salespeople to enter an order through their computer, transmit it over phone lines to the home office, have the order reviewed and approved electronically, and shipped, if needed, within 24 hours.

Order Shipment. In simple terms, order shipment is the movement of the product from seller to buyer. If a company chooses to use its own transportation system, it must decide what and how many vehicles (trucks, railroad cars, barges) to own and how to schedule their use. If neither the seller nor the buyer provides transportation, a third party enters the picture: a transportation firm (Kansas City Southern Railroad, Consolidated Freight Shippers). The customer often specifies the type of transportation preferred and even the company to provide it. Salespeople have an opportunity to help customers avoid costly and frustrating errors when making that decision.

DISTRIBUTION DECISION AREAS

Two important decision areas regarding physical distribution management are storage and transportation. These areas cannot be managed separately; storage decisions and transportation decisions affect each other. For example, choosing to store a large quantity of a product at a single, centralized warehouse can reduce warehousing and inventory costs, but it can also force a company to use faster and more expensive modes of transportation to reach far-flung customers quickly. In making decisions in each area, the distribution manager needs to consider their impact on costs and customer service and on other decisions.

Storage. Product storage is needed when demand or supply is uncertain and when demand or supply is seasonal. For example, Macy's does not know how many television sets, shirts, or electric mixers it will sell on a given day; so it buys a quantity large enough to meet expected demand for several weeks or a whole season and stores those products until they are all sold. Heavy-equipment manufacturers are dependent on the supply of steel available to them. They stockpile steel when shortages are threatened due to possible strikes in the steel industry.

Transportation. Transportation decisions initially involve the choice of transportation mode: railroads, trucks, waterways, pipelines, and airplanes. Salespeople should understand the cost and service characteristics of each in order to make realistic delivery promises to customers or advise customers when they specify the transportation mode to be used.

Choosing the lowest-cost or best-service transportation mode depends on the products being shipped and the distances and locations involved. Salespeople should be able to help customers make a wise decision. Salespeople should have some idea of the shipping costs and times from the company's warehouse to each major customer, and know when increased weight and bulk or special handling characteristics make shifting from one mode to another desirable. And, when in doubt, utilize the services of the company's traffic manager. It may even be appropriate to use intermodal methods of transportation. Railroads load truck trailers on flat cars (piggyback service) and transport them by rail as far as possible before shifting them to a truck tractor to be delivered to the customer's door. Ships, combined with trucks, offer a similar "fishyback" service.

EMERGING TRENDS IN DISTRIBUTION

The worldwide competitive environment of the 1980s forced manufacturers and middlemen to join together to develop and implement cost-saving distribution strategies. The new strategies place primary emphasis on manufacturers responding as rapidly as possible to market requirements. The ideal vision is that a product would never be manufactured or a component purchased until a customer order is received. Components or materials necessary to support production or assembly are purchased to arrive at the specified production plant as needed and in the exact quantity required. Prime attention is directed to quality control to assure that products are produced with "zero defects" the first time, thereby eliminating reruns. The manufacturer, therefore, would receive materials and component parts "just-in-time" for production runs. Similarly, wholesalers and retailers would place orders and receive them "just-in-time" to meet market demands. Hence, the label of "just-in-time" manufacturing and distribution strategies has emerged as a means of reducing substantially the costs of warehousing and inventory holding.

SUMMARY

In order for salespeople to be experts, they must know industry origins, current developments, and future potential. This requires product, manufacturer, and market research.

Prices are extremely important to buyers and salespeople. Prices can be set above the market, below the market, or as close to the competition as possible. Quantity discounts are offered to customers in return for buying in large volume. Trade discounts are offered to middlemen. Cash discounts are offered as an incentive for customers to pay early. Credit management depends on character, capacity, capital, and conditions.

Salespeople must know their product's features, physical attributes, brand names and trademarks, and packaging. Salespeople must also be familiar with their competition and its products. While needing to have a full knowledge of all of this, the salesperson should not overburden his or her prospect with a lot of technical data. He or she, however, must be able to answer the prospect's questions.

Product distribution channels can be either direct or indirect. Direct channels go directly to the end user, while indirect channels use middlemen. Physical distribution refers to the actual flow of goods. Maximized customer service and minimized costs are the goals of physical distribution management. Intensive distribution is used when the seller sells through every available outlet, while exclusive distribution refers to selling through one or two outlets in an area.

KEY TERMS

sales books	conventional discount store
product research	distressed discount store
terms of sale	franchising system
distribution channels	leased departments

REVIEW QUESTIONS

1. Why is knowledge so important to salespeople?
2. What industry characteristics should be understood by salespeople?
3. Which is more important: reputation with consumers, or trade reputation? Why?
4. What is the difference between list price and net price?
5. What does FOB mean? Why is it important?
6. Why are quantity discounts given?
7. What is the purpose of a cash discount?
8. Why must salespeople be attuned to credit and collection issues?
9. What is a trademark?
10. How do merchant wholesalers and merchandise agents differ?
11. Why have manufacturers set up sales branches and offices?
12. How has the growth in popularity of discount stores influenced other retailers?
13. Why are voluntary and retailer cooperative chains organized?
14. What is a franchise?
15. How do salespeople influence the order cycle?
16. List the three major product storage decisions.
17. What are the different responsibilities of salespeople under intensive versus exclusive distribution?
18. How do salespeople act as substitutes for wholesalers and retailers?

DISCUSSION QUESTIONS

1. Can you think of any salespeople you have interacted with or observed recently? In your opinion, were they knowledgeable? What was it about those salespeople that influenced your opinion in such a manner?
2. Why do people care about the seller's financial condition, standing in the industry, and growth potential?
3. What types of information and supporting materials are provided to salespeople by the manufacturer? How can salespeople use these materials and information to make a sale?

4. Why do some manufacturers use intensive distribution while others use exclusive distribution? List three products distributed with each method.

CASE 5-1   GULF COAST METALS*

Gulf Coast Metals is a distributor of specialty metals with its home office located in Pensacola, Florida. The sales staff includes the sales manager, Steven Blake, and five salespeople. The market area served includes five states—Texas, Louisiana, Mississippi, Alabama, and Florida. A branch sales office with limited warehousing space is located in Baton Rouge, Louisiana. Approximately 70 percent of their product mix is aluminum and stainless steel. Other metals they sell include bronze, cast iron, nickel alloy, brass, and copper. These metals are sold in the following forms: sheet, plate, bar, and custom-machine shapes. Industrial customers are the primary market for specialty metals. Customers include machine shops, ship-building plants, pulpwood processors, chemical plants, electrical-generating utilities, metal-fabricating shops, and the government.

One of Gulf Coast Metals' sales representatives, Jim Franklin, just found out he lost a major customer—one whose orders had averaged over $100,000 annually for the three years Jim serviced the account. When he called the purchasing agent to find out why they stopped buying from Gulf Coast Metals, the agent said, "I'll be quite frank. Reynolds Metals quoted me a lower price and I couldn't afford to pass it up. After all, specialty metals are the same no matter where you get them."

When Jim told his sales manager about the problem, he suggested they review a customer survey that was recently conducted by a consultant for Gulf Coast Metals. A random sample of 400 interviews was conducted with customers and noncustomers of Gulf Coast Metals using a telephone survey approach. The chart below, taken from the consultant's report, shows the criteria customers use in selecting a specialty metals supplier and how Gulf Coast Metals compares with their major competitors.

Respondents were asked to rate seven factors in terms of their importance (from "0" for "not important" to "10" for "highly important"). They were also asked to rate suppliers (from "0" for "not competitive" to "10" for "highly competitive"). The average results of this survey are shown in the table below.

The sales manager asked Jim to use the information to come up with ways to regain a competitive advantage over Reynolds.

---

*Case prepared by Sandy Franklin. Used with permission

EXHIBIT 5-1 IMPORTANCE OF FACTORS AND COMPETITOR RATINGS

Factor	Overall Importance	Rating by Company			
		Reynolds	Gulf Coast Metals	Blanchard	O'Neal
Service	9	8	10	5	5
Competitive Price	9	9	3	4	6
Delivery Schedule	8	8	9	4	4
Inventory	7	9	7	4	6
Sales Force	6	5	8	7	9
Credit Policy	5	8	6	9	6
Cutting Capability	4	6	6	9	8

CASE QUESTIONS

1. Using this data and Lotus, create comparisons among the firm by (a) finding the product of importance and firm rating on each factor, and (b) summing the ratings for each firm.
   - Which company has the highest rating?
   - Which has the lowest?
2. Copy your Lotus table to another sector of the spreadsheet, and change the factor importance ratings for "competitive price" to a "2," and the factor importance rating for "cutting capability" to a "9."
   - Which company now has the highest rating?
3. How would you use the consultant's report to develop a more effective sales presentation?
4. Based on the information provided in the consultant's report, what could Gulf Coast Metals do to counteract the effects of Reynolds Metals' lower price?

CASE 5-2 INSTITUTIONAL EQUIPMENT AND DESIGN*

Institutional Equipment and Design (IE&D) is a wholly owned subsidiary company of Piccadilly Cafeterias, Inc. It was established in the early

---

*Case prepared by Bob Powell. Used with permission.

1970s when Piccadilly began adding new cafeteria units at a much faster pace. Between 1970 and 1990 Piccadilly opened 92 new cafeterias in 14 states in the South and the West. IE&D was responsible for the design, layout, and interior decoration of the cafeterias, and for the fabrication of kitchen equipment.

In early 1990 a consultant was hired to evaluate the feasibility of setting up an outside sales force for IE&D. The consultant's report indicated there were many other companies providing the same products and services as IE&D, but only a few were as large and as knowledgeable. Like IE&D, the other companies design all types of machinery and accessories for large food operations.

There are two primary market segments for companies like IE&D: (1) commercial operations such as restaurants, hotels, and cafeterias, and (2) institutions such as hospitals, schools, and nursing homes. Although there is little difference in the types of products/services offered, the quality of the equipment, its durability and reliability, and the follow-up servicing are very important considerations in deciding whom to buy from.

Prices in both the commercial and institutional market segments are very competitive. The market leader, however, with about 24 percent of market share, prices its products about 15 percent above other competitors. Their salespeople justify this by saying that their products are more durable and more reliable than their competitors'.

IE&D management met recently with the consultant to decide what their differential competitive advantage would be. They had already decided they did not want to price their products at the low end of the market, and, like the market leader, might choose to be higher than many other competitors. The consultant indicated that to be successful they would have to offer one of the following: (1) superior products and/or services, or (2) more effective sales and/or advertising strategies.

IE&D felt their products/services were superior, or at least very comparable, to the market leader. Also, they had spent a lot of time planning an excellent approach for servicing their customers. But they believed their real opportunity was in developing more effective sales and advertising strategies to communicate their message to the market.

CASE QUESTIONS

1. Should IE&D set up an outside sales force to serve the commercial and institutional markets? Should only one segment be pursued at first?
2. Who are some of IE&D's prospects?
3. What kind of service approach do you think they have developed?
4. What should be emphasized in IE&D's sales/advertising messages?
5. Who should the sales presentation be made to?

CHAPTER 6
Promotional Sales Support

After studying this chapter, you should be able to:

- Tell what advertising is and identify the groups engaged in advertising

- Suggest how salespeople can benefit from the advertising their firms do

- Discuss the differences between sales promotion for dealers and sales promotion for ultimate consumers

- Describe the elements in a promotion program

A company's promotional support system refers to those activities the company engages in to help communicate its product to the consumer. A consumer who has prior knowledge of a product before speaking to a salesperson will probably be easier to sell to. To accomplish this task, sellers have available to them three direct promotional strategies. The first, **personal selling**, is the subject of this book. Personal selling is a "push" technique, which entails pushing a manufacturer's products down through the distribution channel.

The second direct promotional strategy is **advertising**. Manufacturers may direct some of their advertising to wholesalers and retailers. In addition, they may direct some to certain professional groups (architects, dentists) whose members influence certain purchases. Most advertising, however, is addressed to ultimate consumers. Advertising is a "pull" technique, because it urges consumers to ask for and buy advertised brands by pulling those brands through the channels of distribution.

The third direct promotional strategy consists of a group of auxiliary activities labeled **sales promotion**. These activities enhance personal selling and advertising strategies. Sales promotion can influence retailers and stimulate the purchase of the manufacturer's products by ultimate consumers. Examples of sales promotions include coupons, rebates, displays, deals, and contests.

Another ingredient of the promotional mix is an indirect strategy called **publicity**. There are two types of publicity: (1) information about a firm or product considered news by communication media and reported by that firm to the public at no charge, and (2) two or more persons conversing about a seller or the seller's product, referred to as "word-of-mouth" promotion.

Personal selling, advertising, sales promotion, and publicity are all part of the promotional mix. Each seller faces the challenging problem of combining them in what will be the most effective promotion program. Most medium and large sellers of consumer products use all five promotional activities. These companies talk individually with some buyers through their salespeople, communicate impersonally with large groups of buyers through advertising, use the amounts and types of sales promotion desirable, and build publicity schedules to appear in media.

THE PROMOTION MIX

Promotion programs must be planned. Management sets up goals or objectives, the major ones involving sales, share of market, and profit. Management next develops strategies for attaining its goals. Time, effort, dollars, and personnel are budgeted. The result is the promotion mix of the firm.

ADVERTISING

The mass communication of an offer of satisfaction is generally referred to as advertising. Advertising can be designed to achieve three objectives: to inform, to persuade, and to remind. The *content* of advertisements should give buyers the facts about the benefits of products/services, which will help them make better buying decisions. The various *forms* advertisers employ to communicate a seller's story allow them to reach millions of consumers quickly. Because advertising is mass communication, it can have a low cost-per-prospective-buyer impression if a firm is selling to the mass market. But since it is a form of impersonal communication, it is much more easily ignored than are salespeople.

Advertising is best suited for preselling. Preselling involves creating awareness and interest for the product/service. When a manufacturer's advertising presells middlemen on products and/or services, salespeople have an easier job selling to those middlemen. When the manufacturer's advertising presells consumers, the selling done by retailers is made easier. In preselling, advertising introduces products/services to prospective buyers. In subsequent contacts, buyers recognize the products, their brand names, and the manufacturer's name. If this recognition is favorable, buyers often will buy one of the items when the purchase is recommended by a retail salesperson or suggested by a friend.

Despite its preselling feature, advertising lacks personal contact and the impact of a salesperson's personality. Thus, advertising alone seldom "makes" the sale unless it is a low perceived risk product/service.

GROUPS INVOLVED IN ADVERTISING

There are four major components involved in the advertising process: advertisers, buyers, media, and advertising agencies. Each plays an active and coordinated role in presenting a company's message to the public.

ADVERTISERS

This chapter will emphasize the manufacturer as the advertiser. Of course, many of the principles and techniques of creating effective advertising apply equally to retailers and other middlemen. For manufacturers of consumer items such as soap, cereals, beverages, and automobiles, the typical promotion mix is one that involves advertising to ultimate consumers and salespeople calling on wholesalers and retailers. Manufacturers of industrial products and sellers of industrial services usually direct advertising and personal selling efforts toward either industrial buyers or middlemen.

BUYERS

Within the ultimate consumer group of buyers, the advertiser recognizes four types of customers. One group consists of persons who do not consume the advertiser's kind of product. For example, a thin person would not use a weight-loss product. A second type is composed of people who use the advertiser's kind of product but who buy competitors' brands. The third type are those who buy the advertiser's brand but do not buy as much as the advertiser might wish; and the fourth type are those who buy as much of the advertiser's product as they need but need to be reminded of its benefits from time to time. Advertisements are constructed and transmitted with these four consumers in mind.

MEDIA

Advertising media are the third component involved in the advertising process. One group of these media sells space and uses print promotion through newspapers, magazines, outdoor billboards, and public transit systems such as space on buses and subways. The other group of media sells time. Radio broadcasts audio promotion and television combines audio and visual promotion.

ADVERTISING AGENCIES

Advertising agencies make up the fourth component involved in the advertising process. These specialized firms have two principal functions: (1) to design effective advertising campaigns for their clients, and (2) to contract with advertising media to execute the advertising campaigns.

TYPES OF ADVERTISING

There are three common classifications of advertising: primary versus selective, brand versus institutional, and direct-action versus indirect-action.

PRIMARY AND SELECTIVE ADVERTISING

The demand for a type or class of product or service, such as wine, leather, insurance, or investment counseling, is called **primary demand**. Primary advertising, therefore, promotes a generic product or service, not any one brand. Seldom does a salesperson's company engage, by itself, in primary advertising. Instead, the typical sponsor of primary advertising is an industry trade association whose members unite in the hope of achieving something beneficial to the entire industry. For example, the California Raisin Growers made a big splash with its award-winning "I Heard It Through the Grapevine" commercial, which used animated singing and dancing raisins made of clay. This ad aided such companies as SunMaid and Del Monte.

The individual seller is concerned mainly with the stimulation of **selective demand**. The seller wants consumers to buy a particular brand within a broad class of products. Whereas primary demand determines the total market, selective demand determines each competing seller's share of the market. To each seller, the selective demand for a particular brand is a segment of the primary demand. Most salespeople are more concerned with selective demand and selective advertising than with primary demand and primary advertising.

BRAND AND INSTITUTIONAL ADVERTISING

Product-promoting or brand advertising seeks to promote the sales of a specific brand. Thus, it is essentially the same as selective advertising. Brand advertising tries to differentiate a particular brand from other similar brands and to endow that brand with a favorable image. A **brand image** is the consumer's impression and evaluation of a certain branded product.

Institutional advertising does for the company what promotional advertising does for the brand. It attempts to develop a favorable **corporate image** for the firm. Corporate image is the buyer's picture of the character and personality of that corporation.

DIRECT-ACTION ADVERTISING AND INDIRECT-ACTION ADVERTISING

Some advertising is designed to stimulate immediate response on the part of the buyer. An advertisement containing an inquiry coupon is an example of a **direct-action advertisement**. Manufacturers use these advertisements to stimulate inquiries about a product(s), while retailers use them to persuade consumers to visit the store promptly to look for or buy some specific merchandise.

Some salespeople work for firms that employ only **indirect-action advertisements**. This type of advertising has long-range goals. Its objective is to influence buyer attitudes rather than stimulate immediate action. Much television and magazine advertisement is indirect in nature. It encourages the development of respect for and confidence in a certain product. Of course, the advertiser hopes eventually for buying action brought about because of the influences attitudes have on action. Much of Kodak's advertising is designed to stimulate warm feelings toward Kodak and its products, which eventually should result in purchase of their products.

ADVERTISING MANAGEMENT

Advertising management is the process by which the advertiser develops advertising campaigns, prepares schedules, determines budgets, and evaluates advertising.

ADVERTISING ORGANIZATION

A company's advertising may be managed by the firm's own in-house department, by an outside advertising agency, or by a combination of the two.

IN-HOUSE ADVERTISING DEPARTMENTS

Many in-house advertising departments conduct marketing research, particularly on advertising problems. In-house departments maintain records, design ads, place media, and check the appearance of scheduled advertisements. They also maintain relationships with outside advertising agencies for situations that cannot be handled effectively on an in-house basis. Basically, in-house advertising departments perform the same functions and services as do outside advertising agencies.

ADVERTISING AGENCIES

An advertising agency is a group of external advertising specialists plus marketing, merchandising, public relations, communication, behavioral, and other related specialists. Advertisers (usually called clients) use agencies when they do not have in-house advertising capabilities. Advertising agencies study their clients' advertising needs, draft and recommend advertising programs, design the advertisements, schedule the advertisements, and contract with the advertising media to transmit those advertisements.

ADVERTISING PLANNING

To be effective, advertising campaigns must be planned. A campaign is a planned, unified series of advertisements. It has its own objectives and themes. The advertisements look or sound similar in their intent. They start on a certain date and end on a certain date. Campaigns vary in length, size, and cost. Salespeople need to be acquainted with the firm's advertising campaigns because they can help them to sell, and because buyers will ask about them.

An advertising campaign is not a one-time event, but a continuous process of planning, implementation, evaluation, and replanning. The ultimate goal is to create a high level of continuity beginning with the identification of marketing problems all the way through the development of the creative strategy. All parts must blend together like a family, with individual members bearing a striking resemblance to each other, but functioning in separate roles. Figure 6-1 shows a ten-step process for advertising planning.

MEDIA SCHEDULING

The number of buyers "reached" by advertisements during a certain period of time is aptly called **reach**. The advertiser obviously wants to reach 100 percent of the audience it hopes to persuade and influence.

The number of advertisements run during a certain period of time is called the **frequency**. Radio is probably the medium offering the highest potential frequency. Just as advertisers want complete coverage, most, if not all, feel that high frequency is desirable. There is an inevitable trade-off between the two, however. Frequency usually wins this trade-off, because it is better to achieve high recall among a smaller group with frequency than to have a high reach and low recall.

BUDGETING

Many times the manufacturer's salespeople are asked how much their firm is spending on advertising. Some of their customers complain about how small that figure is, others about how large it is. How do advertisers determine how much to spend for advertising?

There are four basic approaches. In the **percent-of-sales approach**, the advertiser estimates next year's net sales, picks a multiplier (perhaps 3 percent), multiplies one by the other, and that is the amount of the advertising budget. The second method of estimating is the **objective/task approach**. In this case, the advertiser first develops advertising objectives for the next year, then determines the advertising tasks necessary to attain those objectives. In the third step, the advertiser estimates the cost of an advertising program that will achieve the objectives. Once advertising budgets are determined they must be broken down by sales

STEPS IN THE ADVERTISING PLANNING PROCESS

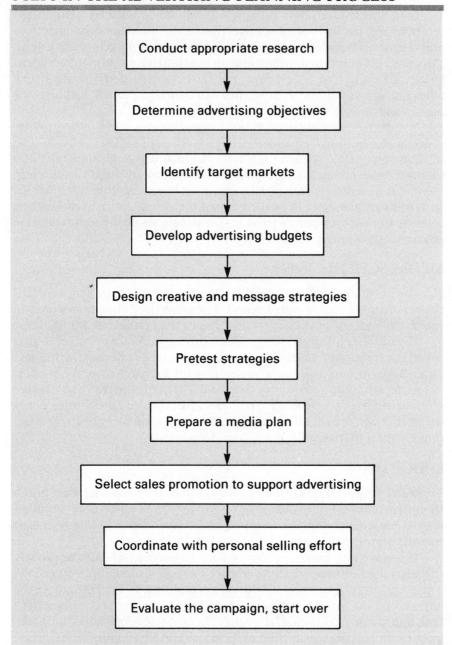

Figure 6-1 Advertising is not a separate activity. It must be coordinated with the firm's sales promotion and personal selling functions.

territory, product, customer, advertising medium, and time period. The third method is the **competitive parity approach**. This approach is a copy-cat approach. That is, the advertiser spends as much as the competition on advertising; thus, neither has an advantage. Finally, some companies do not have the money, interest, or expertise to use complex budgeting approaches. Instead, they must use the **affordable approach** and spend whatever they can afford on advertising.

EVALUATION

The final stage in managing an advertising campaign effectively involves a variety of evaluation techniques. The **pretest** evaluation, for instance, uses **checklists**, which are made up of the values an advertisement should have—attention value, comprehension value, conviction value, memory value, attitude change value, etc. Proposed advertisements are checked against the list and scored. If an advertisement is weak on attention value, then back it goes for revision. Advertisements are often pretested by **focus groups**, which are small groups of representative buyers who look at proposed advertisements and say what is good and bad about them.

Another technique, **concurrent evaluation**, is most often used in the broadcast field. Telephone calls are made to a sample, say, between 7 P.M. and 9:30 P.M. to learn if the TV is on and, if so, to which station. Commercial marketing research firms do this research.

Readership studies, on the other hand, are a **post-test**. The number of inquiries received, samples requested, contest entries received, or incoming telephone calls are post-tests. Without question, the greatest handicap in advertising is the absence of a measure that indicates the effect advertisements have on sales. But with the emergence of scanner data and point-of-sale information, companies will soon be able to do this. For example, A. C. Neilsen sells a service called Scantrack, which is based on supermarket scanner data. It monitors sales of over 100,000 products sold in supermarkets in the top-50 markets. These data are then sold to companies such as Procter & Gamble, Nabisco, and Quaker Oats, which use them to determine market share, the impact of various promotional campaigns, and so forth.

ADVERTISING AND PERSONAL SELLING

Advertising and personal selling can each contribute significantly to the more effective functioning of the other. Advertising can presell merchandise and stimulate demand for the salesperson's products. Advertising that invites inquiries from interested buyers also can locate prospects for salespeople.

When it is effective, advertising does a superb job of increasing a salesperson's sales power. Advertising can build buyer confidence in salespeople and give a product prestige, which results in more sales calls, shorter presentations, and higher sales success. Presentations sound stronger to buyers because points which were only seen or heard once are now reinforced by the salespeople. Because advertising can increase consumer demand, many retailers view the amount of advertising a company does to support a product as a major factor in their decision to carry a specific product in their stores. A final way in which advertising increases sales power is to help keep customers sold between sales calls. The advertising buyers see during these intervals reduces the chance the salespeople will be forgotten.

Advertising efforts can be aided by the sales manager and staff. First of all, the sales force helps stock wholesalers and retailers before an advertising campaign breaks. The sales staff also can provide feedback information to keep the company's advertising slanted in the proper direction. Salespeople often are in a position to supply some of the raw materials from which advertisements are fashioned—such as case histories, experiences, testimonials, and product information not previously known by the company.

"SELLING" ADVERTISING POLICY TO MIDDLEMEN

Salespeople have an obligation to understand the company's advertising policy and to be able to make a credible case for it. Obviously, a company can adopt one of two general policies: it can do no advertising, or it can incorporate that activity into its promotion program. Salespeople for manufacturers that do not advertise usually contrast their products with advertised products of higher price and comparable quality. These salespeople might stress that their lower prices permit wholesalers and retailers to sell the unadvertised lines at lower prices than they can sell the advertised lines, and that dealers will have greater freedom in pricing the merchandise and avoiding price wars. If the company does advertise, its salespeople might stress that advertising builds consumer demand for the product. In addition, salespeople might also stress high turnover and ease of selling for the retailer, because the manufacturer has presold the merchandise through advertising. Salespeople might point out that markdowns, dealer advertising expenses, and inventory can be reduced as a result of the manufacturer's advertising. These reduced expenses can mean greater profits for the middleman.

SALES PROMOTION BASICS

The term *sales promotion* is used widely and somewhat loosely in marketing. We define sales promotion as a limited-time, special-offer pro-

Figure 6-2 A trade show is an example of how advertising helps salespeople sell more effectively.

gram directed toward consumers, the trade, or the sales force, which is designed to achieve quick response. Examples include trade show exhibits, distribution of new-product samples, coupons redeemed for discounts, contests, sweepstakes, and display allowances.

Sales promotions are used by many different industries for many types of products. Manufacturers of drugstore and supermarket products are among the most frequent users but so are marketers of consumer durables, such as automobiles, refrigerators, and television sets. Retailers are the heaviest users of sales promotions, but wholesalers and manufacturers use them, too. It is estimated that over $105 billion was spent on sales promotion activities in 1989. This was slightly less than that spent on advertising, which was estimated to total almost $120 billion in that same year.

Sales promotion is not a replacement or substitute for either advertising or personal selling. Instead, it supplements them and makes them more effective. Most manufacturers promote their products with salespeople and advertisements year after year, but most sales promotion activities are short-lived.

OBJECTIVES OF SALES PROMOTIONS

As part of a seller's overall sales effort, sales promotion obviously is intended to influence buyers. Sales promotion offers prospects an additional reason for buying the product. It suggests to middlemen, especially to retailers, that they buy and promote the manufacturer's product. It suggests to ultimate consumers, sometimes to purchasing agents, that they examine and try the manufacturer's brand. If successful, a sales promotion can convince some habitual users of other brands to try out a different brand. Sales promotion also encourages salespeople to give a stronger effort to sell a certain product, usually the company's new products or those that go through seasonal slumps.

Sales promotion can be used in an aggressive manner when a new product is put on the market. It also can be used to respond when competitors are promoting their brands heavily. Keep an eye on Burger King the next time McDonald's introduces a special deal. Burger King often will counter immediately with their own deal.

Some buyers may be encouraged by sales promotions to buy a new type of product (a CD player, for example). If the trial is a happy one, repeat purchases are probable. Sales promotions can also motivate buyers to purchase more of a satisfactory brand than they did in the past. This can be true if the seller shows that the item can be used in various ways. Sales promotions can back up and strengthen what the seller's salespeople and ads claim.

Sales promotion techniques can influence retailers to begin carrying and selling a manufacturer's brand. They also can motivate wholesalers and retailers to buy and stock more than they have in the past. Some promotions are designed to increase the number of consumers in stores, and ultimately their purchases. Others may be used to obtain a better display for a manufacturer in a retailer's store.

TRADE PROMOTIONS

Some sales promotions are directed toward wholesalers and/or retailers that distribute the advertiser's product. These promotional activities, usually called **trade promotions**, are designed to improve distribution, motivate a build-up in stock, or encourage special selling effort.

Salespeople must "sell" wholesalers and/or retailers on the sales promotion techniques the manufacturer wants to use. The manufacturer explains the program's details to the salespeople well before the start of a sales promotion program. The sales promotion manager, sales manager, or marketing manager makes sure that the salespeople know how advertising and sales promotion activities contribute to the total sales effort, and that they know what techniques to use in "selling" the firm's promotional program to middlemen. Sales meetings usually are used for this purpose.

A major decision in planning trade promotions centers on what kind of incentives to offer wholesalers and/or retailers to encourage them to participate. The following represent the major types of trade promotion incentives.

TRADE ALLOWANCES

The most widely used incentive in trade promotions is a temporary reduction in the price of the product. The price reduction may be offered through an extra percentage off the regular price of a purchase during a specified promotion period—for example, a 10 percent discount on all purchases of suntan lotion in April to encourage stocking for the summer months. Another approach could be to offer an extra discount above a specified minimum quantity—for example, a 10 percent discount on orders of more than five cases of suntan lotion. A third method is to give free merchandise. For example, the manufacturer might give one free case of suntan lotion for every ten purchased.

POINT-OF-PURCHASE PROMOTION

Advertising materials that retailers display near the point of sale are called **point-of-purchase advertising**. Such materials include window displays, counter displays, floor displays, and items for wall, ceiling, and exterior displays—ad reprints, banners and streamers, decals, and posters. Some point-of-purchase materials are really considered part of fixtures and equipment. These items include racks, stands, clocks, store signs, thermometers, and cabinets.

Point-of-purchase promotions back up the manufacturer's advertising efforts at the most crucial point: the point of sale. Point-of-purchase promotions give the manufacturer a last chance to communicate with the customer in the store before the purchase; they stimulate impulse buying and reminder buying. Point-of-purchase promotions are important because many of the persons reached with preselling tactics are close to the act of buying.

Some manufacturers ship their point-of-purchase items directly to the retailer either packed with the merchandise or sent separately. Often such direct shipment is made only upon the retailer's request. But the manufacturer may have invited the request by sending the retailer an inquiry advertisement through direct mail or trade papers. Occasionally a manufacturer makes use of an installation crew, especially with costly items. In most cases the crew is from a commercial firm specializing in this type of work.

The salesperson plays a key role in the company's effective use of point-of-purchase advertising. In fact, the most common method of distributing point-of-purchase materials is through the salesperson. First, the salesperson must see that the retailers are stocked with enough merchandise to justify their use of the company's materials. Selling retailers on the company's point-of-purchase program is a continual effort. In many instances, manufacturers give the display to the retailer as an incentive. By persuading more retailers to use more of the items for greater lengths of time, the salesperson helps the company reduce waste. The salesperson tries to encourage retailers to coordinate their point-of-purchase activities with the promotion schedule of the company. The salesperson always tries to obtain the most desirable locations for the materials, and reports to the company on the use of the various items. The salesperson reports to the sales promotion manager on the company's point-of-purchase program, the programs of competitors, and the thinking of customers.

COOPERATIVE ADVERTISING ALLOWANCES

In their promotion programs, manufacturers may encourage dealers and/or retailers to advertise their products by offering to pay part of the advertising cost. The manufacturer designs the advertising program, establishes the rules and controls, prepares the ads, and encourages retailers to use them. The most common arrangement for sharing costs of cooperative advertising is for manufacturer and retailer to split the costs equally. The manufacturer might limit the amount it pays on the basis of the retailer's yearly purchases. For example, if the amount is equal to 5 percent of the retailer's yearly purchases and the retailer's purchases amount to $100,000, the manufacturer will match the retailer dollar for dollar up to $2,500, one-half of the limit of $5,000.

OTHER TRADE INCENTIVES

Consultation on managerial decisions is another incentive used in trade promotions. Retailers may be given recommendations about store location, layout, equipment, and organization. Guidance also may be provided in such areas as buying, pricing, credit, and control. Certainly, middlemen should be able to obtain from the sales promotion department all the assistance they need in the areas of personal selling, advertising, and display.

Some manufacturers design contests for their middlemen, administer the contests, and then award prizes to the winners of the contests. Others place ads in trade publications (e.g., *Progressive Grocer, Hardware Retailer*) to stimulate sales by manufacturers' middlemen. These ads stress sales and profit potentials. Typical trade ads urge retailers to stock and push the line, announce new products or policies, or promote the manufacturer's consumer promotion program.

In addition, manufacturers offer special concessions, or **deals**, to middlemen. The deal usually can be earned if the middleman places a large order. These concessions take many forms. For example, middlemen might receive free goods, reduced prices, a promotional allowance, or some exceptional point-of-purchase display. Sometimes the deal involves more liberal credit-dating, billing, or terms. The manufacturer might also include middlemen's names and addresses in ads, particularly in regional magazine ads.

Another form of incentive manufacturers can offer deserving middlemen is the **executive gift**. This is given in appreciation for past business and in anticipation of future business. Popular for short-run consumption are steaks, theater or sports events tickets, and fruit baskets. Popular for long-run use are cameras, glassware, and luggage. Some gifts are delivered by salespeople.

SALES PROMOTION FOR ULTIMATE CONSUMERS

If consumers can be presold on a manufacturer's brand of merchandise, retailers will want to stock or feature that brand. Therefore, sales promotion activities often are directed toward ultimate consumers. To that end, manufacturers usually work with retailers in sales promotion activities, such as contests for which the retailer makes entry blanks available. Sales promotion activities targeted to ultimate consumers should induce trial by new purchasers and increase purchase frequency by existing customers.

Designing an effective incentive for consumers is not easy. The incentive must be sufficiently attractive and different from competitive offers to motivate consumers to purchase a product. Some of the more widely used consumer incentives are discussed below.

CONTESTS

Some goals of contests are to build greater retail distribution, increase store traffic, persuade consumers to try a product for the first time, increase the units of purchase, and stimulate new uses for old products. Many different kinds of contests are used. Some are based on word-building, others on slogan-writing. Some ask the contestants to add the last line to a poem or limerick, others are based on puzzles, and many ask for a written statement or letter. Execution of contests poses many problems. For example, the contest designer is responsible for obtaining retailers' cooperation and must determine the length of the contest, the number, nature, and size of prizes, the contest rules and legal aspects, and the judging.

SAMPLING

Samples may be given away free or may bear a small charge. The virtue of sampling lies in the claim that nothing promotes the consumption of a good product as effectively as a trial of that product.

Like contests, sampling presents problems for the manufacturer. Is the product one that can be sampled satisfactorily? What is the optimum size of the sample? Should the offer be a free one? If not, what charge should be made? What method or methods of distribution should be adopted? Should retailers be given a role in the project? Retail cooperation is usually most desirable, and seeing that retailers are well stocked is usually the first step in a sampling operation.

Sampling is used primarily with new products or improved products. It is most often used when product differences can be appreciated

TRADE PROMOTION

TRADE PROMOTION
Tartar Control Aqua-fresh Introductory Deal

Retailers:

	Tubes				Pumps	
	2.5 oz.	4.3 oz.	6.0 oz.	7.6 oz.	4.3 oz.	6.0 oz.
500+ Case Cost	$31.48	$30.45	$39.87	$48.89	$37.50	$48.89
500+ Unit Cost	$ .87	$ 1.27	$ 1.66	$ 2.04	$ 1.56	$ 2.04
Off Invoice Allowance	$ 3.90	$ 3.75	$ 4.85	$ 5.95	$ 4.50	$ 5.95
Early Buy Allowance	1.10	1.05	1.40	1.70	1.55	1.70
Ad Allowance	2.15	2.10	2.75	3.35	2.50	3.35
Roto/Display Allowance	1.05	1.00	1.35	1.70	1.20	1.70
Total Allowances	$ 8.20	$ 7.90	$10.35	$12.70	$ 9.75	$12.70
% of List	26.0%	25.9%	26.0%	26.0%	26.0%	26.0%
Unit Dead Net	$ .65	$ .94	$ 1.23	$ 1.51	$ 1.16	$ 1.51

— Ship dates: 5/23/88
— Extended Dating 2%, 60, net 61

Retailer Displays:
1. We'll have open stock floorstands for each of the merchandising sizes of Tartar Control Aqua-fresh: 4.3 oz. tubes, 6.0 oz. tubes, and 4.3 oz. pumps.

CONSUMER PROMOTION
1. **High Value Coupons**
    —A 75¢ introductory Tartar Control Aqua-fresh coupon will be distributed to 49.5 million households via a full-page FSI on 7/10/88, seven weeks after the start of shipments, generating 3,960M redemptions or 385M stat cases.

    —We will distribute a follow-up 50¢ coupon to 49.5MM households via a full-page FSI on 8/28/88, seven weeks after the first coupon, generating 2,970M redemptions or 300M stat cases.

2. **On-Pack Couponing**
    —Also, to generate repurchase, introductory volume of all Tartar Control Aqua-fresh tube SKU's will carry 20¢ coupons good on the next purchase of Tartar Control Aqua-fresh — nearly 100 million coupons in all!

3. **In-Store Advertising**
    —Coinciding with the first coupon, Tartar Control Aqua-fresh will be featured in-store for four weeks, 8/08-9/04/88, via Act Media shopping carts in Food stores and ShelfTalk in Drug stores to provide reminders of our new product.

4. **Trial Size Event**
    —A Tartar Control trial size event will be fielded in August. 0.9 oz. Tartar Control Aqua-fresh tubes pre-priced at 39¢ will be available in 120-count floorstands. This will provide 3 million trial opportunities and be an on-going item.

2379M-2

Figure 6-3 Many manufacturers, like Beecham, offer early buy, special stocking or display, promotional offers, and advertising allowances to trade members.

Source: Courtesy of Beecham Products USA.

only through trial. The major drawback to sampling is the cost. Companies that use sampling must pay both the cost of the product and of its distribution.

PREMIUMS

For the many consumers who at any given time are close to buying and trying a manufacturer's product, only a small incentive is needed to induce trial. The incentive needed is often a premium—something of value given to the consumer at no cost or at a very low price—which can take many forms. Premiums can be merchandise packed inside the containers that hold the manufacturer's products; for example, a fancy designer container for butter. They may be products offered free or at a small price with a combination purchase or a certain amount of purchase from the seller.

A good premium should be attractive and, if practicable, not available in the consumer's local shopping area. A quality brand name also helps make the premium seem desirable. If the consumer must pay for the premium, the premium should be worth at least twice the amount charged. The premium should be useful, dependable, not instantly consumed, up-to-date, and in good taste.

TRADE CHARACTERS

The growth of television encouraged manufacturers to explore the creation and promotional use of trade characters. Ronald McDonald and the California Raisins are two well-known trade characters.

Some trade characters are masculine, some feminine. Some are popular cartoon characters. Each is a unique personality, able to move, act, and talk. Some are named, some are not. Most deliver advertising messages for their sponsors.

ADVERTISING SPECIALTIES

Promotional novelties dominate the advertising specialty group. Their main goal is to build goodwill. Of the many wall, desk, and pocket calendars given away, three fourths are used. Other examples of novelties are thermometers, pens, rulers, and ashtrays. Novelties are distributed by mail, by retailers, through advertising offers, and by salespeople.

CONSUMER DEALS

There are two major types of consumer deals—price deals and package deals. Consumer price deals save customers money when they purchase the product. Package deals provide customers with something extra in the package.

Cents-off coupons are one type of price deal. (See the example of a cents-off coupon for Aqua-fresh in the color insert of this text.) Consumers commonly receive these coupons through the mail, in a newspaper or magazine ad, or in the package of a product. When the shoppers buy the promoted brand, they present the coupon and are given a price reduction.

Cents-off packages are a second kind of consumer price deal. Here the manufacturer features the price reduction on the package of the product. A jar of instant tea, for example, might bear a "25 cents off regular price" label. The price reduction is given by the retailer at check-out.

There are two types of package deals—bonus packages and banded packages. A bonus package is larger than the standard package. They are commonly used in the food, cleaning, and health and beauty-aids product categories. For example, extra pieces of chewing gum or cough drops may be included for the same price, or the shampoo container might be 20 percent larger. Bonus packaging is often used to introduce a new larger-size package.

A banded package involves selling two or more units of a product at a reduced price. Sometimes the products are physically banded together, such as with toothpaste, deodorant, razor blades, or candy. Sometimes a smaller size of the product is attached to the regular size. Other times a related product is attached—dips for chips or other snacks, for example.

REFUNDS

A refund is an offer by the manufacturer to pay a certain amount of money to the purchaser when the product is purchased separately or in combination with other products. Refunds are a long-established and heavily used consumer incentive. Refunds are most often used to increase purchase quantity and/or frequency. But in recent years they have become very popular as a method of inducing trial through the use of rebates on automobiles and appliances.

Refund incentives are mainly distributed through print media and direct mail. Occasionally, they are in or on the product package, or on tearpads at the point of purchase. Consumers usually are required to submit labels or package certificates as proof of purchase to receive the refund.

SALES FORCE PROMOTIONS

A third type of sales promotion is directed toward wholesalers' and/or retailers' sales personnel. Its purpose is to encourage salespeople to intensify their sales effort for a particular manufacturer's products. Sales promotion programs for salespeople may include sales manuals, sales training courses, films on selling, and/or sales instruction given by the manufacturer's salespeople. Salespeople may be offered cash payment (called PMs, or push money) to encourage their support of the manufacturer's merchandise. Gifts, discounts, and contests are other possible means of sales promotion manufacturers use to stimulate a middleman's sales force.

COST-SAVING SALES SUPPORT TECHNIQUES AND ACTIVITIES

According to a study by the Laboratory of Advertising Performance (LAP), a division of McGraw-Hill Research, the cost of personal selling increased by 160 percent between 1977 and 1987,[1] and this rate of increase was expected to continue throughout the 1990s. By 1989, the average cost of a business-to-business sales call was almost $300. For selling complex and/or technical products, which involve more time and more highly compensated salespeople, the cost of a single sales call exceeded $400, and is expected to top $600 by 1991.

Many companies have been forced to adopt alternate means of communicating with customers and supporting the sales effort to offset these rising costs. They include telemarketing, direct mail, demonstration centers, sales or technical support staffs, and customer service representatives. These new methods allow salespeople to be more effective doing what they do best; interacting with people and making sales. Each of these methods is discussed in the following section.

TELEMARKETING

Telemarketing employs the telephone as a marketing tool along with other marketing and communication techniques to make salespeople more efficient. Telemarketing can be used to generate sales leads, qualify prospects, manage customer accounts, and improve customer service. Some companies have even been successful completing the entire sales process, including closing the sale, via telemarketing.

DIRECT MAIL

Direct-mail approaches are not new, but have been used more often in recent years to sell to manufacturers and other businesses, as well as to ultimate consumers. In many cases direct-mail brochures, catalogs, and fliers are combined with telemarketing to form an inexpensive combination of oral and visual sales presentations.

Direct-mail promotion consists of sales letters, cards, folders, circulars, booklets, broadsides, and catalogs sent by the manufacturer directly to buyers. Much of a manufacturer's direct-mail promotion is aimed at middlemen, so this type of promotion often is assigned to the department in charge of dealer relations. Some of the possible uses of direct-mail promotions are:

1. To locate prospects.
2. To send precall information to buyers or request it of them.

---

[1] *Marketing News* 22, no. 19 (September 12, 1988): 5.

3. To make appointments.
4. To follow up a salesperson's call and to maintain contact with buyers between calls.
5. To help keep the goodwill of customers and to help keep them sold on the manufacturer's product.
6. To sample and answer inquiries.

DEMONSTRATION CENTERS

Many companies that have found it very expensive to visit each and every customer in person have set up demonstration centers. These demonstration centers are similar to retail outlets because they give the customer a chance to see and try out equipment. Salespeople can answer customer questions and demonstrate complex equipment that would be too difficult to bring into a customer's place of business.

Demonstration centers are very popular among manufacturers of small business equipment such as copiers and computers. International Business Machines (IBM), for example, has one such center located just outside of New York City in Paramus, New Jersey. Considering the hundreds of thousands of businesses in the New York-New Jersey metropolitan area, it was a very smart decision on IBM's part to provide a central location where prospective customers could come to IBM, rather than to spend the money itself to find those customers.

Figure 6-4 An IBM demonstration center helps the sales force to sell more effectively.
Source: Courtesy of IBM Corporation.

SALES OR TECHNICAL SUPPORT STAFFS

Ideally, companies that sell technical products like to hire salespeople who not only have a technical college degree, but also are able to interact in a business environment. However, these people are in short supply, and people with technical degrees often prefer to work alone and are less likely to enjoy persuasive communications with customers. Thus, many companies hire graduates with business degrees and train them on the technical aspects of the product.

A salesperson selling to a systems engineer is at an obvious disadvantage when talking about the inner workings of a computer. Though capable salespeople do know their product inside and out, no customer should expect them to be experts on information that requires years of training, experience, and education to acquire. A technical support staff serves as a safety valve when salespeople are unable to satisfy the customer's technical questions. Salespeople can include a technical support person in their call with a customer, or can have the technical support person follow up their initial sales call. The former is considered to be the better option, because the sales representative maintains contact with the customer, provides immediate answers to the prospect's questions, and avoids the image of being unqualified.

The support staff provides assistance to make salespeople more effective. IBM employs a sales support staff made up largely of college interns who instruct the customers on how to use the product properly after it has been sold. This enables sales representatives to maximize their selling time, while ensuring that the customer is satisfied.

CUSTOMER SERVICE REPRESENTATIVES

A common complaint among many salespeople is that they have to handle customer complaints or service requests, which can take up much of the salesperson's valuable time. To help maximize the salesperson's selling time and still satisfy the customer's problems, companies have developed customer service departments. It is the customer service representative's job to satisfy customer complaints, questions, and service requests. The salesperson's time is then freed up to concentrate on making sales.

Telemarketing, direct mail, demonstration centers, sales and technical support staffs, and customer service representatives are some of the new communication techniques that corporations are utilizing to make the salesperson's job easier and more productive.

PUBLICITY

Sellers do not want a single month to pass in which they receive no publicity. They want good publicity, not bad publicity. A television newscast that reports on and shows the wreckage of a large plane of a major airline is an example of bad publicity. Editors of newspapers, magazines, television, and radio decide which firms get publicity, so publicity directors are eager to have a good relationship with editors. This is best achieved by supplying the editors with material that is truly newsworthy. News releases, press conferences, and feature stories are common.

Another form of publicity, word-of-mouth promotion, can help or hurt a firm. Its influence is particularly powerful. Sellers hope opinion leaders like them, the company, its personnel, and its brands, and they hope that the opinion leaders will pass these attitudes on to opinion followers.

SUMMARY

There are three direct promotional activities available to sellers: personal selling, advertising, and sales promotion. Publicity is an indirect promotional strategy.

Advertising is a nonpersonal mass communication that is meant to be informative and persuasive, and its purpose is to presell the prospect. Primary advertising promotes a generic product, while selective advertising promotes a specific brand. Advertising may be managed by the firm or by an outside agency. An advertising manager's main concerns are reach, frequency, and cost. Reach refers to the number of potential buyers exposed to the advertisement during a certain period of time, while frequency is the number of times that potential buyer will see the advertisement during that same period. Advertising budgeting methods that may be used include the percentage-of-sales approach and the objective-task approach. The salesperson has an obligation to understand the company's advertising policy and be able to make a credible case for it.

Sales promotions are nonpersonal incentives that are designed to encourage immediate action on the part of the consumer, trade member, or sales force. Point-of-purchase displays are a sales promotion that retailers place right at the point of sale.

KEY TERMS

personal selling	direct-action advertisement
advertising	indirect-action advertisement
sales promotion	reach
publicity	frequency
primary demand	percent-of-sales approach
selective demand	objective-task approach
brand image	competitive parity approach
corporate image	affordable approach
pretest evaluation	post-test
checklists	trade promotions

focus groups   point-of-purchase advertising
concurrent evaluation   deal
readership studies   executive gift

REVIEW QUESTIONS

1. Why is advertising a "pull" technique?
2. List some limitations of advertising.
3. What is the difference between direct-action advertising and indirect-action advertising?
4. What is an advertising campaign?
5. How does advertising increase sales power?
6. List four ways that a salesperson can take advantage of the firm's advertising.
7. What is the purpose of sales promotion?
8. What are the advantages of direct-mail promotion?
9. How is cooperative advertising used?
10. What problems are involved in product sampling?
11. List four examples of consumer deals.
12. Name several methods of preevaluation of a sales promotion.

DISCUSSION QUESTIONS

1. Describe a familiar ad campaign that you thought was successful. Why was it successful?
2. Some television advertisers use commercials that are irritating. Why do they use such ads when they know the ads will upset viewers?
3. Give an example of each of the following: a primary, selective, brand, institutional, direct-action, and indirect-action ad. Can an ad be of more than one type?
4. Some advertisers use well-known people such as actors and sports stars to promote their products. Is this more effective than using unknown people? Does it enhance the image of the product?

CASE 6-1   MARSHA FEINMAN: INSURANCE SALESPERSON*

Marsha Feinman is a salesperson for one of the nation's largest insurance firms. The company offers a complete range of business and per-

---

*Case prepared by Daryl McKee. Used with permission.

sonal insurance policies and advertises them heavily in business publications, in consumer publications, and on television (including the
sponsorship of shows on public television). It even sponsors a major professional golf tournament.

Feinman graduated from college last year and is still learning the
ropes from the experienced salesperson who was assigned to conduct
her on-the-job training. Feinman is receiving a salary right now, but
when she completes her training program all her income will come from
commissions on the policies she writes. She's a bit concerned because
she thinks that the commissions are a little low. She wonders out loud
one day while eating lunch with the senior salesperson why the company
can't spend much less on advertising and use the money saved to pay
higher commissions. She concludes by saying, "I don't see how advertising can help at all. Salespeople are the only ones who can persuade the
prospect to buy, so why shouldn't we get all that money that's being
wasted on advertising?"

EXHIBIT 6-1 COMBINED EFFECT OF SALESPEOPLE AND ADVERTISING

Total Sales	Advertising Effect	Salespeople Effect	Combined Effect	Total
Initial Situation				
Variable Values	$120	6	720	
Reg. Weight	2.5	75.5	0.5	
	$300.00	453	360	$1,113.00
Total Investment in Salesforce				
Variable Values	$0.00	10	0	
Reg. Weight	2.5	75.5	0.5	
	___	___	___	___
Total Investment in Advertising				
Variable Values	$300.00	0	0	
Reg. Weight	2.5	75.5	0.5	
	___	___	___	___
Equal Salesforce/Advertising Split				
Variable Values	$150.00	5	750	
Reg. Weight	2.5	75.5	0.5	
	___	___	___	___

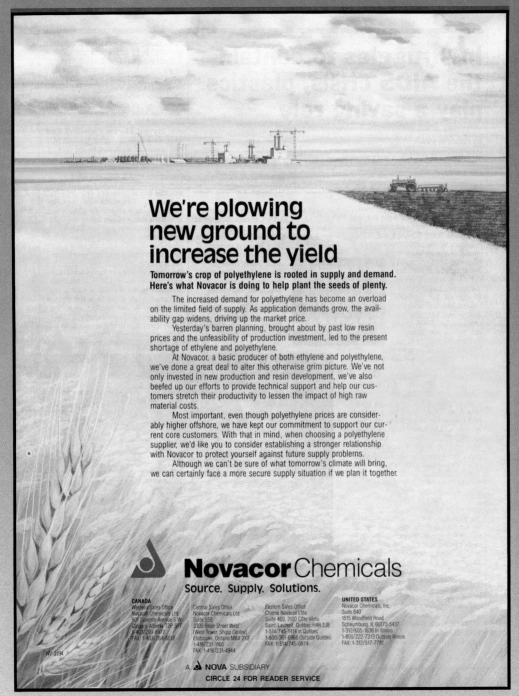

We're plowing new ground to increase the yield

Tomorrow's crop of polyethylene is rooted in supply and demand. Here's what Novacor is doing to help plant the seeds of plenty.

The increased demand for polyethylene has become an overload on the limited field of supply. As application demands grow, the availability gap widens, driving up the market price.

Yesterday's barren planning, brought about by past low resin prices and the unfeasibility of production investment, led to the present shortage of ethylene and polyethylene.

At Novacor, a basic producer of both ethylene and polyethylene, we've done a great deal to alter this otherwise grim picture. We've not only invested in new production and resin development, we've also beefed up our efforts to provide technical support and help our customers stretch their productivity to lessen the impact of high raw material costs.

Most important, even though polyethylene prices are considerably higher offshore, we have kept our commitment to support our current core customers. With that in mind, when choosing a polyethylene supplier, we'd like you to consider establishing a stronger relationship with Novacor to protect yourself against future supply problems.

Although we can't be sure of what tomorrow's climate will bring, we can certainly face a more secure supply situation if we plan it together.

Novacor Chemicals
Source. Supply. Solutions.

CANADA
Western Sales Office
Novacor Chemicals Ltd.
801 Seventh Avenue S.W.
Calgary, Alberta T2P 3P7
1-403/290-8977
FAX: 1-403/264-6012

Central Sales Office
Novacor Chemicals Ltd.
Suite 550
3300 Bloor Street West
(West Tower, Shipp Centre)
Etobicoke, Ontario M8X 2X2
1-416/231-1160
FAX: 1-416/231-4944

Eastern Sales Office
Chimie Novacor Ltée.
Suite 460, 3100 Côte Vertu
Saint-Laurent, Québec H4R 2J8
1-514/745-1414 in Québec
1-800/361-6966 Outside Québec
FAX: 1-514/745-0874

UNITED STATES
Novacor Chemicals, Inc.
Suite 840
1515 Woodfield Road
Schaumburg, IL 60173-5437
1-312/605-1836 In Illinois
1-800/222-7213 Outside Illinois
FAX: 1-312/517-7781

NV 3194

A **NOVA** SUBSIDIARY

CIRCLE 24 FOR READER SERVICE

Company Knowledge is Vital Information for the Salesperson.

TARTAR CONTROL AQUA-FRESH

"DOMINOES II"

LENGTH: 30 SECONDS

COMM'L NO.: BEAF 9073

(MUSIC UP)

ANNCR: (VO) You are about

to be knocked over

by Tartar Control Aqua-Fresh.

Because it does a lot more.

Besides reducing ugly tartar build-up,

Tartar Control

Aqua-Fresh goes on . . .

to also help

remove plaque for healthier gums and more.

It has flouride to fight cavities

and has the taste

that knocks over the leading brand.

Get great Tartar Control,

great taste,

and a great deal more. Tartar Control Aqua-Fresh.

A Storyboard for Aqua-Fresh.

Coupons are One Form of Consumer Promotion.

HAND AND BODY LOTIONS

- *Hand and Body Lotion category is $465MM annually in* F/D/MM *(1986 Nielsen)*

- *90% of women use hand and body lotions for soft skin*
  - — 60% use lotions <u>at least once a day</u>

- *Profitable —*
  - — Trade margins average 20%-30%

- *Growing —*
  - — Plus $150 million last 5 years

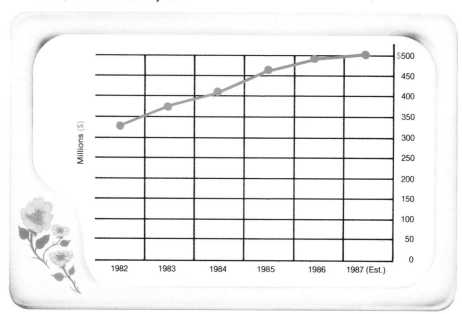

Market Research Data on Hand and Body Lotions.

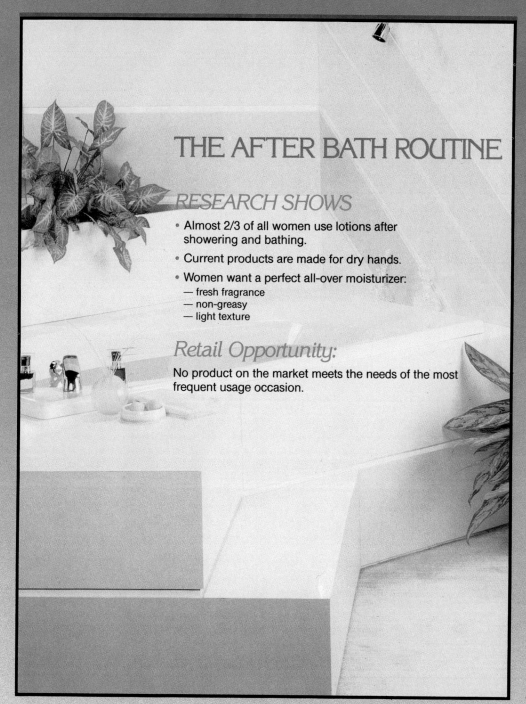

THE AFTER BATH ROUTINE

RESEARCH SHOWS

- Almost 2/3 of all women use lotions after showering and bathing.
- Current products are made for dry hands.
- Women want a perfect all-over moisturizer:
  — fresh fragrance
  — non-greasy
  — light texture

Retail Opportunity:

No product on the market meets the needs of the most frequent usage occasion.

Introductory Information.

Strong Consumer Support

Television and Print

- $3.5MM annualized TV plan breaks in October

- $2MM annualized print plan breaks in October

- TV Support
  Reach: 87
  Frequency: 4.0
  GRP's: 350
  Commercials per week: 25

Coupons

- November 1988 — Full page print ads with 50¢ coupons in Vogue, Cosmopolitan, Woman's Day, and People.

- December 4, 1988 — Full page 50¢ FSI coupons delivered to 50 million households.

- December 1988 - February 1989 — 3 million 25¢ cross-ruff coupons carried on Calgon Bath products.

$1.50 Refund Offer

- Point-of-purchase refund offer for two proofs: one on Calgon Moisturizing Foam Bath and one on Calgon After Bath Lotion.

  Consumer receives:
    — $1.00 Cash
    — Two 25¢ coupons good on Calgon Moisturizing Foam Bath and Calgon After Bath Lotion.

Promotional Plan for Calgon AfterBath Lotion.

CALGON ®
AfterBath Lotion
Introductory Offer

5% Early Buy Allowance
+
15% Stocking Allowance
+
10% Performance Allowance

Plus Extended Dating

Order Dates _____

Ship Dates _____

Performance Period _____

Normal to Dry

Extra Dry

	Normal to Dry	Extra Dry
Regular Cost		
Less: Early Buy Allowance		
Less: Stocking Allowance		
Less: Performance Allowance		
Net Cost		
Suggested Feature		
Feature Profit		
After Sale Retail		
Retail Profit		

SHIPPING SPECIFICATIONS:

6 oz. Normal to Dry/6 oz. Extra Dry

Case Dm.	8⅝ x 6½ x 7¾
Case Wt.	8.5 lbs.
Case Cube	.251
Pallet Pattern	34 x 5
PC Dm.	3³/₁₆ x 1¼ x 7½

RECOMMENDATION

Distribution _____
_____

Shelving _____
_____

Merchandising _____
_____

Pricing _____
_____

8D-010CL (retailer)   **BEECHAM PRODUCTS USA**, Pittsburgh, PA 15230   Printed in U.S.A.

Introductory Price Deal and Feature Pricing Terms.

Unsurpassed Consumer Support!

T.V. Advertising

- $30MM TV Intro (7/1/88)
- Reach: 92% of HH
  Frequency: 5.2 times/month
  GRP's: 480/month
- 29 commercials/week

- 49.5MM 75¢ introductory FSI (7/10/88)
- 49.5MM 50¢ follow-up FSI (8/28/88)
- 10 MM 20¢ introductory tube on-pack coupons
- Over 300M 50¢ targeted in-store coupons (9/12-10/23/88)
- 4-week Act Media campaign on shopping carts (8/8-9/4/88)

Professional Dental Program

- 1MM free samples to dentists May, 1988
- Print ads in all major dental journals

Team-Up With Tartar Control Aqua-fresh In The Race For Profits

Item	Regular Cost	Dead Net	Suggested Feature Price	Feature Profit	After Sale Price	After Sale Profit	Suggested Order
Tubes							
2.5 oz.							
4.3 oz.							
6.0 oz.							
7.6 oz.							
Pumps							
4.3 oz.							
6.0 oz.							

Company Proof of Advertising Support.

The marketing research department at Marsha's firm recently analyzed the relationship between sales and expenditures on advertising and the number of salespeople employed for each division. A predictive method called regression analysis was used. Regression analysis is a technique that market researchers can use to understand, for example, the extent to which the amount spent on advertising, salespeople, or both influences sales.

Exhibit 6-1 shows the company's current sales (in thousands of dollars), the present number of salespeople, and the level of advertising expenditures (in thousands of dollars). The regression weights show the influence of each variable (advertising, sales, or both combined) on sales. The regression weights are based on past experience of the company.

CASE QUESTIONS

1. Using Lotus, complete the table on p. 202 showing what would happen if: (a) $300,000 were spent to employ ten new salespeople at $30,000 each; (b) the $300,000 were spent totally on advertising; and (c) the money were divided evenly between using $150,000 to employ five salespeople and $150,000 on advertising. Then answer:

   * Which situation results in the lowest level of sales? Why?
   * Which situation results in the highest level of sales? Why?

2. If you were the senior salesperson, how would you answer Marsha's question?

CASE 6-2   LAMAR OUTDOOR ADVERTISING*

Sandy Franklin is National Accounts Executive for Lamar Outdoor Advertising, a division of the Lamar Corporation, one of the largest independently owned outdoor advertising companies in the United States, with annual gross sales in excess of $75 million. The Lamar Outdoor Advertising division serves more than 550 markets in 13 southeastern states.

Sandy was Account Executive with Lamar for three years, and was recently promoted to National Accounts Executive. She expects to earn almost $40,000 this year. Her compensation package consists of base salary, commission, bonus, car allowance/expense reimbursement, and benefits.

---

*Case prepared by Kevin P. Reilly, Jr., and Tommy Teeple. Used with permission.

Shortly after being hired by Lamar she was given training on how to sell outdoor advertising. In addition to information on company policies and procedures, she was taught the characteristics of the major media she would be selling against as well as basic selling approaches. A summary of the content of the training program on media follows.

TELEVISION

Television is not a highly selective medium. It offers neither the geographic selectivity of newspapers nor the demographic selectivity of specialized magazines. Television's greatest strength lies in its ability to reach a mass audience. Today, almost 98 percent of all homes have one television and more than half have multiple sets. The amount of time spent viewing television far exceeds the time spent with any other medium. Older adults, women, and preschool children are frequent viewers. Individuals with higher incomes and more education watch considerably less television. On average, members of TV households typically spend almost seven hours a day viewing television programming.

RADIO

Radio offers less of a mass audience than television, but it permits the advertiser to aim the message more precisely to the target audience and deliver it more often. While radio does not have the creative impact of television, it does offer creative flexibility and the opportunity to personalize the message. Today there are over 480 million radios in use in the United States, an average of almost 5.5 per household, and 123 million automobiles have radios. Over 8 million walkabout radios are in use and 56 percent of all adults have a radio at work. The average person over 12 years of age listens to radio nearly 3.5 hours a day, second only to television. Radio listenership is highest during the daytime, but selected audiences can be reached better in the evening. Two time periods have very high listenership. They are referred to as "drive times" and are the early morning from 6 A.M. to 10 A.M. and the late afternoon from 4 P.M. to 7 P.M. on weekdays. Listenership is very heavy at these times because people use the radio to wake up to, as background during breakfast and dinner, and as entertainment while driving to and from work.

NEWSPAPERS AND MAGAZINES

Newspapers, the largest of the advertising media, are particularly important to local advertisers and retailers. But they can also be valuable to some national or regional advertisers. Of the major media, newspapers are the least selective on a demographic basis because their audience is not restricted to a particular class of consumers. The audience reach of a single issue of a newspaper is very high compared to most media. In fact, on an average weekday almost 70 percent of all adults read a daily newspaper. Newspapers are strictly a visual medium, and are therefore not good for advertisers who wish to demonstrate how a product or service works. Color reproduction is possible, but because of its limitations is not used very often. As a medium, newspapers are very cluttered because a single advertiser's message must compete with a great many competitive messages.

Magazines, like newspapers, are a major print medium. For the most part, magazines are a more specialized medium in terms of both readers and advertisers. Some magazines, such as *Reader's Digest* and *TV Guide*, have mass appeal. But most magazines are much narrower and more specialized in their audience appeal. For a single magazine the reach is low, even for larger magazines. Also, magazines do not deliver the frequency of impressions that other media do. Newspaper ads can be run every day and radio commercials every 10 to 15 minutes, but magazines are published once a week or less. Magazines are a visual medium with more creative possibilities than newspapers, but less than television. Like newspapers, they have a lot of competitive advertisements and thus are a very cluttered medium. The distinctive advantage of magazines is their long life (they are usually retained in the home or office for several days or longer and are read by several people). Readership studies suggest that the typical magazine reader spends an hour or more over a period of two to three days reading an average magazine issue.

OUTDOOR ADVERTISING

Outdoor advertising is typically referred to as billboards. There are two basic types of outdoor advertising—the poster panel and the painted bulletin. The standard **poster panel** is approximately 12 feet high by 25 feet long, whereas the standard **painted bulletin** is nearly three times larger, measuring 14 feet high by 48 feet long. Bulletins are individually painted by skilled artists. Posters are first printed on special paper and then are pasted on the panel by a billposter. Outdoor advertising is a mass audience medium rather than a selective medium. Several billboards located in high traffic areas and distributed throughout the market area will reach nearly every adult in the market. Billboards also enjoy high frequency. A person going to and from work may pass two or three of an advertiser's billboards, and over a one-month period a typical outdoor buy could easily reach over 80 percent of the adult audience with a frequency of more than 20 times. The average recall for the various major media is as follows:

Media	Average Recall
Radio	16%
Television	23%
Newspaper	36%
Magazine	44%
Outdoor	
Poster Panels	63%
Painted Bulletins	71%

Source: Telcom Research & Burke Market Research.

The average costs per thousand impressions for the major media are shown below:

Media	Cost per Thousand
Radio	$ 4.30
Television	$12.01
Newspaper	$11.90
Magazine	$ 8.50
Outdoor	$ 2.09

Source: Media Market Guide, 1989.

SALES CALL ON PICCADILLY CAFETERIAS, INC.

This past Tuesday, Sandy made a sales call on Brian Von Gruben, the Director of Marketing for Piccadilly Cafeterias, a chain of restaurants with over 140 cafeterias. Its home office is in Baton Rouge, Louisiana, but its cafeterias are located in 13 southern states and California. Annual revenues were expected to top $300 million in 1990. Some advertising programs are suggested on a local level by the cafeteria managers. But most advertising campaigns, including media selection and schedules, are planned by the director of marketing. Sandy spent a great deal of time learning about the cafeteria chain and planning her presentation because she knew the potential for a large sale was possible. Shortly after her presentation began, Mr. Von Gruben interrupted her and said: "We believe television and newspaper advertising are much more effective for our audience. We only have two or three billboards for all our cafeterias!"

Sandy has decided to show Mr. Von Gruben the impact of using different media on his budget by preparing a simple income statement. Beginning with an existing budget, Sandy has prepared new columns showing the cost of 500,000 impressions using each of the media (see table below). For example, under the existing budget (which uses mostly television advertising) the total advertising expense is $9,000.

EXHIBIT 6-2   SALES CALL ON PICCADILLY CAFETERIAS EXAMPLE OF COST OF 500M IMPRESSIONS BY VARIOUS MEDIA

	Existing Budget	Radio	Television	Newspaper	Magazine	Outdoor
Sales	$1,000,000	$1,000,000	$1,000,000	$1,000,000	$1,000,000	$1,000,000
Cost of						
Food Products	$370,000	$370,000	$370,000	$370,000	$370,000	$370,000
Labor	$270,000	$270,000	$270,000	$270,000	$270,000	$270,000
Advertising	$9,000					
Overhead	$215,000	$215,000	$215,000	$215,000	$215,000	$215,000
Total Costs	$864,000	$855,000	$855,000	$855,000	$855,000	$855,000
Profit	$136,000					
Media CPM		$4.30	$12.01	$11.90	$8.50	$2.09

CASE QUESTIONS

1. Using Lotus, complete the table for Sandy showing the change in advertising cost of 500,000 impressions, and the resulting impact on profits, using each of the media mentioned above.
2. How would you respond to Mr. Von Gruben's concluding comment?

PART 3

Preselling Activities

CHAPTER 7
Prospecting and Qualifying

After studying this chapter, you should be able to:

■ Explain the importance of the prospecting function for the salesperson

■ Understand why each prospect must be qualified

■ Use the five qualifying questions to separate prospects from leads

■ Give examples of both sources and methods of prospecting

■ Classify prospects to maximize your effectiveness as a salesperson

The **selling process**, shown in Figure 7-1, is a series of actions by which a salesperson attempts to locate a potential customer, plans and presents her or his product offering, satisfies any customer questions, makes the sale, and establishes a long-term buyer-seller relationship. In this chapter we will examine the first step in the selling process, prospecting and qualifying.

THE IMPORTANCE OF PROSPECTING

A **prospect** is any potential customer for the company's product. The activities involved in locating these prospects are called prospecting. The importance of prospecting to the sales process is obvious: no sale can be made unless there is a customer.

THE BEGINNING OF THE SALES PROCESS

The first step in determining who needs the company's products is to make exhaustive study of the product line. In other words, the salesperson must first find out what his or her company's products/services can do before determining who can benefit from their purchase.

Once the salesperson has learned what the products do, it is possible to determine what kinds of customers the products can help. For example, personal computers can be purchased and used by both small and large businesses, financial, medical, and educational institutions, as well

210

THE SELLING PROCESS

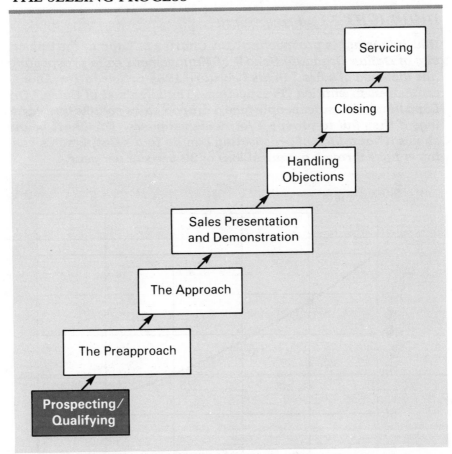

Figure 7-1 The sales process is a series of steps, of which prospecting and qualifying is the first.

as homeowners. These are all prospects for the personal computer salesperson to consider.

THE NEED FOR PROSPECTS

Prospecting is necessary for any salesperson to be successful, because it supplies a constant source of new sales. Salespeople cannot count on the customers they are currently doing business with to be there forever. These customers can die, retire, go out of business, move away, switch to the competitor's product, or enter a different line of business. As most sales representatives will tell you, prospecting is not fun or glamorous. The salesperson must work hard to find prospects, and usually there is no immediate reward for finding them. However, in the long run, these prospects can be cultivated, hopefully as repeat cus-

HIGHLIGHT 7-1   *Prospecting*

How important is prospecting? Dr. Charles L. Lapp at the University of Dallas Graduate School of Management calls prospecting "the lifeblood of sales." In his February 1984 article in The American Salesman entitled "Prospecting—The Lifeblood of Sales," Dr. Lapp notes that salespeople face a drop in sales volume and earnings if they fail to prospect for new customers. The chart below shows what a lack of prospecting can do to a salesperson's customer base through a natural loss of 20 percent per year.

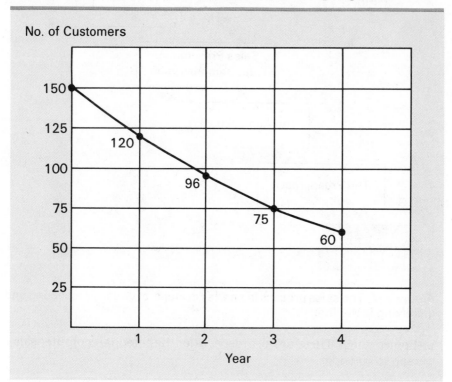

No. of Customers

In this example, the salesperson's business has been cut in half in just three years. Thus, it is important for salespeople to work just as hard to find new prospects as they do to sell those prospects.

Source: Dr. Charles L. Lapp, "Prospecting—The Lifeblood of Sales," *The American Salesman* (February 1984): 10-13.

tomers, which would benefit both the salesperson and the company for a long time. Highlight 7-1 illustrates what a lack of prospecting can do to a salesperson's client base.

QUALIFYING PROSPECTS

Salespeople should remember one rule of thumb concerning potential buyers: not all prospects are "real" prospects. Just because someone has been referred to you, or made an inquiry to your company, does not mean that that person is really a prospect for your product. Salespeople can avoid wasting time, and increase their productivity by qualifying all prospects prior to attempting to sell them. **Qualifying questions** are used to separate prospects from those who do not have the potential to purchase. The following five questions will determine who is a real prospect, and who is not:

1. Does the prospect have a need for my product or service?
2. Can the prospect make the buying decision?
3. Can the prospect afford my product or service?
4. Is the prospect eligible to buy my product or service?
5. Will the prospect give me the opportunity to sell them?

DOES THE PROSPECT HAVE A NEED?

The most basic criterion for determining whether or not someone is a prospect for your product is a discernible need that is not being satisfied. The salesperson should consider prospects with recognized needs first, but should not discount prospects who have not yet recognized they have a need. An informed prospect may realize that a need does exist. However, using high-pressure selling tactics to force a product on someone who does not need or want it will only produce negative results. First, the prospect will resent having been forced into the purchase. Second, the prospect will have nothing but negative feelings for the salesperson and the company. And finally, the salesperson will have lost a potential long-term customer.

Determining whether or not a prospect has a need for your product is not an easy task. Industrial goods salespeople usually will do a preliminary interview with a prospect to determine whether their company can solve the prospect's need. Even after the need has been established it will take a number of calls to determine if they have a product to solve the prospect's need or if they must customize a product to meet the need. Consumer goods salespeople, on the other hand, must question the prospect to establish if any intangible needs exist. Intangible needs such as status and prestige are hard to detect but often play an important role in the purchase of consumer goods. There are some products for which almost everybody is a prospect. For example, magazine salespeople call on every home in their territory because almost everyone reads magazines.

CAN THE PROSPECT MAKE THE BUYING DECISION?

Finding the person within the prospective organization who is responsible for making purchasing decisions is of utmost importance to the salesperson, but is often very difficult. Sometimes talking to an influential person in the organization other than the prospect's purchasing agent reaps some benefit, but usually a salesperson's time is more productive when talking directly to the one who has the authority to buy. The salesperson must ask the purchasing agent who is responsible for the final purchase decision. In some cases it will be the purchasing agent, in others it will be someone else in the organization. The salesperson may have to ask several people within the prospective organization for this information, as purchasing agents tend to hold on to power that they do not have. The salesperson cannot rely on the purchasing agent's word. Instead the salesperson should make sure the information is correct.

CAN THE PROSPECT AFFORD TO PAY?

The third criterion the salesperson should consider is whether the prospect is financially able to pay for the product. For example, automobile salespeople check prospects' credit history to determine whether the bank will approve their request for a loan. The automobile salesperson does not waste time with a prospect who will not be able to get a loan.

Industrial salespeople can check a prospect's financial standing by reviewing Dun & Bradstreet's credit report or Moody's Industrial Manual. These rating services keep track of the financial status of companies and rate them based on their ability to repay debt. Financial information on a prospect also can be obtained from the Better Business Bureau (BBB), local credit agencies, and other salespeople who do business with that prospect.

DOES THE PROSPECT HAVE THE ELIGIBILITY TO BUY?

Eligibility is the fourth criterion used to qualify a prospect. For example, a prospect for life insurance must pass a medical examination before being allowed to buy, regardless of whether or not they pass the other criteria.

Salespeople are often restricted as to which prospects they can call on, and which prospects are assigned to other sales representatives. One of these restrictions is the salesperson's territory. Companies will not allow a sales representative to call on prospects in another salesperson's territory, regardless of a potential buyer's eligibility as a prospect for any other salesperson. Another restriction is the type of buyer the salesperson can call on. For example, manufacturer's representatives who call on

Figure 7-2 Once a prospect has been qualified, the final sale can be made.

retailers exclusively are not supposed to call on wholesalers, and vice versa.

IS THERE AN OPPORTUNITY TO SELL?

Many prospects will not give a salesperson the opportunity to sell to them even if they have a recognizable need. For example, some prospects maintain a strict policy of refusing to see salespeople, while others, because of their stature within the prospect's organization, will see only salespeople who have achieved a similar stature within their profession. These people are usually eliminated as potential prospects because the salesperson recognizes that chances of getting an appointment and the opportunity to sell to them are very slim.

WHERE TO FIND PROSPECTS

Because of the lack of sure-fire methods for prospecting, most companies will suggest that their salespeople try numerous methods to locate potential customers. Some of these methods require investigating internal records and outside publications, and keeping one's eyes and ears open, while others require a more aggressive approach. This text refers to the former as *sources for prospecting*, and the latter as *methods for prospecting.*

SOURCES FOR PROSPECTING

INQUIRIES

The most viable source of prospects for most companies is the inquiries generated by a firm's advertising and promotional efforts. Inquiries are also known as **sales leads**. These sales leads usually come into the company in the form of a letter, a card, or a telephone call.

Many companies that advertise in trade magazines include their corporate address within the advertisement, and encourage those seeking more information to write to the company. One problem with this approach is that most prospects will not go to the trouble of writing a letter and sending it, unless they are very interested in the product or company. In an effort to facilitate the inquiry process for the prospect, some companies will include a self-addressed, postage-paid postcard insert along with their advertisement. Then all the interested prospect has to do is fill out the card and put it in the mailbox.

Another method of encouraging prospect inquiries was created by the telecommunications boom of the late 1980s. Companies, both small and large, began advertising an 800 number, which allowed prospects from all over the country to call the company requesting information. The call is free to the prospect, and provides immediate response to both the prospect and the company. Prospects get the information they are seeking, and the company learns of potential customers.

When a sales lead comes into the office, either through the mail or over the phone, it is noted on a **lead sheet**. The lead sheet is a form that contains pertinent information about the prospect, such as:

* Name
* Address
* Phone number
* Company name
* Prospect's position
* The date of the inquiry
* The product of interest
* Where he or she learned about the product (which advertisement?)

The telemarketing representative or marketing support person is trained to gather as much of this information as possible or to **qualify** the prospect. The sales lead sheet is then given to the salesperson who covers that prospect's territory. Some companies have computerized their sales lead sheets so they can input the data into their database under the salesperson's territory. When salespeople want the lead sheet information they just activate their territory code and the information appears on their computer screen. An example of the computerized sales lead sheet they use is shown in Figure 7-3.

LISTS

Some companies supply their salespeople with prospect lists. These lists are compiled by the company from external sources such as Chamber of Commerce directories, classified telephone directories, newspapers, public records, club membership lists, and professional or trade publication lists. Companies can also hire the services of a **list broker** to provide them with a prospect list. A list broker acts as a sales agent and rents mailing lists from one company to another company. List brokers can represent the buyer or the seller, or both. The broker's main responsibility is to negotiate a price for the list. The negotiation is based on the following factors: the number of names being sold, the quality of those names (large companies/wealthy consumers or small companies/poorer consumers), the strength of the prospect's interest in that type of product, and the recency of their inquiry or interest. Brokers receive a commission from the sellers for their service. These lists provide the salesperson with a virtually ready-made prospect list. However, even a prepared prospect list does not relieve the salesperson of the duty of using ingenuity in looking for prospects.

TRADE SHOWS

Many companies participate in trade shows, professional conventions, state exhibitions, or automobile shows. These shows provide participants with seminars and exhibits to learn and update their knowledge, and also give them the opportunity to view new products. Sales representatives attend shows to display and demonstrate their company's products, and to answer the questions of those attending.

Trade shows can be an excellent source of prospects, many of whom cannot be contacted regularly by the salesperson. For example, a textbook publisher's sales representative would attend the National Educators Association's convention in order to talk to teachers and department heads, who are often busy teaching when textbook salespeople make calls. Companies are afforded the luxury of having a large number of prospects come to them, rather than having to seek the prospect out. Also, the educational nature of these shows usually attracts the key decision makers in the buyer's organization. This allows the salesperson to establish many quality contacts in a relatively short period of time.

Most trade shows have a large number of attendees, so salespeople usually have only a few minutes to speak with each prospect. Thus, their main responsibility is to qualify these prospects, and, if possible, set up a follow-up appointment. Many companies have developed structured qualifying forms so salespeople can get the necessary information and

A COMPUTERIZED SALES LEAD SHEET

NAME AND ADDRESS INFORMATION	PROSPECT STATUS DETAIL SORTED BY CUSTOMER	PROFILE AND STATUS INFORMATION

BAUSCH & LOMB   PERSONAL PRODUCTS DIVISION
1400 NORTH GOODMAN STREET   ROCHESTER   NY 14692   BAU1469201

01 GEORGE SMAGLO   CLASS: A   IND: PHARM. PREPARAT IND2:   DALE GRAFTON
STS: QUOTED PROS50%   TERR: DALE GRAFTON

11/21/--   INQUIRY   FUP ON "A" LEAD NAFM INQUIRY
SOURCE: FORMAL/BUDGETARY   QUOTATIO   PROD:
QUOTED AN NAFM SW-10 ON OCTOBER 21. TOTAL PRICE QUOTED IS $375,000
LEADTIME IS 6-7 MONTHS. PRODUCT IS OPHTHALMIC SOLUTIONS. FOR FURTHER
DETAILS REFER TO QUOTATION.

PRODUCTS OF INTEREST	STATUS	POTENTIAL	ACTUAL
NAFM NAFM MACHINERY	IN NEW INQUIRY	0	0
	TOTALS:	0	0

BECTON DICKINSON CONSUMER
ONE BECTON DRIVE   FRANKLIN LAKES   NJ 07417   BEC0741701

01 THOMAS DRAGOSITS   MGR SYRING DEV   CLASS: A   IND: PHARM. PREPARAT IND2:   GEORGE WELKER
STS: PROJECT QUOTED   TERR: GEORGE WELKER

02/20/--   INQUIRY   FUP ON "A" LEAD NAFM INQUIRY
SOURCE: FORMAL/BUDGETARY   QUOTATIO   PROD:
QUOTED A SW-8-SP TO SLEEVE TO SECURE NEEDLE COVER THUS PROVIDING T/E
TO SYRINGES   SAMPLES REC'D AT NAFM (NC)
TOTAL PRICE OF SYSTEM $460,000

PRODUCTS OF INTEREST	STATUS	POTENTIAL	ACTUAL
NAFM NAFM MACHINERY	IN NEW INQUIRY	0	0
	TOTALS:	0	0

BEECH NUT NUTRITION CORP.
CHURCH STREET   CANAJOHARIE   NY 13317   BEE1331701

01 GERALD SELIGMAN   PROD. SUPV.   518-555-3251   CLASS: A   IND: IND2:   GEORGE WELKER
STS: QUOTED PROS50%   TERR: GEORGE WELKER

03/06/--   MISC F/U   NO FOLLOW-UP
ALL INTEREST SHIFTED TO MR. MATTI TORNIAINEN
12/14/--   MISC F/U   FOLLOW UP IN 60 DAYS ACTIVE PROJECT. WELPAK TO CONTINUE FOLLOW UP
07/24/--   INQUIRY   'C' LEAD LITERATURE
SOURCE: FOOD AND DRUG PACKAGING 3 PROD: TRA MACH. 4/30 APPOINTMENT.
INTERESTED IN COMBINATION TRP SLEEVE LABEL. DISCUSSED CMS THOUGHTS
ON HIGH SPEED SHRINK LABELING FROM FLAT WIDTHS IN GENERAL. WOULD BE
INTERESTED IF WE CAN HAVE MATERIAL COST AND REASONABLE MACHINE
PRICING BALL PARK FIGURE OK. WE WILL NOT

Figure 7-3 A lead sheet contains pertinent information about a prospect.

Figure 7-4 Trade show exhibits include the product, easy-to-read summaries of features, and an informed sales representative to answer questions.

not waste time. Also, special promotions such as giveaways can build a strong list during a trade show.

COMPANY RECORDS

Information present in a firm's files and records can be used in prospecting. One source is correspondence with buyers. Another is records in the service department that identify owners who are prospects for the replacement of old models with current models. Records in the credit department can be used not only to reduce credit risks, but to identify inactive customers who buy only part of the selling firm's product assortment but could buy more.

SALESPERSON'S CONTACTS AND OBSERVATIONS

Friends and acquaintances of salespeople can supply prospect leads, either in casual conversation or in conversation directed specifically toward uncovering prospects. If a salesperson's friend is also a friend of the prospect, so much the better. Salespeople often ask friends and relatives to act as "bird dogs" or "spotters"; that is, keeping their eyes and ears open to help uncover someone who could use the salesperson's product. For example, a salesperson selling telephone systems might ask his friend, the photocopier salesperson, to be on the lookout for companies interested in changing their telephone system. The photocopier salesperson is in the perfect position to do this because she is in and out of office buildings all day long. In return, the telephone systems salesperson may pay the friend a fee if the lead turns out to be a bona fide prospect and a sale is made. Salespeople generally ask only those who sell unrelated products for names of prospects.

A salesperson's own powers of observation can help in the search for prospects. For example, a thermopane window salesperson who sees ground being broken for a new house needs no better clue to a likely prospect. An even earlier lead could be found from a list of approved building permits. Another example is the encyclopedia salesperson who finds leads by observing swing sets and tricycles in residential areas.

METHODS FOR PROSPECTING

THE ENDLESS CHAIN METHOD

The **endless chain method** of prospecting can be quite successful at generating names of potential buyers. Salespeople who use this method ask satisfied customers or former customers to suggest individuals who could use the product being sold. Customers are inclined to be cooperative with salespeople who work hard to serve them. The objective of this method is to get at least one prospect lead from each person spoken to.

THE REFERRAL METHOD

The **referral method** goes beyond the endless chain method of asking customers to supply names of prospects. In the referral technique, customers may give the salesperson a personal card or note of introduction for the suggested prospect. They might recommend the salesperson to a prospect through a telephone call, perhaps trying to set up an appointment for the salesperson. They might also arrange to introduce the salesperson personally to the prospect.

To get referrals, a salesperson has only to ask for them. Requests for referrals can be made upon completion of the first sale, on the next call, or after allowing a reasonable length of time for the customer to become accustomed to the product or service. When asking for referrals, salespeople must be specific in their requests. For example, a salesperson might ask, "Do you know of any of your colleagues who might be interested in saving money on their long-distance charges?" Customers are less likely to draw a blank than when a salesperson asks, "Do you know anyone who needs a new telephone service?" Customers usually cooperate with the salesperson for various reasons. Some want their friends to know of the wise purchases they have made, and most feel that their decisions and actions carry weight with their friends. For these reasons, most customers will supply the salesperson with enough information to qualify the lead, thus saving time for the salesperson.

There are several advantages to the referral technique. Prospecting time and approach time are minimized, permitting more face-to-face selling time. Appointments are more easily arranged, and they are generally made with likely prospects because the customer's recommendation serves as a screening procedure. The main advantage, however, is that referrals carry more weight with the prospect because they contain the customer's vote of approval. Highlight 7-2 provides an example of the referral technique in practice.

HIGHLIGHT 7-2   *Referral Tips*

Marie A. McConnell is the president of Marie A. McConnell Realty, Incorporated of Mobile, Alabama. In her article entitled "Build Your Referral Business" (Real Estate Today, May 1986), Ms. McConnell notes that contacts are very important for developing prospects, "but it is referrals that multiply sales volume."

Ms. McConnell's article offers some tips for building a referral business. First, Ms. McConnell recommends the use of personalized, handwritten notes to friends, acquaintances, etc., to announce that you are in business in the area. Next, update these people every three months or so with brochures, cards, letters, or notes. Of course, the list of people on your mailing list should grow once the phone calls start coming in.

A third tip from Ms. McConnell is to reward those referrals that end in a sale. She sends a gift and a note to those referring the customer, which naturally encourages them to keep sending names to her.

When dealing with competitors, Ms. McConnell suggests lending a hand whenever needed, and sharing any relevant information you might have, even if it involves sending the customer over to the competition. Ms. McConnell reasons that everyone will benefit from your referral of the prospect to the competition. The customer will be satisfied, your profession's image will be enhanced, your competitor will not only make a sale, but will respect you, befriend you, and will want to repay the favor.

Referrals are the building blocks of the future. These tips will help you make the most of your referrals.

THE CENTER OF INFLUENCE METHOD

The **center of influence method** also can be used to obtain the names of prospects. The center of influence is anyone who has influence over other individuals, and who can provide the salesperson with information about these other individuals. For example, home-improvement salespeople seek out the most influential person on the street, and then offer them their services at a discount. The salesperson is hoping that the customer's neighbors will see the improvements being done, and will inquire about the salesperson's services for their home. In effect, the salesperson relies on the tendency of neighbors to "keep up with the Joneses" to make further sales. Lawyers, doctors, ministers, public officials, and business executives all serve as centers of influence for their friends, employees, neighbors, associates, and relatives.

Centers of influence do the job of referral, but they also do more. For example, they may supply all the prospect information the salesperson needs. They may make appointments and then go on to recommend the salesperson and the proposal to the prospect. Sometimes they are even present at the selling interview.

Centers of influence are more likely to function for the salesperson's benefit if the salesperson keeps them fully informed about prospect developments and expresses appreciation for their help.

THE COLD CANVASSING METHOD

Some salespeople use the **cold canvassing method** to obtain prospect names. This method is also known as cold prospecting and cold calling. The salesperson locates prospects by contacting people who may or may not be prospects and about whom very little, if anything, is known. Those who are not prospects are then eliminated. Usually the salesperson starts by knowing the type of individual to whom sales can be made. Next, it is necessary to find how and where that type of person can be located. Then the salesperson talks briefly to many people to identify those who are real prospects.

Door-to-door selling is a prime example of cold canvassing. Another example is the photocopier salesperson who begins on the top floor of an office building and calls on every company seeking qualified prospects until they reach the bottom floor. Because the salesperson can do nothing to pave the way for a call on a person whose name is not known, the qualifying and need determination must be done after meeting a prospect.

THE TELEMARKETING METHOD

The method of using the telephone to prospect for and qualify new accounts is referred to as **telemarketing**. (This is the same method used by Lisa Brown in Chapter 1.) Sales representatives save time and money with this method, because they typically can contact five to ten prospects in the time it would take to travel from one prospect to another in the field. By using the phone, salespeople can quickly identify prospects, gain their interest, and then make appointments, allowing the salespeople to travel efficiently from one customer to another. Also, telemarketing eliminates the limitation of distance in prospecting; a buyer 100 miles away can be reached as easily as one 100 yards away.

Many companies are using telemarketing staffs for prospecting. For example, telemarketers for insurance companies qualify the many leads that are generated by their advertising, and then pass these prospects along to their independent sales agents to follow up. Some insurance companies have recorded a 70 percent closing rate using this method because the salesperson spends less time prospecting, and more time selling. Using a telemarketing staff to prospect for new customers is popular with companies in the home-improvement industry as well. The president of one home-improvement company has said that if the telemarketing staff can produce one "hot" prospect for every 25 they call, the benefits will far outweigh the cost.

One business machines company relies on the telephone for prospecting and requires their copier sales trainees to make at least 500 prospecting calls before they step out into the field. The trainees first qualify each prospect and identify the decision makers. The trainees then send out product literature via direct mail, and make a second call to set up an appointment. Only after this process is complete do the sales trainees go out and demonstrate their copiers. To keep the cycle going, sales trainees are expected to continue making another 25 prospecting calls each week.

Sales representatives should prepare a plan prior to prospecting via telemarketing. Some prospects prefer to talk to a salesperson on the phone and not in person, but many prospects do not take telemarketers seriously. The effectiveness of telemarketing depends on the salesperson's ability to keep the prospect interested in what he or she is saying. This is not always easy because the prospect has the advantage of being able to hang up on the salesperson without incurring any risk. Prospects

Figure 7-5 A telemarketing staff generates many leads for sales agents.
Source: ROLM Corporation

are much more likely to reject a salesperson during a telephone call than in a face-to-face meeting.

The salesperson should utilize the following telephone prospecting procedure in order to avoid having their conversation terminated by the prospect:

1. **Develop a prospecting plan.** Prospects generally spend only a short time on the telephone with salespeople. Therefore, salespeople should prepare their messages carefully so that every word counts. The salesperson cannot waste time with idle conversation, or bore the prospect with an uninteresting message. The sales representative must maintain interest and get the prospect involved in the conversation. The salesperson should prepare a script to get the message across quickly and efficiently. A list of prospects should also be prepared, so that the salesperson can move quickly from one call to the next.

2. **Make a strong opening statement.** The first 15 to 30 seconds of a prospecting call are vital in determining whether or not the prospect will grant the salesperson an appointment. Salespeople must introduce themselves and their company in a way that will build interest and excitement within the prospect. Salespeople should always include the prospect's name in the introduction so they are sure that they are talking to the right person.

3. **Ask questions to qualify the prospect.** After the introduction, and when the salesperson senses genuine interest, the prospect should be qualified. Using the same qualifying questions discussed earlier in the chapter, the salesperson will determine whether this prospect should be given priority over other prospects. The salesperson's efficiency depends on calling on those larger, or more interested prospects first, and then the smaller, or less interested prospects afterward.

4. **Create interest with a benefit statement.** Once the prospect has been qualified, the salesperson should use a benefit statement to further the prospect's excitement. The benefit statement is usually a "teaser," whereby the sales representative convinces the prospect that allowing the salesperson the opportunity to make a presentation would be of tremendous benefit to the prospect in the long run.

5. **Ask for an appointment.** If the salesperson is successful in getting the prospect's interest, an appointment is inevitable. However, if the prospect still has reservations, the salesperson will have to ask carefully for an appointment. In doing so, the salesperson should assure the prospect that the presentation will be brief, to the point, and, again, of major benefit to the prospect. One approach to requesting an appointment is to assume that the permission has been granted and that a time needs to be set: "Would first thing Friday morning be good for you, or would you prefer just after lunch?" Once the ap-

pointment has been set, the sales representative should thank the prospect, confirm the date, time, and location, and close the conversation. A follow-up letter is a pleasant way of expressing the salesperson's appreciation and developing goodwill prior to the meeting.

THE DIRECT MAIL METHOD

Some companies use **direct mail** to locate prospects. They send promotional fliers, brochures, and catalogs to select groups or areas and wait for a response. The mailed items often contain a coupon, which, when returned, provides evidence of a person's interest in the company's products. The company responds by sending additional information. The coupons also provide addresses and phone numbers of prospects.

KEYS TO SUCCESSFUL PROSPECTING

Qualifying prospects is vital to maximizing a salesperson's productivity, but a salesperson also must consider other key factors to successful prospecting.

CLASSIFYING PROSPECTS

A salesperson's effectiveness depends on maximizing the time spent with those prospects who are ready to buy now, and cultivating those prospects who need more time to make a decision. By classifying qualified prospects based on the strength and immediacy of their need and interest, a salesperson can call on the "hot" prospects first, and bring along the "cooler" prospects slowly. The salespeople who do not classify their prospects run the risk of losing a prospect who is ready to purchase by giving priority to a prospect who needs time to gather more information.

DEVELOPING A PROSPECTING PLAN

Prior to setting out to locate prospects, the efficient salesperson sits down and develops an organized prospecting plan. A well-prepared prospecting plan greatly reduces wasted time, confusion, and frustration. Inexperienced sales representatives generally have difficulty organizing their time and records. They must learn about the company, its products and competition, and their customers, while at the same time, adjust to their territory and learn how to sell. All of these new responsibilities often overpower beginning salespeople, causing them to be disorganized and inefficient at the start. With experience salespeople gain an appreciation for organization, and usually develop an efficient system for maintaining prospect records.

Efficient prospecting plans rely on the salesperson's ability to execute the following tasks:

- Maintain clear, detailed prospect files
- Establish prospecting quotas
- Evaluate performance objectively
- Try new methods
- Follow through

MAINTAIN PROSPECT FILES

The key to maintaining good prospecting records is determination. Most salespeople hate paperwork. They would much rather be out in the field talking with people and trying to make deals than sitting at a desk shuffling a stack of papers. However, successful salespeople recognize the value of detailed, easy-to-understand records when trying to call on a large number of prospects. These salespeople use determination to force themselves to keep good records. Most companies ease the difficulty of good recordkeeping by providing their salespeople with prospecting forms. These forms contain all the vital information salespeople need to know about their prospects. All the salesperson has to do is to fill out the form.

ESTABLISH QUOTAS

Just as a sales volume quota is used to determine a salesperson's selling effectiveness, so can a quota be used to determine the salesperson's prospecting effectiveness. A weekly or monthly prospect quota is nothing more than a goal that salespeople set for themselves. Salespeople know they need a steady supply of new prospects to call on in order to maintain sales and profits within their territory. By attaching a quota to prospecting, salespeople are reminded of the importance of this activity. For example, a salesperson may set a quota of calling on 100 prospects from the day's trade show.

EVALUATE PERFORMANCE OBJECTIVELY

When sales are good there is a tendency for salespeople to spend more time selling and to forget about prospecting. Mature salespeople know that sales can decrease just as fast as they increase. They must fight this tendency to ease up on prospecting and keep evaluating their prospect files. This includes upgrading the emphasis on those getting ready to buy, and eliminating those who are never going to buy.

TRY NEW METHODS

There are no "best" methods in sales. Though many of the techniques used in sales are sound, different people and unique situations demand innovation. To be able to adjust to anyone and any situation, salespeople should practice an assortment of techniques and should always be willing to try new methods. This is as true for prospecting as it is for any other function. Salespeople who rely strictly on the center of influence method may not be getting the right kind of prospects. Instead, salespeople should use as many methods and sources as they can on a regular basis.

FOLLOW THROUGH

One of the biggest complaints sales managers have about their salespeople is that they do not follow through on their leads. From the salesperson's point of view, it is much easier to call on someone who is a customer, or who is on the verge of buying the product, than on a prospect who may or may not even know how to use the product. Effective prospecting requires dedication and the will to follow up on all prospects without fear of rejection.

SUMMARY

Successful salespeople must continually prospect for new customers to replace those lost for one reason or another. Sources for finding prospects include inquiries, lists, trade shows, company records, and the salesperson's contacts and observations. Methods for finding prospects include the endless chain method, the referral method, the center of influence method, cold canvassing, telemarketing, and direct mail. Successful prospecting depends on evaluating prospects and establishing an organized prospecting plan.

Qualifying prospects refers to asking questions that determine whether prospects are good ones. Qualifying questions should seek to determine the prospect's need, ability to pay, authority to make the purchase decision, eligibility to buy, and willingness to be approached.

KEY TERMS

selling process	list broker
prospect	endless chain method
prospecting	referral method
qualifying questions	center of influence method
sales leads	cold canvassing
lead sheet	telemarketing
direct mail	

REVIEW QUESTIONS

1. Why wouldn't a salesperson be more effective concentrating on closing sales instead of spending time prospecting?
2. What are the five qualifying questions?

3. Why should a salesperson qualify prospects before calling on them?
4. What are some of the devices companies use to generate sales leads?
5. How does the *referral method* improve on the *endless chain method*?
6. How does the *center of influence method* improve on the *referral method*?
7. How can telemarketing increase the salesperson's prospecting efficiency?
8. Why is a prospecting plan necessary for success when prospecting via telemarketing?
9. How does classifying prospects improve the salesperson's chances for success?
10. Which is the best method or source for prospecting?

DISCUSSION QUESTIONS

1. "Salespeople get paid for closing sales." What effect does this statement have on the salesperson's motivation to prospect, and what changes would you use to place more emphasis on prospecting?
2. Salespeople may feel awkward asking prospects the five qualifying questions, because they do not want to "turn off" the prospects. Who else can salespeople talk to in order to qualify those prospects?
3. You are working a trade show as part of your responsibility as a PC sales representative for Apple Computer Company. In your booth there are six prospects. Three of them are "just looking", two are seeking information regarding what your Macintosh computer does, and one is asking how they can finance the purchase of a new Macintosh computer, laser printer, and assorted software. How should you handle the situation?

CASE 7-1   GALLAGHER OIL COMPANY*

Gallagher Oil Company is one of the largest producers of propane in the United States. The company is a major player in two of the more lucrative propane markets in the nation—the Midwest and the Northeast—where demand is generated from agricultural, residential, and industrial sources.

Unfortunately for Gallagher and its competitors, the propane market in the United States has provided decreasing returns to producers in

---

*Case prepared by Brad O'Hara. Used with permission.

recent years. Price-competitive substitutes and excess production (some propane is a byproduct from gasoline refining) have caused the erosion of once lucrative margins. Associated with this has been an upswing in buyer power. In the past, retailers paid essentially what the producer asked. Today's buyers, however, have several supply sources at their disposal and can negotiate a more price-sensitive deal. "As far as propane is concerned, there is no difference," according to one retailer. "National industry specifications mean that Gallagher's propane is no different from that produced elsewhere. As a result, price is most important to me. Fortunately, the abundance of propane in North America has turned this market around—retailers are crazy if they don't beat the bushes to secure the lowest price possible."

One market that has provided relatively consistent returns for Gallagher has been the Michigan-Northwestern Ohio market. In this region, the company's state-of-the-art production facility provides customers with a consistent, price-competitive supply base, unlike that offered from other sources (refineries), which have a history of being unreliable during peak demand periods. This has allowed Gallagher to develop a somewhat loyal customer base, composed of important multinational retailers (who also do business with Gallagher in other areas), and small "mom-and-pop" operations. In an effort to maintain this broad base of customers, marketing department personnel have joined both the Ohio and Michigan Propane Gas associations.

The recent termination of a long-term contract between Gallagher and a local utility for ethane has made available a pipeline that is connected with Gallagher's production facility. Company officials, determined to expand propane sales, are seriously considering adapting this pipeline for propane sales by constructing a truck terminal at the Gallagher terminus in Central Ohio. Marketing personnel are hopeful that construction could start within the next four months, with possible completion within six months of ground breaking.

John McCormack, Gallagher's most successful sales representative, has been charged with the job of investigating possible sales associated with this venture. McCormack is hopeful that the terminal's location will be attractive not only to some of Gallagher's existing customers in Northwest Ohio, but, more important, to a new set of clients in Central and Southern Ohio. One problem with this possible expansion of Gallagher's market area will be a new set of competitors from areas south of the planned Central Ohio truck terminal, which will require expanding the company's "marketing intelligence" base.

CASE QUESTIONS

1. How should McCormack develop a list of possible customers?
2. What important questions should McCormack ask in deciding the suitability of clients for this terminal?

3. What sorts of questions should McCormack initially anticipate from contacts he makes?

CASE 7-2   C. L. FOSTER COMPANY*

Martha Sullivan has just received her Associate of Arts Degree from Anderson College. Her new job is as a sales representative with the C. L. Foster Company in Columbia, South Carolina. C. L. Foster Company is the largest office supply distributor in South Carolina and offers four product lines: office equipment (electronic typewriters, computers, copiers), office furniture, general office supplies, and printing services. Martha is responsible for selling Olivetti electronic typewriters and A. B. Dick copiers to businesses in the Columbia metropolitan area.

Martha spent her first week on the job in a sales training course with three other new sales representatives who will be selling office equipment in other cities. The sales manager of the office equipment division, Judith Thompson, called Martha into the office on Friday afternoon to discuss Martha's strategy for the next week when she will begin selling in "the real world."

JT: Martha, there is a lot of competition in the Columbia area among office equipment dealers—especially for typewriters and copiers. How do you plan to "get your foot in the door," so to speak, and get the customers to notice your product over competitors' products?

MS: I had hoped to get some leads from the reader service cards in magazines. In general, though, I plan to spend about 60 percent of my time prospecting for customers by phone. The other 40 percent will be spent making cold calls.

JT: What you are telling me is basically all right. However, neither Olivetti nor A. B. Dick uses much, if any, magazine advertising and I haven't seen many leads come in from those reader service cards in the past. Also, telephoning and cold calling are good ways to identify leads but sometimes it is difficult to get through to the person you need to see. Have you thought about using the mail to introduce yourself and the products?

MS: Not really. What suggestions do you have as far as using the mail?

JT: It would probably be best to start with a small area, like downtown, and read through the directory to find com-

---

*Case prepared by Elizabeth Wilson. Used with permission.

panies that might have a strong interest in office equipment. Send packets to all of the law firms, for example, since the legal industry uses a lot of office equipment. Also, consider insurance firms, banks, accounting firms and any other companies that seem likely candidates.

CASE QUESTIONS

1. Given the suggestions of the sales manager, what specific strategy should Martha use to increase her chances of being asked to make a sales presentation to a company in her territory?
2. What can Martha do to get her foot in the door? That is, what small request can be made that may encourage agreement with the larger request to present the typewriters in a formal demonstration?

CHAPTER 8

Planning the Sales Presentation— The Preapproach

After studying this chapter, you should be able to:

- Understand the necessity of conducting a thorough preapproach
- Discuss the "mental states" approach to preparing a sales presentation
- Describe the three major tasks that constitute the preapproach
- Discuss the five buying decisions
- Show how salespeople should plan for the first "no"

Salespeople need plans for their presentations, just as motorists need road maps for their travels. In planning a sales presentation, the salesperson researches each prospect's personality, experience, and motivation; the circumstances of the moment; the prospect's attitudes toward the salesperson's product and competing products; and the prospect's purchasing preferences and problems. Through this research, the salesperson seeks the best approach to use in adapting the products or services to each individual customer. This preparation enables the salesperson to pinpoint the customer's need, develop a plan to show how the product's utility outweighs its price, identify probable objections and gather the facts to counter those objections, and put together a presentation that is both believable and complete enough to close the sale.

Empathy, an important quality for all salespeople to have, is valuable in planning the sales presentation. Empathy in selling refers to the salesperson's ability to see and feel the buyer-seller relationship from the prospect's viewpoint. Salespeople who have empathy will be sympathetic to the preferences, perceptive about the attitudes, sensitive to the hopes and fears, receptive to the ideas, and appreciative of the objectives and values of every prospect.

232

THE SELLING PROCESS

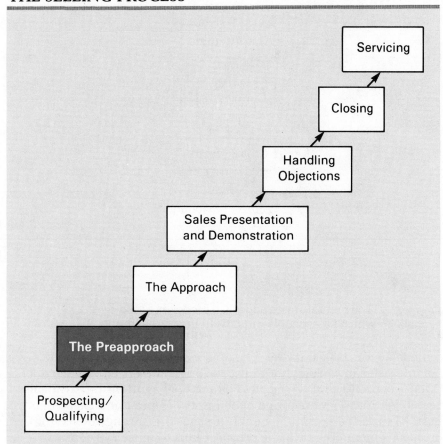

Figure 8-1 The *preapproach* is the second stage of the selling process.

AN OVERVIEW OF THE STEPS IN SELLING

The traditional view holds that a salesperson makes a sale by leading the prospect through five steps. This view is based on a theory known as the **mental states approach** to selling (see Figure 8-2). In using this approach, the salesperson must get the prospect's attention, gain the prospect's interest, create the prospect's desire for the product, secure the prospect's conviction that a purchase should be made, and, finally, get action from the prospect in the form of a purchase. The salesperson must construct every presentation in such a way as to have these five effects.

ATTENTION

The salesperson must get and then hold the prospect's attention if a sale is to be made. The prospect's problems and other interests often

THE MENTAL STATES APPROACH

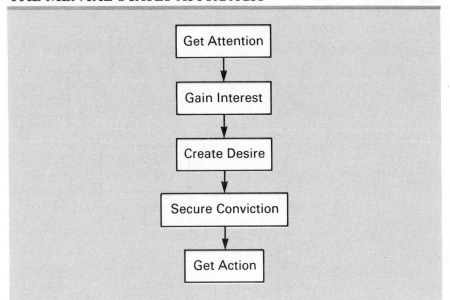

```
Get Attention
      ↓
Gain Interest
      ↓
Create Desire
      ↓
Secure Conviction
      ↓
Get Action
```

Figure 8-2 The mental states approach proposes a step-by-step hierarchy of goals on which salespeople must base their presentations.

complicate this task, however. The prospect may have the attitude, "I'm not interested in you or what you are selling. I don't need your product." Often prospects will close their minds and not pay attention to the salesperson because they are afraid of being sold something instead of buying it. The salesperson might be able to sense this through observing the prospect's mannerisms. If the prospect fails to make eye contact, or is preoccupied by other objects in the office, it is likely that the salesperson has not yet gained the prospect's attention.

INTEREST

A prospect can be said to be interested in the salesperson and the salesperson's products when the prospect asks to hear more of the salesperson's story. The best start the salesperson can make toward gaining the prospect's attention and interest is to use effective attention-getters, because they help shift attention into interest. Also effective are the salesperson's expressions of interest in the prospect. Because prospects are interested in themselves, salespeople should plan to listen and talk about prospects' interests—their hopes, problems, possessions, families, accomplishments, and such. This approach encourages prospects to link together thoughts about their needs, the product, and its price. The prospect who does this is interested.

Figure 8-3 A sure sign of a prospect's interest is when he or she starts to handle or sample the product.

Source: Photo courtesy of SCM Corporation.

DESIRE

The way to sell is to present a sales story that makes the prospect want to buy the product. A product or service is desired only if it will do something the individual wants done. To establish a need or want, the salesperson must help the prospect "see" the benefits of the product/ service. This requires considerable tact if, in effect, it asks the prospect to admit carelessness, ignorance, or that decisions or purchases made earlier were mistakes. Then, of course, it is necessary to get the prospect to agree that the salesperson's product seems a desirable answer to a need or want.

CONVICTION

A salesperson has succeeded in this fourth stage when the prospect admits a desire to buy. The prospect now sees a problem or situation about which something must be done. The prospect agrees that the salesperson's product will do the job better than any other product. The prospect realizes the price of the product is reasonable when related to the satisfaction resulting from the purchase. No longer bothered by doubt, the prospect agrees to buy.

Figure 8-4 The salesperson must create desire within the consumer in order for the sale to be made.

PURCHASE

The prospect's agreement to purchase the product or service represents only partial success for the salesperson. There can be only one act that will make a salesperson's undertaking a complete success. This, of course, is a purchase by the prospect, now. The salesperson's presentation is the tool that sells merchandise.

PROBLEMS WITH THE MENTAL STATES APPROACH

The mental states approach is a good way of looking at the prospect's internal thought processes during a sales presentation, and the smart salesperson will try to influence these processes to his or her best advantage. However, there is a problem in using the mental states approach. How does the salesperson know when the prospect has moved from one mental state to the next? Obviously, there are no neon signs on the prospect's forehead that flash the prospect's current mental state. Moreover, most professional buyers are highly skilled in hiding their intentions. Thus, this approach requires salespeople who are highly skilled at "reading" their prospects, and who can detect even the slightest changes in the prospects' appearance or attitude.

THE PREAPPROACH

The example shown in Highlight 8-1 illustrates the importance of conducting a thorough preapproach. The **preapproach** is the salesperson's

HIGHLIGHT 8-1   College Textbooks, Inc.

Billy Taylor is the Louisiana and Texas sales representative for College Textbooks, Incorporated. He went through the company's one-month training program, which centered on product information for all of CTI's textbooks, their competitors' textbooks, and on certain selling techniques. When it was completed, Billy felt comfortable that he was prepared to make his first sales call on South Central Louisiana College. This is how the call started:

Salesperson: Hello, Dr. Williams?
Buyer: Uh, that is Ms. Williamson.
Salesperson: Oh yes, sorry. My name is Billy Taylor and I am your new College Textbooks sales representative. I understand you are using our Johnson & Johnson text for your Principles course.
Buyer: Uh, no longer. Our department chairman chose to adopt the Mitchell text for this year.
Salesperson: Oh, I didn't know. What other courses are you teaching this semester?
Buyer: Personal Selling.
Salesperson: Oh, we have a fantastic new text called Professional Selling Techniques.
Buyer: Yes, I know. I wrote it!
Salesperson: Oh, yeah. Williamson. That's right.

Obviously, Billy Taylor was not as prepared as he thought for this sales call. He mispronounced the professor's name, was unaware that the professor did not possess a doctoral degree, did not know that the department had dropped his company's text for the Principles course, had no idea what other courses the professor taught, and did not even realize that the text he was promoting to the professor was actually written by that professor.

Billy should have updated his information prior to making the call. He could have checked the school's class schedule, where he would have noticed that "Williams" was really "Williamson," and that besides Marketing Principles, she was also teaching Personal Selling. Next, Billy could have checked the campus bookstore to see which texts were being stocked for Ms. Williamson's classes. In doing so, he probably would have noticed that his company's text had already been ordered for the Personal Selling class, and that the author's name was the same as the professor's name. Taking note of the coincidence, Billy might have then investigated the preface of the text and seen that the author was a professor at South Central Louisiana College, did not have her Doctorate, and more than likely, was the same Williamson that he was about to approach.

preparation for the coming sales presentation. To be more specific, the preapproach is the salesperson's way of finding the prospect's basic problem, or need, which the product will solve, and then planning the best way to present the problem and its solution when talking to the prospect. The preapproach gives the salesperson a clear and detailed picture of each prospect so that a personalized presentation can be built for each one. While the major emphasis is on the salesperson's getting ready emotionally, mentally, and physically for the call, there will be certain instances in which the preapproach includes some preparation of the prospect to hear the sales story. In every instance, the purpose of the preapproach is to establish the best possible foundation for a sale.

A salesperson does most of the preapproach groundwork before ever seeing the prospect. Once the salesperson has a qualified prospect there are three major tasks to complete before making the presentation. These tasks are the **customer profile**, the **sales call objectives**, and the **customer benefit plan**.

To round out the customer profile, the salesperson collects information about the prospect and the prospect's organization. The second task requires developing objectives for the sales call. In other words, what does the salesperson hope to achieve during the first visit? The third task of the preapproach is to prepare an appealing sales presentation. This involves determining what prospects' needs are and what benefits they are seeking. Then, the product's features must be related to those benefits to satisfy the prospect's needs.

THE CUSTOMER PROFILE

The most important research in the preapproach concerns the problems, needs, and wants of the prospect and any special circumstances that have a bearing on the salesperson's presentation. The salesperson performs this research prior to developing the sales presentation in order to tailor the presentation regarding which product or products to recommend and the quantity to suggest.

The customer profile is an analysis of both the individual purchasing agent and the buying organization. The personal preferences of each prospect are as important as the buying philosophy and practices of the organization. All of the principal decision makers should be identified at this time. Figures 8-5 and 8-6 show the types of information included in the customer profile.

HOW AND WHERE TO OBTAIN THIS INFORMATION

A salesperson develops most of the customer profile before even meeting the prospect. Much of this information is obtained from the salesperson's prospect records. If the salesperson is already doing business with this person and/or company, the customer files may be re-

INFORMATION ON BUYER'S ORGANIZATION
USED IN CUSTOMER PROFILE

Business information that the salesperson will want to obtain may include the following:

1. Name of company
2. Type of business
3. Size of business
4. Location and most efficient route of reaching business
5. Product line
6. Markets served
7. Organization
8. Type of management
9. Credit rating
10. Prominent executives and other key personnel
11. Policies
12. Pertinent routines and procedures
13. Terminology
14. Major income and expense items
15. Competition
16. Previous experience with the salesperson's company
17. Problems
18. Future prospects
19. Where, how, when, why, and by whom the products will be used
20. Volume possibilities
21. Frequency of purchase
22. What the prospect now does about the salesperson's type of product

Figure 8-5 A salesperson's customer profile should contain all of the above types of information concerning the buyer's organization.

viewed for this information. Sometimes, however, certain information is omitted during the initial prospect search or is missing from the customer files. In these cases, the salesperson may have to question people close to the prospect or customer. These sources include the customer's secretary, friends and business associates, other people in the buying company, noncompetitive vendors the prospect purchases from, and the salesperson's competitors and customers.

SALES CALL OBJECTIVES

When the salesperson has a good understanding of who the customer is for a particular sales call, the next step is to set specific objectives for that sales call. Sales representatives should have at least one objective for every sales call they make; otherwise, the sales call will have no focus.

Sales call objectives should be set with the intent of getting the customer to commit to some type of action. In other words, the focus should be on what the customer will do as a result of the sales call, not on what the salesperson should do on the sales call.

INFORMATION ON INDIVIDUAL BUYER USED IN CUSTOMER PROFILE

Personal information that the salesperson will want to obtain may include the following:

Objective Information

1. Name (including initials, spelling, and proper pronunciation)
2. Age and birthday
3. Home address and telephone number
4. Ownership of specific items, such as houses or automobiles
5. Education and background
6. Purchasing power
7. Marital status
8. Family data (including names, schools, and interests of spouse and children)
9. Social circle
10. Reputation
11. Organization memberships (including fraternal, civic, political, and religious ties)
12. Job (including company name, job title, nature of work, responsibilities, approximate salary, training, experience, years with the company, and years on the present job)
13. Daily routine

Subjective Information

1. Character
2. Beliefs
3. Personality type
4. Traits
5. Interests
6. Likes and dislikes
7. Buying problems
8. Aspirations

Figure 8-6 A salesperson's customer profile should contain all of the above types of information concerning the individual buyer's organization.

Finally, sales call objectives should be measurable so salespeople can determine if objectives are accomplished. As a district sales manager for Beecham once said in a sales class, "It costs us $35 to put that sales rep in the store. They had better accomplish something tangible, or else we've just thrown $35 out the window."[1] Examples of specific objectives that different types of sales representatives might set are shown in Figure 8-7.

---

[1]Miles Faust, Sales Manager, Beecham Products, in a presentation to a "Buyer-Seller Communications" class at Louisiana State University.

EXAMPLES OF SPECIFIC SALES CALL OBJECTIVES

Consumer Packaged-Goods Sales Representative

Objective 1: Convince the customer to provide an extra shelf facing for our toothpaste brand.

Objective 2: Have the customer commit to providing distribution and two shelf facings for new deodorant roll-on in store.

Objective 3: Encourage the customer to commit to a 50-case end-of-the-aisle display, and the lowest category price in the store through the use of a $1-off-per-case deal.

Pharmaceutical Sales Representative

Objective 1: Encourage nurse to use our diet supplement guide for low-cholesterol patients.

Objective 2: Get nurse to recommend me and my products to the doctor in order to get a 10-minute presentation.

Objective 3: Get the doctor to commit to prescribing our low-cholesterol drug.

Industrial Sales Representative

Objective 1: Get the purchasing agent to listen to my 15-minute presentation.

Objective 2: Get the purchasing agent to allow me to compare our refractory insulation material with what they are currently using.

Objective 3: Get the purchasing agent to allow me to make a bid for the contract.

Figure 8-7 Sales call objectives will differ depending on the type of products the salesperson sells and the situation under which the sale is taking place.

THE CUSTOMER BENEFIT PLAN

Once the objectives for the sales call have been set, the salesperson then analyzes the **customer benefit plan** (also known as the **FAB sheet**). The FAB sheet gets its name from the fact that it describes which *features* (F) are important to this particular customer, the *advantages* (A) the features have over the competition or what the prospect is currently using, and how the prospect will *benefit* (B) from the features.

The customer benefit plan enables salespeople to structure their presentations in the most persuasive fashion possible. The customer benefit plan also helps to highlight the most compelling buying motives of the prospect. Knowing this helps salespeople determine the type of demonstration and closing to use, as well as the possible objections that may be raised. The example shown in Table 8-1 shows the FAB sheet that might be used by the Frito-Lay sales representative covering the Orlando, Florida, territory when trying to gain distribution of their Cajun-flavored Ruffles brand potato chips in a grocery chain.

Virtually all companies publish information concerning their products and services in order to educate their salespeople and their customers. The salesperson should review this information and condense it into a customer benefit plan.

AN EXAMPLE OF A CUSTOMER BENEFIT PLAN OR FAB SHEET

Feature	Advantage	Benefits
New Cajun flavor	New consumer trend toward flavored chips, especially Cajun	Increased store traffic Increased demand/sales Increased consumer satisfaction
Frito-Lay name	#1 market share of all snack foods in Orlando area	Increased store traffic Enhanced store image
Free-standing insert: $.25 introductory coupon to be dropped in insert section of Sunday newspaper	Increased consumer awareness No cost to retailer	Increased store traffic Reduced advertising costs Increased demand/sales
$15-million advertising budget in the first year, with ads featuring famous Cajun television chef, Joleen Wilcox	Increased consumer awareness No cost to retailer	Reduced advertising costs Increased store traffic Increased demand/sales

Table 8-1 Customer benefit plans help salespeople structure their presentations.

Many consumer packaged-goods manufacturers, such as Procter & Gamble, Beecham, and Carnation, provide their sales representatives with product pamphlets to help support the salesperson's customer benefit plan. These pamphlets usually run anywhere from six to eight pages and typically contain some or all of the following information:

- Information on the product category:
  - total projected sales for the product category
  - who competes in the market
  - market shares for product category competitors
  - any segmentation that might be present in the market
  - any trends that are presently occurring, or are in the foreseeable future
  - growth potential for the product category
- Information on the competition:
  - who the competitors are
  - what brands they market in that product category
  - their strengths and weaknesses in relation to our brand
  - their positioning strategy in the product category
  - their prices and pricing strategy
  - their advertising and promotion strategies and tactics
  - in which stores they are currently in distribution
- Market information for our brand:
  - target market
  - positioning strategy
  - market research data
  - advertising strategy
  - sales promotion strategy
- Pricing terms and other information:
  - early buy discount
  - early payment discount
  - promotion allowance
  - invoice buying allowance
  - shipping information
  - packaging information
  - regular cost
  - suggested manufacturer's everyday retail price
  - everyday profit
  - suggested manufacturer's feature retail price
  - feature profit

An example of the introductory product pamphlet used by Beecham Products of Pittsburgh, Pennsylvania, when they introduced their Calgon After Bath Lotion is shown in the color insert of this text.

BENEFITS OF THOROUGH PREAPPROACHES

In a preapproach, it is essential that the salesperson consider a future sales presentation from the prospect's point of view. Certainly, the salesperson must see, think, and feel as the prospect does before being successful in getting the prospect to see, think, and feel as the salesperson does about the salesperson's products. A thorough preapproach limits the number of facts a salesperson takes for granted; the selling strategy can be developed out of a firm background of knowledge.

The presentation the salesperson makes reveals the planning that went into it. Thorough preparation increases not only the salesperson's confidence, but also helps convince the prospect of the salesperson's competence in making buy recommendations. Preapproach work results in sounder selling efforts and in shorter, more successful calls. By completing the three preapproach tasks, the salesperson has laid the foundation for the plan of attack and can begin implementing it. Figure 8-8 shows a "Sales Call Planner," which can be completed during the preapproach. This planner can help ensure that salespeople are thoroughly prepared and have fully analyzed their presentations ahead of time.

THE FIVE BUYING DECISIONS

No purchase is ever made, whether the product is a candy bar or a car, until the buyer has said "yes" to five specific questions. The salesperson's basic job in any sales situation consists of identifying which of the five decisions the prospective customer is uncertain about, and then securing a favorable verdict on each.

The five questions are: (1) Is there a definite *need* for certain advantages, benefits, or satisfactions that I, the prospect, do not now enjoy?; (2) Is a specific *product* the best answer to that need?; (3) Is a specific *source* the best one to patronize?; (4) Is the *price* acceptable?; and (5) Is now the *time* to buy?

There is no standard sequence in which prospects make the five buying decisions. This means, for example, the source may be selected or the price determined before the need is acknowledged. Similarly, prospects often have no time schedule for making the decisions. Seconds or months may elapse between any two decisions. These two uncertainties make it possible for a prospect to have made one or more of the decisions before the salesperson comes into the picture and to make the other decisions in any order they may choose.

If you run a classified advertisement in a newspaper saying that you want a baby carriage, sellers start with Buying Decision No. 1, need, already made in their favor. If you have been wearing Nike jogging shoes for years and have no intention of changing, then Buying Decision No. 2,

SALES CALL PLANNER

SALES CALL PLANNER

Account name: _WINN DIXIE_

Person to contact: _JOHN SMITH_   _STORE MGR_
                   (NAME)   (TITLE)

1. **OBJECTIVE**   (What do you want customer to do?)

   SELL THE PERIOD SALES PROGRAM

2. **OPENER**   (Attention—Interest—A pivot into your sales story)

   DISCUSS HOW WELL CURRENT PROGRAM IS SELLING

3. **BENEFITS**   To the customer or their company. What can you supply to answer needs or wants—business or personal?

   ADDED SALES, ATTRACTIVE DISPLAYS IN STORE, COUPONS

4. **PROOFS**   That reinforce or dramatize the BENEFITS . . . including data, studies, "Third Party", etc.

   SALES FIGURES FOR PREVIOUS MONTH

5. **OBJECTIONS**   You can anticipate:

Customer Objection	Your Answer (Listen—Don't Argue!)
1) LACK OF ROOM	SUGGEST MOVING SLOWER PRODUCTS
2) CURRENT PRODUCT FULL	SUGGEST RE-BOXING THE PRODUCT

6. **THE CLOSE**   Recheck your OBJECTIVE. What can you ask to learn if you've accomplished your objective?

   WHEN CAN WE SEND THE DELIVERY, QUANTITY

Figure 8-8 Sales call planners such as the one illustrated enable the salesperson to be focused when he or she walks into the customer's office.

product, is settled, at least for the time being. If you have been buying your clothes at Neiman Marcus for years and plan no change, Buying Decision No. 3, source, is already made. If you have decided that $200 is the right amount for you to spend on a suit, then Buying Decision No. 4, price, is settled before you see the salesperson. Finally, if you walk up to a retail salesperson and say that you must have a birthday gift today, Buying Decision No. 5, time, clearly has been made.

Salespeople cannot assume that prospects really mean what they say relative to the buying decisions. Prospects may say they have no time to spend listening to the salesperson when actually they have no money to spend. Much of the time, however, a prospect's comment or question will throw light on the missing buying decision. Clearly, no need is detected in the observation, "My car is only three years old; it's certainly good for two more years." There is an objection to the product in the exclamation, "I hate them!" The prospect's feeling about source must be changed if the reply is, "But I've bought all my insurance from State Farm." Price is the objection when the prospect asks, "What's it made of, gold?" And, finally, there is a refusal to make the time decision when the salesperson is dismissed with, "See me next week."

By determining quickly which buying decisions the prospect is uncertain about—and these are the ones that must be won before the sale can be closed—the salesperson avoids wasting time on any matter upon which the prospect has already decided in the salesperson's favor. The salesperson also avoids spending time on a topic that needs no attention and thus reduces the risk of irritating or antagonizing the prospect.

To determine how the prospect feels about the five buying decisions, the salesperson relies heavily on two techniques: first, analyzing the prospect's voluntary comments, particularly the objections; and second, sounding out the prospect—indirectly, if possible—on each decision.

BUYING DECISION NO. 1—NEED

In Chapter 3 we recognized that all voluntary behavior of ultimate consumers—including their voluntary purchases—is intended to either protect or enhance one's self-concept. Therefore, individuals always have needs. Let's see how a salesperson for a textbook publishing company secures an affirmative buying decision concerning need. The prospect is the coordinator for the textbook committee for the city of Newark, New Jersey Board of Education. The New Jersey State Board of Education has just ordered that all schools within the city of Newark must use the same mathematics textbook series for grades 9 through 12. The reason for this judgment is the poor scores attained by Newark students on the mathematics section of the Scholastic Aptitude Test (SAT) over the past five years. Students in Newark often switch high schools when their families move. Since all schools are using different texts, and few texts are alike, students often miss instruction on important topics that are covered on the SATs. The State Board thinks this is the reason for the low scores.

The salesperson for the McGraw-Hill Publishing Company is aware of the order put forth by the State Board of Education, and he is hoping to present his mathematics series as the solution to Newark's need. The salesperson is new and has never met the prospect before. The prospect is familiar with McGraw-Hill, having purchased English and social studies books from the company in the past. The salesperson's objective for this call is to secure a positive response from the coordinator for a full hour-long presentation to all eleven members of the textbook committee.

Salesperson: Ms. Turiello, my name is Carl Ponti and I am the new sales representative for McGraw-Hill Publishing Company in northern New Jersey. I would like to talk with you about your need for a new mathematics series for grades 9 through 12.

Prospect: Well, Mr. Ponti, I do not really have the time to talk with you, and anyway, the committee is already considering presentations from three of your competitors.

Salesperson: Ms. Turiello, would you mind telling me which three companies the committee is considering?

Prospect: No, I do not mind. The committee is considering Random House, MacMillan, and Prentice-Hall.

Salesperson: Well, Ms. Turiello, I am aware of the new order sent down by the New Jersey Board of Education and the reason for it. Did you know that our new mathematics series is the only one on the market that is accompanied by a schedule showing the teacher how many days to spend on each topic, and how to schedule their instruction throughout the semester?

Prospect: No, I did not know that.

Salesperson: Ms. Turiello, this schedule was developed for school systems like Newark's that need a high degree of structure in their curriculums because of the constantly changing flow of students within the city's schools. With this schedule, every student in grade 12 will be learning the same material in week 8, no matter which of the nine high schools they are in. Thus, if a student switches schools he or she will not miss out on any necessary instruction.

Prospect: Well, Mr. Ponti, this schedule seems to be exactly what our school system needs.

Salesperson: Great, Ms. Turiello! Do you think you could convince the committee to give me an hour of their time so I can present all four textbooks for grades 9 through 12?

Prospect: Yes. I have the authority to set up such an appointment.

Salesperson: Good, would later in the week, say Friday, be good for you or would you prefer to wait until next Monday?

Prospect: No, Friday would be fine. The committee has their weekly meeting at 4 P.M. and I can guarantee everyone will be there and McGraw-Hill will receive full consideration.

Salesperson: Fantastic! I will see you Friday afternoon at 4 P.M., Ms. Turiello. Thank you so much for your time. Bye.

BUYING DECISION NO. 2—PRODUCT

Once need has been established, the next step is to show how the product fills that need. If the prospect is buying for personal use, the salesperson points out the satisfaction desired by the prospect and found in the product, such as safety, comfort, economy, approval, affection, and prestige. If the prospect is buying for resale, the salesperson points out how and why the product will make more money for the prospect. Here is an example of how a salesperson obtained the second buying decision from the prospect. We will continue with our example—Carl Ponti, the school textbook sales representative—to illustrate this point.

Salesperson: Well, committee members, I am sure Ms. Turiello has explained to you why she has granted me this presentation. The main feature of our mathematics series is that it includes a teaching schedule that plans the teacher's semester and ensures that all students in the city are on the same topic on the same day. No other publisher includes such a schedule in their series.

Member #1: That's all well and good, Mr. Ponti. However, can you assure us that the level of instruction in your texts is satisfactory for our school system? We have some very bright students in our schools; however, many of them are well below the national averages.

Salesperson: Sir, our texts are loaded with problems for the students to solve. I am sure that you are aware that below-average students need a lot of reinforcement when it comes to mathematics. Our texts have over 150 problems per chapter for the students to practice on.

Member #2: What about teacher's manuals?

Salesperson: I am glad you asked that question, Mrs. Ross. I have provided each of you with a copy of our teacher's manual. You should find it there on your desk. If you open it up to page 5 you will see the course schedule that I have told you about. If you thumb through the rest of the manual, you will notice that it contains solutions for all of the problems given in the text, as well as additional problems to be used for tests.

Member #3:   Did you say solutions for all of the problems?

Salesperson: Yes, sir. All 150 problems in each chapter. And I know none of my competitors can say the same.

Ms. Turiello: I think we can all agree that this series is by far the most comprehensive product we have seen. Anyone disagree? No? Okay, Mr. Ponti. We are satisfied that your product is a good one.

BUYING DECISION NO. 3—SOURCE

From the prospect's point of view, the source decision may involve one, two, or three types of sources. The first type of source is the salesperson. The prospect must approve of the salesperson before the purchase is made. A second type of source is the middleman. Individual consumers give approval to retailers by patronizing them, and the customers of other middlemen, notably wholesalers, do the same. The third type of source is the manufacturer who must be accepted before purchases are made.

Member #4:   You seem to be very knowledgeable, Mr. Ponti. How long have you been in this business?

Salesperson: Well, sir, I have been with McGraw-Hill Publishing Company for seven months; however, before joining the company, I spent 12 years as a mathematics teacher in the New York Public School System. New York's Board of Education ordered this very same decision throughout all its public schools five years ago.

Member #2:   So you have had experience using these texts?

Salesperson: Actually, no, Mrs. Ross. This series is less than a year old. I used the Random House text. But it was this series that encouraged me to stop teaching and start selling for McGraw-Hill. The McGraw-Hill series is by far the best on the market and its potential is unlimited!

Ms. Turiello: It sounds to me like we not only have an intelligent salesperson here, but also a quality company.

Salesperson: The committee should know. They have been purchasing our English and social studies texts for years.

BUYING DECISION NO. 4—PRICE

The fourth buying decision is made when the prospect deems the price is acceptable. This decision on price is closely related to those concerning need and product. Only after the prospect has decided on those two matters can the product's satisfaction be related to its price. Then, of course, the prospect compares the product's satisfaction with the satisfaction that could be obtained from another product bought for the same amount of money. The greater the satisfaction and value the salesperson has built up, the more easily and promptly the prospect is able to approve of price.

Ms. Turiello: Mr. Ponti, you realize that we are working with a very limited budget in Newark? How much will this series cost the city?

Salesperson: Ms. Turiello, as you know, McGraw-Hill has a reputation for providing excellent value for the money.

Ms. Turiello: Yes, Mr. Ponti, I am aware of your company's reputation. However, we need to know specific prices.

Salesperson: Each hardbound textbook costs $25. We will provide one complimentary text and a teacher's manual for every 30 ordered. Now I know this price is lower than both Random House and MacMillan, and only $1.50 more than the Prentice-Hall series.

Member #5: Yes, but $1.50 per text adds up when you're talking about 50,000 students. That's $75,000!

Salesperson: I realize that is a lot of money, Mr. Calvin, but the Prentice-Hall series provides far less in terms of instruction and problems, and they do not have our course schedule. Let's face it, you are getting a lot for that extra $1.50! Also, we can provide the city with financing so it will not seem like such a heavy commitment.

Ms. Turiello: That sounds very good to me, Mr. Ponti. What about the rest of you? Are you satisfied?

BUYING DECISION NO. 5—TIME

When the salesperson makes a bid for the time decision, it is an attempt to close the sale. When the decision is an affirmative one, the prospect buys. However, uncertainty may still remain about the purchase. For example, the prospect may want the salesperson's product because it will fulfill a desire, but also knows that a choice must be made between this product and other items that are needed. Our textbook example continues and demonstrates how Mr. Ponti handles the situation.

Salesperson: Well, if there are no more questions, when can I have these textbooks delivered to you?

Ms. Turiello: Mr. Ponti, before we can answer that question, the committee and I would like to talk things over. After all, we are talking about a $750,000 purchase decision, and your text is a little more expensive.

Salesperson: Fine, Ms. Turiello. Would you like me to wait outside?

Ms. Turiello: If you would not mind. I do not think we will be more than 30 minutes.

(20 minutes later)

Ms. Turiello: Mr. Ponti, we have decided to go with your textbook series and we would appreciate it if you could deliver the texts next week to the different schools. Mrs. Ross will give you a breakdown of the number of texts we will need for grades 9, 10, 11, and 12, and how many of each should be delivered to each of our nine schools. Do you think you can handle that?

Salesperson: You bet, Ms. Turiello. I will make sure all the texts are delivered to the right schools on time. Thank you very much! You will not be disappointed!

ADOPTING THE PROSPECT'S POINT OF VIEW

One of the most critical questions a salesperson must answer in planning a sales presentation is where the emphasis should be placed. For example, should the sales effort be centered on the prospect or on the product? The answer is clear: on the prospect. Letting the prospect be the focus of attention requires the salesperson to fashion his or her own thoughts, words, and actions accordingly. It means locating the prospect's buying problems, then finding solutions for them. This is sometimes called taking the "you" point of view. The salesperson gets in step with the prospect and stays there. Another phase of the "you" attitude consists of putting a strong service flavor into each presentation. Instead of selling to the prospect, the salesperson helps the prospect make a sound purchasing decision by providing information to help in the decision-making process. In developing a sales presentation, the salesperson must remember that the efficiency of a product, its inexpensiveness, or its style appeal mean little to a prospect until the effect of these features can be seen. As the salesperson gives the sales presentation, it is the satisfactions the product will or will not bring that enter the prospect's mind.

The salesperson's adoption of the prospect's point of view demands that the prospect be encouraged to do some of the talking during the sales interview. By intentionally arranging to do some listening, the salesperson ensures the prospect a chance to take part in the interview and to express opinions.

Prospect participation in the conversation helps the salesperson in several ways to understand and adopt the prospect's point of view. First, conversation helps the salesperson recognize early in the presentation the buying motives that seem dominant. Second, an unhampered exchange between prospect and salesperson can be had only if the prospect tells the salesperson what is needed. The prospect is encouraged to do this if the salesperson is tactful, receptive, and respectful of confidences. Third, the salesperson who listens to the prospect's ideas and opinions is held in high regard by the prospect; the prospect feels that the salesperson understands and respects the prospect's opinions. Fourth, by talking and listening, the salesperson keeps a close check on the prospect's thinking. The salesperson can tell what the prospect takes exception to and what is accepted. Finally, the prospect's comments provide the salesperson with clues, which enable the salesperson to adapt the sales story so as to personalize as much as possible.

SUMMARY

Salespeople must develop a plan for each sales call in order to maximize effectiveness. The preapproach consists of three major analyses: customer profile, sales call objectives, and customer benefit plan. The customer profile is background information about the prospect's personality, experience, attitudes, and problems. Sales call objectives help the salesperson measure his or her effectiveness, and the customer benefit plan refers to those features and benefits the salesperson needs to stress to this particular prospect. Sales presentations should focus on the prospect, not the product, and should actively involve the prospect. Thorough preapproaches lead to more sales calls of higher quality with better prospects.

Five buying decisions must be made before a customer will purchase: Is there a need? Will this product satisfy the need? Who is the best source for this product? Is the price acceptable? Is this the right time to buy?

KEY TERMS

empathy
mental states approach
preapproach
customer profile

sales call objectives
customer benefit plan
FAB sheet

REVIEW QUESTIONS

1. List the five mental states that salespeople lead prospects through to make a sale.
2. How can salespeople gain the prospect's interest?
3. What problem does the salesperson encounter in using the mental states approach?
4. What is the purpose of the preapproach?
5. What information is contained in the customer profile?
6. Where is the information from the customer profile obtained?
7. What guidelines should the salesperson consider when developing the sales call objectives?

8. What does "FAB" stand for?
9. How does the customer benefit plan help salespeople structure their presentations?
10. What type of information is contained in the product pamphlets given to their salespeople by many consumer packaged-goods manufacturers?
11. How do salespeople benefit from thorough preapproaches?
12. List the five buying decisions.
13. Is there a standard sequence of the five buying decisions?
14. Describe the "you" point of view.
15. Why should salespeople adopt the "you" point of view?

DISCUSSION QUESTIONS

1. You are a new sales representative for the Sunshine Company. Explain how you would go about developing a preapproach for a customer who has done regular business with your company for the past 20 years. Next, explain how you would develop a preapproach for a prospect who has never purchased from your company. How do the two situations differ in your development of the preapproach?
2. Review Table 8-1 for a couple of minutes. Notice that the Frito-Lay salesperson is selling to a retailer based on the benefits that the retailer would receive from reselling the potato chips. Now assume that you are the salesperson, and you are selling the potato chips door-to-door directly to the consumer. What benefits would the normal consumer receive from purchasing the potato chips?
3. Before any sale is made, the customer must answer "yes" to five buying decisions. How would you explain impulse purchases then, when a purchase is made practically on a whim with no real conscious decision making?

CASE 8-1   PICCADILLY CAFETERIAS, INC.*

This past week Brian Von Gruben, Executive Vice President and Director of Marketing, Piccadilly Cafeterias, Inc., attended the annual conference of the Chain Operator's Exchange, in Orlando, Florida. At that meeting he was the keynote speaker—his speech was on "Pitfalls in Serving the 55-Plus Market Segment." The speech focused on Piccadilly's marketing strategy for appealing to this fast-growing segment. Following his presentation there was a reception where he had the opportunity to talk to

---

*Case prepared by Brian Von Gruben. Used with permission.

many of the people attending the conference. One of those people was Ms. Sandy Franklin.

Ms. Franklin is a National Accounts Executive for Lamar Outdoor Advertising. Lamar Outdoor Advertising is a division of the Lamar Corporation, one of the largest independently owned outdoor advertising companies in the United States, with annual gross sales in excess of $75 million. The Lamar Outdoor Advertising Division serves more than 550 markets in 13 southeastern states. Its home office is in Baton Rouge, Louisiana.

Ms. Franklin joined Lamar Outdoor Advertising as an Account Executive a little over three years ago. At that time she was living in Lexington, Kentucky. She was quite successful in selling outdoor advertising for Lamar, and was recently promoted to her present position of National Accounts Executive. This promotion required a move to the home office in Baton Rouge. In this position, her responsibilities are to sell outdoor advertising to national accounts such as Procter & Gamble, R. J. Reynolds Tobacco, Brown-Forman Distilleries, and General Motors Corp. Sometimes she makes personal calls on these accounts, but most of the time she sells over the phone. She had wanted to call on Mr. Von Gruben since moving to Baton Rouge, and the chance to meet and talk with him informally at the conference seemed like a very lucky break.

During the conversation she gathered a great deal of information that she felt would be helpful in making a sales call on Mr. Von Gruben. Piccadilly Cafeterias is a chain comprised of more than 140 cafeterias. Its home office is in Baton Rouge, Louisiana, but their cafeterias are located in 13 southern states and California. Annual revenues were approximately $350 million in 1990. In addition to the cafeterias, the corporation also owns eight fine seafood restaurants in Texas and Louisiana, a seafood processing plant, and a construction company which designs and builds its new restaurants.

She also gathered information on the residential market within a three-mile radius of several Piccadilly Cafeteria locations (Exhibit 8-1). From this, she began to develop an estimate of the market by age group served by each location (labeled A, B, C, and D in the exhibit). For example, there are 89,611 people within three miles of location A. About .303 of these people are in the 18–28-year-old age groups, but only .023 frequent Piccadilly. So the 18–28-year-old market around location A numbers only about 624 people (.303 × .023 × 89,611).

All marketing programs, including most advertising campaigns, are planned by Mr. Von Gruben. The corporation does work with the Bauerline Advertising Agency of New Orleans, Louisiana, to plan and execute corporate-wide campaigns. Also, some advertising programs are suggested on a local level by the cafeteria managers, but they must be approved by the Regional Manager and the Director of Marketing. At

EXHIBIT 8-1
PICCADILLY CAFETERIAS INC. RESIDENTIAL MARKET
ESTIMATE FOR FOUR LOCATIONS

Proportion of Population by Age Group

Age Group	Cafeteria Locations			
	A	B	C	D
18-28	0.303	0.308	0.293	0.244
25-29	0.135	0.133	0.134	0.153
30-34	0.099	0.089	0.118	0.163
35-44	0.126	0.106	0.155	0.200
45-54	0.115	0.101	0.125	0.118
55+	0.222	0.263	0.175	0.122
Total	1.000	1.000	1.000	1.000

Proportion of Patronage by Age Group

Age Group	A	B	C	D
18-28	0.023	0.054	0.045	0.030
25-29	0.054	0.080	0.075	0.068
30-34	0.119	0.061	0.098	0.090
35-44	0.183	0.198	0.178	0.222
45-54	0.220	0.097	0.189	0.182
55+	0.401	0.510	0.415	0.408
Total	1.000	1.000	1.000	1.000
3-Mile Population	89,611	104,361	46,116	65,979

Market by Age Group

18-28	624
25-29	653
30-34	1,056
35-44	2,066
45-54	2,267
55+	7,977
Total	483,260

present, Piccadilly is using mostly newspaper and direct mail to communicate with its target customers, but they are also using some billboards and radio. During the next three months, Mr. Von Gruben will be coordinating the preparation of the annual corporate marketing plan.

CASE QUESTIONS

1. Using Lotus, determine which markets have the greatest potential. How could Ms. Franklin use this information to make a formal sales call on Piccadilly?
2. What other information did Ms. Franklin learn that could be useful in preparing to make a formal sales call on Piccadilly Cafeterias, Inc.?
3. What other types of information should she try to find out?

CASE 8-2   GULF COAST OFFSHORE SUPPLY AND SERVICES*

Raquel Cortez hung up the phone and frowned. She was worried. The purchasing manager for her best customer, Petrol Energy, Inc., had just called to advise Cortez that he was preparing to write a new supply agreement with a competitor on a six-month trial basis. Cortez had known for some time that a new competitor was trying to take away the Petrol account, but it was distressing to have the news confirmed.

GULF COAST OFFSHORE SUPPLY AND SERVICES

Raquel Cortez was the top salesperson for Gulf Coast Offshore Supply and Services, Inc. (GCOSS). GCOSS operated in a five-state area, supplying offshore and downhole-drilling operating companies with a variety of specialty repair and replacement parts for drilling platforms—fittings, gaskets, bearings, valves, and other parts. In the previous year GCOSS had generated revenues of $65 million. Petrol Energy was the largest single account of GCOSS with sales exceeding $8 million each year over the past six years. Raquel Cortez was the sole account representative for GCOSS at Petrol Energy. She felt that she had very carefully developed and nurtured the relationship between the two companies. Now, that relationship was in jeopardy.

THE OFFSHORE/DRILLING INDUSTRY

GCOSS enjoyed a reputation as a top supplier to the offshore drilling industry. Offshore drilling platforms are expensive to operate. Safety and continuity of operations are paramount since only a few hours of downtime can cost thousands of dollars in expenses and lost revenues. Consequently, a tradition of supplying repair parts and services on short notice had been established by reputable suppliers. GCOSS was considered to

---

*Case prepared by Chuck Nielson. Used with permission.

be one of the best. The company kept large local inventories of critical parts and material. As a distributor, they contracted only with manufacturers of the highest-quality products. GCOSS maintained contracts with helicopter transport companies for 24-hour, on-call delivery service. Company technical specialists were available from the headquarters of GCOSS for customer troubleshooting services.

Cortez used all these services in developing her majority supply position at Petrol Energy. She had studied Petrol's operations and installation and critical repair part requirements. She prided herself on knowing all the key operations personnel at Petrol's platform. She had also developed a very close relationship with the purchasing manager at Petrol, Jeff Boudreaux. When Boudreaux announced his retirement six weeks earlier, Cortez was not pleased. Boudreaux's replacement, Jesse Nugent, had been promoted into the purchasing manager's position from his operations job at a different location in another state. Cortez was just getting to know Nugent.

THE COMPETITION

For several years, Cortez had had to deal with only one competitor, Bradley Distributors. Bradley supplied not only the offshore and downhole-drilling segments of the oil industry, but pipeline and refinery operations as well. Bradley could not concentrate its services on the platform business as did GCOSS, and consequently was only a minor supplier to Petrol Energy. Boudreaux had traditionally given Bradley a 15-to-20-percent position to provide for back-up supply and, as he would jokingly tell Cortez, "to keep GCOSS honest."

However, six months earlier a major European offshore supply and services company, Consort, Ltd., announced their entry into the U.S. market. Consort stated that they intended to penetrate the Gulf Coast area first. A local manager had been hired and local warehouse and logistics operations were being established. They had advised several of Cortez's customers that their plan was to "beat out" GCOSS on price and secure a significant share of the Gulf Coast market. Cortez was certain that Consort was the competitor that Nugent intended to award the trial contract to.

All of these thoughts passed through Cortez's mind as she reviewed her sales strategy for the next day's meeting with Nugent. She knew she was up against a strong competitor and must have a well-thought-out sales plan before the meeting.

CASE QUESTIONS

1. Cortez believes she has established a strong base of goodwill at Petrol Energy. Do you think that she has? Why?

2. How will Cortez's goodwill benefit her in the current problem at Petrol Energy?

3. What should Cortez's sales plan be for her meeting with Nugent? Include in your answer a discussion of price, service/supply, her position regarding Consort, and how she might best approach Nugent, recognizing that their relationship is just getting started.

CASE 8-3   McDONALD REALTY*

Peggy Rogers has recently been promoted to district sales manager of an insurance firm and is in the process of relocating. Her husband, Jerry, has also found a position at the town's junior college. They have two school-age children and want to purchase a house rather than rent. A fellow salesperson referred Peggy to Donna Parker, a relatively new associate working with McDonald Realty.

Donna has not had a chance to meet with Peggy and Jerry prior to their appointment at 10:00 A.M., but has talked with Peggy over the phone. The sales presentation occurs as follows.

Peggy:	Donna?
Donna:	Yes, hello. You must be Peggy Rogers.
Peggy:	Yes, and this is my husband Jerry.
Donna:	Jerry, it's good to meet you. I hope you and Peggy had a good flight.
Peggy:	Yes, it went smoothly, but I'm really rushed for time. I have an appointment with my sales representatives at 11:30.
Donna:	I'd hoped that you would have more time to look at the houses that I have found. I'm sure you realize that buying a house is a complex process.
Peggy:	Of course, but today this is the most time I can allot. Jerry will go with you to look at the ones we agree interest us. We have already decided that he will do our preliminary screening and then I will go with him to look at the ones he really likes. I know that we can depend on you to locate just what we're looking for.
Donna:	Let's get right to work then. I've picked out five homes in the size and price range that you indicated were appropriate when I talked to you on the phone. Three of them are in the northern part of the city and the other two are in the eastern suburbs. That puts them within easy driving distance of Jerry's school and yet allows you to get to work easily.

*Case prepared by Jim Boles. Used with permission.

Jerry:	Good, let's see them.
Donna:	Well, first I want to show you pictures of them and give both of you some basic information. Some of these houses may not be what you are looking for and by doing this, we can eliminate them from the start and not waste time looking at them.
Jerry:	That makes sense.
Donna:	The first two homes are located in a subdivision near Park Heights School. Both of these are ranch-style homes with approximately 2,000 square feet of living area, three bedrooms, two baths, central air/heat, and a garage.
Jerry:	(Examining pictures of the homes) Those look good, don't they, Peggy?
Peggy:	Yes, they are attractive. Donna, what kind of schools are in that area for our children?
Donna:	(Referring to a city map) Well according to the map, East Heights Elementary, Byron Junior High School, and Washington Senior High are all located within two miles of the houses you are looking at.
Peggy:	Are those good schools?
Donna:	I really don't know. Are good schools important to you?
Jerry:	Oh yes. The quality of the schools will be the primary determinant of which house we purchase.
Peggy:	Which schools are the best in the area?
Donna:	Well, I really don't know. Let me show you the other houses and then, once you've found one you like I can check on the schools in that area.
Peggy:	If you remember our phone conversation, I clearly said that the quality of schools was very important to us.
Donna:	Everyone says that, but not many people are really that concerned. If the house they like is in an area with good schools great, if not, it's usually no big deal. Usually the location is not as important as the house.
Jerry:	For us, school quality is the important factor since both our children will be in school. Education is very important to our family. It's the one thing that people can always carry with them.
Peggy:	(Looking at her watch) Donna, I've got to go pretty soon. Instead of looking at the houses you have selected, why don't you find the best schools and then pick out some houses near those sites to show us. When you get a new list, contact me and we will come in one weekend and look at what is for sale in those areas. As we have told you, the quality of schools is the most important factor in the location of a house for our family.

Donna: Certainly, I'll get right on it and call you. I only wish my first
                list had been more acceptable. Would Thursday or Friday
                be a better day to catch you and set up an appointment to
                show you what I have found?

CASE QUESTIONS

1. What type of work has Donna already carried out, prior to meeting
    with Jerry and Peggy? Did she do enough? What else might she have
    done?
2. Who appears to be the key decision maker of the family? Is there one?
    Why do you say that?
3. Evaluate the planning that went into developing the list of houses to
    show.
4. The art of listening is critical in sales presentations and in dealing
    with customers. How did Donna fail in this area? If schools are al-
    ways mentioned as important, yet seldom enter into the final pur-
    chase decision, was Donna wrong in basically ignoring Peggy's
    statement that school quality was very important?
5. What would you do differently if you were the salesperson in this
    example?

PART 4

The Selling Process

CHAPTER 9

Securing and Opening the Sales Call—The Approach

After studying this chapter, you should be able to:

- Identify the problems involved in securing sales calls with prospects
- Relate what takes place in the approach
- Evaluate the importance of the first moments of sales calls
- Use the SPIN approach effectively to establish the prospect's need
- Point out common difficulties salespeople may experience on first calls

Having planned the sales presentation, the salesperson's next concern is to deliver it to the buyer for whom it was prepared. Before the presentation can be made, the salesperson naturally must meet with the buyer and must have permission from the buyer to make the presentation. The first portion of this chapter deals with securing the buyer's approval to meet and talk with the salesperson. Later parts of the chapter discuss techniques for getting the presentation off to a good start.

SECURING A SALES CALL

The chances of securing a sales call are improved if the salesperson (1) contacts the proper person in the organization, (2) selects the proper time to set up a sales call, (3) understands the importance of making appointments, and (4) is prepared to handle barriers to securing the sales call.

WHOM TO SEE IN A BUSINESS

For many kinds of selling, particularly in selling to ultimate consumers, the question of whom to see is readily answered. In many organizations the person to talk to is also easy to determine. For example, many industrial companies employ professional buyers called **purchasing agents**. Purchasing agents are highly visible within an industrial organization as the ones through whom the salesperson must pass in

THE SELLING PROCESS

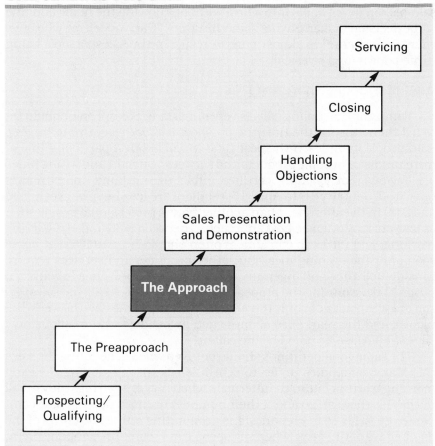

Figure 9-1 The *approach* is the third stage of the selling process.

order to get to the "real" decision makers. For most small orders, the purchasing agent is the only decision maker. In some business selling, however, identifying the proper person to be contacted in a certain business can pose a real problem. For example, does the credit manager of a corporation order the typewriters used in the credit department or does someone else order them? In other words, who is the real decision maker?

The salesperson naturally wants to deal with the person who has the most influence over the purchase of the product. This individual will be the one most interested in the advantages to be gained from making the purchase, will be more likely to take the time to hear the salesperson's presentation, either makes the decision or has strong influence on the decision, and is most able to grasp the benefits that will be gained from buying. The salesperson who has qualified prospects adequately should know the name of the person to contact for a sales call. The well-prepared salesperson never walks into a firm without knowing the name and title of the decision maker. Saying something like, "Can you tell me who buys your typewriters?" is almost sure to result in the salesperson's being turned down for a sales call.

WHEN TO SET UP A SALES CALL

Timing or scheduling calls is very important. Salespeople should try to tell their story at the time the prospect is most receptive to buying. Salespeople must learn the best time to call about a particular line of merchandise. For some products and services, the right and wrong times are obvious. For example, certified public accountants are extremely busy from January 15 to April 15; retailers are less busy between 1:00 and 3:00 in the afternoon than at other hours; professional people such as lawyers may often be best approached between 8:30 and 10:00 in the morning; and ultimate consumers often should be contacted at home soon after the evening meal. But other products and services require considerable time and ingenuity to determine the best time to contact a buyer. In determining the proper time to set up a sales call, the salesperson must consider not only the time of day but also the day, the week, the month, and the year. Special days such as holidays and religious holy days should also be noted before calling.

The same considerations should be given when scheduling the sales call. Many companies prefer to schedule salespeople during the early morning hours or late in the afternoon when they are getting ready to call it a day, so they can go about their business uninterrupted. Some companies go so far as to prepare signs designating only a few hours of the day, or days of the week, when salespeople may come on company premises to make presentations. The salesperson should always find out such regulations and make note of them in the customer files when doing the customer profile. Companies generally are more receptive to salespeople who adhere to the company's procedures. Salespeople, while noting all of these considerations, should also realize that they are providing the customer with important opportunities. Salespeople are entitled to see the buyer, and need not feel as though they are beggars.

MAKING APPOINTMENTS FOR SALES CALLS

Some salespeople find the selling-by-appointment technique impracticable, if not impossible. For instance, appointment making is not easily adaptable to house-to-house selling or selling in retail stores. In contrast, other salespeople sell only to people with whom they have appointments. For example, salespeople in the insurance field, missionary salespeople, and salespeople selling to purchasing agents almost always make appointments. Between these two extremes is a large group of salespeople who can, if they wish, make some use of appointments to see specific buyers. Undoubtedly, more salespeople can make profitable use of the appointment technique than do. Generally speaking, appointments are easier to arrange with customers than with prospects and are easier to arrange for subsequent calls on buyers than for first calls.

ADVANTAGES AND DISADVANTAGES OF MAKING APPOINTMENTS

Making appointments saves the salesperson's time and energy. Appointments reduce wasted activity and make it possible to obtain more interviews that are productive. The most significant advantage of making appointments is that an appointment helps get the actual sales interview off on firm footing. The buyer recognizes that the salesperson understands the value of the buyer's time. With an appointment, the salesperson is expected by the buyer and is more inclined to give the sales presentation a better hearing. By agreeing to an appointment, the buyer has agreed to listen courteously if not sympathetically to the salesperson.

Making appointments also benefits buyers. First, it gives the buyer greater latitude in seeing salespeople because calls can be scheduled so they will be most convenient. Buyers appreciate the salesperson's consideration in not wanting to interrupt them at inopportune moments. In addition, each buyer is allowed to get ready for a salesperson's visit. The buyer can do any surveying or checking needed, can have facts and questions ready, and can confer with other departments and arrange schedules as needed. These advantages are particularly helpful when the buyer is already a customer of the salesperson.

This technique of making appointments does have some disadvantages. Perhaps the most significant is the risk of refusal when the salesperson asks for an appointment. It is easier for buyers to refuse to see a salesperson who is calling or writing for an appointment than it is if the salesperson appears in person and asks to see the buyer. A second drawback is the possibility of being late for an appointment or not being able to keep the appointment at all. While a salesperson can telephone the customer if he or she will be late or cannot keep the appointment, the customer may not appreciate allocating time that could have been used for someone or something else.

SUGGESTIONS ON HOW TO MAKE APPOINTMENTS

A salesperson who intends to make appointments for interviews must decide whether to use direct mail, telephone calls, or face-to-face requests. It is always wise for the salesperson to review the prospect or customer file prior to asking for the appointment. This preparation allows the salesperson to target the "right" person for the call. Asking for the purchasing agent or buyer by name, rather than by title, gives the salesperson a greater chance for success.

One simple method of arranging appointments is to send an announcement card to buyers, giving the date of a forthcoming sales call. Supplementary literature may accompany the card. An example of an announcement card is shown in Figure 9-2. In a few cases, a mutual friend may make the appointment, although friends normally prefer to limit their cooperation to an introductory card or even to an anonymous identification of prospects. Regardless of the technique the salesperson uses to make appointments, those appointments made well in advance have a greater chance of success.

The right locale for a sales call can be especially beneficial for the salesperson. Scheduling the appointment for the salesperson's office enables the salesperson to avoid interruptions and offers the perfect setting to introduce the buyer to products, individuals, and facilities. The salesperson also may derive a psychological advantage from arranging the appointment in this manner. If the sales call is held at the salesperson's place of business, the buyer may be more inclined to join in the salesperson's way of thinking. The buyer's role as an invited guest may influence buying actions, as the buyer may feel a sense of obligation due to the salesperson's hospitality.

AN EXAMPLE OF AN ANNOUNCEMENT CARD

Sharon Forbes: 5/23/--

Just dropping you a note to let you know that I'll be in your area next Monday, May 30.

I hope that you'll be able to find about 15 to 20 minutes to meet with me to discuss our new Psychology textbook. How does 9:15 sound? I know that is your free period, and I will try to be quick so you will still have time to prepare for your next class.

I'll call Friday to verify this appointment with you. Look forward to seeing you next Monday. Thanks.

Patricia Venkman

Patricia Venkman
College Books, Inc.

Figure 9-2 Announcement cards can simplify the process of making appointments.

HIGHLIGHT 9-1

Roy Schwartz, in his article "Telephone Sales Tips" in the May 1987 edition of **The American Salesman,** *offers the following advice when calling for an appointment:*

For first time calls:

*The seven-second rule: **Get to the point quickly. Identify yourself, your company, and your reason for calling.**

*Imply existing relationship: **Use your precall analysis information to give the impression that you know the person and you belong.**

*Sincere request to help: **Be sincere in your desire to provide assistance.**

*Get rid of yourself: **Accomplish your objective, thank them for their time and get off.**

For subsequent calls:

*Summarize: **Save prospects the embarrassment of having forgotten their call to your company, or the discussions you have had already.**

Salespeople can improve their efficiency dramatically by making frequent use of the telephone. The telephone has become such a vital tool to the sales profession that many companies are installing cellular phones in their sales representatives' cars. This allows salespeople to stay in constant contact with their buyers and the sales office. Should the salesperson be stuck on the road, a quick call to let the buyer know may save a customer. Salespeople also can call to confirm that the buyer has not forgotten their appointment before they make the trip to the buyer's location. Finally, salespeople can make appointments for later in the week while traveling between calls. In this way, salespeople increase their efficiency and make more calls, which should result in increased productivity.

HANDLING BARRIERS

People who have the responsibility of seeing that the prospect's time is not wasted are known as **barriers**. Barriers are supposed to stop salespeople when it appears that such salespeople will not be beneficial to the company and/or the buyer. Sometimes the barrier has reasonable evidence that the salesperson would not be beneficial—if the company does not have a need for the product, for example, or has recently committed to another product. Other times, the barrier's decision may be purely judgmental. Switchboard operators, receptionists, secretaries, junior employees, partners, and even family members can be barriers. The most frequent excuses for not allowing the salesperson to see the prospect are that the prospect is not interested, not open to buy, or not available. After being stopped, the salesperson may or may not be asked to leave sales literature or to call again.

The job of barriers is to bar only the salespeople who do not qualify for some of the prospect's time. Barriers are instructed to admit any salesperson whose product or service would probably benefit the prospect. For example, a pharmaceutical representative trying to present a line of prescription drugs to a doctor must first go through the receptionist, and then through the nurse. The salesperson's job is to present the company's products to the buyer, who in this case is the doctor who prescribes the drugs. Usually, the only way this salesperson will get any time from the doctor is if the nurse has recommended the salesperson to the doctor. This will not happen if the salesperson has been rude and condescending to the receptionist and/or nurse, or has used "bully" tactics to get into the doctor's office. Therefore, the salesperson should always spend a little time developing and cultivating a relationship with these barriers, in order to get on their "good side."

The following six techniques are proven ways of handling barriers with positive results: (1) delivering a requested item, (2) depending on the company's prestige, (3) revealing something of the mission, (4) providing a benefit, (5) using a "referred" lead, and (6) being confident in expecting cooperation. Although these techniques will be helpful, nothing is more basic or more effective than collecting and analyzing as much information as possible about the prospect. The more information the salesperson has in advance, the better the chance of seeing the prospect. No tricks are warranted in gaining admission to see the prospect. Such tricks are often resented, usually remembered, and often damaging to the salesperson's chances of making a sale.

DELIVERING A REQUESTED ITEM

If the prospect has written to the salesperson's company for product information or product samples, the salesperson can deliver the requested item and use it to get in to see the prospect.

DEPENDING ON THE COMPANY'S PRESTIGE

Some highly prestigious companies instruct their salespeople to start the request for the interview with a statement such as, "My name is Patricia Lewis, and I am the local sales representative for Holland Enterprises." These companies feel that the mention of the company name frequently is sufficient to ensure getting some of the prospect's time.

REVEALING SOMETHING OF THE MISSION

When a barrier is particularly difficult to overcome, a salesperson may find it necessary to reveal part of the sales mission to the barrier in order to see the prospect. However, the salesperson should guard against making too much of the sales presentation to the barrier.

PROVIDING A BENEFIT

Another approach with a particularly difficult barrier is to provide a benefit to a barrier or buyer, or both. This may be as simple as convincing the barrier that the product/service is so beneficial the buyer will be pleased with the barrier for admitting the salesperson, or it may involve a free sample, a coupon, or a small gift. The salesperson must be careful to avoid giving the impression that anything unethical is involved here.

USING A REFERRED LEAD

Another useful method of handling a barrier may be through the use of a "referred" lead. This involves letting the barrier know that someone referred them to the buyer. To work, the referred lead clearly must be someone the buyer knows and respects.

BEING CONFIDENT IN EXPECTING COOPERATION

One of the best ways of overcoming barriers is to exhibit a good appearance and a confident, pleasant manner. If the salesperson looks and acts professional the chances are the salesperson will receive an appointment. The salesperson's obvious conviction in the product or service is the best assurance of making it past the barrier.

THE APPROACH

The approach refers to the first few minutes the salesperson is in the buyer's office. The salesperson must greet the potential buyer, and initiate the sales call. The approach determines how receptive the prospect will be to the sales presentation, and any future calls or presentations, and how difficult or easy the close will be.

There are several different ways the salesperson can "approach" the customer. This section of the chapter will first consider a *tailored approach* versus a *standard approach*. Next, the *SPIN approach* is described. Then the basic principles of an effective approach are reviewed, and finally, items which should be checked just prior to opening the interview are listed.

TAILORED VERSUS STANDARD APPROACH

A **tailored approach** is one designed specifically for the selling situation and the prospect. A **standard approach** is a single approach used with all prospects.

All salespeople should recognize the advantages and limitations of both the tailored and the standard approach. There are strong arguments supporting the use of both techniques. The tailored approach is generally favored because no single approach fits all prospects and all selling situations, particularly when considerable differences exist among prospect groups. Also, no single approach fits the personality of every salesperson.

Supporters of the standard approach, however, feel that it is more effective because it has been carefully developed, tested, and proved. The standard approach tends to produce more uniform and predictable results. This approach is more beneficial to inexperienced salespeople because it reduces the chances of their making mistakes in attempting to tailor the opening of the sales presentation.

Each salesperson will probably want to experiment with tailored and standard approaches to discover which works best under certain conditions. It may be desirable to develop a single "best" approach for each prospect classification. If it is decided to use a standard approach, the salesperson should have prepared at least one service approach and one selling approach. The service approach begins with the offer of a favor to the prospect in the hope of obtaining goodwill so that the sales presentation can be made later. In the selling approach, the salesperson begins the sales presentation immediately after contacting the prospect by stressing the product's features and how the product can benefit the prospect. The selling approach is most effective when the salesperson knows the prospect.

MULTIPLE QUESTION APPROACH

In addition to the tailored or standard approaches, some salespeople use a third approach, referred to as the **multiple question approach**. This approach combines both the tailored and standard approaches to provide the salesperson with a framework of questions that can be tailored to each individual prospect. Multiple question approaches utilize a series of questions, usually to confirm the precall analysis or to substantiate the salesperson's reason for being there. One multiple question approach that is used by Xerox is the **SPIN approach**.

SPIN stands for **S**ituation, **P**roblem, **I**mplication, and **N**eed, and relies on asking a series of questions to (1) put the customer into a situation, (2) determine what problem the customer has, (3) show the negative implications of the problem, and (4) establish a need in the customer's mind. The sales psychology in using this approach is that once the salesperson has established a need in the customer's mind, the product or service can be introduced as the solution to the customer's need. It is imperative that the salesperson not mention the product during the SPIN, because until a need has been established in customers' minds, they are likely to discount the product as something they do not need.

The following dialogue is an example of the SPIN approach being used by a salesperson for a national advertising firm:

Salesperson:	Mrs. Johnson, I understand you are currently using a local firm for your advertising, is this true? **(Situation)**
Prospect:	Why, yes. We are using the firm of Wilson, Wilson, and Wilson.
Salesperson:	Since you contacted our company, I assume you are not satisfied with their work. What problems are you having? **(Problem)**
Prospect:	Well, I just feel that their work is too narrow-minded for us.
Salesperson:	Why is this a problem? **(Implication)**
Prospect:	The image they have developed for us is just too "small-town." It's not creative at all!
Salesperson:	Mrs. Johnson, it sounds to me like you need a large, national advertising firm that can provide you with creative ideas, and can develop a fresh, innovative image for your company. **(Need)**
Prospect:	Well, you may be right. Tell me a little something about your company.

The salesperson is now ready to introduce the company's advertising expertise as the solution for this prospect's problem.

PRINCIPLES OF AN EFFECTIVE APPROACH

Regardless of whether a tailored approach or a standard approach is used, the salesperson should follow certain principles during a sales call. The salesperson should make maximum use of advance information, never call "just to be calling," ask questions if necessary, secure control at the beginning of the interview, keep in step with the prospect, observe the law of self-interest, promise the buyer a benefit early, show sincere interest in the prospect's welfare, and be personable. Each of these principles is discussed in the following sections.

Figure 9-3 Many sales are made or lost during the approach. The sales-person must take charge early and command the prospect's attention.

MAKE MAXIMUM USE OF ADVANCE INFORMATION

A salesperson who knows the needs and goals of the prospect and recognizes these in the sales approach will be more apt to receive approval to tell the complete sales story. The prospect, seeing that individual buying circumstances have been considered, is inclined to listen to the entire presentation. (Methods for acquiring advance information were reviewed in Chapter 7, Prospecting and Qualifying.)

NEVER CALL "JUST TO BE CALLING"

There should be a definite reason and a definite goal for each call. The salesperson should start moving toward that goal from the first moment.

ASK QUESTIONS IF NECESSARY

In many cases, the salesperson will need data that was unavailable prior to the sales call. Thus, the salesperson will find it helpful to ask tactful questions. It is not enough just to ask questions, though. The salesperson also must listen actively to the buyer's responses, for it is the prospect who often tells the salesperson exactly what is wanted.

SECURE CONTROL AT THE BEGINNING OF THE SALES CALL

The salesperson wants to secure control of the sales presentation and to hold that control throughout the visit. The approach should connote authority, but the salesperson must be subtle in attempting to lead the prospect to the desired way of thinking.

KEEP IN STEP WITH THE PROSPECT

The salesperson's thinking and conversation must be synchronized with both the direction and the speed of the prospect's thinking. The salesperson keeps in step with the prospect by listening and observing nonverbal communications, and by responding appropriately.

OBSERVE THE LAW OF SELF-INTEREST

All prospects are motivated by self-interest. For this reason, the salesperson should do and say those things that will appeal to the prospect.

PROMISE THE BUYER A BENEFIT EARLY

Prospects listen only to those salespeople who promise advantages to them, so the salesperson wants to appear immediately as one who will help the prospect in some way.

SHOW SINCERE INTEREST IN THE PROSPECT'S WELFARE

One of the best ways to gain acceptance is to have and demonstrate a sincere interest in being of assistance to the prospect. The salesperson can indicate by attitude and expression a desire to know the prospect better in order to be of greater assistance.

BE PERSONABLE

The salesperson should strive to be easy to talk to and pleasantly mannered throughout the approach and, later, the sales presentation. The salesperson should be mindful of the prospect's feelings and ideas and should approach the prospect with understanding. The salesperson does this by showing empathy for the prospect.

CREATE AN IMAGE

Salespeople should try to establish an image for themselves and their company either through their appearance—the way they carry themselves—or the way present themselves and their materials. The salesperson does this through proper attire, posture, and professionalism. Figure 9-4 demonstrates how salespeople can use words to create an image.

CREATING AN IMAGE WITH WORDS

Whether you are talking about your product, your profession, your competition, or yourself makes no difference. The words you use conjure up images in the minds of prospects. The words you use will either turn them on or turn them off.

"Cheap"	Do you mean to say least expensive or worst quality? *Inexpensive* may be a better word for you to use.
"This stuff"	No salesperson sells "stuff" and no customer buys "stuff." The salesperson should show more respect for the product by identifying exactly what it is.
"This racket of mine"	Is this an appropriate description for your profession? Salespeople create their own image by building status into their position.

If there is to be any downgrading of the competition, let the prospect initiate it. Avoid the use of Hollywood-type superlatives. Avoid verbosity.

Source: Russell Jacobs, "Words That Turn Prospects Off," *The American Salesman* 31 (June 1986): 16.

Figure 9-4 Using the wrong words can create an unfavorable impression.

THE SALESPERSON'S FINAL CHECK

Four matters deserve a final check by the salesperson as part of the approach: physical appearance, mental attitude, equipment and supporting materials, and the plan for the sales call.

PHYSICAL APPEARANCE

The first 30 to 60 seconds of a sales call often determine the outcome of that call. Thus, it is essential that the prospect's immediate reaction to the salesperson be favorable. Everyone tends to judge strangers on the basis of first impressions. If a salesperson's physical appearance does not impress the prospect, it is difficult for the buying proposal to do so.

MENTAL ATTITUDE

The outlook the salesperson should maintain in leading up to the presentation should be one of optimistic confidence. The salesperson must expect to be received courteously and listened to with interest. The prospect's business is very important to the salesperson; therefore, the prospect should be made to feel important.

EQUIPMENT AND SUPPORTING MATERIALS

Whatever the salesperson needs in the way of equipment and supporting materials should be checked before the presentation begins. This may consist of vital facts and figures, diagrams, pictures, product samples, testimonials, price lists, an advertising portfolio, or contract forms. Salespeople naturally will want to have at hand all the equipment and materials needed, though they should hold down the bulk as much as possible. All equipment and materials should be arranged for quick reference and easy handling. If there is any special equipment intended for a particular prospect, the salesperson should give this special attention.

PLAN FOR THE SALES CALL

A final item to be checked is the plan for the sales call. The salesperson should intend to make every minute count toward achieving the objective of turning the prospect into a customer. The salesperson should review what seem to be the best buying motives to appeal to, the best procedure to use in doing this, the buying proposal to make, the points which should be stressed, the proof to be offered, the prices to be quoted, and the time to ask for the order.

SELLING IS SOLVING BUYERS' PROBLEMS

When planning a sales call, the salesperson should be thinking as a problem solver. Of fundamental concern should be identifying buyers' problems and then working with the buyers toward solving them. Salespeople should communicate this concern to buyers promptly.

The first step in problem solving is to wonder if (or sense that) something is not right. This kind of thinking—observing the present state of affairs—leads one to the gathering of facts. The salesperson's first responsibility is to determine the nature of the problem about which the buyer makes buying decisions.

Once the problem is established, the problem solver (salesperson) tries to analyze and classify the problem, by defining it, limiting it, and clarifying it. The salesperson tries to evaluate what the buyer will gain from solving the problem.

The next step demands creativity on the part of the problem solver. Here the salesperson develops a number of possible ways to solve the problem. The salesperson estimates the time each solution would require and its cost. Good salespeople identify many problems and develop many alternative solutions.

Of course the prospect expects only the best solution, not a group of them. Therefore, after comparing the solutions (maybe experimenting

HIGHLIGHT 9-2

The approach one Fortune 500 company teaches in its sales-person orientation course is described below:

The first few moments in the prospect's business are the most criti-cal. The interest and imagination of the prospect must be captured in this short span of time. One must appeal to the prospect's inter-ests by first discussing general benefits that are synonymous with improved business practices, then relating these benefits to the company's system.

The course also advises salespeople to use company literature, tes-timonials, and past experiences to lend credibility to their claims. Salespeople must be aware of signals given by the prospect that show interest or skepticism. If the prospect is interested, the sales-person must maintain the prospect's positive frame of mind. If the prospect is skeptical, the salesperson must stop and reinforce his or her credibility.

Other approach tips used by the company include:

- *Displaying a keen interest in whatever the prospect says or does.*
- *Being a good listener.*
- *Allowing the prospect the opportunity to speak freely.*
- *Being patient, and sometimes accepting an interim objective in order to have another opportunity to achieve the final objectives.*

with two or three), the salesperson discards those not worthy of con-sideration and, from what remains, selects the best one as the winner.

The final step is the verification. The selected solution is tested and results are evaluated.

THE FIRST MOMENTS OF THE PRESENTATION

Salespeople should begin to control the selling situation within the first few seconds. Salespeople must be leaders, and guide prospects toward a purchasing decision that will help the prospect. Control is secured most easily when the salesperson makes the call a gesture of sincere, personal interest, and identifies that the intent of the call is to discuss the benefits of the products/services with the prospect, rather than forcing these benefits on the prospect.

SURVEYING THE SELLING SITUATION

The first phase of surveying the selling situation involves sizing up the prospect. This early appraisal will help to guide the rest of the sales call. The salesperson observes the prospect to gain clues as to what type of person the prospect is and what the prospect is thinking. Throughout the entire call, the trained, alert salesperson will continue to follow the prospect's reactions as they are expressed in looks, tone of voice, and actions.

The second phase of the survey involves the quick inspection of physical surroundings when the sales call is at the prospect's home or place of business. External elements can be indicators of important matters such as purchasing power, tastes, interests, and needs.

The third phase of the survey is to determine as quickly and accurately as possible what the prospect really needs. This will help to identify the prospect's buying problems.

THE SALESPERSON'S ATTITUDE

A salesperson must be relaxed and confident. Good salespeople have many reasons for feeling confident. They know what their company has done and is doing. They know how their product has helped other buyers in the past. They know that they have made themselves experts in solving prospects' problems. These salespeople are not fearful or timid, because they know more about their product than the prospects do. They have a sincere belief in the ability of their company, their product, and themselves to help their prospects.

Viewed from another angle, good salespeople have a positive attitude that assumes they will be welcome, that their story will be heard, that their prospects will realize the desirability of the product, and that a purchase will be made. These are the assumptions that prevent the salesperson from being defeated before going in.

By inviting and inspiring the confidence of prospects, the salesperson puts prospects in the mood to discuss and explain their problems. This often must be done before the salesperson can attempt to ascertain a prospect's needs. Prospects must have confidence in the salesperson and the salesperson's propositions before they are accepted. Prospects must feel that the salesperson is both honest and well informed.

THE INTRODUCTION

When first meeting the prospect, most salespeople state their name and the name of their company. This constitutes a formal introduction. In some selling situations, however, salespeople may give only their company's name and not their own. Salespeople who make house-to-house calls, for example, might not use a formal introduction. The formal introduction can also be dispensed with when salespeople are calling to generate, retain, or increase goodwill or when their company's identity is more significant than their own. Every salesperson needs to establish a feeling of friendliness and confidence. The introduction should be adapted to the type of prospect, the type of sale, or the image of the salesperson's company. The formal introduction, for instance, is straightforward and allows the prospect to concentrate on what the salesperson has to say instead of wondering who the salesperson is.

CAPTURING THE PROSPECT'S ATTENTION

The prospect must be attentive to understand the full significance of the salesperson's presentation. The salesperson must have the prospect's undivided attention to obtain and hold control of the sales call. If the prospect tunes in to the salesperson's message and grasps the meaning of what the salesperson has to say, then the salesperson has the prospect's attention.

Having secured the prospect's attention, the salesperson is next ready to gain the prospect's interest. This is done by relating the product to one of the prospect's needs, problems, or hopes. As the salesperson promotes the prospect's self-interest, the prospect becomes an attentive listener to the salesperson's story, becoming curious enough about the salesperson's product to hear the salesperson. Indeed, the prospect feels that both the visit and the salesperson's proposal are important.

PRINCIPLES OF OPENING THE CONVERSATION

One of the first things to remember in opening the selling conversation is that it is generally undesirable to ask specifically for permission to tell the complete sales story. For example, a salesperson might need a minimum of 45 minutes to make a complete presentation, yet the prospect would probably refuse to allow that much time if the salesperson asked for it. The best procedure in most cases is to begin the sales story, then sell the prospect on the desirability of listening to the whole story only if the prospect tries to shut the salesperson off.

After the first few sentences, the salesperson should pause to gauge the prospect's reaction. If there has been no comment, or if the prospect has given a polite and obviously formal comment, interest has not been aroused. If the reaction is clearly good or bad, the salesperson can judge what action to take next.

EXAMPLES OF OPENING REMARKS

Some salespeople have more or less standard opening remarks that they use with certain types of prospects. These standardized remarks are particularly helpful for cold calls when the salesperson has little or no information about the prospect. A refinement of this technique is to have a predetermined set of opening remarks for each prospect type and to vary these remarks only as suggested by the conditions encountered at the meeting. Some examples of ways to open a sales presentation are shown in Figure 9-5.

WAYS OF OPENING THE SALES CALL

1. Show the prospect something immediately and begin talking about it.
   "Have you seen our new plastic container? It's guaranteed not to break."
2. Render some free service to the prospect, and let that favor be the basis for opening a conversation. This can be done easily by salespeople who sell to retailers, and often no authorization or permission will be needed. Where the prospect must approve in advance, the offer of the service or favor can be the opener.
   "Here, let me clean those glasses for you. Have you considered prescription sunglasses?"
3. Point out current conditions which your product can be helpful in improving.
   "I notice the new department head is in favor of using PC-compatibles."
4. If a single buying motive is obviously predominant, appeal to it in the opening remark.
   "I realize the main feature you are interested in is performance. Well, here are the test results showing our product out-performing all the others."
5. Ask the prospect a question. Tactful questioning is permissible, particularly for determining a prospect's needs. If questions are to be used, however, certain rules should be observed. Do not apologize for asking the questions. Do not ask too many questions. Ask personal questions only when they are absolutely necessary. Do not ask for information the prospect can't supply. Do not collect vague, general information, because it is of little or no value. As was shown by the multiple question approach and SPIN, questions can be a very good method of gathering information and convincing prospects of their needs.
   "Sir, may I ask you why you are dissatisfied with your current supplier?"
6. Relate a case history which may point out either something the prospect wants or wants to avoid.
   "Let me show you what we were able to provide XYZ Company with for their Christmas party."

7. Where the prospect has requested something from the salesperson's company or made a request of the salesperson on the last call, the conversation can be opened in the following manner:
    "Ms. Smith, here is the textbook you requested. While I am here, let me show you our new workbook that accompanies that text."

Among the worst, absolutely inexcusable openers are these:

"Hot enough for you?"
"About ready to give us some business?"
"What's new?"
"What do you know?"
"How's business?"
"I would like to interest you in a money-making proposition."
"Just happened to be out this way and thought I'd drop in."

Figure 9-5 The opening statement is crucial to the success of the approach.

After each sales call, salespeople should evaluate the success of the opening remarks. In this way, they can learn which openers were most effective and which should be avoided in the future.

COMMON FIRST CALL DIFFICULTIES

One common difficulty encountered by salespeople on first calls to prospects is the prospect's natural fear of strangers. Uneasiness in the presence of a stranger may make prospects suspicious, particularly if they have been the victim of some unethical salesperson in the past.

A second difficulty is that of getting a full hearing. Thirty minutes may be needed to make the presentation, yet only ten are granted. What should a salesperson do when the time a prospect specifically allots is obviously insufficient? The salesperson may feel forced to spend at least part of the time allotment in "selling" the value of a longer interview. Seldom can a 30-minute story be condensed into 10 minutes and still be effective. If the needed time cannot be granted at the moment, the salesperson should ask for another appointment. This indicates that the salesperson means business, and the prospect may reconsider and grant the full amount of time.

Prospects who say they are busy pose another problem. In this case, the salesperson must earn some of the prospect's time, which is often best achieved by offering helpful ideas and suggestions or something of value to the buyer. For example, when selling to middlemen, offering merchandising ideas is especially helpful. Salespeople should check the displays, stock arrangements, selling techniques, advertising, and sales

HIGHLIGHT 9-3   *What Buyers Dislike*

In a recent study, buyers and purchasing agents were asked, "What do you most dislike in the general manner of any salesperson who has called on you?" The following responses were among those given by the buyers surveyed.

One salesperson was too darn nonchalant. His lounging, slouching manner seemed to imply he didn't think I was a particularly important person.

Her eyes were shifty and evasive. I didn't like the way she kept them narrowly slitted.

One salesperson's eyes were unfocused and dreamy. I didn't like their blank stare. I didn't like the phony smile. It was either a forced smile . . . or the kind of a half-smile you see on the face of a baby about to have a gas burp.

That particular salesperson's whole manner was that of an order hawk rather than of someone sincerely trying to help me. I got the impression that getting an order from me meant he was adding another scalp to his belt.

I didn't like the bored, impatient way the salesperson listened when I talked. Her manner seemed to say: "For heaven's sake, will you ever pipe down and let a smart person talk."

I didn't like the liberties he took, like placing a soiled hat on my papers, balancing a lighted cigarette on the edge of my desk . . . and then, later on, knocking the ashes off into the little jar that holds my paper clips. I didn't like the pompous, bombastic way in which he orated his sales talk.

He fingered his lips as he talked, so his words sounded like someone drinking coffee out of a moustache cup.

I didn't like the presumptuous, back-slapping way the salesperson breezed into my office and took the initiative in shaking my hand.

The salesperson's manner implied he was a wiser, better man than I am.

She was full of nervous mannerisms that distracted my attention.

I didn't like the salesperson's obvious attempts at flattery.

The salesperson's manner was too oily, too clever. My reaction was: "I don't want to play poker with this city slicker!"

She was too synthetically pleasant. I like salespeople to be sunny but I don't want to get freckled.

promotion of each merchant they call on in search of good ideas that they can pass along to other prospects.

Sometimes prospects who say they are busy are merely stalling. To minimize this, salespeople should have a businesslike manner, which shows they value both their time and that of their prospects. If a prospect really is too busy, the salesperson should try to make a later appointment. When the prospect is preoccupied, the salesperson's story obviously is not going to register. Thus, the salesperson should offer to return and should sell the prospect on the desirability of having proper conditions for the sales presentation.

A fourth common difficulty centers on prospects who sincerely claim they are not interested. The salesperson must remember that each prospect is interested in something. The task is to find the prospect's most important buying motives. In cases of uncertainty, the salesperson can sometimes ask for a few minutes in which to determine whether the product can be of any aid and, consequently, of any interest to the prospect.

It is inexcusable to be arrogant or impertinent in the face of disinterest on the part of the prospect. Once in a while it might be permissible to meet this type of resistance with an aggressive, independent attitude, but that is a risky course to follow.

SUMMARY

Securing a sales call is more likely if the proper person is contacted at the right time through an appointment with proper handling of barriers. Salespeople should contact the person who has the most influence in making the purchasing decision. Prospects use barriers to ensure time is not wasted and prefer appointments set by direct mail, telemarketing, or face-to-face requests.

The approach refers to the first minute or two of the sales call. The first impression the salesperson makes can determine the success or failure of the sales call. Physical appearance, positive mental attitude, and a carefully developed sales call plan are all vital for "getting one's foot in the door."

Tailored approaches are preferred over standard approaches because they are more personalized. The multiple question approach uses standardized questions that are tailored to each prospect. The SPIN is one such approach.

Common objections during the approach are that the prospect is not interested, is busy, or does not like to deal with strangers. The salesperson must overcome any objections and should try to control the sales call from start to finish.

KEY TERMS

purchasing agent   standard approach
barrier   SPIN approach
tailored approach   multiple question approach

REVIEW QUESTIONS

1. Which person in an organization should be sought for a presentation?
2. List three advantages of appointments.
3. How should the salesperson prepare for making an appointment?
4. What are some of the devices used to make appointments?
5. What is a barrier?
6. Why are tailored approaches generally preferable to standardized approaches?
7. What does SPIN stand for?
8. Why is it wise for the salesperson to ask questions and listen actively during the approach?
9. What should the salesperson check before beginning the presentation?
10. What are the five steps in problem solving?
11. What are the six principles for opening the conversation?
12. How can the salesperson capture the prospect's attention quickly?
13. What are some typical first call problems?

DISCUSSION QUESTIONS

1. You are trying to call on a person you know is a prospect for your product. However, the prospect's secretary will not give you the time of day. In fact, the secretary will not even ask if the prospect wants to see you. How do you reach that prospect?
2. You are a sales representative for Cellular One car phone company. Your friend, a computer salesperson, is angry. She has lost sales because her office was unable to reach her on the road. She wants you to approach her boss with the idea of installing a cellular phone into each sales representative's company car so that salespeople can be contacted when customers need them. Develop a set of SPIN questions to establish this need in her boss's mind.
3. Give three examples of prospects with whom it would be desirable to obtain an appointment. Give three examples of prospects with whom it would not be desirable to obtain an appointment. Explain why you put each prospect into its respective category.

CASE 9-1 GULF SOUTH PAPER*

Gulf South Paper is a distributor of paper and plastic products in a four-state market. Gulf South commands a strong market share and presence with a sales force of 24 representatives. Andy Johnson, the General Manager and part-owner of Gulf South, recently committed his company to sell 500,000 pounds of a new paper container for the upcoming fiscal year. The new product is a dense-bodied paper capable of withstanding temperatures of 400° F for 45 minutes as well as being microwaveable. Since almost any size container can be made, this new container would be ideal for restaurant takeouts. Mr. Johnson shared this commitment with his sales manager, David Bruce, and asked for an all-out blitz of the marketplace to ensure movement of this revolutionary product. Like most innovations, this new paper container would cost almost twice as much as paper containers currently available.

First thing Monday morning, David Bruce began his usual sales meeting by explaining the details of this new product to his sales force. To help push this new product the company is offering an incentive bonus to the salesperson with the highest sales volume for this product in the upcoming month.

Bill James, Gulf South's top salesperson, listened carefully as he thought of his number-one customer, Swanson's. Swanson's is a family-style restaurant operating 100 stores in a seven-state market. The daily average of sit-down meals is 800 per store as well as 150 takeout meals. Bill's mission was clear: create a need for this new paper container within Swanson's and he would be a shoo-in for the sales promotion bonus. Bill already sold Swanson's all of their paper products, including napkins, paper cups and containers, plastic takeout bags, styrofoam containers, and some cleaning products.

Bill arranged a meeting with Roberta Gavel, Purchasing Agent for Swanson's. The meeting couldn't have come at a more opportune time because Roberta had just been asked by Swanson's president to come up with a new takeout bag. Excited about the opportunity, Bill emphatically began to sell—pointing out to Roberta how Gulf South was going to revolutionize Swanson's takeout business. Roberta patiently listened to Bill but she knew that they really needed to talk about the takeout bag. Finally Roberta interrupted, stressing that maybe down the road Swanson's could look more closely at the container, but right now she was interested in having a new takeout bag designed to open flat on the bottom as well as being printed with Swanson's newly designed three-color logo. She further stressed that she needed prices as soon as possible.

---

*Case prepared by Henry Fourrier. Used with permission.

Roberta also asked about a dispenser to hold cups for a new soft-serve ice cream product Swanson's was introducing company-wide.

When Roberta was finished, Bill acknowledged her requests concerning the takeout bags and dispensers and ended on a final note concerning the new takeout container. After leaving, Bill tried to figure out where he failed on his presentation of the new takeout container because Swanson's didn't order any. Disappointed, he approached his sales manager David Bruce with the dilemma. They both decided it would be best to visit the plant in Chicago where this new product was manufactured to learn as much as they could so they could create a need within Swanson's.

As the week went by, Roberta Gavel was catching heat from Swanson's president because there still was no new takeout bag or any price information. Swanson's was preparing this year's budget and wanted a newly designed takeout bag as long as prices were not too high. A small increase in price would definitely impact profits when ordering 5 million bags. Roberta had been calling Bill for days but he still had not returned her calls. Despite her loyalty to Bill James and Gulf South's excellent track record of service, Roberta called another source. The representative was at Swanson's three hours later with a prototype of the new bag and prices for production and printing. When ordered in the large quantity which Swanson's required, the new bag could be purchased from the new supplier for about the same cost as the old bag. For the good of Swanson's and the security of her job, Roberta placed the order for the new takeout bag with the new source.

The following Monday, Bill James showed up at Swanson's with several of the new paper containers and a briefcase of information on how Swanson's could benefit from this innovation. When he was done, he told Roberta that he would have prices and a prototype for the new bag by the end of the week. At that time Roberta informed Bill that he had lost the contract for Swanson's takeout bags. Naturally, Bill left dejected and angry at Roberta.

Bill felt the new bag he carried might save Roberta three cents off the existing bag cost and that the new bag she adopted might cost as much as three cents above the existing cost. Using a profit analysis (below) as a base, Bill wanted to show the profit impact of these changes over 150 takeout meals a day at 100 stores, 365 days a year. For example, under the existing bag price (eight cents per bag), the organization made more than $14.3 million a year profit from takeout meals (based on 150 meals at 100 stores for 365 days a year).

EXHIBIT 9-1
GULF SOUTH PAPER PROFIT ANALYSIS
FOR TAKE-OUT MEALS

	Existing Bag Price	3 Cents Less Per Bag	3 Cents More Per Bag	6 Cents More Per Bag
Average Price/Meal	$6.95	$6.95	$6.95	$6.95
Cost of Ingredients	$2.15	$2.15	$2.15	$2.15
Labor	$0.95	$0.95	$0.95	$0.95
Package (bag)	$0.08	————	————	————
Allocated Overhead	$1.15	$1.15	$1.15	$1.15
Total Cost/Meal	$4.33	$4.25	$4.25	$4.25
Average Profit/ Meal	$2.62	————	————	————
Annual Profit From Meals	$14,344,500			
Profit Impact of Bags	————	————	————	————

CASE QUESTIONS

1. Who should Bill be angry at?
2. What could Bill have done differently?
3. What is the one thing, as a salesperson, Bill forgot to do?
4. At what point did Bill go astray?
5. Using Lotus, complete Bill's table showing the impact of his bag (at three cents less per bag), the competitor's bag (at three cents more), and a situation where the bag cost six cents more. Show annual profits for the total organization (i.e., from 150 meals at 100 stores for 365 days) and profit impact of each alternative compared to the existing bag price.
    Given these results:
    • What arguments should Bill make?

CHAPTER 10
Making the Sales Presentation

After studying this chapter, you should be able to:

■ Discuss the psychology of each sales call from the salesperson's point of view

■ Explain the types of sales presentations and their advantages and disadvantages

■ Compare the types of sales presentations and determine in what situations each should be used

■ Trace the advantage-proof-action sequence for telling a sales story

■ Summarize six useful types of proof

■ Explain some of the difficulties encountered when making sales presentations

This chapter looks at the sales presentation through the eyes of salespeople; their objectives, tactics, techniques, and strategies, and the reasons behind their actions. The chapter also covers the mechanics of delivering a sales presentation, factors that cause problems during the presentation, and ways of dealing with the competition during a presentation. In reading this chapter, students should remember that salespeople can be effective only if they are meeting customer needs. The techniques discussed are ways to better solve customer problems and satisfy needs, not to manipulate them to meet the sellers' need to sell.

THE PSYCHOLOGY OF THE SALES PRESENTATION

Good salespeople know several objectives must be met in order for their sales presentations to be successful. First, salespeople must grab the prospect's attention. Next, salespeople must establish a rapport with the prospect and at the same time build credibility for themselves. Once this has been accomplished, salespeople must collect information so they can identify the prospect's needs. Once the prospect's problems and needs

THE SELLING PROCESS

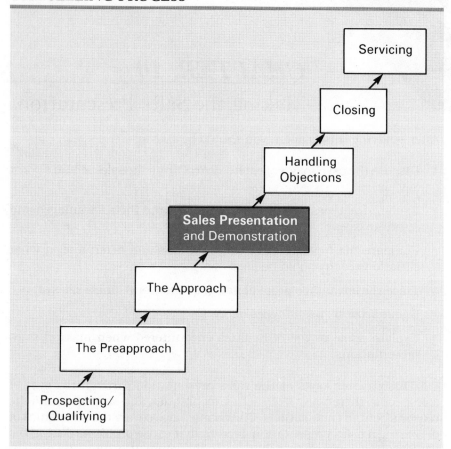

Figure 10-1 The *sales presentation* (and demonstration) is the fourth stage of the selling process.

are identified, salespeople can begin to develop a strategy designed to solve those problems and satisfy those needs. Naturally, salespeople are going to present their products as the answer to the prospect's problems, and in doing so they must relate the features and advantages of their product to the benefits the prospect will receive. Finally, salespeople must get a commitment on some type of action from the prospect. These internal objectives, which fuel sales presentations, are shown in Figure 10-2. In reviewing these internal objectives, students must remember that the overriding goal is customer satisfaction, and that these internal objectives are interim steps to achieving this goal.

GETTING THE PROSPECT'S ATTENTION

In the previous chapter, the approach was described as occurring during the first two minutes of the presentation. Recall that the goal of

THE SALESPERSON'S INTERNAL OBJECTIVES FOR SALES PRESENTATIONS

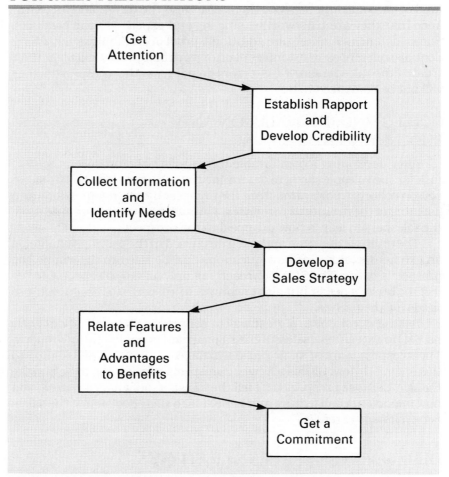

Figure 10-2 The salesperson has six general objectives to achieve in order for any sales presentation to be effective.

the approach is to get the prospect's attention and interest. If an approach fails to command the prospect's attention, the rest of the presentation will fall flat.

DEVELOPING RAPPORT AND BUILDING CREDIBILITY

Success in grabbing the prospect's attention results from the approach the salesperson uses, and in part from the impression the prospect gets from the salesperson. Salespeople know that if they cannot maintain the initial impression they will soon lose the prospect's interest. Thus, the salesperson's objective is to enhance the impression by developing rapport with the prospect and proving her or his credibility.

Rapport and credibility start to develop immediately. Salespeople should always offer a confident appearance, a strong handshake, some kind of personal link between themselves and the buyer, and an assurance that they are trustworthy, sincere, and experts on the products. Some customers may require additional proof of credibility such as credentials, references, or examples of prior work before they will place their trust in the salesperson. If customers do not trust the salesperson, they will not be convinced to buy.

COLLECTING INFORMATION AND IDENTIFYING NEEDS

After developing a comfortable rapport with the prospect, the next task for the salesperson is to determine the prospect's needs. The salesperson collects information from the prospect by asking questions and listening to the prospect's responses. Through two-way communication, the salesperson learns how to appeal to the prospect.

The multiple question approach discussed in the previous chapter is an excellent example of how questions can be used to determine the prospect's needs. The SPIN approach not only allows salespeople to detect the buyer's needs, but also encourages prospects to recognize those needs for themselves.

Asking questions is a great way to get prospects to talk about their needs. However, it is useless if the salesperson is not listening properly. The salesperson must show prospects the consideration of listening to their point of view. Ultimately, what prospects say is going to help make the sale, because prospects will tell the salesperson what they need, and how important each feature and benefit is to their decision, if the salesperson listens carefully.

DEVELOPING A SALES STRATEGY

At this point, salespeople should have the prospect's attention, interest, and respect. Through effective questioning and listening, they have been able to determine the prospect's needs. While listening, salespeople should be developing their strategy for presenting their product in an appealing manner. This involves determining which type of presentation would be best for a particular prospect.

There are three general types of presentations used to sell a product: the memorized, or "canned," presentation, the story plan, and the program presentation.

THE MEMORIZED PRESENTATION

The question of whether a memorized sales talk—usually called a **canned presentation**—is superior to an extemporaneous one is open to debate. The canned presentation is one that a salesperson memorizes word for word and delivers exactly as memorized. In its extreme form, a single presentation is memorized literally from beginning to end. In a less extreme form, the salesperson memorizes elements or sections but uses some discretion in deciding which sections to include and which to omit from the presentation for a specific prospect. The memorized presentation is based on the **stimulus-response theory**, which says the salesperson should provide the buyer with the proper stimulus in order to get the desired response. The vacuum-cleaner salesperson who dumps dirt on the homemaker's carpet (stimulus) gets a shocked expression from the homemaker (response). When the salesperson vacuums every bit of dirt off the carpet (stimulus), the homemaker is pleasantly surprised by the machine's strength (response), and agrees to the sale.

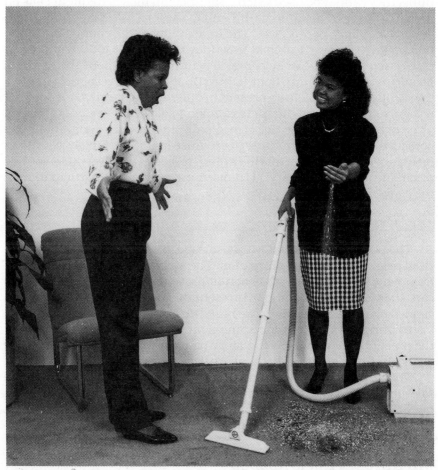

Figure 10-3 Memorized or canned presentations are common in door-to-door or "in-home" selling.

There are some strong arguments in favor of canned presentations. One is based on the logical assumption that canned presentations have been well constructed. This should be the case, because the person who prepares the presentation can test it and identify and eliminate the parts that are weak. The phrasing of the canned presentation can be superior to the phrasing a typical salesperson would use in making a sales presentation extemporaneously. Another argument is that the sound construction of the presentation gives salespeople confidence, particularly inexperienced salespeople. There also should be fewer questions from prospects to bother the salesperson because of the completeness of the presentation. All important points are included, and they are arranged in the most effective sequence. Careful preparation of canned presentations can avoid undesirable repetition or omission of important facts.

Canned presentations have several limitations, however. For one thing, they cannot be used when a salesperson makes frequent calls on the same buyers. They are also difficult to use for a salesperson who handles a wide range of products. The inflexibility of the canned presentation makes it impractical in at least four respects: (1) it does not recognize that a prospect can be completely uninformed about the product, hostile toward it, or impatient to buy; (2) it does not recognize motivational differences, which are present in different prospects; (3) it does not recognize the obvious differences among sales calls—such as length, place, or atmosphere. The lack of originality in canned presentations can bore prospects, and their rigidity can cause irritation. Finally, countless recitals of the same presentation are apt to lead to a delivery that sounds mechanical and listless; and (4) it discourages prospect participation in the conversation.

THE STORY PLAN

The position of this text is that salespeople should not use a memorized presentation but a **story plan**. The story plan is the raw material from which the salesperson's actual presentation is fashioned. At its core, the story plan is a standard presentation in much the same way as a canned presentation is. Both are based on an established sequence and tested phrasing. When circumstances pressure the salesperson to tailor the presentation, however, the story plan proves to be superior to the memorized presentation, because its flexibility is planned.

The story plan is based on the **need-satisfaction theory**, in which salespeople must first help prospects recognize and understand their needs, and then present their products as the satisfiers of those needs. (The SPIN approach discussed in Chapter 9 is an example of the need-satisfaction theory.)

WHY A STORY PLAN IS NEEDED

Regardless of how a salesperson feels about memorizing a presentation, the duty of organizing the presentation cannot be avoided. If organization is lacking, the salesperson's approach will lose its potential for cumulative strength. More important, a random presentation may serve only to confuse the prospect. Clearly, erratic selling is unsound selling. No sales call can be planned adequately if conscious study has not been given to the organization of the presentation.

A well-planned presentation enables any salesperson to make a more favorable impression than would otherwise be possible. Instead of hoping the sales presentation will achieve the desired results, every salesperson must know how to ensure the desired results. This requires planning and personalizing the presentation.

The more personalized the presentation, the more convincing and persuasive it will be. If Prospect A places great importance on comfort, the organized salesperson concentrates on that particular motive. If Prospect B ranks economy as the most desirable feature, the salesperson emphasizes the economy of the product. Personalizing the presentation demands from the salesperson the ability to diagnose accurately and to modify skillfully on short notice. Without these abilities, the salesperson had better stick to the standard presentation.

DEVELOPING A STORY PLAN

To develop a story plan, a salesperson must identify and memorize specific areas of a prospect's need:

- buying motives
- product advantages (e.g., less expensive, easier to use)
- product appeal (e.g., comfort, approval, safety)
- objections

The first requisite to any purchase is a motive. Identifying the buying motives establishes the focal point of the story plan. The salesperson proceeds to build the framework of the presentation around the motives. For instance, once the advantages of the salesperson's product are matched with the prospect's buying motives, the salesperson determines the sequence by which those advantages will be presented to the prospect. In some cases, this can be done best by making a memory scheme of the initials of the buying motives. For example, the code word might be C-A-S-H-E-D, as in:

Comfort   **A**pproval   **S**afety   **H**ealth   **E**conomy   **D**urability

Nothing is perfect, however. According to statistics, out of every 100 presentations, approximately 40 prospects will object to the price of the product and 20 will always want to "think it over." Acknowledging this pattern helps the salesperson to prepare for opposition. The salesperson's final preparations of the story plan involve experiments to discover and memorize key phrases that answer and overcome a prospect's objections.

THE STORY PLAN IN OPERATION

When planned intelligently, the story plan offers the salesperson several advantages:

1. The basic presentation is sound. No strong selling points are omitted; there is no repeating or backtracking unless the salesperson intends to do so; and there is no overemphasizing or underemphasizing.
2. The presentation can be tailored to each prospect. This permits the product to be described in terms of the hopes and dreams of each individual prospect. Because the salesperson can construct a complete, specific presentation for each prospect seen, the presentation is more impressive and persuasive. Tailoring the presentation allows the salesperson's initiative, imagination, and resourcefulness to operate and grow.
3. The presentation is made in the salesperson's own words. As a result, the salesperson delivers a natural presentation, not an awkward or artificial one.
4. With a story plan in mind, the salesperson can concentrate on prospect reaction and watch for indications of how the presentation is being received without any sacrifice of effectiveness.
5. The story plan encourages two-way communication between the buyer and seller, which leads to a better understanding of the buyer's needs and the seller's offerings.
6. The presentation provides the salesperson the flexibility to drift from the outline to satisfy a buyer's questions, rather than being held to a memorized monologue.

One drawback of the story plan is that it requires salespeople to "think on their feet." The trouble is, some salespeople are not able to think quickly and provide quick responses to the buyer's questions. When this problem exists, the company is either hiring the wrong kind of salespeople or not training them well enough. Salespeople also may develop the tendency to not prepare as well as they should because there is no memorization required.

AN ALTERNATIVE POINT OF VIEW

Some sales managers do not like planned sales presentations. Because some students may go to work for companies that hold this view, this perspective is presented.

Sales managers opposed to story plans do not like to outline a sales talk because they say that no two calls are alike. Their approach is to give each salesperson information about the product, prospects, and how the company operates, and they may even indicate points to be brought up in the sales call, but they stop there. They feel this information is sufficient for the sales call if the salesperson is intelligent, familiar with the merchandise, aware of current market conditions, and encourages two-way communication with prospects by listening and responding. Experience, they say, will enable the salesperson to handle sales calls satisfactorily.

The authors of this text believe that in many situations a story plan is needed, particularly for new salespeople. Virtually all new salespeople should write out several presentations, revise and improve them, and then learn the best. Role-playing and rehearsing in this manner results in a strong, confident presentation until the day when the experienced salesperson may want to improvise. Even if the memorized presentation is never delivered, it inevitably renews and increases belief in the product/service, and this conviction will be present in whatever presentation is made. It should be noted that when using a story plan listening is still very important because often adjustments are needed. The goal of the story plan then is to help the salesperson be prepared, to stimulate two-way communication, and ultimately to satisfy the buyer's needs.

THE PROGRAM PRESENTATION

The **program presentation**, also known as the *survey*, is a written sales presentation developed from a detailed analysis of a prospect's business. It has its foundation in the **problem-solution theory**. The backbone of this theory is a strong interaction between the buyer and the seller. Together, the buyer and seller determine the buyer's problem and customize a solution to the problem. This type of presentation is widely used in selling consulting services, creative advertising services, computer systems, trade selling, and the sale of industrial and office equipment.

The program presentation is often referred to as the survey because it usually involves conducting a survey and detailed analysis of the buyer's business operations prior to making the presentation. There are really two sales involved in this type of presentation. First, salespeople must sell the prospect on the idea that their service can benefit the prospect if they are allowed to survey and analyze the prospect's company. This is usually done by presenting case histories of companies whose problems have been solved and whose business has improved as a result of the product or service.

After conducting the survey and analyzing the information, salespeople prepare a written proposal of how they plan to solve the problem. The second sale involves presenting the proposal. This is a full-scale presentation that may include flipcharts, slide shows, videos, role-playing, and play-acting.

The advantages of the program presentation are: (1) it places emphasis on the "needs" or "problems" of the buyer, and the survey allows for strong verification of the problem's existence, (2) plenty of time is given to secure and analyze information, and (3) it results in a highly professional presentation that enhances the seller's reputation and image.

The obvious disadvantage of the program presentation is that it is very time consuming and costly, and for that reason it is only used for big-ticket sales. Other disadvantages include the buyer's skepticism of studies, and subsequent reluctance to open the company's operations to strangers. The chart in Table 10-1 shows each type of presentation, tells what it is, how it is implemented, gives its advantages and disadvantages, and lists which salespeople would use it.

RELATING FEATURES AND ADVANTAGES TO BENEFITS

You have already learned that people do not buy merchandise but rather satisfaction, which is composed of many separate advantages. The way to attract a buyer's attention and interest in a sales presentation is to promise advantages or benefits. Because most buyers are somewhat inclined to doubt salespeople's promises, salespeople usually find they must support their promises with proof. Then the salesperson tries to get action from the buyer in the form of a commitment to buy.

In Chapter 8, the customer benefit plan (FAB sheet) was described as one approach for planning the presentation. Now the salesperson must implement the FAB sheet. One technique that is used to implement the FAB sheet is the **advantage-proof-action technique**. The salesperson relates the features and benefits to the customer; however, it is the advantages that sell the product. Many products have the same features and provide the same benefits. What separates one from another are its advantages; why that product is superior to its competition's. The customer will buy the product that has the most advantages.

As with any claim, salespeople must support advantages with proof. Once the prospect is convinced that a product is superior (has more advantages), the salesperson tries to get the prospect to commit to an action (purchase).

STATING ADVANTAGES/BENEFITS

Stating an advantage or benefit to be gained from buying the salesperson's product or service is actually an appeal to a buying motive. For each buying motive to which the salesperson plans to appeal, it is necessary to have in mind several advantages/benefits to stress. Salespeople can isolate the specific advantages of a product or service by studying it, reading advertisements for it, reading material supplied by the company, and being alert for comments about the product/service from other individuals. By understanding the fundamentals of buying behavior and by placing special emphasis on the buying motives that are mainly responsible when a prospect investigates buying this type of product/service, salespeople can isolate those advantages/benefits that will probably be most important to each particular prospect. This can be done by analyzing the advance data obtained on the prospect and by observing the prospect before and during the sales presentation.

Sources of Advantages.   The prospect is the most productive single source of advantages the salesperson will need. The first step toward identifying the advantages is for the salesperson to study human behavior and motivation, placing special emphasis on the buying motives that are mainly responsible when a prospect thinks about, investigates, buys, and is happy with the salesperson's type of product. A second method of using the prospect as a source of advantages is to analyze the advance data the salesperson has on the prospect. The salesperson should look at the product from the prospect's point of view and then decide what motives will cause that particular individual to buy. A third and final way of learning from the prospect what advantages to use is through observation. Before and during the presentation, the salesperson has a good opportunity to observe the prospect. The salesperson can talk with and even question the prospect, thus gaining much information about the prospect from what he or she has to say.

HEADLINING

Prospects are not equally interested in the same advantages or motivated by the same desires. Yet selling is easiest when it is based on each prospect's strongest interests, and when the salesperson can make major appeals to the prospect's dominant buying motives. Faced with a large collection of product facts and buyer benefits, the salesperson needs some method of selecting the major points and advantages to be stressed.

The tactic known as **headlining** may often be what the salesperson is looking for. In headlining, the salesperson absorbs and masters a two- or three-sentence summary for each major advantage. The sales story is opened with a quick, impressive summary of the chief benefits of the sales proposal and a brief outline of the major reasons for buying. For example, the salesperson might give a thumbnail sketch of what the product will do in the areas of appearance, safety, and ease and economy of operation. As a product's major attributes are covered, the salesperson observes the prospect's reactions, listens to remarks made by the prospect, and analyzes the situation for clues as to which attributes to stress.

The salesperson hopes to strike a responsive chord or to draw a comment from the prospect. The salesperson wants the prospect to look at the headlined preview of the story and to respond in such a manner as to indicate the sections that he or she wants to know more about. The salesperson hopes the prospects will select the topics for the ensuing conversation just as one glances over the front page of a newspaper and

A COMPARISON OF THE THREE TYPES OF SALES PRESENTATIONS

Presentation	Memorized	Story Plan	Program
What is it?	A sales story that is memorized and presented word for word.	A framework in outline form presenting the major selling points the salesperson wants to cover.	A written sales presentation developed from a detailed survey and analysis of a prospect's business.
How is this presentation implemented?	The sales story is built via experimentation. Parts are tested and either strengthened or eliminated until the story is smooth and covers all selling points. The salesperson memorizes and presents it word for word.	After the need is identified, the salesperson: 1. Identifies buying motives. 2. Relates benefits to each buying motive. 3. Determines the best sequence for presenting these benefits. 4. Develops key phrases for describing the product and handling objections.	1. Get permission to do the survey. 2. Gather information and analyze the facts. 3. Prepare a written proposal. 4. Present the proposal.
Advantages	1. All sales points are covered. 2. Phrasing is well-planned to sound smooth.	1. Well planned. 2. Can be tailored to each individual customer.	1. Emphasizes needs or problems. 2. Verifies customer's "real" needs.

3. Provides confidence.	3. Sounds natural.	3. Plenty of time to gather and analyze information.
4. Objections are handled within the sales story.	4. Allows salesperson to concentrate on customer's reaction.	4. Highly professional and polished presentation.
5. Eliminates repetition and omission of important facts.	5. Encourages two-way communication.	
	6. Very flexible.	
Disadvantages		
1. Cannot be used with regular customers.	1. Salesperson may not be able to think quickly and respond smoothly.	1. Very time consuming.
2. Assumes prospect is interested in the product.	2. Tendency for salespeople to be lazy since less work is required, relative to program approach.	2. Very expensive.
3. Does not recognize that customers have different motivations.		3. Customers may be skeptical of studies.
4. Does not recognize differences in sales interviews.		4. Customers may be reluctant to open up to strangers.
5. Discourages customer participation.		
Who uses it?		
Inexperienced salespeople. Door-to-door salespeople. Telemarketers.	Any sales rep who does not need to customize a product or service for a customer.	Consulting, advertising, office and industrial equipment, computer and trade sales.

Table 10-1 The salesperson decides which presentation to use by questioning and listening to the prospect.

decides, from the headlines, which story to read first, which to read next, and so on.

When the prospect responds with enthusiasm, the salesperson can emphasize those product features and benefits that tie in with the prospect's interest. The sales presentation should emphasize the services and benefits that have created the prospect's enthusiasm. The salesperson can point out advantages and offer proof relating to the prospect's individual buying motives.

PRINCIPLES OF PRESENTING PROOF

The first step in the advantage-proof-action technique secures the prospect's attention, gains the prospect's interest, and kindles a desire for the product. The objective of the second step—giving proof for the advantages claimed—is to convince the prospect that a purchase will perform as described and satisfy the prospect's need. Salespeople must expect skepticism from prospects. They cannot be asked to believe without proof, and for this reason salespeople must have proof for all product claims made. Salespeople must prove each advantage to the prospect until the prospect feels that it is possible to attain that advantage.

General claims of product excellence usually cannot be regarded by the prospect as legitimate grounds for buying. Concise facts are more interesting than vague claims, and specific evidence is superior to generalizations. Prospects prefer to prove claimed advantages to themselves; but, where this is impractical, their second choice is proof from an authority. The following sections describe six useful methods of proof.

Logical Reasoning.   Logical reasoning appeals to the prospect's judgment, common sense, and experience. It is a positive form of proof if the product does not lend itself well to demonstration. It can be forceful and easily grasped if it is kept simple and direct. Logical reasoning has two limitations: (1) it will seldom overcome prejudice, defective thinking, or emotion; and (2) its effectiveness is limited by the prospect's mental capacity.

The simplest and weakest form of logical reasoning used as proof is made orally by the salesperson. Oral statements may be somewhat stronger, however, when they come from a salesperson who has extensive knowledge of and experience with buyers' problems. The prospect may accept the printed form of logical reasoning more readily than oral statements, because of an inclination to believe the printed word more than the spoken. A third type of logical reasoning is found when the prospect and the salesperson sit down together and calculate on paper what will result if the prospect buys. This third form is superior to both the previously discussed forms of logical reasoning used to prove a sales point.

Company-Supplied Proof.   The salesperson's company may supply proof in a variety of forms. First, the company may have run tests, the results of which can be used to support the salesperson's claims. A product guarantee is another way to prove that the product is of some quality. Third, in talking to middlemen, the company's advertising support of the product may be used as evidence of the market for the product. In discussing advertising support, the salesperson will find it desirable to know the number of dollars earmarked for advertising, the media to be used, and the total circulation of those media. An example of how a company's advertising support is presented to middlemen is shown in the color insert. A fourth example of company proof consists of statistics, such as data on dealers or consumers, supplied to the salesperson by the company. This is shown in Figure 10-4. A fifth example of company-supplied proof could be the findings from a survey that the salesperson made of the prospect's circumstances.

Independent Research Findings.   This third type of proof consists of data secured from impartial sources outside the salesperson's company. An example of such proof would be the results of an analysis of the salesperson's product, together with an account of the experiments conducted by an independent, commercial testing laboratory, such as Underwriter's Laboratories. A second example would be the results of market studies made by some unrelated concern—consumer preference studies made by newspapers or magazines, for example, or studies published in *Consumer Reports.* A third type might consist of related statistics a salesperson has acquired, such as the probability and expectancy tables of insurance companies, or the sales and expense figures for department stores collected by the NRMA (National Retail Merchants Association) or some other impartial agency.

Testimonials.   Although testimonials have been abused as a selling technique, they can still be effective, particularly when the nature of the product does not allow demonstration. The person who delivers the testimonial may be: (1) an expert in some field whose position demands the prospect's respect; (2) a prominent person from the society, sports, or entertainment world; or (3) a so-called ordinary individual whose testimonial may be more acceptable because the individual is an everyday person like the prospect. A sample testimonial is shown in Figure 10-6.

Case Histories.   Case histories are similar to testimonials, in that they are built around a third party whose experience the prospect is inclined to believe, because the third party is not biased, as the salesperson is, toward the product. In using case histories as a form of proof, it is generally best to build them around a customer as much like the prospect as possible. The ideal situation is to use a case history involving someone in the prospect's locality, perhaps even someone the prospect knows and can call for verification of the salesperson's statements.

DATA SUPPLIED TO SALESPERSON BY THE COMPANY

Figure 10-4 Many companies provide their salespeople with brochures that outline the promotional campaign that is being used to support the product and product facts that enable the salesperson to develop better sales presentations.

Source: Courtesy of Beecham Products USA.

Demonstration.   The best type of proof a salesperson can use is a demonstration of the product. Demonstration shows how the product is constructed and how it will perform. Sometimes, of course, the nature of the product is such that it cannot be demonstrated easily. Examples of demonstrations include those given by the salesperson during the sales presentation, distribution of product samples, selling on approval, trial offers and trial orders, and placing the product in the prospect's hands to experience what it will do. Because the art of demonstrating a product effectively is so important in selling, the next chapter will be devoted to it.

GETTING THE COMMITMENT

In delivering the sales presentation, the action the salesperson wants is agreement. Specifically, the salesperson first wants the prospect to agree with each point made and to accept each advantage presented and proved. Then the salesperson wants a "yes" to each of the five buying decisions, including the decision to buy immediately. If the salesperson is to succeed in achieving these decisions, the prospect must agree voluntarily and without reservation. Getting some form of action early from the prospect helps to make the prospect "action-minded" from the start of the presentation. Then the act of purchasing will not seem so much like a brand-new idea at the end of the presentation. When a prospect withholds agreement, the salesperson knows that more advantages must be presented.

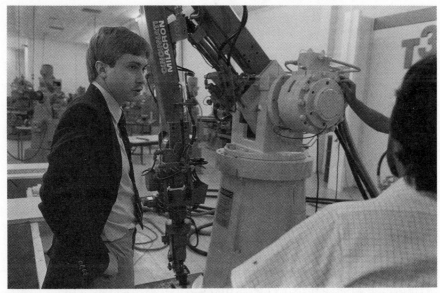

Figure 10-5 Demonstrations allow the customer to sample the product or see it in use prior to purchasing.

A SAMPLE TESTIMONIAL

JOCK UNIVERSITY ATHLETIC DEPARTMENT
1313 Mockingbird Lane   Centerville, Ohio 09876

June 30, 19--

Ms. Bonnie Taylor, Sales Representative
Touchdown Uniforms, Incorporated
37 Football Road
Passerville, Ohio 12345

Dear Bonnie:

I would like to thank you and your company for your professionalism in
handling our order, and for the excellent quality of your uniforms.
Everyone involved in the football program here at Jock U. is very
pleased with the fine quality and styling of the uniforms we purchased
this past summer.

I thought I would let you know that we have just won the Middle Ohio
Conference championship, and we owe it, in part, to the enthusiasm and
motivation created by your uniforms. I also would like to say that since
every single uniform stood the test of a grueling ten-game schedule, we
are able to put our excess monies toward recruiting for next year.

Please feel free to use my name as a supporter of Touchdown Uniforms,
and we look forward to continuing a strong business relationship with
you and your company. Thank you.

Sincerely,

Kathy Naugle
Kathy Naugle
Athletic Director

KN/ec

Figure 10-6 Testimonials show the customer that others have tried your product and are satisfied.

Action is secured by asking questions throughout the sales presentation—questions constructed so as to secure from the prospect a favorable commitment to each selling point and advantage. Even with difficult prospects, the salesperson usually will continue to ask questions until the prospect says something that can be interpreted as a "yes." By asking frequent questions, the salesperson observes one of the cardinal rules of selling: to take up a second point or advantage only after the prospect has accepted the first one. Occasional violation of this rule is permissible when a prospect feels lukewarm toward a particular advantage. In such cases, the salesperson should attempt once or twice to get a commitment and then move on.

In periodic checks on the prospect, the salesperson is always alert for enthusiastic agreement on an advantage because it is a signal to try at once for a commitment on the buying decision. An enthusiastic agreement on one of the buying decisions may be a signal to try to close the sale.

Here are a few questions that can be used to assess commitment:

"Could your firm benefit by using this product?"
"Would this feature help you complete your work faster?"
"Would you find this feature useful?"
"That would help you do a better job, wouldn't it?"
"That's what you want, isn't it?"
"You'll enjoy that, won't you?"
"Your friends will certainly enjoy this, won't they?"
"A 10 percent increase in sales sounds good, doesn't it?"
"You'd like to cut delivery costs 17 percent, wouldn't you?"

A salesperson should always be ready for unfavorable action by having some reserve selling ammunition ready. If beauty, comfort, performance, and economy fail to sell an automobile, for example, the salesperson can still talk about dependability and safety. Any attempt to get action must be so executed that a negative response will not bar the salesperson from continuing the sales presentation. In trying to achieve agreement, the salesperson should not try to trap the prospect. Instead, what is desired is the confirmation of a sound conclusion that two individuals have reached by a free discussion of mutually recognized facts. Agreement must be strong and sincere, especially in the case of the first buying decision—need. Until this type of agreement is secured, the salesperson must continue to add more advantages.

MECHANICS OF DELIVERING THE PRESENTATION

A sales presentation should be simple, yet complete. It should contain positive statements of what the product will do rather than negative statements of what the product will not do. A confident delivery is a valuable asset in the presentation. The poised salesperson makes a presentation that is characterized by assurance, smoothness, and finesse. The objective is to deliver a presentation that convinces and persuades the prospect to make a buying decision beneficial to both parties.

CONSIDERATION FOR THE PROSPECT

Because the prospect expects a presentation from a salesperson, the salesperson should start the sales story right away. The prospect resents the salesperson's wasting too much time on weather, sports, politics, and other unnecessary conversation. The salesperson should get down to business promptly, and after making the presentation, leave promptly.

A salesperson must be careful not to offend prospects by the manner in which the presentation is made. Most prospects find it irritating to be interrupted while asking a question or making an objection. Further, following up by arguing or contradicting not only antagonizes the prospect, but also makes the prospect defend any resistance. Any tactics the prospect considers objectionable are to be avoided, such as pestering, wisecracking, dictating, begging, or being too persistent. The salesperson should keep a respectful distance from the prospect. At the same time, the salesperson must not be so aloof as to talk *to* prospects rather than *with* them. Prospects do not care to be overwhelmed with the salesperson's personal opinions on products or controversial subjects such as labor unions, religion, politics, or the danger of war. Such opinions had best be expressed only when the prospect requests them. Attacking the prospect's present choice of product, or arbitrarily making a decision or selection for the prospect are unreasonable presumptions.

The salesperson's main objective during the sales presentation should be to serve the prospect. This attitude will be reflected in a concern for the prospect and a sensitive response to the prospect's interests. Adopting the role of an interested friend, the salesperson will strive for the prospect's goodwill by being agreeable and by demonstrating courtesy and tact. Anything that annoys or upsets the prospect works against, rather than for, the salesperson.

NECESSITY FOR SOCIAL INTERACTION

Social interaction is the salesperson's most useful approach to influencing a buyer's opinions and purchase decisions. Social interaction takes place when the salesperson and the buyer exchange information, feelings, attitudes, and ideas; it is two-way communication. The superior salesperson is sensitive to each buyer's likes and dislikes. The salesperson can strengthen the social relationship by recasting the buyer's comments, asking the buyer questions, or soliciting the buyer's opinions.

The more satisfaction or value (appreciation, agreement) the buyer receives from a salesperson, the more the buyer is inclined to do what the salesperson wants done. When the salesperson and the buyer identify and interact with each other, they are thinking as a team.

WORDS ARE TOOLS

A salesperson needs a large vocabulary, and must be able to use it effectively. Choosing the most appropriate words can be more impressive as well as more precise. Concepts and suggestions can be expressed in a concise manner, and greater conciseness contributes to greater success in influencing the thoughts and actions of buyers. While it is true that a salesperson should appeal to more than just the buyer's sense of hearing, one can nevertheless contend that words are a salesperson's basic tools. They are depended on most heavily in communication with buyers.

In selling situations where a buyer's background, intelligence, and education are above average, the need for an outstanding vocabulary becomes even more important. Salespeople must distinguish themselves when their buyers are not ordinary buyers, but are highly sensitive and responsive to salespeople's speech. The better their mastery and use of words, the better the salespeople sell.

VOICE AND RATE OF DELIVERY

How one delivers a message can add significantly to the impression one makes on a prospect. An authoritative voice does more than allow a salesperson to be heard. It garners respect and forces a prospect to take notice of what is being said. This type of respect increases a prospect's confidence in the salesperson, which, consequently, leads to a higher sales volume. The authority of one's voice can be improved through practice. Vocal inflection and tone of voice can mean the difference between an irritated prospect and a satisfied customer. In general, a low-pitched voice is more pleasing than a high-pitched voice.

The rate of delivery of the sales presentation must be adjusted according to the prospect's ability to comprehend. If the salesperson rushes the presentation by talking too fast, some points will not register with the prospect and will not be understood. If the salesperson talks too slowly for the impatient prospect, the prospect's attention will wander. The more common error is for salespeople to talk too fast because they know their presentations so well.

The salesperson's delivery should be animated and not monotonous. By dramatic use of pauses, by executing accompanying gestures, and by changing the voice's pitch and volume, the salesperson is able to maintain a more interesting pace. Although speed of delivery should be varied for emphasis and variety, the flow of the story should be so smooth that salesperson and prospect stay mentally in step with each other.

USES OF SILENCE

Silence can be a great ally to a salesperson. A salesperson should practice recognizing the meaning of silent pauses. A few examples of the uses of silence follow:

1. Silence gives buyers an opportunity to make a comment, ask a question, or voice an objection.
2. Silence offers buyers a welcome change of pace from salespeople who talk too much.

3. Silence establishes rapport and contributes to social interaction.
4. Silence focuses attention on a product through visual dramatization of a special feature.
5. Silence emphasizes the last point the salesperson made, encouraging buyers to accept it.
6. Silence permits buyers to cool their hostilities.
7. Silence influences purchases by allowing buyers to think matters over before they decide to buy.

THE SKILL OF CREATIVE LISTENING

Most of the time the salesperson is not talking should be spent in **creative listening**. Why? To get information, to bid for buyers' goodwill, and to compliment buyers are just three good reasons. To be an active listener, that is, one who is interested in and alert to buyers, a salesperson must acquire the skill of listening. As a skill, listening can be improved.

What do salespeople who are good listeners do? They maintain eye contact with the buyer, which shows attention and interest. They permit themselves little relaxation of posture or facial expression. Good listeners concentrate attention on what the buyer says and does, never faking that attention. This is quite an achievement for most individuals, because listeners usually think much faster than speakers talk. Good listeners note changes in a buyer's tone and inflection, and try to interpret what the buyer does not say. They hope to think ahead of the buyer, focusing on main ideas and striving to understand what the buyer is actually communicating.

Salespeople who listen well do not hesitate to ask questions for clarification and confirmation, but do not interrupt. They also do not run out of patience; do not reveal any lack of interest in what the buyer says; do not allow themselves to be distracted by a buyer's personality, appearance, grammar, or delivery; do not harbor bias or prejudice; and do not allow themselves to react emotionally to "red-flag" words such as taxes. The goal of creative listening is to assure effective two-way communication.

ASSURING TWO-WAY COMMUNICATION

Sales presentations are more satisfactory if both the salesperson and the buyer participate. Thus, it is desirable for the salesperson to encourage each buyer to contribute ideas, questions, and reactions. It is particularly wise for a salesperson not to monopolize the conversation when the buyer is expertly informed and qualified in buying, as many purchasing agents are. The salesperson may find a sales call with such a buyer an excellent opportunity to acquire valuable information. There is also a much better chance of making the sale if the buyer is encouraged to talk.

The proper level of buyer participation is difficult to define and just as difficult to control. The buyer who talks too much is just as much a problem as the buyer who says too little. Somewhere between these two extremes is a satisfactory balance. Even while listening, the salesperson's facial expressions, movements, and actions can influence how much the buyer talks and can guide what is said.

Not all successful salespeople encourage questions and comments from prospects. Some salespeople prefer to present their proposals without interruption. This does not seem to be as sound a policy as that of welcoming questions and objections from the prospect. When prospects express their views, salespeople gain a measure of progress because they know what the prospects are thinking. Prospects who take part in the conference generally have greater interest in the presentation. The questions salespeople ask should supply any needed information. These same questions can be used to challenge the prospect and to plant ideas. If prospects are so agreeable as to make salespeople suspicious about the penetration and actual acceptance of the story, questions such as the following can be helpful:

"Where within your operation do you feel you will get the most benefit from my product?"

"Are you looking to cut costs or increase your production capacity?"

USING QUESTIONS

There is an art to asking questions just as there is an art to listening to a buyer's conversation. Strategically, the salesperson can use questions to help discover what a buyer needs or wants from a product. The questions can be phrased to help a buyer recognize these needs or wants. The right questions can identify the topics which should be discussed and those which should be avoided or at least handled cautiously.

There are also several tactical jobs that questioning can perform. First, it is the simplest technique for ensuring two-way communication. Second, it can be used to recapture a buyer's attention and to create interest. Third, a salesperson can determine how well the sales story is being understood by asking questions. Fourth, buyers appreciate and are favorably impressed by questions about their ideas and attitudes. Finally, a question-and-answer session is one way of getting a buyer's agreement to portions of the sales proposal on record.

REHEARSING THE PRESENTATION

A quick and painless way to become proficient in presenting a sales story is to rehearse. Members of the clergy, politicians, public speakers, and actors all know the value of rehearsals. These people understand that running through a sales story aloud is the best preparation and training for acquiring poise and confidence. Salespeople are advised to write out a sales story, and then read and reread it—editing, revising, and improving it on each pass. Then comes the rehearsing. At first this can consist of nothing more than reading or speaking the story aloud. Next, the salesperson can talk before a mirror. After this, the presentation can be made to someone else, perhaps an accommodating friend. Two salespeople can take turns playing the role of salesperson and buyer. Eventually, the salesperson will progress to the point at which a presentation can be rehearsed mentally, which permits rehearsal in a variety of places and circumstances.

Certain matters should get particular attention in rehearsals. One is the salesperson's manner of speaking. The objectives here should be correct pronunciation, pleasant tone of voice, clear enunciation, proper inflection, and a change of pace which lends variety and emphasis to the presentation. Another matter to be tried and tested, which is closely related to speech, includes the key words and phrases of the sales story. Finally, the salesperson should eliminate extremes in the presentation. Anything overdone or underdone—whether it is emphasis, enthusiasm, contrast, speed, or length of story—handicaps the salesperson.

Figure 10-7 Rehearsing the presentation in front of a mirror may help to detect weaknesses in delivery or physical appearance and can also provide the self-confidence needed to make the presentation.

DIFFICULTIES ENCOUNTERED IN THE SALES PRESENTATION

Almost all salespeople encounter some difficulties or obstacles in any given sales presentation. The most common difficulties are external interruptions, interruptions by prospects, and difficult prospects who may be inattentive, silent, indifferent, undecided, skeptical, or hostile.

EXTERNAL INTERRUPTIONS

One of the most troublesome experiences encountered by salespeople is external interruption of their presentations. The external interruptions a salesperson must cope with are usually of three types: the prospect may receive a telephone call, may be called away from the presentation, or may be visited by someone else. These external interruptions break the prospect's train of thought by calling attention to other matters. Interruptions reduce the cumulative force of the presentation, consume the salesperson's time, and give the prospect an excuse for ending the presentation or for not buying.

On the positive side, the salesperson can use the break caused by an external interruption for a quick mental review of what has been said up to that point. This will enable the salesperson to plan the rest of the presentation soundly. When the prospect resumes the presentation, the salesperson should not act as though nothing has happened. Instead, the salesperson should summarize the points made prior to the interruption to remind the prospect of the ground that was covered, and check for understanding and attention.

In the case of lengthy interruptions, particularly those from which the prospect seems to return in a worried or distracted frame of mind, the salesperson should try to regain control and continue the presentation. If unsuccessful, the salesperson should make an appointment for an early return call. When external interruptions are either too long or too numerous, it is usually advisable to make a later appointment.

It is often possible to avoid or reduce external interruptions. The shorter the salesperson's presentation, the less time there is for interruption. Also, there will be fewer interruptions if the salesperson calls during hours that are not especially busy for the prospect. Sometimes a direct, courteous request to go to a quiet place is sufficient. Finally, if the salesperson can convince the prospect that the presentation is important and should not be interrupted, the prospect is likely to cooperate.

INTERRUPTIONS BY PROSPECTS

Every question that a prospect asks interrupts the salesperson's story, whether the question is a request for information, an objection, or a willful attempt to derail the salesperson from the sales talk. There are two broad methods of handling a question: to deal with it at once, or to postpone answering it. If the salesperson elects to handle the question immediately, he or she should do so with firmness and conviction. The reply should be brief, yet satisfactory to the prospect. The salesperson should attempt to resume the presentation immediately.

If an instantaneous answer to the prospect's question would be awkward, the salesperson should try to postpone handling the question. Should the question be an objection, the salesperson may find it desirable and possible to delay an answer with a reply such as:

"I'm coming to that."
"I'll take up that point in a minute."
"Yes, I can see your point."
"Yes, I'll cover that later."
"Perhaps you're right."

The preceding responses allow the salesperson to resume the presentation.

We know that the sales story should be built around the product's advantages rather than the weaknesses of competitive products, for this approach makes it more persuasive. If the prospect insists early in the presentation that the salesperson's product be compared with a competitive brand, perhaps the brand the prospect then owns, the comparison should be executed immediately and fairly.

Another way of avoiding interruptions is to keep the discussion of prices in the background in the initial stages of the presentation. Price is a relative factor that depends on what the buyer gets; it is important only in terms of value. Prospects cannot judge price fairly without knowing what the product or service will do. A price quoted too soon always sounds high because the salesperson has not had time to establish the value. For these reasons, an early inquiry about price should be side-tracked, perhaps with a diverting statement such as, "The price varies with the product purchased. Let's find out first which can best meet your needs and then I can tell you the price."

(Chapter 12 is devoted to discussing the most troublesome form of interruption by prospects, the objection.)

THE DIFFICULT PROSPECT

Sometimes a salesperson encounters a prospect who for some reason is difficult to handle. Six causes of such difficulty are discussed in the following sections.

INATTENTIVENESS

When the prospect's attention wanders away from the presentation, the salesperson should try at once to determine the cause. It may be that the sales story is so vague that the prospect cannot or will not spend the effort required to follow it. It may be that the salesperson's method of presentation is failing to interest the prospect. It may be that the prospect's attention is intermittently, yet irresistibly, drawn to other matters.

One possible course of action is to mention the prospect's various wants, if the salesperson knows them, in the hope of finding a clue to the prospect's most powerful buying motives. A second, somewhat similar possibility is to summarize what the product delivers, all the while looking for clues. A third approach to recapturing the prospect's attention is to startle the prospect by enthusiastically presenting a new slant, a new case history, or a new advantage. Another way is to offer proof that is more meaningful than any yet given. A fifth option is to pause in the presentation until the prospect's attention returns. Finally, in serious cases when the prospect is too inattentive, the salesperson may frankly ask for more attention. If none of these techniques succeeds in recapturing the prospect's attention, the only resort left is to ask for a later appointment.

SILENCE

Being met by silence is not so serious as it might seem, because the prospect who listens can be sold. The proper procedure is to feed advantages and proof slowly to the prospect and to make sure the prospect is listening. If questions such as, "That's true, isn't it?" are interspersed, the salesperson is taking positive action to draw out the prospect. An occasional question that cannot be answered by "yes" or "no" will help the salesperson check the progress being made.

INDIFFERENCE

One of the most exasperating hurdles a salesperson must overcome is prospect indifference. The difficult job here is to convince the prospect of need, without the prospect becoming aware of being on the road to buying. To do this, the salesperson must keep the presentation informal and frictionless. The salesperson must make the presentation a casual dialogue and, ignoring the prospect's apparent indifference, continue to add advantage to advantage.

INDECISION

The salesperson must confront indecision when the prospect's uncertainty and hesitation cause postponement of the purchase. The salesperson must take the initiative by demonstrating friendly but firm guidance. By taking a positive, decisive attitude, the salesperson helps the prospect make a decision. Questions should be asked throughout the presentation to build up a series of commitments by the prospect, and the close should not frighten the prospect. Relating case histories can be an effective method of dealing with the indecisive prospect.

SKEPTICISM

Skeptical prospects are usually people who have been deceived by a salesperson or who know other people who have been deceived. Instead of making the skeptic back up claims, the salesperson should go ahead with the presentation and keep piling up facts backed by reliable proof. By being intentionally conservative, the salesperson makes it difficult for the prospect to voice disagreement. Above all, the salesperson must remain poised in dealing with the skeptical prospect and must refuse to argue.

HOSTILITY

When salespeople encounter prospects who are decidedly antagonistic, they must try to change that attitude. Such an attitude can have far-reaching, harmful effects on the salesperson's company and the salesperson. Also, a hostile prospect tends to become a good customer once an erroneous opinion of the salesperson and the salesperson's company has been corrected. The worst course of action the salesperson can take is to argue. The prospect will naturally become defensive, even if proven wrong, and will usually be too irritated to buy. Instead, the salesperson should listen sympathetically, thank the prospect for the information, and promise to investigate and try to remedy the cause of dissatisfaction.

SELLING AGAINST STRONG COMPETITION

To sell effectively in a competitive environment, a salesperson must (1) have the proper attitude toward competitors, (2) know who the competitive salespeople are and what their sales presentations are like, and (3) avoid unsound ways of handling information about competitors.

PROPER ATTITUDE TOWARD COMPETITION

One feature of the salesperson's attitude toward competitors should be respect for them and their products. In many lines, one brand of product is just about the same as other brands, and prospects know this. Furthermore, competition involves companies, salespeople, and products that have both good points and loyal supporters. A prospect may buy or use a competing product. In view of this, it is a mistake to show lack of respect for competition in front of the prospect. The tactful salesperson shows respect for all competitors by giving them credit for their selling efforts and their products.

A second characteristic of a proper attitude toward competitors is fairness. Salespeople lower themselves in the prospect's estimation when they do or say anything that smacks of unfair treatment or criticism of the competition. Resentment may be particularly strong when no defenders of competitors are present or when a direct comparison requested by the prospect is not made fairly. All questions and comparisons call for an honest treatment. Exhibiting fairness affords the salesperson the good feeling that results from operating ethically, and ensures more enthusiastic customers.

Confidence is a final ingredient in developing a proper attitude toward competition. It is comforting to know that one has nothing to fear from any product comparison. However new salespeople often develop unrealistic fears about the competition.

The first fear develops when a salesperson is unduly impressed by a competitor's good qualities, or gets an exaggerated idea of who the competitors are and what they are doing. This fear often leads new salespeople directly into a second, self-defeating effort based on this fear—taking unwise action in response to the competition.

Salespeople sometimes misuse their selling efforts by spending too much time hunting for competitive weaknesses when faced with stiff competition. Instead of being frightened at the thought of learning too much that is good and bad about the competition, the successful salesperson collects and uses information about competition in a purposeful manner. A salesperson's efforts should be devoted to studying both the merits of the salesperson's own product as well as those of the competition.

COMPETITORS' SELLING ACTIVITIES

In assessing competitors' selling activities, the salesperson will want to obtain information on competitive salespeople and on competitive presentations.

COMPETITIVE SALESPEOPLE

The first thing to know about competitive activities is who the competitive salespeople are. Personal facts about the people who represent competitors might include their names, background, where they live, their interests and tastes, their avocations, and their social circles. Business facts might include the length of time they have been with their companies, what they did previously, their various duties, and how long they have worked in their territories.

More specific and relevant information about competitors' salespeople concerns their sales personalities. Their personal characteristics are worth knowing. Their concepts of the duties of a salesperson and their patterns and methods of operation should be valuable. How their prospects and customers rate them as salespeople, what prospects like and dislike about them, and whether they are considered personal friends as well as sources of supply are bits of information that can be used to advantage. For example, relying too heavily on friendship to hold present customers makes for an insecure relationship. Such a situation invites another salesperson to move in with more quality, more service, lower prices, or better selling efforts, because these are the things that will get and hold customers away from competition in the long run.

The more similar competing products are, the more the emphasis shifts away from merchandise features and toward the salesperson as an individual. In some lines, a given product can be bought on the buyer's specifications from two or more vendors of equally satisfactory standing at the same or approximately the same price. In such cases, the purchaser has little on which to base a choice except differences in competing salespeople. Hence, a salesperson needs to know who as well as what the competition is.

COMPETITIVE PRESENTATIONS

As far as competitive presentations are concerned, a salesperson is particularly interested in two things: what was said and how it was said. The "what" is the proposition offered by competing representatives to the prospect. Salespeople must determine whether or not the item recommended by the competition adequately meets the prospect's requirements. The price quoted by the other representatives, as well as terms and allowances, also should be learned.

Another consideration is "what" the competing salespeople say about their products and about your products. Particularly desirable is information about the selling points stressed. Which features do competitive representatives emphasize? Which are not mentioned? What word-of-mouth publicity is being given to your products? Do competing salespeople take a dim view of some of the features of others' products? If so, can that view be converted from a drawback into an effective advantage for the buyer?

A final consideration in analyzing what competing representatives say is to determine their most effective selling techniques. For each individual prospect, a salesperson benefits from knowing those features of competitive proposals that have strong appeal. Similarly, the features that most often impress prospects in general are good to know. Add to these persuasive features the closing appeals that often secure orders, and the result is a collection of data that better enables salespeople to select and emphasize the features of the proposition which will counteract competitive features.

The second aspect of competitive presentations that salespeople are interested in is "how" the presentation is made. This is important because the more a salesperson knows about the type of presentation made by each competitor, the stronger the salesperson's own presentation can be. The visual aids used—the models, samples, charts, catalogs, reports, equipment such as video and computer, and survey findings—are all part of the presentation. If demonstrations are used, especially when they are impressive, one cannot afford to be uninformed about them.

Collecting information about competitive sales personnel and their presentations is very helpful to salespeople. Some companies, mostly larger ones, do this for their salespeople. But most do not. When the company does not provide this information salespeople must listen and continually ask questions so they can get as much of this information as possible.

HANDLING INFORMATION ABOUT COMPETITORS

Selling against strong competition takes tact, judgment, and control. Every product, service, salesperson, and company has its good points. Each salesperson will stress those points. Prospects buy the product or service they believe will provide the greatest amount of satisfaction. Because selling against competition is at best a difficult matter, some suggestions about what not to do should be helpful. If the errors shown in Figure 10-8 are avoided, the salesperson will more effectively handle the competition in a sales presentation.

HOW NOT TO HANDLE THE COMPETITION

1. Do not include any reference to competition in constructing the sales presentation because it is not sound strategy to recognize it in that manner. In putting your presentation together, be like the runner who eyes the tape, not the other runners.
2. Never initiate the subject of competition. If it is to be mentioned, let the prospect make the first reference. Furthermore, do not compare your product with another unless the prospect demands it. Competition should not be discussed except to answer a direct question.
3. Do not stray or be maneuvered away from the primary task, which is to explain what your product will do for the prospect. Do not be dragged into a discussion of competitive topics.
4. Have no ambitions to win mudslinging contests. Most prospects detect and resent any disparaging remarks made by competing sales representatives.
5. Never make a statement about competition before checking its accuracy.
6. Do not expose flaws in competition in the hope of making sales through this tactic.
7. Don't welcome gossip. If you must listen to it, don't repeat it.
8. Never criticize the competition. Criticism is poor sales technique. Prospects know that you are not impartial and thus may have difficulty believing you. Prospects may like and have faith in the other brand, and they will resent any belittling of it.

Figure 10-8 By following these suggestions, the salesperson can more effectively handle strong competition during the presentation.

SUMMARY

Salespeople have six objectives they try to achieve during a presentation: (1) grab the prospect's attention; (2) establish rapport and credibility; (3) collect information and identify needs; (4) develop a sales strategy; (5) relate features and advantages to the benefits the prospect will receive; and (6) get a commitment.

The salesperson must not be afraid to approach prospects and grab their attention. Developing rapport and credibility depends on a confident appearance, a strong handshake, the establishment of a link between buyer and seller, and the assurance that the salesperson is trustworthy, sincere, and expert on the product/service being sold.

The SPIN approach is a method used to collect information and identify needs. There are three types of presentations discussed in the text that can be used once the prospect's needs have been discovered. The memorized or "canned" presentation is a sales story memorized and presented word for word. The story plan is an outline of selling points arranged to make a favorable impression for the product. The program or "survey" presentation is a written presentation developed from a detailed survey and analysis of the prospect's problem.

The longest segment of the presentation is when the salesperson relates the features and the advantages of the product over the competition's to the benefits the prospect will receive. Finally, the salesperson must get some type of response or feedback from the prospect at the conclusion of the sales visit.

Two-way communication makes sales presentations more effective because it gets the prospect actively involved. Rehearsing makes the presentation more effective because it makes the salesperson more confident and gives him or her preparation in handling objections. Other skills that need to be strengthened are the salesperson's interaction, vocabulary, vocal, and listening skills.

KEY TERMS

canned presentation
story plan
need-satisfaction theory
program presentation
stimulus-response theory

problem-solution theory
advantage-proof-action technique
headlining
creative listening

REVIEW QUESTIONS

1. What are the six objectives that a salesperson tries to achieve on every sales call?

2. What is meant by "developing credibility?"
3. What is the stimulus-response theory and which presentation is based on it?
4. Which theory is the program presentation based on?
5. How is the program presentation implemented?
6. List at least six of the suggestions for stating advantages.
7. Why is proof presented to buyers?
8. List three effective types of proof.
9. Why is social interaction necessary in the sales presentation?
10. What do salespeople who are good listeners do?
11. How can salespeople minimize the effects of external interruptions?
12. Describe the proper attitude toward competition.
13. What should a salesperson know about the competition's salespeople and their presentations?

DISCUSSION QUESTIONS

1. Explain how a thorough preapproach can be used to help the salesperson establish a good rapport with the prospect.
2. You are a salesperson selling Diet Coke. What features, advantages, and benefits would you consider in developing a sales presentation for a grocery store? What SPIN questions would you use to convince them they needed to stock Diet Coke on their shelves? What types of proof would you offer to support your advantages? What type of action would you be seeking?
3. A cardinal rule of selling is never argue with a customer. How can a sales manager persuade an argumentative salesperson who has been complained about by a customer to stop arguing?

CASE 10-1   GLOBAL MUTUAL LIFE INSURANCE COMPANY*

Chris Armstrong is a young salesperson with the Global Mutual Life Insurance Company. One day a friend mentioned to Armstrong that another friend, Edna Carmichael, was having trouble saving money. Armstrong learned that Carmichael is a service technician with Cablevision, the local cable TV company, is 28 years old, has a husband and one child, and a trade school education. She has worked well for Cablevision and is in line for promotion. With this information, Armstrong telephoned Carmichael one Friday at Cablevision.

*Case prepared by Gordon D. Ellis. Used with permission.

Salesperson: Ms. Carmichael, I'm Chris Armstrong. Joe Craig and I were talking earlier this week. Joe said something that led me to believe you might be interested in a plan to save some money. I know a good way to save money and would like to tell you about it. May I drop by your house tonight—about 7:30?

Prospect: We'll be real busy tonight packing for a two-week vacation, which starts tomorrow.

Salesperson: I wish you would spare me a few minutes tonight. It could be well worth your time.

Prospect: No, I can't, and I've told you why.

Salesperson: Then after you get back?

Prospect: Maybe.

Salesperson: Today is Friday, July 8. How about three weeks from tonight, July 29 at 7:30?

Prospect: Oh, all right.

Salesperson: Fine. See you then.

On Friday, July 29, Armstrong knocked on Carmichael's door at 7:20 P.M.

Salesperson: Ms. Carmichael? I'm Chris Armstrong. Three weeks ago I phoned you at work and set up an appointment for tonight to talk about saving money.

Prospect: What's this? Who are you? I don't remember any appointment.

Salesperson: We set this up the day before you went on your vacation.

Prospect: Well, maybe so. Come in.

Salesperson: I hope Mr. Carmichael is here.

Prospect: He went out a few minutes ago to the service station.

Salesperson: Ms. Carmichael, if a person earns $22,000 a year on the average from age 28 to age 65, that's a total of $814,000. A lot of money, isn't it? What do you think your average earnings will be from now to the age of 65?

Prospect: I don't know. Maybe $25,000.

Salesperson: $25,000 multiplied by 37 years equals $925,000. Part of that should be yours to keep. But, too often, the size of the savings account goes up and down like a yo-yo. Edna, just how much do you think you could save each month— $150? $100? $75?

Prospect: I guess I could save $75 a week.

Salesperson: Here's a plan where you save only $50 a month. It covers all three possibilities: first, that you live and complete the plan; second, that you die before reaching your goal; and third, that you quit the plan somewhere along the way before completing it. At 65, you can have $136,881 in a lump sum, or you can choose to get a monthly check for life to supplement your other retirement income. If you should die before reaching your goal, $36,589 will be paid to your beneficiary.

Prospect: Wait a minute! What you call a savings plan sounds like life insurance to me. Is it?

Salesperson: Well—uh—it's both. But let me finish. If you quit the plan somewhere along the way, the policy will provide you the cash value it has built up or an amount of fully paid-up insurance. So, you see, this plan takes care of you and provides if you live, if you die, or if you quit. Now, how would you prefer to make your premium deposit? (At this moment Mr. Carmichael enters through the front door.)

Prospect: Bobby, this is Chris Armstrong. I think he's been saying we should save money and then spend it for insurance.

Husband: Hi. We must tell you, Mr. Armstrong, we won't be buying any insurance now.

Salesperson: Well, thanks for your time. See you later. Goodnight.

CASE QUESTION

What errors did the salesperson commit?

CHAPTER 11
The Demonstration

After studying this chapter, you should be able to:

- Indicate the psychological value of demonstrating
- Recognize when and what to demonstrate
- Argue successfully that advance preparation is necessary
- Outline the principles of effective demonstrating
- Describe the use of showmanship in demonstration

Though not all sales presentations include a product demonstration, an impressive demonstration can increase the likelihood of its success. **Demonstrations** can be used for many purposes. They can be constructed to capture the interest of the prospect and move the prospect toward desire, conviction, and, hence, action. They are particularly effective in achieving conviction, by showing what the product will do for the prospect. They prove that the product is the solution to one of the prospect's problems. They prove the salesperson's points by presenting external evidence to back up assertions. They make the story sink in and stick. They translate words into action. They can be used to teach the prospect how to use the product or the merchant how to sell it. Finally, they can be real time-savers, because one simple demonstration can often be the equal of a flood of oral eloquence.

PSYCHOLOGICAL VALUE OF DEMONSTRATING

When a salesperson delivers only an oral sales presentation, prospects may instinctively adopt a defensive role and confront the salesperson as an opponent. But when the salesperson demonstrates, prospects feel involved. The prospect no longer sees the salesperson as an adversary. Instead, salesperson and prospect are joint participants in a situation or an exercise. If the expression "seeing is believing" is true, then smelling, touching, or tasting is learning. The more complicated the subject, the more demonstration facilitates learning.

THE SELLING PROCESS

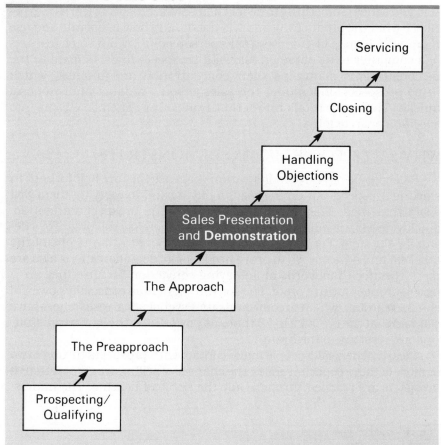

Figure 11-1 Many, but not all, sales presentations include demonstrations. Demonstrations can make for a more effective sales presentation.

To get the maximum psychological impact from a demonstration, the salesperson must do some research. The salesperson must identify the major benefits in order to demonstrate them and must devise the most persuasive way to communicate those benefits. The demonstration must be as simple, clear, and dramatic as possible. Prospect participation is essential. If these requirements are met, rapport will be maximized and the demonstration will be psychologically strong.

WHY PROSPECTS LIKE DEMONSTRATIONS

Prospects like demonstrations because they prefer to trust their own senses rather than a salesperson's promises. They would rather taste than be told how something tastes, rather touch than be told how something feels, and rather operate a product than hear a description of the process. When prospects take part in the demonstration, their participation gives them something to do for themselves. Prospects learn by experience what the product will and will not do, and how to operate and use it properly. Figure 11-2 shows a salesperson pointing out some features of a computer to a customer. Allowing prospects to participate in the demonstrations maintains their concentration and interest, which helps prospects understand the salesperson's product and proposal quickly. They convert talk into action, translating general concepts into specific, concrete form.

WHY SALESPEOPLE LIKE TO DEMONSTRATE

Salespeople rely on demonstrations because they are helpful both in starting prospects out on the road to buying and in carrying them well down that road. They reach out and grab the prospect's attention, quickly develop it into interest, and usually increase the prospect's desire for the item. For many products the demonstration is one of the quickest and surest ways to prove need. Visual demonstrations also are more effective than words at achieving conviction because they are a much stronger form of proof. The sense of sight is an especially powerful channel through which to communicate. Psychological researchers have claimed that the eye is 22 to 25 times as powerful as the ear in transmitting impressions to the brain.

Clearly, when salespeople make contact with prospects through two or more of the prospects' senses, the chances of selling are greater than if prospects are reached through only the sense of hearing. The impres-

Figure 11-2 Demonstrations are very effective in retail selling.

sions salespeople make with demonstrations are deeper and more vivid. The points made are remembered longer because they penetrate further. *Belief* in the product is more likely because prospects have a firmer grasp of the product and its advantages when they see it. Retailers know the impression a demonstration can make, especially when selling cosmetics, as shown in Figure 11-3.

Effective demonstrations tend to reduce buyer opposition by focusing attention on the product's benefits. In that way, prospects cannot deny what the salesperson is demonstrating. Moreover, the salesperson does not seem to be selling—just operating, explaining, and showing. The prospect and the salesperson are partners in executing and watching the demonstration. As a result of their involvement, customers are less likely to be interrupted by ringing telephones, external noises, or other activities going on in the office.

Finally, demonstrations simplify the salesperson's job, giving the salesperson more time and confidence. Demonstrations are used not only to impress, startle, and even amaze, but also to steer prospects whose attention is prone to wander. It is difficult to quarrel with the claim that every sales story ever composed can be strengthened by the addition of demonstrations.

THE NECESSITY OF ADVANCE PREPARATION

Considerable advance preparation is needed if demonstrations are to be powerful and persuasive. The demonstration must be constructed care-

Figure 11-3 Customer participation enhances the demonstration.

HIGHLIGHT 11-1   *An Inevitable Sale*

THE FAR SIDE   By GARY LARSON

9-25   ©1987 Universal Press Syndicate   Larson

**Darren's heart quickened: Once inside
the home, and once the demonstration
was in full swing, a sale was inevitable.**

fully and thoughtfully. Planning the demonstration is just as important
as planning the sales story.

WHAT TO DEMONSTRATE

The salesperson's first responsibility is to have a plan. This involves
deciding what features to demonstrate, what features to omit, and the
most effective sequence for presenting these points. Any products that
are to be shown, operated, or used in any manner should be inspected

before they are exhibited. A malfunctioning product is certain to ruin the chances of making a sale. The appearance of items should be checked periodically to ensure they look as presentable as possible under the harshest conditions. Even the best salesperson cannot sell a product that has a poor appearance.

HOW TO DEMONSTRATE

Sometimes what is to be demonstrated is decided by the prospect. Therefore, salespeople must be able to demonstrate every product feature that a prospect finds interesting. This fact of selling means salespeople must master several methods of demonstrating the outstanding points of their products. This is not to say that salespeople should go through their entire assortment of demonstrations on every call. As we will learn, a more effective plan is to discover the prospect's exact needs and interests, then concentrate the demonstration on the features of the product that most closely relate to those needs and interests.

Yet there will be times when little or nothing is known that would aid in tailoring the demonstration to an individual prospect. In that case, the salesperson should have a standard sequence of steps to follow in the demonstration. The emphasis each step deserves and the timing of the delivery of each point must be predetermined. To demonstrate every feature with equal emphasis ignores two basic truths: (1) product features are not of equal importance, and (2) prospects are not alike. If Prospect A is mainly interested in safety and the salesperson is embarked on a long demonstration of comfort, it is fairly certain Prospect A would become restless and irritated to the point of voicing objections to buying.

WHEN TO DEMONSTRATE

The decision of when to demonstrate is often made during the advance preparation stage. Careful planning should reveal enough about the prospect to help the salesperson determine the appropriate time and place for the demonstration. In general, salespeople find demonstration useful at any time. Some salespeople use demonstrations to open the interview, or to follow an introductory sales talk. When used as openers, demonstrations are usually only partial demonstrations, which are employed only to get the prospect's attention. A demonstration that follows an introductory sales talk is usually accompanied by its own oral presentation.

PRINCIPLES OF DEMONSTRATING A PRODUCT EFFECTIVELY

The all-encompassing principle of effective demonstration is that the salesperson should not tell a prospect something when the prospect can be shown the same thing. The demonstration should involve all of the prospect's senses—sight, touch, taste, and smell. Demonstrating to senses other than the sense of hearing is a more subtle way of showing prospects something they might resent being told. Demonstration allows the product to appeal to whichever sense or senses are most appropriate.

USING VISUAL AIDS

The product is not the only item the salesperson can show to the prospect. Maximum use should be made of **visual aids** that help to picture the sales proposition. Examples of visual aids include advertisements, cross-sections of the product, models, and samples.

COVERING IMPORTANT PRODUCT/SERVICE FEATURES

The standard demonstration should include all features of the product or service that are important to the prospect to avoid the dangers of omission. The first danger is that the feature omitted may be of particular interest to the particular prospect. Second, competitors may be stressing their comparable feature in talking to that prospect. Thus, be prepared to neutralize competitors' claims, or at least offset them. Third, competitors may be telling the prospect that a particular feature of their product is more outstanding. Sometimes the salesperson must take the product apart in order to demonstrate its important features, as is shown in Figure 11-4.

Figure 11-4 Demonstrating the product's important features can offset competitors' claims.

Source: Photo courtesy of Hewlett-Packard Company.

Salespeople who sell to retailers need to demonstrate all of the important benefits that will accrue to the retailer as well as the benefits the retailer's customers will enjoy. In other words, the salesperson's demonstration to the retailer should emphasize those features/benefits that are important not only to the retailer, but also to those who will buy the retailer's products/services.

MAKING THE SALES TALK INTERPRET THE DEMONSTRATION

One of the first things salespeople must learn to do is to synchronize a spoken message with each phase of the demonstration. An accompanying sales talk permits salespeople to continue their selling efforts, which often involve helping prospects to interpret the demonstration. A second purpose served by this sales talk is to prevent awkward periods of silence.

The initial part of the talk normally precedes the demonstration itself. The purpose of this preliminary part of the talk is to build up the demonstration in the prospect's mind, selling the idea of a demonstration. The body of the talk takes product features and converts them as they are demonstrated into advantages of owning and using the product. These advantages can make a strong impact on the prospect because any spoken claim is instantly backed up by product performance.

MAKING THE PRODUCT LOOK ITS BEST

In all demonstrations, both the salesperson and product must make a good impression from the first moment. The product must be displayed in its best possible light. This calls for staging the demonstration when and where it will be most effective. Every distraction that will compete for the prospect's attention should be eliminated. The product should, of course, be tested in advance to see that it will work perfectly. Salespeople should practice giving demonstrations point by point until everything is done perfectly and naturally.

MAKING THE DEMONSTRATION CLEAR

Because one purpose of the demonstration is to clarify what the salesperson says, care must be taken to see that it fulfills this function. The salesperson begins by making sure that the prospect understands the purpose of the demonstration. Then the salesperson demonstrates one point at a time so that the prospect can completely absorb each one. Though brevity aids in making the demonstration clear, one should not sacrifice completeness for brevity. Do not attempt too much in any one demonstration. Displaying too many products or making too many points often results in confusion. Clarity sometimes demands that the salesperson perform some activity rather than depending on the prospect to perform it; for example, figuring out costs or savings. Under some circumstances it may be desirable or even necessary to repeat a demonstration several times.

MAKING THE DEMONSTRATION TRUE TO LIFE

It is not enough for the salesperson just to point to each part or accessory of the product and name it. Instead, the salesperson must show why each was developed and what each means in the day-to-day use and operation of the product. This can be done best if the product is demonstrated in circumstances of actual use. When conditions and atmosphere are realistic, the prospect's feeling of confidence in product and salesperson is increased.

TAILORING THE DEMONSTRATION

The salesperson fits the demonstration to the prospect by dramatizing those features that seem to be of particular interest to the prospect. When an installation is to be used for the demonstration, the one selected should be as nearly like the prospect's circumstances as possible.

In some ways, salespeople prepare for the demonstration exactly as they do for the sales story. They plan it in advance and then modify it only when modification will make it better fit the individual prospect. The job of tailoring the demonstration also includes scheduling it to suit the prospect's convenience, determining its length in the light of the same consideration, and executing it at the proper rate of speed for the prospect.

ENCOURAGING PROSPECT PARTICIPATION

A basic feature of demonstrating is to let the prospect take part as much as possible in the demonstration. Encouraging the prospect to actually work with the product can often do more to bring about a purchase than just talking to the prospect about the product. By using the product, the prospect becomes better acquainted with the product's features and remembers them longer. Handling the product gives the prospect the feel of ownership.

ACHIEVING PROSPECT AGREEMENT

After demonstrating each product feature, the salesperson should check to see that the prospect understands and agrees with the features being demonstrated. If not, further explanation may be needed.

APPEALING TO ALL SENSES

The best demonstrations are those that maintain the prospect's total concentration. Appealing to all senses, not just sight and sound, totally immerses the prospect in the demonstration. Allowing the prospect to feel the product and, if appropriate, taste and smell the product encourages them to pay total attention to the product, the salesperson, and the presentation. This will facilitate the salesperson's attempt to close the sale.

MAINTAINING CONTROL

Control must rest with the salesperson during the demonstration. It is unwise to turn the product or any visual aid over to the prospect if such a step gives up control of the demonstration. An example of this is the prospect who is allowed to leaf through a portfolio or catalog while the salesperson is talking. In such situations, the prospect's attention is focused away from the sales presentation, which decreases the salesperson's effectiveness. By maintaining control of the situation, the salesperson can also prevent the prospect from making mistakes that might be embarrassing. An illustration of this might be the prospect who accidentally breaks the product sample.

Occasionally, a salesperson wanders away from the planned sequence of the demonstration and its objectives. It is not wise to digress from the demonstration to interject such things as local gossip or opinions on matters not connected with the sales interview and demonstration. Instead, conversation should relate to the advantages being shown by the demonstration.

DEMONSTRATIONS INVOLVING PRESENT CUSTOMERS

Sometimes a salesperson of installation products will demonstrate the merchandise using units that have been bought by and installed for satisfied buyers—previous prospects that have been converted into buyers. This might be true, for example, of a heating and air-conditioning system for a house. When the salesperson's demonstration involves present customers, several rules should be kept in mind. First, those customers should be inconvenienced as little as possible. The salesperson should call them well in advance, choose a satisfactory time for the visit, and not stay too long. Second, the customer should be put to no expense. Third, the salesperson should do as much as possible to get things ready for the demonstration and should leave the scene as it was before the presentation. Fourth, the salesperson should express appreciation for any testimony the customer gives the prospect and for answers the customer gives to the prospect's questions. Finally, if the demonstration causes inconvenience or expense for the present customer, compensation or reimbursement may be necessary. Of course, this must never appear as if the favorable testimony is being paid for or that ethics are being compromised.

FOLLOWING UP THE DEMONSTRATION

There should be no hesitation at the conclusion of the demonstration. In most cases, the salesperson will sum up the demonstration and try to complete the sale at that point. If the prospect hesitates, the salesperson should try to find out the cause so that objections or misunderstandings can be clarified and overcome. Thus, if the sale is not made this time the salesperson can improve for the next presentation.

DEMONSTRATION INSTRUCTIONS

A company outline of a suggested demonstration usually is well tested, represents the organized experiences of the company, and often is the cream of successful field trials. Highlight 11-2 shows the instructions one Fortune 500 company provides its salespeople. These instructions provide advice for three different demonstration settings: in the company's district office, in the prospect's place of business, and in the user's business place.

HIGHLIGHT 11-2   *General Suggestions a Fortune 500 Company Provides Its Sales Representatives*

DEMONSTRATING IN THE DISTRICT OFFICE

A demonstration in the district office has many advantages, provided you have made the proper arrangements.

The office personnel should be informed you are not to be disturbed by district personnel or phone calls during the demonstration. It is very important that you have checked the equipment, have all necessary forms and supplies, and the equipment to be demonstrated is carefully cleaned. It is imperative that all necessary details be checked prior to the demonstration, for nothing will detract from your demonstration more than to have to stop and search for a key, a form, or something else that is needed.

Many sales representatives use a checklist of all necessary things to do and the necessary supplies to be used prior to their demonstrations.

1. *Make a definite appointment.*
2. *Ensure privacy and be certain there will be no interruptions.*

3. *Have the right equipment, and make sure it's clean and working properly. (Check for paper, keys, etc.)*
4. *Use a visual listing of the weaknesses of the present system and the features, functions, and benefits of the proposed system.*
5. *If possible, have the equipment the prospect is now using available so a comparison can be made.*
6. *Practice the demonstration. You should know the operations procedures so well that your attention is not divided between the prospect and the system.*
7. *Be prepared to use order forms, leasing forms, and universal agreement forms.*
8. *Dramatize your presentations.*

DEMONSTRATING IN THE PROSPECT'S PLACE OF BUSINESS

For various reasons, many demonstrations must be made in the prospect's place of business. This can be an efficient way of demonstrating, if properly planned.

When the prospect consents to a demonstration in his or her place of business, there is a tendency to bring in the equipment and immediately start to explain what the machine will do. To do the job properly, the sales representatives should prepare for this type of demonstration just as thoroughly as they would plan for a demonstration in the district office.

Several factors must be considered when demonstrating in the prospect's place of business:

1. *The demonstration should be given at a time which will not conflict with the prospect's peak business activity.*
2. *Place the equipment to be demonstrated in a location that assures maximum privacy.*
3. *Make sure all necessary forms and other material needed are available. (Many salespeople have made demonstration kits to be used for such demonstrations, thereby eliminating the failure to have the right material when needed.)*
4. *Make use of audiovisual aids.*

DEMONSTRATION IN A CUSTOMER'S BUSINESS PLACE

Sometimes effective demonstrations are made in a satisfied customer's place of business. Many experienced salespeople have learned the tremendous value of taking a prospect to a customer's business for a demonstration, especially if the prospect has a doubtful attitude toward the company.

The purpose of the demonstration is to prove to the prospect that your proposed system will fill the prospect's needs best. There is no better way to prove your point than to have the prospect see or hear the results of an actual installation from a satisfied customer. The benefits of taking a prospect to a user are twofold:

1. *The prospect can see the benefits of the system and the simplicity of operation. They can see in a few minutes what would probably take hours to present.*
2. *The prospect is more willing to accept the statement of the user regarding the benefits that have resulted from the installation of our equipment. It is natural for a prospect to question certain claims that salespeople make about their products, but very convincing if the claims are substantiated by a satisfied user.*

The advantages of demonstrating in a user's place of business are possible only if you make the proper arrangements with the user. Keep the following points in mind when planning a user demonstration.

1. *Select a user in the same line of business.*
2. *Select a user who formerly used the same type of equipment you are trying to replace, if possible.*
3. *Call on the user sufficiently in advance to make the appointment and briefly outline a few pertinent facts about the prospect.*
4. *Select a user who is also a good "salesperson." Many users are thoroughly sold on all the benefits of our equipment but outwardly are not enthusiastic about these benefits. You should select a user who outwardly praises his or her equipment and does an enthusiastic job of getting all of the important points across to the prospect. When you have that type of user, let the user do most of the talking, and you confine your efforts to merely guiding the demonstration.*

USING SHOWMANSHIP IN THE DEMONSTRATION

If the demonstration is the dramatization of the sales story, **showmanship** can be considered the dramatization of the demonstration. Showmanship makes the demonstration picturesque instead of allowing it to be commonplace. A salesperson who jumps up and down on a suitcase to prove its durability is using showmanship. The salesperson who does no more than list reasons for buying in black ink and objections in red is using showmanship. Handling the product with obvious respect is also showmanship.

The purpose of showmanship is to make the demonstration more effective and to draw the prospect's attention to the product or service. Showmanship enables facts to be presented and actions to be executed in such an unusual way as to secure attention, increase prospect receptivity, make proof more spectacular, and bring about conviction. Showmanship makes a definite impression on the prospect's emotions. Because the prospect buys on both emotion and reason, a message with emotional appeal can often be just as persuasive as a statement of fact.

Two additional, minor uses of showmanship are to entertain prospects while prescribing for their needs, and to demonstrate to merchants the showmanship they can use to secure sales.

Much of the salesperson's thinking and talking, and use of showmanship, must be tailored to the prospect. The major tailoring job in the area of showmanship, however, is fitting it to the salesperson. Two salespeople can be quite successful and yet not be able to use the same types of showmanship. Instead, each salesperson must experiment to identify what can be used in the area of showmanship that will be in harmony with his or her own personality.

WHERE SHOWMANSHIP IS MOST USEFUL

Some form of showmanship can be used with almost any product and by almost any salesperson. There are certain areas in which showmanship is more suitable and effective than in others, however. First, new products will benefit more from showmanship than will established products. The sale of a new product demands a change in the prospect's thinking pattern before the buying pattern will change, and showmanship can help accomplish this big task. Second, specialty products offer better opportunities for the salesperson's imagination to be translated into showmanship than do staple items. This should not be interpreted, though, as meaning that the selling of staple products disallows the use of showmanship. Third, intangibles need showmanship more than tangibles do. Fourth, as price and quality increase, so does the possibility for using showmanship. Finally, there is greater use of showmanship in selling to ultimate consumers than in selling to purchasing agents and middlemen, and more opportunities for showmanship in selling to retailers than in selling to wholesalers.

CAUTIONS ABOUT USING SHOWMANSHIP

Salespeople should remember a number of important cautions about the use of showmanship. First, it is no substitute for a thorough preparation for selling that includes product or service information, prospect information, and the principles of selling. Second, showmanship must not be gaudy, insincere, or undignified, because this not only fails to make a sale but also gives a bad impression of the salesperson, the company, and the product or service. Third, showmanship must be used only to get sales and not to show off. A salesperson's showmanship must not call attention to itself or distract the prospect's attention from the advantages of the product or service.

ATTITUDES TOWARD SHOWMANSHIP

Sales managers often have conflicting attitudes toward showmanship. Based on these attitudes, sales managers might be classified into three groups. The first group consists of those who do not want their salespeople to use any showmanship. They want a sound, businesslike presentation. They also want a salesperson to appear to the prospect as an earnest individual who knows the business thoroughly and is keenly interested in customers' welfare. Some of these managers feel that both advertising and sales promotion need showmanship, but personal selling does not.

Sales managers in the second group feel that showmanship can be helpful but is not essential, arguing that some salespeople cannot develop the art of showmanship, no matter how hard they try. These sales managers prefer their salespeople to work on developing a forceful personality instead of a knack for using showmanship.

The third group of sales managers considers showmanship an essential ingredient in a good salesperson. They consider the use of showmanship one of the most important phases of a salesperson's presentation, largely because people have become accustomed to dramatic presentations through advertising on radio and television and in magazines. They contend that prospects respond more readily to showmanship and that dramatized selling is thus essential. In this situation, dramatized selling means an approach that stirs emotions and/or imagination deeply, and has a striking yet positive effect on the prospect.

SUMMARY

The proliferation of media advertising has made it necessary to use drama in selling. Salespeople should appeal to senses besides hearing as often as possible. Visual aids, combined with an oral presentation, allow the prospect to both see and hear the presentation.

Demonstrations get prospects involved and make them partners in the presentation. More than advertising the existence of products, demonstrations capture prospects' attention and interest, provide them with information, and achieve conviction. Prospects like demonstrations because they can see for themselves the product's benefits.

Demonstrations require careful planning and advance preparation. Each demonstration should be tailored to the prospect and planned to encourage the prospect's involvement. The salesperson who controls the demonstration, follows the plan he or she has established, and uses showmanship will leave a lasting impression on the prospect.

KEY TERMS

demonstrations
visual aids
showmanship

REVIEW QUESTIONS

1. To get the maximum psychological impact from a demonstration, what kinds of things must a salesperson research?
2. What advantages do buyers get from demonstrations? How do salespeople benefit?
3. Should all product features be stressed equally? Why or why not?
4. What kind of preparation should salespeople make in advance of their demonstrations?
5. How should prospects be prepared for a demonstration?
6. Why should a sales talk interpret the demonstration?
7. What should the salesperson do to make the demonstration clear?
8. Why should the salesperson try to make the demonstration true to life?
9. How can a demonstration be tailored to each individual prospect?
10. What advantages are there to encouraging prospect participation in demonstrations?
11. What are some signs that the salesperson has lost control of the demonstration?
12. List four important elements of demonstrations involving present customers.
13. When is showmanship most effective?
14. How can showmanship hurt a presentation?
15. Describe three possible attitudes of management towards showmanship.

DISCUSSION QUESTIONS

1. Assume you are making a presentation that will include a demonstration using flip charts, a tape recording, and a videotape program. What characteristics of the room the presentation will be given in interest you as you prepare?

2. Assume you are selling stereo systems in a stereo shop. How would your demonstration to a young adult differ from one to a middle-aged couple?

3. It has been suggested that a good salesperson involves the prospect in the demonstration whenever possible. Would it be even more beneficial if the prospect were just given the product to try for a short time without a normal demonstration?

CASE 11-1   ALCAS CUTLERY CORPORATION*

Alcas Cutlery Corporation, located in Olean, New York, is a medium-sized manufacturer of very high quality household cutlery sold under the brand name CUTCO cutlery. Alcas sells its products in all 50 states, as well as in Canada, Japan, and the Philippines.

Alcas was founded in 1949 as a joint venture between Alcoa and Case Cutlery. In 1982, Alcas was purchased by its officers and became privately held. Alcas has three basic product lines: Household Cutlery, Sporting Knives, and Professional Cutlery. All products are considered high quality and are at the top end of the product class. The CUTCO household cutlery line accounts for over 92 percent of the total sales volume. The CUTCO line consists of 50 separate cutlery items with an average retail price of U.S. $35 per item. The largest complete set costs approximately $600. All products are manufactured in the Olean facility.

CUTCO products are sold in the United States by the direct selling method. Sales presentations are arranged by reference and appointment, and the product is demonstrated in the home on a one-on-one basis. At any one time, as many as 5000 independent contractors are making sales presentations direct to the consumers, usually in the home. Cold calls are not made.

The CUTCO sales program is conducted by a wholly owned subsidiary, Vector Marketing Corporation, and its independent contractors. Vector has more than 125 offices nationwide, each with its own direct sales organization. Living up to CUTCO's 40-year tradition as the world's finest cutlery, all CUTCO products feature the award-winning Universal Wedge Lock handle and the exclusive Double-D recessed edge. CUTCO's typical production takes 10 to 12 weeks and over 75 production and inspection steps to produce a single knife. CUTCO features a wide variety of household knives to accomplish most of these tasks: Parer, Trimmer, Butcher, Carver, Slicer, French Chef, Turning Fork, Carving Fork, Petite Carver, and Spatula Spreader. Under normal use CUTCO knives stay sharp for years rather than weeks. The unique selling features include

---

*Case prepared by Scot Burton, Donald Lichtenstein, and Nancy Ridgway. Used with permission of the authors and Alcas Cutlery Corporation.

the patented, ergonomic design and construction of the handle and the high-carbon stainless steel blade with its double-durable cutting edge.

The Vector Marketing Division is organized into four regions in the United States—the Western, Central, Northeast, and Southern regions. District Manager Mitch Leger started in the Southern region as one of the college sales representatives. Before selling, all representatives complete a three-phase training program. The first phase is a three-day training seminar. The second phase is practicing, in which trainees actually go into the field and sell. The third phase is advanced training.

Product information is presented on the first day of the three-day training seminar. It includes lectures, demonstrations, information pamphlets, and a videotape on the factory production story of all CUTCO products. After viewing the videotape, a recently trained sales representative makes a sales presentation for the group of trainees. The presentation includes the technical aspects of cutlery, the product craftsmanship and guarantees, and a demonstration. From the presentation, trainees are able to see the progress that can be made in a short period of time.

The second day of training is on the psychology of selling. The first topics are prospecting, planning, presentation, meeting objections, closing, and follow-up—specifically for CUTCO products. Next, they cover competitors and the industry, pricing information, buyer behavior, and the ways that buyers typically react when you try to close the sale. Finally, trainees are taught what to expect customers to tell them and how to respond to their questions and comments.

The third day trainees are taught how to write up an order correctly and how to explain the financing plans the company offers. In the final part of the three-day training, trainees role-play an entire presentation.

During the second phase of the training program, trainees actually practice selling in the field. This allows them to practice what they have been taught in the three-day training session. After practicing for about a week, the trainees attend an advanced training session. During this session they can ask questions that have come up. Also, discussions are held and a videotape is shown to demonstrate the importance of "asking for the sale."

The company provides continuous training to sales representatives in weekly sales meetings, advanced training seminars, and sales conferences. These also help to keep salespeople informed about what is happening in the company, and they provide an opportunity to present new selling ideas and approaches.

CASE QUESTIONS

1. How would you find prospects for CUTCO's Cutlery?
2. Is the training program complete?
3. Outline a presentation for CUTCO Cutlery.
4. What are some effective ways to demonstrate CUTCO Cutlery?

CASE 11-2   TIMBERLAND COMPANY*

The Timberland Company is a premier manufacturer of casual footwear, apparel, and accessories. Through its commitment to authenticity, Timberland produces high-quality, high-performance products that work in tandem with the great outdoors, whether they are protecting a Wall Street executive from a blizzard or a world-champion sailor from the high seas.

The Timberland Company began as Abington Shoe Company in 1952, when Nathan Swartz bought one-half interest in the company. Three years later, Swartz bought the remaining half and brought his two sons into the business. For the next ten years, the Swartz family manufactured shoes under a private label for several leading national brand manufacturers.

In 1965, the company redirected its efforts toward manufacturing quality shoes and introduced injection-molding technology to the footwear industry. This new technology, which directly attached soles onto a leather upper without stitching, produced the first truly waterproof boots and shoes. After much success with the new process, they decided to manufacture footwear under their own brand name. In 1973 they designed a rugged, waterproof, insulated boot and began marketing it themselves under the name Timberland. That same year, a subsidiary was set up in New Hampshire to produce Timberland boots.

The company marketed the new Timberland boots to upscale stores, such as Bergdorf Goodman. Boot sales took off, and it soon became apparent that the subsidiary was running the parent company. In 1978, with more than 80 percent of the footwear being produced under the Timberland name, the Timberland Company became the successor to Abington Shoe Company and discontinued manufacturing unbranded products.

From the start, the Timberland Company established itself as an innovator. In addition to designing the first injection-molded boot, in 1985 the company also developed a patented "tap sole" on its dress shoes to bring increased flexibility, durability, and traction to traditional leather soles. In 1988, Timberland developed an exclusive Gore-Tex® Leather® liner technology for its footwear line.

Timberland also can claim a number of firsts in the boat shoe product category. The company pioneered the scuppered sole in 1981 to reduce hydroplaning; it introduced the quick-drying mesh upper to the boat shoe industry in 1985; and in 1988 it developed the first self-bailing boat shoe, the Hydro-Tech, which actually drains water away from the foot and out of the shoe through vents in the midsole.

---

*Case prepared by Scot Burton and Donald Lichtenstein. Used with permission.

Today, Timberland manufactures and markets a wide collection of premium-quality footwear, apparel, and accessories for men and women, including insulated leather boots, dress, casual, and boat shoes, shearling leather coats, foul-weather gear, hand-knit sweaters, and water-resistant leather luggage and accessories.

Timberland products are distributed in the United States through approximately 3,000 accounts consisting of department stores, specialty stores, shoe stores, and athletic outlets. A sales force of 36 salespersons sells to these accounts which are located in all 50 states. Outside the United States, Timberland has company-owned subsidiaries in England, France, and Germany, and 13 distributors in other countries.

Andrea Haynes was recently hired as a salesperson in the new Apparel Division of Timberland. Seven of the 36 salespeople are in the Apparel Division. Her job involves calling on retail accounts in six southeastern states—Louisiana, Arkansas, Mississippi, Alabama, Georgia, and Florida. Approximately 50 percent of Andrea's time is spent on what she calls administration. This includes paperwork, planning sales calls, telephone contacts with accounts, and in general servicing the accounts. About 30 percent of her time is spent on showing apparel products, actual selling, and conducting clinics (training sessions) with retail employees to help them know the products and sell them better. The remaining 20 percent is spent traveling between retail accounts. Andrea says her job is demanding, as are all sales positions. Fortunately, she believes it is easier to sell the Timberland apparel lines than it was to sell the apparel lines she sold for her previous employer. The reason is the long established, high-quality image and reputation of Timberland footwear.

Another new salesperson, Rick Warner, is responsible for selling Timberland's shoe line to retail accounts for the Footwear Division. He calls on accounts in the same six southeastern states that Andrea does. Rick estimates that his time is spent in a manner similar to Andrea's.

CASE QUESTIONS

1. What are the major points that Rick should emphasize in selling the Timberland footwear lines? What should he cover in his training sessions with retail employees?
2. What are some things Rick can do to most effectively demonstrate his footwear lines?
3. What are the major points Andrea should emphasize in selling her apparel lines? What should she cover in her training sessions with retail employees?
4. What are some things Andrea would do to demonstrate most effectively her apparel lines?

5. From talking to his customers, Rick has discovered that he and Andrea often call on the same retail accounts. He feels that this leads to some duplication of effort and feels that he could sell Timberland's apparel and accessories products in addition to its footwear line. What would be the advantages and disadvantages of reorganizing so that each salesperson sold the entire range of products manufactured by Timberland, including footwear, apparel, and accessories?

CHAPTER 12

Answering Buyers' Objections

After studying this chapter, you should be able to:

- Show why buyers offer opposition to buying

- Discuss the proper attitudes toward objections

- Differentiate between excuses and objections

- Summarize the principles of handling objections

- Name five techniques for handling objections

- Explain how to prevent objections

Salespeople encounter **resistance** from prospects for many reasons. Regardless of whether the resistance is active or passive, expressed or implied, overcoming prospect resistance requires skillful, effective selling techniques. In everyday selling, salespeople frequently meet resistance that acts as a barrier between them and sales.

By opposing purchase suggestions, prospects hope to get rid of the salesperson without buying. Prospects also try to avoid an obligation that will lead to a purchase. An objection does not mean that prospects do not need or want the product offered. In the majority of cases, prospects object because they lack information. They may not be conscious of a need that the salesperson's product will fill, or they may need help in justifying the purchase, to either themselves or others. Furthermore, they want assurance that what they are doing is correct, and this often means that a doubt must be dispelled by the salesperson. This chapter investigates the next stage of the selling process—handling the objections presented by the prospect.

THE ART OF FRICTIONLESS DISAGREEMENT

Disagreement between a salesperson and a prospect is understandable, universal, and inevitable. Objections are both evidence and causes of disagreement. Because the salesperson must be able to disagree without being disagreeable, we must preface our study of objections with a look at

THE SELLING PROCESS

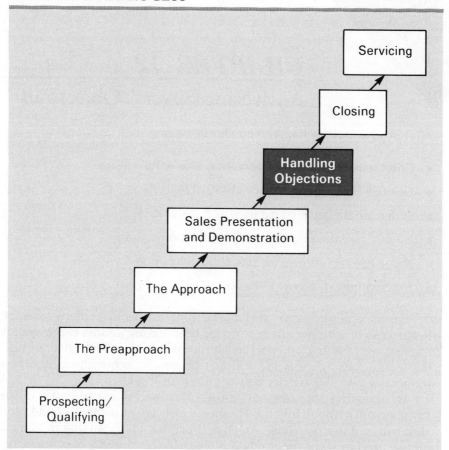

Figure 12-1 Handling objections is the fifth stage in the selling process.

some facets of disagreement. Some guidelines on how salespeople should handle disagreement are shown in Figure 12-2.

COPING WITH PROSPECT HOSTILITY

A very small proportion of prospects are hostile and become antagonistic as they discuss certain objections with salespeople. When this occurs, the salesperson must handle the situation carefully. If a hostile prospect is not handled properly, it can really hurt the salesperson, the product, and the company. The salesperson's objective is to avoid generating hostility, but, when hostility is encountered, to handle it satisfactorily. Figure 12-3 provides suggestions for coping with prospect hostility when it is encountered.

GUIDELINES FOR HANDLING DISAGREEMENT

1. Establish the facts. Should the prospect be in error, establish that fact with tact and diplomacy. **Show that you are right, not that the prospect is wrong**. Give the prospect every opportunity to save face.
2. Agree with the prospect on as many points as possible, introduce them into the dialogue, and get the prospect to acknowledge them as points of agreement. Examples include experiences, hobbies, and backgrounds. When the prospect learns how much the two of you have in common, hostility begins to wane and rapport begins to develop.
3. Disagreement must not be allowed to lead to argument or a tense, emotional confrontation. Remember, "Lose the argument and you lose the sale—win the argument and you lose the customer."
4. Often you can reword the prospect's statement of disagreement to show that your recommendation and the prospect's best interests are in harmony, not in conflict.
5. Sometimes you can switch the conversation smoothly to a topic on which you both agree.

Figure 12-2 Disagreement is inevitable. These guidelines are designed to help the salesperson solve the disagreement while keeping friction at a minimum.

SUGGESTIONS FOR COPING WITH PROSPECT HOSTILITY

1. Above all, listen courteously and sympathetically without interrupting. Try to remain poised, to be friendly, and to stay in control of the situation.
2. Explore to see if the prospect has any justification for his or her belligerence. If you, your product or service, or your firm is at fault, agree to that fact, apologize, and try to right what is wrong.
3. Ask the prospect questions. Then sit tight and listen to the prospect's gripes and resentments. Indulge the prospect by being an attentive and interested audience.
4. On extreme occasions, end the presentation on some pretext (you need to get additional information, for example) and schedule a future call.
5. If the prospect's hostility is aimed at you, stop calling. You cannot afford to yield and defer beyond the limit of your self-respect.

Figure 12-3 Some customers can be hostile. These suggestions can aid the salesperson in handling buyer hostility.

WHY PROSPECTS OFFER OPPOSITION

All salespeople meet resistance and opposition. Success in selling requires disposing of resistance. There is nothing more basic in selling than for salespeople to encounter resistance in the form of silence, questions, or objections. Since opposition will be a problem as long as salespeople sell, salespeople should learn as much as possible about it and become skillful in handling it.

Most resistance is the result of prospects' not knowing enough about their needs and the products or services that might fulfill those needs. They must have more information before they can grasp the salesperson's ideas about needs and benefits. They require more understanding of their needs and of the benefits the salesperson promises before they can appreciate the salesperson's product for what it really is and does. Sometimes the information a prospect has is not accurate. Sometimes there is not enough of it. However lacking the information may be, prospects who do not understand the sales story will probably offer opposition to buying. Such difficulty is most often the salesperson's fault. When prospects do not understand, the salesperson must find out why and try to promote understanding.

Another form of resistance lies in the reluctance of people to change their habits. They tend to adopt a way of life and to stick to it, repeating the same actions time after time. They are not interested in making a change. For some prospects, raising objections has itself become a habit. These prospects give all salespeople at least some token opposition, whether or not they are going to buy.

Some opposition is presented in order to check on the salesperson's knowledge of the product and ability to answer objections. Sometimes prospects are really asking for justification for the purchase they want to make. Or, at the other extreme, they may be trying to justify not buying now.

Personal preference and prejudice also can cause resistance. Differences of opinion exist in prospects' minds about the quality and suitability of various products or services. Some prospects believe that certain competing products/services are superior to the one the salesperson is selling, and such beliefs cause opposition.

Finally, prospects are often afraid to buy. They fear that the product/service may not perform as the salesperson claims, or that the salesperson will benefit more from the transaction than they will. They fear that soon after the purchase they will see a new product/service which they should have waited to buy.

THE PROPER ATTITUDE TOWARD OBJECTIONS

Instead of fearing objections, the salesperson should welcome them and encourage the prospect to speak up. The objections a prospect voices can be helpful to the salesperson. Viewed in one light, they are the pros-

WHY DO PROSPECTS OBJECT?

"Sorry, I need more information."

"No, I really don't need your product."

"Could you explain what you mean by that?"

"I'm sorry, I'm not interested . . . I don't care what you are selling, I'm still not interested."

"Are you sure this product will do what you said it would?"

"Listen, I don't like your product and I don't like you!"

"No, I'm going to wait. I'm not satisfied that this product will satisfy my needs, and I don't want to waste my money!"

Figure 12-4 Determining whether an objection is real or if it is an excuse depends on the salesperson's ability to *read* the prospect.

pect's way of asking for more information and of pointing out areas that need more coverage by the salesperson. As requests for information, prospects' objections give the salesperson opportunities to explain what the product/service will do for the prospect and why the prospect should purchase immediately.

Selling is made easier when the prospect objects, because the prospect who talks is easier to deal with than the prospect who is silent. The most dangerous objections are those that are not disclosed. When a prospect refuses to take part in the conversation, the salesperson is in the dark about what the prospect thinks, about points that need amplification, and about the buying motives to appeal to. Careful observation of a prospect's objections will reveal which of the five buying decisions are missing before the attempt to close the sale is made.

Objections also offer salespeople a way of gauging their progress toward completion of the sale. Prospects who object in some way generally are giving some thought to the salesperson's presentation. It is fairly safe to say that almost all sales are made after the prospect has voiced some objection.

Clearly, the salesperson's proper reaction is to welcome objections. All questions and negative statements should be treated as requests for information, and objections should be used to plan the future course of the sales presentation. In handling objections, the salesperson should be courteous so as not to antagonize the prospect. The salesperson should be poised and tactful and should have a sympathetic understanding of what an objection really is.

EXCUSES VERSUS OBJECTIONS

Before a salesperson can close a sale, real obstacles that stand between the prospect and a purchase must be identified and removed from the prospect's mind. The hostile statement or objection the prospect makes may or may not be the real barrier preventing the purchase. Frequently, apparent objections are only excuses. Rather than admit feeling unable to afford the product/service, the prospect may tell the salesperson that the color is wrong. Similarly, rather than admit to being a procrastinator, the prospect may ask to talk things over with someone else. Thus, one of the salesperson's first objectives is to identify and isolate the real reason why the prospect refuses to buy. Those obstacles that are really excuses merely waste the time of a salesperson who handles them in detail. If one excuse is answered sincerely, the prospect merely thinks up another.

THE EXCUSE

An excuse is a type of resistance offered by prospects. Sometimes it is an attempt to dismiss the salesperson. Sometimes the prospect is rationalizing resistance to buying—for example, the prospect who buys a lower-priced item and hates to admit it, does not have the authority to buy, or is not carrying enough money to buy. Sometimes the excuse is only a buying defense erected by the prospect who feels obligated to offer some resistance even when planning to buy. Standard excuses are often voiced by prospects, many of whom tend to repeat what they have heard from someone else.

THE OBJECTION

An objection is the real reason the prospect has not said "yes" to one of the five buying decisions. It points to the buying decisions that still must be made by the prospect. The objection represents valid resistance, and it must be handled before the prospect will buy.

PRINCIPLES OF HANDLING OBJECTIONS

The basic principles of handling objections that a salesperson should learn and remember are: (1) clarify the objection if necessary; (2) classify the objection; (3) maintain control at all times in handling the objection;

HIGHLIGHT 12-1

In the Xerox Corporation's "Professional Selling Skills III" Program, two types of objections are noted. One is misunderstandings due to a lack of information about the company's products and services. The other is drawbacks that result from the inability of the product or service to satisfy the customer's needs.

Xerox advises handling a misunderstanding in the following manner:

1. *Use questions to confirm the customer's need.*
2. *Use a support statement to clear up the misunderstanding.*

To overcome a drawback, Xerox recommends minimizing the importance of the drawback in the customer's mind. That is, use the previously accepted benefits of your product or service to outweigh the drawbacks the customer has. This is done by:

1. *Reminding the customer of the previously accepted benefits.*
2. *Probing to uncover needs.*

For example, the customer objects to your price being too high. You could respond, "Granted our price is high; however, you said you were looking for the fastest product on the market, and that's us."

(4) don't argue with the prospect; (5) be diplomatic in answering the objection; (6) fit the answer to the prospect; (7) minimize, not maximize, the objection; and (8) capitalize on the objection if possible.

CLARIFYING THE OBJECTION

Before attempting to answer any objection, the salesperson must have a clear understanding of just what the prospect means. A difficult problem is presented when the prospect hides behind excuses such as "not interested," "not in the market," or "no time to see you." One way to find out the real objection is to urge prospects to discuss fully what they have on their minds. Another way is to ask diplomatically what, where, who, how, and why concerning the objection. A third course consists of alert observation until the real objection is identified. In clarifying the objection, it is often desirable for the salesperson to restate the objection. This assures the prospect that the difficulty is understood and gives the salesperson a few seconds in which to analyze the objection and determine what might be the best method of answering it.

CLASSIFYING THE OBJECTION

The act of buying requires that the buyer make five affirmative decisions, and objections point out negative buying decisions. The salesperson can thus tell from the type of objection which buying decisions are still to be made favorably.

Some objections clearly indicate that the prospect does not recognize any need or does not want to admit the existence of need. In other cases, the objection implies a belief on the part of the prospect that no personal needs demand immediate attention.

Some prospects show through their resistance that they believe competing products/services are better than the salesperson's product/service. Moreover, the prospect may decide that the services accompanying competing products are superior. Resistance of this nature indicates that the salesperson has not successfully established need and matched the product or service to that need.

Opposition to source usually implies a lack of confidence in the seller. Perhaps the prospect does not have complete confidence in the salesperson as an individual, or perhaps the prospect has doubts about the salesperson's company.

Objections to price mean that the salesperson has not built up an acceptable amount of value or satisfaction for the price quoted. More selling effort may be needed on the buying decisions of need and product.

When a prospect objects to the decision concerning time, it means only one thing: the salesperson must obtain more enthusiastic agreement on the first four buying decisions.

MAINTAINING CONTROL

Every salesperson needs to acknowledge that there are some prospects who will hide behind a host of objections. These objections must be treated calmly, necessitating control. The salesperson who stops talking after answering an objection, or worse, asks if there are any other questions or matters causing the prospect difficulty easily loses control. Instead of pausing, a better course of action is to try to close the sale, and, if not successful, continue the sales presentation. This does not prevent checking with the prospect to determine understanding and agreement, however.

AVOIDING AN ARGUMENT

A salesperson should never argue with a prospect. If the salesperson wins the argument, the prospect's goodwill is lost. If the salesperson loses the argument, the sale is lost. Because it is hopeless to antagonize someone and at the same time try to gain influence, it is never wise to take issue with prospects. Even when the salesperson is right, contradicting the prospect is running a great risk. Rebuttal by the salesperson intensifies opposition. Blanketing the prospect with questions in order to divert negative thoughts and to bring out the weakness of the objection is more effective than arguing.

BEING DIPLOMATIC

Challenge, contradiction, or direct attack increase prospect opposition, no matter how sound or logical the salesperson's answer. Salespeople should never disagree with the prospect in such a way as to cause offense. A flippant or belittling answer, a blunt statement that the prospect is wrong, and a condescending attitude are all likely to cause unfavorable reactions from the prospect. Diplomacy demands that the salesperson tactfully remove incorrect beliefs and replace them with accurate ones.

FITTING THE ANSWER TO THE PROSPECT

The salesperson must give the objecting prospect a new concept to accept as a substitute for a former opinion. The salesperson's chances of success are increased if the answer is molded to fit the prospect. This task has two phases. In the first phase, the salesperson makes certain that the prospect's real difficulty is understood and convinces the prospect of that understanding. The second phase consists of phrasing the reply in whatever manner seems most appropriate to the prospect's nature. Answers will be more persuasive if they are adapted to the prospect's own personality. The prospect's attitudes, not the salesperson's, should be the guide in shaping the reply.

MINIMIZING OBJECTIONS

Objections should be minimized. To accomplish this, the salesperson should go to no greater length than is necessary in handling an objection. The salesperson should make sure that the prospect understands and agrees and then should immediately move on in the presentation. In saying just enough to dispose of the objection to the prospect's satisfaction, the salesperson avoids dwelling on it and thereby exaggerating its importance.

An attempt to avoid an objection completely may magnify its importance. Prospects may attribute undue significance to an objection that the salesperson does not answer. When objections will be answered logically later in the presentation, it may be helpful to delay responding. But usually it is best to tell the prospect you will be talking about that objection later in the presentation.

CAPITALIZING ON THE OBJECTION

Every objection should be used constructively to bring out as many benefits as possible. The salesperson can capitalize on an objection by translating it into a justification for purchase. Each objection can thus be used to bring the prospect closer to the purchase.

In taking advantage of an objection, the salesperson may find it wise to clarify some or all of the sales points that already have been made. A second approach is to review all the advantages the product offers that are related to the particular objection. For example, when a prospect complains of high price, the salesperson points out all the product features the buyer will enjoy for that price. A third method of capitalizing on the objection is to offer more facts to the prospect. A fourth technique is to isolate the buying motive that gave rise to the objection and then build up as many benefits as possible for that one motive.

To capitalize effectively on an objection, the salesperson should attempt a trial close after answering an objection. If the trial close does not succeed, or if the salesperson feels that it is too early to attempt to close, then he or she should continue the presentation.

WHEN DO OBJECTIONS OCCUR?

Quite simply, objections can occur at any point during the sales presentation. To illustrate this point further, let us divide the selling process into three vital stages: the *approach*, the *presentation*, and the *close*.

APPROACH

It is likely the salesperson will encounter some resistance when trying to set up an appointment, thus reducing the salesperson's chances of making a presentation. This is especially true when the salesperson is selling an intangible product, idea, or service, such as insurance, creative advertising, or financial services. For this reason, some companies prefer that their salespeople not set up an appointment, and instead "cold call" their customers. These companies reason that it is harder for the prospect to object to an appointment to the salesperson's face than if the salesperson were to call on the phone.

PRESENTATION

The salesperson can expect a series of objections during the presentation. Objections that are raised at this point are very favorable to the salesperson because they show that the prospect is listening and paying attention to the presentation. Also, when prospects object, they are telling the salesperson exactly where they stand. That is, "I do not understand that point you just made. However, if you explain it to me, I will be more receptive to buying." On the opposite end, prospects who are silent and emotionless throughout the presentation have not offered any indication that they understand a word that was said. In this situation, salespeople have no idea of how effective their presentations are.

CLOSE

Prospects often object to the seller's price during the close. Sometimes prospects want to feel as though they are getting a "deal," or "pulling one over on the salesperson." Objections during the close must be handled carefully, because this is the decision point. No matter how effectively the objections were answered through the first two stages, if salespeople cannot satisfy objections presented at the close, they will not get the sale.

In conclusion, knowing when objections are likely to occur can help salespeople prepare effective answers for them, and be ready to use those answers when the objection arises. If a large number of objections arise, it is very likely the salesperson has not prepared a strong presentation.

WHEN TO HANDLE OBJECTIONS

There is no single, speedy test to separate objections from excuses. Likewise, there is no single technique for coping with either. In one sense, every excuse or objection should be handled. This does not mean that each should be answered, and most certainly it does not mean that the excuse or objection should be featured. Each of the general methods listed below will be effective in some situations. Unless otherwise specified, throughout the rest of this chapter the word *objection* will be used to include both real objections and excuses.

FUTURE HANDLING

It is not always necessary to answer an objection immediately. Instead, the salesperson may choose to disregard the objection the first time it is made. In passing up the objection, the salesperson can make no comment at all, simply appearing not to hear it, or the salesperson can say "yes" with no change of facial expression and continue the presentation.

Ignoring the objection is one way of separating the real from the artificial. If the prospect's objection was an excuse used to change the subject or to interrupt the salesperson's story, it probably will not be mentioned again. Indeed, if it was phony, there is no reason for the salesperson to answer it.

In some cases, the prospect gets the idea that the objection was not important enough to have any impact on the salesperson. By not stopping to handle it, the salesperson keeps the objection from appearing to be a big issue and thus tacitly suggests that it not be brought up again.

Sometimes when an objection is raised, the salesperson can ignore it and immediately make recommendations on the quality and price for the prospect to order. This technique may antagonize the prospect, however, and can result in a lost sale. There is one thing the salesperson can count on when an objection is ignored—if the prospect is serious, he or she will repeat the objection.

Postponing the answer to an objection may help the salesperson in more ways than one. Resistance, when set aside for a few moments, often evaporates. Also, the delay allows the salesperson to establish more benefits before taking up a negative matter, thus reducing its significance. Finally, by postponing the handling until some later moment, the salesperson maintains control of the interview and is confronted by the obstacle at the time of his or her own choosing. As has been mentioned, postponement must not resemble evasion.

IMMEDIATE HANDLING

Under the right circumstances, an immediate, *direct answer* is the proper method of handling objections. One significant advantage of this technique is that it convinces the prospect of the salesperson's sincerity. In addition, it prevents any inference of evasion or inability to answer. A third advantage is that quick, deft handling accompanied by courteous and intelligent consideration often kills objections before they establish themselves in the prospect's mind. Once prospects realize the objection was really baseless, they can concentrate completely on the rest of the salesperson's story. Finally, quick handling keeps the salesperson off the defensive. However, smiles and tact are essential to success.

The *indirect answer* is probably the most widely recommended, the most widely used, and the most effective method of handling objections. It is versatile, flexible, and safe. Basically, it involves two steps. The first is for the salesperson to agree with the objection with a remark such as, "That's true" or "Yes." The second is to follow up with "but" or "however" as a point of departure into a different area for consideration, an area that leads right back into the selling story.

The salesperson's "yes" implies an attitude of respect for the prospect's viewpoint, and the "but" suggests that the salesperson has certain related facts that may not have come to the prospect's attention. The salesperson agrees with the prospect as much as possible, admitting that there may be some truth in what the prospect says, and then points out some other factors that must be considered. After giving some ground in opening the reply, the salesperson then tactfully proceeds to show the prospect how this particular case is different.

The principle of this technique is that concession on the salesperson's part will influence the prospect to be more receptive. By expressing an understanding of the prospect's position, the salesperson encourages the prospect to listen. Figure 12-5 lists a number of techniques that can be used for handling objections.

TECHNIQUES FOR HANDLING OBJECTIONS

1. **The "Yes, but" Technique.** A very good way of handling most resistance is the indirect answer known as the **"Yes, but" technique.** This method avoids argument and friction by respecting the prospect's opinions, attitudes, and thinking. It operates well where the prospect's point does not apply in a particular case. Examples: (1) "Yes, I can understand that attitude, but there is another angle for you to consider."; or (2) "Yes, you have a point there, but in your particular circumstances, other points are involved, too."

2. **Boomerang.** The **boomerang technique** allows the salesperson to agree with the prospect and then to show how the prospect's objections should not prevent a sale. It involves agreeing with the objection and then making another statement that translates the objection into a reason for buying.
    Example: Prospect: "Your product is too new to this area. My customers will not buy something they have never heard of before." Salesperson: "You're right that we just started selling in this area last month. So, in order to promote our product, we will be launching an extensive advertising program in the area."

3. **Ask Questions.** The "why" question is of value in separating excuses from genuine objections and in probing for hidden resistance. The same question is useful in disposing of objections. Probing or exploratory questions are excellent in handling silent resistance. They can be worded and asked in a manner that appeals to the prospect's ego. In making the prospect do some thinking to convince the salesperson, questions of a probing nature get the prospect's full attention.

4. **Deny.** One way to respond to an objection is simply to point out that the prospect is wrong. When using the **denial technique,** salespeople must make sure they can support their denial with facts. Also, denial approaches must be used cautiously because they may upset prospects. The salesperson may win the argument but lose the sale.
    Example: After listening patiently to the prospect's objection, the salesperson might say the following: "I'm not sure I understand what your objection is. Could you tell me again?" If the prospect repeats the same incorrect objection the salesperson can then say: "I'm not sure where you got your information, because, as you see, *Consumer Reports* rates our product as being superior to the others in terms of performance."

5. **Hearing the Prospect Out.** Some prospects object because they have been wronged in the past. Often they just want to release

their negative feelings. If the salesperson allows them to vent their frustration, the end result is likely to be a new and refreshed perspective.

Example: "I realize you have been taken advantage of before, and I know it feels very unpleasant, but I assure you that my company will guarantee our product for a full three years."

Figure 12-5 These suggested techniques can help the salesperson effectively handle objections. The salesperson should experiment with these to determine which ones work best and in which situations.

EXAMPLES OF HANDLING OBJECTIONS

This section consists of examples of objections that are frequently encountered and answers that will, at times, be appropriate and successful. The objections are divided evenly among the five buying decisions.

OBJECTION TO NEED

EXAMPLE NO. 1

Situation:	The thermopane window salesperson has an appointment at the prospect's home.
Prospect:	"I'm really not interested in new windows. The ones I have are fine."
Comments:	This may mean that the prospect is not willing to make the sacrifice that buying would demand. It also may mean being unaware of needs, or uninformed about what the salesperson's product will do. Often it is a mere excuse. The comment, "I'm not interested," definitely cannot mean that the prospect is not interested in health, wealth, popularity, economy, comfort, safety, and convenience. So the salesperson's job is to find where product satisfaction touches and stimulates one or more of the prospect's buying motives.
Technique:	*Agree and counter, relating the product to the prospect's buying motive.*
Salesperson:	"I understand. But what I would like to do is determine how much my windows could reduce your monthly energy bill, and then give you a chance to consider them. To do this I need some information. Would you help me by telling me what your typical monthly energy bill is?"

EXAMPLE NO. 2

Situation: The potato chip salesperson is trying to convince the grocery chain's head buyer to carry a line of Cajun-style potato chips.

Prospect: "Listen, we've got potato chips coming out of our ears. There just is no shelf space to give to your product. Besides, how do I know that Cajun potato chips will sell?"

Comments: When retailers tell a salesperson that they will handle the merchandise only after there is a demand for it, they are usually just trying to get rid of the salesperson. It may not be too far from the truth to say that no retailer has, or can, become a successful merchant by waiting to get calls before stocking a product. Also, few retailers can say that every product on their shelves provides maximum profits for that space. The "boomerang" technique converts an objection into a reason for buying. It demands skilled handling and a friendly manner. It should be used sparingly.

Technique: *Boomerang.*

Salesperson: "Mrs. Delany, I understand your shelf space limitations and that is one of the reasons you should try our product. Our firm recognized the limited shelf space in most stores so we developed a 2-foot-by-3-foot corner aisle display. We can put one in and you can evaluate the performance of our Cajun potato chips without any reduction in shelf space and without any risks. Further, if you do not receive positive results in two weeks we will take back the unsold chips and remove the displays."

EXAMPLE NO. 3

Situation: The advertising salesperson for KRAM-FM radio is calling on a local delicatessen owner.

Prospect: "My business is doing fine. I really do not need to advertise."

Comments: Prospects often do not know they lack something. It is risky to take issue with them over whether they need the salesperson's product. Instead, the salesperson should provide examples to the prospects, relating the experiences and case histories of impartial, similar third parties. In this way prospects may recognize the similarity between their own needs and those of the salesperson's satisfied customers. Need must be established before any other consideration can be discussed seriously.

If an individual cannot use the salesperson's product to his or her advantage, that person does not need it and, hence, is not a prospect. When a salesperson has the misfortune to spend time on a person only to find that need does not exist, then the only thing to do is to start a search for a person who is a prospect.

Technique: *Agree and counter, using a case history.*

Salesperson: "Mr. Marinaro, I'm glad to hear that your business is doing so well, but before you make a final decision against advertising let me tell you about Sal's Pizzeria on Fourth Street. Sal was very skeptical about radio advertising because he did not feel people really listened to the radio. I was able to persuade him to advertise with us because we targeted the teenage and young adult crowd, who are his customers! Sal's business is up 20 percent over this time last year, and he's still advertising with us."

OBJECTION TO PRODUCT

EXAMPLE NO. 1

Situation: The used-car salesperson is talking to a prospect who has had a bad experience in the past with a certain make of automobile.

Prospect: "Don't talk to me about that make of car. The last one I had was a complete lemon. I'll never buy another one."

Comments: When a prospect is bitter toward the salesperson's make or brand, the salesperson has a difficult job. The salesperson must be conciliatory and in harmony with the prospect, yet dare not appear disloyal to the company represented and its merchandise. Sometimes the salesperson can point to product changes that make the prospect's criticism no longer valid. Sometimes the changes have been not in product but in circumstances, with the same result. Sometimes the salesperson should encourage the prospect to get rid of resentment by letting off pressure and to unburden personal feelings before an audience by airing the complaint completely. At the same time, this performance aids the salesperson in two ways. It obligates the prospect to listen to the salesperson's reply, and it provides tips and clues as to what that reply should be.

Technique: *Hearing the prospect out.*

Salesperson: "Tell me all about it."

EXAMPLE NO. 2

Situation: The salesperson is trying to convince the owner of a chain of beauty salons to purchase his computerized point-of-sale terminals for her salons.

Prospect: "John, I'm just not interested in replacing my cash registers with your terminals."

Comments: As was explained in an earlier example, the comment "I'm just not interested" is usually an excuse. The salesperson must probe to get to the real problem.

Technique: *Ask questions.*

Salesperson: "Miss Brocato, there must be some reason why you won't consider my new computerized point-of-sale terminals. Could it be our warranty? Is it the payment terms? Do you feel you do not need to keep information on each sale, such as the type of service used, or the average sale?"

EXAMPLE NO. 3

Situation: The copier salesperson has encountered a prospect who has been given false information by a competitor.

Prospect: "Well, what you say is all well and good, but Tom Snyder with Kodak Office Copiers says his copiers are faster and provide better quality than yours."

Comments: This objection must be handled tactfully. You do not want to downgrade your competitor or get involved in a mudslinging competition. You do, however, need to set the prospect straight in a professional manner.

Technique: *Deny, using a product comparison.*

Salesperson: "Sir, Mr. Snyder has some fine copiers, but his comparisons are just not true. I will be happy to compare the speed and quality of my copiers with his and let you be the judge."

OBJECTION TO SOURCE

EXAMPLE NO. 1

Situation: The salesperson from a small company is meeting resistance as to the size of their company.

Prospect: "Your company is too small."

Comments: Sometimes a diverting move benefits the salesperson. One way to switch the prospect's mind away from the objection is to pass the conversational ball back in the form of a question. The salesperson can use the question to be certain to have a clear understanding of the nature of the prospect's resistance and, thus, know where more selling is needed.

Technique: *Ask questions.*

Salesperson: "Does the size of my company really matter? Would you like to talk to a few of my customers to see how satisfied they are with our service?"

EXAMPLE NO. 2

Situation: The retailer is concerned about the seller's ability to provide the service being offered.

Prospect: "Jim, I'm concerned about how quickly your company can restock my shelves if we have a rush on a product."

Comments: What a manufacturer does to win new customers is always good news to retailers.

Technique: *Boomerang.*

Salesperson: "I understand your concern about avoiding stockouts. Two years ago we installed a computerized ordering system to help us respond to unexpected demand. Since installing the system we can guarantee to have the product on your shelves within 36 hours. If you would like to talk to some of our customers about this system I would be glad to give you some names of people to call."

EXAMPLE NO. 3

Situation: The salesperson is not going to be able to replace the prospect's current supplier, and so will try instead to become a second supplier for the prospect.

Prospect: "I've been giving all my business to the Arrow Shirt company for years and see no reason to change now."

Comments: Prospects who are fiercely loyal to their present suppliers can be approached because of just that characteristic. Friendship between buyer and seller can be a very difficult factor for the salesperson who is hunting for concrete, clear proof that the prospect should take on a new vendor. The problems involved in buying from friends, the healthful effect of competition on present suppliers, the importance of not being dependent on a single source of supply, the desirability of a wider inventory, and the relatively greater importance of product over maker are possible lines of approach. Intelligent selling technique demands that the salesperson find why the prospect is so loyal and prefers to deal with the Arrow Shirt company.

Technique: *Agree and counter by showing the benefits of using multiple suppliers. Asking questions may be helpful, too.*

Salesperson: "That's fine, because Arrow is a good company. You might find, however, that if Arrow had a bit of competition, you would stand to benefit. And the danger of putting all your eggs in one basket is something to think about."

OBJECTION TO PRICE

EXAMPLE NO. 1

Situation: The prospect is showing resistance to the price of the automobile.

Prospect: "$15,000 is far too much money to pay for this car."

Comments: It is always good for the salesperson to build up, as early as possible, a large mass of value against which the prospect can measure price. The larger the mass and the lower the price, the more attractive the ratio seems. The salesperson should never apologize for a high price. Instead of taking the defensive, the salesperson should point out how modest the price is in relation to what it buys. Some prospects relax a bit when they are told that instead of spending money, they are making an investment. Other prospects like to be told that what they will save will pay for the item. Purchase price is often minimized when reduced to small amounts by, for example, spreading the cost over the life of the product.

Technique: *Agree and counter by spreading the cost over a period of time.*

Salesperson: "I realize that $15,000 is a lot of money, but if we spread the note out over 60 months I'm sure I can keep the monthly cost down around $250."

EXAMPLE NO. 2

Situation: The salesperson is trying to convince the owner of a small business to replace the old copier.

Prospect: "I just can't afford a new copier right now."

Comments: So-called easy terms of payment are an effective answer to objections of high price. Features stressed are low down payment, small periodic payments, long pay period, low charge for the privilege, and, in general, the philosophy of paying out of income. This should be balanced with other features such as increased employee productivity.

Technique: *Boomerang, using installment terms. Counter with product advantage.*

Salesperson: "I agree that the monthly payment on this machine is higher than your present one. But with the terms of sale we're offering during this promotion period we can keep the increase to a minimum and spread the cost over three years. This should be more than offset by the increased productivity of your secretary."

EXAMPLE NO. 3

Situation: The salesperson has several different models of point-of-sale terminals to present to the owner of the company.

Prospect: "Before we take up any of each other's time, how much will each point-of-sale terminal cost?"

Comments: It is neither desirable nor possible to ignore the fact that price is a tremendous obstacle for higher-priced products. The sooner the salesperson has to take up the topic, the greater the salesperson's disadvantage. When the salesperson has to quote a rather high price early in the presentation, it seems all the higher because there has not been time to describe all that the product/service will do for its user. The more firmly the salesperson establishes the benefits before referring to price, the more price becomes merely a detail.

Technique: *Postponing.*

Salesperson: "I have them from $300 to $2,000, so I can't quote a price to you until we see what model you need."

OBJECTION TO TIME

EXAMPLE NO. 1

Situation: The prospect is postponing a decision, probably because she or he is afraid of the circumstances.

Prospect: "I'd better think this over."

Comments: This may come from a postponer of decisions. It may come from one who was not actually sold on need for the product. Some of the salesperson's points may not have been clear to the prospect, or they may have been misinterpreted. Technically, the objection is evidence of inadequate interest more than it is a real objection. The salesperson may elect to move for an immediate close by finding out what it is the prospect wants to think about and handling it then and there. In this event, the advantages of buying now will be stressed. If unsuccessful in this attempt to close the sale, the salesperson may choose to leave with the prospect a checklist against which the prospect can test the brands under consideration. Because the list is drawn up for comparison purposes, it will certainly include every characteristic or feature that is exclusive with the salesperson's product.

Technique: *Ask questions.*

Salesperson: A general response might be: "What is it that you are still undecided about?" More specific responses include: "Have I adequately explained our training program to ensure your employees know how to use our product?" "Did you realize we could deliver and install the machine tomorrow?"

EXAMPLE NO. 2

Situation: The salesperson wants Eckerd Pharmacy to carry their new line of cold medicine.

Prospect: "I cannot do it at this time. Business has been bad, and I already carry eight or nine brands."

Comments: One way to try for an immediate purchase is to describe and emphasize the enjoyment that begins with possession. This enjoyment usually consists of added satisfaction, added savings, increased profits, increased sales, or a combination of all of these.

Technique: *Agree and counter, stressing the savings and profits that could immediately be achieved.*

Salesperson: "I know times are tough right now, but you cannot afford to let this deal pass. By purchasing now you can take advantage of our introductory offer, plus you will immediately be making profits from product sales."

Technique: *Boomerang.*

Salesperson: "I know times are tough, and I realize you already carry nine other brands. I have evaluated the sales of those other brands in other stores and my study shows our sales are higher."

EXAMPLE NO. 3

Situation: The last computer this company purchased became obsolete within two years.

Prospect: "I'm going to wait to be sure of what we are buying. Two years ago we purchased a computer system and it is no longer any good to us. We cannot afford to keep throwing money away like that. No, next time I'm going to be very, very sure!"

Comments: In this situation, the salesperson is best off letting the prospect get everything off his or her chest. There is still the opportunity of a sale here because the prospect is not anti-computer, just very hesitant. Let the prospect speak his or her peace, get the prospect relaxed, then resume the sale.

Technique: *Hearing the prospect out.*

Salesperson: "I can understand your reason for wanting to be sure. Why don't you tell me how you are using your present computer? Then I can explain our trade-in policy as well as the ways to upgrade and expand the models we are now selling to meet your future computing needs."

PREVENTING OBJECTIONS

Despite the advantages salespeople can gain through a careful examination of prospects' objections, there are several very good reasons for attempting to prevent objections. Preventing objections keeps the prospect from doing any negative or unfavorable thinking and talking. Second, voicing of an objection at an awkward moment is avoided. Third, prevention makes more time available to the salesperson for use in presenting a complete sales story. Fourth, the salesperson appears completely fair in cases where objections are both raised and answered by the salesperson or the answer is woven into the presentation. Fifth, and most important of all, the prospect is prevented from taking a position. Once an individual states a position, there is pressure to stick to this commitment and to defend it. Most people hate to appear easily influenced, to allow their minds to be changed with little trouble, because that is close to admitting they were wrong.

The best way to avoid objections is to prepare a complete sales story; one that includes all the information the prospect will need. Then in telling the story, the salesperson should check with the prospect to make sure that each point is clear.

The salesperson should note and list the most frequent and most troublesome objections encountered in interviews. The salesperson should then work into the sales presentation the most effective answers to these most common questions, complaints, and criticisms. The answers should be in the form of positive selling points. The sales story certainly should include the strongest points about product features, which competitive salespeople tend to discount in order to put some doubt in the prospect's mind. It is this type of product feature which must be covered fully and favorably in the sales story.

The clearer, more logical, and more complete the sales story, the less important a prospect's objections become. If the prospect's attention is monopolized by a mountain of positive points and a small pile of negative points, the prospect will be inclined to consider the objections planned as too insignificant to mention.

SUMMARY

Disagreement between salespeople and prospects is inevitable, especially when the prospect's purchasing power is limited. Frequently, objections are nothing more than excuses given because the prospect is reluctant to accept change or the products that lead to change.

Objections can arise at any time during the sales presentation. The salesperson's first job is to identify the real reason behind the prospect's refusal to buy—an excuse or an objection. Next, the salesperson should follow basic principles for handling objections. These include: (1) clarifying the objection; (2) classifying the objection; (3) maintaining control; (4) avoiding arguments; (5) being diplomatic; (6) fitting the answer to the prospect; (7) minimizing the objection; and (8) capitalizing on the objection.

The following techniques are often used in handling objections: (1) agree and counter ("Yes, but"); (2) boomerang; (3) question; (4) deny; (5) hear the prospect out; or (6) postpone the answer until later in the presentation.

The salesperson should encourage objections. If their objections are handled successfully, then customers are generally better satisfied. Often, a well-constructed and complete sales story can help prevent the negativism of an objection.

KEY TERMS

resistance	boomerang technique
misunderstandings	ask questions technique
drawbacks	denial technique
"yes, but" technique	hear-customer-out technique

REVIEW QUESTIONS

1. Why is frictionless disagreement desirable?
2. List three ways to deal with buyer hostility.
3. List four reasons why buyers offer objections.
4. Why should the salesperson welcome objections?
5. What is the basic difference between an excuse and an objection?
6. How can the salesperson use objection classification as a sales tool?
7. Why shouldn't a salesperson ever argue with a prospect?
8. How can salespeople capitalize on objections?
9. What are the advantages of a direct answer?
10. What is the best way to prevent objections?

DISCUSSION QUESTIONS

1. Assume you are a sales manager training a new sales representative. The sales representative is young, bright, straight out of college, and ready to tackle the world. What advice would you give him or her on handling objections and maintaining a high level of motivation?

2. What problems will a salesperson using a memorized presentation encounter when trying to answer objections?

3. Assume you are a sales representative and have just been given an objection that you do not know the answer for. Do you bluff that you know and lie, or do you honestly admit that you cannot answer their question? Why?

CASE 12-1   UNIVERSITY SUPPORT CORPORATION (USC)*

University Support Corporation was established in February 1989. In conjunction with Louisiana State University, Baton Rouge, and the LSU Alumni Association, it has the exclusive rights to sell outdoor advertising on attractive, high-quality waste receptacles on the campus. The only other methods of directly targeting this unique market are the school newspaper (*Daily Reveille*), fliers distributed on campus or posted on bulletin boards, direct-mail efforts from a list of students, university directory yellow pages, football stadium scoreboard ads, and baseball stadium billboards.

The USC advertising program involves the placement of a two-part advertising message on the opposite sides of metal waste containers. The message rotates monthly to several of the 240 possible locations on campus, providing reach and frequency for a firm's message to a broad cross-section of the student body, as well as faculty, staff, and campus visitors. The top portion of the message is changed quarterly and can be directed toward specific promotional campaigns for each company. The lower portion is 16 inches by 21 inches; the top rotating message is 5 inches by 21 inches. Contracts for placement of the ads on the waste containers are signed for a six-month period. Exhibit 1 shows a typical waste container.

A unique aspect of the USC advertising program is they have agreed to pay the University a 25 percent commission on all revenues. This commission will be placed in a trust fund and will be used annually to provide scholarships for students.

The LSU campus represents a substantial marketing opportunity because of the high concentration of student consumers in a small, well-

---

*Case prepared by Colleen Terro and Jerry Richard. Used with permission.

EXHIBIT 12-1
TYPICAL WASTE CONTAINER

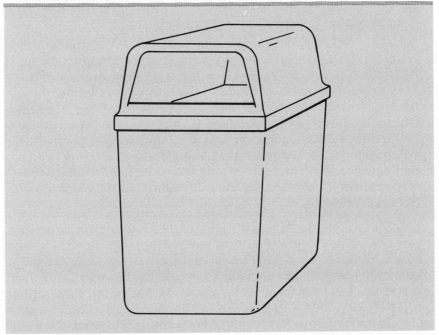

defined target area. Prior to selling the initial advertising space, USC contracted with Advanced Strategic Research, a market research firm based in Baton Rouge, to conduct an independent, objective assessment of the characteristics of the college consumer market and, more specifically, the LSU campus market. The following is a summary of the findings of that report:

LSU, the flagship institution of the LSU system, is a nationally recognized research institution with diverse educational, recreational, and cultural opportunities. LSU is considered to be a sports capital of the South and operates a broad intercollegiate sports program for men and women in 16 sports. In addition, an extensive amount of special events are held on campus each year. They include sorority/fraternity and other organization functions, banquets, political events, musical concerts, lectures, instructional workshops, short courses, correspondence courses, seminars and conferences, and hundreds more. LSU supports 31 religious organizations, 186 professional, honorary, and miscellaneous organizations, and 39 Greek activities. The student body represents 64 Louisiana parishes (counties), 50 U.S. states and 104 different countries. The daily population with faculty and staff hovers around the 32,000-plus mark.

College students represent a significant and important market because of their high current and expected future income, their special lifestyles, and their influence on attitudes in the broader culture. The students, faculty, and staff of LSU have over $137 million of discretionary income annually. Specifically, the students account for $95 million and the faculty and staff spend approximately $42 million each year. When you consider the large number of visitors to the campus, in addition to the normal population, these figures represent one of the most attractive consumer markets within the entire state of Louisiana. On a larger scale, Baton Rouge is the capital of Louisiana, the site of the fifth largest port in the U.S., a major petrochemical, financial, and industrial center, with a metro population of more than 500,000 people. It is estimated that 80 percent of the visitors that come to Baton Rouge include a visit to the LSU campus.

Exhibit 2 is an overview of the LSU market. Exhibit 3 is a rate sheet for the USC waste-receptacle outdoor advertising program. Exhibit 4 is a sample contract. As a basis of comparison, the cost per thousand (CPM) customer impressions for available media are the following: USC waste receptacles—CPM = $.91 ($165/two boards, including production); *Daily Reveille*—CPM = $18.52 ($352/full page ad); Football stadium scoreboard ads—CPM = $142.86 ($50,000+ annually); Baseball stadium billboards—CPM = $19.04 ($2,000+ annually); University directory yellow pages—CPM = $29.95 ($1,348/full page).

Robbie Powell is a student at LSU. He and two other students were recently hired for the summer by USC to sell ads. Of the 240 possible locations on campus, approximately 125 have already been sold, some for six months and others for one year.

CASE QUESTIONS

1. Who are the prospects for this unique new form of advertising?
2. What methods would you use to identify and locate these prospects?
3. What are the main selling points that would be emphasized in the sales presentation?
4. What objections are likely to be raised? How would you overcome these objections?
5. Using Lotus and the information in Exhibit 3, create a table to show the cost-per-thousand-customer impressions for each of the number of two-panel contracts (i.e., what are the cost-per-thousand-customer impressions for two two-panel contracts, for three, and so on). How can this information be used in the sales presentation?

EXHIBIT 12-2
LSU MARKET OVERVIEW

Fall enrollment:	27,000–28,000
Spring enrollment:	21,000–22,000
Faculty:	1,277
Support staff:	3,200

Age distribution:	17–21	42%
	22–24	30%
	25–older	28%

Population:	Freshmen	8,303
	Sophomores	4,742
	Juniors	4,274
	Seniors	5,905
	Graduate Students	4,480
	Faculty/Staff	4,523

Disposable Income:	$137 million annually
	$ 95 million—students
	$ 43 million—faculty/staff

- 91% have checking accounts
- 77% have savings accounts
- Baton Rouge student living with parents or on campus spends $1,600 in addition to fees, rooms, and meals per school year
- Out of town student living off campus spends $5,200 per school year on food, clothes, cleaning, books/supplies, transportation, entertainment, etc.
- Married students spend approximately $11,550 per school year
- Housing and meals:
  on campus—$425 - $935 per semester
  fraternity/sorority houses—$925 - $1,525 per semester
- Approximately 30% of entire LSU population lives on campus
- Almost 50% LSU undergraduates have part-time employment, loans, and scholarships
- 20% hold jobs on campus (part-time)
- 38% hold jobs off campus (part-time)
- 40% obtain loans and scholarships
- 50% of graduate students receive assistantships, fellowships, or work as graduate trainees
- 65% of LSU students receive funds from scholarships, grants, fellowships, loans, and student employment

EXHIBIT 12-3
USC RATE SHEET

UNIVERSITY SUPPORT CORPORATION
Louisiana Business and Technology Center
LSU South Stadium Drive
Baton Rouge, Louisiana 70803
(504) 388-3994

CAMPUS RECEPTACLE PROGRAM
For the Campus of
LOUISIANA STATE UNIVERSITY

R A T E   S H E E T
Effective January 1989

Number of Two-Panel Contracts	Monthly Cost Each Panel	Monthly Cost Each Contract
1	$82.50	$165.00
2	76.00	152.00
3	75.00	150.00
4	74.00	148.00
5	73.00	146.00
6	72.00	144.00
7	71.00	142.00
8	70.00	140.00
9	69.00	138.00
10	67.00	134.00
11 plus	65.25	130.50

24-Hour Exposure for a Three-Month Contract — $495.00

Price Includes

1. All production costs
2. Top message change after three months
3. Two colors on white background (additional colors $10.00 each/contract)
4. All maintenance
5. Rotation of panels each month
6. Strategic placement throughout campus

EXHIBIT 12-4
SAMPLE CONTRACT

PILOT PROGRAM ADVERTISING SPACE AGREEMENT
UNIVERSITY SUPPORT CORPORATION (USC) & _____
_____ ("ADVERTISER") HEREBY AGREE & CONTRACT AS
FOLLOWS:

1. Copy Content

USC and LSU Alumni Association reserves the right to determine if copy and design are in good taste and within the moral standards of the individual communities in which it is to be displayed. Further, USC and LSU Alumni Association reserves the right to reject or withdraw any copy, either before or after posting.

2. Placement

Each client can choose from the many rotation schedules depending on availability at the time the contract is signed. This includes the Pilot Program.

3. Contract Definition & Dimensions of Printing Area

The Pilot Program entails the placement of a two-part advertising message on opposite sides of top of the line waste receptacles. These messages will rotate monthly in accordance to the schedule agreed on by USC and the client.

Seasonal message—6 inches by 21 inches
Logo message—16 inches by 21 inches

4. Camera Ready Ads

We will build your ad as long as we are provided with color separated PMT (Photo Mechanical Transfer) logos and special PMT artwork. If the client cannot provide camera ready art, we would provide this service at cost. No extra charge for typesetting normal typestyles Helvetica, Times Roman, etc.

5. Mechanicals

Artwork is placed on black and white PMT positive on clear velox, color separated, typeset and fully laid out to print at 100%. All messages are printed on baked, enamel coated 24-gauge steel panels and durable white outdoor vinyl material. Inks are top of the line Nazdar paints used with printing screen mesh of 196 holes per square inch.

Additional production charges for special screens or special colors that are not standard are available upon request.

6. Layout

Composition and minor revisions for ads provided normally at little additional cost. Quotes for design, illustration, and extensive production or revisions will be provided. Rates available upon request. We do not guarantee exact PMS colors, however, every effort is made to match standard colors requested by the client. Responsibility is not assumed for art, Velox prints, mechanicals or other advertising materials not called for by the advertiser within 15

calendar days after publication and posting. In any case, University Support Corporation shall have no financial responsibility for any such items lost while in the company's possession.

7. Liability and Claim for Errors

Please check your copy carefully. We make every effort to avoid errors in advertisements before production is begun. USC is not responsible for incorrect copy submitted by the advertiser after copy has been released for production or for copy changes made by phone. All ad materials produced by USC remain the property of USC and will not be released. If a panel should be lost during the period of display, a panel of equal advertising value will be substituted and time credited for loss of service.

8. Contract terms (Pilot Program only)

Each contract consists of 3 (three) consecutive months.

9. Contract dates

Begin with effective posting date (normally on the first day of the month).

10. Credit

Advertisers who do not have approved credit are required to pay for advertising in advance.

11. Invoices/When Due

Invoices are mailed upon publication and are due 15 days after rendering. Any account not paid within 15 days is considered delinquent, and a service charge of (1 1/2%) per month shall be due on any unpaid balance. If a delinquent account is placed with an attorney for collection, Advertiser shall be liable for all costs associated with the collection of said account, including 25% of all principal and interest due as attorney's fees.

12. Make all checks payable to University Support Corporation.

13. Identification

The advertiser agrees to assume sole responsibility for statements contained in his copy and to protect USC against any and all liability, loss or expense arising out of claims of libel, unfair trade practices, unfair competition, infringement of trademarks, names of patents, copyrights, and all violations of the right of privacy resulting from publication of the advertiser's copy.

14. Effect and Terms

This contract shall remain in effect throughout the advertising relationship between USC and Advertiser. The rate charged for advertising by USC shall be controlled by the rate card of USC then in effect.

15. Representative Capacity

The undersigned representative of Advertised, hereby declares that he or she duly authorized to act on behalf of Advertiser.

I hereby authorize you to begin production for advertising on the campus of LOUISIANA STATE UNIVERSITY for a period of

_____ (months) at a rate of _____ ($) for _____ (#) two panel

contract(s). Date contract begins _____ and ends _____

University Support Corporation   Advertiser _____ Date _____

By _____   Authorized by: _____ Title _____

CHAPTER 13
Closing the Sale

After studying this chapter, you should be able to:

- Discuss the psychological problems that face salespeople when closing

- Point out how prospects feel about attempts to close sales

- Indicate why and when salespeople should try to close sales

- Relate closing clues to trial closes

- Describe various techniques of closing sales and when they should be used

- Compare activities after successful sales calls with those after no-sale calls

- Discuss the scheduling and handling of callbacks

The close is the final stage of the sales presentation, as shown in Figure 13-1. The salesperson has told the sales story, demonstrated the product, disposed of resistance, and wants the prospect's commitment to purchase.

THE IMPORTANCE OF CLOSING

Closing is the capstone of what the salesperson and the company are working toward. The company's goal in developing a product or service is to make a profit and satisfy customer needs. But profit cannot be realized, nor can customers have their needs met, until the product or service is sold. The ultimate goal of the salesperson is to sell products that satisfy customer needs and bring in profit to the company. If the salesperson fails, so does the company, because money does not come in to pay for the effort that goes into making the sale.

To close the sale the salesperson must ask the buyer for a commitment to purchase the product or service. If the salesperson does not ask for the sale, the sale will not be made. Only in rare cases will buyers be in such dire need for a product or service that they will ask to purchase. In

THE SELLING PROCESS

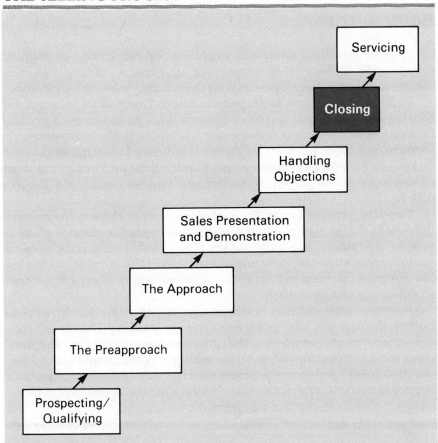

Figure 13-1 Closing, the act of asking for the sale, is the next-to-last stage of the selling process.

today's highly competitive marketplace there are too many alternatives available to buyers for them to be so dependent on a single supplier. If you don't ask, your competitor will. And your competitor will be the one to make the sale.

Closing the sale is important to salespeople for several reasons. First, all of their efforts in the earlier stages of the selling process are meaningless if they have not succeeded at closing. Salespeople spend their time prospecting, qualifying, preparing, approaching, presenting, demonstrating, and asking questions for the sole purpose of closing the sale. If they succeed, all of the effort and long hours are worthwhile. If they fail, however, salespeople will feel as though they have just been wasting their time, and will become frustrated and scared of rejection.

Though most salespeople are compensated based on their sales performance, their performance is not judged by the quality of their presen-

HIGHLIGHT 13-1

Joseph Vaccaro, assistant professor of marketing at Suffolk University's School of Management in Boston, Massachusetts, claims the best salespeople employ the adage, "always be closing."

In his article, "Best Salespeople Know Their ABCs (Always Be Closing)" in The Marketing News *(March 28, 1988), Vaccaro argues that one of the primary reasons for lost sales is the salesperson's inability to ask for the sale, or to close. Vaccaro bases his argument on survey results that show approximately 60 percent of the time salespeople either forget or knowingly choose not to ask for the order.*

Vaccaro goes on to say the best closers start closing the minute they meet the prospect. Now granted, salespeople cannot close a sale for a product they have not yet presented. Vaccaro focuses on establishing a winning attitude at the start of the interview. Closing the prospect on the idea that you, the salesperson, are a winner and worth doing business with.

Vaccaro also advises salespeople to close on minor selling points throughout the presentation. By gaining the prospect's agreement on minor points, the salesperson should find the final close to be nothing more than a formality. In other words, the prospect has been sold on the product and the salesperson throughout the presentation. This will make "asking for the order" seem like a natural conclusion to the salesperson.

tation, or how well they answered the prospect's objections, or by the number of sales calls they were granted. Instead, sales performance is judged the same way as ability, on the number of sales they have closed, and the dollar and volume size of those sales. The "best" salespeople earn the most money because they close the most and/or the largest sales.

PROBLEMS IN CLOSING

Many of the difficulties experienced at the close are caused by circumstances prior to the close. For example, an inadequate opening of the interview and delivery of the presentation will not capture a prospect's attention, which certainly makes closing nearly impossible. The presentation may be weak because the salesperson lacks sufficient information about the prospect. The weakness may be in the sales story itself. Closing is also hampered when the salesperson's handling of objections or the demonstration is faulty.

Sometimes the salesperson is unsuccessful in obtaining an affirmative buying decision because of flaws in the close itself. Prospects are often taken aback when a ceremony is made out of the close. Another cause of buyer resistance is an awkward or anxious salesperson during the closing. Successful closes are also jeopardized if the salesperson fails to steer a middle course between too much and too little aggressiveness. If the close is incorrectly worded or ill-timed, the sale is not likely to be completed.

SALESPEOPLE'S ATTITUDES TOWARD THE CLOSE

Given the obvious benefits of asking for the sale (success, fame, fortune), why wouldn't every salesperson try to close every sale, every time? The answer is simple: fear. Think of the time you were in high school and you wanted to ask a boy or girl that you had a crush on out for a date. Do you remember that feeling? Nervous, jittery, butterflies in your stomach. Why? Because there was the possibility that you would be rejected. Salespeople go through these feelings whenever it comes time to close. Successful salespeople learn to cope with these feelings by developing an inner confidence in their abilities.

Salespeople must develop the professional philosophy of doing one's job to the best of one's ability. If salespeople perform each task of the selling process to the best of their ability, and the prospect refuses to purchase, it is not the fault of the salesperson. Some prospects just will not buy, for whatever reason. Salespeople should remember not to take the rejection personally; it is business. They should go right out and try to close the next prospect. Successful salespeople are those who are confident in their abilities, and who won't let rejection get in their way.

PROSPECTS' ATTITUDES TOWARD THE CLOSE

The thought of buying has both positive and negative aspects for prospects. They would obviously not be prospects unless they could somehow benefit from buying. On the other hand, they cannot have all the things they want, and they cannot prove in advance that they will not regret their decision to buy the particular product under consideration. Reluctance to buy, then, is normal and expected. Prospects feel the urge to conserve their purchasing power and avoid making a commitment.

What prospects need most in the close is assurance. Confidence in their decision to buy must be great enough to override their doubts. To convey this assurance adequately, the salesperson must show the proper amount of self-confidence. The negative feelings that invade the thinking of some salespeople as they prepare for the close are contagious. They can ruin the closing because they influence the prospect's attitude and ultimate decision.

What the salesperson tells prospects is as important as attitudes and actions in assuring the prospect. Prospects want to hear statements that will dismiss their indecision. They want to be told that the decision to buy is the correct decision. In the closing remarks, the salesperson should remove from the prospects' shoulders as much decision making as possible. The salesperson should make positive, constructive recommendations instead of provisional suggestions. The salesperson should describe what is going to happen after the purchase, not what will happen *if* they buy. The salesperson strengthens prospects' resolution to purchase by telling them that they are demonstrating common sense, that they can feel proud of their action, and that they can feel confidence in the salesperson and the company represented. In some situations, the prospect will feel a need for reasons that can be used to justify the purchase to others. These reasons can be an important part of the close.

WHEN TO CLOSE THE SALE

The major part of a successful closing is the preliminary work done in the early stages of the presentation. If a sound presentation is made from the outset and the prospect agrees with the points the salesperson makes, the close will almost take care of itself. Thus, the salesperson should start moving toward a close the moment the sales presentation is opened.

The salesperson should secure understanding and agreement from the prospect as each selling point is made. Unless the prospect agrees with the salesperson's analysis and recommendations, no attempt at closing will be successful. If prospects go along with each benefit as it is presented, they must logically accept the aggregate of the benefits at the end by agreeing that the only thing to do is to buy immediately. Each earlier agreement reduces the magnitude of the final agreement—the final decision becomes just one (the last) of a number of decisions. The prospect will not be surprised and shocked by an attempt to close. The salesperson can assess the prospect's understanding through the use of questioning.

CLOSING CLUES

Closing clues, or **buying signals**, are the cues indicating that a close should be attempted by the salesperson. They alert the salesperson to the fact that the prospect may be ready to buy. Salespeople who study the prospect's reactions can learn to spot closing clues, though this diagnosis can never be completely accurate.

Prospects give some indication when they are near the act of buying. As a matter of fact, there may be several of these clues or signals in a single presentation. This is possible because a prospect can get near buying, back away, and then once again be on the verge of making a purchase—all in the same presentation. Because reactions show when the prospect is ready for the salesperson's attempt to close, they are ex-

HIGHLIGHT 13-2

The salesperson orientation course at one Fortune 500 company calls closing the logical conclusion to the completion of all the steps of the selling plan (process), provided you have built up an attitude of willingness to buy in the previous steps.

If you have not created this willing attitude, your attempts to close will fail, because you cannot hope to secure orders from people who are not willing to buy.

The company offers the following factors as the keys to success when closing:

- **Product and business knowledge** — When you do not know the industry or your product, prospects lose confidence.
- **Knowledge of human nature** — People are different, so are prospects. Learn as much as you can about the different types of prospects you will encounter.
- **Enthusiasm** — Enthusiasm breeds excitement.
- **Aggressiveness** — Take charge, but don't overstep your bounds and be overly aggressive.
- **Confidence** — You must develop a winning attitude to overcome fears. People want to deal with winners. So do prospects.
- **Be thorough** — Do not leave a stone unturned. Explain all the benefits of the product, and completely outshine the alternatives, whether it be the competition or their present system.

If salespeople successfully adhere to these factors, there won't be any reason for them to be afraid to close.

tremely valuable to salespeople. Nothing is more important in closing than for the salesperson to learn to spot these signals and to act on them.

There are also physical closing clues. For example, when prospects repeatedly operate a product or sample its usage they are sending signals or clues that they are highly interested. When a customer starts working on figures on a calculator, or intently reviews the product literature or support material, it is a strong notice to the salesperson to ask for the sale. Verbal closing clues may be comments or questions like those shown in Figure 13-2.

TRIAL CLOSES

A trial close is an attempt by the salesperson to see if the prospect is ready to make a purchase; it sounds the prospect out. If the prospect's

EXAMPLES OF VERBAL CLOSING CLUES

1. I've been satisfied with your products in the past.
2. What kind of financing do you have available?
3. Can you deliver the product to me by Friday?
4. Will you come in and set up the displays?
5. Which model do you think will satisfy my needs?
6. I haven't seen anything yet that surpasses your product.
7. Can you come in and train my sales clerks?

Figure 13-2 Sometimes prospects will give the salesperson verbal clues that they are ready to buy.

response to the trial close is favorable, the salesperson goes ahead at once and tries to complete the sale. If the prospect's reaction clearly shows that the prospect is not yet ready to buy, the salesperson continues the sales presentation.

The trial close serves two purposes. First, it is a safe and simple way of asking the prospect to buy. If it succeeds, it can result in an immediate purchase. Second, it is an inoffensive check on what prospects are thinking. Are they reacting favorably? Are they convinced yet? Are they ready to buy? The trial close sheds light on these matters.

Verbal trial closes are usually phrased in the form of questions, which call for decisions on minor points. A verbal trial close customarily asks the prospect to make some choice. Some sample questions for a trial close are shown in Figure 13-3. It takes only a glance at these examples to see that the prospect who gives a direct answer to the question has in effect agreed to make the purchase.

Physical trial closes are those in which the salesperson starts to execute the physical phases of the sale without asking permission to do so. For example, the salesperson could pick up an order book and start to write out the order. When a trial close, either verbal or physical, fails to complete the sale, the salesperson analyzes why the prospect is not ready

SAMPLE TRIAL CLOSES

1. When do you need it delivered?
2. Will you be trading in your old one?
3. Do you want this delivered to your home or to your office?
4. Will you be paying with cash or with credit?
5. Is a dozen enough?

Figure 13-3 The trial close is a way of "testing the waters" to see if the prospect is ready to buy.

to buy and then works on the difficulty. Figure 13-4 shows when a trial close may be appropriate.

In the use of trial closes, the salesperson must not stimulate the prospect's buying defenses. Instead of asking for a decision on the major issue at that time, the salesperson will bypass it in favor of a lesser decision. Also, the salesperson must never close the door to more discussion or make it possible for the prospect to do so. If the salesperson detects a closing clue, executes a trial close, and then finds that it was not a clue, it should be possible to resume the sales story.

WHEN TO ATTEMPT THE CLOSE

A sound rule for closing is to do it as early as possible, for more sales are lost by trying too late than by trying too early. A salesperson's objective is to close a sale, not to present a complete sales story just because one is prepared. A closing attempt made too early will find one or more of the five buying decisions missing. However, the salesperson who talks past the first closing opportunity may lose the sale by not having tried to close when the prospect was favorably inclined toward buying.

Salespeople used to think that only one moment for closing ever occurred during a presentation, and the salesperson had to make an attempt to close at exactly that moment if a sale was to be made on that call. Authorities on selling now believe that this so-called psychological moment is a myth. They believe there may be several high spots of conviction during the selling conversation and purchase might easily be made at any one of them. Resistance and opposition are at a minimum at these points, objections are not raised, and the prospect seems sold on the salesperson's proposal. The salesperson might even miss on the first, second, and third high spots but be successful in closing the sale on the fourth one. The general rule is for the salesperson to make an attempt at closing whenever it appears the time to close is right. Obviously, expe-

WHEN TO USE A TRIAL CLOSE

1. When the prospect gives a closing clue.
2. When the prospect gives enthusiastic agreement on one of the selling points or one of the salesperson's leading questions.
3. When the prospect accepts proof of the product's advantages in a convinced manner.
4. When the salesperson has just completed an effective demonstration of the product.
5. When the salesperson has disposed of some objection in an effective way.

Figure 13-4 Knowing when to use a trial close is half the battle to completing a successful close.

rience is a great help in learning to sense when the conditions for closing are most favorable.

TECHNIQUES FOR CLOSING THE SALE

No salesperson closes every sale. It must be pointed out, however, that one mark of a successful salesperson is a high percentage of sales made in difficult situations. Mediocre salespeople get orders from prospects who are ready and waiting to buy, but expert salespeople can succeed in selling to almost anyone who qualifies as a prospect.

No specific technique of closing is effective in all cases. The first closing approach attempted may be logical and often successful. But frequently the salesperson will have to use other closing approaches before finally making the sale. A number of methods of closing that have proved valuable to salespeople will be discussed in the following sections.

No matter which closing method the salesperson chooses, there is one piece of advice: close and be quiet! Once the salesperson has asked for the sale, it is up to the prospect to answer. If the salesperson is the one to break the silence, he or she has just forfeited that opportunity to close.

THE CHOICE CLOSE

The technique of closing on a choice is probably the most often used closing technique because it is the most versatile and the most likely to be successful. This technique is also referred to as the technique of **closing on a minor point**, the **double-question method**, the **selection close**, and the **split-decision close**.

The salesperson takes for granted that the prospect is going to buy; but at the same time knows that the prospect is reluctant to concede. The prospect, in effect, is saying, "Yes, you win—you've sold me—I'll buy." So what the salesperson does is ignore and avoid the major buying decision, which is to buy or not to buy, by posing a minor decision for the prospect to make.

Closing on a choice is particularly appropriate when the prospect is having trouble deciding because it narrows the choice down to two. This makes the process of choosing less complicated and, hence, less confusing. The device is also good when a new salesperson is reluctant to press for a close.

In using the technique of closing on a choice, the salesperson asks the prospect which of the two products is preferred. The difference between the two may be a matter of model, color, size, material, or some other product feature. The salesperson frames the choice by asking a question such as, "Do you prefer the full-color assortment or the single-color assortment?" The prospect makes the choice, and either alternative chosen represents a closing of the sale. The question the salesperson asks should be framed so the choices offered will be of equal utility and suitability, and so either choice will be satisfactory to both prospect and seller.

THE ASSUMPTION CLOSE

In the **assumption close**, both salesperson and prospect have a specific product in mind; both are thinking about the same model, color, size, material, and price. The prospect may have narrowed the field down to the one product, or the salesperson may have selected the most appropriate item for that particular prospect.

The assumption close is a result of the salesperson's doing and saying things throughout the presentation that indicate the major buying question is settled. The closing question assumes the prospect's acceptance of the salesperson's recommendations and inquires only about some minor point. The question asked and the choice presented are quite similar to those used in the choice close, except the question now concerns an auxiliary matter and not the product itself. Thus, the salesperson may ask questions such as the following:

1. Would you like this delivered today?
2. How much do you want to pay as a down payment?
3. How do you want this shipped?
4. When do you want this to become effective?

CLOSING ON THE OBJECTION

Sometimes a prospect gives honest agreement to every point the salesperson makes except one, and that one obstacle prevents the purchase from being made immediately. Perhaps everything is satisfactory except the price; perhaps the prospect feels obligated to buy from some other vendor; or perhaps the prospect fears the cost of operating the product.

The first thing the salesperson should do is to get the prospect to agree that the objection raised is the only thing holding up the purchase. The salesperson may ask: "Is that the only objection you have about my product? Or is there another reason why you are not willing to buy?" If there is no other reason for that prospect not to buy, then the solution is simple: satisfy that objection and then close on it! For example, the salesperson might say:

"Mr. Jones, I realize that our price is a little higher than theirs, but does theirs contain a full 2-year warranty on parts?"

"No, it doesn't."

"Don't you feel more secure in knowing that with our product if something breaks in those first two years it will be replaced free of charge?"

"Why, yes I do."

"Then, that security should warrant the additional $5 in price, right?"

"I guess so."

"Well then, would you like me to deliver it today or tomorrow?"

THE SUMMARY CLOSE

After covering most of the benefits the salesperson thinks will appeal to the prospect, the moment has come to try to close the sale. A method of closing that may be effective—especially when the prospect will have to defend the purchase to family, friends, or employer—is a review of each advantage the salesperson has mentioned. The collection of advantages may be impressive enough to persuade the prospect to buy immediately. If any one or two of the benefits seemed to be of particular interest to the prospect as they were initially described, they should be stressed in the summary.

The summary should be simple and informal and may be prefaced by a remark such as, "Let's review the benefits I've mentioned so we won't forget any that might be of special interest to you." The salesperson will ask the prospect for agreement on each benefit so that if there is an objection to one, it can be disposed of immediately. When there is complete agreement, the salesperson assumes that the prospect is ready to buy and goes through the mechanics of closing. Generally, following the use of the summary close the salesperson uses another close, typically the assumption close, to actually close the purchase.

REVIEWING THE FIVE BUYING DECISIONS

As we have learned, prospects make a purchase only when they are positive there is a need for something, a certain product will fill that need, a particular salesperson or company is the proper source, the price is satisfactory, and the time to buy is now. One course the salesperson can follow in closing the sale is to review these five decisions and obtain the prospect's approval on each one. Until the prospect actually buys, only one conclusion can be drawn: agreement is still missing on one or more of the five decisions. If this is true, the salesperson brings in additional facts and supplies more convincing proof until the missing decision is made affirmatively.

THE STANDING-ROOM-ONLY CLOSE

People want what other people want and what other people have. They want anything that is hard to get. This is the reasoning behind the **standing-room-only close**.

A salesperson who tells a prospect a price increase is due next week, the doctor turned down one of the prospect's friends when he applied for insurance, the supply of a product is limited, or a premium offer expires

HIGHLIGHT 13-3

The following are some "Do's" and "Don'ts" that salespeople should remember when closing a sale.

DO'S

Do display a friendly manner at the close, even if there is disagreement. This helps to avoid arguments.

Do be sure to have all materials and equipment that will be needed. Misplaced order blanks, obsolete price lists, and faulty pens can lose sales.

Do realize that begging for a sale makes you and your offer look bad; it also disgusts the prospect.

Do ask the prospect to "OK" or approve the order rather than sign it.

Do make buying as easy and painless as possible.

Do try for privacy at the close. Telephone calls and third parties distract.

Do study each prospect to learn their primary buying motives. Then adapt your presentation/close to appeal to these motives.

Do lead the prospect to think as the owner of the product from the very beginning of the interview.

Do put the order book and pen in a conspicuous, convenient spot long before attempting a close.

Do remember that meeting customer needs is the salesperson's primary objective.

DON'TS

Don't be apologetic, particularly in quoting price.

Don't make written or even oral promises unless authorized to do so.

Don't make a ceremony out of closing, lest the prospect become frightened.

Don't give the prospect an excuse or an opportunity to back away from the purchase.

Don't ever ask the prospect for the buying decision in such a way that it is possible to answer with a "no."

Don't make it difficult for the prospect to complete the purchase quickly if desired.

Don't let the prospect miss seeing that you expect a purchase.

Don't make it easier for the prospect to refuse than to buy.

THE ART OF THE DEAL

Figure 13-5 The Art of the Deal
Source: Drawing by R. Chast; copyright © 1990, The New Yorker Magazine, Inc.

soon is using the standing-room-only close to stimulate the prospect to buy. This device should be held in reserve until late in the interview because it can weaken the presentation. There is often a temptation to use this close unethically to get rid of slow-selling merchandise.

THE SPECIAL-DEAL CLOSE

In using the **special-deal close**, the salesperson offers the prospect an inducement for acting at once. The most common inducement is a cut in the price originally quoted. For some product lines, the salesperson might offer something free to the buyer; for example, a retailer might be given a dozen free items for each ten dozen bought immediately. In selling to wholesalers and retailers, there also may be some allowance, such as an advertising allowance equal to 5 percent of the merchant's purchases, which can be given if certain minimum quantities are purchased immediately. The trial order can also be a form of concession because the salesperson agrees to settle for the purchase of a smaller, trial quantity instead of the quantity originally suggested.

There are other types of special inducements. A trade-in allowance can be revised upward, or the down payment reduced. A manufacturer may offer **PMs** (push money) to a retailer's salespeople to push the manufacturer's brand or might offer the retailer more elaborate **POP** (point-of-purchase) displays than the retailer has been getting. Premiums, free accessories, extra discounts, and longer pay periods are other examples of special inducements that might be offered.

Special deals should not be offered until the last moments of the interview, and even then there are dangers in using this technique. The prospect may keep pressing for more concessions once the salesperson starts offering them, or the prospect may begin to wonder about the product's value and desirability if deals must be made to sell it. Deals also reduce the seller's profits. Finally, the salesperson must not play favorites among buyers.

THE T-ACCOUNT TECHNIQUE

The **T-account** can be an effective closing device. The salesperson draws a large T. On the left side the salesperson lists reasons for the prospect to buy and on the right side reasons for not buying. Obviously, there must be more weight on the left side than on the right side, for example:

PRO (Buy)	**CON** (Don't Buy)
Save $100 per month	Large investment required
Less duplication	Prices have been dropping
Reduce overtime	
Better control	
Salesperson's machine works faster	

THE CONTINGENCY CLOSE

Sometimes, the salesperson can get the prospect to commit based on the satisfaction of a **contingent promise**. In other words, the prospect will buy if the salesperson promises to satisfy a particular request. For example:

"Mr. Smith, if I can guarantee that your order will be in your warehouse first thing Friday morning, will you agree to buy?"

The contingency close is very effective because it shows prospects you are willing to go out of your way to satisfy them.

THE REQUEST FOR AN ORDER

When a salesperson has recommended a sound solution to a problem and the prospect seems to be in agreement, the salesperson is entitled to ask for an order. The salesperson can imitate the political candidate who asks a voter, "Will you vote for me?" When the time has come to write up an order, the salesperson may say:

"I'll appreciate your business. Will eight dozen be about right for you?"

"Fine. Then let's go right ahead. How many do you want and when do you want them?"

"Approve this order and you'll get delivery by Wednesday of next week."

All of these closing methods are sound techniques that salespeople have been using successfully for years. Figure 13-6 offers advice regarding the best situation in which to use each of the various closing methods.

WHEN TO USE EACH TYPE OF CLOSE

Technique	"Best" Situation
The Choice Close	This closing method is best used with prospects who are indecisive, and need to be reminded of the alternatives.
The Assumption Close	Salespeople may employ this technique with prospects who have difficulty making decisions, or who are afraid of taking risks.
Closing on the Objection	Prospects who need to be assured of specific points, often only one or two, are prime candidates for this technique.
The Summary Close	The summary close would be best in situations where many selling points and considera-

	tions need to be reviewed before a decision can be made.
The Minor-Points Close	This closing method should be used when the sale is for a very large or expensive order and many decisions must be made prior to the final decision.
Reviewing the Five Buying Decisions	Salespeople should use this technique when there is a question as to the prospect's need, the product's ability to satisfy the need, the credibility of the source, the price, or the timing of the purchase.
Standing-Room-Only Close	Use this technique only when the prospect highly desires the product but is putting off the decision.
The Special Deal Close	This method is generally best when used as a promotion to get rid of excess product or to match a competitor's promotion.
The T-Account Technique	Analytical prospects warrant this technique because they like to see all the pros and cons compared on paper prior to making the decision.
The Contingency Close	Salespeople should use this method with prospects who have special needs or who need to feel pampered in order to buy.
The Request for an Order	Can be used anytime, but is most effective when dealing with professional buyers who are direct in their approach to purchasing.

Figure 13-6 There are many closing techniques one could choose from. Some work better than others depending on the situation.

THE SALESPERSON'S POSTSALE ACTIVITIES

Whether or not the prospect buys, the salesperson always thanks the prospect at the end of the interview for the consideration given and tries to leave the prospect favorably disposed toward the product and the company represented. The salesperson makes certain that the prospect has his or her name, address, and telephone number, as well as some literature or other material about the product. There are also more specific activities that the salesperson will perform depending on whether the prospect buys or does not buy.

ACTIVITIES FOLLOWING A SUCCESSFUL SALE

If a seller is to avoid ill will, complaints, demands for adjustments, cancellations, and unfavorable word-of-mouth publicity, customers must use the products they buy, like them, and continue to buy them. The time to start converting a first-time customer into a regular, satisfied one is just after the first sale has been made.

The first thing, of course, is to thank the prospect for becoming a customer. This should be sincere, yet crisp, and must never be allowed to become casual. A compliment can be paid to the prospect's good judgment, and assurance given that the product will live up to expectations.

A second activity is to try to make certain that the prospect will use the product to maximum advantage. The prospect should understand the operation and care of the product in order to benefit most. If appropriate, the prospect should be impressed with the importance and necessity of following directions and with the continued service the seller makes available.

A third activity is to see if any other sales possibilities are at hand. If the salesperson is handling a family of products, perhaps there are other items that might benefit the customer. It may be observed that opportunities for more business will be coming up in the future. The customer may allow the salesperson to take before and after pictures to use in other solicitations. The new customer may be asked to help the salesperson by agreeing to be a source of testimonials. Or the customer might be able and willing to supply the names of, and other facts about, people who are prospective buyers.

Extreme care should be used in writing up the order. Errors and omissions should be avoided, particularly on the first order. For example, forgetting to obtain any data that will be called for by some department of the company, such as the credit department, will delay the delivery of the product. In writing up the order, the salesperson may ask several questions, even though the answers to them are known. This helps to keep the buyer from being idle and wondering if the purchase was wise. As a matter of fact, it lets the buyer help close the sale. The salesperson might repeat the terms or figures being written on the order blank or sales contract. This prevents awkward periods of silence and eliminates the possibility of misunderstanding between seller and buyer over quantity bought, price, delivery date, method of shipment, and such. This time of writing up the first order is most suitable for making certain that the new customer knows the terms of the seller and also understands why they are important. After making the sale, there are certain mistakes salespeople should avoid. These are listed in Figure 13-7.

The time immediately after the first sale is the right time to begin learning as much as possible about the former prospect who is now a customer. The salesperson must keep an individual, detailed record of each customer, much like a prospect file. All transactions should be noted on the record, as should a list of all products bought. These records should be studied thoroughly, systematically, and often. They reveal which items the salesperson sells with ease and which with difficulty. They indicate what buying decisions have been troublesome, and supply clues as to what revisions or adjustments are needed.

ACTIVITIES FOLLOWING NO-SALE CALLS

When the sale is not closed on a particular call and the prospect is to be visited again, the salesperson should spend the final moments of the presentation in building up goodwill and paving the way for a return visit. Any needed information is secured so that a more appropriate and beneficial proposal may be presented later. The salesperson inquires whether there are any facts to be obtained or any favor that might be done for the prospect before the next call. Sincere appreciation is expressed for the time the prospect has given.

MISTAKES TO AVOID AFTER A SUCCESSFUL SALE

1. Talking too much, especially about the purchase, or talking down to the buyer.
2. Staying too long, wasting both parties' time. This is very important to remember if the buyer is a purchasing agent.
3. Acting like the "winner," for that implies that the buyer lost.
4. Thanking the buyer too profusely.
5. Giving the impression that sales are novel and infrequent.
6. Relaxing too obviously.
7. Being casual to the point of appearing indifferent.
8. Leaving so abruptly that you forget to compliment the buyer.
9. Failing to assure the buyer of the salesperson's availability and continuing interest.

Figure 13-7 Once the sale is made, the salesperson should quickly and tactfully exit to avoid making any mistakes.

Immediately after leaving the prospect, the salesperson begins to prepare for the return call. Everything learned about the prospect is jotted down so that the salesperson will have a record to review before calling again. What took place in the conference is summarized. Any mistakes made are listed with possible means of correcting them. A matter that must not be overlooked is that of the objections encountered. This should be done while the call is still fresh, because thoughts may come to mind about how to handle such obstacles better. Buying decisions should be classified into two groups, those made in the affirmative and those still missing. The salesperson must note and file away information on prices quoted, deliveries promised, or any other commitments. These notes should be made to avoid possible misunderstanding in the future or failure to fulfill promises. Finally, the salesperson must enter the callback date in his or her calendar.

The causes of failure to sell must be handled in some systematic fashion if the number of failures is to be reduced. Some companies require that a **lost-order report** be filed with the sales manager. Figure 13-8 shows a typical lost-order report.

Another method is for the salesperson to start a **lost-order checklist**, which will indicate the deficiencies that resulted in an incomplete sale. The assumption is, of course, that the salesperson's product and its price are satisfactory and that the prospect has a real need and can afford to buy. Items such as appearance, product knowledge, and approach may appear on a checklist. See Figure 13-9 for an example of such a checklist.

SCHEDULING AND HANDLING CALLBACKS

There will be times when prospects refuse to commit themselves, because they are either actually unable to buy or unwilling. It may be that before giving a final decision, someone else's permission for the purchase must be secured or certain matters that are involved in the sale must be arranged. Regardless of the reason, prospects may postpone buying for what to them is a real and justifiable cause. When the salesperson is certain that the prospect is determined to delay the purchase, the only thing to do is to suggest a later visit. In essence, the salesperson must close by scheduling a second visit. For some products, the decision involves such great importance or is so expensive that the salesperson knows from the start that it will require several sales calls. For these situations, the salesperson's objective for that call may only be to inform the prospect about the product and to set up a second sales call.

By recognizing that many sales require more than one call, experienced salespeople leave gracefully as soon as they are positive that another call will be necessary. This avoids antagonizing the prospect by pressing for an immediate decision and also minimizes the time the salesperson spends in ineffectual conversation. The best plan is to agree

A LOST-ORDER REPORT

Lost-Order Report

1. Name of sales representative _____
2. Name of prospect/buyer _____
   Address _____
   _____
   _____

   Has the above firm ever bought from us? _____
   If so, when? _____
   Was the firm satisfied with our product(s) and service? _____
   If not, why not? _____
   _____

3. Product(s) quoted on:

Product	Quantity	Unit Price	Total Price

4. To what company was the order given? _____
5. Did you see the competing product(s) the company is now using?
   _____

   If yes, name the product(s) _____

6. State your reasons for losing this order _____
   _____
   _____

7. How can we help you with this account? _____
   _____
   _____

8. When do you expect to make another call? _____
9. Date report filed _____
10. Signed _____

Figure 13-8 Many companies will have their salespeople file a report when they lose an order so that salespeople will learn from their mistakes.

at once on a definite time for the next meeting in which the salesperson hopes to review the buying decisions already made, obtain favorable decisions on the missing ones, and close the sale.

Making a specific appointment for the **callback** has a number of advantages. First, it avoids wasting the salesperson's time because it ensures the prospect will see the salesperson on the second call. Second, the salesperson can suggest a date for the callback which will fall as closely as

LOST-ORDER CHECKLIST

Check YES or NO to diagnose why your order was lost. The more NOs, the harder it was for the prospect to say YES.

		YES	NO
1.	I prepared for the interview	___	___
2.	My appearance was good	___	___
3.	I felt confident	___	___
4.	I was enthusiastic	___	___
5.	I showed sincere interest in the prospect	___	___
6.	My approach was well chosen	___	___
7.	I inspired the prospect's confidence	___	___
8.	I awakened the prospect's interest	___	___
9.	I concentrated on the sales points that most interested the prospect	___	___
10.	I made the prospect realize his/her needs	___	___
11.	I questioned the prospect intelligently	___	___
12.	I could answer the prospect's questions about the product	___	___
13.	I was careful not to interrupt	___	___
14.	I anticipated the prospect's objections	___	___
15.	I handled objections well	___	___
16.	My talk was arranged in logical order	___	___
17.	I stuck to the facts	___	___
18.	I demonstrated my talk	___	___
19.	I backed up what I said with examples, figures, and visible proof	___	___
20.	I boiled everything down to a few definite, simple sales points	___	___
21.	I tested the prospect's agreement on one point before going on to the next one	___	___
22.	My sales presentation was a good length	___	___
23.	I used showmanship	___	___
24.	My interview was free of argument	___	___
25.	I asked for an order	___	___

Figure 13-9 It is important to take note of the reasons why a close failed, so that next time the mistakes can be corrected.

possible to the next time the prospect will be in a position to buy. Third, this technique calls the prospect's attention to the salesperson's interest, expectation of getting the order, and desire to be of service. Fourth, the prospect can look forward to a second, scheduled visit from someone who wants to be of assistance. Finally, arranging an appointment may mean the prospect can block out interruptions during the next conference, thus giving full attention to the salesperson.

Callbacks demand special preparation. In getting ready for the next visit, the salesperson should carefully review the prospect card and what took place at the previous meeting. The salesperson who promised to bring something back to the prospect, such as information or samples, should be sure to have them. Because the prospect's attention has been devoted to many matters in the interim between the two calls, the salesperson must be prepared to revive the prospect's interest and reestablish contact. The salesperson cannot expect the prospect to remember all that was said on the last call. In some instances, the prospect may have developed a negative attitude toward the sales proposal. Pressure, then, is on the salesperson to have some message for the prospect that is new and important.

In executing the callback, the salesperson must offer a justification for the repeat visit. Whenever new facts of value to the prospect are used as an introduction to the callback, the chances of a friendly welcome are good. Whatever introduction is used, the salesperson must capture the prospect's interest quickly and place the presentation on firm ground. The salesperson should personalize the conversation, show particular interest in the prospect's problems, and offer definite advantages to the prospect just as would be done on any first call.

SUMMARY

The close is the final stage of the presentation. Closing means asking the prospect to buy the product. Successful closing requires salespeople to look beyond their fear of rejection and to develop an inner confidence.

The salesperson must take note of verbal and physical closing clues in order to spot an opening for a trial close. Once the opening is spotted, the salesperson has several closing techniques from which to choose, including: (1) closing on a choice; (2) assuming the sale is made; (3) summarizing product benefits; (4) getting the prospect's agreement on lesser points; and (5) offering a special deal.

Regardless of whether the sale was made, the salesperson should develop goodwill by thanking the prospect for taking the time and consideration and pave the way for future sales visits.

KEY TERMS

closing	double-question method
buying signals	selection close
choice close	split-decision close
closing on a minor point	closing on the objection

summary close   point-of-purchase (POP) display
assumption close   T-account
standing-room-only close   contingent promise
callback   request an order
special-deal close   lost-order report
push money (PM)   lost-order checklist

REVIEW QUESTIONS

1. What does the word *closing* refer to?
2. Why is closing important?
3. How does the salesperson usually feel about closing?
4. What are closing clues?
5. What is the purpose of a trial close?
6. When is the best time to try a trial close?
7. What is meant by closing on a choice?
8. Why is the minor-points close effective?
9. Who or what situation is best for using the T-account technique?
10. List four things that a salesperson should do after a sale has been made.
11. When does preparation for a return call begin?
12. What information should be generated and recorded after an unsuccessful call?
13. What are the advantages of making a specific appointment for a callback?
14. How should a salesperson arrange and prepare for a callback?

DISCUSSION QUESTIONS

1. Assume that you are sales manager for a furniture distributor. It has come to your attention that one of your salespeople has been unsuccessful because he is intent upon playing out his entire presentation rather than closing the sale. How would you try to help this salesperson?
2. Assume you are selling textbooks and you are calling on the department chairman of English at a very large high school. He likes your product, but he insists that he cannot buy now and must use his current books because classes start next week and he is afraid that you cannot get the books to him in time for the start of classes. Which closing method do you use? Give an example of how you would use it.
3. Assume that you are the sales manager for a company that sells door-to-door. One of your salespeople has become very frustrated and hesitant because she keeps getting the door slammed in her

face. She now has a very low degree of confidence. How do you try to help her?

CASE 13-1   CITATION COPY MACHINES—A*

Steve Sanders is a sales representative for the Citation Copy Machine Company. Today he is calling on Hannah Harwell, a partner at Interstate Investments, a small firm specializing in commodity options and futures contracts. Steve has just entered Hannah's office.

Steve:	Good morning, Hannah. I'm Steve, Steve Sanders. Citation Copy Machines.
Hannah:	Good to meet you, Steve.
Steve:	(Handing Hannah a brochure.) When we were talking on the phone, this is the model I was telling you about: the Citation C-9000. Top of the line. It'll run off 200 copies a minute in color or black and white.
Hannah:	That's pretty fast.
Steve:	Best in the industry. And take a gander at page four. The C-9000 averages 320,000 copies before needing a major overhaul. None of the top-of-the-line models made by our competitors average more than 275,000. That's quality.
Hannah:	It looks big.
Steve:	Sure is. Six feet by four. Built right. Built tough.
Hannah:	But we only have 400 square feet of office space.
Steve:	How 'bout that little refreshment area you have in the back? We could fit it in there.
Hannah:	We'd have to take out the table where we eat our lunch.
Steve:	That'd do it. Look at page two, Hannah. Comparable models run between $7,000 and $8,000. We've got better quality, better reliability, and you can have the C-9000 for only $6,795.
Hannah:	$6,795? I could buy a car for that kind of money.
Steve:	Maybe a used one or a little puddle-jumper. Not a new one that'll do 200 in color.
Hannah:	I'm afraid it's more than we can afford right now.
Steve:	(Pulling out a calculator and punching in some numbers.) Tell you what, Hannah. We're having a sales contest this month and I'd like to win it. If we can sign the contract today, I can let you have it for $6,495.
Hannah:	Steve, we've only been in business for a couple of months. There's just no budget for a capital expense item like that.

---

*Case prepared by Bob Kimball. Used with permission.

Steve:	You drive a hard bargain, Hannah. OK, what will you give me for one? Would you pay $6,000?
Hannah:	It might as well be six million. There's no way.
Steve:	All right then, no problem. Tell you what: we don't normally do this, but for you I'll make an exception. We'll lease it to you for $250 a month.
Hannah:	Two hundred and fifty dollars? A month?
Steve:	Well, that's a one-year contract. If you'd agree to a two-year contract, it would be just $225. That's a savings of $25 every month. Would you be more interested in the two-year lease?
Hannah:	I don't know. We're not spending anywhere near that now.
Steve:	Hannah, I'll beat any competitive deal. What kind of copier do you have now?
Hannah:	We don't have one.
Steve:	What are you using, carbon paper?
Hannah:	No, there's a copy center two doors down right here in the mall. We just go down there.
Steve:	What a hassle! All that walking! All that waiting!
Hannah:	It's right around the corner. And they've got eight self-service machines. We've seldom had to wait more than a minute or two.
Steve:	But don't you get tired of having to go back and forth all day long?
Hannah:	No, the secretaries usually do it. The only time my partner or I have to go is when one of the two secretaries is out of the office and the other one is covering the phones.
Steve:	What's it costing you to run off your copies at the copy center?
Hannah:	Let's see. We do, oh, thirty or forty copies a day at $.10 each. About three or four dollars a day.
Steve:	(Punching in numbers on his calculator.) So about $65 to $85 a month.
Hannah:	Sounds about right.
Steve:	How much time every day do your secretaries spend going back and forth to the copy center?
Hannah:	Oh, maybe twenty or thirty minutes a day.
Steve:	Each of them?
Hannah:	No, both of them combined.
Steve:	How about on a real busy day when things are getting all backed up at the copy center?
Hannah:	That doesn't happen very often.
Steve:	But when it happens, how much?
Hannah:	I'd say forty, forty-five minutes.

Steve:	Maybe fifty?
Hannah:	That'd be on the high side.
Steve:	So let's say an hour a day. Including all the fringe benefits, Hannah, what do you pay your secretaries?
Hannah:	It would probably come out to around eight dollars an hour.
Steve:	(Punching in numbers on his calculator.) Hannah, do you realize it's costing you as much as $176 a month for your secretaries to run to and from the copy center? When we add in the cost of the copies themselves, that's $241 to $261 a month.
Hannah:	(Looking through a computer printout on her desk.) No, last month it was $74.40.
Steve:	But that doesn't include your secretaries' time. You've got to count that.
Hannah:	Not really. We have to pay them anyway. They'll be paid the same whether they're in the office or at the copy center.
Steve:	Then think of the convenience. This way you'll have a copy machine ready to use seven days a week, 24 hours a day. What would happen if you needed copies and the copy center was closed?
Hannah:	They're always open when we are.
Steve:	What about late nights and weekends?
Hannah:	We only work when the markets are open.
Steve:	I'll bet they don't make color copies over there, though, do they?
Hannah:	I'm not sure. We've never needed color copies.
Steve:	That's just because you've never had color capability. Once you've had color, you'll wonder how you ever lived without it. It's like a microwave oven.
Hannah:	Like a what?
Steve:	A microwave oven. Do you have one at home?
Hannah:	Yes, we do.
Steve:	Now that you have one, I'll bet you'd never want to have a home without one.
Hannah:	I can't say. I don't use it that much.
Steve:	Believe me, Hannah, you'll love it. Well, if you don't have any more questions, I've got one for you. Can I have your order?
Hannah:	I don't know. I'll have to talk this over with my partner.
Steve:	What's there to talk over? Let's wrap this up today and you can be rolling in color tomorrow.
Hannah:	I'm just not sure. Give me a call in a couple of days.
Steve:	Hannah, let me ask you this: What have I got to do to get your order today?

Hannah:	I'm not going to make a decision today.
Steve:	OK, no problem. How 'bout if I call you the first of the week?
Hannah:	That'll be fine.
Steve:	Have a good day. I'll talk to you then.

CASE QUESTIONS

1. Rate Steve's sales presentation on a scale of 1 to 10 (1 = terrible sales presentation; 10 = excellent sales presentation).
2. What things did Steve do well in identifying customer needs, selling the benefits of his product, and involving Hannah in the presentation? What could he have done better?
3. What things did Steve do well in handling Hannah's objections? What could he have done better?
4. How effective was Steve in his attempts to close the sale and get the order? What could he have done better?
5. Beginning with the initial assumptions below, use Lotus to complete the remainder of the table showing the impact on total cost of copies if: *(a)* the office down the hall starts charging 15 cents each; *(b)* it were discovered that secretaries were really using a full hour a day getting copies made down the hall; and *(c)* it were discovered that, on average, the managers spent fifteen minutes a day going to the copier down the hall.

EXHIBIT 13-1
ANALYSIS OF COST OF USING AN OUTSIDE COPIER

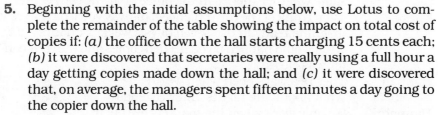

	Initial Assumptions	Increased Copy Cost	Increased Secretarial Time	Management Copy Use
Copies per Day	40	40	40	40
Cost per Copy	$0.10	$0.15	$0.10	$0.10
Secretarial Time (Hrs.)	0.5	0.5	1	0.5
Secretarial Salary (per Hr.)	$8.00	$8.00	$8.00	$8.00
Manager Time (Hrs.)	0	0	0	0.25

Manager Salary (per Hr.)	$50.00	$50.00	$50.00	$50.00
Total Cost of Copies for 30 days	$240.00	_____	_____	_____

- How can Steve use this information in his presentation?

CASE 13-2   CITATION COPY MACHINES—B*

Barb Brownlee is a sales representative for the Citation Copy Machine Company. Today she is calling on Rod Russell, a partner of Interstate Investments, a small firm specializing in commodity options and futures contracts. Barb has just entered Rod's office.

Barb:	Good morning, Mr. Russell. I'm Barb Brownlee from Citation Copy Machines.
Rod:	Rod Russell. Good to meet you, Barb.
Barb:	You're new here in the mall, aren't you?
Rod:	Yes, we are. We've just been open a couple of months.
Barb:	Is this a new business, or just a new location for you?
Rod:	New business. My partner and I had each worked at Standard Securities for over five years. Decided it was time to take the plunge and go into business for ourselves.
Barb:	I'll bet this is an exciting business.
Rod:	Exciting is an understatement. Most of the time the commodities market is frantic. And dog-eat-dog. It can be rough.
Barb:	What kind of investors do you normally work with?
Rod:	Very different from a full-line brokerage firm. We only deal in commodities, so we don't cater to little old ladies or small investors. Our clients are the high rollers who'll move in and out of the markets with hundred-thousand-dollar trades.
Barb:	You have a more affluent clientele, then.
Rod:	Definitely. You can't effectively play the commodities market with money you can't afford to lose. It's high risk,

*Case prepared by Bob Kimball. Used with permission.

	high reward. Not for the little guys, and not for the faint of heart.
Barb:	Interesting. So, what's the most important benefit you offer to prospective clients?
Rod:	In a word, Barb, professionalism. We know commodities. We're experts. And a close second to that is timing. In this field, you've got to know when to buy, when to hold, and when to fold.
Barb:	You've got decisions to make every day, then.
Rod:	Every day? Every hour! Every minute!
Barb:	Really?
Rod:	You bet. We see it all the time. Five minutes either way can be the difference between fortunes made and fortunes lost.
Barb:	Sounds fascinating.
Rod:	It sure is.
Barb:	Well, Rod, I believe that we may be able to help you and your business.
Rod:	How can you do that?
Barb:	Just by having you answer a few questions. First of all, do you presently have a copy machine in your office?
Rod:	No, we don't.
Barb:	Do you ever make copies at a location outside the office?
Rod:	Yes.
Barb:	Where would that be?
Rod:	There's a copy center just two doors down from us right here in the mall. We really lucked out. It's very convenient.
Barb:	Good. About how many copies do you run off on an average day?
Rod:	Oh, thirty, maybe forty.
Barb:	So, any time you need to run copies, you just walk down there?
Rod:	Well, usually I don't. My partner and I have two secretaries. Generally, we just send one of them.
Barb:	One of them is always free to do that?
Rod:	Most of the time. Unless one of them is at lunch or on an errand or something.
Barb:	What do you do then?
Rod:	My partner or I will cover the phones and send the other secretary to the copy center. Once in a while, we just go ourselves.
Barb:	How many times a day does someone from your office go over to make copies?
Rod:	Probably four or five times.
Barb:	Do you have to wait a lot when you go down there?

Rod:	Not very often. They've got eight self-service machines. We've seldom had to wait more than a minute or two.
Barb:	How often do you have to wait more than that?
Rod:	Not very often. Maybe once or twice a week.
Barb:	About once or twice a week. . .
Rod:	Yeah, sometimes they just get real busy all of a sudden.
Barb:	Any idea how much you're spending on copies?
Rod:	Let's see. They're $.10 each, so it's about three or four dollars a day. (Looking at a computer printout on his desk.) Last month it was $74.40.
Barb:	And how much time a day do your secretaries spend going back and forth to the copy center?
Rod:	Oh, maybe twenty or thirty minutes a day.
Barb:	Each of them?
Rod:	No, both of them combined.
Barb:	Including all the fringe benefits, Rod, what do you pay your secretaries?
Rod:	It would probably come out to around eight dollars an hour.
Barb:	(Pulling out a calculator and punching in some numbers.) According to your estimate, then, it's costing you between $59 and $88 a month for your secretaries to go to and from the copy center.
Rod:	Not really. We have to pay them anyway. They'll be paid the same whether they're in the office or at the copy center.
Barb:	That's a good point. When they're in the office, what sort of things do they do?
Rod:	Well, as I said, they handle the phones. And they maintain all the client files and billings. Then, when clients are in the office, they meet and greet them and get coffee or soft drinks. Many times, they'll sit in on the meetings with clients to transcribe conversations and prepare contract orders.
Barb:	The professional touch.
Rod:	Precisely.
Barb:	And when they have to be out of the office, wouldn't you agree that you're not getting $59 to $88 worth of professionalism for the time your secretaries are going to and from the copy center?
Rod:	Maybe not.
Barb:	And for your clients . . . You were saying how a few minutes could be critical in the commodities market. Do you think some of your clients might not care to have to wait even a few minutes to have copies run off?

Rod: Some of them.

Barb: And wouldn't you agree that it would look a lot more professional and be much more convenient to run them off right here in the office?

Rod: It might.

Barb: For the copies you're doing now, how many do you do in color and how many in black-and-white?

Rod: They're all in black-and-white.

Barb: Do you think that color capability might be useful to you?

Rod: I don't think so.

Barb: How about in preparing presentations or other materials for yourselves or your clients?

Rod: Not really.

Barb: Then, you'll want to consider our C-2000, C-3000, and C-4000 models. These are the finest black-and-white copiers made. Is a collating feature important to you?

Rod: We need it sometimes, not all the time.

Barb: You said you were running about thirty or forty copies a day. Do you anticipate that number being higher or about the same in the future?

Rod: Probably a little higher as our business grows.

Barb: And you'll need collating more often in the future, too?

Rod: I expect so.

Barb: (Handing Rod two brochures.) I believe that either the C-3000 or the C-4000 would best suit your needs, Rod. The C-4000 is a floor model equipped with a collator, and the C-3000 is a desktop model onto which we can adapt a collator now or later. The C-3000 runs ten copies a minute and the C-4000 runs twenty. Both of these models can be yours on either a lease or purchase plan.

Rod: As I said, Barb, we're new here. There's just no budget for a capital expense item like that.

Barb: Then let's talk about leasing. On a one-year lease, the C-3000 with collator is $80 a month and the C-4000 is $105. (Punching in some numbers on her calculator.) Including paper and toner, the C-3000 will total about $130 a month and the C-4000 about $155.

Rod: That's about twice what we're paying now.

Barb: In direct costs, yes. But the difference comes out to only about three or four dollars a business day. If you consider your secretaries' time, it's about even.

Rod: Well, maybe.

Barb: And as you were saying, your most important product is professionalism. Wouldn't you rather have those eight-dollar-an-hour secretaries providing professional services to you and your clients rather than running to and from the copy center?

Rod: Makes sense.

Barb: And won't your office seem even more professional when you can run off a copy here instantly instead of having to cover the phones for even a minute or two while the secretary goes out?

Rod: Yes, I guess it would.

Barb: Where do you think would be the best location for a copier in your office?

Rod: We only have 400 square feet of office space. There isn't a lot of room in here.

Barb: So the smaller, desktop model might be more convenient. Tell me, Rod, would ten copies a minute be fast enough for you, or do you really need to have a model that will do twenty?

Rod: Ten's fine.

Barb: Then it looks like the C-3000 is a winner all around. If you'll just initial this agreement, we can install it today.

Rod: How long will it take to install it?

Barb: About fifteen minutes. Is now a good time, or would later in the day be more convenient?

Rod: I've got an important meeting in about an hour.

Barb: I'll do it right now, then, and be out of your way in plenty of time.

Rod: Sure will be nice not to have to go down to that copy center any more.

CASE QUESTIONS

1. Rate Barb's sales presentation on a scale of 1 to 10 (1 = terrible sales presentation; 10 = excellent sales presentation).
2. What things did Barb do well in identifying customer needs, selling the benefits of her product, and involving Rod in the presentation? What could she have done better? What were the major differences between this case and the prior case, Citation Copy Machines—A?
3. What things did Barb do well in handling Rod's objections? What could she have done better? What were the major differences between this case and the prior case, Citation Copy Machines—A?
4. How effective was Barb in her attempts to close the sale and get the order? What could she have done better? What were the major differences between this case and the prior case, Citation Copy Machines—A?

PART 5

Basic Selling Responsibilities

CHAPTER 14
Providing Service and Goodwill After the Sale

After studying this chapter, you should be able to:

- Suggest guidelines for scheduling calls on established customers

- Understand how salespeople build repeat business and increase the volume bought by customers

- Argue that salespeople should try to secure customer support and influence customers' merchandising policies

- Answer questions about salespeople's meetings with customers

- Outline what salespeople can do when dealing with customers' complaints, cancellations, and returned goods

- Show a grasp of credit and collection problems

So far, our journey through the selling process, as shown in Figure 14-1, has concentrated on convincing prospects—those who are potential customers—to buy our product. Once the salesperson has successfully closed the sale, that prospect becomes a customer.

The relationship between the salesperson and the buyer changes once the prospect becomes a customer. The salesperson is no longer trying to get commitment. Instead, he or she is trying to ensure the obligations agreed upon during the pre-sale are met. The salesperson's goal also has changed from a short-term perspective (making the sale) to a long-term perspective (a strong, long-term buyer-seller relationship). This is not to say that the salesperson stops selling. Nothing could be further from the truth. It is just that the relationship is different. The preapproach is already done and only requires updating. The approach is smoother because a rapport and credibility has already been established. The rest of the selling process, however, will remain the same because the salesperson will be selling different products, or updated and improved versions of the product that was originally sold. Thus, you can see in Figure 14-2 that the selling process is really an ongoing cycle.

THE SELLING PROCESS

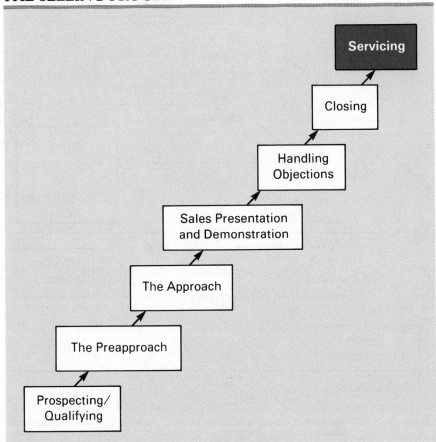

Figure 14-1 The last stage of the selling process is *servicing*.

THE IMPORTANCE OF BUILDING SOUND RELATIONSHIPS

The salesperson who works constantly to see that each customer derives the maximum benefit from purchases lays the foundation of a sound customer relationship. The salesperson should be guided by the customer's circumstances and make only sound purchasing recommendations. A sound relationship means that the customer respects the salesperson both personally and as a source of quality products and services.

The rewards of working systematically with customers in order to build sound buyer-seller relationships are many. One of the most obvious rewards of satisfied customers is that repeat sales lead to increased sales volume. Another reward is that the cost of maintaining an existing

THE SALES CYCLE

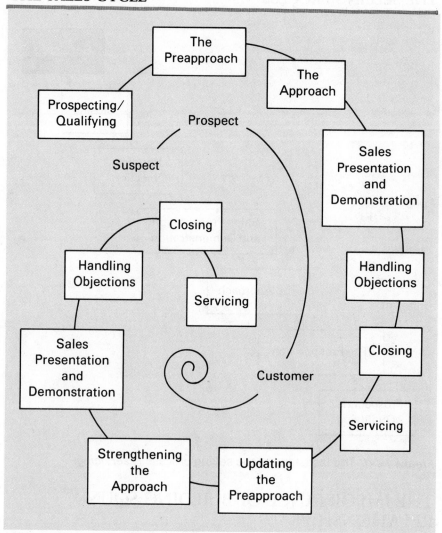

Figure 14-2 The selling process is a never-ending cycle. Successful servicing of an account will lead to repeat purchases.

customer is much less than that of gaining a new one. Satisfied customers also are valuable sources of a number of kinds of information: case histories, solutions to common business problems, testimonials, suggestions of new uses for the salesperson's products, and names of new prospects. Finally, satisfied customers provide favorable word-of-mouth publicity.

Providing quality products and services in a timely fashion helps salespeople build sound relationships with their customers. In this chapter we will point out ways to do this. These include the following:

- appropriate scheduling of calls on customers
- building repeat business, increasing the volume of accounts
- handling inactive accounts
- securing customer support
- profitably influencing customers' merchandising policies
- aiding customers by holding informative meetings with them
- dealing effectively with customer complaints, order cancellations, and merchandise returns
- regaining lost customers
- handling the problems of credit and collection

These services together with quality products build enduring goodwill.

SCHEDULING CALLS ON ESTABLISHED CUSTOMERS

After the first purchase that makes a prospect a customer, the salesperson should schedule an early return visit to see that the new customer is satisfied with the purchase. On this visit, the salesperson should make sure that the order was filled correctly and that the customer is using the product properly. Instructions about use and maintenance may be repeated, and any questions that have come up since the initial sale should be answered. If anything has gone wrong with the purchase, the salesperson can use this early return visit to find out what happened and take appropriate action. The call also can be useful in continuing to sell the customer on the benefits that may be derived from the purchase. Finally, the visit may help lay the groundwork for future purchases and may result in obtaining a testimonial for the product or some leads and preapproach information about new prospects.

After this early return call, the salesperson is faced with the problem of deciding how often to visit the new customer. Calling too often wastes selling time and money and may irritate the customer. Informed customers recognize that too many calls are being made, and this tends to make them question the salesperson's judgment and managerial ability. If the calls are scheduled too far apart, there may also be difficulties. The customer resents being given inadequate service and thus begins to wonder about how much dependence can be placed on the salesperson. Furthermore, infrequent calls are an invitation to competition to move in and steal the account. Good salespeople will manage sales call frequency so that their time and the company's limited resources are used most efficiently.

CLASSIFYING CUSTOMERS FOR SCHEDULING PURPOSES

No one interval between visits will fit all customers. Some demand a short interval between calls, while others require fewer calls. One of the most efficient solutions to this problem is to classify customers according to their importance in terms of sales volume. Three or four classifications should be adequate for most selling situations. The classifications shown in Figure 14-3 are typical.

PROBLEMS IN HANDLING SMALL ACCOUNTS

A concept often referred to as the **80-20 principle** is useful with the above classification of customers: 20 percent of the customers account for about 80 percent of the sales. For the salesperson, the problem is what to do about scheduling calls on the 80 percent of the customers who account for only about 20 percent of the sales volume.

Some small accounts will eventually grow into Group A accounts, and some, of course, will become even smaller and eventually disappear. No seller wants to cut off a small account just because it is small and perhaps is being handled at little profit under current conditions. Salespeople who do will have an almost impossible task trying to recapture it later. But regardless of the potential growth of a small account, its profitability at the moment must be considered. No salesperson can continue indefinitely to call on a small customer whose patronage does not result in some profit. So, the salesperson must evaluate each customer's present volume and future possibilities versus the cost of continuing the account. For the individual salesperson, the best policy is probably to work with small customers in an effort to develop them into large ones, and to continue this practice until convinced that it is not possible to increase the account to a profitable level. Figure 14-4 offers some specific suggestions for handling small accounts.

HANDLING GROUP B AND GROUP C ACCOUNTS

Group A accounts should not be serviced to the neglect of Group B and Group C accounts. Almost all Group A accounts were at an earlier time Group C, then Group B accounts. The salesperson who wins out over competition at the B or C level will be better able to maintain this position when the buyer becomes an A account. In some instances, it may be possible to capitalize on a competitive supplier's problem to secure additional business from a B or C account. When the salesperson can solve an immediate crisis, a longer-term commitment may result.

In servicing Group B and Group C accounts, the salesperson must do everything possible to ensure ease of buying for the ultimate consumer. The salesperson tries to persuade the B or C customer to do those things that will enable the product or product line virtually to sell itself. Thus, the salesperson tries to see that the merchant has a balanced stock and that products are displayed so as to invite consumers to examine them.

CUSTOMER CLASSIFICATIONS

GROUP A
- Most Important Customers
- Call on Them Once a Month
- Give Utmost Personal Attention

GROUP C
- Small, Less Profitable Customers
- Call on Twice a Year
- Can Use Some Telephone and Direct Mail

GROUP B
- Solid, Substantial Customers
- Call on Them Every Other Month
- Give Plenty of Personal Attention

GROUP D
- Least Valuable Customers
- Small & Expensive to Call on
- Strictly Telephone and Direct Mail

Figure 14-3 Customer follow-ups and service calls should be scheduled according to the importance of the account.

SUGGESTIONS FOR HANDLING SMALL ACCOUNTS

1. Service no account buying less than a certain amount. (While this may work toward eliminating unprofitable customers, it will drive some customers to competitors.)
2. Adopt a service fee for small orders. (Both establishing and collecting such a fee is difficult. Suggestion No. 3 is often more acceptable.)
3. Establish a system of quantity discounts; price small volume orders to recover overhead costs.
4. Educate small customers about the costs of handling small accounts.
5. Raise the size of the average order through better selling.
6. Classify small customers into two groups, the promising and the unpromising, and give the former most of the time and attention available for small customers. This time will be determined by such factors as how many of these customers the salesperson has, how often they are in the market to buy, and how often they need merchandising assistance.

Figure 14-4 For the individual salesperson, the best policy is probably to work with small customers in an effort to develop them into large ones and to continue this practice until convinced that it is not possible to affect this growth.

Salespeople assure quality service by monitoring timely delivery of goods, quality of product and packaging, proper invoicing and other documentation, and the performance of the product(s).

Specific selling techniques that have proved effective elsewhere are passed on to the merchant and the sales force. Periodic reference to customer records will show how well the salesperson is succeeding with any customer and guide the salesperson in allocating time to that customer in the future.

BUILDING REPEAT BUSINESS

A salesperson often spends much time and money calling on a particular prospect before obtaining an order. Furthermore, the first order is often not large enough to equal the expenses incurred up to that time; in some cases, three, four, or even more orders will be required to equal the development cost of the account. A customer who switches to a competitor must be replaced at the further expenditure of the salesperson's time and money. Thus, salespeople must not let accounts slip away. Except for the relatively few salespeople who sell products that are purchased infrequently (houses, for example), the salesperson looks to repeat orders for the bulk of sales volume.

Because satisfied customers are hard to take away from their present source of supply, and personal standing with customers is so important, the salesperson should be careful in handling all transactions and contacts with customers. The salesperson should win and keep a customer's complete confidence concerning honesty, judgment, and discretion. The salesperson should not ask favors of customers except in emergencies.

The salesperson must be alert for any signal that might indicate a deterioration in the buyer-seller relationship. Such a signal may be financial: a customer's sales may drop or some change may be made in financial policy. A second signal is of a personal nature: the customer may be increasingly influenced by someone hostile to the salesperson, may pay less attention to business matters, or may allow associates to handle more business responsibilities than they formerly did. Finally, outside events may change good customers into poor ones: legislation, product obsolescence, and physical changes such as the rerouting of traffic flow are examples. Any one of these signals demands the salesperson's examination because they could affect the amount of repeat business obtained from any one customer.

As part of an annual analysis of their own performance, salespeople should study each account acquired during the previous year and make definite plans for holding it. Each account retained and each account lost during the period also should be examined in detail. In determining the cause of the loss, it may be found that the merchandise did not sell well in a certain area, the dealer failed to handle the line properly, the dealer's margin was inadequate, the salesperson's company gave poor service, or the salesperson was somehow at fault. Once the cause has been identified, an appropriate program to regain desirable accounts should be started.

INCREASING THE VOLUME OF ACCOUNTS

It is not enough for the salesperson to acquire and then hold an account. Each account must be built up to its full potential in sales volume. The aim is to develop the account until the customer is buying and selling or using as much of the salesperson's product as possible. Among the more important reasons for increasing the volume of an account are:

1. Additional volume means additional income for the salesperson's company.
2. Less time and money is required to build up the volume of established customers than to obtain the same dollar amount by converting prospects to customers.
3. The customer who ought to be buying the salesperson's complete line but buys only part of it is not completely supplied. This customer

should appreciate suggestions regarding how to better provide for requirements.

OBSTACLES TO INCREASING THE VOLUME OF AN ACCOUNT

Certain obstacles make increasing accounts a challenging job. One obstacle is the reluctance or even refusal of a buyer to change buying habits. Some buyers divide their purchases among vendors to keep a close check on the prices and quality of various vendors. Others do this in an attempt to ensure a source of supply in case something should happen to any one supplier. Reciprocity influences still others. There can be powerful pressures on buyers not to switch their patronage from current sources of supply, because other salespeople are working just as fiercely. Salespeople should anticipate these obstacles and plan ways to overcome them. Several methods of overcoming these obstacles were covered in Chapter 12.

For whatever reasons, no salesperson is ever able to secure as great a share of every customer's total business as desired. This does not excuse the salesperson from estimating a realistic share in each case, however, and making appropriate plans to obtain it.

SUGGESTIONS FOR INCREASING THE ACCOUNT

Salespeople should be neither too conservative nor too aggressive in trying to increase the customer's volume of purchases. Overly conservative salespeople give competitors an opportunity to pursue and obtain orders they could have had. Overly aggressive salespeople, in their haste to effect changes and realignments, can close doors in their own faces permanently. Too often salespeople are determined to write up a large order without proper consideration of the customer's needs. The best strategy is to follow a moderate course by holding on to current business while gradually taking over other products and/or product lines.

The methods listed in Figure 14-5 may prove helpful in increasing the dollar volume of a customer's purchases. Not all of the methods will be appropriate in every situation, but each will be effective for certain customers on certain occasions. Explanations of each method are given in the following paragraphs.

IMPLEMENTING A SYSTEMATIC DEVELOPMENT PROGRAM

Be systematic about the development program. A carefully thought out master plan is needed to increase sales volume. This plan should consist of definite programs for building up the business of each individual customer.

SUGGESTIONS FOR INCREASING THE VOLUME OF ACCOUNTS

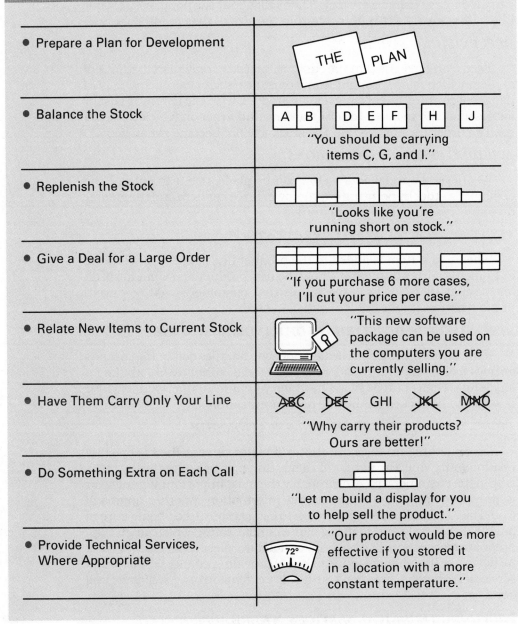

Figure 14-5 Once a customer has been sold, the salesperson's job is to try to increase the account's sales volume.

IDENTIFYING MERCHANDISE FOR BALANCED STOCK

Identify merchandise that the customer does not carry but should carry for a good balance of stock. Then talk about the popularity of your line in that area, its turnover rate, and the size of the potential market.

REPLENISHING STOCK

Keep alert for signs that the customer needs to replenish the stock of an item which is now bought from someone else. A customer who is in danger of running out of a particular product, with the resulting cost or loss, is most apt to listen to your warning and to act on it by letting you rush an order through so that the stock will not become exhausted.

AVOIDING SPECIAL CONCESSIONS

Whenever a special concession can be made, use it to enlarge the customer's order by pointing out the lower price per item and the greater discount resulting from a larger order.

RELATING NEW ITEMS TO CURRENT STOCK

When a new item is added to the product line, relate it to what the customer is currently buying. Show the new product and what it will do for the customer. Good salespeople also ask customers what new products or services might fulfill unsatisfied needs.

STRESSING THE DESIRABILITY OF HANDLING A SINGLE LINE

If the customer is a split dealer (one who handles competing brands or buys from competing vendors), stress the desirability of handling a single line. Then point out ways in which your line is superior and why it deserves to be chosen as the line for concentration.

CEMENTING THE BUYER-SELLER RELATIONSHIP

Do something on each call that will better cement the buyer-seller relationship. While the nature of this action may be suggested by referring to the customer's record, probably the most important type of favor is providing valuable merchandising information. Another approach would be to provide a personal touch to each account, but being sure to handle it tastefully and tactfully. For example, salespeople can give appropriate recognition for a birthday or holiday. Salespeople must be careful not to use the personal touch in lieu of providing quality products and services. Personal expressions are a polite extension of a job already well done.

PROVIDING TECHNICAL SERVICES, WHERE APPROPRIATE

For products that are technical in nature or are used by industrial firms, the provision of on-site technical services and product information is often of great value to the customer. Examples of **product infor-**

mation include product specifications, typical quality, allowable conditions for use or exposure, limits on service life or operating conditions, and performance under typical operating conditions. Examples of *on-site and in-plant technical services* include operations troubleshooting, hands-on training in use of product, and meetings with customer manufacturing and/or technical personnel in designing new or modified products, or changes in packaging or design.

HIGHLIGHT 14-1

Three tactics that can be used to increase the volume of accounts and improve customer relations are customer service representatives, newsletters, *and* team selling.

In her article entitled "Customer Service Reps Are Ideal For Marketing Team," in The Marketing News *(May 23, 1986), Sheila N. Haverty calls the customer service representative "a valuable support for outside sales and supplier of marketing research information."*

Ms. Haverty, president of Haverty & Associates, advises companies to train their customer service reps in these skills:

- *Upgrading orders*
- *Cross-selling*
- *Determining additional product applications*
- *Introducing new company products*
- *Uncovering competitive products*
- *Uncovering customer's buying criteria*
- *Opening new accounts*
- *Reactivating former accounts*
- *Referring large accounts to outside reps for development*
- *Managing and developing marginal accounts from the inside*
- *Following up and qualifying direct-mail leads*

The result of this training should be the development of the customer service department as a valuable marketing resource.

G.A. Marken, president of Marken Communications, Incorporated, is convinced that newsletters are a great way of staying in contact with clients and building sales.

*In his article "Newsletters Are Good Way to Build Sales" (*The Marketing News, *November 7, 1986), Marken says a company can improve relations with both prospects and customers by producing and distributing a well-edited newsletter. He also claims that this newsletter need not be expensive.*

Newsletters can improve a company's visibility in its market in the following manner:

- *Making readers more aware of the company and its products*
- *Building interest by discussing past successes*
- *Introducing satisfied customers to the readers*
- *Informing readers of all of the product's uses*
- *Showing proof of the product's claims through testimonials*
- *Instructing readers on the proper usage of the product*
- *Informing readers of trends, new product developments, and additional services*
- *Showing the company's commitment to provide the market with better products and services*

Marken advises not to turn the newsletter into an "I-oriented" selling piece, but rather to present the facts on topics that the customer or prospect wants to hear about your company, its products and services, and the industry as a whole.

Team selling is the use of your company's executive, technical, manufacturing, or other staff personnel in assisting the salesperson to service the customer. In appropriate circumstances, team selling can make a lasting impression on the customer. To be effective, team members must adopt the attitude that they are also salespeople and that the customer comes first. When used judiciously, and where justified by sufficient volume of business, team selling is a useful tactic for the salesperson to employ.

INACTIVE ACCOUNTS

The kind of inactive account about which the salesperson can do little or nothing is the former customer who ceases to be a prospect. An example would be the industrial firm that begins to manufacture all it requires of some part it used to buy from the salesperson. Some customers are lost who still buy, but they buy from a competitor. Other customers may become inactive (lost for the short run) for various reasons, such as misunderstanding, sellers' mistakes (especially in order filling, delivery, and billing), weak selling, a specific product complaint, and lower prices offered by competitors.

To prevent inactive accounts, the salesperson should practice effective communication, watch each customer's order size, and stay sensitive to any hint of customer dissatisfaction. When trouble develops, the salesperson should determine the facts promptly, usually in person. It is important to correct misunderstandings and remove causes of friction. Salespeople should be as generous as possible. Point-by-point comparisons against competition may be helpful. In addition, the salesperson may look for some unique benefit to offer.

SECURING CUSTOMER SUPPORT

Up to this point we have been discussing aid and assistance in one direction—from seller to buyer. Now it is time to examine and evaluate the customer as a possible source of help to the salesperson.

The phrase **customer support** is used to describe the most desirable and sought-after service the buyer can render the seller. At the start, the individual is a prospect and nothing more. The prospect places the first order and becomes a customer. The final step in the process of development is taken when the customer becomes an enthusiastic and loyal supporter.

In this relationship, the customer is actively and enthusiastically in favor of the salesperson, company, products, and service. For example, customers who are retailers make sure the salesperson's line of merchandise is always stocked in adequate volume, is favored in the display treatment given it, and is pushed by personal selling as much as practicable. Calling to alert the salesperson to an unexpectedly large order, or suggesting new ideas for new products and services are ways that nonretail customers help out salespeople. In a sense, the customer is actually selling for the salesperson. Most important, the customer looks on the salesperson almost as a partner. The customer asks the salesperson's opinions on a variety of matters, some broader than just the salesperson's line, and often relies on the salesperson's judgment. Because the salesperson is regarded as an expert, the customer relies on the salesperson's advice.

HOW TO OBTAIN CUSTOMER SUPPORT

There are several possibilities for obtaining support from customers. One is to develop an agreeable, pleasant personality, and then use it. Salespeople should be on a friendly basis with the customer and with the customer's employees. A friendly relationship, not undue familiarity, is the goal.

Frequent contact, even if only a reminder postcard, is desirable. Make each visit special by always having a good reason for calling, such as a new product, model, sample, plan, or bit of information. Don't ever give the customer the impression that you "just happened by," or "just dropped in to see how things are going." By indicating that a special call is being made, you flatter the customer and encourage cooperation.

Be more than just a salesperson. Never stop accumulating knowledge, particularly about your products and the art of selling. Be aware of what's happening in the field of sales, not just locally, but nationally and internationally. Learn about your customer's business and industry. Read business journals, the *Wall Street Journal*, or the trade press to keep abreast of recent trends and developments in new products, com-

Figure 14-6 The Wall Street Journal can provide the salesperson with a wealth of information on both customers and competitors.

petitive activity, government regulation, and so on. Discuss these developments with your customers. Be able to interpret and justify your company's decisions and policies. Your grasp of general business conditions, causes, and trends must expand continuously. To the maximum extent, be a dependable source of current information about such matters as collections, advertising, and legislation.

Serve the customer's best interest by providing wise guidance and helpful service. The customer should never have to ask about something new or wait for something due. No customer should ever be given cause or opportunity for losing enthusiasm. Never allow anything to happen that would encourage questioning of any buying decision.

Do as many favors for the customer as possible. Any help, sound advice, valuable information, or personal assistance obligates the customer just that much more, and by implication asks for reciprocation by increased patronage and support. Whenever practicable, locate customers and prospects for your customers.

Show the customer the benefits of giving you support and loyalty. It may be that some policy of your company helped the customer to weather a price war, to maintain a certain margin, or to cash in on a special event.

In addition, you may show actual figures that prove how other customers have increased sales in the past by tying their efforts in with those of your company. Finally, always point out how the customer will gain by cooperating in the future.

HOW CUSTOMERS HELP SALESPEOPLE

We mention here six areas in which customers can assist salespeople. The first is case histories—experiences customers have had which are of interest or value, but which did not involve any particular problem. One merchant put Brand X tires on his delivery trucks, got exceptionally good mileage out of them, and was delighted. Or an individual provided for her child's education through insurance. Or a retailer installed a certain system of lighting with gratifying results.

Second, solutions to common problems may be passed along. A retailer revised business hours, a wholesaler installed a new system of stock control, and each change was an improvement.

Testimonials are a third type of assistance. For example, the customer may describe the benefits of the salesperson's product. The salesperson then may write a conservative, appropriate statement for use over the customer's signature on the customer's letterhead. An example is provided in Figure 14-8. A slightly different kind of testimonial, one that salespeople can construct without having to obtain anyone's permission, is a list of their customers.

A CARD THANKING THE CUSTOMER FOR PURCHASING

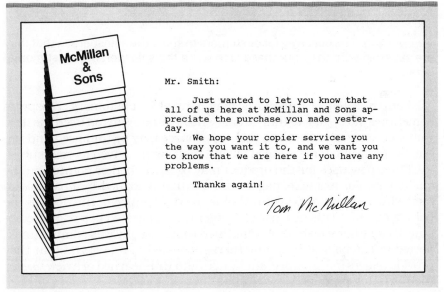

Mr. Smith:

Just wanted to let you know that all of us here at McMillan and Sons appreciate the purchase you made yesterday.

We hope your copier services you the way you want it to, and we want you to know that we are here if you have any problems.

Thanks again!

Tom McMillan

Figure 14-7 Thank you cards are an excellent way of showing customers that their business is appreciated.

TESTIMONIALS ARE A FORM OF CUSTOMER SUPPORT

NORTHSIDE COMMUNICATIONS, INC.

23 July, 19--

To Whom It May Concern:

I am writing this letter in support of Jim Flatley and the Gulf Coast
Office Products Company, from whom I have recently purchased a Ricoh
facsimile machine. Jim and the rest of the people at Gulf Coast have
been very instrumental in teaching us the many uses of a facsimile machine and in showing us how to save money.

From the beginning, Jim went out of his way to ensure that all of my employees with access to the machine were fully trained in its efficient
and effective operation. This required many hours of Jim's time, much of
which were spent outside of normal business hours.

We at Northside Communications, Inc., have nothing but the utmost
respect for Jim Flatley and the Gulf Coast Office Products. Both are
very dependable and true to their word.

I would like to conclude by highly recommending Jim Flatley as a sales
representative, and Gulf Coast Office Products as a supplier of facsimile machines. I know that you will be as pleased as I am in making
this business decision. Best of luck!

Sincerely,

Harry T. James

Harry T. James

Figure 14-8 The best way for customers to show the salesperson that they are satisfied with their purchase is to write the salesperson a testimonial letter.

Fourth, a list of references may consist of customers. Prospects sometimes like to talk to individuals who have bought and used the item under consideration, feeling that this source may be unbiased and impartial. Many customers enjoy having their names given as references.

Fifth, new uses for the product may be furnished or pointed out by customers. For example, pagers are frequently loaned by hospitals to men whose wives are expecting babies so they can be notified when the baby is coming. This new use of a pager was suggested to a paging company by a father who had to be notified that his baby was coming unexpectedly. The paging company then suggested to a hospital that they provide pagers free to expectant fathers and thus learned of a new use for their existing product.

Finally, customers may supply the names of new prospects for the salesperson to investigate and cultivate. In some instances, background

information may supplement a name and address. Or a letter of introduction may be volunteered by the customer in special cases. Once in a
while, the customer will even make an appointment for the salesperson
with the prospect.

INFLUENCING CUSTOMERS' MERCHANDISING POLICIES

In this section, the word *merchandising* means advertising, display, and
personal selling. Good salespeople are able to help shape and guide the
merchandising activities of their retail customers and, in so doing, ultimately help determine merchandising policy.

It must be emphasized at this point that the job of influencing a
customer's policies requires skill and tact. The overall objective of such
influence is to maximize dollar profits for customer and salesperson. The
salesperson wants the customer to handle the full line and to maintain
adequate stock at all times. This permits balanced sales, including sales
of higher-priced, high-profit items. The salesperson would like every customer's place of business to be a model of enthusiasm and efficiency. In
this atmosphere the salesperson's product(s) would be the most preferred, favored, and pushed—to the extent that a retailer can afford to
push a single line.

With the proper approach, customer buying patterns can be influenced. A starting point is to analyze a customer's orders. Once a pattern
has been identified, it can be compared with that of the salesperson's
best customer in order to locate weak spots. Advertising policies can be
influenced, too. One approach is for the salesperson to persuade the customer to plan and schedule merchandising activities to coincide with
the complete promotion program of the salesperson's company. Along
this line, the salesperson should convince the customer of the desirability of using all available company promotional material that is suitable.

The salesperson may get the retailer to encourage suggestive selling
and trading up, increasing the amount of the average sale and the average selling price per item. The salesperson tries to get the customer to do
an effective advertising job, both for the customer's entire business and
for the salesperson's own merchandise. Salespeople should never be too
important or too busy to lend a hand in setting up displays, dressing
windows, or doing other merchandising jobs. Finally, the salesperson
needs to make constructive suggestions that will help ensure profitable
operation.

INFLUENCING ADVERTISING ACTIVITIES

Before attempting to influence a customer's advertising policies,
salespeople should clearly understand (1) the general nature of advertis-

ing, (2) the more specific nature of their company's advertising, and (3) their customers' advertising problems.

In regard to the first point, salespeople need an appreciation of the role advertising plays in the overall marketing process and an awareness of its potential benefits and limitations. Sometimes they will have to defend advertising as a selling tool, especially as it is used by their companies, and explain to nonadvertising customers how they may be handicapping their business operations by not advertising. An effective strategy for convincing the nonadvertising customer to use advertising is to show the total potential demand that could be reached within the trading area by advertising.

As far as their companies' advertising efforts are concerned, salespeople must first know what company policy is and how to justify it to customers. Smaller customers may criticize a company that advertises extensively, claiming that those dollars should instead be spent in giving greater discounts to dealers. Salespeople who have a sound understanding of their companies' advertising policies should have little trouble in satisfactorily answering these objections. They also should have complete information about their companies' current and future advertising efforts: what campaigns are running, which media are being used, how large the advertising budget is, what the results of a particular campaign were, and what new campaigns are scheduled. They should know what their companies will do for customers in the way of advertising. Customers surely would be interested in knowing if the company identifies its dealers in selected advertisements, if advertising materials are supplied to them, if a cooperative arrangement operates between company and customer, and if direct mail pieces with or without the dealer's imprint can be obtained.

A third method of influencing a customer's advertising activities is based on understanding customers' advertising problems. To fully understand a customer's advertising problems, salespeople must be familiar with the sequence in planning advertising, which is shown in Figure 14-9.

The salesperson must be willing and competent to advise the customer on each of the phases shown in the figure. Then, and only then, is the salesperson in a position to encourage the customer to use advertising in adequate volume. The plea will be for a well-balanced, continuous program. The salesperson must continue to educate the customer on the benefits of advertising until the customer realizes advertising is not a luxury to be denied when volume drops, it must not be scheduled according to whims or to the persuasiveness of advertising salespeople, and it must be undertaken with full knowledge that its effectiveness is reduced when turned on and off like an electric light.

THE ADVERTISING PLANNING SEQUENCE

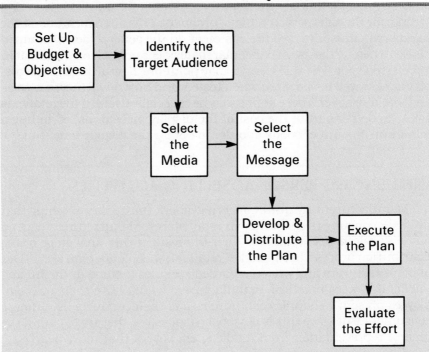

Figure 14-9 **Salespeople can help their customers with advertising advice; however, this requires a strong knowledge of the advertising planning sequence.**

INFLUENCING DISPLAY ACTIVITIES

Salespeople have two definite obligations in promoting the use of display. One is to keep the customer completely informed about what is available from their company and on what terms, what display materials should be used, and how these materials should be used to get the best sales results. The second obligation is to know at all times what their customers are actually doing about general display and the display of their products.

With the growth of self-service merchandising, retail merchants necessarily must use display as effectively as possible. The importance that manufacturers attach to good display is indicated by their competition for prominent positions for their respective brands, positions that will increase sales and profits. Many prefer favorable store position over mention of their products in local newspaper, radio, or television advertisements.

Salespeople should check continuously to see that their customers are using display as an extra sales force—first, in a storewide way, and second, for the salesperson's line of products. This often means that the salesperson must first sell the customer on the general idea of planned display, then on the use of particular materials, and then on placing it in a preferred spot. The salesperson may point out how attractive the display is, how well it was rated when tested, and how it will increase sales and stock turnover. These points may be especially useful if the retailer is asked to defray part of the cost of the display piece or asked to buy a minimum amount of goods in order to obtain the display item.

INFLUENCING PERSONAL SELLING ACTIVITIES

Manufacturers are quite concerned about the quality of selling that ultimate consumers encounter in retail stores. Manufacturers depend on retail salespeople to handle their interests at this final stage of the distribution process. In this sense, retail salespeople are representatives of manufacturers and are so regarded by at least some of the buying public. If it were practical, manufacturers would have their own employees present to handle each purchase of their products by ultimate consumers. But since this is obviously impossible, they try to obtain the kind of representation from retailers' employees that most nearly approximates the ideal.

There is a second, broader phase of the manufacturer's interest in retail selling. Manufacturers want their retailers to be profitable so that they qualify as excellent outlets for their merchandise. Progressive, prosperous merchants typically sell a better-than-average amount of the manufacturer's merchandise. Thus, the manufacturer's first step is to influence the merchant to raise the quality of selling in a general way so that the store becomes a better store. The second move is to help get more sales power for the manufacturer's own lines from the retailer's sales force.

Salespeople must be extremely tactful in trying to upgrade retail selling. An effective method of bringing to the minds of retailers the significance of their employees' selling activities is to ask about the training program, thereby calling their attention to the subject and setting the stage for further discussion of it. A second method is to note what happens when a retail salesperson meets a retail prospect in an actual sales situation and then to use these observations to open the conversation. Salespeople also may show retailers or their salespeople how the product should be demonstrated. Still another possibility is to pass on to retailers ideas about selling techniques that have proved effective in other stores. If the salesperson's company provides training materials, the task is to see that they are used in retail stores.

HIGHLIGHT 14-2   *Qualities That Make Salespeople Tops*

Readers of Purchasing Magazine, *mainly industrial buyers and purchasing managers, were asked to choose the three traits that make top salespeople.*

Willingness to go to bat for the buyer within the supplier firm, 65%

Thoroughness and follow-through, 56%

Knowledge of his or her product line, 56%

Market knowledge and willingness to keep the buyer posted, 39%

Imagination in applying his or her product to the buyer's needs, 24%

Knowledge of the buyer's product line, 23%

Preparation for sales calls, 16%

Regularity of sales calls, 8%

Diplomacy in dealing with operating departments, 7%

Technical education, 6%

Note: Percentages total 300 because respondents were asked to check three outstanding characteristics.
Source: *Sales and Marketing Management* (August 20, 1979): 38.

HOLDING MEETINGS WITH CUSTOMERS

Some salespeople (e.g., those selling automobiles, insurance, or home insulation) will never have occasion to hold a meeting in connection with their selling activities because of the nature of their sales transactions. Other salespeople will conduct meetings, but before doing so will be trained specifically and thoroughly for that job, and will then be supplied by their companies with everything they need. This section on holding meetings is included not particularly for the benefit of these two groups of salespeople, but instead to help the salespeople who, when they begin selling, need to work with customers by scheduling and conducting meetings without much assistance from any source.

PURPOSES OF MEETINGS

Holding meetings with customers can be an extremely worthwhile undertaking, but to do so demands time, patience, and thorough planning from the salesperson. The overall purpose of any meeting is to increase profits for the salesperson and the company by increasing the customer's volume of sales and profits on the salesperson's products. The purpose of any single meeting, however, is much more specific. Here are some topics the salesperson might choose to discuss in a meeting:

1. **Customer matters:** how to get new customers, how to hold customers, how wholesalers build up retail accounts, what to do about small orders, or how to revive dormant accounts.
2. **Product matters:** how merchandise should be demonstrated, the manufacturer's support and promotion plans, how to launch a new product, or a study of the advantages of the salesperson's product.
3. **Selling matters:** how to prove product claims, how to handle objections, how to obtain the five buying decisions, or how to close the sale.

In most cases, the salesperson's audience will consist of either a wholesaler and staff, a retailer and staff, a group of wholesalers, or a group of retailers. When the meeting is with a wholesaler or retailer and staff, the staff may be limited to sales employees. Meetings should be scheduled when and where they will do the most good. The better accounts—those that do the most outstanding selling jobs—are the ones entitled to benefit from the time and money spent on meetings.

Figure 14-10 Sales meetings are vital to the salesperson's continued improvement and for keeping up-to-date.
Source: INTERNATIONAL MULTIFOODS CORPORATION

PRINCIPLES OF CONDUCTING MEETINGS

Below are some principles for holding meetings that have proven effective:

1. Have a definite reason for the meeting and publicize the reason beforehand. Describe in advance how the meeting will be of value to customers—this helps sell all prospective attendees on being present.
2. Schedule only one topic for each meeting. This will assure shorter meetings, more complete treatment of a certain subject, and increased understanding on the part of customers.
3. Have a definite timetable for the meeting. Start it on time, run it according to schedule, and do not allow the tempo of the meeting to drag.
4. Stay in control of the meeting, but make provisions for group discussion.
5. Make it as easy as possible for the audience to understand and retain the message by distributing printed material—such as an outline of the meeting and summary of the major points to be made—and by making maximum use of audiovisual aids.

PREPARING FOR THE MEETING

Thorough preparation is always needed for effective meetings. Participants quickly recognize whether or not time and thought have been spent by the salesperson in getting ready for the gathering. A definite written schedule of a complete program should be made in advance. It should name a specific day, place, and hour so as to maximize the chances of success. The written schedule will outline what topics are to be treated, how much time will be devoted to each, and the method of presentation, including the props to be used.

Particular preparation is needed for meetings where group participation will require some flexibility in handling and fitting the meeting to the time schedule. If a schedule is not established and agreed to prior to the meeting, the salesperson will frequently experience postponements, absence of key individuals who were to take part in the program, lack of coordination, and even failure. The junior salesperson may be more relaxed with prepared opening remarks, questions for discussion, and closing thoughts. While in the presence of the audience, the salesperson should do no more reading from notes than is absolutely necessary.

If it appears that a considerable amount of time will be required, several short sessions should be scheduled rather than a few long ones. Maintaining a high degree of interest throughout a long meeting is difficult.

Before the meeting takes place, case histories, experiences, and other happenings from the meeting locale should be assembled. For instance, a new sales technique that was originated nearby, or the experience of some local merchant who successfully tied promotion efforts in with those of the manufacturer, gets and holds the interest of the group. Facts, figures, impartiality, and tact are needed in using such information.

DEALING WITH POSTSALE PROBLEMS

Occasionally, the salesperson will need to deal with problems that occur after completion of the sale. These problems can include customer complaints, cancellations and returned goods, and lost customers.

CUSTOMER COMPLAINTS

All salespeople can expect some complaints from dissatisfied customers, and the effective handling of complaints can do much to build sound customer relationships. Some companies have a separate department to assist in handling complaints because the effective and timely resolution of complaints is critical in building and maintaining customer trust. Often, the identification of, and solution to, the actual problem exceeds salespeople's immediate resources and they must call on others in the company for assistance. In many companies, salespeople are responsible for handling complaints because they are in contact with the customer most frequently, know the most about the customer's problems and buying situation, and are the people to whom the customer looks for satisfaction. Further, salespeople grow in stature with the customer by handling complaints effectively. If a complaint is received, it must be handled expeditiously, firmly, and with tact. At the very start, salespeople should convey to the customer that their company will be fair and courteous in discharging its responsibility. Salespeople should not display doubt or suspicion as to the validity of the complaint and should reaffirm the customer's faith in the company, thus encouraging the customer to accept the company as one that stands by its customers. When the salesperson or the company is at fault, the responsiblility for the problem should be acknowledged and followed up with prompt and satisfactory action.

In discussions with the customer, salespeople should determine the exact nature of the problem, which may have a cause unrelated to the company's product or service. These discussions provide the customer with an opportunity to let off steam and demand satisfaction. All the while, the salesperson is collecting information, saying nothing until all the facts are in. Once the facts are in hand, the salesperson must identify the nature of the problems(s), e.g., billing errors, product deficiencies, delivery or packaging. Only after the problem is properly defined can the salesperson return to the company for solutions. By taking immediate, personal action, the salesperson increases the customer's confidence in the company.

If the salesperson is unwilling or unable to handle the complaint, the reasons should be explained clearly to the customer. In discussions with customers, the salesperson should review company policies and procedures for handling complaints, assure prompt and proper attention, and continue to follow up to ensure action.

In some instances, successful resolution of complaints can work in the salesperson's favor. The customer will perceive the salesperson and the company as fair and reliable, one that provides honest treatment and deals squarely. If the adjustment or action exceeds the customer's expectations, goodwill can be particularly enhanced.

CANCELLATIONS AND RETURNED GOODS

Closely related to the problem of customer complaints are the problems of cancellations and returned goods. The handling of these two problems increases a seller's expenses. Their presence means that the original selling job was a failure and that the same merchandise must be sold a second time, sometimes at a lower price. Sellers always run the risk of losing a good reputation if they are at fault in the case of cancellations or returned goods.

Buyers cancel orders and return merchandise for several reasons. A salesperson may have sold the wrong quantity or the wrong quality. The buyer may have been oversold on the privileges of canceling orders and returning unsatisfactory goods. Sometimes an order is filled incorrectly, or the merchandise is defective or damaged when it arrives. Sometimes the shipment does not arrive by the promised date. Prices may drop, or a competitor may make a more attractive offer. The buyer's need may disappear. Sometimes the person who placed the order is overruled by someone else, and the purchasing decision is canceled. Good judgment is required in deciding to accept or reject the customer's reasons.

Salespeople obviously must not contribute to these causes of cancellations and returns. They must always try to raise the quality of their selling efforts, work especially hard to identify need accurately, and then sell the buyer completely on the product to fill that need. They must be careful to recommend the exact quality and quantity the buyer should order, and they must stay away from unrealistic promises. Usually the salesperson should go over the order and terms with the buyer so that the buyer understands them clearly, particularly in regard to the conditions under which orders can be canceled and goods returned. If two or more people have a voice in the final buying decision, the salesperson should usually talk to them as a group and sell all of them on the soundness of the sales proposal. The same is true if there is a strong buying influence in addition to the buyer.

LOST CUSTOMERS

Customers who used to buy, but who do not buy at the present time, may well be good prospects. Of course, if their needs or conditions have changed so as to make a product no longer of use to them, they are not prospects. When customers discontinue buying either because of dissatisfaction or because a more persuasive competitor took them away, it may well be worthwhile to try to get them back as customers. Each case should be examined to see why, how, when, and to whom the account was lost. The answers to these four questions will point out the techniques that should be used in attempting to regain the account. Usually, many of the techniques of handling complaints are equally appropriate and effective here.

HANDLING CREDIT AND COLLECTION PROBLEMS

Companies differ in their methods of dealing with credit and collection activities, some making extensive use and others making little use of their salespeople. Salespeople should be informed about credit management, regardless of the extent to which they are involved in their firm's credit and collection activities.

CREDIT INFORMATION NEEDED

Before a seller opens a credit account for a customer, these questions must be asked:

1. Can that customer pay for your firm's product(s)?
2. Will that customer pay for your firm's product(s)?
3. What maximum credit limit should be given?

These questions must be answered for each account because customers vary in their ability to pay, in their determination to pay, and in the limit they should be allowed to owe the seller at any one time. Before these questions can be answered, the seller must have facts.

The seller needs information about the customer's capital circumstances—financial situation and strength. The seller needs a picture of the prospective customer's assets, liabilities, and net worth. No business is solvent unless assets are greater than liabilities; no business is liquid unless there are dollars today to pay tomorrow's bills.

The seller needs information about the customer's financial capacity, and the customer's ability to sell a satisfactory amount of merchandise at satisfactory prices. The sales and earnings records of the business can suggest what future sales and earnings may be. Respectable capacity reflects sound, able management.

The personal character of the customer can be an important credit factor. Sellers prefer to deal with businesses that are honest and trust-worthy. They hope their credit customers have a fierce determination to pay their debts because they think it is right to pay what they promised to pay. The greater a buyer's sense of obligation and integrity, the less moral risk is involved.

These three credit influences—capital, capacity, and character—must be considered in the light of current circumstances. For example, competitors' policies and practices of the moment affect a seller's policies and practices. One must always take into consideration the present stage of the business cycle. In bad times, one can defend certain actions which would be difficult to defend in good times. A third consideration is the safety-risk standard the seller is observing for credit sales. Here the seller determines the minimum safety standard—the maximum accept-able risk limit. A fourth and final matter is current policy on collection. The stricter the seller is in collecting what is owed, the lower the safety-risk standard can be set.

SOURCES OF CREDIT INFORMATION

The firm itself is a prime source of information about its own credit rating. Standardized financial statement forms are available that sellers can ask customers to fill out. These forms provide a large amount of credit information, and feature the balance sheet and the income statement.

Many manufacturers ask their salespeople to collect certain credit information on prospective customers and on present customers. By na-ture, of course, the typical salesperson is not a credit reporter. However, salespeople have a vital and continuing interest in customers' credit and in their firm's credit management. In the process of collecting credit in-formation, the salesperson gets to visit with the customer, know the manager personally, see the business in operation, and sense how sales are going.

A seller's own records contain valuable credit information about present customers and former customers. This information is contained in the file set up every time a new account is opened. Prominent in this file is the customer's ledger record.

Then, of course, there is Dun & Bradstreet, Inc., which reports on the credit standing of businesses. Twice a year the agency issues credit ref-erence books, state by state, in pocket size. Credit managers and sales-people make much use of these handy and informative reference books.

As for miscellaneous sources of credit information, there are banks, attorneys, public records, references supplied by businesses, and other (usually noncompetitive) sellers.

THREE CREDIT MANAGEMENT SUGGESTIONS

Credit information has both quality and quantity. In terms of quality, one asks how good the information should be: if the information is accurate, current, and basically relevant. In regard to quantity, one asks how much information one should collect. Collecting a large amount of information can demand much time and money and can cause customer resentment. Collecting less information is more speedy and economical but more risky.

A second suggestion is that **credit management** be seen as having two major objectives. One is to maximize sales; the other is to minimize credit expenses. Credit expenses include clerical costs, interest on capital invested in accounts receivable, collection costs, and bad debts. If credit management is too lax, the seller maximizes sales volume but reduces the percentage of accounts receivable collected. If credit management is too strict, sales volume and earnings suffer.

Finally, the seller must recognize that credit and credit management demand continuous attention and analysis. The management of a business can change. Market potentials may increase or decrease. The business cycle is either going up or down. Any one customer can improve or slip as a credit risk as time passes. So, each credit customer's credit rating must be checked regularly and the credit limit revised if needed. Sellers should try to anticipate changes in a customer's credit condition before they take place.

COLLECTION

Because a period of time passes between the date of a credit sale and the scheduled date of payment, some credit customers will not pay all they owe when they owe it. Credit sales become actual sales only when the buyer pays in full for the merchandise bought. Unless the seller gets the money due, merchandise is not being sold—it is being given away.

When does the collection period start? The moment the credit period runs out. If a customer agreed to pay on or before May 10 but does not, the collection period starts May 11 because the account becomes past due on May 11.

WHY CREDIT CUSTOMERS DON'T PAY

It is important to understand the reasons why cash selling poses no collection problems, whereas credit selling does. The following seven situations reveal how changes, uncertainties, faulty predictions, risks, mistakes, and disappointments affect a customer's ability to pay.

SITUATION 1

The customer does not understand the seller's credit terms. The best way to prevent this is to see that all details are clear to the buyer at the time of the first sale.

SITUATION 2

Because the balance owed is small, the customer prefers to postpone payment until it is larger. This is a tough one for which there is no magic answer. Vigorous collection attempts would be costly and would irritate the customer. Maybe this is one that the seller simply has to learn to live with.

SITUATION 3

The customer is slow in paying because of habit. Seldom does this customer pay any supplier before receiving one or more collection notices. This situation calls for considerable and firm collection effort. The seller may be wise to check the expense of selling to this account against the gross margin made. This type of customer can easily be unprofitable as well as unpleasant.

SITUATION 4

Some customers are merely careless. When customers overlook or forget, they should be reminded that their accounts are overdue.

SITUATION 5

Every now and then buyers run short of cash for the moment. Maybe they overbought, their accounts receivable paid below expectations, or they suffered some accident. The first move in this type of situation is to verify the tight condition. The next step is to adjust the debt and to extend the pay period, if at all justifiable.

SITUATION 6

What about the business that is experiencing rough going? Maybe the management has deteriorated. Maybe the market has shrunk. Maybe the customer is experiencing trouble because of other causes. The basic question here is whether or not the customer can become profitable in a reasonable period of time.

SITUATION 7

If customers turn out to be dishonest, turn the account over to a lawyer or a collection agency.

BUILDING GOODWILL

Salespeople need and want the goodwill of their customers. Salespeople build enduring goodwill by providing quality products, timely and useful services, and prompt delivery. Goodwill is enhanced when the customer trusts the salesperson's competence and integrity. Salespeople enjoy goodwill when their customers like them, think well of them, and communicate these complimentary opinions.

It is clear why salespeople work so hard for the goodwill of their customers. The first sale is often made only after good customer relations have been established. Repeat sales rarely are forthcoming unless the customer feels goodwill toward the salesperson. A customer's account cannot be increased to its maximum potential without goodwill. Finally, the customer's continuing support, loyalty, and cooperation will not be so great as they might be unless there is goodwill.

To get goodwill, nothing is so essential as a program of helping customers. Helping them in business ways will increase the customer's sales, reduce the customer's expenses, or both. Helping them in personal ways results in the customer's securing more personal satisfaction.

Goodwill is earned when salespeople let themselves be guided by their customers' interests and goals. To accomplish this, salespeople must learn their customers' circumstances and take a position in sympathy with them. Salespeople must make sound recommendations and then take pains to see that the customers understand fully what the results will be if they buy and if they do not buy.

Salespeople also earn goodwill by their ethical conduct. They keep promises; they are fair and honest, they demonstrate the fact that the Golden Rule is good business as well as good behavior.

Finally, salespeople earn goodwill by liking each of their customers personally. They learn to do this by knowing and understanding customers and by being a real friend to them. Salespeople show this liking in many ways. They appreciate any favors done by a customer and are prompt to repay in generous measure. They ask their customers for advice, opinions, and suggestions. They take the time and effort to adapt to the customer's mood of the moment, respecting the customer's right to have both good and bad days. They supply the customer with related information, keeping the customer well posted on the latest happenings in various fields. They may entertain certain customers on special occasions. At holidays, birthdays, and anniversary times, salespeople will certainly remember customers in appropriate ways. They will congratulate the customer on the birth of a baby, and will mail a get-well card when the customer is ill. All this takes time, but it is well worth the effort.

SUMMARY

The selling process is not complete when the prospect agrees to buy, because selling activities are divided into two categories: (1) dealing with prospects, and (2) dealing with customers. Repeat sales, important and useful information, and favorable word-of-mouth communication between buyers are a few of the rewards of maintaining good customer relations.

Usually, 20 percent of the customers account for about 80 percent of a salesperson's sales. Because this repeat business is very profitable, the salesperson should visit the customer soon after the sale has been made to ensure that everything is satisfactory. After an account has been sold, efforts should be made to increase its volume, thus turning a small customer into a large customer.

Inactive accounts may be caused by misunderstandings, sellers' mistakes, weak selling, specific product complaints, and lower prices elsewhere. All salespeople must expect to deal with complaints and should handle them as skillfully and tactfully as possible. Salespeople can avoid complaints by being honest with the prospect during the presentation.

KEY TERMS

80-20 principle
product information
customer service representatives
newsletters

team selling
customer support
credit management

REVIEW QUESTIONS

1. What is the 80-20 principle?
2. Why is account classification necessary?
3. How can salespeople handle small accounts economically?
4. Why is repeat business the most profitable?
5. List three obstacles to increasing the volume of an account.
6. List five suggestions for increasing the volume of an account.
7. How can salespeople gain the support of customers?
8. List four ways customers can help salespeople.
9. What must the salesperson understand before trying to influence customers' advertising?
10. What two obligations do salespeople have in regard to displays?
11. How can salespeople assist their customers in improving the effectiveness of their personal selling?
12. How can salespeople avoid complaints?
13. How can salespeople limit complaints, cancellations, and returned goods?
14. What must the seller know about a customer before granting credit?
15. List four reasons why customers don't pay their bills.
16. How can salespeople build customer goodwill?

DISCUSSION QUESTIONS

1. Explain what happens to the salesperson's goals and perspectives when the prospect becomes a customer.
2. The sales cycle shows the change in the salesperson's activities as the buyer-seller relationship is extended beyond the sale. Does this imply that the salesperson has grown beyond their need to do future prospecting? Why or why not?
3. What is the difference between customer support and goodwill?
4. Explain how customer service reps, newsletters, and team selling can help the salesperson increase the volume of accounts and improve customer relations.

CASE 14-1   COMMUNITY COFFEE*

Community Coffee is a regional coffee company headquartered in Baton Rouge, Louisiana. The company roasts and distributes coffee and related products in Louisiana, southeast Texas, southern Arkansas, and southern Mississippi. Despite its relatively small distribution area, the company is the twelfth largest distributor of coffee in the United States. The success of the company stems from its unique understanding of coffee tastes in Louisiana and surrounding states where it dominates the ground roast coffee market with market shares as high as 80 percent.

The company was begun in the early 1900s by Norman "Cap" Saurage, Sr., as a sideline to his grocery store. As demand for Cap's Community Coffee increased, Cap hired his brother-in-law, Albert Dupuy, as the first salesperson. Cap continued to roast, grind, and package the coffee while Albert sold and delivered it directly to the grocer's shelf. This distribution system enabled Community Coffee to maintain consistent quality and freshness, which has been critical to the success of Community Coffee. Today, Community still delivers its coffee directly to the supermarket, instead of selling it through supermarket distribution centers, which is unique to the coffee industry.

Throughout its history, Community has been an industry leader. In the early 1980s Community was the first U.S. coffee company to "vacuum pack" its bagged coffee products. This process removes the air from the bag resulting in a hard, brick-like product, which extends the shelf life of the product from six weeks to six months. This allowed Community to

---

*Case prepared by Ron Roullier. Used with permission.

expand its marketing area to include new markets that had insufficient demand to support a direct store-delivery system. The longer shelf life of the new product also meant the company could use a warehouse distribution system in expansion markets and still maintain its standards for freshness.

Vacuum-packed bags offered other benefits. The process reduces the dimensions of the product, making it much more efficient in utilizing space than either traditional bags or cans. With these efficiencies shelf stock could be increased, reducing the likelihood of out-of-stocks and lowering handling and storage charges.

To maintain market share in current markets and to evaluate market potential in expansion markets, Community Coffee is setting up an information base using scanning technology. This new technology has been installed in many supermarket chains in the past five years and is expected to be in all but small independent stores in the next couple of years. Jason Mori recently was hired as the company's first market analyst. His job is to analyze information available from supermarket scanning equipment and develop ways to improve marketing and sales programs. Information available from scanning includes how much of the product is sold in a specified period (usually a week), the average retail price, the advertised sales price where appropriate, and how much competitors are selling, including a market share analysis.

Community Coffee's sales force has 80 route salespeople who call on supermarkets. These salespeople both sell and deliver coffee directly to the supermarkets. To assist the route salespeople there is a merchandising manager who works with large supermarket chains like Albertson's, Winn-Dixie, A & P and Delchamps. The merchandising manager works to make sure Community Coffee gets good shelf space and he also negotiates prices. The route salespeople are managed by five branch managers. The one exception is the Houston, Texas, market where there are five salespeople who sell to national accounts. Thus, in Houston, distribution is through the supermarket's warehouse rather than directly to the individual stores.

Jason's first task as market analyst is to develop information which will help the sales force sell more effectively. He has been working on an information packet for the past four months. He has just finished the first sales packet containing sales information and intends to schedule a training session with the sales force to explain it. An example of the types of information to be included in the sales packet is shown in Exhibit 14-1 on page 440.

In addition, as part of his analysis, Jason analyzed the sales for coffee packaged in two ways—in brick bags and canned—on a month-by-month basis. The first part of his analysis is shown in Exhibit 14-2.

EXHIBIT 14-1
MARKET SHARE FOR MAJOR COFFEE BRANDS

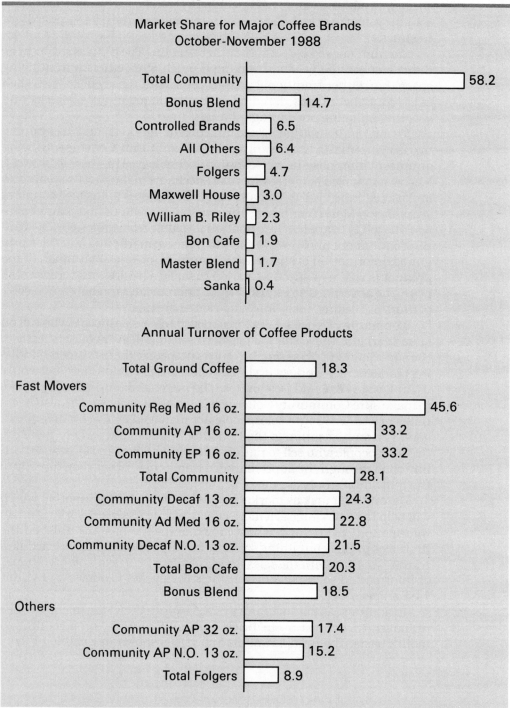

Market Share for Major Coffee Brands
October-November 1988

Brand	Share
Total Community	58.2
Bonus Blend	14.7
Controlled Brands	6.5
All Others	6.4
Folgers	4.7
Maxwell House	3.0
William B. Riley	2.3
Bon Cafe	1.9
Master Blend	1.7
Sanka	0.4

Annual Turnover of Coffee Products

Total Ground Coffee	18.3
Fast Movers	
Community Reg Med 16 oz.	45.6
Community AP 16 oz.	33.2
Community EP 16 oz.	33.2
Total Community	28.1
Community Decaf 13 oz.	24.3
Community Ad Med 16 oz.	22.8
Community Decaf N.O. 13 oz.	21.5
Total Bon Cafe	20.3
Bonus Blend	18.5
Others	
Community AP 32 oz.	17.4
Community AP N.O. 13 oz.	15.2
Total Folgers	8.9

EXHIBIT 14-2
COMMUNITY COFFEE SALES BY MONTH

Month	Brick Bag Sales	%	Can	%
January	$1,658,851	7.78	$119,461	_____
February	$1,935,048	9.08	$113,696	_____
March	$1,989,514	9.33	$114,303	_____
April	$1,909,106	8.96	$117,217	_____
May	$1,815,622	8.52	$122,713	_____
June	$1,650,203	7.74	$112,749	_____
July	$1,752,540	8.22	$112,417	_____
August	$1,672,207	7.84	$114,675	_____
September	$1,736,458	8.15	$113,692	_____
October	$1,693,385	7.94	$112,760	_____
November	$1,750,621	8.21	$112,424	_____
December	$1,752,479	8.22	$130,787	_____
Total	$21,316,034	100.00	$1,396,894	100.00

CASE QUESTIONS

1. Using Lotus, complete the table for Jason, then answer the following:
    - Which months have the heaviest coffee consumption?
    - Which months have the lightest coffee consumption?
    - Does the pattern of coffee sales vary by type of container?
2. If you were a salesperson for Community Coffee, do you think the information Jason is obtaining from scanning would help you sell more? Why?
3. How would you use the information to provide better service to your customers?
4. Could this information be used to help establish and maintain goodwill? How?

CASE 14-2   COMMUNITY COFFEE ADDS TEA PRODUCTS*

Community Coffee Company is expanding its traditional product line to include tea products. Since the company lacks experience in tea products, it decided to introduce the line of tea products into four test

*Case prepared by Ron Roullier. Used with permission.

markets. This would help the company learn how to best market its tea products prior to launching products into the entire marketing area. The markets were selected to represent each of Community's selling areas. The test markets selected were Lafayette and Shreveport, Louisiana; Jackson, Mississippi; and Beaumont, Texas.

In order to better evaluate the test market results, Community purchased A. C. Nielsen Custom Audit Data for each of the test markets. After 12 months of data was collected, Community's marketing analyst presented the following analysis of key business findings in each market:

Lafayette, Louisiana:
1. The Lafayette market is extremely price sensitive. When Community featured its 100-count package of tea bags at $1.39, overall tea consumption increased by 18 percent. Community tea sales volume and market share also increased when priced at $1.89 per 100-count package, indicating that other higher price levels may be possible.
2. Lafayette stores have a higher tendency to display tea, but use it as a feature item less often than in other markets. As a result, features may have a greater impact in the southern Louisiana market while displays may be less effective.
3. High-impact promotions with lower prices and higher levels of feature support increase overall tea sales with less noticeable post promotion decline in sales.

Shreveport, Louisiana:
1. In Shreveport, competitive tea brands appear to be ignoring retailer pressure to increase coupon values above $.50. Retailers prefer all coupons to be above $.50 since many stores double coupon values that are below $.50.
2. The features price on the Community, Lipton, and Luzianne brands has to be below $1.49 to be effective.
3. Advanced buying by retail outlets as well as consumer loading (stocking up during sales) are problems in Shreveport.
4. Shreveport has a distribution problem on Community 6-ounce loose tea.

Jackson, Mississippi:
1. Community tea did not increase the overall sales of all tea products.
2. The majority of Jackson tea sales are in nonmerchandised periods.
3. Lipton is reducing the Community/Lipton price differences (Lipton had been higher).

Beaumont, Texas:
1. Seasonal consumption patterns are much more noticeable than in other markets.

2. Heavy coupon activity characterizes the Beaumont market. Only regional brands are using coupon values over $.50.
3. There appears to be an out-of-stock problem with Community tea. This is a result of volatile swings in promoted product movement and inadequate shelf space.

CASE QUESTIONS

1. The decision has been made to introduce the tea product line into Community's four marketing areas. Based on the test market information, develop a sales story for each of the four marketing areas.
2. How are your sales plans different for each of the marketing areas?

CHAPTER 15
Self-Management

After studying this chapter, you should be able to:

- Differentiate among the techniques of scheduling

- List the techniques of routing

- Illustrate how the telephone can be a timesaver

- Discuss the new technology that affects the salesperson's time management

- Suggest what records salespeople should keep

- Tell what salespeople can do to evaluate their sales performance

Self-management is essential to profitable selling. There are really only two ways to increase sales volume: the salesperson can do more selling, and the salesperson can do more effective selling. Self-managed salespeople succeed in both these areas. They arrange to put in more hours talking with prospects than do other salespeople, and they are constantly trying to raise the quality of their selling efforts. The objective of all self-management activity is to spend the maximum amount of time possible on productive selling activities, and this objective can be attained only if self-management techniques are utilized to their fullest potential.

Salespeople's selling efforts must be well planned and systematically performed according to a program or schedule. Here are some benefits enjoyed by salespeople who plan their work:

1. Systematic planning helps salespeople become more familiar with all aspects of their jobs, because planning starts with a study of their problems and objectives.
2. Through planning, salespeople are able to concentrate their sales efforts on the most promising markets and prospects. They are able to minimize the time spent with prospects who can't use their product, and spend more time with prospects who potentially will be repeat clients—it is better to see four buyers two times each than to call on the same person eight times.

444

3. Planning minimizes lost time; and this is important, as time lost is time that could have been spent selling.
4. Systematic planning reduces mistakes and oversights and results in more consistent success.
5. Planning helps improve the quality and effectiveness of the actual sales presentation.

EFFECTIVE TIME MANAGEMENT: SCHEDULING AND ROUTING

Salespeople's time is very valuable to the company and to themselves. The old adage "time is money" is especially true when talking about a salesperson's time. Because most salespeople's pay is tied directly to sales, it is important for them to maximize their selling time through time management. Time management is a matter of **scheduling** and routing, and taking advantage of today's new technology designed to provide quick information and communication. In this section, we will discuss effective scheduling and routing.

SCHEDULING

Four basic elements determine the makeup of the daily schedule: (1) the number of calls the salesperson hopes to make that day on present customers, old prospects, and new prospects; (2) the expected sales volume for that day; (3) the number of hours of work planned that day; and (4) the salesperson's own energy and initiative.

SCHEDULING PRELIMINARIES

Salespeople should start with the amount of time they consider available for budgeting. Then they can list all the demands that will be made on that time. They should consider how much time to allot for selling and how much for nonselling activities; they should plan how much time to spend on each market covered and how much on each prospect and customer in that market; finally, successful salespeople plan their activities with an eye toward producing the sales volume budgeted for that day.

The calls that salespeople make are, thus, planned calls. Salespeople know specifically what they hope to accomplish on each; they have a plan or outline for each interview; and they have all the material they will need arranged in prospect folders. In addition to the selling calls, the day's schedule will often include "in-between" contacts with customers and prospects. These are calculated contacts that are sandwiched between selling calls and may be made by mail, telegram, mailgram, phone, or even in person.

Figure 15-1 Time is money. Effective time management leads to in-creased sales, which means more money.

PRINCIPLES OF SCHEDULING

The schedule for each day should be constructed around the most important prospects and customers for that day. The following princi-ples will prove helpful in setting up a practical and efficient daily schedule.

Setting Times for the Most Important Calls.   Set a time for each of the most important calls of the day. These important calls may be on buyers who are ready to buy, buyers whom you know to be accessible during this particular trip but who may be out of town or otherwise unavailable during another trip, buyers with whom you have appointments, and buyers whom you were instructed to see. Minor calls should be planned around the major calls.

Setting a Time to Begin Work Each Day.   Have a definite time to start each day's work, and do not stop until the jobs scheduled for that day have been completed.

Laying Out More Than a Day's Work.   Lay out more than the usual day's work, if necessary, to stay busy and meet the quota. Some salespeople schedule one-third more calls than they expect to make. If they hope to make nine calls, a satisfactory quota for the day, they put twelve on the schedule. Then, if interviews go faster than usual or if some of the buyers are unavailable, the salesperson still keeps busy.

Allowing Enough Time for Each Call.   Allow enough time for each call to minimize departures from and disruptions of the schedule. Lay out the calls in sequence.

Reducing Wasted Time with Appointments.   Appointments, where practical, are worthwhile because they reduce pointless calls, waiting time, and the average length of the call. Appointments made for an early hour, 8 to 9 A.M., and for the late afternoon hour, 4 to 5 P.M., help keep the salesperson on the job all day.

Devoting the Most Productive Hours to Selling.   Devote the most productive hours of the day to selling to buyers. Schedule routine jobs, paperwork, and service functions for other hours.

Scheduling According to Routing and the Needs of Customers. Prepare the preliminary draft of the schedule for each day of the coming week or two weeks as a part of routing for that period. The final version of each day's schedule should be written out on the preceding night. Construct the schedule as much as possible according to the needs and wishes of buyers.

Substituting Mail, Telephone, or Fax Contacts for Personal Contacts.   The salesperson will find that each day can be made more productive by sometimes substituting mail, telephone, or fax contacts for certain personal contacts. Duties obviously must not be slighted by depending on the telephone, fax, or mail to do things that should be done in person. It is possible, however, for the salesperson to use these methods to hold onto and even to obtain some new business while visiting other trading areas. Good use of these methods also can be made to deliver advance notice of calls in cases where such notification would increase the effectiveness of interviews.

Being Flexible. There must be a certain amount of flexibility in a salesperson's daily schedule. Changes and cancellations in both travel arrangements and appointments, often on short notice, are inevitable. Schedules must be revised to fit emergencies, and lost time must be made up. No salesperson should adhere to a plan blindly, disregarding such developments. Transportation delays, broken appointments, and inability to get away from buyers on schedule are typical causes of changes in plans.

There are several ways of achieving the needed flexibility. One is for the salesperson to have the right attitude toward unavoidable revisions. Flexibility is partly a frame of mind, and salespeople begin to achieve it when they start cultivating the ability to improvise. A second step toward flexibility is the realization that minutes can be moved about within a time budget in the same way that dollars can be shifted around in a financial budget. Time allotted for paperwork can be used for selling today and replaced tomorrow, for example. A third method of achieving flexibility is for the salesperson to work toward becoming easily accessible to prospects, customers, and the salesperson's own company.

Another suggestion is that alternate plans be established in case there is unexpected spare time. If a certain prospect is out of the office, the salesperson can avoid wasting time by having a second choice of activities, such as canvassing for new prospects, calling to see whether a dormant account can and should be revived, making callbacks, or catching up on paperwork.

Avoiding Time Traps. Effective time management requires concentration on the part of the salesperson. The sales rep must be aware of the **"time traps"** that can waste a salesperson's time. Some of the more common time traps are shown in Figure 15-2.

Setting Daily and Weekly Goals. Goals provide motivation for the salesperson. Daily and weekly goals provide the impetus for salespeople to effectively manage their time. Such goals include the number of calls to be made per day/week, the number of demonstrations, the number of service calls, and the depth of customer coverage.

Classifying Accounts. The depth of customer coverage is an important decision for the salesperson to make. Some accounts require more attention than others. Just as it is important to classify prospects, as was discussed in Chapter 7, it is also important for salespeople to classify their regular accounts. By classifying certain accounts as being "hot", others as being "medium", and the remainder as being "cold", the salesperson knows which ones require immediate attention, and how much attention is needed.

Figure 15-4 shows one such classification. In the illustration, 15 percent of the accounts are shown to represent 65 percent of the sales

COMMON TIME TRAPS

- Poor daily planning
- Poor prospect qualifying
- Inadequate travel scheduling
- Taking a long lunch
- Getting a late morning start
- Improper use of waiting time
- Insufficient use of the telephone

- Too many coffee breaks
- Talking instead of selling
- Excess entertaining of customers
- Walking in without an appointment
- Stopping work early on Fridays

Figure 15-2 Outside salespeople are responsible for monitoring their time. In order to effectively manage their time, they must avoid as many of these time traps as possible.

volume. These are the company's A or "hot" accounts. The next 20 percent, the B accounts, result in 20 percent of the sales volume, and the final 65 percent, the C accounts, represent the final 15 percent of sales volume. Naturally, the salesperson wants to spend the most time with the A accounts, then attend to the B accounts, and finally the C accounts.

ROUTING

Routing is the travel pattern used in working a territory. Well-planned routing increases both the number of calls the salesperson is able to make and the ratio of selling time to nonselling time. Salespeople who use well-planned routing contact the maximum number of buyers when they are most ready to buy, work the territory in a logical, planned, and controlled manner, and cover the territory thoroughly.

GEOGRAPHIC CONSIDERATIONS

Programs and timetables salespeople develop to attain their objectives can be prepared only in terms of the geographic area covered and what it contains. The boundary lines must be clear in the salesperson's mind, for they specify the exact area in terms of which the salesperson must plan and operate, and therefore represent both problems and possibilities.

Most salespeople have clearly defined sales territories assigned to them. Some of the factors that influence the size of the territory are the total number of prospects within a certain area, the buying habits of the prospects, the location of the prospects in relation to transportation facilities, the best frequency-of-call schedule, how often the salesperson is called back to the home office and for how long, the competition present in a given area, and the potential dollar demand present in various markets.

ARE SALESPEOPLE GAINING MORE SELLING TIME?

Sales Management Highlight

Are salespeople gaining more time?

The increased use of telephone selling in order to curb the rising costs of personal selling is underscored in McGraw-Hill's new survey on how salespeople spend their time. A report issued by the company's Laboratory for Advertising Performance last month shows the average industrial salesperson spends 25% of his time in face-to-face selling, 17% selling customers and prospects by phone. A previous survey done in 1977 that reported 39% of the salesperson's time was taken up in face-to-face selling did not include a breakout for telephone contact because of its lesser importance. However, a comparison of other categories suggests that salespeople are gaining more selling time. Traveling and waiting for interviews decreased from 32% of total time in 1977 to 25% currently, and time spent on reports, paperwork, and meetings slipped from 24% to 22%.

9 to 5: How Salespeople Spend Their Day

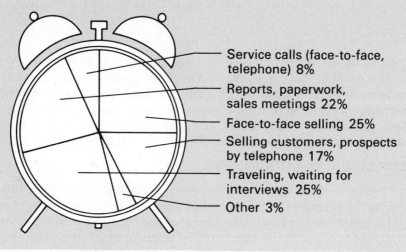

Service calls (face-to-face, telephone) 8%

Reports, paperwork, sales meetings 22%

Face-to-face selling 25%

Selling customers, prospects by telephone 17%

Traveling, waiting for interviews 25%

Other 3%

Figure 15-3   Salespeople need to maximize their face-to-face selling time.

Source: "How Salespeople Spend Their Time," McGraw-Hill, Laboratory for Advertising Performance, in *Sales & Marketing Management* (July 1986): 29.

Salespeople who cover a number of cities or states face the challenge of organizing their sales territories in the most manageable, profitable manner. It often helps if these territories, and even smaller, local territories, can be divided into smaller sections. The salesperson can then think, plan, and work in terms of several individual markets or trading

ACCOUNT CLASSIFICATION SCHEME

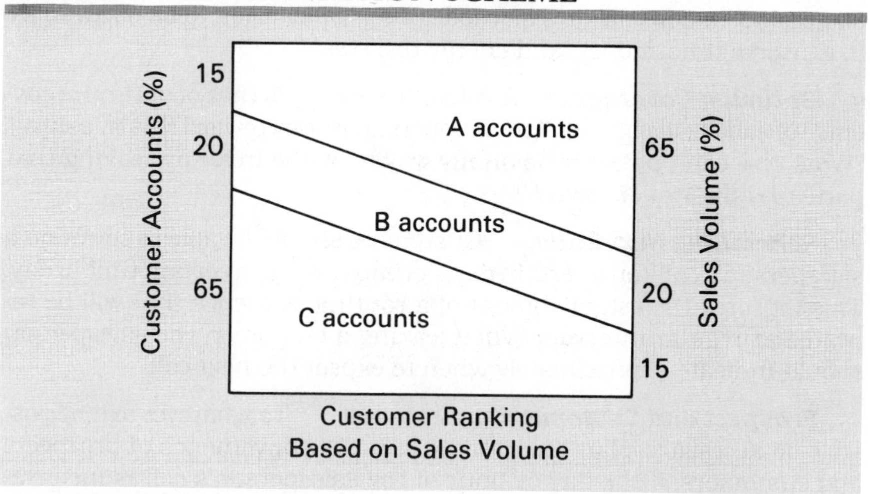

Figure 15-4 "A" accounts result in 65 percent of sales volume.

areas. This enables the salesperson to estimate the need for products and services more accurately and allows the salesperson to be more sensitive to any new market conditions. Selling activities can be adapted to each separate area.

PRINCIPLES OF ROUTING

Good routing ensures that the salesperson covers the territory according to plan. It permits the salesperson to strike the desired balance between intensive and extensive coverage, and it helps reduce traveling costs. When routing permits the prospect to anticipate the salesperson's call, there is more chance that the prospect will be ready to see the salesperson and will require less of the salesperson's time. Routing helps the salesperson better achieve company performance standards.

Geographic Area.   Study the geographic area thoroughly. Plot the cities or markets on a map and trace the most economical ways to get to each. Then do the same type of mapping for all prospects and customers to be contacted within each city or market.

Face-to-Face Time.   Routing should provide the greatest amount of face-to-face time with the most profitable customers. Therefore, salespeople should plan the straightest route possible between their starting point and destination. This will allow for shorter travel distances and a greater number of calls.

Future Planning.   Make up the routing plan for the most suitable future period, generally for the coming week. This permits the designation of a mailing or telephoning point for the company, prospects, and customers. In determining methods of transportation to be used, strive to conserve time, money, and energy reserves.

Optimum Coverage.   A valuable concept is that of optimum coverage of each trading area. The salesperson moves toward this by asking, "What else can I possibly do on my way to, while in, or on leaving that particular district or town?"

Scheduling Next Calls.   Customers should be able to count on a salesperson's calls on a certain day, perhaps even at a certain time of day. This requires the establishment of a routing sequence that will be repeated at regular intervals. When leaving a customer, the salesperson should indicate approximately when to expect the next call.

Prospect and Customer Convenience.   To whatever extent possible or necessary, plan the route to suit the convenience of prospects and customers. If the day or hour of the salesperson's call is inconvenient, additional resistance is faced. This means that in some cases it might be possible for a salesperson to spend more time traveling, see fewer prospects and customers, yet find that the time spent has increased in effectiveness.

Experimentation.   Experimentation is essential to successful routing. Only through trial and error can the best routing plan be determined.

THE TELEPHONE AS A TIMESAVER

Because salespeople must work toward a certain degree of economy in both time budgeting and expense budgeting, they should think of the telephone as a supplementary selling tool. Some customers, particularly retailers, like to order by telephone for reasons of speed and simplicity. Certain products that are simple and routinely purchased can be sold successfully by telephone.

The salesperson can call a customer almost anywhere, at any chosen hour. Because geography is no limitation, the number of calls possible during a day is high. Contact by telephone is almost instantaneous. This means that salespeople can send urgent information to whomever they need to reach. Also, some prospects will talk to a salesperson on the telephone even if they might not see one who calls in person.

Even though few salespeople find telephone calls a complete substitute for face-to-face calls, most are well advised to remember the difference in costs between the two. For some salespeople, the typical personal call costs 20 times as much as the typical telephone call. Telephoning permits the salesperson to get in touch with important customers often, particularly between personal calls, and permits more effective market coverage.

Figure 15-5 The telephone has become an integral part of the selling effort because it is far less expensive than a personal sales call.

USES OF TELEPHONE CALLS

Salespeople find that telephone calls can be timesavers in making sales, making appointments, delivering news; cultivating customers' goodwill, handling customer problems, and doing prospecting and preapproach work. Each of these uses will now be briefly discussed.

MAKING SALES BY TELEPHONE

Salespeople can obtain regular orders by telephone; increase mail orders by trading up or by suggestion selling of related or timely merchandise; and obtain follow-up orders and move odd lots, job lots, end-of-season merchandise, and discontinued items. Salespeople also can sell hard-to-see and impulsive customers by telephone. After a first personal call which went well but did not result in a purchase, a salesperson may telephone a customer to encourage immediate buying action. In these calls, the salesperson can repeat and support what was said in person.

MAKING APPOINTMENTS BY TELEPHONE

A major use of the telephone by salespeople is for making, confirming, and rescheduling appointments. By making appointments, the salesperson is able to cover more territory, make more sales calls, and give more service to customers. Sometimes customer information can be obtained when phoning for an appointment, but the salesperson should not try to do any selling at that time. Telephone calls requesting an appointment may be preceded by a mail communication. After the appointment has been made, the salesperson may send a confirming note, reminding the customer of the date of the appointment.

USING THE TELEPHONE TO DELIVER NEWS

Because it permits instant contact, the telephone helps a salesperson keep customers posted on matters involving products, their prices, promotion efforts, and company policies. A manufacturer may be launching a major advertising campaign in which retail customers will be interested. Perhaps a price rise is coming, but customers can place orders immediately at the present price. Perhaps delivery can be made to an impatient customer earlier than originally promised. If certain ordered items cannot be shipped, the salesperson may telephone to tell the customer that they have been back-ordered and when to expect them.

USING THE TELEPHONE TO CULTIVATE CUSTOMER GOODWILL

The telephone can be used to keep the customer-seller relationship on a personal, friendly basis. For example, a call can introduce a salesperson to a new purchasing agent before the salesperson's first visit in person. Salespeople can telephone to congratulate customers on promotions and achievements. They can call to thank customers for first sales calls, first orders, testimonials, referrals, and case histories. Telephone calls let the salesperson keep in touch and check up on customer service. The fact that a salesperson is concerned enough to take the time to telephone is flattering to most customers. Of course, telephoning can be overdone. It often becomes annoying to customers.

USING THE TELEPHONE TO HANDLE CUSTOMER PROBLEMS

In handling customer problems, the personal touch of a telephone call can often give quick and satisfactory results. When a written complaint or a cancellation reaches the salesperson, a telephone call may be appropriate. Certain collection matters also can be better handled by telephone than by letter. Calls can reveal why a good customer quit buying; they can be effective in reviving dormant accounts; and they can be used to obtain approval for a substitution in an order.

USING THE TELEPHONE FOR PROSPECTING AND PREAPPROACH WORK

Cold canvassing from a directory is possible by telephone. Customers can be asked for leads. Salespeople telephone to qualify prospects, to build a prospect list, and to obtain the data needed for evaluation of customers. Calls can identify the real prospects on a company mailing list, the buying influences, and those who are open to buy or are seriously considering a purchase.

USES OF THE TELEPHONE

- Making Sales
- Making Appointments
- Delivering News
- Cultivating Goodwill
- Handling Problems
- Prospecting and Preapproach

Figure 15-6 Salespeople can use the telephone for many different functions, all of which are less expensive than making a personal visit.

HOW TELEPHONING AFFECTS ROUTING

Some salespeople have incorporated the use of the telephone into what they call skip-stop routing. Suppose that a salesperson has 20 markets in which some personal calls must be made. The salesperson numbers each market and constructs two circuits. On the first circuit, the salesperson visits all odd-numbered markets and telephones certain buyers in even-numbered markets from the closest odd-numbered market. On the second circuit, the salesperson visits all even-numbered markets and from them telephones buyers in the odd-numbered markets.

Other salespeople build their routes on key towns. Under this plan, a salesperson divides markets and buyers into two groups: those deserving personal calls and those who must be handled in a more economical manner—namely, by telephone. Individual customers in the second group are reached by telephone when the salesperson is in the closest key town. It is not unusual for a salesperson to telephone certain small customers who reside in key towns, or to alternate telephone calls with personal calls in handling certain accounts of modest size.

SUGGESTIONS FOR CONDUCTING THE TELEPHONE CONVERSATION

The salesperson should generally begin the call with identification by name and company, and then follow with justification for the call. The salesperson should immediately give the customer a reason for staying on the phone rather than ending the conversation. This reason may be based on curiosity or on information of interest and benefit to the customer. It is virtually impossible for the salesperson to get to the point too quickly because revealing the goal of the call may prevent the customer's losing interest and hanging up. Sometimes there is something to which the salesperson can tie the call: a letter sent to the customer earlier, some communication from the customer, the last personal call, the customer's last order, or even an earlier telephone contact.

A pleasant, courteous manner from the outset of the conversation helps make a favorable impression. Most of the principles that are effective in face-to-face selling are equally effective for telephone communication. Some of these principles are shown in Figure 15-7.

For most salespeople, telephoning can never replace personal calls. Use of the telephone should increase, not decrease, the number of personal calls made; and it clearly is not as effective as a personal visit.

USING NEW TECHNOLOGY TO SAVE TIME

Modern technology has brought about a number of new products that can be used by salespeople to save time. The telephone, as was previously mentioned, is an excellent timesaving device. Of course, the basic telephone is not new. The innovation that has made the telephone a more valuable time-saving tool is the **cellular phone**.

Past technology brought the salesperson pagers and two-way radios. Pagers are battery packs that notify the salesperson, through a beeping signal, that someone wants to talk to her or him. The salesperson must still find a telephone in order to call, however. While pagers have become more sophisticated, allowing communication on a regional, national, or international basis, they are starting to lose popularity. Two-way radios allow communication from remote areas; however, the receiver of the message must have his or her own radio, and how many customers can you expect to have a two-way radio? Both pagers and two-way radios are limited in comparison to cellular phones.

PRINCIPLES OF USING THE TELEPHONE

1. Telephone calls should be made at times convenient to the customer.
2. Customers should be addressed by name and made to feel important.
3. Salespeople should refrain from interrupting the customer, arguing, or monopolizing the conversation.
4. Salespeople must make every word contribute to their goals as they convert product features into customer benefits.
5. They must not be so aggressive and push so hard as to close the door on a subsequent call.
6. They should experiment with various presentation plans and should also keep records of the calls they make.
7. They should not let the customer feel that the call is a routine one and that the salesperson is unwilling to call in person.

Figure 15-7 Salespeople will have better results if they simply follow these principles of using the telephone.

CELLULAR PHONES AND AIRFONES

So, what are cellular phones, and why are they becoming so popular? Cellular phones are mobile telephone and/or portable pack units that allow salespeople to make and receive calls from their automobiles, boats, or elsewhere. Cellular phones work through a network of antennas that are divided into cells. Each cell represents a service area, and a switching office takes the call in and switches it from the calling cell to the receiving cell. This network of antennas makes the cellular phone a wireless communications system. The user can thus talk while driving. Cellular phones also allow communication with virtually every metropolitan area as well as major interstate corridors because of the sophistication of the antenna networks and switching stations. In several studies, cellular phones have been credited with increasing a salesperson's sales.

Cellular phones can be used to confirm appointments, let the customer know of a delay, prospect, preapproach, communicate with the sales manager or home office, and, in some cases, even close sales. Thus, wasted time is reduced, last-minute changes can be made, and the salesperson's productivity ultimately will increase.

Another new communications technology, **airfones**, allows the salesperson to make a call while traveling on an airplane. A phone unit is built into the wall of the plane. The salesperson inserts a credit card, the phone detaches from the wall, and calls can be made from the salesperson's seat. Airfones are not yet perfected, however. There are some problems with interference, busy phone lines, and weak signals that need to be worked out.

PERSONAL COMPUTERS

Throughout this text personal computers have been mentioned as a major innovation aiding the salesperson. Many salespeople are making use of personal computers and portable PCs that can be carried in a briefcase. Salespeople can use these PCs to store all of their account records. The salesperson can put all information relating to each account on a storage disk, and can later access this information to schedule calls, route travels, and do paperwork. PCs can also be used for sales presentations. The salesperson can use the PC to check pricing, delivery, and inventory information in the customer's office. The PC also can be used to develop graphic presentations using charts, graphs, tables, and illustrations.

The personal computer's **electronic mail** function enables salespeople to send and receive messages no matter where they are, as long as they are connected to telephone lines via a modem. The salesperson just types in the message and the computer sends it through the phone lines to the receiver's computer. The advantage of electronic mail over a regular call is that the receiver or a secretary need not be there to answer the phone. Messages could be sent and received after working hours and will be shown on the computer monitor when the receiver uses an access code.

FAX MACHINES

Finally, as was mentioned earlier in this text, facsimile or "fax" machines are also becoming very popular among salespeople as time-saving devices. Instead of mailing or personally delivering a price quote, the salesperson can now fax price quotes over telephone lines. Customers receive the price quote almost instantaneously on their fax machine. Fax machines are becoming so popular among salespeople that companies are starting to develop portable and public pay fax machines.

Figure 15-8 Public pay fax machines have made it more convenient for salespeople to send important documents to their customers.

Source: Photo courtesy of FAX-IT.

RECORDKEEPING

Information on customers and selling techniques is of limited value until it is organized into readily usable records. The amount of time required in keeping records is justified by the improvement in the quality of the salesperson's selling. Salespeople depend heavily on the organization provided by records for self-management. Daily accomplishments must be gauged if salespeople are to make their quotas.

As an example of the tactical use of records, the salesperson can use them to shorten calls and permit more calls to be completed each week. On call-backs, for instance, records relieve the salesperson of spending time in finding out at what point the last visit ended. The salesperson can stress only those points that need stressing and avoid needless repetition.

MECHANICS OF KEEPING RECORDS

No record is worth keeping unless its information can be used to advantage. Records that demand too much paperwork generally contain much useless detail. Records that are simple yet complete are the ones that should be kept up-to-date and used.

If possible, the salesperson should complete any daily reports or orders immediately after each call. By following this practice, the records will contain fewer mistakes, fresher facts, and more complete information. This practice also saves time, permits quicker feedback to the home office, and means that the salesperson is reasonably caught up with records if any emergency should arise. Orders and reports should be sent to the home office promptly after they have been checked for clarity and completeness. Records can be sent electronically by computer, with facsimile machines, through the mail, or they may be called in.

RECORDS THAT SHOULD BE KEPT

This section will point out the major areas in which most salespeople will need to keep some type of record. Obviously, salespeople will keep whatever records their company requires, whether the information is for the use of the sales department or for other departments. In addition to those required, any other records that contribute to the salesperson's success are worth keeping and using.

PROSPECTS AND CUSTOMERS

These two sets of records are similar, each consisting of a card or file which contains a complete history of the salesperson's attention to and experience with each individual buyer. Each file will contain the prospect information the salesperson collected about the customer, any other facts the salesperson finds useful, an account of the salesperson's work on and progress with the customer, and plans for the next sales call. Time spent in keeping these records is extremely well invested.

DAILY CALLS

The daily call record is a basic record used by virtually all salespeople, and shows the number of attempts to sell. It notes any prices quoted and any promises made; shows the results of each call; and when sales are lost, gives a brief reason for the failure to sell. Any suitable facts can be transferred from the daily call record to prospect and customer records. Highlight 15-1 shows a typical daily record.

SALES

There are many breakdowns for sales volume. The total dollar figure may be classified according to product line if the salesperson handles more than one product, or to price line if more than one price line is sold. The breakdown may be by day, week, and month, by size of order, by type of customer, or by type of sale, to name just a few examples. Each salesperson must select which to compile and maintain.

EXPENSES

If expenses are to be kept in an acceptable ratio to sales volume, they need to be carefully controlled. This demands records. Considerable itemization is needed so that the total figure will not be questioned and so that the various items can be analyzed and compared with benchmark figures. A balance is needed, however. If the groupings are too broad, control and comparison are difficult, but if the salesperson's expense groupings are too detailed, they require too much time.

TIME

Time records are designed to log hour and minute utilization for each day. The immediate result is that the salesperson learns just how much time is being spent on each activity. The long-range result of time records should be more time spent in the presence of customers and less time wasted.

TICKLER FILE

A date tickler file is particularly valuable as a reminder of whom to see and what to do on each day of the month. By referring to prospect and customer records, the salesperson knows how each prospect should be approached.

SELF-EVALUATION OF SALES PERFORMANCE

Plans, sales objectives, and records are of little value unless salespeople check the results of their selling efforts against what they schedule for

HIGHLIGHT 15-1   *Daily Record*

This is a typical daily record kept by a salesperson for a Fortune 500 consumer packaged-goods company.

ACME SOAP COMPANY

Salesperson: Willie Lanier   **Territory: Wilkes-Barre, PA**
Date: January 3

Call #	Account/Address	Contact	Activity
1	Sumio's Supermarket Rt 309, Dallas, PA	Joe Sumio	Rotated product; sold extra facing to support coupon-drop; took order for 5 cases.
2	Weis' Market Dallas Hwy, Dallas, PA	Sam Harris	Will accept coupons, but refused extra facing; took order for 3 cases.
3	IGA Supermarket Dallas Hwy, Dallas, PA	Bill Reese	Sold extra facing, plus 6 cases; rotated shelf; took in 1 case of damaged product.
4	ACME Supermarket Lake Street, Dallas, PA	Donna Nahlis	New customer; got 1 facing and an agreement for more if product sells well; sold 1 case; they will accept coupons.
5	Stapinski Drugs Dallas Hwy, Dallas, PA	Ron Stapinski	Sold 2-ft display and 2 cases; will not take coupons.
6	Cook's Pharmacy Dallas Hwy Shavertown, PA	Wilma Cook	Sold 1 case; rejected display and coupon.

themselves. The basic question is, "What do I have to show for my management of myself and my territory?" To answer this question, salespeople must have certain performance standards. Yet, the very nature of selling makes the establishment of absolute standards of achievement difficult. How, for example, can missionary salespeople or other "goodwill" representatives measure their performances? In spite of this handicap salespeople are still under pressure to check their accomplishments. This can be done by constructing quantitative and qualitative standards.

QUANTITATIVE STANDARDS

Quantitative standards are not difficult to construct. Standards for volume of sales, number of calls, new customers, and expenses are examples. Quantitative standards are based on a comparison of the salesperson's current performance with previous performance or with some budget figure or quota. The standards can be used for both control and incentive purposes.

If the question is raised of how many quantitative checks are necessary to measure a salesperson's performance, an argument for having only one check might be made. This one standard would be net profit from the salesperson's selling activities, since selling activities are directly reflected in the net profit figure. But this is a short-run view. Activities that result in the highest net profit today might not do so tomorrow. Thus, some checks are necessary to make sure the salesperson does things that help in the long run also, such as selling new products or calling on new accounts.

QUALITATIVE STANDARDS

Qualitative standards are more difficult to construct because of their subjective nature. Examples of these somewhat inexact standards are those for goodwill, customer loyalty and esteem, and the salesperson's planning ability and initiative. Outstanding or unsatisfactory performance in these areas soon shows up in matters that can be quantitatively measured, such as sales.

Qualitative evaluation of a salesperson's performance also involves matters that influence net profit. But these matters are more elusive than are the quantitative checks. Some fairly typical questions that may be used as qualitative standards are shown in Figure 15-9.

Because the salesperson will no doubt find it impossible to evaluate objectively his or her own performance on such scores, an unbiased third person should be asked for an impartial rating.

PERSONAL RATING CHART

Beginning salespeople sometimes find they can benefit for a considerable period of time from daily use of a personal rating chart. The purpose of the chart is to enable the salesperson to check quickly on points of personal strength and weakness so that steps can be taken to maximize strengths and minimize weaknesses.

While it is true that each chart must be built to fit the particular salesperson, the elements of such a chart will probably follow a consis-

QUALITATIVE SELF-EVALUATION CRITERIA

1. How much growth has the salesperson shown in ability to plan and to administer?
2. How much goodwill does the salesperson create, and how much is it worth?
3. How does the salesperson react to the creative phase of the job and the demands for imagination, tact, and versatility?
4. How much allowance should be made for changing conditions in evaluating job performance—changes in sales potential, the business cycle, competitors' activities, or the policies of the salesperson's own company?

Figure 15-9 One way salespeople can measure their performance is through qualitative self-evaluation criteria.

tent pattern. The specific items can be one-word characteristics or qualities, or they can be structured in the form of questions. Qualities that might be included are appearance, alertness, courtesy, enthusiasm, honesty, loyalty, obedience, and tact.

Examples of questions that might be included on a personal rating chart are:

- Did I make today's decisions on the basis of facts?
- Did I follow up today's leads promptly?
- Did I spend some time hunting for new prospects?
- Did I organize my hours and duties and then follow my plan?
- Did I waste any time?
- Did I waste any of the company's money or my money?
- How can I do more and better tomorrow?

The salesperson can use percentages, letter grades, numbers, yes and no answers, or any other appropriate system.

AFTER-CALL ANALYSIS

Regardless of whether or not a sale was made, the salesperson should analyze each sales call in a critical fashion. This can best be done if a record of each call is faithfully kept. Salespeople will find these records extremely valuable sources of information about buying motives, objections, the effect of different sales approaches, and other vital matters. The record should be made as soon as possible after the salesperson leaves the customer, while the details of the call are still fresh and a note can be made of each important aspect. The main concern of the salesperson is what was well done, what was done badly, what changes of a general nature should be made, and what should be done the next time that customer is called on. After-call analysis benefits not only the novice; more experienced salespeople can keep out of undesirable ruts and avoid forming bad habits only by giving careful scrutiny to their performances.

SELLING SLUMPS

All salespeople experience slumps along with periods of success. Smart salespeople accept periodic slumps as normal and do not make excuses for them. But can anything be done about slumps?

Because of the relationship between health and energy, good mental, emotional, and physical health must be a priority. Good physical condition requires regular medical exams, recreation, rest, exercise, and a proper diet. Moderation should govern recreation, rest, exercise, and diet.

A positive attitude is needed to come out of a slump, because attitude affects selling performance. Negative thinking, doubts, worries, fears, and self-pity consume energy and emotional resources. Enthusiasm is contagious, and thinking success encourages success. Salespeople must have belief and pride in themselves. They need confidence, affirmative feelings, and solid convictions about their company, their customers, and their products.

Figure 15-10 Successful selling requires that the salesperson be both mentally and physically fit.
Source: Virginia State Travel Service.

Most important in working out of a slump is action. Salespeople must act: they may hurry to see the next buyer on the call schedule, visit with the sales manager, or make notes on the services that can be rendered to buyers. Good salespeople check and improve plans, and then carry them out.

THE EXPERIMENTAL ATTITUDE

Successful salespeople must develop an experimental attitude. An experimental attitude can be described as the determination to find new and better ways of doing things through thought and study, testing and experimentation, and adaptation to change. In this way, salespeople will always adhere to the most fundamental commandment in selling: "Never think you are so good that improvement is impossible."

SUMMARY

Effective self-management maximizes the time spent on productive selling activities and results in profitable selling. Planning helps salespeople prioritize customers, travel from customer to customer efficiently, maintain proper records, and manage their personal time.

Effective sales call scheduling and routing that includes a degree of flexibility enables salespeople to effectively maximize their time. Proper use of the telephone, whether for prospecting, collecting preapproach information, making appointments or sales calls, handling customer problems and cultivating goodwill, or skip-stop routing, is a great timesaver.

New technology such as cellular phones, airfones, personal computers, and facsimile machines help salespeople to be more efficient and more productive. Recordkeeping and other methods of self-evaluation, based on either quantitative or qualitative standards, lead to self-improvement and higher productivity.

KEY TERMS

scheduling	cellular phone
time traps	airfones
routing	electronic mail

REVIEW QUESTIONS

1. What is the objective of self-management?
2. What does effective time management rely on?
3. List three elements involved in creating a schedule.

4. Why is careful routing important?
5. List four factors that influence the size of a sales territory.
6. List the principles of effective scheduling.
7. List the principles of effective routing.
8. List four uses of the telephone in selling activities.
9. What are some of the new innovations available to help salespeople save time?
10. What kinds of information should salespeople keep in their records?
11. List three quantitative and three qualitative standards that a salesperson might use to measure effectiveness.
12. What factors should a salesperson consider in after-call analysis?
13. How can selling slumps be broken?
14. What is meant by an experimental attitude?

DISCUSSION QUESTIONS

1. Should sales calls be made on customers only when you expect to make a sale?
2. React to the following: "Paperwork should be done in the evenings and on weekends."
3. Suggest some guidelines concerning travel, time allocation, and approaches to prospects when developing a new territory.
4. How can a salesperson build up the self-confidence that is vital for successful selling?
5. Think of some innovations that have just been or are about to be released. How can they help the salesperson to be a better time manager?

CASE 15-1   WZZZ RADIO*

George Ferrell is a salesperson for WZZZ Radio Station in Pittsburgh, Pennsylvania. In selling, he competes not only with other radio stations, but also with other media, including TV, newspapers, billboards, and magazines. The competition among media salespersons has never been greater in the Pittsburgh market. Within a 50-mile radius of Pittsburgh there are 18 AM stations and 31 FM stations, and new stations are expected to enter the market in the near future.

George has been selling for WZZZ for two years. He is paid on a commission basis so he has to make good use of his time. The station gives him a list of potential customers. Some are established businesses which have purchased radio air time regularly in the past and others are

---

* Case prepared by Ronald F. Bush. Used with permission.

new businesses. He also makes some cold calls. The stations recently hired a time-management consultant to help the sales force. The consultant first asked the salespeople to complete a time log for two days each week over a four-week period; time logs were to be completed on different days of the week so they would be more representative of typical work patterns. Exhibit 15-1 is an analysis of how George spends his time compared to the other salespeople at WZZZ Radio Station. George and the rest of the salesforce were each given a report like this. They were then asked to attend a training session. At the training session the consultant discussed the importance of managing your time and ended by handing out a list of ten time-saving tips. Each of the salespeople was asked to review the list and then talk about it.

EXHIBIT 15-1

	Percent of Time	
Activity	**George**	**Other Salespeople**
Face-to-Face Selling	22%	31%
Telephone Selling	5	14
Account Paperwork	33	11
Traveling	24	18
Sales Meetings	4	5
Prospecting	7	11
Self Improvement	0	6
Other	5	4
Total	100%	100%
Average Hours Per Day	11.25	10.02

EXHIBIT 15-2
10 TIMESAVING TIPS

1. Set goals. Write specific, measurable goals you want to complete each day and each week.
2. Make a "To Do" list. List all the things you have to do and organize them by day and week.
3. Get the big picture. Develop priorities for your "To Do" list so you work on the things that give you the biggest payoff.
4. Create time tools. Keep equipment, forms, checklists, and information handy, organized, and in their place.
5. Make a plan. Select which customers to call on when. Select the best route.

(continued on next page)

6. Develop time blocks. Schedule blocks of uninterruptable time to work on projects that require concentration.
7. Avoid late starts and early quitting, and make use of waiting time.
8. Don't take long lunch hours.
9. Use the telephone effectively.
10. Take the "One-Minute Test." Periodically take a minute to ask yourself, "Am I doing things in the best possible way to meet my goals and the company's goals?"

CASE QUESTIONS

1. Is George Ferrell making good use of his time?
2. How should George change the way he is spending his time?
3. Review the ten timesaving tips. What are the three most important ones for George to follow?
4. Assume you are a salesperson for WZZZ Radio. What time-saving tips do you think you would have a hard time following?
5. What are some ways to avoid disregarding these tips?

CASE 15-2   WTEX TELEVISION*

WTEX Television, Channel 11, is located in Dallas, Texas. It is owned by the Texas Television Broadcasting Corporation, and is an affiliate of the ABC network. For the last four years, it has been the number one TV station in the Dallas market.

The sales department at WTEX TV has three managers, eight account executives, four sales support people, and two interns from the local junior college. There is a general sales manager, a national sales manager, and a local sales manager. The national sales manager makes all sales to customers whose home offices are outside the Dallas-Fort Worth area. The local sales manager manages the eight account executives who sell to businesses located in the Dallas-Fort Worth area. New account executives are given a list of customers who already buy TV air time from WTEX. They call on them as well as develop new customers. As one might expect, there is a large number of potential customers who might use television advertising in the Dallas-Fort Worth area. Consequently, salespeople must learn how to divide their selling time between established customers and new prospects. The sales manager periodi-

*Case prepared by Mark Johnston. Used with permission.

cally reviews each account executive's customer list so two salespeople are not calling on the same customer. The sales support team includes a political sales coordinator, a national sales assistant, a computer specialist, and a copywriter/creative specialist. The interns assist the account executives in prospecting for new customers and in gathering market research information.

Each month the general sales manager schedules a sales training seminar to help the account executives improve their sales. This past week Professor Raymond LeForge from Oklahoma State University was

EXHIBIT 15-3
STRENGTH OF POSITION

Strong	Weak
Segment 1	**Segment 2**
Attractiveness:	*Attractiveness:*
Accounts are very attractive since they offer high opportunity and sales organization has strong position	Accounts are potentially attractive since they offer high opportunity, but sales organization currently has weak position with accounts
Sales call strategy:	*Sales call strategy:*
Accounts should receive a high level of sales calls since they are the sales organization's most attractive accounts	Accounts should receive a high level of sales calls to strengthen the sales organization's position
Segment 3	**Segment 4**
Attractiveness:	*Attractiveness:*
Accounts are somewhat attractive, since sales organization has strong position, but future opportunity is limited	Accounts are very unattractive since they offer low opportunity and sales organization has weak position
Sales call strategy:	*Sales call strategy:*
Accounts should receive a moderate level of sales calls to maintain the current strength of the sales organization's position	Accounts should receive minimal level of sales calls and efforts should be made to selectively eliminate or replace personal sales calls with telephone calls, direct mail, etc.

Source: Raymond W. LeForge, Clifford E. Young, and B. Curtis Hamm, "Increasing Sales Productivity through Improved Sales Call Allocation Strategies," *Journal of Personal Selling and Sales Management* (November 1983): 53-59. Used with permission.

hired to present the seminar. He is a well-known expert on sales techniques. His sales training seminar suggested that salespeople could sell more effectively if they used his *Sales Call Grid Analysis.* His grid analysis indicates that companies should categorize their customers into four segments, as shown in Exhibit 15-3. Segment 1 is what most companies call a key account. Segment 2 is considered the most attractive potential customer or prospect. Segment 3 is a stable account, and Segment 4 is a weak account.

CASE QUESTIONS

1. Would the *Sales Call Grid Analysis* help the WTEX TV account executives?
2. What kind of information would the account executives need to use this grid analysis, and where would they get it? Do most companies have this information?
3. Can you think of a better way to plan sales calls?

CHAPTER 16
Legal, Ethical, and Social Responsibilities

After studying this chapter, you should be able to:

- Describe the major laws affecting salespeople
- Show how these laws apply to pricing and other selling practices
- Identify behavior by salespeople that could be considered unethical
- Tell how the ethics of salespeople could be improved
- Comment on the social responsibilities of salespeople

Salespeople must sell, but they have other responsibilities as well. They must obey the laws that govern company policies and their own actions. They should have a strong sense of what constitutes ethical conduct, because there is growing recognition that the sales force plays an important role in helping the company fulfill its social responsibilities.

LEGAL RESPONSIBILITIES

Salespeople must know what laws prohibit and require and how laws apply to their actions. The salesperson, however, is not expected to be a lawyer. A cardinal rule is: when in doubt, don't. Consult your supervisor or your legal department.

LAWS AFFECTING A SALESPERSON

A salesperson is affected by federal legislation and by state and local laws.

FEDERAL LEGISLATION

The major federal legislation affecting selling activities includes the Sherman Act (enacted in 1890), the Clayton Act (1914), the Federal Trade Commission Act (1914), and the Robinson-Patman Act (1936). Although none of these laws are new, their interpretation by the courts and their enforcement by administrative agencies have broadened their impact on selling activities.

The Sherman Act. The Sherman Act is the oldest of the antitrust laws. One major purpose of the act was to outlaw monopolies or attempts to monopolize. This rarely applies directly to the sales force. A second major purpose was to outlaw actions that were in "**restraint of trade**." That is, it sought to prevent activities that lessened competition. **Price-fixing** is the best-known activity in restraint of trade, but agreements not to sell, to sell only in certain markets, or to sell only to certain customers are also included within this act. Except in seeking remedies in court cases, it makes little difference whether the agreements are written or oral, explicit or implicit, intentional or accidental.

The Clayton Act. The Clayton Act had the same intent as the Sherman Act, but was an attempt to clarify the Sherman Act by making specific practices illegal. Of particular concern to a sales force are provisions restricting **exclusive dealing** and **tying arrangements**. Exclusive dealing, which is illegal, involves requiring that buyers of one product not buy certain products from another seller. A tying arrangement is the practice of requiring the buyer to purchase one product in order to be allowed to buy another.

The Federal Trade Commission Act. The Federal Trade Commission Act extended the Sherman Act by outlawing unfair methods of competition and deceptive practices. It also established the **Federal Trade Commission (FTC)**, whose job it is to see that all of these laws are observed. In 1938, the Wheeler-Lea Amendment to the Federal Trade Commission Act was passed. This allowed the FTC to take action against deceptive practices regardless of whether competition had been harmed.

The Robinson-Patman Act. The Robinson-Patman Act, passed during the Great Depression, grew out of concern that large and rapidly growing chain retailers would demand and get price discounts which would allow them to drive small retailers out of business by underpricing them. Thus, the Robinson-Patman Act was passed to outlaw price discrimination between buyers for products "of like grade and quality" if the price discrimination tended to harm competition. Price differentials are permitted for products of different quality, when costs of doing business with certain buyers can be proved to be lower than with others, in order to match competitors' prices, or when the buyers are not in competition with each other. It is not easy for a firm to interpret how the law applies to it because it can never be sure what a judge will accept as evidence of justifiable price differentials.

The Robinson-Patman Act also outlaws providing various merchandising and promotional aids and allowances in a discriminatory manner, if this would tend to harm competition. These aids and allowances must be provided in a "proportionately equal" manner. It is often the salesperson's responsibility to inform customers of the availability of these aids and allowances.

LAWS AFFECTING SALESPEOPLE

The Sherman Act outlaws:	Price fixing.
	Agreements not to sell.
	Agreements to sell only in certain markets.
	Agreements to sell only to certain customers.
The Clayton Act outlaws:	Exclusive dealing.
	Tying agreements.
The Federal Trade Commission Act outlaws:	Unfair methods of competition. Deceptive practices.
The Robinson-Patman Act outlaws:	Price discrimination. Disproportionate offering of promotional aids and allowances.
The Federal Trade Commission:	Oversees the enforcement of these laws.

Figure 16-1 Salespeople must be aware of those laws that restrict their activities.

OTHER LAWS

The range of legislation dealing with contracts, consumer protection, and personal selling is wide.

The Uniform Commercial Code. The Uniform Commercial Code, which deals in part with the laws of contracts, may treat a sales representative as an agent of the company, authorized to make commitments for the company. Thus, an offer made by a salesperson and accepted by a customer could, in effect, bind the salesperson's company to a contract the company may not have intended. Similarly, comments made by a salesperson about the suitability of a product for certain purposes may be construed by the courts as the equivalent of warranties or guarantees.

The Uniform Commercial Code also recognizes a sale as being made only when title passes from the seller to the buyer, as well as noting that oral agreements between buyer and seller are as binding as written agreements.

Consumer Protection Legislation. Some state and local governments have passed what are known as **Green River Ordinances** (after one of the places where they were first passed—Green River, Wyoming). These laws restrict the activities of certain types of salespeople (notably door-to-door salespeople) by requiring that they apply for and receive a license before they can sell in that area.

Door-to-door selling (and sometimes telephone selling) is often restricted in other ways by state and local laws. For example, salespeople

Figure 16-2 Some businesses and private residences clearly state that they do not want salespeople knocking on their doors.

may not attempt to get a foot in the door by claiming that they are taking a survey when the survey is only incidental to their real purpose—to sell. Salespeople must also inform customers who have signed contracts about a **cooling-off period**, a time (often three days) during which the customer can reconsider and cancel a contract.

Truth-in-lending legislation requires that the seller inform the buyer of the effective rate of interest and the amount of the carrying charge for any credit purchase. The intent of the law is to inform the buyer of the costs of buying on credit.

APPLYING THE LAWS

The laws affecting selling are complex, and their interpretation is difficult. Nevertheless, some actions are illegal, while others are merely unethical. Some of the problem areas are discussed below.

PRICING ACTIONS

Pricing actions such as price-fixing, **predatory pricing**, and **discriminatory pricing** are illegal. Paying bribes and accepting kickbacks are also unethical and can affect prices.

Price-Fixing. Price-fixing is a civil and criminal offense. The company can be sued and a salesperson can go to jail for participating in price-fixing. In fact, even the semblance of price-fixing may be illegal. Thus, not only must salespeople be careful not to agree with a competitor's salesperson to charge a certain price to a customer, they must even avoid exchanging price information with a competitor because it may appear that there was some unspoken agreement to fix prices.

How does this translate into action? Don't discuss prices with competitors at a trade association meeting. Don't respond to questions about price from a competitor, even if your prices are published in price lists and are common knowledge to your customers. If, by chance, you overhear a competitor's salespeople discussing their own prices, there is nothing wrong with listening, but you may not join the conversation. In addition, it must be clear that their allowing you to overhear the pricing information was not intended to be a way of communicating the information to you. There is nothing wrong with getting information about competitors' prices from a customer, on the other hand, as long as you haven't arranged to use the customer to transmit information about price.

Requiring that your distributor or retailer charge certain prices to their customers is illegal. Again, the salesperson must be careful not even to give the impression that the distributor or retailer must charge a certain price.

Figure 16-3 It is not wise for a salesperson to compare prices with competitors because such an act may be construed as collusion to fix prices.

Price-fixing is rarely a concern of retail or direct-to-home (e.g., door-to-door) salespeople. For advice about a specific situation, you should generally rely on your company's lawyers.

Predatory Pricing.   The opposite of price-fixing is predatory pricing. This practice, also illegal, involves intentionally lowering prices below costs so as to drive a competitor out of business. Thus, price competition that is too vigorous may be as bad as agreeing not to compete on a price basis. The outcome of a lawsuit charging predatory pricing may depend on the perception of the company's intent by a judge or jury. Statements made at a sales meeting or to a customer may provide evidence of intent. Statements like, "We're going to drive _____ out of business" or "The way we're pricing, they don't have a chance" may build morale at a sales meeting or impress a customer, but they may also impress a judge or jury—in the wrong way.

Price Discrimination.   Price discrimination is also illegal, under the Robinson-Patman Act. The safest way to avoid legal problems is to sell at the same price to everyone. You cannot sell at a lower price to a customer you like or who is important to you. Therefore, you must know when charging lower prices to certain customers is legal and when it is not. In addition, a buyer who encourages or knowingly accepts a price that is lower than appropriate can be guilty of price discrimination. Once again, when in doubt, consult your company or its attorney.

Price discrimination is not an issue when the product you are selling to a customer is not of like grade and quality to that which you are selling to other customers. In other words, if you sell custom-made products or services, you are probably safe. Nor is price discrimination an issue if the customer to whom you are planning to sell at a lower price is not in competition with those customers to whom you sell at a higher price. This may occur when the customer is in a different industry or a different geographical area.

You can justify different prices to customers in the same industry for your standardized product when it is less expensive to sell to certain customers—that is, when there is a cost basis for the price differential. You can also justify different prices when your customer can show that a competitor is selling at a lower price. You can meet the prices that your competitor is charging, but you cannot lower your prices below your competitor's in this situation. **Quantity discounts**, a popular way of encouraging and rewarding large orders, also must be justified in the same way as any other price differentials.

Free goods or product displays as allowances for promoting a product are governed by the Robinson-Patman Act. These are not illegal, but because they offer the possibility of discriminating on the net cost to a customer, they must be made available on a "proportionately equal" basis. You must inform all your customers of their availability.

Paying **bribes** and accepting **kickbacks** are as much ethical matters as they are legal ones. Bribes are money or valuable gifts given to buyers to obtain their business. Kickbacks occur when a broker working for and paid by the buyer receives a payment from the seller for making the decision to buy from that seller.

CHANNEL/MARKET RESTRICTIONS

Channel/market restrictions are illegal. The first of these channel/market restrictions involves deciding not to sell to certain customers. Often the idea is to avoid head-to-head confrontations: A competitor may say, "If you don't leave my customers alone, I'll come after yours." If you agree, you may be part of channel/market restriction. Channel/market restrictions occur when competitors agree to split up the market, one selling in one area and the other selling in another. Restriction may also be initiated by a customer who says, "I'll buy this product from you if you'll agree not to sell it to my competitors."

When you are selling to a distributor who will resell your products, the legality of certain actions is less clear-cut. For example, it may or may not be illegal for that distributor to ask you not to sell to another distributor. You will have to consult your lawyers for advice.

Nothing said so far implies that you cannot refuse to sell to a customer who has proved unsatisfactory to deal with. Such actions are usually viewed as a prerogative of the selling company.

Exclusive dealing and tying arrangements are other channel/market restrictions. Both are specifically outlawed by the Clayton Act. You may not require a customer to buy only from you or not to buy a competitor's products (exclusive dealing), although the customer may make that decision independently. You may not force a customer to buy a product that is not wanted in order to get one that is wanted (tying arrangements).

Reciprocity may also be considered a channel/market restriction. It violates both the Sherman Act and the Federal Trade Commission Act. You may not suggest that the buyer will lose sales of a product (business machines, for example) to your company if the buyer does not buy your product (electronic parts, for example). Similarly, you cannot promise that your company will buy a product if the seller agrees to buy from you.

OTHER ILLEGAL PRACTICES

Other illegal practices include **disparagement** of competitors, **harassment** of competitors, and **misrepresentation** of your company's products and policies.

Disparagement. Disparagement is criticizing a competitor's product without proof that what you are saying is true. To avoid being charged with this practice, some companies go so far as to require that their salespeople not even mention competitors' products in their sales presentations.

Harassment.   Harassment takes various forms. It occurs when a grocery products sales representative takes a competitor's products off the store's shelves or moves them to a less desirable location without the store manager's approval, lets the air out of a competitor's tires, and persuades friends to complain to the store manager about the quality of the competitor's products. Individually, these actions are merely unethical, but together they may be an unfair method of competition under the Federal Trade Commission Act.

Misrepresentation.   Misrepresentation involves lying or hiding the truth. It may be intentional or the result of oversight. In any event, it is illegal and to be avoided. The salesperson may be viewed as a legal agent for the company and, therefore, must be particularly careful about making commitments that the company does not intend to back. For example, promising a delivery date or guaranteeing the performance of a product may create a legal commitment for the selling company. Thus, knowing the company's policies and products is important not only for effective selling, but also for legal selling.

ETHICAL RESPONSIBILITIES

If legal responsibilities seem unclear, a salesperson's ethical responsibilities may be even more so. Sometimes unethical practices are also illegal, but sometimes they are not. Business firms and their salespeople must frequently decide what constitutes ethical behavior. The following are areas in which behavior is often viewed as unethical.

UNETHICAL BEHAVIOR

To discover what unethical behavior is, we must first consider what ethical behavior is. Dictionaries can help. A look at several of them produces phrases like the following for the word "ethics": "rules or standards of a group or profession"; "moral principles"; "actions based on conscience, or a sense of right and wrong"; and "codes of behavior." Thus we might say that unethical behavior for salespeople is behavior that violates the rules or standards of a firm or selling profession, or it is behavior that goes against one's conscience.

The concept may still be difficult to grasp and apply. To help, let's look at some specific examples of what might be considered unethical behavior:

- Submitting the receipts from personal lunches in one's business expense report.
- Requesting blank receipts and filling them in for more money than was actually spent.

- Selling product samples without reporting them, and pocketing the cash.
- Bad-mouthing competitors or their products to a customer.
- Offering preferential treatment to certain customers and not to others.
- Passing off a defective product as being in perfect condition.
- Accepting a bottle of liquor or free tickets to a football game in exchange for free products.

Now, consider three general areas where salespeople have the opportunity to behave unethically: high-pressure selling, conflicts of interest, and confidential information.

HIGH-PRESSURE SELLING

This, unfortunately, is what many people think of when they think of effective selling techniques. They view selling as high-pressure practices that manipulate individuals by playing on their fears and unrealistic desires, or practices that sell customers something they do not need or cannot afford. High-pressure selling (not to be confused with factual and persuasive selling) is as unnecessary as it is undesirable. Factual and

Figure 16-4 Consumers fear salespeople because of high-pressure selling tactics. High-pressure tactics should be avoided and replaced with factual and persuasive selling.

persuasive selling will be effective with properly qualified prospects who have the need for your product and the ability to buy it.

CONFLICTS OF INTEREST

A **conflict of interest** exists when a salesperson must choose a course of action and the course of action that will benefit the salesperson most is not the one that will benefit the buyer most. Bribes and kickbacks are conflicts of interest, and even the appearance of a bribe or kickback is to be avoided. Most companies suggest that accepting things of value is unethical except for low-cost gifts and entertainment (a country ham or an appointment book as a Christmas gift, a business dinner, or tickets to a World Series game) that are commonly found in the industry. The ethical dilemma usually occurs for most salespeople when they are trying to determine when a gift is too expensive or entertainment is too lavish. Timing is also an issue: A gift received just prior or subsequent to a sale seems suspicious. Similarly, most companies suggest that offering bribes or expensive gifts is equally unethical. Bribes and kickbacks may, of course, be illegal as well.

CONFIDENTIAL INFORMATION

Salespeople are often in situations which expose them to confidential information: they know about their firm's marketing plans before they are implemented; they may be told about or allowed to observe a customer's manufacturing process or see financial records of a company; they may be exposed to confidential information at trade association meetings, during calls on customers, when changing jobs, or even in an elevator. Because they also come in contact with individuals and firms who would like to have this information, salespeople may be asked to pass this information along. In an effort to maintain or raise the ethical standard throughout the industry, more and more companies are instructing their employees not to pass along such information.

IMPROVING THE ETHICS OF SALESPEOPLE

The pressure to be unethical grows when you or your company are not doing well. It may seem that personal or corporate survival takes precedence over ethics. For this reason, and because there will always be unethical persons in any profession, it is unlikely that unethical conduct can ever be eliminated. But unethical conduct can be reduced, and the solution starts with individuals who make or influence selling-related decisions or carry them out. Reduction has at least three stages: (1) increased sensitivity, (2) development and strengthening of a personal code of ethics, and (3) more responsive, responsible interactions with other members of the sales team, customers, and competitors.

SENSITIVITY

Increased sensitivity leads the way to heightened awareness of the ethical dilemmas facing salespeople. A salesperson seeking to be ethical should identify possible ethical dilemmas and consider in advance what actions are appropriate. Salespeople should seek out and be open to the opinions of others in these matters.

CODES OF ETHICS

In developing a code of ethics, the individual should consider not only what not to do, but also what actions should be taken. To accept responsibilities is a part of ethical conduct. You owe your company certain things (loyalty and hard work, for example) and your customers other things (honest advice, good service), and if you fail to provide them, you have acted unethically.

A code of ethics may be informal—it need not be written down or framed on a wall. A code is necessary even if it is incomplete and a bit unclear. Difficulties will always exist when trying to be specific, but it should be possible, at least for the experienced salesperson, to develop guidelines for behavior by looking at many possible situations. Highlight 16-1 suggests some broad areas that might be used as a starting point for a code.

HIGHLIGHT 16-1   *Code of Ethics*

As a sales representative I have an obligation to uphold the standards of my profession;

To always conduct myself in an acceptable professional manner;

To endeavor, to the best of my ability, to serve my employer's best interest;

To realize that it is not good business to recommend a product for a purpose for which it is not suitable;

To keep myself fully informed about the latest technology in my field;

To deal fairly with my customers and prospective customers;

To render service to my customers—to serve as I sell.

In order to judge ethical implications, it may be necessary to ask questions about every course of action. Your list of questions may be different, but those that follow are worth considering:

1. Would I want someone else to act this way toward me?
2. What do I owe my company in this situation?
3. What do I owe my customers in this situation?
4. How would I explain my actions to someone else?
5. What are the long-term implications of this action?

Actions which pass the test implied by these questions are likely to be ethical. Those which do not pass the test are unethical.

RESPONSIVE, RESPONSIBLE INTERACTIONS

Salespeople don't have to stop with personal codes of ethics. They should work hard to see that their companies and industry have sound codes of ethics, too. When all salespeople act in an ethical manner, the temptation to be unethical is reduced.

SOCIAL RESPONSIBILITY

Social responsibility is a controversial topic. It includes being legal and ethical, but it is often taken to mean something more—that salespeople should consider the impact of their actions not only in a narrow context (company, competitors, customers, themselves) but also in a broader context, a social context that considers the impact of the salesperson's actions on many elements in society.

In viewing a firm's social responsibility, some suggest that the social responsibility of a firm is to make a profit for its stockholders. Viewed in a similar manner, a salesperson's social responsibility would really be an economic one—to make sales, to hold down expenses, to sell products with good gross margins. Others suggest that the enlightened self-interest of firms and their employees, including salespeople, requires that they do what they can to consider the impact of their actions on the larger environment in which they work.

Thus, what constitutes socially responsible behavior and the reasons for being socially responsible may rest on both pragmatic and more noble grounds. Pragmatically, acting in a socially responsible manner will likely minimize government intervention. More nobly, businesses and their representatives are powerful forces in society, and power implies responsibility. In either event, the salesperson can have much to say and do that will influence the way the company is perceived.

We can divide the possibilities for acting in a socially responsible manner into three categories: actions taken as a good company representative, actions taken as a good company citizen, and actions taken as a good community citizen.

THE COMPANY REPRESENTATIVE ROLE

Here we include the responsibility to avoid the possibly unethical and illegal actions mentioned previously. We also include the salesperson's responsibility to use energy resources wisely; to avoid discrimination on the basis of sex, race, or age; and to build good public relations for the company.

THE COMPANY CITIZEN ROLE

As a salesperson, you must also take a look at your company's policies and practices. Those that are socially irresponsible should not be ignored if there is a chance to improve them. This does not mean that you should become a reformer to the detriment of fulfilling your selling responsibilities to the firm. But it does mean that you should use appropriate opportunities to raise the sensitivities of your colleagues, to question socially irresponsible policies, and to suggest ways to improve them, such as biodegradable packaging or encouraging the hiring of minorities as sales representatives.

THE COMMUNITY CITIZEN ROLE

Last, but certainly not least, is the role that the salesperson plays in community organizations, such as civic clubs, political groups, and community service organizations. Activity in these organizations may not be a requirement of the job, but this activity does affect the image others have of salespeople and the companies they represent.

SUMMARY

Salespeople must be aware of the laws that apply to their activities. They should assume a high level of ethical responsibility to their customers, company, and themselves.

The Sherman and Clayton acts, the Federal Trade Commission Act, and the Robinson-Patman Act outlaw activities designed to restrain trade, including price fixing, deceptive practices, exclusive dealing, and price discrimination. To reduce the risk of breaking one of these laws, the salesperson should avoid exchanging price information with competitors, pricing to harm a competitor, quoting different prices to different customers, and offering or accepting bribes.

High-pressure selling, conflicts of interest, and passing along confidential information are all considered unethical practices. The pressure to be unethical is strongest when personal or corporate survival is at stake. The salesperson also holds a social responsibility to represent and be a part of the company, as well as in being a part of the community.

KEY TERMS

restraint of trade	predatory pricing
price fixing	discriminatory pricing
exclusive dealing	quantity discounts
tying arrangements	bribes
Federal Trade Commission	kickbacks
price discrimination	disparagement
Green River Ordinances	harassment
cooling-off period	misrepresentation
truth-in-lending legislation	conflict of interest

REVIEW QUESTIONS

1. What should salespeople do if they are in doubt about the legality of a certain action?
2. What law is the oldest of the antitrust laws?
3. How did the Clayton Act clarify the Sherman Act?
4. What law was passed to outlaw price discrimination?
5. How does the Uniform Commercial Code affect the salesperson?
6. How can a salesperson avoid charges of price-fixing?
7. What is predatory pricing?
8. List several circumstances in which different prices may be justified.
9. Define unethical behavior.
10. What steps can salespeople take to reduce unethical behavior?
11. List five questions that can be used to test whether a course of action is ethical.
12. What roles can a salesperson play in order to be socially responsible?

DISCUSSION QUESTIONS

1. Make a chart of the federal laws that affect salespeople, and identify the actions they restrict or prohibit.
2. Assume that you are a sales representative at a trade show. A customer offers you a $10 bill for an $11.95 product. What is your responsibility as a salesperson to your company? To yourself? To the customer?

3. Would a code of ethics for an insurance sales agent be different from a code for a retailer or an industrial sales representative? Give reasons for your opinion.
4. What do you think are the social responsibilities of a salesperson?

CASE 16-1   REED APPLIANCES*

Reed Appliances is a locally owned specialty retailer dealing in major kitchen appliances and home entertainment equipment. Until recently most customers were walk-in traffic. Due to an increase in media advertising, however, approximately 25 percent of all orders are now taken over the telephone. In the past, only about 10 percent of Reed's appliance sales were conducted over the telephone.

Jerry Weeks has been working with Reed Appliances as a salesperson for three months. His job involves retail sales of appliances to the general public. He is quite happy with his sales record and has been meeting or exceeding his weekly sales goals. Tara Clinton, general sales manager for Reed also has commented favorably on Jerry's progress. Yesterday, however, Ms. Clinton called Jerry into her office and said that Jerry needed to put more effort into selling service contracts to his customers.

These contracts extend the warranty of the products beyond the normal six-month guarantee offered by many manufacturers of major appliances. Ms. Clinton noted that all salespeople were expected to sell extended warranties to approximately 30 percent of their customers. Revenue from these contracts helps offset the costs of maintaining a service department.

At present, Jerry gets only about 15 percent of his customers to include the extended warranty in their purchases. His customers often say that if the product is so poor that it requires an additional warranty then they probably should not buy it. In response to comments of this type, Jerry assures them the product is of the best quality but that the service contract provides additional security to the consumer. If they say that the extra protection is not needed, he drops the subject and continues to write up the sale.

Jerry agrees with Clinton that he needs to promote the service contracts more aggressively but is unsure how. He has personally never bought one on a major appliance and does not necessarily believe in them. Seeking guidance in the matter, he asks Jane Britt. Britt has been the leading appliance salesperson for Reed each of the last two years. She also leads in percentages of service contracts with over 45 percent of her customers choosing to purchase an extended warranty.

---

*Case prepared by Jim Boles. Used with permission.

Jerry finds that Jane has an easy solution to his problem. "Jerry, it's easy to sell the contracts," says Britt. "You just include them in each phone order."

Jerry is puzzled by Jane's statement. "How do you get the customer to agree to the contract over the phone? I think that selling the extended warranty over the phone is more difficult than in person."

Britt chuckles and responds, "Who said anything about selling it? I just automatically include it. If the customer gets upset when the bill comes in, I just apologize and tell them that so many people buy the service contract that I assumed they wanted it as well.

"You would be amazed," Britt continued, "how many people never realize that it is included in their billing. If you need to improve your sales levels on the service contracts, that is the easiest way, and it probably helps the customer in the long run. If anything goes wrong with the product during the first two years, it gets repaired for free."

Jerry agrees that it is a good idea to help the customer and moves away to assist a customer looking at washing machines.

CASE QUESTIONS

1. What should Jerry do to increase his sales of service contracts?
2. What do you think about Jane Britt's idea for helping Jerry meet his service contract quota? Is it good for business in the short run? In the long run?
3. In Jerry's place, what would you do?
4. Is there anything illegal about Britt's approach? Do you think some salespeople would agree that this is a good method to reach a goal?
5. Jerry doesn't believe in buying service contracts himself. How strongly should he recommend them to his customers?

CASE 16-2   RIVER CITY FLEET TIRE SERVICE*

River City Fleet Tire Service is located in Memphis, Tennessee. Because of its central location in the mid-South and the intersection there of several interstate highways, Memphis is a major transportation and distribution center. Several interstate trucking firms are headquartered or have maintenance facilities in the area. River City Fleet Tire Service manufactures retreaded truck tires for large, 18-wheeler trucks.

Tires are a major investment for trucking firms. A set of 18 tires for one truck can cost five to six thousand dollars. Assuming normal usage, a truck may use several sets of tires per year. To minimize the expenses

---

*Case prepared by K. Randall Russ. Used with permission.

associated with buying new sets of tires each time the tread wears out, trucking firms often recycle the old tires by having them retreaded. This can be done for approximately $100 per tire versus $300 for a new tire. As long as the sidewalls and other parts of the "casing," or worn tire, are in good condition, the tire can be retreaded. Given proper quality control during the retreading process and scheduled maintenance of the tires (i.e., maintaining proper air pressure), retreads provide the same amount of mileage as the original new tire. So for a fleet of several hundred trucks the annual savings from buying retreads can be quite substantial.

The market for retreaded truck tires in Memphis is quite competitive. Contracts are normally put out for bid between several suppliers. Trucking firms typically issue a single contract for several thousand retreads to one retread area. At $100 per retread, these contracts can be quite lucrative for the retread firm. Retreads covered by a given contract usually are delivered in large quantities (several hundred) and on a frequent basis. Since most suppliers of retreaded truck tires use similar manufacturing technology and produce retreads of comparable quality, the decision on which firm to use often comes down to price. The individual responsible for placing orders for retreaded tires at the trucking firm is usually the fleet maintenance manager. Companies that sell retreads normally have several field salespeople who call on the fleet maintenance manager and president of trucking firms.

Jimmy Lopez is a sales representative for River City Fleet Tire Service. Jimmy recently joined the company after working as the manager of a Firestone Tire Center located at a local shopping mall. His list of prospects includes MUDD Trucking, a large trucking firm with a fleet of 900 trucks. This is the largest account in Jimmy's territory. Having called on MUDD Trucking on three different occasions, Jimmy has gotten to know both the president, Kyle Mudd, and the fleet maintenance manager, Ralph Goode. However, Jimmy has yet to secure an order.

On his most recent trip, Jimmy was waiting for an appointment with Ralph Goode in an office near the fleet terminal area. He was looking out the window facing the loading dock area where retreaded tires are usually delivered. What he saw was quite disturbing. A truck loaded with retreaded tires from Rocky's Retreads pulled up to the dock and Ralph Goode greeted the driver with a big smile and a handshake. The driver went around to the back of the truck and unloaded a microwave oven and a shotgun. Ralph motioned to a car near the dock and gave the driver a set of keys. The driver unlocked the trunk of the car and placed the items inside. Jimmy assumed that the car belonged to Ralph Goode. Now Jimmy began to understand why he wasn't receiving any orders.

Ralph walked into the office and apologized to Jimmy for being a little late for the appointment. They went into Ralph's office and sat down. Jimmy started to talk about the quality and delivery capabilities of

River City Fleet Tire, but Ralph seemed to be uninterested and preoccupied with something else. Ralph stopped Jimmy in mid-sentence and said, "Jimmy, you know hunting season is right around the corner and Kyle has just bought a new camp down on the river which we use to entertain customers. He has put me in charge of getting all the gear we need for the season." Jimmy acted as if he didn't understand what Ralph was getting at. Ralph continued, "Kyle and I would be most pleased if you could help us out. In fact, we usually take our suppliers down there for a little fun during the season." A grin came over Ralph's face as he said, "Oh, I forgot, you're not a supplier yet! We haven't given you an order!" With that comment the phone rang, Ralph winked at Jimmy and motioned for him to go back into the waiting area. Jimmy knew what Ralph was trying to get across. To get an order from MUDD Trucking meant providing "help" in outfitting the company hunting camp. Jimmy did not know what to do. He had never faced this situation before, and to make matters worse, River City Fleet Tire Service had no formal policy to give him direction.

CASE QUESTIONS

1. What is the basic problem facing Jimmy Lopez?
2. What are Jimmy's options in this situation?
3. How should Jimmy proceed? Why?
4. What could River City Fleet Tire do to make decision making in these situations less difficult for salespeople?

PART 6

Special Types of Selling

CHAPTER 17

Selling to Organizational Buyers

After studying this chapter, you should be able to:

- Discuss the steps of the organizational buying process

- Explain how the salesperson can be influential within the organizational buying process

- Name and explain the features of organizational selling

- Describe the nature of organizational buyers

- Detail the buying patterns of purchasing agents

- Explain value analysis

- Discuss purchasing contracts and their effects on the selling process, and the salesperson

- Make suggestions about securing and opening organizational sales interviews

- Contrast selling to a group with selling to an individual

Both products and services are sold to the organizational market. The product may be an entire plant, such as a factory or warehouse; heavy equipment, such as a bulldozer or mainframe computer; light equipment, such as word processors, copiers, and hand tools; raw materials, such as cotton and tobacco; processed materials, such as flour and steel; fabricating materials, such as batteries and packages; operating supplies, such as stationery and soap; or services, such as transportation and insurance. Typically, the products are used in the manufacture of other products or in the firm's operation. They differ from consumer products more in use and buying procedures than in physical features. An organizational buyer of products and/or services usually buys for one of three groups: business firms, institutions, or governmental units. Wholesalers and retailers make up a fourth group, but mostly when purchasing operating supplies or light equipment, as opposed to purchasing merchandise for resale.

FEATURES OF ORGANIZATIONAL BUYING AND SELLING

The eight stages in the **organizational buying process** were discussed in Chapter 3. The sequence of these stages is reviewed in Figure 17-1. Recall that the first step toward an organizational buyer's purchase, as is true of any purchase, is the recognition of a need. For example, a firm may realize that it must replace obsolete machinery or expand its plant facilities. It is quite possible, however, that as many as half of all organizational purchases fill needs that were undiscovered until salespeople pointed them out.

The next step in the procurement sequence is a tentative decision on the type of product to fill the need. Sometimes the buying firm will draft **product specifications** for the product it has decided to buy. More often, though, the purchasing office will select several potential sources of supply and begin negotiations. The purchasing agent may even keep lists of approved suppliers for various products the firm buys. Negotiations begin with a discussion of the product needed, the time frame within which the product is needed and terms of delivery. Negotiation often ends when each of the suppliers submits a proposal, including the bid or price charged for the product. The buyer analyzes each proposal and may select the best one, or suppliers may be recontacted for clarification or further negotiations.

Once the source of supply has been selected and negotiations completed, the buyer issues a purchase order, making the transaction official. This process includes determining the best delivery method, the order routine, and the financial terms. Next, the goods are received, inspected for correctness, quantity, and quality, and checked into inventory. When the seller's invoice has been checked and found in order, payment is authorized and made, and the transaction is completed.

Though the transaction is complete at this point, the buyer will take note of the product and the supplier's performance through periodic evaluations. These evaluations will help the buyer determine whether future purchases of the product should be made from this supplier.

THE SALESPERSON'S ROLE IN THE ORGANIZATIONAL BUYING PROCESS

The salesperson plays a very important role throughout this process. As was noted earlier, salespeople often recognize that buyers need their product and, because they are the ones recognizing the need, they often are in a position to influence the product's definition and specification development stages.

When salespeople point out the need to the buyer, they are usually guaranteed that their company will be one of the suppliers considered.

STAGES OF THE ORGANIZATIONAL BUYING PROCESS

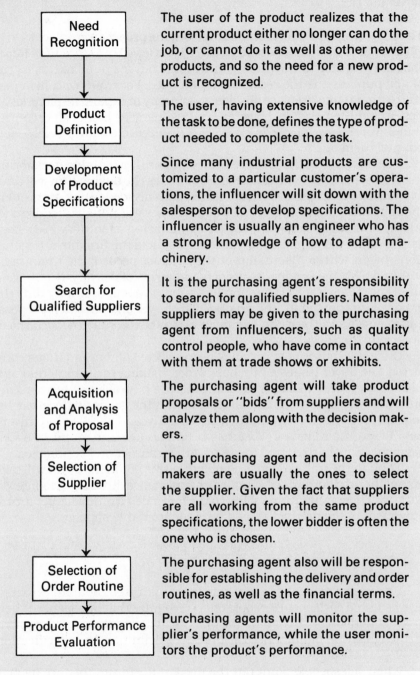

Need Recognition	The user of the product realizes that the current product either no longer can do the job, or cannot do it as well as other newer products, and so the need for a new product is recognized.
Product Definition	The user, having extensive knowledge of the task to be done, defines the type of product needed to complete the task.
Development of Product Specifications	Since many industrial products are customized to a particular customer's operations, the influencer will sit down with the salesperson to develop specifications. The influencer is usually an engineer who has a strong knowledge of how to adapt machinery.
Search for Qualified Suppliers	It is the purchasing agent's responsibility to search for qualified suppliers. Names of suppliers may be given to the purchasing agent from influencers, such as quality control people, who have come in contact with them at trade shows or exhibits.
Acquisition and Analysis of Proposal	The purchasing agent will take product proposals or "bids" from suppliers and will analyze them along with the decision makers.
Selection of Supplier	The purchasing agent and the decision makers are usually the ones to select the supplier. Given the fact that suppliers are all working from the same product specifications, the lower bidder is often the one who is chosen.
Selection of Order Routine	The purchasing agent also will be responsible for establishing the delivery and order routines, as well as the financial terms.
Product Performance Evaluation	Purchasing agents will monitor the supplier's performance, while the user monitors the product's performance.

Figure 17-1 The organizational buying process is more involved than the consumer buying process because the product being sought may have to be customized.

Good salespeople, knowing that at this point they have an "in" with this particular buyer in negotiations, should make use of questions to determine what the buyer's budget for making this purchase will be. This type of information allows the salesperson to prepare a bid within the buyer's price range and should serve to give that salesperson and her or his company an edge.

The salesperson, having prepared a very competitive bid, is now in line to make the sale. If the sale is made, the salesperson should ensure that the product is in good working condition, with all additional parts included, and is packaged and ready to be delivered on time. Once this is done the salesperson should make sure that payment is received in full.

Figure 17-2 Salespeople who help the customer recognize the need usually have an edge on the competition when the customer is selecting possible suppliers.

Finally, throughout their follow-up service, salespeople should ensure that the customer is fully satisfied with both the products and their performance.

MARKETING CHANNELS IN ORGANIZATIONAL SELLING

In the marketing of organizational products, there is much direct selling from manufacturer to user. Sometimes the product involved must be tailored to a specific buyer's needs and is bought on the buyer's specifications, thus eliminating the need for any middleman. Sometimes the buyer needs technical advice which can come only from the manufacturer of the product; sometimes a small manufacturer needs technical advice from a larger firm that will be using the product. Finally, the large amount of money involved in many organizational transactions makes direct selling the most practical.

There is, of course, some indirect selling—used mainly when the product involved is low in price, standardized, and widely used by small, geographically scattered buyers. The middlemen may be merchant middlemen, such as industrial wholesalers, or they may be agent middlemen, such as brokers, manufacturers' agents, and sales agents. Organizational middlemen operate only at the wholesale level.

THE NATURE OF THE ORGANIZATIONAL SALESPERSON'S JOB

The organizational salesperson's duties differ in several respects from those of many other salespeople, particularly those who sell merchandise to middlemen for resale and those who sell to ultimate consumers. It is common for a manufacturer of organizational products to have fewer salespeople than would a manufacturer of consumer products. Organizational salespeople make fewer calls per month than do consumer goods salespeople, and each call is longer because they usually must see several people in each company contacted. Because these individuals often are located in different departments and on different management levels, great demands are made on the salesperson's human relations abilities. The organizational salesperson is responsible for fewer buyers or accounts than is the salesperson of consumer products, and few organizational salespeople are supported by the advertising and sales promotion campaigns that stand behind many consumer products salespeople.

Organizational selling requires a high degree of creative selling, particularly when the salesperson must uncover a need or problem of which the buyer is unaware in order to sell a new product or the new use of an established product. Organizational salespeople must be competent, honest consultants to purchasing agents. A large amount of technical

HIGHLIGHT 17-1   Special Features of the Organizational Market

Certain special features of the organizational market make it different from other markets for products and services:

1. **The typical unit of sale in the organizational market is much larger, both in dollars and in units, than that in the consumer market.**
2. **Organizational demand is derived, fluctuating, and often postponable; it is much influenced by the business cycle.**
3. **Unlike consumer markets, organizational markets ignore population distribution; they may be concentrated geographically and may consist of relatively few buyers.**
4. **Purchasing agents, in contrast to ultimate consumers, are trained, professional buyers. They indulge in little or no emotional buying.**
5. **Often the purchasing agent is not the only buying influence affecting purchasing decisions, and the identification of those other individuals can be a real challenge. Selling to a group can be quite different from selling to one individual.**
6. **Some prices in organizational selling are negotiated by the buyer and vendor together. Some orders go to the lowest bidder, and often a comparison of prices can be difficult.**
7. **Brand names play a lesser role in organizational buying than in consumer buying because of purchasing on specification and on the basis of performance.**
8. **Much time may elapse between a salesperson's first call on an organizational buyer and the first sale to that buyer. In some cases, salespeople must first convince the buyer to allow them to survey the buyer's operations before purchasing recommendations can be made.**

information about their own products or services as well as about the requirements of customers also is needed.

Organizational salespeople need accurate and complete information about the products and services they are selling, and must be able to make effective comparisons with their competitors' products and services. In addition, they must be well acquainted with their own company's background, position in the industry, and all issues affecting buyers. The nature of the **vendor company** is an important factor in purchasing agents' buying decisions.

Figure 17-3 The relationship between organizational buyer and supplier is usually a long one with both parties being dependent on each other. The salesperson would be wise to be cordial, trustworthy, and as helpful as possible.

THE NATURE OF ORGANIZATIONAL BUYERS

Organizational salespeople locate customers in several ways. Sometimes a buyer directs an inquiry about some specific product to that product's manufacturer or to its salesperson. The buyer's communication is occasionally nothing more than a description of a problem on which assistance is needed. Sometimes satisfied customers refer salespeople to prospects who later become customers, and often satisfied customers are good prospects for other products the salesperson handles. These sources, however, must be supplemented by what is probably the greatest customer-producing activity of all: the discovery by a salesperson of a need, a problem, or a use for which the product represented can be successfully recommended.

BUYER INFORMATION NEEDED

Organizational salespeople are under pressure to know as much as they possibly can about the operations of their prospect's company. They benefit from knowing what goals that company seeks to attain and what plans and problems are involved in reaching them. Because the product they sell must contribute to or sometimes become a component part of what the purchasing agent's firm sells, they must acquaint themselves with a prospect company's marketing efforts as well as with its production efforts.

Salespeople need to know the size of a prospect's company, its financial standing, and the location of its plants and buying offices. Knowledge of purchasing policies, procedures, and personnel also is valuable: how the company buys, who does the buying, who influences the buying, when and where key people can be seen, and what their backgrounds are. Before making a sale, salespeople must learn what the prospect currently does about the problem which the salesperson's product can solve. This influences what the buyer thinks about the salesperson's particular product and competing products.

What sources of buyer information are useful to organizational salespeople? A study of the buyer's end product—done perhaps by the research staff of the salesperson's company—can be revealing, especially to sellers of raw materials and fabricating parts. If retailers handle that end product, their opinions can be helpful, and advertising for the end product can also supply useful information. Sometimes firms related in some way to the buying company can contribute to the organizational salesperson's information about a buyer. So can noncompeting salespeople.

A particular problem is caused by the presence of a need in the buyer's company that is unrecognized by the buyer, or a need existing in a department not visited by the salesperson. This suggests that the salesperson would benefit from a tour of the buyer's facilities. Talks with production personnel might reveal an impending product or plant change, production improvements needed, or troublesome problems. By examining, listening, and questioning, salespeople often can identify specific requirements which might lead to sales.

BUYING INFLUENCES

Buying influences are those people in the buying firm whose attitudes carry some weight in the firm's buying decisions. These buying influences range from users and operators all the way through top management. The purchasing agent usually issues the purchase orders and generally wields a great deal of power in buying decisions, but there are others in the company whose influence is felt. For example, a salesperson selling plastics would want the approval of people in design, research, production, and sales, as well as those in purchasing; someone selling a new packaging material would get involved with the product development, sales, advertising, production, legal, customer service, and purchasing departments. Quite often, depending on the size of both the purchasing firm and the purchase, members of top management participate in the decision; in many companies they are a more powerful buying influence than the purchasing agent.

It is important for salespeople to find out the names and titles of the buying influences who can help or hurt their causes. This is not always easy, however, because of the continuous changing which takes place among the buying influences within the company. People are promoted and transferred; their titles and duties change; they join other firms; they retire; they die. It is quite possible that less than 50 percent of key buying influences stay put throughout one year. Another complication stems from the fact that a job title—plant engineer, for example—does not mean the same thing from company to company. In fact, a person's name and title are only a start—ideally, the salesperson also would like to know the interests and motives of all the buying influences and the best ways to cultivate them.

Sometimes a team, a **buying group**, or a committee is set up to make a large purchase. Getting in touch with each member is not easy, especially if all members are not in the same locality. The same is true for operating and technical advisors, whom organizational salespeople may never see at all. If a salesperson must sell a certain number of buying influences in a company, and if, in that same company, two-thirds of all buying influences seldom or never see salespeople (and these assumptions are realistic), then we can understand why some salespeople feel they have done a very good job if they get in touch with one-third of the buying influences in the organizations they visit.

WHAT PURCHASING AGENTS BUY

Buying patterns of purchasing agents typically are based on quality, service, and price—generally in that order.

QUALITY

Unless a product is correct for the use to which the buyer will put it, it should not be purchased. In this sense, quality refers to technical suitability. Just as a superior tool can do a better job in the production process, a superior package can increase the dealer and consumer acceptance of a brand. Evaluation of quality also involves the salesperson and the salesperson's company. For example, the purchasing agent wants to deal with reputable salespeople and companies that are financially responsible.

SERVICE

Just as they must buy satisfactory products from vendors, purchasing agents must buy satisfactory service. Suppose that a particular transaction involves the purchase of heavy equipment. Prepurchase service could start with a survey of the buyer's needs. Survey findings would then be studied and, after thorough analysis, become the basis for a report and recommendations which constitute a purchasing proposal. If a purchase results, postpurchase service might consist of installation of the equipment and then lead to the training of those employees who will be using or operating the equipment. Other postsale activities could include maintenance and repairs.

Another feature of service that purchasing agents buy is dependability of supply. Organizational buyers must be able to count on a vendor's delivering exactly what was ordered when it is scheduled to be delivered. Buyers also welcome services which help them sell their finished products. Service of this sort is especially appropriate when the seller's product is an identifiable part of the buyer's end product.

PRICE

Obviously, the firm buying a salesperson's product or service is in business to sell some other product or service at a profit; and the price charged for that product or service influences the dollar volume of sales and the gross margin. Certainly, purchasing agents want to buy at low prices—at the lowest prices, under most circumstances. The qualification "under most circumstances" must be included because a purchasing agent can be too powerful in prevailing upon sellers to cut their prices. A purchasing agent who pressures a supplier to cut prices to a point where the supplier loses money on the sale almost forces the supplier to skimp on the quality of the product in the hope of breaking even. The purchasing agent also may, in effect, force the supplier to quit selling to him or her and this means a new source of supply will have to be found.

An organizational salesperson must be extremely effective in getting buyers to see that quoted prices are meaningless apart from other considerations, such as suitability of the product, quality of the product, service, and nature of buyer-vendor relations. In attempting this, many salespeople shift the buyer's attention from price and focus it on long-run cost, including costs for storing, handling, rejections, and use.

WHAT BUYERS DEMAND OF ORGANIZATIONAL SALESPEOPLE

Buyers make certain demands of organizational salespeople, and some of the more important aspects of their demands include the following:

THOROUGH PRODUCT KNOWLEDGE

Purchasing agents obtain much of their product knowledge from salespeople. Quite naturally, they come to depend on all salespeople to a degree and on some salespeople most heavily as sources of information about new products, improved products, and new uses for established products. The purchasing agent's main interest, of course, is in receiving the greatest product benefits. In this way, organizational salespeople function as product consultants and experts. If the salesperson can deliver enough product information, the purchasing agent will be able to explain and defend purchases should this become necessary.

OUTSIDE IDEAS

Because of their many diverse contacts, organizational salespeople can and should bring ideas to purchasing agents and report to them on changing conditions and new developments outside their firms—changes within their own companies, in companies which compete with their firms, and in retail stores if applicable. They can even report on what the purchasing agent's competitors are doing, provided they do not reveal anything told to them in confidence.

These outside ideas may pertain to economic conditions, pricing practices, trends within the specific industry, and even business trends in that company's market. It would not be improper for an outstanding salesperson to recommend new markets for the purchasing agent's firm, or even new products that the firm might consider producing.

ASSISTANCE ON PROBLEMS

The problem on which a salesperson works most quickly and with the greatest concern is a problem the customer has in using the product. But purchasing agents also welcome help on other problems. These problems include those which the purchasing agent may not recognize. The salesperson who is interested in buyers' problems, who acquires an intelligent understanding of them, and who takes the initiative in hunting for better solutions is particularly appreciated. Such a salesperson is always looking for cost-cutting steps that purchasing agents can take, and is always alert to see that customers receive all the service to which they are entitled. For example, the conscientious salesperson following up a customer's order involving a series of deliveries would make sure that exactly what was ordered was delivered on schedule and in the most efficient and cost-effective manner.

CONSIDERATE TREATMENT

Purchasing agents expect organizational salespeople to be thoughtful, proper, and understanding. Salespeople must understand, for example, that purchasing agents must budget their time carefully and therefore cannot engage in much general conversation at the beginning or end of sales interviews. Salespeople are expected to act properly in regard to any confidential information about competing companies; they must also avoid the impropriety of offering purchasing agents substantial gifts, lavish entertainment, or expensive favors. Salespeople should be informed about the needs, personnel, procedures, and concerns of the purchasing agent's company; this includes going through the proper channels in contacting buying influences. Most purchasing agents expect salespeople to get in touch first with purchasing office personnel. Contacts with production and engineering personnel, or any other company personnel, can then be made through the purchasing agent.

SECURING AND OPENING ORGANIZATIONAL SALES CALLS

Most purchasing agents are readily accessible to those salespeople who deserve to see them. It is not uncommon for a purchasing agent to contact two or three salespeople when searching for a source of supply for a soon-to-be-made purchase. Many organizational sales calls are made on an appointment basis. Both letters and telephone calls are used to make appointments. The letters can be sent by the salesperson or by the salesperson's company. Sometimes a salesperson can schedule the next call when leaving an interview, and sometimes appointments can be arranged at trade shows. Appointments are particularly appropriate if the salesperson's presentation is long, if he or she calls on others in the purchasing agent's company, or if the purchasing agent involved prefers scheduling calls by appointment.

Unless the salesperson and the purchasing agent have known each other for some time, the salesperson should open the presentation with personal and company identification. The salesperson should do this in successive calls on the same purchasing agent, remembering that that individual may have seen scores of salespeople since their last meeting. From that point, the organizational salesperson conducts the sales call in a fashion similar to that of any other salesperson. When the salesperson knows the buyer is not ready to buy, the presentation may be opened with information helpful to the buyer or with questioning the salesperson intends to develop in a way that will benefit the agent and the agent's company.

Frequently, the first call an organizational salesperson makes on a prospective customer is not opened by an attempt to sell a product. Instead, the objective is to sell the buyer on giving the salesperson permission to make a survey of the buyer's circumstances. A life insurance salesperson might offer to examine the policies held by a company; a point-of-sale terminal salesperson might offer to study how cash sales, credit sales, payments on accounts receivable, and payouts are currently being handled in a retail store. Usually the survey is free and does not obligate the prospective customer. Occasionally the buyer will help defray the costs of the survey.

The purpose of the survey is to obtain current, correct, and complete information about the buyer. Salespeople must be particularly alert to spot any problem for which their products or services will be solutions. They want to determine whether buyers can make advantageous use of their products and, if so, exactly how the buyers can use the products.

While the survey is being made, the salesperson may draw on the personnel and facilities from his or her own company, particularly if the survey is extensive and quite technical. In addition, the salesperson usually works with people other than purchasing personnel in the buyer's organization because their participation in the survey may be mandatory.

Once the survey has been completed, its findings are analyzed and then interpreted. If the buyer has no problem requiring action, there is no second step in that particular instance. Most of the time, survey findings constitute a sound foundation for a sales presentation. By knowing how things stand, the salesperson can make an effective comparison between present conditions and better conditions which will exist once the buyer has followed the salesperson's recommendations. The next step, then, is selling the proposal to the buyer.

ORGANIZATIONAL DECISION-MAKING TECHNIQUES

Having secured and opened a sales call, the salesperson needs to be familiar with some of the organizational decision-making techniques used by many companies. Two of the most common are discussed below.

VALUE ANALYSIS

Value analysis, pioneered by the General Electric Company, is a problem-solving technique for reducing unnecessary costs without decreasing a product's usefulness, appeal, or sales. Value analysis (VA) is a systematic analysis and evaluation of products and their component parts to see if changes in design, materials, or construction will reduce the cost without damaging the performance of a product. Basic assumptions of VA are: (1) a high-priced product may be the best value, and (2) a low-priced product may not be the best value.

VA is done by a team usually headed and coordinated by the purchasing agent, who frequently must sell the idea of VA to people in other departments. Other members of the team may include the executives heading engineering, research and development, production, and sales.

If the firm is to maintain and even increase a product's utility while decreasing its selling price, it must ask questions, accumulate existing information, brainstorm for worthwhile ideas, settle on one course of action, execute that program, then evaluate the results. Sample questions are:

1. Just what jobs does this product and each of its component parts do? Does it have any unneeded features?

2. Can we combine several parts into one and, in this way, reduce assembly cost?
3. Which special component parts now specified can be replaced with standard parts?
4. Should we switch from making a part to buying it or vice versa?

Most organizational salespeople must understand the basics of value analysis and be able to deal with purchasing agents who use it. Such buyers are always asking salespeople how costs can be reduced—and expecting salespeople to have suggestions. When creative, imaginative salespeople build into their presentations helpful answers to VA questions, the rewards can be great.

PURCHASING CONTRACTS

One common buying technique employed by organizations is the **purchasing contract**. Purchasing contracts are used with products that are purchased often and in high volume. In essence, the purchasing contract allows the buyer to routinize the decision on this particular product, while promising the salesperson a sure sale. Thus, the advantage of purchasing contracts to the buyer is a quick, confident decision, and to the salesperson, reduced or eliminated competition.

Figure 17-4 The purchasing agent uses value analysis much in the same way a consumer would comparatively shop in order to get the best deal.

The two most common forms of purchasing contracts are the **annual purchasing contract** and the **blanket purchasing contract**. The annual contract provides a discount schedule for purchases over the period of the contract. The company's purchases are accumulated during the year. The more the company buys throughout the year, the greater the discount it receives.

The blanket contract, on the other hand, engages the supplier to provide "X" amount of product each month through the course of a year at one set price. Each year the contract and the price are renegotiated.

SELLING TO A GROUP

Many organizational sales presentations are made to groups of individuals who constitute a buying committee. Most sales presentations to a group start with the salesperson's making the presentation to one person—a presentation designed to get that person to approve and schedule a meeting between the salesperson and the group. A four-member group might consist of the vice-president for production, the general superintendent, the general supervisor, and the purchasing agent. In some ways, the group behaves as a unit; but at the same time, each member is an individual buying influence.

Figure 17-5 Selling to a group of decision-makers at one time is not unusual in organizational selling.

Presentations to groups are made in various places. Most are made in a conference room or an office at the buyer's location. But sometimes the seller designs an event in order to accommodate the buying influences and provide for product displays and demonstrations.

GENERAL SUGGESTIONS FOR GROUP SELLING

Let us examine how a typical organizational salesperson might go about the task of selling to a buying group. Before meeting with the group the salesperson would like to do a preapproach on each member of the group to determine needs, preferences, prejudices, plans, and interests, and to discover what each member likes and dislikes about this product and competing products. If there is one person who is clearly a leader (and this is typical of most groups), the salesperson may be wise to try to see that person before the group meets in the hopes of making an ally ahead of time.

The salesperson then goes about preparing the presentation. As the sales story is drafted, advantages and proof are stressed and backed up with appropriate visual aids. Organizational salespeople have found the following visual aids to be particularly effective: samples, models, sketches, slides, photographs, movies, testimonials, advertisements, and performance records. Thorough rehearsal of the sales story and the use of visual aids is strongly recommended.

The final plan can then be drawn. The salesperson knows what will be needed in a physical way and assembles these items. The salesperson lists the questions and the most probable objections, with answers for each, and sets up in order the steps or phases of the presentation. Finally, each step or phase of the presentation is clocked and a timetable is established.

Once the presentation starts, the well-rehearsed salesperson should maintain almost continuous eye contact with the group, watching facial expressions and movements in order to sense reactions. If at all practicable, the salesperson can encourage members of the group to interrupt with comments and questions, once again alert to developments. Seldom, however, should the salesperson ask for agreement as when selling to an individual. Nor should one benefit be stressed too much, because the various buying influences comprising the group have different interests and operate under different pressures. Benefits should be fully explained and presented in a thorough manner.

During the presentation, the organizational salesperson has a difficult job in respect to the leader of the group. The salesperson wants to win the leader, but at the same time, no other member of the group should be given cause to feel slighted. The salesperson hopes to appear impartial even while referring and deferring more to the leader than to any other member. Salespeople should remember that the leader often can be influenced—even won over—by the rest of the group.

When responding to one group member's question, comment, or objection, the salesperson must answer in a manner which includes other members. This helps all members feel that they have a part in shaping the ultimate decision. The salesperson tries to avoid arguments with the buying group, and among members of the buying group. Control of the session may be more easily maintained if a top official of the prospect company shares the stage with the salesperson. In some situations the salesperson will want to arrange for the members of the group to talk among themselves privately. If literature or other printed material is to be distributed, this is best done after the salesperson has made the presentation and just before the question-and-answer period, if one has been scheduled.

PROBLEMS IN GROUP SELLING

When the buying group is made up of persons from different levels of management, the salesperson faces the problem of communicating with individuals who differ in background, training, personality, and goals. Each member has a motivation pattern, which may differ from the others. A complete sales story is probably the best solution to this problem.

Another problem, as has been mentioned, is that of identifying the leader of the group. The leader may be the oldest person, the one with the most impressive title, the one who asks the best questions, the one with the most definite ideas, or the last person to join the group. Sometimes the salesperson must simply try to sense who the leader is. The leader is not always the most vocal, the most active, or the most prominent person.

Should the organizational salesperson selling to a group bring in one or more people to help make the presentation? Sometimes there is no choice: a demonstration may require more than one person, or sometimes the buying group requests the presence of an additional person. The use of a two-person selling team can offer flexibility. Salesperson A can interrupt Salesperson B, ask questions, or take over occasionally. One salesperson can take notes or just observe the group while the other is making the presentation. Of course, the selling team ought not be so large that it appears to overwhelm the buying group.

Questions directed to the salesperson before the scheduled question-and-answer period pose another problem. Premature questions should be discouraged, and any treatment of them should be brief. Closing at the end of the presentation can be awkward, also; it is normally impractical to ask an entire buying group for the order.

TEAM SELLING

The size and complexity of some projects and contemplated purchases means that several specialized departments within the firm are involved. Such projects and purchases are too big for one salesperson to undertake, too broad for one salesperson to master, too varied for one department to handle. In these situations, **team selling**, in which each member has particular interests and asks special questions, is useful.

A selling team may include technical specialists from marketing, production, purchasing, finance, and accounting. Frequently, if there is a production specialist on a buying team, that person is matched by a production specialist from the selling firm; a marketing specialist on the buying team is matched by a marketing specialist on the selling team; and so on. The captain of a selling team is an executive salesperson or sales engineer who coordinates the team and serves as a communication channel between the buying and selling teams. This person designs the selling effort and directs the presentation.

The selling team permits a strong selling effort to be made. The prospect gets a great amount of information about all the aspects of the seller's proposal from a group of experienced specialists. Analyses, solutions, and recommendations are sound, made by a balanced team of experts.

SUMMARY

Organizational markets consist of businesses, institutions, and governmental units who buy products and services. Organizational sales require extensive direct selling activities such as customizing products, providing technical expertise, and arranging for financial assistance.

The organizational buying process starts with the recognition of a need, the definition of a product and specifications, and a search for a supplier to satisfy that need. Next, the organization acquires and analyzes a proposal before selecting a supplier. Finally, the company settles on a delivery method, order routine, and financial terms which are ultimately evaluated along with product performance.

Organizational selling differs from other selling in that sales staffs are smaller, and they make fewer but more lengthy sales calls which require more creativity and information. Purchasing agents are the organizations' buyers; however, there are many others in the organization who influence the decision, from users and operators through top management. Purchasing agents use value analysis and purchasing contracts to ease their decision-making duties.

Salespeople are required to make appointments for organizational sales calls, which are usually held at the buyer's place of business. Sometimes, the salesperson must make presentations to buying committees consisting of several individuals. It is important that the salesperson give special attention not only to the leader, but to all of the committee's members.

KEY TERMS

organizational buying process	value analysis
product specifications	purchasing contract
vendor company	annual purchasing contract
buying influences	blanket purchasing contract
buying group	team selling

REVIEW QUESTIONS

1. What groups make up organizational buyers?
2. Why is there direct selling to organizational buyers?
3. List the stages of the organizational buying process.
4. List three special features of organizational buyers.
5. How do the duties of an organizational salesperson differ from those of most other salespeople?
6. What kinds of information should organizational salespeople have?
7. What is a buying influence?
8. What is value analysis?
9. What are some difficulties often encountered in selling to groups?
10. When is team selling likely to be necessary?
11. What are some advantages of team selling?

DISCUSSION QUESTIONS

1. Compare the benefits that you would use to sell a purchasing agent a telephone system with those used to sell a store manager on carrying your brand of cheese-flavored popcorn.
2. Are the interpersonal skill requirements higher for a salesperson selling to a group than are the requirements of one selling to a single buyer?
3. Why must organizational salespeople be expert problem solvers?
4. React to the following statement: "Because organizational demand is derived and postponable and there may be hidden buying influences, the organizational salesperson has less control of the factors that lead to sales than does a salesperson selling to wholesalers or retailers."
5. Assume that you are an organizational salesperson selling cardboard cartons to a large printing firm. What information should you research before making your first sales call, and what information would you gather in the first sales call?

CASE 17-1 ALPHA BUSINESS SYSTEMS*

Alpha Business Systems, Inc., was an authorized Canon copier dealer with its main headquarters located in Orlando, Florida. It had grown rapidly since its inception in 1976 through a strategy of strong personal selling and emphasis on the Canon name. The company's marketing decisions were controlled by Fred Cady, the marketing director, and Emi Dolan, the president. With the 1991-92 fiscal year (which begins in July) approaching, the two principals found themselves assessing the Central Florida market situation and the company's promotion needs for the coming year.

The geographic boundaries of the market corresponded roughly to the Orlando Metro Area (Metropolitan Statistical Area), which includes Orange, Seminole, and Osceola Counties, as well as Volusia County (Daytona Beach) and Brevard County (Cocoa Beach and Melbourne). The area had experienced rapid economic growth from 1970-1991, initially as a result of tourism anchored by Disney World, but more recently in the form of light industry, construction, retailing, banking, high-tech firms, government contractors, and a wide array of other medium- and small-sized enterprises.

The extremely rapid growth of the area had fostered some unique marketing circumstances. For instance, municipal building regulations had caused the downtown area to become a mixture of mostly high-rise financial services office buildings and original architecture refurbishments. Numerous suburban communities had become commercial centers networked and partially linked with a system of congested highways, including Interstate 4, running north-south, and the Orlando Expressway, running east-west. Morning and afternoon traffic invariably clogged all major highways as business commuters sought to move to and from their places of work.

Orlando acted as a magnet to new businesses and a professional work force, drawing national headquarters relocations and a wide cross-section of branch offices seeking tax benefits, life-style gains, and growth opportunities stemming from the rapid expansion of the population and economy. The special situation was both a blessing and a bane to Alpha. It insured constant growth in the need for copy machines while, at the same time, bringing an ever-changing set of prospects who were unfamiliar with Alpha and attracting a growing list of competitors.

Alpha was a sales-oriented company that had built its success on a young, eager sales force. Salespeople were expected to push aggressively the firm's products, usually with a mix of appointments and cold calls, and would sometimes join forces to "blitz" local office buildings. They were paid on a straight commission basis. Commissions were set as a

---

*Case prepared by Alvin C. Burns. Used with permission.

percentage of gross margin, with the individual salesperson given some leeway in negotiating prices. Although a number of salespeople earned in excess of $50,000 per year, turnover among the sales force was fairly high. Alpha provided the sales force with little formal training. They did provide a variety of promotional support materials and sales leads generated through a direct mail campaign.

The company sold a line of twelve copiers, ranging in quality, price, and features from the most basic to the top of the line. Alpha had also recently added a line of facsimile equipment. About 60 percent of company revenues came from servicing copiers after they were sold, as well as from parts and supplies. Alpha offered customers a number of different service contract options, and paid salespeople a commission when they sold one of these contracts.

The basic sales philosophy at Alpha was that "everybody's a customer." The firm had made sales to a wide cross-section of organizations in Central Florida, including hospitals, insurance agencies, hotels, law firms, schools, municipal government offices, retailers, construction companies, and many more. No formal attempt had been made to track customer sales patterns, and only recently was a program instituted to coordinate copier sales with service sales.

The copier market in Central Florida was dominated by one competitor, Copymasters, Inc., which was estimated to have almost a 50 percent market share compared to 25 percent for Alpha. Cady and Dolan were uncertain of why Copymasters was the dominant company. In their analysis both companies offered equivalent copy machines at competitive prices. In fact, Alpha offered more support services to customers than did Copymasters. Both had been in business for about 12 years. Mr. Cady claimed that much of the difference was due to Copymasters' radio advertising campaigns, which were launched four years ago and continued to be an important part of its promotional mix.

Alpha historically had adopted a different promotional strategy. To support the personal selling effort, which relied on referrals and cold calls, Alpha had invested heavily in billboard advertising all across the five counties comprising Central Florida.

Cady and Dolan agreed on the overall marketing objective for 1990-91 to increase market share from its current level of 25 percent to at least 30 percent. They disagreed, however, on the advertising objectives and strategy. Dolan contended that the billboard advertising had been successful in creating Alpha's name recognition and should remain the mainstay of the 1990-91 strategy. Her rationale was based on the heavy commuter traffic patterns in Orlando and the obvious high exposure value of strategically placed outdoor ads. Cady, on the other hand, felt that Copymasters' radio advertising should be a model, since they had come to dominate the market. The advertising could have more impact, in his opinion, especially if a catchy jingle were used. He also felt radio would be useful in generating sales leads, especially if the ads emphasized Alpha's toll-free and local telephone numbers.

Both agreed that it was time to invest in some marketing research in order to gain a better perspective on what was happening in the copier industry, and specifically to Alpha and Copymasters. They contacted a local marketing research company for assistance. After a series of meetings, Dolan, Cady, and the marketing research company came to agreement on precisely what information would be useful. The research objectives were finalized as follows: (1) to determine the relative effectiveness of different media in creating copier dealer name awareness; (2) to determine the present level of awareness of various copy machine vendors in the area; (3) to determine prospects' copier needs for the next year; and (4) to determine prospective customers' buying behavior characteristics.

The survey method involved the design of a telephone questionnaire which was administered to 500 companies randomly selected from a master list of about 6000 company names in Central Florida. This sample frame was purchased from a listing service. Interviews were conducted with the "person who makes the copier machine purchase or lease decisions" in the company.

The final report contained many tables and figures summarizing the findings, but Cady and Dolan agreed that a few tables succinctly related to the basic questions addressed. Selected findings are presented in the table below.

Cady and Dolan began to analyze these particular findings by calculating a "recognition factor," consisting of the percent of respondents mentioning that Alpha appeared in the advertisements they saw minus the percent who mentioned any copier company.

Once they had a chance to review the marketing research results carefully, Dolan and Cady prepared the advertising campaign and budget for next year. They decided to retain the same amount of billboard space, but to triple the amount of radio advertising. They also decided to buy a full page of the Yellow Pages instead of the single line listing they

EXHIBIT 17-1
RECALL OF LOCAL COPIER COMPANY ADVERTISING

Medium Mentioned	Percent Mentioning Any Company	Alpha	Recognition Factor
Radio	69%	59%	–10%
Direct Mail	55%	22%	_____
Sales Call	52%	28%	_____
Television	43%	11%	_____
Word of Mouth	30%	9%	_____
Yellow Pages	28%	7%	_____
Billboards	11%	4%	_____
Newspaper	5%	11%	_____
Magazine	5%	2%	_____

had used in the past. Finally, they agreed to hire the services of a telemarketing company which would make calls to all prospective clients in the Greater Orlando area during the first quarter of the year. Leads generated from this effort would be turned over to the sales force to follow up.

CASE QUESTIONS

1. Using Lotus, complete the "recognition factor" column in the table that Cady and Dolan started. What are the implications of these results for their advertising strategy?
2. Assess the relative effectiveness of the promotional strategies, both advertising and sales force, for Copymasters and Alpha Business Systems.
3. What changes in personal selling strategy should Dolan and Cady make so it will complement the advertising campaign and be more effective over the next year?

CASE 17-2   EPI TECHNOLOGY*

"I can't believe we lost another order at Olivetti Digital Systems," exclaimed Donna Stallings. "It's just not fair. We had the competition beat!" Donna Stallings is a salesperson for EPI Technology, a manufacturer of electronic circuit board assemblies for computers and other electronic equipment. Circuit board assemblies are the primary component in most electronics. Thus, EPI's quality and reliability of delivery on new boards, as well as speed of service on defective assemblies, is critical to their customers.

EPI Technology, founded by several electrical engineers, has been in business for three years in the Dallas-Fort Worth area. EPI Technology markets its products nationwide, mainly in areas with high concentrations of electronics companies. The company is an upstart in the marketplace and employs young, aggressive personnel in all areas: engineering, production, and sales. Donna started with the company as a customer service representative after receiving her Associate of Arts degree from a community college. She initially handled customer inquiries concerning the status of orders and price quoting over the telephone. Recently, Donna was promoted to outside sales and given the Dallas-Fort Worth territory.

The competition in her territory consists of four other firms, each of which has been in business longer than ten years. One firm in particular, Control and Information Systems, Inc. (CIS), has served the local market for over fifteen years. CIS has developed solid long-term relationships with many of EPI Technology's potential customers. Donna previously quoted against Control and Information Systems on several orders and

*Case prepared by K. Randall Russ. Used with permission.

knows that CIS is the firm to whom she lost this most recent order at Olivetti Digital Systems. Olivetti is one of the largest users of printed circuit board assemblies in Donna's territory, but she has yet to "crack" the account.

Donna enters the office of Paul Carnaggio, the sales manager for EPI Technology and blurts out, "CIS never has the lowest price, yet they have won every order from Olivetti that we have bid on. I just can't take this any more! I'm going to call the purchasing manager to find out what's going on!"

Prior to calling Ms. Johnson, the purchasing manager at Olivetti, Donna recalls the day she made the sales presentation which detailed EPI Technology's approach to supplying the computer boards for the new Olivetti personal computer. She remembered that the buyer and Ms. Johnson, in addition to the managers of engineering, production, finance, and quality assurance, were all in attendance at the meeting. Donna had never met any of them. She had only dealt with Ms. Johnson and the buyer on the project. She recalled that all the managers were much older than she, so she assumed they had been around the electronics industry for some time. Each manager was favorably impressed with EPI Technology's modern plant, young, well-trained personnel, rapid growth, and impressive client list. However, they didn't give her the order. Losing a $1.5 million sale really hurt both the company and Donna's ego.

Donna picked up the phone and dialed the number for the purchasing department at Olivetti. "Hello, Ms. Johnson? This is Donna Stallings with EPI Technology," said Donna. Ms. Johnson replied, "Hello, Donna, how's it going? I guess Jill Bostick, the buyer for the PC project, informed you that you guys missed this one." Donna was trying to keep her cool as she remarked, "That's the reason for my call. We at EPI just can't understand why we keep losing orders. Jill mentioned to me that we had the lowest price." "I know," said Ms. Johnson, "but you need to understand that we all took a vote on this one, it was such a large order. None of us wanted to go out on a limb. Actually, Donna, the vote was split three for CIS and two for EPI Technology. After we discussed this thing all afternoon we decided to stay with CIS. We wish you all the luck next time and hope that we can do business in the future." As Donna hung up the phone she still could not understand why the order was lost.

CASE QUESTIONS

1. If you were Paul Carnaggio, Donna's boss, what reasons could you give for losing the sale?
2. Is there anything that you feel Donna could have done to salvage this order?
3. What steps could Donna take in the future to try to get that first order from Olivetti?

CHAPTER 18
Selling to Ultimate Consumers

After studying this chapter, you should be able to:

- List the duties and responsibilities of retail salespeople
- Classify and comment on the information needed by retail salespeople
- Trace the steps in retail selling
- Compare trading up, substitute selling, and suggestion selling
- Make suggestions about postsale behavior
- Show how retail salespeople can build sound customer relationships

THE NATURE OF RETAIL SELLING

Although the fundamentals of selling are universal, the job of selling in retail stores differs from other kinds of selling in several respects, as shown in Figure 18-1. In retail selling, potential buyers come to the salesperson. These buyers are thus physically, financially, and emotionally closer to buying than are most of the buyers contacted by other kinds of salespeople. Buyer attention and buyer interest in some type of merchandise are strong enough to have motivated the person to visit a particular store. Even though retail customers are not usually so well

CHARACTERISTICS OF RETAIL SELLING

- Buyers come to the seller (retail outlet).
- Buyers are more attentive and interested because they sought the outlet.
- Salespeople are responsible for a wider variety of products.
- Greater number of buyers.
- Salespeople do very little prospecting.

Figure 18-1 The job of selling in retail stores differs from other kinds of selling.

informed as the buyers organizational salespeople visit, they generally know something about the store they choose to visit, about the merchandise they are seeking, and perhaps even about the salespeople themselves.

The retail salesperson is typically responsible for selling a wider variety of products than is the organizational salesperson. The number of buyers encountered is also considerably greater. Yet, the retail salesperson does not have the organizational salesperson's range of choices of when, where, and to whom to sell. Retail salespeople also do little prospecting for customers, unlike organizational salespeople. Instead, their stores' advertising, displays, and reputations draw people in.

Customers judge a store largely by its sales staff, and the customer who makes a purchase is really buying a package comprised of product, salesperson, retailer, manufacturer, and follow-up service. The customer is the person most dependent on the retail salesperson, but the retailer is dependent to a great degree on that same salesperson. Wholesalers, manufacturers, and facilitating firms are also quite dependent upon retailers' sales forces. Most of their merchandising efforts mean little unless retail salespeople succeed in their selling efforts.

DUTIES OF RETAIL SALESPEOPLE

Retail salespeople have three principal types of duties or responsibilities. The most important, obviously, is the duty to sell (**selling duties**). Salespeople sell merchandise to the mutual benefit of the customer and the store, and this includes writing up sales slips, wrapping merchandise, operating point-of-sale terminals, verifying and executing credit card sales, and making change. Satisfactory performance in this area depends on the salesperson's knowledge of the merchandise, customers, selling techniques, and store procedures.

Retail salespeople have various **nonselling duties**. Some receive and mark incoming merchandise and participate in taking inventory. Most are responsible for getting their departments ready for the selling day and closing them at closing time. They make sure their department stock is adequate and neat. Some build counter, floor, or window displays. A few compare merchandise in competing stores. Senior salespeople may act as sponsors and trainers for new employees. Other nonselling duties involve customer service, which often includes giving merchandise instructions to the buyer, helping the customer when a purchased item needs servicing, handling customer complaints, handling merchandise exchanges or returns, and giving directions to customers within the store.

Finally, salespeople have certain responsibilities to their employers. They should plan ways to make a maximum contribution to the store's profitable operation; determine to minimize mistakes, waste, and expenses; make constructive suggestions and pass along customer feedback to store management; and reflect a loyalty to and a pride in the store. The job requirements and duties for a typical position in retailing are shown in Figure 18-2.

THE REWARDS OF RETAIL SELLING

Retail selling offers many rewards and opportunities for those who have the drive and determination to succeed. There are many avenues for

RETAIL JOB REQUIREMENTS AND DUTIES

Below are some typical job requirements and duties for a sales position at a high-profile department store.

Division: Apparel.
Job Title: Sales—Women's and Misses' Dresses.
Duties: (A) Sales—Sell dresses through intelligent use of size, style, and fashion information; must explain washability, cleaning requirements, advantages through certain design features which tend to enhance the customer's figure; meet objections to certain competitive stores' claims and price advertisements; be familiar with sizing by manufacturer so as to provide merchandise which will fit well with a minimum of alteration. Try to be certain when selling merchandise that the item is one that will not be returned because of a hasty decision, that the item is tried on so that the customer will have an opportunity of seeing as well as feeling the fit and style advantages.
(B) Stock—Fill in sizes as required, help keep section stock in order by replacing in proper racks and in correct size sequence items which have been shown but not sold. Assist in maintaining section orderliness, straightening chairs, picking up hangers, etc.
Previous Experience Requirements: At least six months' dress or similar selling experience.
Educational Requirements: High school minimum.
Working Hours: Regular store hours of 40 hours a week.
Overtime: None except for 48-hour weeks, 4 weeks a year.
Physical Demands: Standing, walking (to fitting rooms, stockrooms), with the usual seasonal rush pressures.
Machines and Equipment: Point-of-sale terminals, charge-card verification machines.
Method of Compensation: Straight commission with guaranteed minimum.

Figure 18-2 Many department stores offer positions in their apparel divisions.

advancement, and because the entry-level requirements are less stringent for retail selling than for other types of selling, highly motivated salespeople can rise to a management position at a relatively young age.

A career in retailing usually begins in sales. The new employee learns about the customers, their wants, and their needs first-hand through sales. This customer knowledge is vital to the employee's development in retailing because of the heavy emphasis placed on customer satisfaction, and the wide variation of customer tastes and opinions that are encountered.

Figure 18-3 shows the career path possibilities facing retail salespeople. In many companies this consists of rotating between store management and merchandising management positions. Companies en-

THE RETAIL CAREER PATH

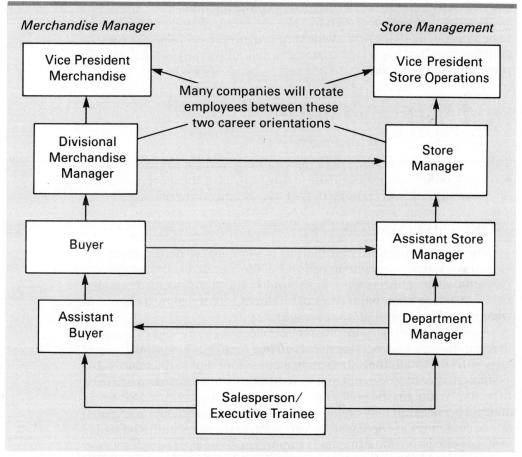

Figure 18-3 The positions available in retail sales offer employees the opportunity to manage people and store operations and to learn how to buy and incorporate new merchandise with existing stock.

courage this type of rotation because it provides employees with the opportunity to manage people and store operations, while also enabling them to learn how to buy and incorporate new merchandise with the merchandise already being offered.

Starting salaries for retail salespeople traditionally have been lower than for other types of jobs. For the trainee going into retail sales on a part-time basis while in high school, the salary is likely to be hourly and not much more than minimum wage. Because many retail companies do not require that their employees have college degrees, the salaries at other sales and lower management positions are also typically on the low side. However, if the employee is willing to sacrifice current salary for future opportunities, good financial rewards can be earned in the long run. Managers at both the merchandise and store levels can earn anywhere from $40,000 to over $100,000 a year, depending on the company, the size of the store, and the method of compensation.

Besides being rewarded financially, the retail salesperson is exposed to new products, styles, and a wide variety of people, and also receives the satisfaction of having served customers well, and of having established a professional reputation.

INFORMATION NEEDED BY RETAIL SALESPEOPLE

To be considered competent as a merchandise adviser, a retail salesperson must be knowledgeable about many aspects of the store, merchandise, and the kinds of customers that may be encountered.

STORE INFORMATION

The most important information a salesperson needs about the store relates to policies and procedures of the store. One of the more significant policies concerns the merchandise the store stocks. The salesperson needs to know what types of products are carried by the store, in what price ranges, and of what general quality.

A second basic policy involves the services the store makes available to its customers. For each service there is a small but essential group of facts without which the salesperson cannot function satisfactorily. For example, if the store does not make credit sales, the salesperson will need to be able to explain the policy and, in certain cases, justify it. Delivery is another service that may or may not be offered. Its frequency and cost, if any, to customers are necessary information to the sales staff. Knowledge of store policies on adjustments is important, too. Here the salesperson must know what the store does about refunds, exchanges, returns, and complaints. Finally, for stores selling appliances, knowledge of product service, including installation, repairs, service calls, and guarantees, is important.

A store's promotional efforts are a third important area salespeople must be familiar with. Retailers, like other sellers, combine the basic marketing strategies of personal selling, advertising, and sales promotion into what they believe will be the most profitable combination. Salespeople must understand the relationships among these three factors. In addition, they always should be aware of what items are currently being promoted and with what forms of promotion.

The fourth area of necessary information is store procedures. Knowledge of merchandise location within the store is a basic element. Another essential element is knowing how to make a charge sale, a task which calls for credit clearing and the writing of a charge slip. For cash sales, the salesperson must be able to operate the point-of-sale terminal and to make change. Finally, salespeople in some stores must be able to wrap a neat, safe package.

MERCHANDISE INFORMATION

Customers expect the sales staff of a retail store to know the merchandise the store carries. Most buyers are willing—even eager—to become better informed about merchandise, and nothing seems more natural than to look to the salesperson for answers to product questions. Many buyers go even further than that when making certain purchases, asking a salesperson for personal views, preferences, or convictions; the buyer assumes that the salesperson is an authority on merchandise.

The retail salesperson needs to know specific product facts, including the identity of the manufacturer, composition of each product, construction, finish, style, price, size, color, and model. The salesperson should also know what the product is used for, how it should be used or operated, its performance and its limitations, the care it requires, and the services, if any, available with its purchase. It is particularly important that the salesperson be able to compare a given product with its closest competitors and to highlight its various points of superiority. While the general rule is that the amount of product information needed increases as the price rises, retailers hope that each salesperson will know one or more influential facts about as many products as possible.

Several productive sources of merchandise information are available to most retail salespeople. The product's label and package can be as informative to those who sell the item as it is to those who buy. Some kinds of products—such as food, clothing, and beverages—can be tried under conditions of everyday use. Salespeople representing manufacturers and wholesalers of the product can be valuable sources of information, as can their product literature, visual aids, and any plant tours made available. Advertising is another source of product information—

the manufacturer's advertisements, those of competing manufacturers, those of competing retailers, and those of the salesperson's own store. Individuals with whom the salesperson deals are still another source. One group, prospects, can tell why they do not use the product; the other group, users, can tell why they do use it. A final major source is the buying personnel of the store. They can make available to the selling staff valuable product information such as merchandise manuals, product specifications, and results obtained from testing bureaus.

CUSTOMER INFORMATION

Retail salespeople do not have much of a prospecting job to do; their stores do the job for them. Advertising is one of the strategies used by stores to attract buyers. The store's window displays issue another invitation. They entice sidewalk or mall traffic into becoming store traffic. Inside some stores are customer services or facilities such as telephones, post offices, automatic-teller bank machines, and lounges. These bring individuals into the store, and some of those individuals become customers. A few stores that can be termed "prestige stores" are found in most large markets. They are so widely and favorably known that they pull buyers in because of their reputations. Finally, some stores are good at obtaining considerable amounts of favorable publicity that recommends, even if subtly, the store as a place to shop.

Because the retail salesperson does not know who the next customer will be, a personalized preapproach is almost impossible. Salespeople can only assume that the next customer is in a buying mood and is curious about and interested in merchandise because of some need or want. The majority of shoppers do not enter stores unless these conditions exist. The salesperson must identify customers' buying motives quickly because contacts are of short duration. Instead of a preapproach, the salesperson is forced to rely on observation and experience. It is particularly helpful for salespeople to note the treatment they get in various stores when they are buying, and to analyze their own reactions to it. This will help them to serve their customers better.

STEPS IN RETAIL SELLING

Selling in retail stores consists of several standard steps. The customer is approached and greeted. The salesperson learns what the customer needs or wants. Suitable merchandise is selected from stock, and it is then shown and described to the customer. Buyer benefits are stressed. After handling any objections, the salesperson closes the sale and attempts some suggestion selling if this seems appropriate. A sincere desire to serve—to help customers buy what they should have—is the most important factor. It is essential to retailing success, which has been described as "selling products that won't come back to customers who will."

GREETING THE CUSTOMER

Before examining particular greetings, it is well to realize that the salesperson's manner of speaking and acting is really more significant than the greeting itself. Customers demand much. They are in the store because of an invitation that, if not direct and specific, is clearly implied. Thus, customers expect salespeople to be alert and to offer quick service when they are ready to buy. If salespeople are talking to each other or concentrating on other duties, an essential customer awareness and promptness is lacking, and this reflects poorly on the store as a whole. Salespeople should always be friendly and polite, and their actions should recommend them to the customer as expert merchandise advisers whose major interest is in the customer's welfare.

When the salesperson approaches, the customer is usually either seeking assistance or looking at merchandise. In the first case, these greetings are acceptable: "May I help you?" "Are you being served?" "How do you do?" "Good morning (or afternoon)." When the customer is looking at merchandise, the salesperson has two choices. One is the silent approach, in which the salesperson steps up, obviously at the customer's service; the customer will almost always make a comment or ask a question to start the interview. The other choice is to use a merchandise greeting, such as: "Very attractive, aren't they?" "This is one of our new spring colors." "These came in just last week from Ireland." "This item makes a most appreciated gift." When salespeople know their customers, they can call them by name and perhaps ask a casual question or make some informal remark as part of the greeting.

DETERMINING CUSTOMER WANTS

One handicap in retail selling is the impossibility of learning in advance what each customer needs and wants. The preapproach work that organizational salespeople perform simply cannot be done for retail customers. Yet, if a sale is to be made, the salesperson must determine fairly accurately what customers want. How can customer wants be determined? Several suggestions follow.

OBSERVING

If the salesperson observes each individual customer's interest in merchandise and watches closely the customer's reactions to various products, some indications of customer needs and wants will be found.

LISTENING

Customers' comments may be vague or inaccurate, or they may be so rationalized that they camouflage the customer's real need. Even so, what the customer says must be analyzed and used. The salesperson may be able to elicit some more concrete, specific comments by placing merchandise in the customer's hands.

HEADLINING

While the customer is examining a particular product, the salesperson can quickly mention the three or four most outstanding benefits the product offers and then watch and listen for reactions. This tactic is called "**headlining**."

QUESTIONING

Restrained, tactful questions can be used to point up the customer's buying problems. Questions about material and style desired by the customer, as well as intended uses, are appropriate. Questions about size are risky, as are questions about price. Answers to questions about price may commit the customer to a price level the store does not have in stock and may handicap attempts at trading up. The smaller the retailer's stock, the fewer questions a salesperson should ask. Salespeople should not ask too many questions early in their dialogue with shoppers—to do so reduces their options.

SERVING CUSTOMERS

Retail salespeople often encounter problems in the first stages of the retail selling situation. The most serious of these concern how to handle decided and undecided customers, how to handle casual lookers, how to handle several customers at once, and how to handle groups of customers.

SERVING DECIDED AND UNDECIDED CUSTOMERS

In dealing with customers who know what they want, the salesperson should strive for a short sales situation. The salesperson should quickly place some merchandise before the customer, avoiding a lengthy presentation, and provide brief, specific answers to questions. If the customer decides to buy a product that would not be suitable, all the salesperson can do is recommend a more suitable product and urge the customer to make a careful comparison of the two items before buying.

Undecided customers who want to buy something but don't know just what need considerable help from salespeople in pinpointing their needs and in selecting merchandise which will fill those needs. Perhaps the soundest suggestion to salespeople dealing with such customers is that they begin showing merchandise as soon as they approach the customer. In this way, the customer can hardly avoid revealing information about prices, uses, colors, and product preferences. While showing the merchandise, the salesperson must attempt to analyze the customer's appearance and manner to help in determining real needs and wants.

Figure 18-4 By showing the merchandise as soon as the customer approaches, the salesperson soon learns what prices, uses, and product preferences the customer has in mind.

SERVING CASUAL LOOKERS

In many stores, well over half the customers are "just looking," and pose a difficult problem to salespeople: How should casual lookers be dealt with? Salespeople can logically make four assumptions about casual lookers: (1) these people are not consciously planning to buy now; (2) their immediate wish is to be left alone to look at and perhaps price merchandise; (3) in all probability, the looker really wants to buy something and can finance the purchase or would not be looking; and (4) it is the salesperson's duty to discover what the looker needs.

Several courses of action may be taken in dealing with casual lookers. One is to leave the customer alone, hoping that examination of the merchandise will sell it. This is appropriate for customers who raise their buying defenses if they are immediately approached by a salesperson. Another course of action is to offer to help the looker inspect merchandise. This is particularly appropriate when products need to be demonstrated and when the salesperson is not busy with other customers. A third possibility is for the salesperson to brief the looker on the general location of merchandise, issue an invitation to feel completely at home, and assure prompt service as soon as it is desired. A fourth technique is to refer the looker to some specific merchandise with a remark such as, "Take all the time you want. You may be interested in seeing our new collection of scarves, right over there." Special sale items, products featured in the day's advertisements, products being pushed by the store's sales staff, and merchandise in window or interior displays all may be referred to.

Regardless of which method is used in dealing with casual lookers, it is the salesperson's duty to work toward achieving their goodwill. When goodwill is achieved, the salesperson may make a serious attempt to close a sale. Whether the immediate goal is achieving goodwill or making

STEPS IN RETAIL SELLING

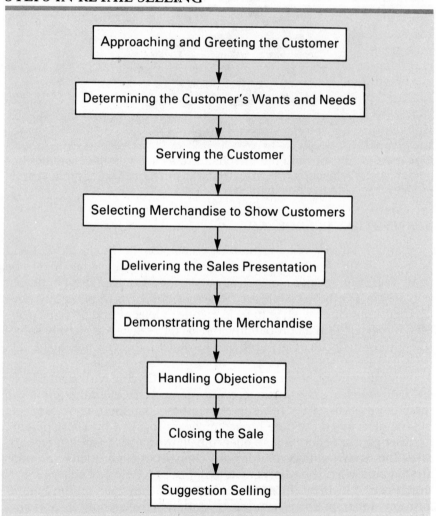

Figure 18-5 In "selling products that won't come back to customers who will," the retail salesperson follows these nine steps.

a sale, the salesperson should observe the casual looker closely and be ready to give service.

DEALING WITH SEVERAL CUSTOMERS AT ONCE

During store rush hours, there may well be several customers needing the attention of the same salesperson at the same time. This creates a problem involving promptness in approaching customers and the sequence in which customers are to be served. The most important principle for the salesperson to follow is that the first customer on the scene has top priority and that other customers must be served in turn. Sometimes the first customer will tell the salesperson to wait on another customer. In other situations, the salesperson may ask if it is all right to wait on someone who is ready to buy. The first customer must not be given cause for feeling neglected or rushed into buying.

When additional customers approach, the salesperson should at least acknowledge their presence and promise prompt attention with a phrase such as, "I'll be right with you." If any of the customers are lookers, the salesperson can solve the problem by permitting the looker to examine merchandise alone, taking care of the customer who is ready to buy, and then returning to the looker.

DEALING WITH GROUPS OF CUSTOMERS

Often the retail salesperson is approached by several customers shopping together. Typically, the group will be composed of a customer and one or two friends or family members. The salesperson should try to determine which member of the group is the dominant one and what merchandise interests are involved; the major sales efforts can then be aimed at that person. As a shopping group is served, the salesperson must remember that people in the group often think highly of their companions' opinions. Members of the group should be given the opportunity to talk among themselves if they desire. If the group members cannot agree on merchandise, the best course is for the salesperson to recommend the item he or she sincerely believes to be the most appropriate.

SELECTING MERCHANDISE TO SHOW CUSTOMERS

Having greeted the customer and made an attempt to determine what the customer may want, the salesperson must select merchandise to show and recommend. If the customer made a specific request to see a certain product, that, of course, is the one the salesperson will show first. If the customer was somewhat vague, then the salesperson must bring out what the customer might like. Here the salesperson is well advised not to lead off with either the highest- or the lowest-priced items. The safest as well as the most ethical guide in selecting merchandise to show is customer satisfaction. If a customer later regrets a purchase, the natural reaction is to blame the store. This usually results in decreased buying at that store and in unfavorable word-of-mouth publicity for it.

TRADING UP

In selecting the merchandise to show, the salesperson must decide whether to attempt **trading up**. A salesperson succeeds in trading up when the customer buys a better-quality item than the customer had planned. Another version of trading up is selling a larger quantity of the product.

The customer who trades up and buys the better-quality suit, for example, gets greater value, or greater satisfaction of some other kind. Salespeople should practice until they can show their superior lines of merchandise smoothly and recommend them naturally.

SUBSTITUTE SELLING

Sometimes the store will not have in stock the item a customer requests. Other times the salesperson may try to redirect the customer's interest to some other product or brand, even though the requested item is in stock. In either case, **substitute selling** is the result. No matter what the reason for substitution, there will be negative aftereffects if either the salesperson or the customer successfully insists on the purchase of a product the customer should not buy.

If the store does not have the requested product in stock, the customer should be told this immediately. If the store has a comparable product in stock, this item should be quickly given to the customer for inspection. The out-of-stock item should not be criticized, nor should the item shown be directly referred to as a substitute. The salesperson can question the customer tactfully while showing the substitute item.

If the store does have the requested item, there must be a sound reason for any attempt at substitution. If the customer intends to buy a product that would be entirely inappropriate, it is the salesperson's duty to try to prevent an unsatisfactory purchase and to recommend a more suitable one. It is often wise to show the more appropriate product along with the customer's request. Many customers will immediately realize that their original preference was not sound.

DELIVERING THE SALES PRESENTATION

Retail salespeople deliver sales presentations that are somewhat different from those delivered by organizational salespeople. One difference is length. Because the store presentation is shorter, the salesperson must make the strongest and most persuasive points at the beginning, or the opportunity to make them may be lost. Another difference is that retail salespeople cannot plan the sales presentation in advance to the degree that the organizational salesperson can. Standard or canned presentations are almost impossible for retail salespeople to use because they sell many different kinds of products, but key words and phrases can be used effectively.

Most of the important principles of delivering a sales presentation discussed in earlier chapters can be applied effectively in retail selling. Customers do not buy until they are convinced that the purchase will be of benefit to them. The customer is entitled to the salesperson's complete attention, and the salesperson can in turn hold or recapture the customer's attention by directing it to the product or by asking the customer to do something with the item. Agreements on small matters should be obtained, and value should be established before price is discussed. If the customer asks the price of an item, the salesperson should quote the price immediately, but should also tell the customer about buyer benefits that justify the price. As the sales interview progresses, the presentation should become more specific and more emphatic.

DEMONSTRATING MERCHANDISE

In retail selling, as in outside selling, the salesperson should show the products when explaining their use. Because the item the customer buys is practically always in the store at the time of purchase, there is rarely an excuse for not demonstrating.

How much merchandise should be shown? This decision must be left up to the salesperson. If not shown enough merchandise, the customer may not feel informed enough to buy. If shown too much, the customer may become confused. Customers should be shown all the items they wish to examine. In every case, the customer should feel that the salesperson has shown, or will gladly show, every bit of the store's merchandise that is suitable. The demonstration phase of the sale rarely lasts very long, although there is usually time to repeat a demonstration, even in greater detail, if necessary.

The rules for product demonstration are applicable in retail selling. Customer participation is desirable and can be enlisted by asking the customer to watch a demonstration of the product, or, whenever practical, to handle or operate the product just as it will be used after purchase. For example, the customer can try on clothing or write with a pen. While this is being done, the salesperson should point out the buyer benefits that the customer is experiencing.

Merchandise should be displayed in its best light and in an impressive yet believable way. Demonstration should be designed to show off the advantages promised by the salesperson. Throughout the sales presentation, the salesperson should remember that the manner in which the merchandise is handled is quite revealing; therefore, respect for the merchandise should always be evidenced. Nothing must destroy or damage the customer's respect for the goods.

HANDLING OBJECTIONS

Most buying resistance that retail salespeople meet stems from the customer's uncertainty about the buying decisions relating to product, price, and time. Few objections are based on need, although need must always be established. Even fewer objections concern source. Thus, the salesperson can expect to deal with customers who are not completely convinced that the product under consideration is the best buy, customers who feel that the price is really more than they can afford to pay, and customers who feel that they must think the prospective purchase over or shop around a bit more before making a final selection.

The general rule here, as in outside selling, calls for the avoidance of objections by explaining them away before the customer raises them. When the salesperson selects the most appropriate merchandise to show, the amount of product objection encountered is reduced. When the salesperson points out the benefits to be obtained from the product, the likelihood of price objections is decreased. Difficulty with the time decision will be less frequent and troublesome as the salesperson successfully handles product and price objections.

Sometimes a customer sincerely feels a need to think about a prospective purchase, or talk it over with someone. In these circumstances, there are several options that the salesperson may choose. He or she may agree with the customer that deliberation is desirable before making the purchase. The salesperson may offer to show the customer even more merchandise; if this offer is not accepted, the customer can be given a summary of product benefits to think about or discuss with others. The salesperson may offer to put the item aside for the customer until a decision is made. Literature on the product or a business card may be offered in an effort to get the customer to return to complete the sale later.

The concealed or camouflaged objection poses the same difficult problem in retail selling that it does in other selling. For example, after a presentation or demonstration the customer may say, "I'm afraid that isn't exactly what I had in mind." In order to determine what affirmative buying decision is missing, the salesperson has little recourse in such a situation but to observe the customer's actions, comments, or facial expressions or to ask tactfully just what the shopper did have in mind. Meanwhile, the salesperson can repeat the most persuasive buyer benefits the product offers; this may cause the unknown objection to disappear. In some cases, the salesperson may directly ask the customer, "Have I failed to make anything clear?" Once the objection has been identified, it should be handled quickly and thoroughly.

CLOSING THE SALE

There are closing clues in retail selling just as there are in outside selling. Verbal closing clues can take the form of questions relating to price, size, or terms, or can take the form of a statement about the product such as, "It would save me time each week." Closing clues may also take the form of changes in facial expression that indicate interest or decision, reading of the product's label, or a movement to one side to see the product from a different angle.

As the salesperson senses the approach of the end of the sales situation, his or her manner should become more positive and forceful. The customer must feel the salesperson's confidence in the product and in the buying recommendation. No new merchandise should be brought out at this stage; other items no longer under consideration should be removed. The salesperson should concentrate on the two or three items of particular interest to the customer and should review the merits of each. The salesperson should ask for customer agreement more often during this stage and should be ready to suggest a buying decision to an undecided customer, but never should the salesperson make it seem that the customer is being rushed into buying.

When a retail salesperson cannot close a sale, a sales supervisor or another salesperson may be called in. The second salesperson and the customer may be more compatible, and the customer may feel a bit flattered by this treatment.

SUGGESTION SELLING

The objective of **suggestion selling** is to get the customer to make unplanned purchases of items over and above those the customer requested. The resulting additional sales volume explains the store's as well as the salesperson's interest in it.

Customers typically want suggestions from the sales staffs of retail stores. Suggestions can remind customers of products they need so that they will run out of these products less often. Suggestions also can help consumers identify needs of which they were unaware. When made in a tactful way, suggestions can be considered helpful hints and are appreciated by customers. Suggested purchases can save both time and money and can increase the customer's personal satisfaction.

When should suggestion selling be attempted? It is usually best for the salesperson to take care of the customer's requests first and to close the sale before suggesting other products. Then, before going through the mechanics of completing the sale physically—writing up the sales ticket, wrapping the merchandise, making change—the salesperson can make suggestions. Once in a while the salesperson can make use of the ensemble technique before the first purchase is made in the customer's mind. The salesperson might bring out a tie to show with a shirt the customer is examining, for example. The tie often helps to sell the shirt; the purchase of the shirt encourages the purchase of the tie.

Because suggestion selling can be executed in such a way as to irritate or even drive customers away, certain rules or principles which have proved sound should be observed. The salesperson's ideal suggestion should prove to be a realistic and suitable solution to a customer problem. If the suggested merchandise is something that will benefit the customer, the salesperson is well on the way to customer acceptance of the suggestion. If the customer is in a hurry, however, the salesperson should avoid suggestion selling.

Another rule is that suggestion selling must be moderate in three ways: in intensity, in the amount of the recommended purchase, and in the number of items mentioned. A salesperson can easily be too aggressive in trying to increase the amount of the sale; this can result in customer resentment. If the salesperson tries to make too large an additional sale, or suggests too long a list of products, it will certainly irritate and may even infuriate the customer.

Still another guide is that suggestions must be definite. The salesperson should not make the mistake of using any of the following questions: "Now, what else?" "Will that be all?" "Anything in socks today?" If the salesperson uses a tone of helpful concern and interest, it helps give the suggestion the appearance of a service to the customer.

Merchandise best suited to suggestion selling includes: related items (suits call for shirts, socks, and ties; computers call for software); specials of the day, which may be new products or old products for which new uses have been found; items currently featured in display and advertising; and merchandise that is timely because of its relation to holidays or seasons.

POSTSALE BEHAVIOR

Immediately after making a sale, the salesperson should record it. As the purchase is wrapped, the salesperson can at the same time assure the customer that he or she made an intelligent decision. A warm "thank you" should always be voiced to let the customer know that the purchase was appreciated, and a sincere personal invitation to return should be issued. If appropriate, the customer's name should be learned and remembered for possible future use. If asked for or appropriate, the salesperson's name or business card should be given to the customer.

When a customer postpones a purchase, the salesperson should continue to be just as courteous and friendly as before the decision. The salesperson should not display any irritation, disappointment, hurt, or resentment. The salesperson should let the customer know that visits to the store are and will continue to be appreciated. Customers should be encouraged to return by the salesperson's manner. Courteous and friendly treatment of all customers builds goodwill for the store.

The customer has two undeniable rights: (1) to postpone a purchase decision, and (2) to shop further before buying. Any attempt to curtail these rights can be damaging to a store. If, therefore, a customer insists

Figure 18-6 Customers appreciate a warm "thank you" and a sincere personal invitation to return.

on asserting one or both of these rights, salespeople can summarize the advantages of their merchandise and ask the customer to investigate competing products on those points, but there is little else that can be done. It is clearly the salesperson's responsibility to see that the customer knows thoroughly and completely before leaving what the store can supply in the product lines being considered. Salespeople should assume that the customer will return and will then buy. They might even try to make a definite appointment for the return visit. In some cases, the salesperson can give the customer a memo, a sketch, some literature, or a business card in an effort to increase the chances of the customer's return.

BUILDING SOUND CUSTOMER RELATIONSHIPS

No thorough attempt at working with customers can be made without reviewing the reasons why customers quit buying at certain stores and from individual salespeople. The indifference of salespeople always ranks high on lists of causes of customer loss. High-pressure or over-aggressive selling tactics can drive customers away. If too many attempts at substitution are made, or if the attempts are too crude and obvious, customers will take their patronage elsewhere. Other customer complaints include the charge that some salespeople are haughty or discourteous; some are not well enough informed about their merchandise to supply the product information required by customers. A more disturbing charge is that some salespeople actually misrepresent their goods. When a salesperson promises something to a customer, such as a delivery date and hour, but fails to comply, the effects are negative. Finally, the mistakes of salespeople may discourage return visits and purchases.

There are certain steps that some salespeople can take in building sound customer relationships. One of the simplest, yet most rewarding, is learning the names of as many customers as possible and addressing those individuals by their names. Another habit well acquired is that of remembering the preferences and prejudices of regular customers. In the higher-priced merchandise lines or services, salespeople often find it worthwhile to develop customer information files (CIF's). A CIF might include the customer's name, the date of the last visit, and the items bought, the birthdate for sending a card, and any other significant facts about the customer. The CIF is usually set up on a personal computer and stored on special software. The computer system can be used to prepare phone or mailing lists and labels. Where installment credit is available, salespeople can keep posted on customers' balances and recommend additional purchases at the appropriate times. Many services, including veterinarians, dentists, and cosmetologists frequently use CIF's to maintain contact with customers, as do many other types of businesses, including clothing stores, banks, car care centers, florist shops, and appliance stores.

HIGHLIGHT 18-1   Why Sales Are Lost

1. *Disinterest—Don't conduct a conversation with a fellow employee or another customer while waiting on someone. Give the customer your complete attention. Deadpan expressions, daydreaming, or "take it or leave it" attitudes result in unsold merchandise.*
2. *Mistakes—If you show the wrong item or make a mistake in change, acknowledge it and make the customer feel you are genuinely sorry.*
3. *Appearing too anxious—Show customers you want to serve their interests. Overinsistence and high-pressure tactics are objectionable to customers.*
4. *Talking down other brands—Talk up the brand you want to sell. Do not make unfair remarks about a competitive brand.*
5. *Arguing—Never argue with a customer. If it appears that an argument might develop, shift the conversation to another topic. There's little profit in winning an argument and losing*

the customer. If a customer makes an absurd statement, don't laugh or argue. You may anger the customer, and an angry customer is a lost customer.

6. *Being too long-winded—A flood of words doesn't make many sales. Some people take time to make up their minds, and silence at the right time allows the customer to think and decide. A good listener often makes more sales than a fast talker does.*

7. *Lack of courtesy—Discourteous salespeople rarely last long on a job; they lose too many customers.*

8. *Showing favoritism—Never wait on your friends or favorite customers before taking care of customers who were there first.*

9. *Being too hurried—Take time to find out what a customer wants and then take time to show the merchandise properly.*

10. *Embarrassing the customer—Never laugh at a person who speaks with a foreign accent or correct a person who mispronounces words or product names.*

11. *Misrepresenting merchandise—Never guarantee any cures or make any claims for products that cannot be backed up by facts.*

12. *Lack of product information—Salespeople who are not well informed cannot expect to build a steady clientele for their store.*

13. *Wasting customers' time—When a customer is in a hurry, finish the sale as quickly as possible.*

14. *Getting too personal—Assume a professional attitude. Be sincere and friendly, but keep a touch of dignity and formality in all customer contacts. Never let familiarity creep into the conversation, for it is usually resented.*

THE PROBLEM OF RETURNED GOODS

A problem of obvious interest to retail salespeople is that of merchandise bought by customers but subsequently returned to the store. Returned goods are a significant element in a retailer's expenses. Returns must be handled, and this involves cost. An item being returned may show evidence of use, abuse, or deterioration; markdown may be necessary. Then, for the time the merchandise was out of the store, it was neither sold nor available for sale. Unless the retailer is out to lose sales, inventory must be large enough to allow for this out-of-stock time. In addition, some returns reflect an increase in customer ill will. Finally, the volume of returns may suggest that buying or selling is less efficient and more expensive than it should be.

Retail salespeople are often responsible for a significant proportion of returned goods. Sometimes a salesperson makes a mistake unknow-

Figure 18-7 A customer's disappointment in merchandise performance, a mistake in order filling, or a delay in delivery are some causes for returned goods.

ingly. Sometimes there is a misunderstanding between customer and salesperson involving just what is being bought or its price. An ignorant, poorly trained salesperson can expect returns. The same holds true for the careless, indifferent salesperson who does not bother to tailor merchandise recommendations to individual shoppers. The high-pressure salesperson can expect returns as well. So can the weak salesperson who urges shoppers to take goods home on approval instead of selling goods to those buyers. Equally guilty is the casual salesperson who allows customers to buy inappropriate items. Customer disappointment over merchandise performance—whether this is a matter of operation, fit, color, or size—often leads to the return of the item.

Of course, some causes of returned goods do not relate closely to the personal selling done by retail salespeople. For example, the reason could be a mistake in order filling, damage en route, or delay in delivery. The item might be inherently faulty. Or the customer may buy, then find the same item available in another store at a lower price.

Retail salespeople have a considerable interest in the returned goods problem if they work in department, clothing, or furniture stores. Because they are determined by their sales volume, salespeople's earnings are usually affected directly. There are more than a few cases where a salesperson made a big sale, spent the commission, and then found the commission account charged because the merchandise was returned. In addition, returns can take up a salesperson's selling time when stores ask their sales staffs to handle returns. Then, too, there is often a makeup or replacement sale which must be made.

If the store has a liberal policy about returns, retail salespeople should be pleased, because such a policy stimulates greater sales. New customers are more easily attracted, and present customers are more easily held. If the store's policy is generous, the salesperson should not fail to emphasize this fact. But, at the same time, this fact does not relieve the salesperson of the responsibility of helping customers make purchases that will not come back.

TECHNIQUES OF SELF-MANAGEMENT

Self-management is not nearly the complicated, challenging, and difficult matter for retail salespeople that it is for outside salespeople. Typically, the store schedules salespeople as to how many hours a week they will work and establishes their duties.

What, then, can or should store salespeople do about managing themselves? They should concern themselves mainly with attitudes and activities. As to attitudes, the starting step is to recognize that improvement is always possible. Salespeople must realize that their present as well as their future depends in large measure on how well they get along with three groups: customers, associates, and the store's executives. Further, they must remember that few customers who quit buying at a store do so because of the store's merchandise, its prices, or its customer services—most quit because they find the salespeople ignorant, incompetent, or disinterested. Salespeople's attitudes must reflect their understanding of the dependence of customers on salespeople and of the customers' need for help and advice; perhaps even more important, they should reflect an understanding of the salesperson's own dependence on the customer, whose continued patronage pays the salesperson's salary.

Activities can be whatever is needed to achieve self-improvement. They include such obvious practices as the analysis of selling attempts in order to identify elements of strength and of weakness. In particular, the well-managed salesperson searches for the causes of lost sales and lost customers. Another activity involves the collection of all information needed; information about merchandise, customers, and how to sell the merchandise to the customer. Still another activity is memory improvement, without which the information about merchandise, customers, and selling techniques will be of limited use. Then there is the matter of developing and even trying to perfect a pleasing personality. These attitudes and activities help salespeople to be of greater help to the real boss: the customers.

DIRECT SELLING

So far in this chapter we have discussed personal selling to ultimate consumers as it occurs in retail stores. But personal selling also is used to sell to ultimate consumers in ways other than through retail stores. This is referred to as nonstore retailing.

NONSTORE RETAILING

Nonstore retailing accounts for almost 10 percent of all retail sales and includes **direct selling**, direct-response selling, and vending machine sales. Direct selling is defined as direct personal sales contact between buyer and seller. Direct sales companies include Amway, Shaklee, Avon, L. L. Bean, Land's End, Mary Kay Cosmetics, and Tupperware. Direct-response selling, sometimes referred to as direct marketing, is a type of nonstore retailing in which a consumer is exposed to a good or service through a nonpersonal medium and then orders by mail or telephone. Direct-response selling involves the use of nonpersonal media such as mail, catalogs, television, radio, newspapers, magazines, telephone or other directories, or personal computers to stimulate customers to place orders. Merchandise is then shipped directly to the consumer or, sometimes, to the local retail store for pickup. Many specialty and department stores issue catalogs to create telephone and mail-order sales and to promote in-store purchases of items featured in their catalogs.

A recent innovation in direct-response selling is the use of computer-based catalogs. CompuServe, The Source, and Applelink are all examples. CompuServe is the largest of the computer-based catalogs, featuring almost 275,000 products in its electronic catalog.

HOME SHOPPING

Among the biggest growth areas in direct-response selling is in home shopping. Home shopping is the use of cable television networks to sell merchandise through telephone orders. Shoppers are given an 800 number to call. Orders are then placed, most often paid for by credit card, and the goods are shipped to the buyers' homes.

Home shopping using cable television networks began with the launching of Home Shopping Network, Inc. in the early 1980s. Numerous competitors have since been started. Today, half of all households with television sets in the United States will on occasion watch one or more home shopping networks, and over 9 percent of those will buy something. In fact, home shoppers tend to be heavy users of this form of nonstore retailing, averaging six orders a year. Some industry experts have predicted that home shopping will exceed $9 billion by 1990.

SUMMARY

Retail salespeople sell more products and deal with more buyers than other types of salespeople. Retail salespeople sell merchandise, conduct nonselling activities, and act responsibly toward their stores and their companies.

Retail salespeople are rewarded through salaries and promotion opportunities. Salaries start low, but there are many advancement opportunities which can lead to higher salaries.

The retail selling process consists of greeting customers, determining their needs, making short presentations, demonstrating the merchandise, handling objections, closing the sale, and providing follow-up service.

Retail salespeople must know their store, their merchandise, and their company's policies, and must be able to control their attitudes and personal activities when dealing directly with consumers in a highly populated environment.

KEY TERMS

selling duties
nonselling duties
headlining
trading up

substitute selling
suggestion selling
postsale behavior
direct selling

REVIEW QUESTIONS

1. What customer-related differences are there between retail selling and other kinds of selling?
2. List three types of duties or responsibilities of retail salespeople.
3. What store information is needed by retail salespeople?
4. What is the first step in retail selling?
5. How can a salesperson determine what the customer wants?
6. What should a salesperson do when confronted with a number of customers?
7. How should the salesperson handle groups of customers?
8. What is trading up?
9. Why is substitute selling done?
10. What is the objective of suggestion selling?
11. If no sale takes place, what should the salesperson do?
12. List three methods for building sound customer relationships.
13. List five reasons why retail sales are lost.
14. What is a customer information file? How can it be used by the salesperson?

15. What are some reasons customers return goods?
16. What aspects of self-management can a retail salesperson control?

DISCUSSION QUESTIONS

1. Much retail selling is done by very young, inexperienced people working part-time. How can such individuals be trained and convinced of the importance of maintaining the same standards of performance that professional salespeople maintain?
2. Discuss the compensation systems most widely used in retail selling. Are they similar to those used by wholesalers and organizational selling firms?
3. Discuss the following statement: "Most retail salespeople are not rewarded for truly outstanding efforts."
4. What closing techniques are especially effective in retail selling?
5. If you were the manager of a retail store, how would you try to convince someone that they should endure a low starting salary in return for relatively quick management advancement?

CASE 18-1   CELLULAR SERVICES, INC.*

Cellular Services, Inc., is a sales agent for BellSouth Mobility, Inc., in the Norfolk, Virginia, metropolitan area. BellSouth Mobility, Inc., owns and operates one of the cellular phone systems in the Norfolk market. Typically, there are two competing marketers of cellular service in each market. The competing system in Norfolk is owned and operated by Cellular One, Inc., of Norfolk. Both Cellular One and BellSouth Mobility have their own sales forces, but they also each have three sales agents who sell mobile phone equipment and service for them. Cellular Services, Inc., is one of these sales agents.

Cellular phone systems provide mobile phone service. The system offers clear, static-free communications to mobile phones. The primary market segment is business people who need phone service in their cars. A secondary market is higher-income people who like the convenience and luxury of a phone in their car. A third market in the Norfolk area is the marine market. Cellular phones offer a primary advantage over marine radio communications in that land-based callers may call a cellular user by simply dialing a number on any telephone. That is, you call a cellular user in the same manner that you would call anyone using a conventional telephone. To make a marine radio call, however, a land-based caller first must place the call through a marine radio operator who then places the call.

---

*Case prepared by Ronald F. Bush. Used with permission.

Most other companies selling cellular service and equipment have concentrated on the automobile market. The sales manager for Cellular Services, Inc., thinks the marine market has been overlooked. She does not know of any cellular phones or service that her sales force has sold to this market, and she also has not heard that any competitors are selling to this segment.

The sales manager's interest is based on an article she recently read on the potential for the marine cellular market in *Mobile Communications Business*, an industry trade publication.

The article indicated that there are three market segments for marine cellular service: (1) owners of offshore oil and gas rigs, (2) offshore oil/gas field service companies, and (3) owners of pleasure boats used in the Chesapeake Bay area, the Atlantic Ocean, and protected coastal waterways. Marketing research indicated there are almost 100 rig owners and service operators in the Virginia, northern California, and Maryland coastal areas. Moreover, there are over 200,000 owners of pleasure boats over 18 feet in length in this same area. A demand forecast included in the article estimated the marine cellular market.

After reading the article, the sales manager called in her two top salespeople—Teri Shafer and Ted Samuelson. She showed them the article and asked them to think about it, ask some questions of people they thought might know something about the marine cellular market, and come back in to talk with her on Friday.

Teri and Ted began by converting the demand forecast in the Exhibit below into an index, so that change in each market segment could be compared directly.

EXHIBIT 18-1
DEMAND FOR MARINE CELLULAR SERVICE

A. Total Cumulative Demand

Segment	1990	1992	1994	1996
Owners/Offshore rigs	140	220	299	495
Service Firms	38	71	117	143
Pleasure Boaters	836	4,179	8,358	14,715
Total Market	1,014	4,470	8,774	15,353

B. Index of Total Cumulative Demand

	1990	1992	1994	1996
Owners/Offshore rigs	100	157	214	354
Service Firms	100	___	___	___
Pleasure Boaters	100	___	___	___
Total Market	100	___	___	___

CASE QUESTIONS

1. Using Lotus, complete the index portion of the table for Teri and Ted. Which is the fastest growing segment? Which is the slowest growing segment?

2. Selling to ultimate consumers does not always occur inside a store, and in some instances may involve services instead of a physical product. How does selling a service to ultimate consumers differ from selling a product?

3. How many cellular phones do you think Cellular Services, Inc., can sell to the marine market in 1992? In 1994? In 1996? What are your assumptions?

4. How would you find out more about this market?

5. Which segment of the marine cellular market would you try to sell to first? Second?

6. What sales appeals would you use? Would a demonstration of this product/service be helpful?

CASE 18-2 McKEE'S CAR CARE CENTERS*

Daryl McKee owns nine car care centers in the Tampa–St. Petersburg, Florida, metropolitan area. He is a local franchisee for Goodyear Tires; they account for about 15 percent of his sales. The remaining sales are comprised of: (a) gas, oil, and accessories (12 percent) and (b) repairs and maintenance (73 percent). The car care centers have a total of 54 bays (a bay is an area to service an automobile); four centers have six bays, three centers have ten bays and two centers have fourteen bays. Average monthly sales volume has ranged from a low of $80,000 to a high of $170,000. McKee's Car Care Centers serve two primary market segments: (1) middle to upscale people who trust Goodyear Tires and McKee's service, and (2) small businesses that own a fleet of cars and/or trucks.

The 1992 sales plan for McKee's Car Care Centers projects a profit of $580,000 based on sales of $14 million—this represents a 15 percent increase over 1991. The expected increase is based on two factors: (1) an ongoing sales and advertising campaign, and (2) the introduction of two new products/services—a Maintenance Plus Program and a Customer Recall Program.

The new programs can be briefly described as follows. The Maintenance Plus Program is designed for the business having a fleet of vehicles

---

*Case prepared by Debbie Easterling. Used with permission.

to maintain. It involves the development of a customer information file (CIF) to assist in selling new business. The Customer Recall Program involves customer follow-up. Specifically, this program involves telephoning customers not only to thank them for their business but also to make sure they are satisfied with the service or products they have purchased. Also planned is expansion of a previous program, the Tire Protection Plan. This particular plan includes free alignment, tire rotation and balancing, and road hazard protection for a nominal charge.

Up until two years ago, McKee's Car Care Centers employed only an inside sales force. These salespeople waited in the Car Care Centers until customers came in the door. They then helped the customers with whatever they requested—for example, tires, batteries, trailer hitches, or repairs. Occasionally, there was some cross-selling of products and services, but it was not very consistent because the salespeople had not been trained to cross-sell. (Note: Cross-selling is a sales technique in which people come to the store to buy one product and the salesperson attempts to sell them other products as well. For example, a salesperson would try to sell tire rotation and balancing to a customer who comes in to purchase tires.)

Recently however, while at a Goodyear Tire Dealer's Convention in Las Vegas, Mr. McKee learned about a programmed training course and bought it for his salespeople. This course included training manuals, a slide presentation, and a timed slide projector with which to show the slides. After returning from Las Vegas and implementing the training, Mr. McKee thought that the training program had worked. However, he wasn't entirely convinced that his sales force remembered all the important points. At present, it's been over a year since the training was initially utilized. Since that time, seven new salespeople have been hired and Mr. McKee has set up a telemarketing sales force at one of the larger Car Care Centers. The newly formed telemarketing division was designed to make sales calls for all nine stores, but has only one salesperson employed.

Mr. McKee thought that perhaps it would be a good idea to hire some new salespeople to assist in selling the new programs, but he was not sure whether they should be inside telemarketers or outside salespeople.

CASE QUESTIONS

1. How can Mr. McKee use the new CIF? What information should be included in it? Will it have to be computerized? Can the CIF be used with products/services other than the new Maintenance Plus Program?

2. Should Mr. McKee hire telemarketers or outside salespeople, or a combination?
3. What kind of sales presentation would you develop for the new products/services?
4. Is the training program adequate? If not, how would you change it?

PART 7

Sales Management

CHAPTER 19
Building the Sales Force

After studying this chapter, you should be able to:

- Break the management process down into the four functions of planning, organizing, directing, and evaluating a sales force
- Describe a firm's promotion budget
- Contrast line organization with line and staff organization
- Contrast the different forms of fragmented sales force organizations
- Distinguish between job analysis, job description, and job specification
- Explain the tools widely used in selecting salespeople
- Discuss training programs for salespeople

For many companies that sell over a wide geographical area, the key employee is the salesperson in the field. The climax of promotional efforts for those companies occurs when a salesperson presents the product line to a buyer. That salesperson is the company to many buyers. Consequently, the salesperson's influence on company-buyer relationships is great.

THE NATURE OF MANAGEMENT

The management process can be divided into four functions: planning, organizing, directing, and evaluating.

PLANNING

Planning is the primary function of sales management, since plans guide all sales and sales force decision making. Sales managers should follow a planning process when developing their sales plans. The steps in this process are shown in Figure 19-1. The planning process should start with a situational analysis. During this stage the sales manager analyzes the environment and identifies potential opportunities and challenges

THE PLANNING PROCESS

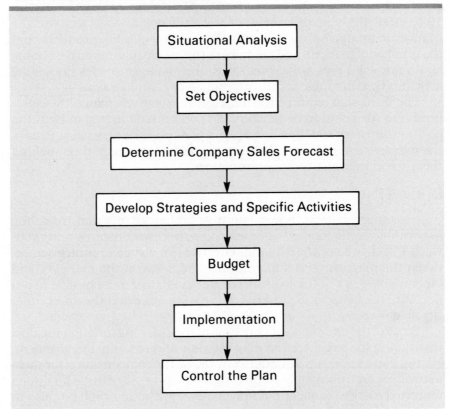

Figure 19-1 The planning process consists of seven steps.

in relation to the sales organization's strengths and weaknesses. Next, the manager should set objectives. Objectives are necessary to provide direction for the organization's efforts. The third step is to determine the industry's sales potential, from which the manager can derive the company's sales forecast. This forecast will be broken down so that each salesperson is responsible for a sales quota.

After developing the forecast, the sales manager must next develop the strategies and specific sales activities to be implemented in order to achieve the forecast. These activities will be budgeted for and added together to represent the company's sales budget. Finally, the plan is implemented by the sales force, while the sales manager monitors and controls the plan's progress.

ORGANIZING

In organizing the sales force, the sales manager is responsible for determining how many sales reps the company should have, who they should be and what they will be responsible for. The organizational process for developing a sales force consists of four steps, as shown in Figure 19-2. First, the manager must review the company's objectives, the number of products they sell and the similarity of those products, and the number of markets and customers they serve in order to determine how many sales reps are needed. Next, the manager divides the selling activities by geographic territory, product, or customer type.

The third step requires the manager to effectively match the salesperson to the position or territory. A good understanding of both the position/territory and the salesperson's personality is necessary. Finally, the manager assigns responsibility to each salesperson, thus making them accountable for their performances.

DIRECTING

Directing consists of administering the planned program. In leading subordinates, the manager guides and supervises, inspires and motivates. Effective directing demands effective two-way communication between the manager and subordinates and between the manager and other managers. For this reason, the sales manager must be able to understand the behavioral patterns of the sales force and the other functional managers.

Some of the more specific concerns of the directing function include: instructing the sales force on effective time and territory management, setting the salesperson's quota, determining the compensation for each, motivating and, ultimately, leading the sales force. All of these functions require the sales manager not only to develop and instruct, but also to monitor the sales force.

THE ORGANIZATION PROCESS

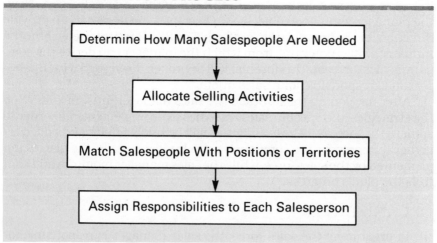

Figure 19-2 Organizing consists of four separate but interrelated steps.

EVALUATING

In evaluating, the manager checks actual performance against planned performance and notes what progress is being made (often by month) toward objectives. If the differences between what was planned and what was actually done are too great, the manager tries to determine why and then takes the appropriate corrective action. This process is known as sales analysis. The sales manager also might conduct a marketing cost analysis in order to judge how profitable and/or productive the salesperson is.

The sales manager is interested not only in whether salespeople achieve their sales objectives and performance standards, but also in how efficient they are. That is, do they maximize their sales volume relative to their sales expenses, or do they waste money?

THE PROMOTION BUDGET

The sales budget is an element of the overall promotion budget. A sales budget is a financial plan that outlines how company resources and selling effort should be allocated to achieve the sales forecast. If the sales budget is too small, the sales forecast will not be achieved. Thus, when the sales forecast is increased, the sales budget should be increased, too. As described in Figure 19-3, the sales budget is a critical tool for the success of the entire company.

Budgeted promotion makes each promotion activity dollar-specific, and the scheduling which budgeting includes makes each time-specific. Proper promotion budgets permit the seller to avoid the extremes of wasted resources and inadequate promotion/sales support. The sales forecast is the basic influence in the setting of promotion budgets. Budgeting for promotion is one of management's most difficult tasks.

Annually, each firm's management must determine the make-up of the next year's promotion mix—how much personal selling, how much advertising, and how much sales promotion to buy and use—in an effort to reach that year's goals. This is a critical decision because the promotion program is seldom changed to any great extent during a year. For many firms the building and managing of the sales force is the largest operating expense.

Once these three budgets have been set, then each is broken down according to: (1) product (how much effort will salespeople put behind Product A vs. Product B); (2) time (should the manufacturer drop TV advertising in the summer as some do); (3) buyer (what point-of-purchase items should be designed for large-volume retailers and what for small-volume retailers); (4) sales territory (New England vs. Pacific Coast); and (5) expense classification (should an ad in a school annual be charged to advertising or to public relations). These breakdowns are essential be-

THE SALES BUDGET

I am a piece of paper, maybe two or more . . .
I am the promise of the future.

I make people dream dreams and wrestle with ideas . . .
I am the catalyst that converts ideas to decisions.

I am increasing in value every year . . .
I am a gauntlet thrown down at the feet of competition.

I create jobs . . .
I maintain jobs.

I am the difference between hard planning and playing it cozy . . .
I declare the right to be met and, if necessary, exceeded.

I am the means by which to further cooperation . . .
I am one way to earn a promotion.

I am a silent enforcer that demands quality action . . .
I am a benchmark that quantifies performance.

I issue a challenge that professional men acknowledge . . .
I am accused, cursed, agonized over—but also indispensable.

I am often cast in concrete, but I really hate the "clay feet" that come
      with such rigidity . . .
I am more agreeable to practical flexibility.

I am the basis on which everything in your company depends . . .
I am not the last word in everything—just the first.

I have to be contended with in the end in any case . . .
I am the sales budget.

Figure 19-3 This poem helps you understand the frustrations in developing a sales budget.

Source: Reprinted by permission of *Sales & Marketing Management*, Copyright: March 14, 1977.

cause of variations in type of product, market potential, share of market now held, competition, stage of business cycle, and so on.

INTRODUCTION TO THE SALES MANAGER'S JOB

The sales manager's main concern and responsibility relate to the firm's sales budget, the first budget in point of time and importance. A business's most basic figure as it starts each fiscal year is the sales forecast, and the attainment of that figure is the sales manager's main objective.

Figure 19-4 The sales manager plays a vital role in maintaining the morale and motivation of the sales force.

All cost and profit forecasts and all planning for purchasing and production are based on the sales forecast.

Based on the sales forecast, the sales manager establishes goals and requests budgets; plans the nature and the direction of the firm's personal selling efforts; organizes the personal selling function; and staffs the sales department and the sales force. The sales manager directs this sales force in productive activities and effective operations, and exercises control to keep the staff on course.

The sales manager's job includes providing support for salespeople and equipping them with selling tools and aids. Examples include samples of the product, catalogs, manuals, visual aids such as photographs and videotapes, the company advertising schedule, and samples of point-of-purchase items available to retailers. Salespeople may need assistance from nonselling employees in the firm. Specialists (engineers, chemists, accountants) can help salespeople analyze buyers' technical problems and select (even help present and demonstrate) the solution to recommend. For certain products, specialists install and then provide maintenance service. The sales manager must see that salespeople get the information they need about their customers and prospects and the geographical markets for which they are responsible. With it, they can work their territories most profitably and increase their performance.

ORGANIZATION OF SELLING ACTIVITIES

The two principal types of organization for any firm or selling division are line organization, and line and staff organization. Line organization is usually found in very small firms; line and staff organization is adopted as a firm grows in size. A third type of organization, fragmentation, also may develop as organizations grow in size.

LINE ORGANIZATION

In line organization, authority flows in a direct line from a top executive to the first-ranking subordinate, from this first subordinate to a second-ranking subordinate, and so on. This is comparable to the military system of organization in which the line of authority may go from major to captain, from captain to lieutenant, and so on. Each subordinate is responsible to only one person on the next highest level. There are no specialists or advisers. The sales manager of a field sales force in a small company is often the head of a sales department organized on the line pattern. All the planning for and administration of the department are done by the sales manager.

This type of organization is relatively inexpensive to implement, results in speedy action and decision making, is fairly simple and clear to operate, and permits good control because authority and responsibility are centralized. Disadvantages of line organization are that it suffers from the absence of specialization and tends to reflect the weaknesses of any one-person situation. Expansion tends to result in too many levels of authority.

LINE AND STAFF ORGANIZATION

As a firm grows, **line organization** often becomes unwieldy, and the need for a line and staff organization develops. With this type of organization, the top marketing executive may no longer be the sales manager, as is typical of small firms, but rather a vice-president of marketing. This individual represents the top of the "line" of marketing authority, and may have a staff consisting of a sales manager, an advertising manager, a sales promotion manager, and a marketing research director. The line of authority goes from vice-president of marketing to sales manager to regional sales manager (if there is such a position in the firm), to field salespeople. The vice-president's staff gives advice and makes suggestions on how best to conduct marketing activities. People holding staff positions have no authority over such line individuals as field salespeople, but they do have line authority over their own assistants. Figure 19-5 provides an example of a line and staff sales organization.

Line and staff organization allows the utilization of experts in a specific area and results in the effective division of effort toward a common goal. Staff members plan and make suggestions; the top executive administers, controls, and coordinates all the activities below him or her in the organization, including both line and staff activities. Responsibility and authority can be clear in a line and staff organization, but mainte-

LINE AND STAFF SALES ORGANIZATION

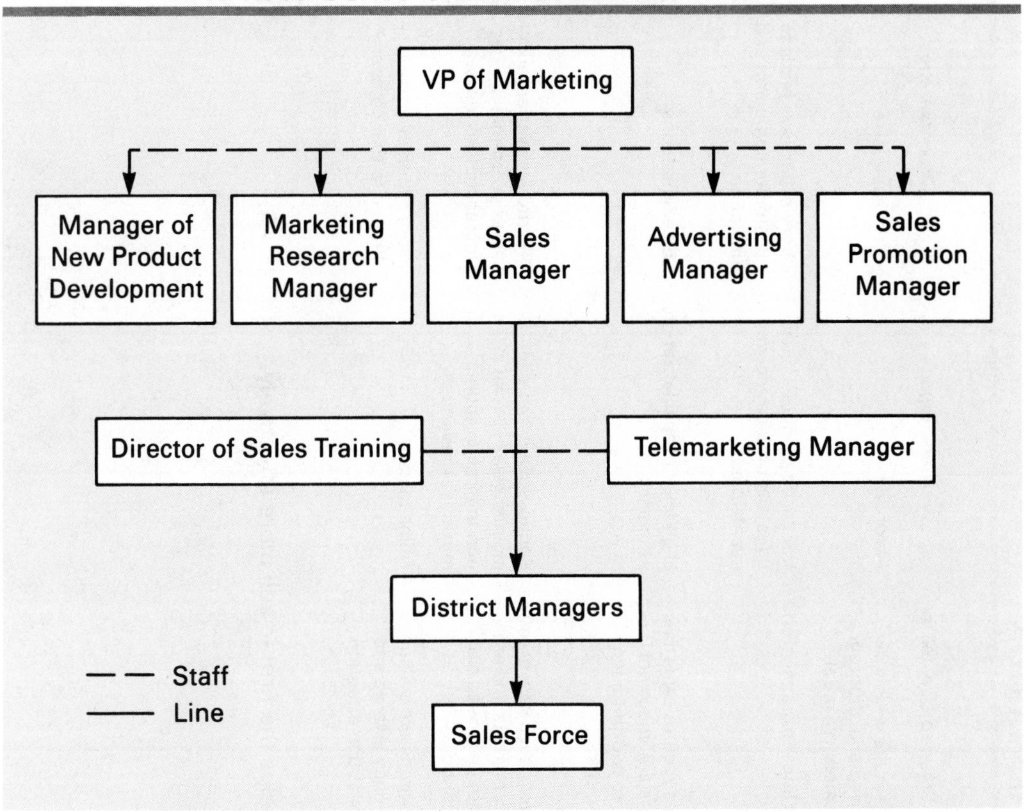

Figure 19-5 **The VP of Marketing manages all line and staff activities within the organization that are marketing related.**

nance of such an organization can be expensive. Troubles can arise if a staff member usurps authority and issues orders to subordinates improperly.

FRAGMENTATION

As a company continues to expand, **fragmentation** may develop. This fragmentation is a subdividing of some already existing phase of an organization. The different bases for organizational fragmentation are summarized in Table 19-1.

GEOGRAPHIC FRAGMENTATION

The most common basis of organization within the sales department is by geography. Most companies are decentralized through the use of regional sales offices separate from the company's headquarters. Other companies have international, as well as domestic offices. The

BASES FOR ORGANIZATIONAL FRAGMENTATION

Basis for Organization	Description	When to Use	Advantages	Disadvantages
Geography	Sales force is broken up into regions and districts with each responsible for itself	Customers are widely dispersed; regional differences in customers are great	Flexibility	Very expensive
Product	Sales force is broken up according to products, product categories, strategies, and product lines	Product line is expensive and complex	Increased product knowledge and problem-solving capabilities	Very expensive; leads to customer confusion and irritation
Function	Sales force is broken up by functions: Servicing current customers Developing new accounts Prospecting and qualifying	Activities require expertise; functions are important enough to warrant such consideration	High level of specialization; efficiency	Size limitations
Market	Sales force is broken up according to the market it serves	Customer needs vary greatly between markets and are large enough to warrant such attention	Reduces customer complaints; gives special attention to large accounts; maximizes revenues	Territories overlap; additional sales personnel are needed; increased expenses
Combination	Combination of the geographic, product-oriented, function-oriented, and market-oriented approaches	Special needs are evident; the company is large and can afford such attention	Tailor-made	Very expensive; use is limited to that company

Table 19-1 Organizational fragmentation often helps the firm to sell more effectively.

company may have several levels of sales managers, such as regional, divisional and district sales managers, as shown in Figure 19-6.

A manufacturer may subdivide the market area geographically so as to have a number of manageable units instead of one large, unwieldy area. Field salespeople in the various territories report to a district or branch sales manager who may be responsible for three or four states. The district sales manager may report to a regional or divisional sales manager who may be responsible for fifteen states and may report to the sales manager in the home office. Just as the district sales manager has line authority over the district's salespeople, the regional sales manager has line authority over the district sales managers.

The advantage of the geographic organization is that it is flexible, thus allowing the company to adapt to the needs, problems, and competitive conditions present in each regional market. The disadvantage of this type of organization is that it is very expensive to establish regional branches and to fill the management positions that are created.

PRODUCT-ORIENTED FRAGMENTATION

Products are a second base on which to divide line authority. The company may organize the sales department in one of four ways: by product division, product marketing group, product specialization, and product managers. The product division organization is used by General Motors. Each of their product divisions, Chevrolet, Oldsmobile, Buick, Pontiac, and Cadillac is run as a separate entity with separate sales outlets and marketing operations. Coca-Cola is organized by product marketing group. All of their products are bottled in the same location; however, each is sold using different marketing strategies. IBM's sales force is organized according to the product specialization format with a separate sales force handling each product category. IBM typewriters are sold by one sales force, personal computers by another, and so on. Finally, the product manager organizational structure is used by Procter & Gamble, with each product having one person in charge of its operation. The product manager is responsible for coordinating the cooperation and resources of the other departments.

The advantage of a product-oriented sales organization is the increased product knowledge and problem-solving abilities of its salespeople. The disadvantages, however, are that it is very expensive because of the high level of specialization, and some customers may have to deal with more than one salesperson from a company, which can create customer confusion and irritation.

FUNCTION-ORIENTED FRAGMENTATION

Many companies choose to organize their sales force according to the functions they perform. These functions include servicing current

A FRAGMENTATION ORGANIZATION

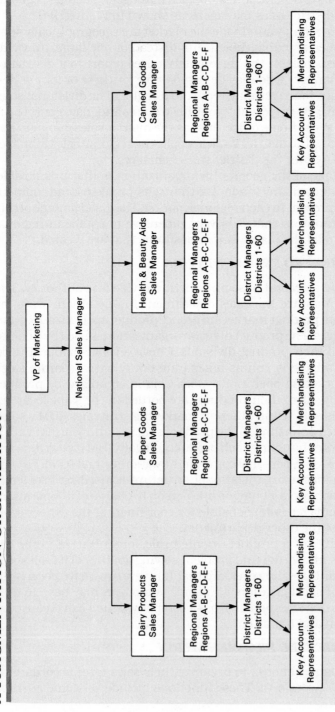

Figure 19-6 Fragmentation organizational structures are typical of most large companies.

customers or obtaining new accounts. Some companies employ tele-marketing staffs to prospect and qualify potential customers, then have other salespeople go in to present and close the sale. Because these functions are all unique, these companies choose to utilize separate sales forces for each.

The advantages of the function-oriented structure are that it offers a high level of specialization among salespeople, and is efficient for performing selling activities. The disadvantage of this structure is that it is limited in its use to certain organizations. Small sales forces lose efficiency with this type of structure, while very large sales forces have so many people performing different functions that it causes confusion and conflicts.

MARKET-ORIENTED FRAGMENTATION

A third basis for subdivision is type of customer. This also can be viewed as a division on the basis of distribution channel. A typical two-way split has one sales manager and sales force selling to domestic customers, with another sales manager and sales force selling to foreign customers. A three-way split might be made by a manufacturer who sells to the industrial market, to the government, and to wholesalers and retailers. A four-way split might find one sales force selling to mass retailers, another selling to foreign customers, a third selling to institutional buyers, and a fourth selling to wholesalers.

An example of market-oriented fragmentation would be the Thomas J. Lipton Company, makers of Lipton Tea, which has two separate sales forces: one for retail sales, and one for what they call "food services." The food services division sells to restaurants, hospitals, schools, and so on.

A company might also choose to separate its sales force according to proximity. For example, one sales force might handle the company's national or key accounts, while another sales force handles strictly local customers.

The advantages of the market-oriented sales organization are that it reduces customer complaints, gives special attention to large accounts, and can maximize and protect their revenues. The disadvantages of this structure are that territories tend to overlap and that it requires additional sales and sales management people, thus increasing expenses.

COMBINATIONS

As companies grow in size and product lines expand, they tend to develop some combination of these fragmentation structures to fit their own special needs. The obvious advantage of this combination is that it is developed with that particular company in mind. The disadvantages are that it is expensive to develop, and its use is limited to that company.

RECRUITING THE SALES FORCE

A very important task of the sales manager is hiring good salespeople. The hiring process starts with recruiting. Since the cost of recruiting has skyrocketed in recent years, sales managers want to find ways to be better recruiters. To do so, they first must set aside enough time to do a thorough job of recruiting. Similarly, an adequate amount of money must be budgeted for this purpose. Finally, the sales manager must keep abreast of the better techniques of recruiting and must make sure that recruiting efforts are planned and systematic. The recruiting process involves doing a job analysis, developing a job description, determining the specifications of the job, and finally, attracting new salespeople.

JOB ANALYSIS

Job analysis is the determination of the responsibilities and assignments that a particular salesperson is expected to have. The establishment of performance standards, rates of pay, and training programs depend on job analyses. In performing a job analysis, a sales manager will generally classify the different types of selling jobs. Then, for each one, some of the following questions may be considered: What do my salespeople do, and how do they go about doing it? What are their problems and difficulties, and how do they handle them? What do the district and regional managers think their salespeople should do? Just what do my salespeople think their jobs should consist of?

JOB DESCRIPTION

A **job description** formalizes the findings of a job analysis. A job description is a written statement of what the salesperson is to do. It represents management's conclusions after executing a job analysis. Typical items on many job descriptions include the official title of the job; the amount of authority the salesperson will have; the salesperson's accountability to others; the relationship of the salesperson's job to other jobs; the salesperson's daily assignments and activities (what products will be sold, the types of buyers to be contacted, the nature of the selling to be done, a breakdown of working time by duty to be performed, routine duties, and self-management and administrative responsibilities); the method of compensation; and the opportunity for advancement.

JOB SPECIFICATIONS

Job specification is a logical extension of job description. A job specification names the personal qualities needed by the individual who is to function successfully in a described job. Items that are often included in job specifications are physical factors, mental factors, environmental factors (such as social class), experience factors (in sales, other business

HIGHLIGHT 19-1   *Components of a Job Description*

Components of a Job Description...

(Panel 1) What will my title be? — Technical Sales Facilitator and Coordinator

(Panel 2) How much authority will I have? — None.

(Panel 3) Who will I be accountable to? — Everybody.

(Panel 4) Where do I stand in relation to everyone else in the company? — At the bottom.

(Panel 5) What are my daily activities? — You will sell all products, to all customers, on a cold-call basis.

(Panel 6) How will I be compensated? — Straight commission. A bag of peanuts for each sale.

(Panel 7) Is there any chance for advancement? — NO! So what do you say?

(Panel 8) I'LL TAKE IT!

situations, and the military), and personality factors (temperament, maturity, persuasiveness, and empathy).

There is, however, disagreement on how various subjective factors should be weighted. How important is age or education? How attractive in appearance should a salesperson be? Is it possible or even desirable to measure motivation or maturity? How much value should be attached to intelligence? Can a person who ranks low in self-confidence or mental ability develop into a superior salesperson? Do high ratings in enthusiasm and health compensate for low ratings in experience and maturity? Finally, because of EEO legislation, subjective factors such as these must be related to performance in the job.

SOURCES OF NEW SALESPEOPLE

A sales manager should experiment to find out what sources of recruits are the most fruitful. Good sales managers identify a number of sources and then set up continuing relationships with them, even when not immediately in the market for trainees.

Figure 19-7 Finding good sales positions requires a lot of effort, as with other careers.

In many circumstances, the sales manager's company can be a productive source of recruits. Nonselling personnel in the sales department, clerical personnel, and engineering and production personnel may have capabilities and knowledge useful in selling jobs. One approach is to ask salespeople and executives to be on the alert for nonselling personnel who might be able to fill selling positions. Seldom, however, does this internal source supply all the needed recruits.

Advertisements, employment agencies, and unsolicited applications are also sources of a considerable number of recruits. Placing "help wanted" ads in the classified section of newspapers and in certain business publications often brings much response, although sometimes of questionable quality. The screening of large numbers of applicants who respond to these ads can be costly. Stipulations in the copy of the ad may aid in screening out undesirable applicants. Some sales managers glance regularly at the "situations wanted" ads placed in newspapers and business magazines by individuals who are unemployed or who want to change jobs.

Some selling firms conduct a recruiting program in which they visit college campuses and interview persons interested in selling jobs. Most recruits from colleges, universities, business schools, or high schools will have had little selling experience, but they can be trained specifically for the selling job in question. Some salespeople also may come from other firms—competitors, allied firms, suppliers, or customers. Over time the sales manager evaluates all sources and then uses the most productive ones for the purpose at hand.

THE SELECTION PROCESS

The selection process consists of determining whether applicants measure up to the firm's specifications, and hiring, if possible, the best who do. Who selects a firm's salespeople? In a small company, the president often does. In a medium-size company, the sales manager usually does. In large companies, a group of sales department executives may do the selecting, aided perhaps by individuals from the personnel department. Even though the sales manager should have the final responsibility and authority for the selection of salespeople, the personnel department may be asked to help in the recruiting, initial screening, and designing of the selection tools. Five basic selection tools will now be discussed: the application blank, personal interviews, references, psychological testing, and physical examinations.

APPLICATION BLANKS

The application blank and the personal interview are the two most widely used selection tools. The application blank supplies background information on the applicant's qualifications and is a record of employment history. Once submitted, it can serve the personnel department as a permanent record. Some firms use a brief preliminary application blank and a brief screening interview. If the applicant is still under consideration after these have been evaluated, he or she is then asked to fill out the firm's detailed application blank. A typical application blank is illustrated in Figure 19-8.

PERSONAL INTERVIEWS

The interview can be used to verify and add to the information contained in the application blank. Also, there is no substitute for face-to-face presence and two-way oral communication when evaluating an applicant on such observable matters as quality of voice, vocabulary and conversational ability, manners, physical characteristics and appearance, ability to impress and persuade, and tact.

One type of interview may be described as a structured interview. Its basis is a standard, written questionnaire which is followed by all interviewers in the firm. The interviewer may read each question directly and record the applicant's answer as it is given, or may memorize the questions and their sequence and record answers only after the applicant has left. Answers recorded after the interview tend to be less accurate than those recorded during the interview.

Another type of interview is described as an unstructured interview, Here the interviewer does little talking, asks open-ended rather than direct questions, appears to exercise little or no control, and encourages the applicant to talk freely.

APPLICATION BLANK

PERSONAL INFORMATION

Name _____

  Last   First   Middle Initial

Address _____

  Apartment No. (if applicable), Street No., and Street

_____

  City   State   Zip Code

Are you a United States citizen?   YES_____   NO_____

EDUCATION

High school attended _____

  Name of School

_____

  City   State

_____

  Years Attended   Did you graduate?

College(s) or univer-
sity(ies) attended   _____

  Name of School

_____

  City   State

_____

  Years Attended   Degree(s) or Hours Earned

_____

  Name of School

_____

  City   State

_____

  Years Attended   Degree(s) or Hours Earned

MILITARY EXPERIENCE

Did you serve in the United States Armed Forces?   YES____NO____

Branch of service _____

Rank attained _____

PROFESSIONAL ORGANIZATIONS

Please list the professional organizations of which you are a member and any offices held or committee assignments in those organizations.

_____

_____

EMPLOYMENT EXPERIENCE

Employers _____

Name of Company

_____

Street Address

_____

City   State   Zip Code

_____

Supervisor's Name and Phone No.

Employment dates: From_____, 19____ to
                           _____, 19____

_____

Last Position Held

_____   _____

Final Salary   Reason for Leaving

_____

Name of Company

_____

Street Address

_____

City   State   Zip Code

_____

Supervisor's Name and Phone No.

Employment dates: From_____, 19____ to
                           _____, 19____

_____

Last Position Held

_____   _____

Final Salary   Reason for Leaving

REFERENCES

References may be business, educational, or character references.
Please supply at least two references.

_____
Name of Reference and Phone No.

_____
Street Address

_____
City   State   Zip Code

_____
Name of Reference and Phone No.

_____
Street Address

_____
City   State   Zip Code

OTHER INFORMATION

Position desired_____

Expected starting salary _____

Figure 19-8 The application blank supplies background information on the applicant's qualifications and is a record of employment history.

Most companies probably conduct interviews which are a combination of these two types. All interviews need to be planned carefully. Rating scales, charts, or forms often are used to organize and summarize the results of and reactions to an interview.

Much college recruiting begins with a short, preliminary interview as the first screening step, sometimes preceding the preparation of the detailed application blank. Often when the more lengthy interviewing starts, a number of interviews may be scheduled. Sometimes the first long interview is at a branch office, with subsequent ones being held at the home office. Generally, there should be more than one interview, and they should be conducted by more than one interviewer.

REFERENCES

It is not uncommon for an applicant to be asked to supply a number of references. Even though no applicant would list people who might provide a bad recommendation, and some may not know as much about the applicant as the sales manager would prefer, the comments of some references may be helpful. References frequently report more freely face-to-face or over the telephone than they would when writing a letter.

Personal references are usually friends of the applicant. Business references are usually former employers. Occasionally they are present or former customers of the applicant. Once in a while, a sales manager is justified in trying to contact neighbors, retailers, teachers, or bankers not mentioned by the applicant.

PSYCHOLOGICAL TESTING

The premise behind the use of psychological testing as a selection tool is that these tests can be used to determine the presence or absence of personal traits essential in successful selling, and the presence or absence of other personal traits found in weak salespeople. There are eight general types of tests in use: intelligence tests, personality tests, vocational interest tests, sales aptitude tests, knowledge tests, polygraph tests, attitude and lifestyle tests, and drug tests.

Figure 19-9 Interviewers almost always question applicants about their applications.

Intelligence tests, or mental ability tests, are used to measure how well the applicant can learn, reason, and solve problems. A high score on an intelligence test is no guarantee that the person being tested will be an outstanding salesperson, however. **Personality tests** are intended to measure purely subjective traits such as confidence and poise. **Vocational interest tests** are intended to identify the vocational areas which appeal to the applicant. **Sales aptitude tests** are designed to measure such selling-related traits as tact, memory, verbal facility, extroversion, persistence, and persuasiveness. **Knowledge tests** attempt to measure how much the applicant knows about a certain product or market. **Polygraph tests**, also known as lie-detector tests, measure the applicant's blood pressure, heartbeat, and perspiration levels as an indicator of personal honesty. Legislation restricts the use of polygraph tests in most situations. **Attitude and lifestyle tests**, used as a substitute for the polygraph test, attempt to assess honesty and to find drug-abusers. An example of the questions used in this type of test is shown in Figure 19-10. Finally, **drug tests** are being used by approximately 50 percent of the **Fortune 500** companies to screen out applicants who may be drug users.

QUESTIONS USED ON ATTITUDE AND LIFESTYLE TESTS

1. How often do you drink alcoholic beverages?
2. How much attention do you pay to your personal appearance and grooming?
3. How often do you daydream?
4. Do you always tell the truth?
5. Do most companies expect employees to always obey company rules and regulations?
6. Do many of your friends and acquaintances use drugs?
7. Do you always tell the truth regardless of the circumstances?
8. How often have you simply thought about stealing something without actually doing it?
9. Most people have tried drugs sometime in their lives. Job applicants usually are either addicted to drugs or have tried them socially or out of curiosity. What kind of person are you? What are your feelings about drugs?

Questions 1 to 8 usually ask the applicant to respond in terms of a five- to seven-point rating scale, such as Never to Very often, or Agree very much to Disagree very much, or Definitely yes to Definitely no. Question 9 is an example of an open-ended question.

Figure 19-10 Questions used on attitude and lifestyle tests are often hard to answer.

It is believed that these tests will become common, and that random testing is apparent in the 1990s.

Psychological testing often can make a valuable contribution to the selection of salespeople. Sales managers act on subjective bases when they rely on their reactions to personal interviews and on the reports from references. Psychological tests—if they are soundly designed, administered, and interpreted—can help supply some objective bases. There is some feeling that psychological tests may be of greater value in screening and rejecting the weak applicant who should not be hired than in identifying the applicant who should be hired. They should never be the sole selection tool used. The personal interview and the applicant's experience as recorded on the application blank are more significant than are test scores. Psychological testing can be a worthwhile aid to, but not a substitute for, the sales manager's judgment.

PHYSICAL EXAMINATIONS

Selling is hard work. Any physical handicap can be quite a burden, and any health problem can be troublesome to both the salesperson and the sales manager. If an applicant cannot qualify physically for the job, this should be determined as soon as possible.

ESTABLISHING THE TRAINING PROGRAM

The need for sales training is common to all sellers. New, inexperienced employees obviously must be taught certain principles and procedures to help them become successful salespeople. But the experienced salesperson also can benefit from training. New types of products appear each year, and the proliferation of brands continues. The increased competition which results calls for more competent salespeople. Because the boundaries of the typical selling job are continually expanding, the need for more effective training also is growing.

A sound training program can justify its cost on several bases. The more expert the sales force is, the larger the sales volume and the greater the gross margin on that volume. Salespeople become productive and profitable more quickly if they are well trained, and their performance approaches their potential sooner than it otherwise would. The better trained salespeople are, the better able they are to control and even reduce direct selling expenses. Good training leads to fewer resignations and fewer dismissals, and the drop in turnover permits reductions in recruiting, selection, and supervisory expenses. The drop also encourages higher morale, makes for more satisfactory relationships with customers, and has a favorable effect on the firm's image.

ORGANIZING THE TRAINING PROGRAM

Each training program must be tailored to the circumstances of the company in question. We have noted various bases of difference among companies. Products can be paper clips or turbines; buyers can be homemakers or purchasing agents; salespeople can merely take orders or they can serve as engineering consultants. Some firms hire only experienced salespeople; others hire graduates with no selling experience. These are just a few of the differences which demand that the training program be tailored to the needs and resources of each company.

The authority and the responsibility for training a firm's salespeople should be given to one person; ideally, this person should be a staff executive who does nothing but plan, organize, train, and supervise. There are, of course, many firms that cannot afford to have an in-house training executive. Usually these firms assign training to a line person—sales manager, district sales manager, or sales supervisor. Outside training organizations are used in certain cases for specific purposes. A firm's personnel department sometimes does some of the training of salespeople (in company history and organization, for example), but the sales manager is usually responsible for what the salespeople are taught about

Figure 19-11 Training programs are important for both new and experienced salespersons.
Source: Alabama Bancorporation 1978 Annual Report.

buyers, products or services, product applications and uses, and how to sell.

Training can be done in the home office, in the field, or in a combination of the two. A strong case can be made for field training. But certain training—training on company history, policies, products, manufacturing processes, etc.—is often more appropriate at the home office in a somewhat formalized school.

INITIAL VERSUS REFRESHER TRAINING

In many firms, there are two types of training, one for inexperienced recruits, and another for salespeople who have been with the firm for some time, often for years. **Initial training**, for new salespeople, is dominated by on-the-job training; the recruits learn by doing, under the supervision of a senior salesperson, a sales supervisor, or a sales manager. They participate in actual selling situations and get critiques, coaching, and counsel on their performances. Mistakes and weaknesses are spotted and corrected; improvement is noted promptly; the recruit gains experience and confidence before taking over the responsibility for a territory. Salespeople with previous experience need less of this training than do typical trainees, but they are scarce and expensive to hire.

Some initial training is done in classrooms. Newly hired salespeople may be given a comprehensive training course before they report to their territories and begin selling, or they may be given a short, fundamental course, receive on-the-job training, and then return to the office for advanced training.

Refresher training deals with such problems as experienced salespeople's drifting into bad habits, and it provides up-to-date information. Any changes the firm makes in the marketing areas of product, distribution, price, or promotion, as well as changes in competition, regulations, availability of raw materials, buyers, problems, personnel, and opportunities, can be announced and explained. Refresher training can amount to continuous training if it is done often—a brief training session every Saturday morning would be an example. Much refresher training is done at sales meetings, and some is done through special courses.

TECHNIQUES OF SALES TRAINING

As was suggested earlier, certain training techniques are appropriate for classroom use, whereas other techniques are more suitable to the field. Lectures have a place in the classroom. Panel discussions and group discussions can be effective classroom techniques. Demonstrations of "how-to-do-it" and role playing also can be valuable in the classroom. Analysis and discussion usually follow demonstration and role playing.

Most sales managers consider on-the-job training essential. Although the classroom is useful for informational training, on-the-job training is better for developing good work habits and breaking bad ones. Some of the more common training aids are described in Figure 19-12.

CONTENT OF TRAINING PROGRAMS

The training program should teach salespeople how best to spend their time. The content of the training program should reflect what salespeople need to know, what they should do, and how they should do it. The program also should show salespeople how to handle common and troublesome problems—customers' problems as well as their own. It should teach them about their customers, their products, and how to sell those products to customers.

The following topics and subtopics are found in most training programs: (1) company—history, organization, and policies; (2) company procedures—credit, shipping, expenses, and complaints; (3) products—manufacturing, features, prices, and uses; (4) buyers—buying motives, buying habits, problems, and attitudes; (5) market—territory, routing, business conditions, and competition; (6) selling—presentation, demonstration, objections, and closing; and (7) non-selling duties—planning, prospecting, customer service, and paperwork.

SUMMARY

Managers perform four functions: planning, organizing, directing, and evaluating. The planning process consists of the situational analysis, setting objectives, determining industry potential, determining the company sales forecast, developing strategies and specific activities, budgeting, implementing, and controlling the plan. The sales budget is a financial plan that outlines how company resources and the selling effort should be allocated.

Organizing refers to determining the number of salespeople needed, allocating selling activities, matching salespeople with positions and/or territories, and assigning responsibilities to each salesperson. In line organizations, authority flows in a direct line downward, with each person responsible to one superior. In staff organizations, staff people have no authority over line employees other than their own assistants.

Recruiting is finding new salespeople for the company. Sources of new recruits include advertisements, employment agencies, unsolicited applications, college recruiting programs, and other firms.

Application blanks and personal interviews are the two most widely used selection tools. Training programs are needed for both inexperienced and experienced salespeople.

TRAINING AIDS

Sales Manuals: May be binders or books that contain information on the company, its objectives, policies, procedures, products, competition, and industry(ies).

Textbooks: Used to teach the finer points of selling and various sales techniques.

Personal Computers: Used to teach selling techniques, sales analysis, sales planning, routing, scheduling, and so forth.

Movies: Usually show salespeople in various situations and how those situations are overcome.

Slide Presentations: Photos usually show the company, its products, and various selling concepts.

Records: Company records can show trends occurring with products and within certain industries.

Charts and Graphs: Usually used within the aforementioned manuals, movies, and slides.

Products: Salespeople can learn a lot just by taking apart, or by using their own products.

Videotapes: Serve the same purpose as movies and slides, but are far easier to use.

Teletraining: Links sales offices with the home office by way of a telephone line and a video link via satellite. Participants in different locations can speak and see each other and the trainer who is located in the home office.

Simulation Games: Computer programs that set up a situation and allow the salesperson to act as the decision-maker. These programs are highly structured and very realistic.

Correspondence Courses: Learn-on-your-own courses that are most effective teaching product data, company policies, and competitive information. These courses do not, however, teach one how to sell.

Interactive Videodisks: Combines video with minicomputers and allows the trainee to control the program. Video segments are combined with the computer's menus and programs. The trainee watches a video presentation, and then does exercises on the computer.

Figure 19-12 Most successful salespeople use several training aids in each sales presentation.

KEY TERMS

Line organization
Life and staff organization
Fragmentation
Job analysis
Job description
Job specifications
Intelligence tests
Personality tests

Vocational interest tests
Sales aptitude tests
Knowledge tests
Polygraph tests
Attitude and lifestyle tests
Drug tests
Initial training
Refresher training

REVIEW QUESTIONS

1. What are the four primary functions of managers?
2. What are the stages of the planning process?
3. What are the steps of the organization process?
4. What are the specific concerns of the sales manager's directing function?
5. What is a *sales analysis*?
6. How are promotion budgets broken down?
7. Describe a line organization structure.
8. Why does fragmentation occur?
9. What are the five methods of fragmentation?
10. List four possible outcomes of unsound recruiting.
11. What must the manager consider when doing a job analysis?
12. What is the difference between a job description and a job specification?
13. List five sources of new salespeople.
14. What is a structured interview?
15. What are the advantages of psychological testing?
16. Why are physical examinations necessary?
17. How can the expense of training programs be justified?
18. What training techniques are best used in the classroom?
19. List five topics usually covered in training programs.
20. List at least seven aids used in training salespeople.

DISCUSSION QUESTIONS

1. Compare the sales forces of two local companies in terms of how they are fragmented (i.e., geographic, product-oriented, function-oriented, market-oriented, combination). Considering the characteristics, advantages, and disadvantages of each structure, why do you think these companies chose the structure they did? Do you feel it is the most effective structure for them? If not, what would be better?

2. How would you respond to a complaint by a senior salesperson that a required refresher training program is just a waste of valuable time that could better be spent on selling?
3. Where is there greater room for ingenuity by the interviewee—in a structured or unstructured interview?
4. From a sales manager's perspective, why do you feel it is necessary to submit applicants to a drug test? Now, from an applicant's point of view, how do you feel about having to take a drug test in order to get a job?

CASE 19-1   MOTOR PARTS, INC.*

The engine electrical equipment industry (SIC 3694) is almost a 2-billion-dollar-a-year industry. In recent years competition has increased from U.S. companies; in 1990 there were 32 companies officially classified as manufacturers of engine electrical parts and accessories for motor vehicles. But the U.S. auto parts industry also is facing strong competition from abroad.

The engine electrical equipment industry is divided into three main segments. Original equipment parts are supplied domestically to Ford, General Motors and Chrysler. Companies supplying these parts are called original equipment manufacturers (OEM's). The second segment is called the aftermarket or replacement parts segment. Aftermarket parts are supplied to wholesalers and retailers of autoparts—to be sold to repair automobiles after they have left the factory. The third segment is called the non-automotive segment—it supplies parts for engines other than automobiles.

Motor Parts, Inc., sells to two of these segments—the OEM (original equipment manufacturer) parts segment and the aftermarket parts segment. Motor Parts, Inc. has been in business for over 30 years and has manufacturing plants in the United States, Canada, and Mexico. Sales are handled by a National Sales Director and ten regional sales representatives. The regional sales representatives line up independent manufacturer's representatives who actually do the selling. The manufacturer's representatives are paid on a commission basis and generally carry products of several non-competing companies. In the last couple of years the regional sales representatives have had a lot of trouble recruiting and keeping manufacturer's representatives. In the past they simply signed them up and they usually stayed with Motor Parts. But three years ago the industry leader, Standard Motor Products, Inc., started taking away their best reps. The National Sales Director could not understand why the reps were going to Standard Motor Products because she thought

---

*Case prepared by Mark Johnston. Used with permission.

their commission schedule for reps was very competitive. She recently ran into one of Motor Parts former reps and asked him why he quit. He said the reason was that Standard Motor Products offered him a sales training class and an extensive sales support package. The former representative indicated that the sales training class was especially helpful because it provided useful information on generating new prospects and minimizing problems with current customers through greater service. The sales support package included information on the following:

- Industry sales by region and state
- Industry sales by customer type
- Industry sales by product line

In addition, the package included general information about the target market by state (exhibit below). To obtain a clearer view of the market by state, company analysts began computing the payroll per employee and the percent of large (over 100 employee) plants.

EXHIBIT 19-1
CHARACTERISTICS OF FOUR-STATE MARKET AREA

Area	Employment	Payroll	Total	Establishments >100 Employees
Georgia	1,405	$31,850,000	15	5
Virginia	451	$7,292,000	9	2
North Carolina	547	$9,379,000	9	3
South Carolina	E	D	4	2
United States	50,577	$1,082,650,000	415	83

E = 1,000–2,499
D = Figures withheld to avoid disclosure

Source: County Business Patterns, U.S. Bureau of Census

PAYROLL AND PLANT SIZE ANALYSIS

Area	Payroll per Employee	Percent Large Plants
Georgia	$22,669	33%
Virginia	_____	_____
North Carolina	_____	_____
South Carolina	_____	_____
United States	_____	_____

CASE QUESTIONS

1. Using Lotus, complete the analysis of payroll per employee and plant size. Which state appears to have the best-paid employees (in this industry)? Which state appears to have the greatest concentration of large plants?
2. What can Motor Parts, Inc., do to keep its reps from quitting and going to work for Standard Motor Products?
3. How could the sales rep use the information provided in the sales support package?
4. What else could be helpful to include in a sales support package?
5. What kinds of things should be emphasized in a training program for a company like Motor Parts, Inc., that employs independent manufacturers' representatives?

CASE 19-2   CITIZENS BANK: INTRODUCING SELLING IN A COMMUNITY BANK*

Bob Newcastle knew he had either the chance of a lifetime, or a challenge too big to handle. The problem was, he didn't know which.

During spring break of his final year in college, Bob had been contacted by Isabel Torres, the new president of Citizens Bank in Austin, Texas. Ms. Torres had just been hired away from a larger downtown bank, and had a reputation for being an aggressive executive who liked to change sleepy departments into dynamic ones. Torres had learned about Bob from his father, who operated his own small accounting firm and was a long-time business customer.

As Bob made the two-hour drive back to campus, he reflected on his conversation with Ms. Torres the day before. During their meeting, Ms. Torres had told Bob that she wanted to make some changes at Citizens.

"Bob, Citizens has been in the Austin community for 50 years. Many of our customers are senior citizens who are very loyal because we provide the finest of service. Our customers feel they have a real relationship with their bank.

"But things in banking are changing. Even small banks like Citizens can't afford to ignore the new opportunities in corporate banking products and services available today. And we certainly can't ignore the threat of increasing competition! We've got to stay competitive ourselves by developing new products and services for the corporate market. And we have to be more aggressive in soliciting new corporate customers. 'Busi-

---

*Case prepared by Barbara Baker Motley. Used with permission.

ness as usual' won't work if Citizens expects to survive and prosper in the future."

Ms. Torres's master plan was to fundamentally change the job description of her corporate banking officers. Instead of simply sitting in the bank waiting for business customers to come and ask for a loan or some other service, she wanted them to go out and prospect for new business customers. She told Bob that her former bank had grown to $800 million in loans from $500 million in just three years after initiating an active corporate business development program. The bank had accomplished these impressive results with a team of 15 young business development officers, all of whom had gone through a two-week intensive financial sales training course offered by the American Bankers Association in Washington, D.C. Bob got the feeling Citizens could be just as successful following the same plan.

"What we really need, Bob, is a sales plan. I was a star sales rep at IBM before going to work for my former bank. We need to train our corporate banking officers to become effective salespeople for Citizens, and then back them up with a solid commission and record-keeping system."

Ms. Torres said she wanted a young, aggressive, knowledgeable person to spearhead her new sales system concept, someone to anchor her "new team of bankers" and "follow in her footsteps." Then she said she'd like Bob to be that person. She was willing to offer Bob a $15,000 base salary, plus a percentage of any new profits resulting from his business development efforts. While Bob and the other five loan officers, ranging in age from 50 to 65, would continue to work directly for Ed Terrell, the 62-year-old head lending executive, Torres would throw all her support behind Bob's business development efforts. She wanted Bob to "set an example" for the other corporate banking personnel.

Bob was flattered, but asked Ms. Torres if he could have two weeks to think about the offer. Ms. Torres agreed, and asked Bob to call her no later than April 30th.

That evening, Bob asked his dad what he thought about the opportunity and about Citizens in general. His dad had some valuable insights to share.

"Well, Bob, I've been a business customer with Citizens for 20 years, and I have always been pleased with the bank. The new president, Isabel Torres, was hired to turn the bank around. But I don't know how well she is accepted by the old guard corporate banking department. You know, they are all older and pretty set in their ways. I can't see them all of a sudden thinking of themselves as sales reps rather than credit people! While I know you like to sell, somehow, I think they see selling as an unappealing activity."

Bob's head was swimming as he unpacked that night in his dorm room. It sounded as though both Ms. Torres and his father agreed that the business development program was necessary. He felt his college coursework made him qualified to sell banking products and services to business prospects. But would the loan officers accept him, or their own new selling responsibilities? And had his courses in sales and sales management prepared him to tackle a new sales job when no real job description existed yet?

He decided that he needed to talk to some more experts. The next day, he made appointments with his personal selling instructor, Dr. Fierro, and the banking professor, Dr. Joseph. Bob felt he could better understand the job ahead of him with some more facts about selling in banks and tackling a new sales position in general.

CASE QUESTIONS

1. What questions should Bob ask his sales professor? What questions should he ask the banking professor?
2. What are some of the problems Bob will face if he accepts this job? List at least five.
3. What might be the rewards of this job if Bob decides to accept Ms. Torres's offer? List at least five.
4. If you were Bob, would you accept the job? Why or why not? Are there additional questions Bob should ask Ms. Torres? What are they?
5. If you were Bob, and accepted the job, what would your new job description look like?

CHAPTER 20
Managing the Sales Force

After studying this chapter, you should be able to:

- Understand the problem of establishing sales territories
- Describe four approaches to sales forecasting
- Comment on establishing sales quotas
- Name and explain the methods of compensating salespeople
- Identify the ways of handling salespeople's expenses
- Recognize the techniques of directing salespeople
- Identify the five leadership styles

The first sections in this chapter deal with establishing sales territories, making sales forecasts, and setting sales quotas. Certain terms are common to each of these topics; before beginning our discussion, it would be well to define these terms.

Market potential is an estimate of the highest possible dollar or unit amount of a product or service that an entire market could be persuaded to buy, from all sellers, during the coming year. **Market forecast** is the realistic estimate of what that entire market will actually buy during the coming year. The **sales forecast** is the estimate of how much of the market forecast a specific firm will sell if it follows a certain marketing program. A company may consider two or three marketing programs, each having its own sales forecast, before adopting a single one.

When **market share** is a projected figure, it is the ratio of a firm's sales forecast to the market forecast. When market share is an actual figure, it is the ratio of the firm's sales for a previous time period to market sales for that period. **Sales quotas** are the portions of the total sales forecast after it has been broken down by buyer; by day, week, and/or month; by sales territory and basic unit; by product and/or product line; or by salesperson. Each salesperson and sales territory will have a quota. A **sales territory** is the specific portion of a firm's total physical market that is assigned to any one salesperson.

With these concepts in mind, let us now look at the sales management activities of establishing sales territories, making sales forecasts, and setting sales quotas.

ESTABLISHING SALES TERRITORIES

A sales territory may be viewed as the geographic area in which a salesperson works—an area ranging in size from a section of a city to a number of states—or it may be viewed as a group of customers assigned to a salesperson. Sales efforts and sales management are much more effective when each salesperson has his or her own territory. The salesperson can budget the appropriate amount of time and selling effort for each customer in the territory, so that no customer is neglected or visited too often. Responsibility is clear when each salesperson is assigned a territory, and this works to reduce the friction among salespeople and between each salesperson and the company. Duplication of selling effort is avoided, and no profitable market is overlooked. Planning and control are more efficient. Each salesperson can be assigned a reasonable quota, and budgeting becomes more precise. Profitable and unprofitable markets can be readily identified.

Perhaps the most important reason for establishing territories in the 1990s is the rapidly rising cost of making a sales call. By establishing territories, the sales manager has eliminated many of the costs associated with overnight travel, and has taken the first step toward making the sales force more productive.

DECIDING ON THE BASIC TERRITORIAL UNIT

The first step in establishing sales territories is to determine the basic unit of which territories will be composed. Ideally, the basic unit will be small, somewhat homogeneous, and have a stable geographic area. Four possibilities for this basic unit are: (1) cities and metropolitan statistical areas, (2) counties and ZIP Codes, (3) trading areas, and (4) states.

CITIES AND METROPOLITAN STATISTICAL AREAS

Once regarded as a prime means of establishing territories, city boundaries have become much less appropriate because of the continuing growth of suburbs. The Metropolitan Statistical Area avoids some of the weaknesses of the city unit. An MSA is defined by the following standards:

- A city of at least 50,000 inhabitants, or
- An urbanized area of at least 50,000 people *and* a total MSA population of 100,000 or more (75,000 in New England).

The Metropolitan Statistical Area is a relatively homogeneous economic unit. It observes county lines but ignores state lines. For example, the Kansas City area consists of four counties in Missouri and two in Kansas. Because it consists of whole counties, much statistical information is available on or can be compiled for this unit. Metropolitan Statistical Areas account for the majority of retail and wholesale sales.

COUNTIES AND ZIP CODES

Other possibilities for the basic territorial unit are counties and ZIP Codes. The boundaries of a county are firm; it is generally a small unit; and much marketing information is broken down by counties. There are over 3,000 counties in the United States. A few of these, Los Angeles County, Cook County (Chicago), and Wayne County (Detroit), for example, are too large to be covered by one salesperson. Most counties are considerably smaller than most manufacturers' sales territories, however.

ZIP Codes also are used as geographical control units. There are approximately 600 ZIP Codes. Some areas are larger than the average county, but they are always smaller than their state. ZIP Codes are a very useful control unit because they frequently can be used to distinguish between affluent and less affluent areas, or with some other distinguishable demographic characteristic.

TRADING AREAS

A third possibility for the basic unit is the trading area for the commodity involved, a natural marketing unit determined by buying and selling patterns. A trading area consists of two elements: the central market or wholesale trading center (usually a large or medium-sized city), and the commercial area dominated by the central market. The boundary of this territory marks how far from home market-based firms sell or how far from the market buyers who concentrate their purchases with market-based sellers are located.

Delineating trading areas is not always easy, and market researchers use various techniques to determine the breaking points between competing central markets. Because breaking points sometimes ignore county lines and because the majority of marketing data are compiled for units no smaller than counties, it is sometimes difficult to locate comprehensive marketing data on a particular trading area. For this reason, many manufacturers delineate trading areas as precisely as possible but make sure they consist only of whole counties.

STATES

Finally, the state can be selected as the basic unit of which sales territories are constructed. The small manufacturer who sells throughout the national market can justify the use of this basic unit perhaps better than anyone else. For other manufacturers, using the state as a basic territorial unit poses problems. States obviously differ widely in geographic area, population, transportation facilities, buying power, nature of their economies, and size and number of cities. Also, trade ignores state lines. Thus, for many manufacturers, the state is too large and too diverse to serve satisfactorily as a basic territorial unit.

ANALYZING THE COMPANY'S ACCOUNTS

After the sales manager has chosen the basic unit for determining territories, an account analysis should be completed. This is done by listing all of the current and potential accounts in each territory and estimating the sales potential for each. Current and potential accounts are located through current and past company records, trade directories, directories of corporations, mailing list brokers, trade books and periodicals, chambers of commerce, and through computerized yellow pages.

After all accounts are identified, sales potential for each is determined. This process is known as forecasting and will be discussed in depth in the next section.

Personal computers (PCs) have become a tremendous tool for accomplishing these tasks. For example, computerized yellow pages can provide thousands of names within minutes. A sales manager also can store and retrieve all of these accounts and have all necessary information within minutes.

After sales potential is estimated, the PC can help the sales manager by classifying each account according to its sales potential. Many companies use an A-B-C classification scheme, where "A" represents a "hot"

Figure 20-1 Many sources of information are available to help salespeople identify prospects and plan their sales calls.

HIGHLIGHT 20-1 *The Salesperson's Workload Analysis*

I. Territory Workload Analysis

A. Estimate Total Sales Time Required

1. *Number of calls*
2. *Frequency of calls*
3. *Duration of calls*
4. *Interval between calls*

Factors to Consider for Any One Account

1. *Expected value of the account in the short run*
2. *Expected value of the account in the long run*
3. *Past history and market share of the account*
4. *Degree and nature of competition*
5. *Buying procedures and organization of the account*
6. *The needs of the account*
7. *Desire of the account*
8. *Expected profitability of the account*

Example:

20	"A" Accounts	12 X/year, 2 hr/call	480
60	"B" Accounts	4 X/year, 1 hr/call	240
150	"C" Accounts	2 X/year, 1 hr/call	300
		Needed sales hours	1,020

B. Determine Sales Time Available

Working days available

×

Number of hours worked each day

×

Percent of time in actual selling

Example:

220 working days × 9 hours/day × 24.7% selling

= 489 sales hours available

C. *Estimate Time Shortage*

Time required – time available

Example:

Required		*Available*	*Short*
"A"	*480 hrs*		
"B"	*240 hrs*	*489 hrs*	*531 hrs*
"C"	*300 hrs*		
	1,020 hrs		

II.   Time Available

Days available in year:		365
Less:		
–weekends	*110*	
–vacation	*20*	
–holidays	*10*	
–personal absence	*5*	*145*
Working days available in year:		*220*

Average Salesperson's Day

	Actual	*Sales Mgr. Estimate*
Customer selling	*24.7%*	*45.0%*
Prospect	*9.1*	*16.0*
Service (Troubleshooting)	*8.2*	*6.0*
Travel	*20.9*	*13.0*
Waiting	*1.0*	*4.0*
Telephone	*8.3*	*5.0*
Paperwork	*10.3*	*2.0*
Sales meetings	*3.8*	*—*
Meals	*9.3*	*4.0*
Follow-up	*2.6*	*2.0*
Quotes	*1.8*	*—*
Miscellaneous	*—*	*3.0*
	100%	*100%*

prospect or customer, with large sales potential, "B" represents a significantly smaller account in terms of sales potential, and a "C" account the least potential. The computer can sort and list all accounts that have a sales potential of $50,000 or more, for example, and label them "A" accounts much faster than the sales manager can by hand. This process was discussed in Chapter 7 from the salesperson's point of view. It is the sales manager's job to estimate these prospects and their sales potential, and the salesperson's job to actually locate them and make that potential a reality.

ANALYZING THE SALESPERSON'S WORKLOAD

The sales manager's next responsibility is to estimate how much time and effort are needed to cover adequately each basic territorial unit. The manager uses the number of accounts, the number of times each must be called on, the length of each call, and the travel and nonselling time needed to do this analysis. This results in a sales call pattern for that territorial unit. Highlight 20-1 shows a workload analysis that has been done for a salesperson handling the Gulf States territory for a manufacturer of refractory insulation materials.

DELINEATING SPECIFIC SALES TERRITORIES

Each territory consists of one or more basic units, and usually consists of many basic units. In delineating specific sales territories, the sales manager must recognize various influences:

1. The basic nature of the product or service and its price.
2. The buyers on whom salespeople will call, including the number of buyers who are prospects and the number who are customers, who they are (purchasing agents, retailers, or homemakers, for example), where they are located, an estimate of the annual purchases per customer, and the number of buyers a salesperson can satisfactorily handle.
3. The sales volume necessary to support a salesperson.
4. The salesperson's call pattern, including the number of calls made each day or week and the frequency of calls scheduled for each group of buyers.
5. Identity of competitors.
6. Transportation facilities.
7. The salesperson's ability.
8. Sales trends.

In the past, sales managers would use one of two approaches, the buildup or the breakdown approach, to accomplish this. A company using the county as its basic unit might select those counties containing large cities and then add to each a county or counties geographically and/or economically related to that particular county.

When using the breakdown approach, the company has two choices. First, the sales forecast can be broken down into quotas for each basic unit. Then basic units can be combined into territories of the proper size for profitable coverage by one salesperson. Second, the company can determine the average sales volume salespeople are expected to achieve for the period, divide that figure into the total sales forecast, and thus determine the number of sales territories needed. Basic units are then combined to produce that number of territories.

Today, sales managers increasingly are using personal computers to perform this task much faster. There are many software packages available to align territories quickly and with no overlapping.

These software packages make the very tedious job of aligning territories evenly into a rather simple one. However, this does not mean the sales manager is no longer needed. Sometimes, the sales manager may construct a territory even with others in sales potential, but inappropriate for a particular sales representative because of his or her physical or mental capabilities. Some sales reps can handle a difficult workload, while others may need a lighter workload. Thus, the sales manager may have to revise territories from time to time.

REVISING SALES TERRITORIES

Sometimes a firm reduces the sizes of some of its sales territories. Perhaps they were incorrect from the start. Or, more often, a territory's potential becomes too big for one salesperson to cover thoroughly, and the workload becomes too heavy. The company reduces the area the salesperson will be covering (and travel costs, too) so as to increase the time spent with individual customers.

Reducing territories usually upsets salespeople. They may fear a drop in earnings. Occasionally, a good salesperson resigns. So, there should be adequate preparation of salespeople if their loyalty, enthusiasm, and morale are not to suffer—even to the extent of the firm's guaranteeing no drop in earnings for a period of time. Similarly, if certain territories are too small, if their sales potentials are inadequate for salespeople to make satisfactory incomes, increases in territory sizes may be necessary.

Companies sometimes withdraw voluntarily and completely from distant, unprofitable markets. In such cases, wholesalers or agent middlemen may be substituted for salespeople in these markets, or the markets may be ignored completely.

Again, personal computers can be used to make the sales manager's job a lot easier. With one of the territory-mapping software programs mentioned earlier, the sales manager can develop several territorial alignments, each prepared according to different criteria.

Figure 20-2 Personal computers enable salespeople to develop their own sales forecasts.

APPROACHES TO SALES FORECASTING

The sales forecast is basic to all company planning. Sales managers who make short-run forecasts are concerned with seasonal matters and developments. Those who make long-run forecasts, perhaps of two to ten years' duration, are interested in trends. Our principal concern in the following discussion will be with the short-run forecast made for the next calendar year. This forecast should be reviewed after at least six months and preferably at the end of each quarter. Some firms choose to check actual sales against budgeted sales every month or even every week. As a general rule, the shorter the forecast period, the more accurate the forecast.

Because sales forecasts are estimates of sales revenue, forecasters try to identify and evaluate the determinants of **demand**. They start by determining the number of buyers (both customers and prospects) who can use the product to advantage and finance its purchase. They compare their products with competing products to learn competitive advantages and disadvantages. They review their firms' marketing policies, particularly those involving pricing and promotion. They investigate the strategies and tactics of competitors. They take a look at the economic state of the industry and at the current stage of the business cycle.

There are various approaches to the establishment of sales forecasts. Four approaches will receive most of our attention: the executives' judgment approach, the salespeople's judgment approach, time-series analysis and correlation/regression analysis.

JUDGMENTAL APPROACHES

Judgmental approaches rely on the expertise of the company's sales executives and salespeople. They are opinionated approaches based on experience and "feel" for the market and its customers.

EXECUTIVES' JUDGMENT APPROACH

In this approach, the views of top company executives are pooled together into one forecast. It may be just the company president or it may include executives from marketing production, statistics, research, and finance. This is a **top-down planning** approach that relies on a **breakdown** technique. That is, top-level management starts with a very large, general figure, and reduces it to a specific company sales forecast. Ultimately, the forecast is sent down to the implementors (sales reps) to be used as an objective for their efforts.

To illustrate how the executives would develop their forecast, let's start with a forecast of general economic conditions. A review of the leading economic indicators can give the sales executive an idea of whether or not buyers will be willing to spend in the upcoming year. The executive's next move would be to estimate the total market potential for that industry. Once the sales executive has an idea of the money being spent within the industry, how much of that money the company should attain can be estimated. This results in the company's sales forecast.

The executives' judgment or opinion approach can be quick, easy, and inexpensive. Data, experience, and judgment usually come from several sources rather than from a single source. But the forecast can be nothing more than an average of guesses. Some of the executives' opinions may be supported by specific facts, while other executives may have formed their opinions on the basis of intuition. Non-marketing executives may be poorly qualified to engage in sales forecasting. Facts and data relating to the market may be grossly inadequate. Breaking this type of forecast down into quotas can be difficult.

Despite all the disadvantages and criticisms, the executives' judgment approach is the most often used sales forecasting technique among small and medium-sized companies. Most times the owner/pres-

STEPS OF EXECUTIVES' JUDGMENT APPROACH

1. Estimate general economic conditions.
2. Estimate industry's total market potential.
3. Estimate company's share of industry's total market potential.
4. Forecast sales.

Figure 20-3 The executive judgment approach is a useful first step in sales forecasting.

ident and the sales manager get together, examine all the facts available to them, and prepare the next year's sales forecast.

SALESPEOPLE'S JUDGMENT APPROACH

Here the sales forecast is made by the sales force rather than by the company executives. This is a **buildup** approach, starting with each salesperson's estimate of what he or she will sell next year. If thought desirable, the salesperson and the district sales manager can develop the forecast together. This is an excellent example of the Management by Objectives (MBO) theory in practice.

Other approaches include having all the field salespeople come up with an overall sales forecast; having all the district or branch sales managers come up with their total estimate; and/or having all the regional or divisional sales managers prepare their total forecast. If the executives still want to make their forecast, they can; then the four can be compared.

Salespeople in the field know their market and their customers' plans and thinking better than anyone else in the firm. The people forecasting are the ones to whom quotas will be assigned; they know they will be expected to sell the volume forecast. The dangers and risks of one-person forecasts are avoided. Finally, operating breakdowns of the forecast by product, customer, territory, and by salesperson should be relatively easy.

But some salespeople are too optimistic; some are too pessimistic; some will underestimate in the hope of getting a smaller quota. Because the method is time-consuming, some salespeople may resent having to participate. And while most salespeople are conscious of current, local conditions, they may not be well informed about broad economic developments and changes.

QUANTITATIVE APPROACHES

Quantitative approaches make use of statistical techniques to provide a relatively unbiased forecast based purely on the "numbers." These approaches have become very popular in recent years because of their objectivity. The two most commonly used methods are time-series analysis and correlation/regression analysis.

TIME-SERIES ANALYSIS

Time-series analysis relies on past sales data to project next year's results. Time-series analysis attempts to locate four characteristics within past sales data and then apply these characteristics to future conditions. These four characteristics are described below.

- **Trends (T).** Trends are sales shifts, either upward or downward, that occur over the course of several time periods, and are due to changes in factors such as population, technology, or capital structures.

- **Periodic (P).** Periodic movements show sales consistencies that occur within a time period, usually a year, and which could be considered seasonal. Retail outlets experience a periodic sales boost every year during the months of November and December due to Christmas shopping.
- **Cyclical (C).** Cyclical movements show irregular occurrences and reoccurrences of a particular condition. These occurrences are usually longer than one year in duration. They may fall off for several years and then reoccur. An example of this would be fluctuations in interest rates or housing starts.
- **Erratic (E).** Erratic movements represent specific, unpredictable, one-time events such as fads, strikes, wars, or fires.

The sales forecast will be a function (F) of the effect of these four characteristics on sales. Thus, sales = F(T,P,C,E). It is important to note that these characteristics and their effects should be separated from all other effects in order to accurately forecast sales.

CORRELATION/REGRESSION ANALYSIS

Correlation analysis shows the relationship between two variables in order to determine whether or not they are related or "move together." Those variables that are positively related will both increase or decrease together. Those that are negatively related will have an inverse effect—when one increases, the other decreases. For example, correlation analysis might find that as production increases, unemployment decreases, thus showing a negative or inverse relationship. A positive correlation might occur between employee satisfaction and sales—as employee satisfaction increases, so do sales.

In Figure 20-4, correlation analysis is shown through the use of scatter diagrams. In the scatter diagram, the vertical axis represents the dependent variable (Y). The dependent variable is the variable that is to be predicted—in our case, sales. The independent variable (X), in this case number of sales calls, is used to predict the dependent variable; it is shown on the horizontal axis. The dots show different occurrences or measures of Y at differing levels of X.

While implying that a relationship does exist, correlation/regression analysis does not try to prove that a cause-and-effect relationship exists. Regression analysis, however, does try to show that an increase in X will lead to an increase in Y. Figure 20-5 uses scatter diagrams to display this idea.

In diagram a, for every increase in advertising (X) there will be an increase in sales (Y). In diagram b, when production costs (X) increase, sales (Y) decrease. Diagram c shows no relationship whatsoever between sales and employee benefits. Regression analysis can be used to determine the relationship between the number of salespeople used, the

SCATTER DIAGRAM FOR CORRELATION ANALYSIS

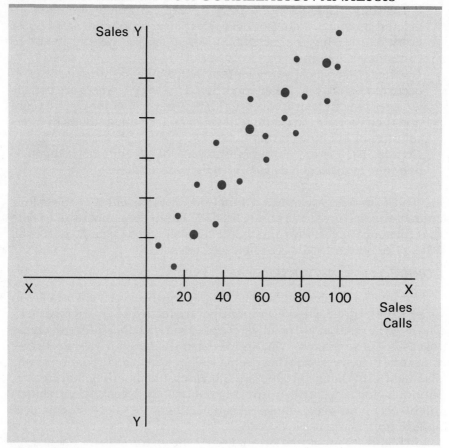

Figure 20-4 Scatter diagrams show how the number of sales calls is related to actual sales.

amount of sales promotion used, or the number of samples given, and sales.

Personal computers can be used to do the number-crunching in these quantitative approaches, thus simplifying this task tremendously for the sales manager. Two computer software programs used to do such analysis are the *Statistical Analysis System* (SAS) and the *Statistical Package for the Social Sciences* (SPSSx).

OTHER APPROACHES

Some forecasters try to base their forecasts on the future behavior of factors which determine demand. The number of births per month

A COMPARISON OF FORECASTING METHODS

	Judgmental Techniques		Quantitative Techniques	
Method	Executive Judgment	Salesperson's Judgment	Time-Series Analysis	Correlation/Regression Analysis
Description	Knowledgeable people within the company make estimates according to the leading economic indicators. The industry's potential is estimated and appropriate adjustments are made.	Each salesperson makes an estimate of what he/she can sell in his/her territory, and all estimates are added together to represent the company forecast.	Past sales data is analyzed to determine trends, and periodic, cyclical, and erratic sales movements. This information is then used to predict future sales.	Relationships between variables are analyzed to identify correlation relationships or cause-and-effect relationships that can be used to predict future sales under varying conditions.
Advantages	Quick and inexpensive.	Sales reps are closest to the market.	Uses several periods of historical sales data.	Very objective.
	Experience comes from many sources.	Sales reps are responsible for attaining the forecast.	Excellent for short-range forecasting.	Causal relationships between two or more variables can be determined.
		Can break down the forecast easily by product, customer, territory, and salesperson.		Easily implemented with the use of a PC.
Disadvantages	Forecast is only an average of guesses.	Sales reps may tend to over- or underestimate forecasts.	Relies on past data.	Often uses information derived from other estimates.
	Forecast may be based on intuition, and not fact.	Sales reps might not be informed about economic developments.	Forecasts may not be indicative of current conditions.	Does not take into account current trends or developments.
	Factual market data may be grossly inadequate.		Method is limited to short-range forecasts.	Complexity of this technique may confuse managers or leave them skeptical.
				Very expensive and time-consuming.

Figure 20-5 Different forecasting techniques are appropriate for different situations.

might well be the most influential factor for a manufacturer of baby foods. The number of four- and five-year-olds could be a major factor for manufacturers of products used in first-grade classrooms. If the seller puts a number of such factors into a composite guide, the resulting statistical maneuvers are far beyond the scope of this text.

Some forecasters include buyer surveys in their overall approaches; these are also called "surveys of buying intentions." Basically, a sample of a buyer group is asked what it plans to buy during some short time period. These surveys probably are of greater value in arriving at market forecasts than in setting sales forecasts.

ESTABLISHING SALES QUOTAS

Sales quotas are sales assignments or goals. They are management's expectations in dollars or units for a specific future period and are assigned to various marketing units. The salesperson and the sales territory form what is by far the most basic of these marketing units. The district sales manager and the district, and the regional sales manager and the region are somewhat similar units. Sales quotas must be set up for each product and/or service. The buyer is another marketing unit that calls for a quota. If salespeople are to meet their quotas, they can do

Figure 20-6 Sales quotas are based on sales forecasts.

so only by selling certain quantities to each of their customers. There can be a quota for sales to the government, for sales to purchasing agents, for sales to wholesalers and retailers, and for sales to foreign buyers. Finally, there is a time variable—the year, the quarter, and the month may each be assigned its own quota.

PURPOSES

Why assign sales quotas? First of all, quotas are established to aid in planning and control. When the sales manager approved the final versions of the job descriptions, what the salespeople's responsibilities were spelled out in a qualitative way; quotas quantify those responsibilities. The sales manager can compare the salesperson's actual sales against the monthly and quarterly quotas to see how sales are going.

Second, the quota can serve as a specific objective or target for salespeople. Some sales managers take the realistic sales forecast for a sales territory, increase it a bit, and assign it as the salesperson's quota for that territory. This may function as an incentive quota. However, if the increase is too great, it does more harm than good.

Third, sound compensation and promotion of salespeople require sound assignments and sound quotas. The quota is usually one of the more important elements in compensation plans and promotion decisions. Quotas can be used to check on the suitability of the sales territories previously delineated by the sales manager. Analysis of salespeople's quotas and sales can suggest that some territories are too large and others too small.

TYPES OF QUOTAS

There are five commonly used types of quotas: (1) dollar volume quotas, (2) unit volume quotas, (3) gross margin quotas, (4) net profit quotas, and (5) activity quotas. By far the most often used quota is that based on dollar volume. For example, a salesperson may be told that during the coming year, sales must total at least $400,000. This is a clear and specific goal. However, sales volume in dollars means little unless it contributes to net profit. A salesperson can reach the dollar quota with an unbalanced and thus undesirable sales assortment and an unacceptable profit showing. Margin and profit quotas urge the salesperson to sell a healthy portion of higher-profit items which are usually higher in price and often harder to sell. These quotas, however, may not be readily understood or accepted by salespeople and also can be expensive to administer.

Gross margin quotas and net profit quotas are linked with expenses—gross margin less expenses equals net profit. In addition to being given an assigned quota, a salesperson typically is told what his or her expense allowance will be, or is offered some sort of reward if expenses do not exceed a budgeted amount.

Activity quotas are based on points rather than on dollar or unit volume; points are awarded for sales and for other accomplishments. Salespeople may earn points for calls made, new customers, product demonstrations, point-of-purchase items installed, missionary sales work, or collections. Activity quotas are designed to ensure that the salespeople are doing their jobs. Thus, the sales manager will set a quota for the number of calls the salesperson must make every day, and will use this information when evaluating the salesperson.

SETTING DOLLAR VOLUME QUOTAS

In thinking about how to set sales volume quotas in dollars, the sales manager visualizes sales territories, each consisting of its own basic units. The basic unit, you recall, is the fundamental geographic unit (MSA, county, state) used in setting up sales territories and forecasting. So what is needed first is the sales forecast by basic unit and by sales territory. If we use the salespeople's judgment approach, we automatically have forecasts by sales territory; if we use one of the quantitative approaches, the sales territory forecast is based on historical data from each basic unit. But we may have followed the executives' judgment approach and have only a total sales forecast. In this case, the total figure must be apportioned over the sales territories (and probably even over basic units) according to some market index. One of the better-known and more widely used indexes of this sort is *Sales and Marketing Management*'s annual "Survey of Buying Power." Regardless of the index used, the odds are great that it will reflect both past sales and market potential.

At this point we have sales forecast by sales territory, and the sum of these territorial forecasts equals the overall company forecast. What we need are sales quotas for the sales territories. Our initial recognition is that in many instances, perhaps even in the majority of instances, the forecast becomes the quota. This makes sense. We commit ourselves to make 100 percent dollar sales next year. But, as suggested earlier, some sales managers might add something to the forecast. These adjustments are referred to as incentive quotas. There are downward adjustments, too. For example, the quota may be tied to the compensation plan in the following manner: a quota of 90 percent of forecast, a bonus for a sales volume of 100 percent, and an additional bonus to salespeople who reach 110 percent.

Quotas can be harmful if they are too high or too low. This argues for a realistic, accurate quota which the salespeople can reach if they work reasonably hard. To be of maximum effectiveness, the quota must be understood and accepted—ideally, even approved—by the salesperson. Salespeople's participation in quota setting may help to avoid the risk of friction, suspicion, and resentment. Sales managers can benefit from reviewing quotas each month and informing their salespeople frequently on how they are doing.

COMPENSATION OF SALESPEOPLE

One of the sales manager's heaviest responsibilities is getting the desired amount of production from each salesperson. Some of the tools used in this endeavor are financial in character. The most direct financial motivation is, of course, money in the form of salary or commission. Indirect financial motivations include insurance, hospitalization, sick leave, paid vacations, and retirement income, and are usually referred to as fringe benefits.

WHAT SALES MANAGERS WANT

Sales managers want a compensation plan that will attract, hold, and develop good salespeople because such salespeople are able to acquire, hold, and develop desirable customers. They do not overload their customers, nor do they skimp on service to them.

The compensation plan must keep costs within reason. Maximum cost to the company is not compatible with maximum pay, which salespeople desire, and a compromise must be reached. The plan must not be too costly to administer—it must not force the company to raise its prices to a noncompetitive level.

Sales managers hope the compensation plan provides them with adequate control over salespeople's efforts and activities. Managers want hard work, done in accordance with approved methods and company policies and procedures. Therefore, the plan should also motivate and stimulate. It should encourage greater, more profitable sales. When making quota depends largely on the salesperson's hard work and the salesperson has few nonselling duties, this incentive element should be prominent.

Finally, sales managers recognize that there are real differences between salespeople, sales territories, products, and customers, so they want compensation plans flexible enough to be tailored to company circumstances, objectives, and problems. They know that the plan for paying salespeople must be in harmony with the plans for paying the firm's other employees.

WHAT SALESPEOPLE WANT

The salesperson's first interest is, of course, amount of income. The salesperson wants an acceptable standard of living and the opportunity to raise it over time. Most salespeople prefer two types of income. First, they want a certain part, perhaps enough to cover basic living expenses, to be regular and steady. This is to provide some security regardless of sales volume, and to prevent wide fluctuations in income. Second, they want an incentive element which rewards them for certain specific accomplishments.

The compensation plan should be simple to understand and compute. Salespeople want to be able to figure correctly how much they earned last week or last month. Finally, salespeople must feel that their compensation was determined objectively and fairly. And they feel unfairly treated if made to wait three or four months for pay they earned.

LEVELS OF COMPENSATION

The term "level of compensation" is applied to what the sales manager must pay in order to hire and hold the type and quality of salesperson wanted. Type and quality can involve such matters as education, training, ability, and experience. Compensation level consists of income plus fringe benefits.

Level of compensation is greatly affected by the job description. From the job description, one can infer the difficulties and unattractive features of the job. From it one can picture the type of salesperson needed and his or her current standard of living.

Another influence is the pay received by competing salespeople or the income range for comparable selling jobs. The gross margin potential of the product involved is also an influence. Closely related is the worth of the salesperson to the firm. Still another influence is what the firm pays other types of employee. Finally, there is the relative bargaining strength of firm and salesperson.

METHODS OF COMPENSATION

The following discussion will examine the compensation methods of straight salary, straight commission, and salary plus incentive. In all three methods, earnings or income are separate from expense allowances or reimbursement.

STRAIGHT SALARY

This method of compensation is fixed. A salesperson is paid a specified amount regardless of sales volume or performance. Several advantages are credited to the straight salary method. It is simple, specific, and economical to administer. Stability of income gives the salesperson security. Straight salary is particularly appropriate when the sales manager wants the salesperson to do a well-balanced sales job. The salesperson's income does not suffer when the sales manager assigns educational, public relations, service, or missionary tasks. When the trainee is new, when the product is new and its initial potential is low, or when the firm is entering a new market, straight salaries are logical.

Straight salary ranks low as an incentive. Consequently, the sales manager must be responsible for stimulating and motivating the salespeople. The sales manager must also pay close attention to salespeople, give close supervision to their activities, and do much checking up.

There are other disadvantages to straight salary, also. Unit selling costs cannot be predicted with confidence because future sales volume is unknown. The ratio of selling costs to sales volume, as a percentage, goes up and down as sales volume goes down and up. There is a problem of fitting salaries to salespeople; older salespeople may be overpaid, and new salespeople may be underpaid. Unless reviewed and revised frequently, the salary structure can become out of date.

STRAIGHT COMMISSION

Under straight salary, sales managers buy salespeople's time. Under straight commission, we see them buying salespeople's accomplishment, paying according to productivity, which is usually measured in sales volume. This is variable compensation.

The great asset of the straight commission plan is its powerful incentive. The more salespeople sell, the greater their income. Under this method, the salesperson enjoys considerable freedom of operation. Straight commission may attract the better salesperson. It can be as simple as 5 percent on net sales, or it can be flexible and tailored. Different rates can be assigned to different products, for different types of buyers, for in-season and out-of-season sales, and to different salespeople and sales territories.

METHODS OF COMPENSATION

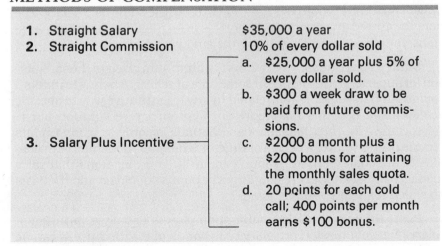

1. Straight Salary	$35,000 a year
2. Straight Commission	10% of every dollar sold
3. Salary Plus Incentive	a. $25,000 a year plus 5% of every dollar sold.
	b. $300 a week draw to be paid from future commissions.
	c. $2000 a month plus a $200 bonus for attaining the monthly sales quota.
	d. 20 points for each cold call; 400 points per month earns $100 bonus.

Figure 20-7 Each company should select which method of compensation is most appropriate for them.

There are, however, several disadvantages to straight commission. The job of setting fair commission rates is not easy. Sales territories often vary in potential, as do assignments of nonselling tasks. Dollar income can fluctuate, sometimes wildly, causing some feeling of insecurity or even some temptation to resort to high-pressure selling. High-pressure selling is bad in itself, but it can also result in the salesperson's neglecting nonselling duties and the firm's interests. House accounts (sold by a company official and ineligible for commissions) can be a cause of friction. If two or more salespeople contribute to making a sale, dividing the commission between them can be a problem.

SALARY PLUS INCENTIVE

Salary plus incentive is by far the most popular of the compensation methods because it combines the advantages of the two plans and avoids many of the disadvantages. There are four principal types of salary-plus-incentive plans: salary plus commission, drawing account plus commission, salary plus bonus, and the point system.

Salary Plus Commission. This is perhaps the most common of the salary-plus-incentive plans and may be appropriate for the salesperson responsible for both selling and servicing. The salary portion can range from 30 percent to 90 percent of the salesperson's total income. The commission may apply either on all sales or only to sales over a certain amount per month.

Drawing Account Plus Commission. A drawing account is a fixed advance of money to the salesperson which is to be repaid from commissions earned. Guaranteed draws do not have to be repaid if the salesperson's commissions for the drawing period are less than the draw. Thus, the guaranteed draw is virtually the same as a salary. The nonguaranteed draw works as a short-term loan against future commissions; the salesperson must repay the amount advanced.

Salary Plus Bonus. A bonus is a lump sum given to the salesperson for superior performance in some area of selling. A bonus is unlike a commission in that it is not related in any quantitative way to specific achievement. A bonus may represent appropriate recognition of the salesperson who has had few cancellations of orders, who submits reports promptly over a period of time, or whose relationships with customers are characterized by much goodwill. Two questions that sales managers must answer are how large the bonus should be, and the basis on which it should be distributed.

Point System. This combination plan is usually a variation of salary-plus-commission or salary-plus-bonus plans. Because it can be extremely complicated to implement, it is not widely used. With this plan, the salesperson earns points for various types of accomplishments. A certain number of points may be earned for every $100 of sales volume and other points may be earned for such things as the number of calls made, point-of-purchase displays installed, and product demonstrations made. There can be penalty points as well as credit points.

FRINGE BENEFITS

Fringe benefits are typically defined as supplementary wage benefits provided salespeople regardless of their performance as long as they remain on the payroll. Most sales managers are pleased with their fringe benefit programs. These benefits boost morale, reduce turnover, and are often essential to attract, hold, and increase the loyalty of desired salespeople.

Federal old-age and survivors insurance (social security), workers' compensation, and unemployment insurance are required by law. Other benefits offered by some companies include: hospitalization, medical, dental, and life insurance; paid holidays and vacations; moving costs; sick leave; loans; stock purchase plans; and educational assistance.

METHODS OF HANDLING SALESPEOPLE'S EXPENSES

A salesperson's business expenses are often sizable, and it is understandably easy for them to get out of hand. Thus, it is important that sales managers carefully watch the expenses of their sales personnel. For an expense plan to be effective, the salesperson's earnings must be handled separately from expense reimbursements or allowances. A salesperson should neither make money nor lose money on an expense account. The company should pay all the legitimate expenses that the salesperson incurs. Most sales managers consider the following to be legitimate business expenses: transportation, out-of-town lodging, out-of-town meals, telephone and telegraph charges, and business entertainment.

Expense plans should be simple and economical to administer, and their design and operation should minimize friction between the sales force and management. Every expense plan must be flexible. It should harmonize with the firm's compensation method, should recognize the nature of each sales territory, and should reflect awareness of the type of buyer the salesperson contacts.

Though selling expenses have increased tremendously, from an average of $250.45 in 1972 to $726.23 in 1985,[1] there has been one re-

---

[1]"Survey of Selling Costs: Onward and Ever Upward," *Sales and Marketing Management* (February 17, 1986): 10.

ADVANTAGES/DISADVANTAGES OF COMPENSATION PLANS

Plan	Advantages	Disadvantages
Straight Salary	Provides security Develops loyalty Increases flexibility (Salespeople not attached to particular territories) High degree of control over the sales rep Easily adapted to market changes Easy to implement	There is no financial incentive High selling costs when sales are low Inequitable (Poor producers are overpaid; good producers are underpaid) Does not encourage excellence
Straight Commission	Income based on productivity Easy to calculate earnings Unlimited earnings potential Money paid only when sales are made Expenses proportionate to sales Eliminates poor performers Provides objectivity	Sales reps may treat customers as though they were "meal tickets" High turnover rate Discourages loyalty Uncertain compensation Neglects nonselling activities Leads to poor buyer-seller relationship No control over salespeople
Salary Plus Incentive	Provides best control over salespeople, because all desirable activities are rewarded Provides security Encourages excellence Provides frequent and immediate reinforcement	Complex Hard to understand Expensive to implement Objectives may not be met

Figure 20-8 In selecting a particular compensation plan, firms should carefully evaluate their advantages and disadvantages.

cent development that may serve to at least slow down this growth somewhat. In 1986, tax legislation was passed allowing only 80 percent of entertainment selling costs to be deducted.[2]

EXPENSE PLAN #1—SALESPERSON PAYS

A few salespeople working on straight commission pay all their expenses. The commission rate is set high enough to allow for expenses that the salesperson will incur. Thus, an 8 percent commission may represent 5 percent for income and 3 percent to cover the salesperson's expenses. Although this method of handling expenses is extremely simple, it is not widely used because it gives management little control and because salespeople may skimp unnecessarily on what they spend, even when the expenditure would enhance sales productivity.

EXPENSE PLAN #2—UNLIMITED REIMBURSEMENT

The most widely used method of handling expenses requires the salesperson to submit an itemized expense report. The salesperson receives an advance and then, when the itemized expense report is approved, he or she is reimbursed if expenses exceed the advance. Any money not spent is turned in. Because each salesperson knows that his or her reports will be examined, the likelihood of padding is reduced.

EXPENSE PLAN #3—LIMITED REIMBURSEMENT

There are two versions of the limited reimbursement plan. In the first version, itemized expense reports are required, and there is a maximum budget figure which cannot be exceeded. The salesperson typically has some freedom within such a budget because there is a ceiling on total expenses but not on any specific item.

The other version includes an additional constraint: it places a ceiling on expenditures for specific items, such as transportation, meals, and lodging. This can be an effective plan if the ceilings imposed are realistic.

EXPENSE PLAN #4—FLAT EXPENSE ALLOWANCE

In this plan, the salesperson receives a certain amount of money each week to cover that week's expenses. There is little administration, and there are no expense reports or disputes about the legitimacy of a certain expenditure. The sales manager must constantly review the flat allowance to see that it is set at the proper level. With this plan, it is easy for the

---

[2]"Corporations to the Party Line," *U.S. News and World Report* (July 14, 1986): 42.

sales manager to determine selling costs. There is always the possibility, however, that salespeople may try to make money on their allowances, or curtail their activities as soon as they have run up expenses equal to the allowance figure.

TECHNIQUES OF DIRECTING SALESPEOPLE

Every sales manager must direct salespeople in such a way that they effectively carry out their assignments, work according to plan, observe company policies, develop their territories as expected, and maximize their own potential. Direction consists of such activities as training, control, encouragement, and guidance.

In smaller firms, the sales manager directs salespeople, mostly from the home office. In larger firms, district sales managers are responsible for direction in the field. Very large companies may have groups of field supervisors or sales supervisors who may do some selling as well as directing. Finally, in some firms senior salespeople may do some directing of junior salespeople. Regardless of title, those who direct salespeople must know how to sell and how to supervise. Many individuals who excel in selling do not have the ability to supervise others.

OBJECTIVES IN DIRECTING SALESPEOPLE

One of the goals of those who direct the work of salespeople is to continue the training of these salespeople. Usually there is an initial training program in the home or branch office. This may be followed by on-the-job training in the field. A second objective is that of follow-up. Someone must see that salespeople understand and follow instructions, that they conform and comply with company policies. A third objective is two-way communication: Salespeople must be kept current and posted on matters which bear on their work, and management needs to stay informed about what is going on in the various sales territories. Fourth, direction is used to achieve better morale. It seeks to encourage the most desirable attitudes toward products, company, buyers, and selling in general. Finally, better planned selling is an objective. Better planning leads to more skillful selling and more productive work. Better routing and better budgeting of time lead to a maximum of face-to-face selling time and a minimum of travel and waiting time.

METHODS FOR DIRECTING SALESPEOPLE

First, because there is no substitute for **personal contact**, sales managers and supervisors spend a considerable amount of time with salespeople. The sales manager may travel with salespeople as they work their sales territory. As the salesperson sells, the manager observes and identifies strengths and weaknesses, and may fill out a rating form on

Figure 20-9 Successful sales managers are sensitive to the individual needs of salespeople.

the salesperson. After a day's work, the two may analyze and discuss the salesperson's efforts. Personal contact makes for understanding and two-way communication. Directing in person is, of course, costly.

Sales managers use various types of **communications** in directing their salespeople. Letters are effective for communicating in some respects, but ineffective in others. Telephone conversations are another type of communication. Periodic mailings, such as house organs and weekly or monthly sales reports, are still another type of communication.

Sales meetings are a third technique useful in directing salespeople. Some retail firms start each day with a brief sales meeting; Saturday morning is meeting time for some sales forces. Quarterly, semiannual, and annual sales meetings are not uncommon. Most meetings address ways of dealing with the salespeople's daily problems; salespeople can exchange experiences and solutions.

A fourth managerial technique in the direction of salespeople is the **conference**. Most are annual, one to three days long, and either regional or national. Conferences can be inspiring and stimulating when they permit salespeople to chat with top management. Training sessions might focus on promotion plans, new policies, new products or services, or better solutions to current problems; these training sessions are often explaining sessions. Plant tours may be scheduled. Salesperson-to-salesperson exchanges of ideas, tactics, and experiences are facilitated. Because big conferences are expensive, because they pull salespeople off their jobs, and because some salespeople attending conferences act as if they are on vacation, teletraining is being considered as an alternative to conferences by some companies.

Reports are a fifth tool employed by sales managers in directing their salespeople. Reports are designed to gather information from and about sales territories, information sales managers use to direct, to control, to supervise, and, often, to rate salespeople's performance. Management's great hope is that a system of reports will encourage salespeople to plan their work and then to analyze their productivity and profitability. There is considerable variety from company to company as to the reports salespeople are expected to submit. Commonly reported matters include daily sales, daily calls made, routing, and expenses.

Contests are a sixth managerial tool. A competitive spirit is almost a prerequisite to even average success in selling. Because so many salespeople are competitive and because salespeople are engaged in competitive situations every week, contests can be a powerful motivating force. Competition can be based solely on the performance during the contest period or on the amount by which contest period performance exceeds some earlier performance.

Every contest needs a purpose or an objective. In most instances, the general, overall purpose is to increase sales volume. The contest must have a theme and a scoring pattern or basis. Boat racing, gold mining, baseball teams, points, wild game hunting, poker hands, and military campaigns are often-used formats. Contest length must be set. Prizes must be determined: cash, merchandise, and travel are the popular types of prizes. The contest must be promoted, executed, judged, and the winners rewarded.

Sales contests have both advantages and disadvantages; managers favor contests more strongly than do salespeople. Those who are enthusiastic about contests stress the stimulating effects of competition and the use of contests to encourage performance along desired lines. Contests can be designed to emphasize certain products or to concentrate sales power on certain types of buyers. Most contests do increase sales volume during the contest period. Special awards to leading salespeople and mention of them in house organs or sales bulletins increase the prestige and feed the egos of salespeople who make an extra effort and achieve greater performance. Contests can show certain salespeople just how much they can sell and bolster their confidence. Contests can make hard work more attractive and acceptable.

Opponents of contests think them childish and undignified. Customers may be overstocked, service to them may be neglected, and future sales may slump. Some contests divert and distract salespeople. Because of technicalities, some people who deserve prizes may fail to get them. Salespeople who don't do well can easily develop a defeatist attitude. Intense rivalry can damage morale and even generate hostility. Some salespeople resent the pressure to win that some sales managers exert on the salespeople's families—for example, a sales manager may attempt to enlist the help of the salesperson's spouse in putting pressure on the salesperson to work harder.

A final managerial technique is that of giving appropriate **recognition** to salespeople. Recognizing superior efforts builds good morale in an organization. The capable sales manager tries in various ways to build each salesperson's pride in achievement, self-respect, and sense of belonging to the sales force and the company. Whether this recognition takes a tangible form—such as a promotion or award announced at a sales convention—or an intangible form—such as private congratulations on a job well done from an executive other than the sales manager—recognition can be an important incentive for a salesperson to work toward better sales efforts.

Finally, an **opportunity to advance** within the sales organization, perhaps toward the sales manager's job, spurs many of the better salespeople to achieve greater performance.

EVALUATING SALESPEOPLE'S PERFORMANCE

Sales managers must evaluate salespeople's performances if total productivity is to be improved. Performance evaluation is essential in determining compensation as well as promotions and transfers, can lead to identification of company policies needing revision, and can be used as a measure of a sales manager's supervisory efforts.

The first step in evaluation is to set up a standard which represents satisfactory performance. Then, actual performance is determined and compared with the standard. The following measures of accomplishment represent one type of standard for evaluating performance: sales volume by product and customer, the relationship of sales volume to quota, gross margin, the relationship of expenses to sales volume, orders classified as to size, and the ratio of sales to calls made. The following measures of activities represent another type of standard: calls per day or week, days worked, product demonstrations made, point-of-purchase displays distributed or installed, or sales meetings held or attended. Qualitative features are a third way of evaluating performance: Customer goodwill, planning ability, imagination and creativity, ambition, product and company information, and appearance are examples of qualitative features.

Evaluation is a prerequisite to the personal growth and development of each member of the sales force. Evaluation is not easy because territories vary, factors other than the salesperson's efforts can have a bearing on sales volume, and some criteria are subjective. But sales managers cannot supervise their salespeople properly unless they know who needs assistance and where this assistance is needed.

LEADING THE SALES FORCE

Sales managers in the field need to have excellent human-relations or "people" skills. They must be able to lead, motivate, and direct their salespeople. This requires a high level of patience and understanding when dealing with seasoned professionals who have, perhaps, lost out on a sale or are facing extraordinary pressures from customers. Salespeople tend to be individualistic, confident, and highly motivated. They may go rapidly from extreme highs to extreme lows. The field sales manager must act as a buffer for these mood swings, and must provide guidance and counseling to the salesperson.

Robert Tannenbaum, et al.[3], have designated five possible leadership styles that sales managers might use in dealing with salespeople. Some sales managers use one leadership style with all of their salespeople, while others adapt their style to each salesperson. Those who are capable of adapting their style are recognized as being more effective because each salesperson has her or his own level of skill and maturity, and needs to be led accordingly.

AUTOCRATIC

The autocratic leadership style is characterized by a "top-down" approach to planning. The sales manager makes all decisions and the salespeople are responsible for implementing the plan. These sales managers use their authority to get results.

Along with this authoritative approach toward salespeople, the autocratic sales manager tends to be interested only in results, and those tasks that were assigned to achieve these results. This approach is most effective when the salesperson is young and inexperienced, or lazy.

PATERNALISTIC

The paternalistic leadership style also utilizes an authoritative approach. However the sales manager takes a more relations-oriented attitude toward the salesperson than with the autocratic style. The sales manager acts as a "father figure" or "big brother" toward the salesperson and uses persuasion to implement the tasks needed to be successful. This style, again, works well with the young and inexperienced salesperson.

CONSULTATIVE

The consultative leadership style takes the salesperson's opinions into account before making the decision. The sales manager using this

---

[3]R. Tannenbaum, I. R. Weschler, and F. Massarik, *Leadership and Organization* (New York: McGraw-Hill, 1961): 24.

style is participative by nature, and generally takes a strong human interest in salespeople and their well-being. The consultative style is most effective with mature and experienced salespeople. They are motivated by the fact that the sales manager values their opinions.

DEMOCRATIC

The democratic leadership style is used when dealing with a small group of experienced sales reps. The sales manager takes a very participative approach, allowing salespeople the freedom to make their own decisions. These sales managers foster group discussion, try to get all salespeople involved, and go with the group's decision.

LAISSEZ-FAIRE

The laissez-faire leadership style allows all salespeople to make their own decisions. It is a very laid-back, "hands-off" type of approach that can only be used effectively with the most skilled and experienced salespeople. The sales manager serves as a sounding board when the salesperson is having trouble, and as a counselor in giving advice about how to achieve goals.

As salespeople develop from trainees into experienced sales representatives, it is not unusual for their sales managers to move through several of these styles. Unfortunately, there are still those managers who use only one style no matter who the salesperson is or how long they have been together.

SUMMARY

Territories are geographical areas in which salespeople work and are composed of cities, Metropolitan Statistical Areas, counties, ZIP Codes, trading areas, or states. Determining these territories starts with an account analysis and a workload analysis, and concludes with a territory definition.

Sales forecasts are estimates of sales revenues over a period of time. Judgmental forecasts can be devised by executives or salespeople. Quantitative forecasts can be determined using Time-Series Analysis or Correlation/Regression Analysis.

Sales quotas are sales assignments or goals used to facilitate planning and control. The five types of quotas are: dollar volume, unit volume, gross margin, net profit, and activity.

Money is the most direct financial motivation. Straight salary, straight commission, and salary plus incentive are the three basic types of compensation plans.

Sales leadership requires excellent "people skills." The five leadership styles are: autocratic, democratic, paternalistic, consultative, and laissez-faire.

KEY TERMS

market potential   buildup
market forecast   personal contact
sales forecast   communications
market share   sales meetings
sales quotas   conference
sales territory   reports
demand   contests
top-down planning   recognition
breakdown   opportunity to advance

REVIEW QUESTIONS

1. What is the difference between market potential and the market forecast?
2. List four factors that influence the size of sales territories.
3. What are the advantages and disadvantages of the salespeople's judgment approach to sales forecasting?
4. What are the advantages and disadvantages of correlation/regression analysis?
5. What are the steps of the territory development process?
6. Why are sales quotas necessary?
7. List five types of sales quota. Which is the most often used?
8. What do salespeople want from a compensation system?
9. What are the advantages of a straight commission?
10. What are the principal types of salary-plus-incentive plan?
11. List three examples of fringe benefits.
12. What are the disadvantages of a system in which the salesperson pays all expenses?
13. List five ways that managers can direct salespeople.
14. Why is the evaluation of salespeople difficult?
15. What are the five leadership styles?
16. What is meant by a relations-oriented manager?

DISCUSSION QUESTIONS

1. Assume that you are the sales manager of a sporting goods company and you supervise ten salespeople. You have set up an excellent training program and otherwise closely manage your subordinates. Your most senior salesperson, who also happens to have the greatest sales volume, has just complained to you that you are supervising him too closely and he feels as if someone is constantly peering over his shoulder. How would you answer this complaint?

2. Generally speaking, employees want the most money possible for doing their jobs while employers or managers try to keep expenses down. What goals do both salespeople and managers share in regard to the compensation system used?
3. Which compensation plan would you prefer to work with—salary, commission, or salary plus incentive? Why?
4. Why are quantitative approaches to sales forecasting becoming more popular?
5. Which leadership style(s) would be most effective with a salesperson just starting to sell vacuum cleaners door-to-door? Why?
6. If you were in charge of making up a selling expense budget, what categories of expense would you include?
7. Assume that your territory includes customers in major metropolitan areas along the West Coast (Seattle, Portland, San Francisco, Los Angeles, and San Diego), that you are on the road 80 percent of the time, and that you spend the same amount of time in each city. Make whatever additional assumptions you need, and then develop a budget for one month. (Your professor may prefer to assign you to a territory nearer you.) For help in figuring out various sales costs, you may wish to consult *Sales and Marketing Management*'s annual "Survey of Selling Costs."

CASE 20-1 SOUTHERN SPORTSWEAR*

Jimmy Jensen is a sales representative for Southern Sportswear, a company which specializes in T-shirts and athletic apparel. Southern Sportswear is introducing a new line of funky T-shirts targeted at college students and other persons in that age group. Because of the students' very limited income, these T-shirts will be priced $10 and under at retail. As part of the introductory sales plan for the new line of T-shirts, Southern Sportswear has scheduled a sales training seminar for all of its sales representatives.

Jimmy Jensen attended the sales seminar last week. He was very excited because he learned several things he felt would help him to sell more. One of the most important things he learned was about estimating market potential. The paragraphs which follow summarize that information.

Jensen learned that salespeople for Southern Sportswear represent the company and its products in a particular geographic location, the sales territory. To effectively manage their territory, the sales representatives need to properly allocate their time according to the market poten-

---

*Case prepared by Bob Kimball and Ronald F. Bush. Used with permission.

tial for their products. Segments of the territory with relatively high potential should be given proportionately more attention. Similarly, segments with relatively low potential should be given proportionately less attention.

Three data sources are utilized to estimate a market's ability to purchase a particular product or service: demographic data, as measured in population by specific age groups; economic data, as measured in numbers of households by specific income groups; and distribution-oriented data, as measured in gross dollar sales by specific outlet categories. The calculated index of a market's ability to purchase is called a buying power index, or BPI. Demographic factors are definitely the most important to the BPI, though economic factors are also significant. Distribution factors are a consideration, but of less importance than demographic and economic factors.

The calculated BPI gives you a relative indicator of a market's potential buying power. Generally, BPI for the Total U.S. is 100, which represents 100 percent of the total potential. However, if you wish to consider only a limited number of markets, you can substitute the total of those markets for Total U.S. in the calculations. In such a case, the BPI of 100 would represent the total of just those markets.

There are four steps used in calculating a custom BPI for a specific product or service. The first step is to identify the population and/or household factors which apply. For example, if your product were headache powders, the 35-and-over group would be your primary demographic target. In other circumstances, you might be concerned just with total population if all persons were equally likely to purchase, or total households if potential sales of your product or service would not be affected by the number of persons residing in any given household. In our example for headache powders,

$$\text{Factor A (Demographic)} = \frac{\text{Market's population over 35}}{\text{Total market population over 35}}$$

Step two is to determine the income group(s) most applicable to your product. For headache powders, the income group of households earning less than $20,000 a year might be most suitable. By contrast, for a premium-priced product, you might wish to use households earning over $35,000 or those earning $50,000 or more per year. In our example,

$$\text{Factor B (Economic)} = \frac{\text{Market's h/h with income} < \$20,000}{\text{Total market h/h with income} < \$20,000}$$

Step three is to identify the appropriate distribution channel(s) for your product. For headache powders, these might be food stores and drug stores. In our example, then,

$$\text{Factor C (Distribution)} = \frac{\text{Market's food and drug sales}}{\text{Total market food and drug sales}}$$

Step four is to determine the relative importance of those factors calculated in the first three steps. In our example, the weighting might be as follows:

Factor A (Demographic):   40%
Factor B (Economic):   45%
Factor C (Distribution):   15%
    (Must add up to 100%)

The BPI is then calculated by multiplying each factor by its weight and adding up the total. In our example,

BPI = 40% of A + 45% of B + 15% of C.

CASE QUESTIONS

1. Do you think the information on the BPI will help Jimmy? How do you think he could use it?
2. Exhibit 20-1A and B contain data from the 1988 "Survey of Buying Power" published by *Sales and Marketing Management*, describing the four-county metropolitan area of Athens, Georgia. Using these data, calculate a BPI for Jimmy's product in each of the four counties, with a BPI of 100 representing the four-county total. Briefly summarize your rationale in selecting the factors and weightings used in calculating the BPI.
3. Rank the counties by this index. Briefly summarize what all this would tell Jimmy about the metro area, and how he could use these findings in managing his territory.

EXHIBIT 20-1A
SOUTHERN SPORTSWEAR:
CALCULATING BUYING POWER

Area	> 35	> $20,000	Food & Drug Sales
Clarke County	28,499	14,625	$165,654
Jackson County	13,953	5,519	$46,848
Madison County	9,559	3,311	$11,564
Oconee County	6,784	3,382	$24,880
Total Market	58,795	26,837	$248,946

EXHIBIT 20-1B
CALCULATION OF BUYING POWER INDEX (BPI)

| | Factor | | | |
	Demographic	Economic	Distribution	BPI
Clarke County	19.39	24.52	9.98	53.89
Jackson County	_____	_____	_____	____
Madison County	_____	_____	_____	____
Oconee County	_____	_____	_____	____
Total Market	_____	_____	_____	____

CASE 20-2   ADVANCED OFFICE SYSTEMS, INC.*

It was 2:30 in the afternoon and Jim Kato and Marci Brown were still sitting at a local restaurant after their long lunch. Both knew they should be out making sales calls—their quota was ten calls per day—but they just couldn't seem to stop talking about how rotten things had become at Advanced Office Systems. Advanced Office Systems sells copiers, fax machines, and personal computers to small and medium-sized businesses. Jim and Marci both left a competitor to join Advanced Office Systems less than a year ago. Their reason for joining the firm was the promise of higher commissions. In spite of the fact that they were earning more money than ever, both were disgruntled and very dissatisfied with the company and their sales manager, Mr. Sanchez.

Jim sarcastically remarked, "We have not had a meeting with Sanchez in over three months. The only contact I've had with the guy lately is in the form of those dumb memos telling me I'm not meeting my activity quota. Doesn't that fool even look at the booked sales figures? We're way over quota in total sales!" Marci responded, "Jim, you're right; in fact, I haven't seen Sanchez much lately, either. In addition to the fact that Sanchez places so much emphasis on that activity quota, I'm really upset about that change in policy concerning expense accounts. We were promised full reimbursement for travel and entertaining expenses when we came on board, and now Sanchez only wants to pay 70 percent. Even though my commission income is up, my total income is actually less because I have to foot more of the bill for expenses!" Marci looked at Jim and said, "What do you think we ought to do: quit or try to talk to Sanchez about these problems?" Jim, looking into his glass, said, "You know, Marci, Sanchez really seems to be a reasonable guy and I really liked him when we first hired on. Maybe he'll be open to some suggestions from us!"

---

*Case prepared by K. Randall. Used with permission.

That idea caused Marci to think about something she had read in a magazine she subscribes to called *Tips for the Salesforce.* "Jim, I remember an article I read not too long ago about the factors that cause friction between the sales force and their company. It said the top seven causes of bad relationships between salespersons and firms are: (1) poor communication, (2) unfair compensation, (3) weak leadership, (4) disagreement with company policies, (5) too much paperwork, (6) inadequate recognition of performance, and (7) personality clashes. Maybe if we identify three or four of the main problems from our point of view, Mr. Sanchez will be open to discussing possible solutions." Jim smiled and said, "Marci, that's the most constructive thing I've heard all afternoon." They both got out pens and began to list on a napkin the things that bothered them at Advanced Office Systems. Next they categorized these problems based on the factors Marci recalled from the article in *Tips for the Salesforce.*

CASE QUESTIONS

1. Even though they were well compensated, what do you think are the short-term and long-term implications of Jim and Marci's dissatisfaction with conditions at Advanced Office Systems?
2. Based on the facts of the case, which of the seven factors leading to friction between a firm and salesforce do you feel are most responsible for the situation?
3. If you were in a position to recommend a solution to Mr. Sanchez, what would you suggest?

GLOSSARY

Adaptive selling A selling technique in which salespeople alter their presentations during a sales call, or use different presentations according to the customer's situation or personality.

Advantage-proof-action technique A technique for implementing the FAB sheet in which salespeople must support advantages with proof. Once the prospect is convinced that a product is superior (has more advantages), the salesperson tries to get the prospect to commit to an action (purchase).

Advertising A direct promotional strategy, said to employ a "pull" technique, because it urges consumers to ask for and buy advertised brands by pulling those brands through the channels of distribution.

Affordable approach An approach used in budgeting advertising, in which the advertiser spends whatever can be afforded on advertising.

Airfones A communication apparatus which allows the salesperson to make a call while traveling on an airplane.

Annual purchasing contract A document which provides a discount schedule for purchases over the period of the contract.

Ask questions technique A technique for handling objections in which the salesperson uses the "why" question to help separate excuses from genuine objections, to probe for hidden resistance, and to dispose of objections.

Assumption close A close in which both the salesperson and prospect have a specific product in mind; both are thinking about the same model, color, size, material, and price.

Attitude and lifestyle tests Tests used as a substitute for the polygraph test in an attempt to assess honesty and find drug-abusers.

Attitudes The views or convictions a person holds about or toward something.

612

Barrier   A person who has the responsibility of seeing that the prospect's time is not wasted by stopping salespeople when it appears that such salespeople will not be beneficial to that prospect.

Blanket purchasing contract   A purchasing contract which engages the supplier to provide "X" amount of product each month through the course of a year at one set price.

Boomerang technique   A technique for handling objections that allows the salesperson to agree with the prospect and then to show how the prospect's objections should not prevent a sale.

Brand image   The consumer's impression and evaluation of a certain branded product.

Breakdown   A forecasting technique act in which top-level management starts with a very large, general figure, and reduces it to a specific company sales forecast.

Bribes   Money or valuable gifts given to buyers to obtain their business.

Buildup   A forecasting approach in which the forecast is made by the sales force rather than by the company executives, starting with each salesperson's estimate of what he or she will sell next year.

Business space   The difference in distance between two parties engaged in business, usually the measure of how far apart they are standing.

Buyer's market   A state of trade in which supply exceeds demand and customers are no longer forced to buy only what the seller offers.

Buying group   A team, group, or committee set up to make a large purchase.

Buying influences   The people in the buying firm whose attitudes carry some weight in the firm's buying decisions.

Buying signals   Cues indicating that a close should be attempted by the salesperson.

Callback   The suggestion of a later visit, when the salesperson is certain that the prospect is determined to delay the purchase.

Canned presentation   A memorized sales talk, delivered exactly as memorized.

Cellular phone   A mobile telephone and/or portable pack unit that allows salespeople to make and receive calls from their automobiles, boats, or elsewhere.

Center of influence method   A method for prospecting which involves the use of anyone who has influence over other individuals, and who can provide the salesperson with information about the other individuals.

Checklists   Lists used in the pretest evaluation of an advertising campaign, made up of the values an advertisement should have—attention value, comprehension value, conviction value, memory value, attitude change value, etc.

Choice close   A close technique used when the salesperson takes for granted that the prospect is going to buy, but at the same time knows that the prospect is reluctant to concede. The salesperson ignores and avoids the major buying decision by posing a minor decision for the prospect to make.

Closing   The act of asking a buyer for a commitment to purchase the product or service.

Closing on a minor point   Another term for the technique of closing on a choice. The salesperson ignores and avoids the major buying decision by posing a minor decision for the prospect to make.

Closing on the objection   A technique used when a prospect gives honest agreement to every point the salesperson makes except one; the salesperson gets the prospect to agree that the objection raised is the only thing holding up the purchase.

Cold canvassing   A method of prospecting in which the salesperson contacts people who may not be prospects and about whom very little, if anything, is known.

Communications   Letters, telephone conversations, and periodic mailings such as house organs and weekly or monthly sales reports, etc., which can be used by sales managers to direct their salespeople.

Competitive parity approach   An advertising budgeting approach in which the advertiser spends as much as the competition does on advertising.

Concurrent evaluation   An advertising evaluation technique in which telephone calls are made to a sample between certain hours to learn if the TV is on and, if so, to which station it is tuned.

Conference   A method for directing salespeople in which salesperson-to-salesperson exchanges of ideas, tactics, and experiences are facilitated, salespeople are permitted to chat with top management, and training sessions take place.

Conference call   A telephone meeting of more than two people.

Conflict of interest   A situation that exists when a salesperson must choose a course of action, and the course of action that would benefit the salesperson most is not the one that would benefit the buyer most.

Consumers   People who buy products and/or services for their own use or for use in their households by household members.

Consumption   The use of goods or services by consumers.

Contests   A method for directing consumers or salespeople and to increase sales volume by using the stimulating effects of competition to encourage performance along desired lines.

Contingent promise   The condition by which the prospect will buy if the salesperson promises to satisfy a particular request.

Conventional discount store   A store that sells brand-name merchandise at prices consumers easily recognize as below traditional prices.

Cooling-off period   A time during which the customer can reconsider and cancel a contract.

Corporate image   The buyer's picture of the character and personality of a given corporation.

Creative listening   A type of listening which is intended to ensure effective two-way communication, and which involves a salesperson's being an active listener, that is, one who is interested in and alert to buyers, in order to get information, to bid for buyers' goodwill, and to compliment buyers.

Creative selling   A type of selling in which the salesperson discovers a customer need of which the customer was unaware, and selling a product as the answer to that need.

Credit management   The act of checking each credit customer's credit rating regularly and revising the credit limit if needed.

Culture   The set of basic values, perceptions, wants, and behaviors that are passed on from one generation to another within a society.

Customer benefit plan   A description of the features important to a particular customer, the advantages the features have over the competition or what the prospect is currently using, and how the prospect will benefit from the features; also known as the FAB sheet.

Customer profile   The salesperson's collection of information about the prospect and the prospect's organization, development of objectives for the sales call, and preparation of an appealing sales presentation through determination of the prospect's needs and the benefits sought.

Customer service representatives   Members of a company's marketing team who provide a valuable support for outside sales and supplies of marketing research information.

Customer support   A relationship between a customer and a salesperson in which the customer is actively and enthusiastically in favor of the salesperson, company, products, and service.

Database manager   A type of software that allows salespeople to put customer files, prospecting cards, past sales records, and other information usually kept in paper files onto a computer disk.

Deals   Special concessions that manufacturers offer to middlemen.

Decoding   The communication process in which the receiver, or "target," of the communication must take the message and interpret it to give it meaning to a situation.

Demand   The number of buyers (both customers and prospects) who can use a product to advantage and finance its purchase.

Demonstrations   A showing of what the product will do for the prospect, presenting external evidence to back up assertions.

Denial technique   A technique for handling objections in which the salesperson, in response to an objection, simply points out that the prospect is wrong.

Derived demand   The result of actual or anticipated buying by consumers.

Detailers Salespeople who work for pharmaceutical firms and who call on doctors to promote prescription drugs.

Direct-action advertisement Advertising designed to stimulate immediate response on the part of the buyer.

Direct mail A method used to locate prospects in which companies send promotional fliers, brochures, and catalogs to select groups or areas and wait for a response.

Direct selling The direct personal sales contact between buyer and seller.

Discriminatory pricing An illegal practice in which a salesperson sells to a customer at a price that is lower than appropriate.

Disparagement The criticism of a competitor's product without proof that what is being said is true.

Distressed discount store A store that offers merchandise that is either damaged, discounted, seconds, irregulars, or used, at substantially below market prices.

Distribution channels The number of middlemen involved in placing the product.

Double-question method Another term for the technique of closing on a choice. In this technique, the salesperson ignores and avoids the major buying decision by posing a minor decision for the prospect to make.

Drawbacks Objections that result from the inability of the product or service to satisfy the customer's needs.

Drug tests Tests used to screen out job applicants who may be drug users.

80-20 principle A term which describes the condition existing in which 20 percent of the customers account for about 80 percent of the sales.

Electronic mail A function of a personal computer that enables salespeople to send and receive messages no matter where they are, as long as they are connected to telephone lines via a modem.

Empathy The salesperson's ability to see and feel the buyer-seller relationship from the prospect's viewpoint.

Employment   The condition of being paid in exchange for work.

Encoding   The attempt by a sender to put ideas in a form that is understandable by the receiver of the communication.

Endless chain method   A sales method by which satisfied customers or former customers are asked to suggest individuals who could use the product being sold.

Exclusive dealing   An illegal activity that involves requiring that buyers of one product not buy certain products from another seller.

Executive gift   A form of incentive offered by manufacturers to deserving middlemen, in appreciation for past business and in anticipation of future business.

Expectancy   Customer's mental sets in which individuals tend to perceive what they want to perceive and what they expect to perceive.

FAB sheet   Another name for the customer benefit plan. It gets its name from the fact that it describes which features (F) are important to this particular customer, the advantages (A) the features have over the competition or what the prospect is currently using, and how the prospect will benefit (B) from the features.

Facsimile (fax) machines   Machines that enable salespeople to send copies of important papers electronically to customers in a matter of minutes.

Family   The most influential reference group, consisting of two or more people who live together and are related by marriage, blood, or adoption.

Federal Trade Commission (FTC)   The governmental agency that was created by the Federal Trade Commission Act to oversee the enforcement of laws concerning unfair methods of competition and deceptive practices.

Feedback   A receiver's response to a message that tells the sender that the receiver has understood the message correctly, or that the receiver interpreted the message incorrectly.

Focus groups   Small groups of representative buyers who look at proposed advertisements and say what is good and bad about them.

Fragmentation   A subdividing of some already existing phase of an organization.

Franchising system   A contractual form of retailing agreed upon by a franchiser and a franchisee.

Frequency   The number of advertisements run during a certain period of time.

Goal-object   A specific item which will help to produce a desired state of affairs.

Graphics software   A type of software that provides salespeople with graphic capabilities and enables them to develop sophisticated sales presentations using graphics such as pie charts, bar graphs, and XY plots.

Green River Ordinances   Laws restricting the activities of certain types of salespeople by requiring that they apply for and receive a license before they can sell in that area.

Harassment   An unfair method of competition that takes various forms, such as having a competitor's products moved to a less desirable location or taken off the store's shelves, having air let out of tires, or persuading friends to complain to the store manager about the quality of the competitor's product.

Headlining   A technique used while the customer is examining a particular product, in which the salesperson quickly mentions the three or four outstanding benefits the product offers and then watches and listens for reactions.

Hear-customer-out technique   A technique for handling objections in which the salesperson allows the prospect, who may have been wronged in the past, to vent his frustration.

Indirect-action advertisement   A type of advertising in which the objective is to influence buyer attitude rather than stimulate immediate action.

Industrial buyers   People who purchase products and services for use in making their own products/services, or for use in their daily operations.

Initial training   Education of new salespeople dominated by on-the-job training; the recruits learn by doing, under the supervision of a senior salesperson, a sales supervisor, or a sales manager.

Intelligence tests   Tests used to measure how well a job applicant can learn, reason, and solve problems.

Items for resale   Products sold to but not for use by the wholesaler or the retailer in the operation of the business.

Job analysis   The determination of the responsibilities and assignments that a particular salesperson is expected have.

Job description   A written statement of what the saleperson is to do; it represents management's conclusions after executing a job analysis.

Job specifications   A listing of names of the personal qualities needed by the individual who is to function successfully in a described job.

Kickbacks   Acts in which the broker working for and paid by the buyer receives a payment from the seller for making the decision to buy from that seller.

Knowledge tests   Tests which attempt to measure how much the applicant knows about a certain product or market.

Lead sheet   A form that contains pertinent information about the prospect.

Leased departments   Retailers that operate departments under a contractual arrangement with conventional retail stores.

Line and staff organization   A chain of command in which staff members plan and make suggestions and the top executive administers, controls, and coordinates all the activities below him or her in the organization.

Line organization   A chain of command in which authority flows in a direct line from a top executive to the first-ranking subordinate, from this first subordinate to a second-ranking subordinate, and so on. Each subordinate is responsible to only one person on the next highest level.

List broker   A person acting as a sales agent who rents mailing lists from one company to another company.

Lost-order checklist   A list that indicates the deficiencies that resulted in an incomplete sale.

Lost-order report   A written record attempting to handle the causes of failure to sell in a systematic fashion.

Market forecast   The realistic estimate of what the entire market will actually buy during the coming year.

Marketing concept   A sales attitude based solely on finding out what consumers want and need, and providing that product or service to customers at a reasonable price.

Market potential   An estimate of the highest possible dollar or unit amount of a product or service that an entire market could be persuaded to buy, from all sellers, during the coming year.

Market share   As a projected figure, the ratio of a firm's sales forecast to the market forecast. As an actual figure, the ratio of the firm's sales for a previous time period to market sales for that period.

Mental states approach   An approach to selling in which a salesperson makes a sale by leading the prospect through five steps—getting the prospect's attention, gaining the prospect's interest, creating the prospect's desire for the product, securing the prospect's conviction that a purchase should be made, and getting action from the prospect in the form of a purchase.

Message   The end result of the communication process, which must be interpreted by the receiver.

Middlemen   Wholesalers and retailers who are in the middle of the channel of distribution, between manufacturers and consumers.

Misrepresentation   An illegal activity in which the salesperson makes commitments that the company does not intend to back. It involves lying or hiding the truth and may be intentional or the result of oversight.

Missionary salespeople   Salespeople working for manufacturers who work to promote their customers' sales, thus increasing their company's sales.

Misunderstandings   Objections due to a lack of information about the company's products and services.

Motivation   An impetus for an individual to act resulting from a recognized need or want.

Multiple question approach   A combination of both the tailored and standard approaches to provide the salesperson with a framework of questions that can be tailored to each individual prospect.

Need-satisfaction theory   The idea that salespeople must first help prospects recognize and understand their needs, and then present their products as the satisfiers of those needs.

Negotiation   The process of working out a purchase and sales program to the point of reaching a mutually satisfactory agreement.

Newsletters   Publications from a company to its customers that present facts about the company, its products and services, and the industry as a whole.

Noise   Anything that causes an incorrect message to be encoded, or a properly encoded message to be incorrectly decoded.

Nonpersonal channels of communication   A form of communication, such as advertising and direct mail promotion, in which there is no direct personal contact between the receiver and the sender.

Nonselling duties   Duties of retail salespeople other than selling for retail. They may include: receiving and marking incoming merchandise, taking inventory, getting the departments ready for the selling day, making sure department stock is adequate and neat at closing time, customer service, and building displays.

Norms   The customary, approved modes of behavior that develop over time as a result of personal interaction within a culture.

Objective-task approach   An approach to budgeting advertising in which the advertiser first develops advertising objectives for the next year, then determines the advertising tasks necessary to attain those objectives. The advertiser finally estimates the cost of an advertising program that will achieve those objectives.

Open-ended questions   Questions which require customers to answer in their own words.

Opinion leaders   People who lead because their tastes tend to be adopted by other members of a reference group.

Opportunity to advance   The chance to move up in rank within the sales organization that spurs some salespeople to achieve greater performance.

Organizational buying process   A series of eight stages in the purchase of a product from a supplier.

Pagers   Portable devices that enable salespeople to maintain contact with the office, a customer, a vendor, or anyone else who knows their number.

Percent-of-sales approach   A determination of the advertising budget in which the advertiser estimates next year's net sales, picks a percentage to use as a multiplier, and multiplies one by the other.

Perception   A process based mostly on stimulus-response relationships. It includes the individual's selection of stimuli for attention, awareness of outside stimuli, interpretation of that stimuli, and the coherent organization of these concepts into the individual's personal world.

Perceptual field   Everything that a person sees or knows about the world.

Personal contact   A method for directing salespeople in which sales managers and supervisors work directly with salespeople, leading to understanding and two-way communication.

Personality tests   Tests intended to measure purely subjective traits such as confidence and poise.

Personal selling   The communication of a company's products, services, or ideas to its customers in either a one-on-one meeting or small group arrangement.

Point-of-purchase advertising   Advertising materials that retailers display near the point of sale.

Point-of-purchase (POP) display   A special inducement for acting at once in which the manufacturer offers the retailer more elaborate displays than the retailer has been getting.

Polygraph tests   Tests, also known as lie-detector tests, which measure the applicant's blood pressure, heartbeat, and perspiration levels as indicators of personal honesty.

Postpurchase dissonance   The customer's questioning the purchase choice when the product fails to satisfy his or her expectations.

Postsale behavior   The continued courteous and friendly treatment of a customer by a salesperson following a sale.

Post-test   Evaluation techniques of an advertising campaign that are employed after the advertisement has run.

Preapproach   A method of preparation for the coming sales presentation in which the salesperson finds the prospect's basic problem or need, and then plans the best way to present the problem and its solution when talking to the prospect.

Predatory pricing   An illegal practice that involves intentionally lowering prices below costs in order to drive a competitor out of business.

Pretest evaluation   An evaluation technique used before an advertisement is run. Proposed advertisements are checked against checklists and scored.

Price discrimination   An illegal activity designed to restrain trade in which a salesperson sells at a lower price to a well-liked or important customer.

Price-fixing   A civil and criminal offense in which salespeople agree with a competitor's salesperson to charge a certain price to a customer, require that a distributor or retailer charge certain prices to their customers, or even exchange price information with a competitor.

Primacy   Placing of the most important idea in the selling message first.

Primary demand   The demand for a type or class of product or service.

Problem-solution theory   A theory calling for strong interaction between the buyer and the seller. The buyer and seller together determine the buyer's problem and customize a solution to the problem.

Product information   Provision of information to the customer such as product specifications, typical quality, allowable conditions for use or exposure, limits on service life or operating conditions, and performance under typical operating conditions.

Production   The creation of goods and/or services.

Product research   The history of the product/service being sold, as well as significant improvements that have been made or are being planned.

Product specifications   A detailed statement of requirements describing the type of product to fill the need.

Program presentation   A written sales presentation developed from a detailed analysis of a prospect's business. It is also known as the "survey."

Prospect   Any potential customer for a company's product.

Prospect file   An individual, detailed record of each of a company's customers.

Prospecting   The activities involved in locating potential customers for the company's product.

Psychic income   A measure of one's level of satisfaction regarding personal growth and development.

Publicity   An indirect promotional strategy using either information about a firm or product considered news by communication media; or "word-of-mouth" promotion by two or more persons conversing about a seller or the seller's product.

Purchasing agent   A professional buyer through whom the salesperson must pass in order to get to the "real" decision makers.

Purchasing contract   A common buying technique used with products that are purchased often and in high volume and which allows the buyer to routinize the decision on these particular products, while promising the salesperson a sure sale.

Push money (PM)   A special inducement for acting at once in which the manufacturer offers money to a retailer's salespeople to push the manufacturer's brand.

Qualifying questions   Questions used to separate prospects from those who do not have the potential to purchase.

Quantity discounts   A price differential that encourages and rewards large orders by giving price breaks to larger orders.

Rationalization   The individual's attempt to justify behavior on logical and proper bases.

Rational motivation   The impetus for which the principal concern is to make a profit by increasing sales volume and reducing costs.

Reach   The number of buyers "reached" by advertisements during a certain period of time.

Readership studies   A post-test of an advertising campaign evaluation that includes the number of inquiries received, samples requested, contest entries received, or incoming telephone calls.

Recency   Placing of the most important idea in a selling message last.

Recognition   A method for directing salespeople by building the salesperson's pride in achievement, self-respect, and sense of belonging to the sales force and the company.

Reference groups   Collections of people consisting of two or more individuals who have something in common.

Referral method   A sales technique by which customers may give the salesperson a personal card or note of introduction for the suggested product.

Refresher training   The education of employees which deals with such problems as experienced salespeople's drifting into bad habits, and provides up-to-date information.

Reinforcement   A reward encouraging the repetition of a particular response to a stimulus.

Reports   A method for directing salespeople which is designed to gather information from and about sales territories. Sales managers use this information to direct, to control, to supervise, and to rate salespeople's performance.

Request an order   A closing technique used when a salesperson has recommended a sound solution to a problem, and the prospect seems to be in agreement; the salesperson is then entitled to ask for an order.

Resellers   Wholesalers and retailers who purchase products in order to sell them for a profit, providing services in exchange for this profit.

Resistance   A barrier between the salesperson and sales in which the buyers oppose purchase suggestions, avoid an obligation, object because they lack information, or want assurance that what they are doing is correct.

Restraint of trade   Activities that lessen competition, such as price-fixing and agreements not to sell, to sell only in certain markets, or to sell only to certain customers.

Retailers   Middlemen who sell directly to ultimate consumers.

Routing   The travel pattern used in working a territory.

Sales aptitude tests   A measure of such selling-related traits as tact, memory, verbal facility, extroversion, persistence, and persuasiveness.

Sales books   Sales information binders containing information about the industry, the company, the competition, and the company's products, promotion, pricing, and distribution strategies.

Sales call objectives   Goals in which the salesperson intends to get the customer to commit to some type of action.

Sales forecast   The estimate of how much of the market forecast a specific firm will sell if it follows a certain marketing program.

Sales leads   Inquiries generated by a firm's advertising and promotional efforts that are a source of prospects for most companies.

Sales meetings   Methods for directing salespeople which address ways of dealing with the salesperson's daily problems. Salespeople can meet and exchange experiences and solutions.

Sales promotion   A direct promotional strategy consisting of a group of auxiliary activities that enhance personal selling and advertising strategies.

Sales quota   The portions of the total sales forecast after it has been broken down by buyer; by day, week, and/or month; by sales territory and basic unit; by product and/or product line; or by salesperson.

Sales territory   The specific portion of a firm's total physical market that is assigned to any one salesperson.

Scheduling   The planning by salespeople of their activities with an eye toward producing the sales volume budgeted for that day.

Selection close   Another term for the technique of closing on a choice. In this technique, the salesperson ignores and avoids the major buying decision by posing a minor decision for the prospect to make.

Selective demand   The buying of a particular brand within a broad class of products.

Self-concept   The way in which a person perceives himself as an individual, influenced by physical traits and moral, social, and mental dimensions.

Selling duties   Duties of retail salespeople, including writing up sales slips, wrapping merchandise, operating point-of-sale terminals, verifying and executing credit card sales, and making change. Retail salespeople sell merchandise to the mutual benefit of the customer and the store.

Selling process   A series of actions by which a salesperson attempts to locate a potential customer, plans and presents her or his product offering, satisfies any customer questions, makes the sale, and establishes a long-term buyer-seller relationship.

Service approach   The missionary salesperson's offer of service such as point-of-purchase materials, help with advertising, teaching about the merchandise, and analyzing the retailer's problems and making recommendations.

Service selling   The finding of buyers who know what they want, and the taking of their orders.

Showmanship   Dramatization of the demonstration in which facts are presented and actions are executed in such an unusual way as to secure attention, increase prospect receptivity, make proof more spectacular, and bring about conviction.

Social class   A relatively homogeneous and permanent segment of society to which individuals and families belong.

Social influences   Buying behavior affected by culture, social class, reference groups, and families.

Social mobility   The movement of an individual from one social position to another, either upward or downward.

Social-style matrix   An approach used to help salespeople adapt their presentations to the prospect through first understanding their own social style before adapting it to the customer.

Special-deal close   A closing technique in which the salesperson offers the prospect an inducement for acting at once.

SPIN approach   A multiple question selling approach, SPIN stands for Situation, Problem, Implication, and Need, and relies on asking a series of questions to: (1) put the customer into a situation, (2) determine what problem the customer has, (3) show the negative implications of the problem, and (4) establish a need in the customer's mind.

Split-decision close   Another term for the technique of closing on a choice. In this technique, the salesperson ignores and avoids the major buying decision by posing a minor decision for the prospect to make.

Spreadsheet analysis   A type of software designed to perform arithmetic calculations and to display these calculations in a grid format (columns and rows).

Standard approach   A single approach used with all prospects.

Standing-room-only close   A closing technique based on using the assumption that people want anything that is hard to get. A warning of impending price increase or limited supply is used to stimulate the prospect to buy.

Stimulus-response theory   The belief that the salesperson should provide the buyer with the proper stimulus in order to get the desired response.

Story plan   A standard presentation similar to a canned presentation, but with more flexibility. The raw material is used by the salesperson to fashion his or her actual presentation.

Stroking   Satisfying the child ego state in order to move a customer into the adult ego state.

Subculture   A grouping of people who exhibit patterns of behavior sufficient to distinguish them from the overall culture or society.

Substitute selling   A salesperson's redirection of the customer's interest to some other product or brand, whether the requested item is or is not in stock.

Suggestion selling   Purchasing in which the salesperson gets the customer to make unplanned purchases of items over and above those he or she requested by recommending these items.

Summary close   A closing technique which includes a review of each advantage the salesperson has mentioned. The collection of advantages may be impressive enough to persuade the prospect to buy immediately.

T-account   A closing device in which the salesperson draws a large T, listing on the left side reasons for the prospect to buy and on the right side reasons not to buy.

Tailored approach   An approach designed specifically for the selling situation and the prospect.

Team selling   The use of a company's executive, technical, manufacturing, or other staff personnel in assisting the salesperson to service the customer. It may also be a group of experienced specialists in which each member has particular interests and asks special questions.

Telemarketing   The use of the telephone in conjunction with traditional marketing methods and techniques.

Terms of sale   The product/service prices, allowable discounts, and the credit and collection policies of the company.

Time traps   Poor management that wastes a salesperson's time.

Top-down planning   A forecasting approach that begins at the top level of management and is then sent down to implementors (sales reps) to be used as an objective for their efforts.

Trade promotions   Sales promotions that are directed toward wholesalers and/or retailers that distribute the advertiser's product.

Trading up   A selling technique in which the salesperson convinces the customer to buy a better-quality item than the customer had planned, or to buy a larger quantity of the product.

Transactional analysis   An approach used to determine the customer's motivations based on the three ego states—the parent, the child, and the adult.

Truth-in-lending legislation   Laws that require that the seller inform the buyer of the effective rate of interest and the amount of the carrying charge for any credit purchase.

Two-way communication   Feedback in the form of customer questions or statements.

Tying arrangements   The practice of requiring a buyer to purchase one product in order to be allowed to buy another.

Value analysis   A systematic analysis and evaluation of products and their component parts to see if changes in design, materials, or construction will reduce the cost without damaging the performance of the product.

Vendor company   The company in the position of selling goods and/or services in a business transaction.

Vertical software   A type of sales-oriented software that provides scenarios or situations that salespeople can review by filling in the needed characteristics.

Visual aids   Advertisements, cross-sections of the product, models, and samples that help to picture the sales proposition.

Vocational interest tests   Tests which identify the vocational areas which appeal to the applicant.

Want book   A notebook, or a computerized order file, in which the retailer lists the items that will soon need to be replenished.

Wholesalers   Middlemen who sell goods, usually in large quantities and below retail price, often for resale.

Word processing   The use of software that helps prepare letters, customer files, and reports.

"Yes, but" technique   An indirect answer technique used to handle sales resistance in which argument and friction are avoided by respecting the prospect's opinions, attitudes, and thinking. It is also called the agree and counter technique.

INDEX